Based on previously-unpublished personal letters and military records, this biography provides a unique insight into the life, ambitions, opinions, and actions of Wellington's most trusted, professional, and thoughtful staff officer, described as 'the only man received into the unlimited confidence of Lord Wellington'. It is a full and frank story of one of the most respected and admired soldiers of his generation, his service in the Low Countries, Ireland, West Indies, and Egypt, and his importance in the Peninsular War. Murray's development of the Quartermaster General's department into an impressively efficient operation, touching on almost every aspect of the Army's movement, topographical and military intelligence, and preparation for battle, was of immense value to Wellington.

More than a fighting soldier and new 'scientific' staff officer, Murray was picked for a number of diplomatic missions and negotiations, where his intelligence, popularity, and ability to relate equally easily to royalty, subordinates, and both enemy and allied officers, marked him out as an invaluable asset in the war against Napoleon.

Murray's personal life and private thoughts are at all times centre stage, and an unlikely, scandalous, and socially damaging love match demonstrates Murray's strong sense of loyalty and duty. These qualities underpinned his lessthan- happy time in politics following Napoleon's defeat. Murray and Wellington faced military and political foes side by side, trusted and admired each other, and were close personal friends for forty tumultuous years. Murray's own story is here told for the first time.

John Harding-Edgar, a Law graduate of Aberdeen University, is a four-times great nephew of Sir George Murray. After ten years working overseas in trade finance, he returned to live in his native Edinburgh to pursue a career as a corporate lawyer. On retirement he began researching the well documented history of the Murrays of Ochtertyre. This soon led to a more detailed examination of the substantial Murray Archive in the National Library of Scotland, comprising Murray's personal and military papers. The temptation to establish the truth of the oft-repeated family maxim that Murray was Wellington's closest friend led to the writing of this book. John lives in Edinburgh with his wife Jennifer and spaniel Sintra, and has three grown up daughters. This is his first published work.

Next to Wellington
General Sir George Murray

The Story of a Scottish Soldier and Statesman, Wellington's Quartermaster General

---

John Harding-Edgar

Helion & Company Limited

Helion & Company Limited
Unit 8 Amherst Business Centre
Budbrooke Road
Warwick
CV34 5WE
England
Tel. 01926 499 619
Email: info@helion.co.uk
Website: www.helion.co.uk
Twitter: @helionbooks
Visit our blog at http://blog.helion.co.uk/

Published by Helion & Company 2018. Reprinted in paperback 2023
Designed and typeset by Mach 3 Solutions (www.mach3solutions.co.uk)
Cover designed by Paul Hewitt, Battlefield Design (www.battlefield-design.co.uk)

ISBN 978-1-804513-88-0

British Library Cataloguing-in-Publication Data.
A catalogue record for this book is available from the British Library.

Contents

List of Plates

Black and White Plates

Colour Plates

List of Maps

Foreword by Rory Muir

The Duke of Wellington had little patience with incompetence. When a newly arrived senior officer failed to impress him in the midst of the Peninsular War he did not conceal his irritation. 'I took care to let him feel that I thought him very stupid', he told his staff; and George Murray, who knew Wellington better than most, commented, 'That must have been by telling him so in plain terms, I have no doubt'. Unlike the unfortunate officer, there was no doubt of Murray's intelligence, and he worked in a close partnership with Wellington, earning his respect by his forethought and calm efficiency. He was the Quartermaster General – the chief staff officer – throughout most of the campaigns in Portugal and Spain, turning Wellington's plans into clear, precise orders that ensured that troops went where they were meant to go without undue delays or starving on the way. Murray sent junior officers to reconnoitre ahead of the army, to see how many troops could pass through the bottlenecks on each road in a day, to discover alternative routes and good defensive positions, and to assess the mood of the local population. He worked out how to distribute the army when it was in winter quarters so that it might be reassembled quickly if active operations were resumed, but was not so crowded in the meantime that the troops were hard to feed or posed an impossible burden on the country. And above all he ensured that the cumbersome machinery of the army worked smoothly and efficiently, averting the natural tendency for military operations to go wrong. The work of a good staff officer, especially a good Quartermaster General, should be almost invisible, and the importance of Murray to the army was never more apparent than in the Burgos Campaign of 1812 when he was in Ireland and the bungles of his replacement led to endless problems. The replacement – Willoughby Gordon – was soon sent home, and Wellington ensured that Murray was back at headquarters before the next campaign opened.

Because his role was so unobtrusive, and because he was so efficient, Murray's role in the Peninsula has never attracted the attention it deserved. That is one reason; but there is another. William Napier, who had served in the Light Division and who wrote the most famous contemporary history of the war, viewed Murray as a potential rival and carefully downplayed his contribution to the victory. Successive historians did little to correct this neglect until S. G. P. Ward examined the workings of Wellington's headquarters in a monograph first published in 1957. Ward, who had himself served as a staff officer in the Second World War, fully appreciated the importance of Murray's role, and started work on a biography of Murray only to be discouraged by the lack of enthusiasm of his publisher and distracted by the demands of other projects.

Now at last, more than two hundred years after the victory over Napoleon, John Harding-Edgar has filled the gap and given us this admirable biography of Murray. The story he tells shows that there was much more to Murray's life than his service in the Peninsula. Murray was one of the leading members of a rising generation of soldiers, shaped by the disappointments of the early years of the war against France, who took their profession seriously, adopting the methodical 'scientific' methods of staff work employed in continental armies. He had a valuable apprenticeship seeing service in the Low Countries, Ireland, the West Indies, Egypt, and Denmark before he set foot in the Peninsula, and worked closely with some of the most capable British soldiers of the day including Sir Ralph Abercromby and Sir John Moore. He was quick to recognize Wellington's ability, although he was never blind to his faults, and took some time to be convinced that his strategy in the defence of Portugal in the months after Talavera could succeed. After the war Murray played an important role in the occupation of France and later in British politics, when he served as a cabinet minister in Wellington's government and appeared for a time to be one of the most promising conservative speakers in the House of Commons. He was also able to marry: and this was the second great story of Murray's life, a tale of romance, intrigue, and considerable difficulty that reveals much about the position of aristocratic women in Regency society, and which brought Murray a great deal of domestic happiness together with some public mortification. One of the most important achievements of this fine biography is that it reminds us that the talented staff officer who worked so closely at Wellington's side was also a warm blooded man who, in his mid-forties, fell head over heels in love and defied society, and who never regretted it.

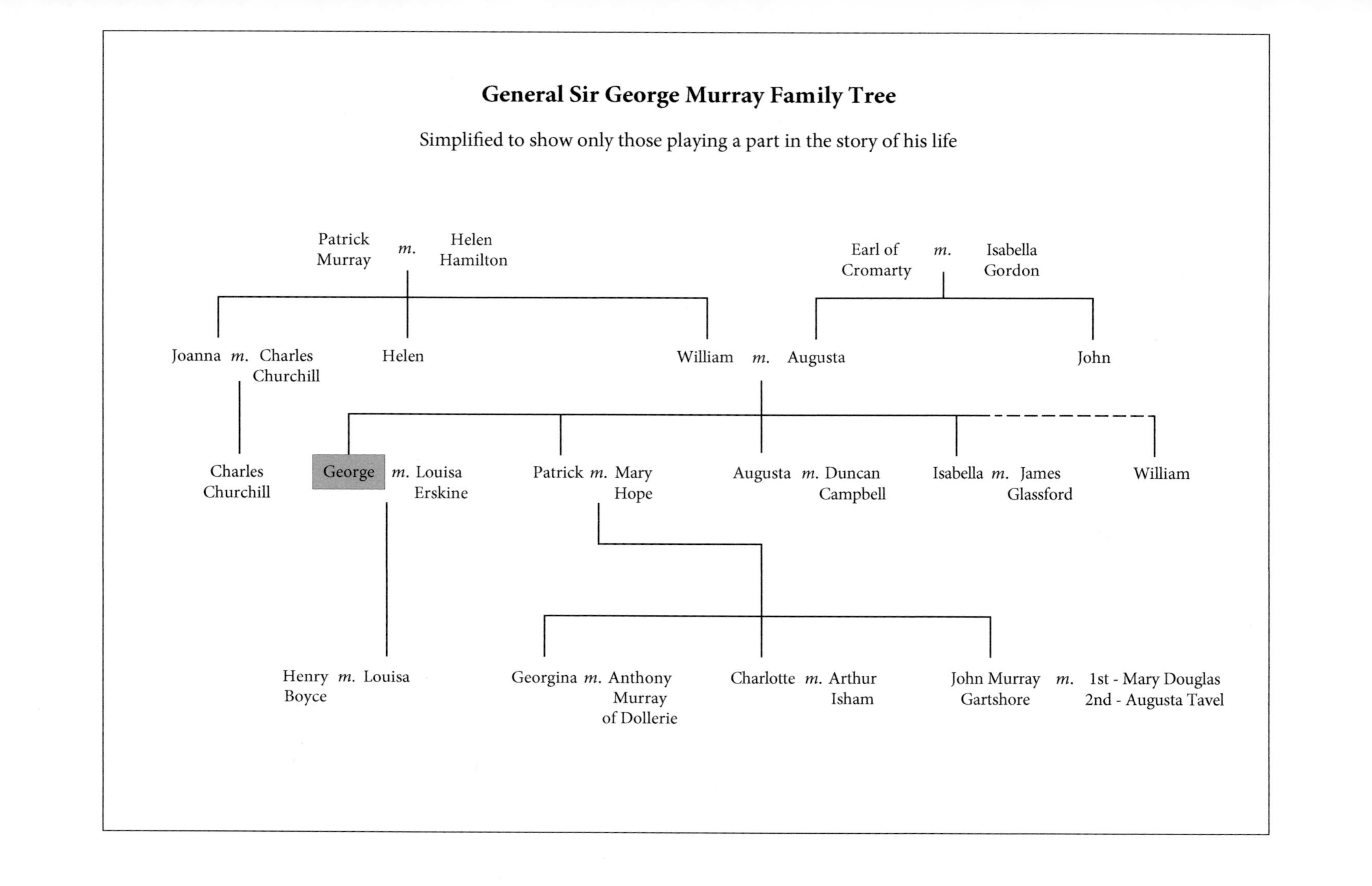
General Sir George Murray Family Tree
Simplified to show only those playing a part in the story of his life
Patrick Murray m. Helen Hamilton
Earl of Cromarty m. Isabella Gordon
Joanna m. Charles Churchill
Helen
William m. Augusta
John
Charles Churchill
George m. Louisa Erskine
Patrick m. Mary Hope
Augusta m. Duncan Campbell
Isabella m. James Glassford
William
Henry m. Louisa Boyce
Georgina m. Anthony Murray of Dollerie
Charlotte m. Arthur Isham
John Murray Gartshore m. 1st - Mary Douglas 2nd - Augusta Tavel

The situation of a Quarter Master General is of so much importance to the interest of an Army as almost equal in that respect and only to be exceeded by that of the Commander-in-Chief. So various and extensive are the duties annexed to this situation and the qualification necessary to fulfil with honour, that volumes might be written on the subject. The QMG should possess a scientific knowledge of everything that comes within the scope of the Military profession. A cool sagacious and penetrating judgement, an active and enterprising spirit, in short a genius capable of taking advantage of every opportunity and of finding resources in every emergency, should distinguish the person holding a situation of such responsibility and importance, and hence proceeds the difficulty in finding persons properly qualified to fill it. It is the particular province of the QMG to attend to the change and distribution of the troops and the arrangement of camps – he is constantly near the Commanding General to receive his orders and accordingly determines the position of every Regiment. To perform these duties with judgement it requires long experience, a scientific knowledge of the ground, the choice of positions and of castramentation.

From *The Elements of the Science of War* by William Mueller,[1] London 1811.

[M]y chief pleasure arises from having abundance of employment. The more I can force myself to application, the more satisfaction do I feel, and nothing makes me so happy as the thought that were several hours added to the day, I should still find occupations sufficient for them all.

(Extract from a letter from Murray to his sister Augusta,
High Wycombe, 22 April 1802)

1 Writer in military and engineering science, the first publicly appointed instructor in Military Science at the University of Göttingen

Introduction

In his will, Sir George Murray directed that all the papers left by him – personal, military and political – should be placed in the charge of his three Trustees. The Trustees knew him well, were conscious of his natural diffidence, and felt it in line with their duties that these papers should be kept private, despite the public nature of his services to the nation. In due course these family papers were entrusted to John Murray Gartshore, one of Murray's nephews, with a view to his indexing them, to make future referencing easier. Letters provided by Murray's sister Augusta, Mrs Campbell of Lochnell, were already in Gartshore's possession. These were mainly letters from Murray to her, her sister Isabella, and their eldest brother Patrick, the 6th Baronet of Ochtertyre, generally addressed as 'Peter'. More papers were later discovered at Ochtertyre, and made over to Gartshore, who took the view that despite the enormous quantity of manuscripts, maps, letters and other official communications on affairs of State, their content would not be of sufficient interest to the outside world to merit the cost of publication.

Gartshore regretted, as we all might, that Murray did not himself write his memoirs. Murray felt he did not want to ask the Duke of Wellington, his lifetime fellow soldier, statesman, and friend, for the use of his papers, although it must be more than likely that the Duke would have agreed, in view of the very close bonds between them. Or maybe these very loyalties were what held Murray back.

Murray was amply qualified to carry out the task of writing an account of the Napoleonic conflicts, particularly the campaign in the Peninsula, as well as the three years following Napoleon's defeat at Waterloo, when Murray was chief of staff to 150,000 allied troops forming the army of occupation in France. He had seen action, much of it as Quartermaster General to the army in Spain and Portugal, almost continuously from 1793 to 1814, although there were significant moments when he was not at Wellington's side, during the whole of 1812 and, notably, at Waterloo.

Murray had left the Peninsular Army early in 1812 to return to London, in the midst of what might be described as a mid-career crisis. Posted to Ireland as Quartermaster General, he was nevertheless soon persuaded to return by entreaties from the Duke of York and Wellington himself. In 1815, Murray was in Canada, acting as Governor General, when Napoleon escaped from Elba, but, despite frantic efforts to cross the Atlantic to join Wellington in his final battle, only arrived in France after Napoleon's defeat.

Not only would Murray have been able to paint a vivid picture of the actions in the Low Countries, Egypt, and the Peninsula by virtue of his own experience, but he possessed the necessary skills in the more academic requirements of writing military history, demonstrated by his significant work in editing *Marlborough's Despatches*, a detailed account of the Duke of Marlborough's campaigns, as well as a unpublished treatise on Caesar's *Commentaries* and their messages for modern warfare. The closest we come to a full description of Murray's military activities in the Peninsula is the introduction he wrote to Wyld's Atlas, published in 1841 and comprising a full set of maps of the campaign, mostly produced by Sir Thomas Mitchell. The introduction contains many orders and memoranda prepared by Murray in the course of the war, in his role as Quartermaster General.

Once, on being urged to write a history of the war in the Peninsula he replied: 'To be an impartial historian I must express disapprobation of some of the Duke's movements. I should not therefore like to publish during the Duke's lifetime'.[1] Another telling remark may also help explain Murray's reluctance to put pen to paper, surely a world away from today's generals and politicians 'I consider it an especial mark of wisdom in the man who contrives to pass through public life without attracting attention to the part he individually takes in it'.[2]

Gartshore came to the following conclusion on limited publication:

> While it is evident that the Trustees have decided wisely, it is hoped that it will not be considered inconsistent with their determination nor presumptuous in one who is not only interested in the subject of the papers but also deeply impressed with a lasting feeling of regard for the memory one of so distinguished yet so gentle, affable, and companionable to all about him, to endeavour to make a selection of some of the papers for the perusal of relations only, who will regard it, as he [Murray] himself wrote of his friend Sir John Moore, more in the light of a tribute of sincere affection than as bearing anything like the testimony so justly due to his merits.[3]

Gartshore was himself a military man, serving in the 42nd Highlanders (The Black Watch) at the time when Murray was colonel of the regiment, and obviously knew Murray well. There are letters in the National Library of Scotland between the two. Gartshore was proud of his uncle's achievements, and clearly also fond of him. There is a manuscript in the National Library of Scotland which contains the early draft of what looks to be somewhat more than just a miscellany of letters and documents, but there is no sign of it having got further than an early scribble, and that limited to the very early years of Murray's career.

Gartshore's daughter, Mary Murray Gartshore, left the family archive, including the Murray Papers and the Ochtertyre Papers, to the National Library of Scotland where they have been preserved and catalogued, thus placing them in the public domain. They provide a wonderful cornucopia of sources. Their greatest value perhaps lies in their personal nature. They provide the reader with a fascinating journey through a life of military and political service, spanning fifty years of Regency and Victorian Britain, which saw immense social

1 Murray Gartshore Papers, Murray Papers, MS 21112.
2 Murray Gartshore Papers, Murray Papers, MS 21112.
3 Murray Gartshore Papers, Murray Papers, MS 21112.

and political change, and positioned the nation, following the defeat of Napoleon, at the heart of a vast empire bedded upon great industrial, naval, and military strength.

The sheer volume of the papers is daunting. The most engaging are the personal letters. Murray wrote regularly to members of the family, often just before and after battles. Given the never-ending duties of a Quartermaster General, one has to marvel at how he found the time and energy to write in the way he did, sometimes driven by a desire to catch the next packet home with his unofficial, and often very pensive, description of events, many of which are now familiar, at least to military historians, as important milestones in the war against Napoleon, just as they were unfolding. Throughout the years of wartime correspondence there flows a familiar theme: 'I seem to manage to write many more letters than I receive'; the sentiments of a man who clearly valued close family ties, eager to be kept abreast of political developments and gossip back in London and Scotland, perhaps to help him keep a sense of perspective in the midst of terrifying carnage and deprivation.

Bear in mind just what the means of communication were: handwritten reports, instructions, letters and memos, and lots of them. Scribbled in pencil on the field of battle or composed during periods of boredom between bouts of action, or waiting to set sail on yet another expedition, the only means to get them to the addressee was to consign them to a departing individual, or to a system that was far from perfect. Hence the practice of numbering letters so that the recipient would know if there was a break in the sequence. Murray would often entrust his precious letters to a fellow officer who was going home on leave, or hastily consign another chapter in the description of the campaign to the packet which was about to sail as soon as the wind set fair. It was not in the least uncommon for these small ships to be intercepted and captured, and, even if they evaded hostile navies, they often had to cross huge stretches of water renowned for storms, which at best delayed the mail by days or weeks, and at worst meant their precious cargoes of descriptions of battles fought and survived, orders from London, or family gossip, sank without trace.

For those at home it meant weeks going by without any idea of what was happening in the war. They barely knew where the soldier in the family was; only that he was engaged in a terrifying conflict, and that casualty rates from disease and injury were appalling among both officers and men. They might, particularly if they were in London, be able to read of a battle fought a few weeks earlier, and be aware that the numbers of dead and wounded were high, but not get firm news of their loved ones' fate for many more weeks. The *Gazette* was the official conveyor of the dreaded news of injuries and death, and of honour gained.

Such delays were unavoidable. Political control of military strategy was continuous, and, in the flow of requests for information and instructions, surprisingly regular – often almost daily. But the politicians did recognise that they needed to give operational latitude to commanders in the theatre of war, which allowed, at times, blame for unfortunate events to be pinned squarely on the military, which may have been more justly ascribed to political shortcomings or lack of understanding of facts at the sharp end, or, as often was the case, lack of supplies, horses, men, or equipment. Equally the generals were not above convenient manipulation, and often wrote their despatches in such a way as to give themselves the best chance of claiming victory, where a no-score-draw might be closer to the truth.

Commanders in the field were often left uncertain as to what orders had got through to their fellow officers. Instructions were duplicated and sent by different routes to increase the chances of successful delivery. There is at least one incident, albeit not in the to and fro of operations, where a more rapid passage of a letter might have had a profound effect on this story. It is probable that had a letter from Wellington, written from Paris, arrived in Murray's hands before he set sail for Canada in late 1814, he would have returned to Wellington's side and played his part in directing operations next to him at the Battle of Waterloo.

So many books have been written around the period. There is a vast pool of material on which to draw should the reader be interested in military events and the long struggle to defeat Napoleon. Very little that is excitingly new is likely to be unearthed. Historians have for many years been concentrating on threads or theories in an effort to bring a little novelty to a well-researched period. And yet if you look at the many volumes that have been published about the Napoleonic Wars you will find only a handful of references to Murray. He could almost be classed as the forgotten general; he certainly has not excited many historians, the exceptions to this being first, S.G.P. Ward, a military historian who spent years after the Second World War researching and writing on Wellington, and whose unpublished material on Murray has been an invaluable source, and, more recently, Rory Muir whose two-volume tour de force, *Wellington – The Path to Victory*, and *Wellington – Waterloo and the Fortunes of Peace* has been my constant companion whilst writing this. The two large volumes comprise an extraordinary work, vast in scope and far-reaching in detail, but delightfully readable, and accompanied by a most useful commentary, available free to all on the internet, which provides an enormous additional amount of material, and demonstrates the lengths Muir has gone to in refining his facts into a brilliant biography of Wellington's military and political years. Both these historians have recognised Murray's valuable contribution to Wellington's success and the close bonds that existed between the two men.

A huge amount of primary source material, both official and family, relating to Murray personally, exists in various libraries. That he and the family kept so much of his correspondence is a huge bonus. If the man himself has never been the subject of close public scrutiny, what is evident is that the very large amounts of material which forms the Murray Papers have provided the backbone of many of the accounts of the Peninsular War written by eminent historians. Much of this material comes straight from Murray's pen, and, of all the senior officers fighting with Wellington, Murray was perhaps in the best position to produce factual accounts of what was going on; after all, one of the many duties of a Quartermaster General was to report accurately on all actions and movements involving the allied forces. These reports were pored over at Horse Guards in London. Throughout his service Murray never attempted to hide his views of the wider canvas – views which differed significantly from his commander's at critical times, and which inevitably would have been fed into the feverish political scene in London, where the course of the war was debated furiously. Support for its continuation, and for Wellington himself, was split along party lines, with the Tories broadly supportive, but barely able to hold their ground in the face of vehement Whig opposition.

Murray was not a glamorous cavalry officer, nor for the most part a controversial character. He was one of a new breed of officer, a skilled professional, who played a significant part at the forefront of events during an extraordinary period. As Quartermaster General with responsibility for the readiness, movement, and billeting of British and allied troops in Portugal, Spain, and France, and their deployment in battle in accordance with Wellington's orders, he developed, as part of his department's remit, accurate mapping and valuable intelligence gathering. The job of Quartermaster General altered radically during Murray's tenure, and assumed an importance and status in the army far beyond anything seen before. On top of his departmental duties Murray was required regularly to play a leading part in a number of highly sensitive negotiations, of great military and political importance, a role in which he seemed to excel.

He was not only as close, literally and metaphorically, to Wellington during the Peninsular campaigns as any man, but he became a trusted colleague and family friend. It can reasonably be claimed that he really was Wellington's right hand man (a title already claimed on behalf of General Rowland Hill and Lieutenant Colonel Alexander Gordon, and quite possibly others).[4] He was Wellington's ideal staff officer – well bred, therefore deemed reliable in an age of insurrection; intelligent; hardworking; seemingly inexhaustible; bilingual; and charming. He was often the go-between when deserving, but perhaps less well connected, officers needed patronage to promote their advancement in Wellington's army, clearly demonstrated in the case of George Scovell who, under Murray, would develop the intelligence, and in particular code breaking, service which played such a big part in the defeat of Napoleon's Peninsular Armies.

Wellington became increasingly dependent on Murray and felt his absences keenly, going to some lengths to bring him back to his side when situations so demanded, notably when Murray had left the Peninsula to return to duties in Ireland in 1812, and in the scramble to face up to Napoleon again after his escape from Elba, when Murray had been posted to Canada at the very end of the so-called War of 1812.

Murray's loyalty was rewarded by a significant political appointment in Wellington's administration after the defeat of Napoleon, as Secretary of State for War and the Colonies and later, under Peel, as Master General of the Ordnance. Murray's skills as a politician have never been regarded as convincing as his military attributes; in fact there is a broad consensus that he simply was not cut out to be a politician. He probably lacked the necessary appetite for the manoeuvrings that were then as much part of each day in the corridors of power at Westminster as they are today. He was never as committed a Tory as Wellington, being very much on the liberal wing, and had more difficulty in supporting him in the political arena than in the field. In fact, given his comments generally, and his attitude to his brother Patrick's and brother-in-law General Duncan Campbell's political careers, whilst he was fighting in the Peninsula, it is strange to think that he took up politics at all, and it is doubtful that he would have been so involved were it not for his loyalty to Wellington, and, perhaps tellingly, his need for a steady income.

Wellington and Murray remained close friends until Murray's death in 1846. Wellington was godfather to Murray's only daughter, and Murray was a frequent visitor to Stratfield Saye, Wellington's country house, and in London, at Number One, London (Apsley House). Belgrave Square, where Murray lived, was well within howitzer range. Wellington attended his funeral, trying to keep as low a profile as possible to avoid inconveniencing the family. A portrait of Murray in his later years by John Prescott Knight was acquired by Wellington to hang at Apsley House, where it still is today.

4 Joanna Hill, *Wellington's Right Hand. Rowland Viscount Hill* (Stroud, Spellmount 2011) and Rory Muir (ed.) *At Wellington's Right Hand. The Letters of Lieutenant-Colonel Sir Alexander Gordon, 1808-1815* (Stroud: Army Records Society, 2003).

Wellington provided the impetus, the masterly military strategy, and the sheer doggedness and determination that attracted the fierce loyalty of his troops, which ultimately overcame the might of Napoleon's armies in Spain and Portugal. Murray was the quiet, reliable, thoughtful 'chief of staff', willing to disagree with his commander and happy to shoulder the responsibility and freedom that Wellington allowed him, which made them, very different characters, a formidable pair. Murray's role was not an obviously glamorous one, but essential in an army engaged in a drawn-out campaign, moving rapidly over large, poorly mapped, distances in pursuit or in retreat, often in brutal weather, in a frequently hostile foreign country, against vastly superior numbers.

In the role of Quartermaster General, Murray developed that department's capabilities well beyond anything that had been seen in the British Army previously. His diplomatic and language skills were recognised early on and put to good use. His contribution to Napoleon's defeat was recognised by both British Royalty, in the award of Knight Commander of the Bath in 1813, at a time when this honour was in the personal gift of the sovereign, as well as numerous decorations bestowed by foreign rulers, which made Murray the most decorated soldier of his time after Wellington.

I approached this project not appreciating the sheer volume of the resources in the various libraries that have long been the raw material of authors and historians producing work on the Napoleonic period. If I have learnt nothing else from my efforts it is to admire the extraordinary detail that needs to be analysed, much of it contradictory or at least opinionated, sometimes deliberately misleading, before a single coherent page can be produced that is worthy of publication and proof against challenge. The volumes and boxes of letters, documents, orders, reports, plans, maps, lists, and tables are seemingly endless, full of sparkling gems and red herrings.

The book focuses on one man, his relationship with the Duke of Wellington, his personal life throughout the Napoleonic wars, and in and out of government, particularly as seen through his regular letters home to his politically active brother and his devoted sister. For the letters to be fully appreciated it is necessary to read them in the context in which they were written. To that end I have spent some time trying to explain a little of the background to the various campaigns and have also recorded, in more detail than might be strictly necessary, Murray's involvement in certain diplomatic and military exploits, one or two of which were distinctly controversial, and which had significant political and military repercussions.

What I have not done is give more than perfunctory descriptions of the battles that Murray was involved in, not because they were anything other than of vital importance, but rather that so many authors have written in staggering detail on them. There is easy access for anyone who might want to delve into this aspect. I have, rather, concentrated on Murray's contribution to the preparations that were required before contact with the enemy, and his often incisive, and always intelligent, ponderings after the battle was done. Anybody who has an interest in military history can glimpse the great volume of detailed planning that was necessary in progressing a campaign of this size and duration, from the multitude of papers, letters, reports, and orders in various libraries, which were written and received by Murray, and kept by him and his department. I have limited their inclusion to just one or two examples to provide a flavour of the work of the man, work that by its nature never ceased, whether the army was stationary, marching, actively engaging the enemy, or embarking for home.

Following his service in the Peninsula, Murray spent a short time in Canada as commander of the British Forces in North America and as interim Governor General, before his vain dash to be at Wellington's side at Waterloo. He served as Chief of Staff to the allied forces of occupation in Paris during the next three years. Further military service as Commander in Chief in Ireland followed. Murray's political career will be covered, his service as a member of Parliament; Secretary of State for War and the Colonies, just as Australia and Canada were opening up; as Governor of the Royal Military College, Sandhurst; Governor of both Edinburgh Castle and Fort George; and finally Master General of the Ordnance. His social life in fashionable London, badly affected by his love affair with the estranged wife of one of his fellow Peninsular generals, with its attendant court proceedings and divorce action, and the birth of an illegitimate daughter whilst hiding away in unfashionable places to escape the glare of publicity, provides us with an insight into a different sort of fierce loyalty.

The most important source of the letters received and sent by Murray that appear in this book, as well as the huge quantity of Quartermaster General's material, and political correspondence, remains the family papers in the National Library of Scotland, the Murray Papers, and the Ochtertyre Papers. Additional items are housed in other libraries including the British Library, the National Archives of Scotland, and the National Archives, Kew, all of which contain numbers of papers relating to Murray, forming part of other collections such as the Hope of Luffness Papers, the Hope of Linlithgow Papers, the Hill Papers, and the Scovell Papers, not forgetting S.G.P. Ward's copious notes at the Hartley Library, University of Southampton.

Ward spent a substantial amount of time examining the family papers, and, based on that research, had embarked on a biography of Murray which was never completed, and remains in a draft state in the Hartley Library.[5] Ward's study of Murray's military career sadly ends in 1810, although the draft does contain chapters on his affair, marriage, and political life. Ward frequently builds on, or adds an interesting angle to, the raw material that he gleaned from the family papers. References to Ward's Draft occur, as one would expect, more frequently than any other secondary source, and I have made every effort to ensure that his material is referenced in an identical manner to other sources that I have drawn from. As this is not intended to be in any way a book that deals with the detailed, operational, side of Murray's military life, except to furnish the necessary background, the vast majority of Ward's material remains an untapped resource that will surely excite some more scholarly author who wants to research, in much greater detail, Murray's career as a soldier, and in particular the development of the role of Quartermaster General under his direction. I am greatly indebted to the Hartley Library who permitted me such full access to the draft.

As a first time author I found it difficult to approach people for help and advice, often not even knowing the right questions to ask. Yet when I did so the response was almost always more generous than I had dared hope. Some individuals merit special mention.

Rory Muir, who encouraged me from the earliest tentative moments, when the book was destined to be nothing more than a relaxed canter through Murray's life for the family. Not

5 See references throughout to Ward Notes and Ward Draft.

only did Rory provide the sort of support that a newcomer such as I could only dream of, but he has always been interested in Murray and his contribution to Wellington's success, which has led to his penning a foreword to the book. I am truly grateful for the time he has spent on my behalf. It goes without saying what a useful resource Rory's major work on Wellington, including the supporting Commentaries, has provided, and I am sure I am not the only one to have marveled at his detailed research.

Iain Gordon Brown and Patricia Andrew, who have given so generously of their time and taken such an interest from the outset, and whose own wide experience of historical writing and research has been generously shared, generally wine glass in hand, always with impatient curiosity.

Will Fletcher, whose own PhD has involved the study of many of the same resources and who proved a breath of fresh air among the dark recesses of academic scholarship, as well as leading me to sources that I would otherwise have missed.

Nick Lipscombe, another who, at an early meeting at a Wellington Congress, greeted the idea of a biography of Murray with infectious enthusiasm and who provided some welcome advice in the later stages of the work.

Kelly Henderson, whose appetite for detail has been extraordinary, and who has steered me down numerous well researched paths with intellectual rigour, particularly where Murray's correspondence involved New South Wales and the Swan River Colony.

Nick Grier who, as a widely respected academic author, understands the ways of that part of the publishing world and offered some excellent advice.

Lawrence James, who I met many years ago and whose own book *The Iron Duke* was one I read ages before I had any idea that I might be writing about Murray, who was very kind in offering me all kinds of assistance as I neared the more serious stage in the road towards publication.

Randall Nicol, who introduced me to Helion, following the great support and encouragement he had received when writing his hugely impressive two-volume book about the Scots Guards in the First World War *Till the Trumpet Sounds Again*.

The staff of the various libraries I visited on numerous occasions, including Karen Robson at the Hartley Library who nudged me back onto the straight and narrow when my enthusiasm threatened to sully necessary scholastic integrity. Those at the National Library of Scotland, in particular Alison Metcalfe who gave her time so readily to reconcile Ward's quoted references with their current system and was ready with help and guidance in large measure.

Willie Mahon, whose excellent book *Waterloo Messenger* got to the finishing line a few months before mine, with whom I shared some heartfelt emails, bits of which are probably best kept from view, but allowed us both to share our bewilderment of the system that we, as new writers, had stumbled into.

Maria and Margarita Catarino who, generously and trustingly, within twenty minutes of an unexpected phone call, laid on a guided tour of Quinta das Longas for me and my wife Jennifer, two total strangers, who had enquired about the house while lunching at a local restaurant.

Andrew Bamford, my commissioning editor at Helion, whose email responses to my ongoing issues were amazingly rapid, extraordinarily detailed, and always immensely helpful and to the point. His patience was, I am sure, often tested, my being such a novice, but his encouragement throughout has been invaluable.

Not forgetting my three daughters Caroline, Louisa, and Georgina who have, as they enjoy pointing out, celebrated most of the more important moments in their lives under the gaze of those blue eyes of Murray's and who have patiently sat through so many kitchen suppers where I have bubbled with enthusiasm over the latest gem unearthed that afternoon in the library. In Caroline's case she also provided invaluable feedback as she diligently read her way through some early drafts.

Lastly, and if somewhat traditionally then no less heartfelt for that, Jennifer, who has lived through the inevitable moments of grumpiness and doubt, who has remained positive throughout, and somehow understood the right moments to climb two flights of stairs with coffee and something from the biscuit tin. That was home service. Overseas duty comprised navigation and engaging the locals in such a manner that doors magically opened to allow us a privileged view of Murray's lifestyle in Spain and Portugal, so beautifully described in his many letters home.

John Harding-Edgar
April 2018

1

1772-1790 – Ochtertyre – Early Life

George Murray was born at Ochtertyre, near Crieff in Perthshire, on 6 February 1772. Ochtertyre was the estate that had been in the Murray family since about 1450 when David Murray, a son of the Earl of Tullibardine, had taken it on lease from the Crown. Full ownership was soon acquired, and the estate passed down through the generations, eldest son to eldest son, for more than 300 years, gradually increasing in size. So the family was, at the time of Murray's birth, a well-established, landowning one, with the inevitable influential connections throughout Scotland, and particularly Perthshire. Murray would in his turn benefit, certainly in the early days of his military career, from these family networks.

He was educated at the High School of Edinburgh between 1781 and 1785, then regarded as the best school in Scotland. Not only the best school but surely the best dressed; the uniform included brown corduroy breeches worn with a coat and waistcoat of the most vivid colours; bright blue, grass green, or scarlet. Blue stockings in summer; white for special occasions. Clumsy shoes with brass or copper buckles completed the image of young men being groomed for important roles in society. Murray and his elder brother Patrick shared a tutor in James Finlayson, later to become Moderator of the General Assembly. In 1785 Murray started at Edinburgh University, reading Lit. Hum. (Literae Humaniores, or Classics), before spending a short time in Geneva perfecting his French 'which he mastered so thoroughly that for the rest of his life he could turn it on and off like a tap, whether writing or speaking'.[1] This was later to prove of immense value in his Army career, when he was involved in a good deal of diplomatic activity, and correspondence with European counterparts.

His father, Sir William Murray, the 5th Baronet of Ochtertyre, having inherited the estate from his own father in 1764, had, in 1770, married Lady Augusta Mackenzie, youngest daughter of the 3rd Earl of Cromarty. Murray's elder brother Patrick, born in 1771, was to become the 6th Baronet in succession to their father. Perhaps unusually for an eldest son and laird, Patrick went on to become an advocate, King's Remembrancer, and later Baron, in the Court of Exchequer, as well as a Member of Parliament for the City of Edinburgh, and held an important political office in London as Secretary to the Commissioners for the Affairs

1 Ward, S.G.P., 'General Sir George Murray', *Journal of the Society for Army Historical Research*, Vol LVIII, No 236. (Winter 1980), p.192.

of India (later to become the India Board of Control). He was very closely involved in the improvement of the public roads all over the country, and especially his native Perthshire. A seemingly gifted lawyer, he also showed a practical interest in both agriculture and landscape gardening, which he employed in the redesign and planting of the estate during his tenure. Murray and his brother remained very close for the rest of their lives, although events prevented them from seeing very much of each other, at least until both were engaged in political life in London. As was so often the case in Ochtertyre history, the financial nous lay elsewhere than with the eldest son, in this case clearly with the younger brother.

George's mother Augusta came to Ochtertyre from an interesting background, having been born in the Tower of London in 1747, where her father the Earl of Cromarty, and her brother, were both imprisoned on charges of treason, following the Jacobite defeat at Culloden a year earlier. Cromarty and two other Jacobite leaders, Lords Balmerino and Kilmarnock, had all been condemned to death. Lady Cromarty, heavily pregnant with Augusta, had begged the King in person, whilst on his way to prayers, to spare her husband's life. A pardon, on condition that Cromarty never return to Scotland, and indeed remain south of the Trent, was granted. Augusta's brother's life was also spared. He later became Lord McLeod and played a key part at the start of Murray's military career. Balmerino and Kilmarnock were not so fortunate and died on the scaffold. Augusta is always depicted as wearing a veil over the back of her head. This was to hide a vivid birthmark which ran across her neck precisely where the axe would have fallen on her father's, complete with red blotches of 'blood' dripping from it.[2]

Augusta's letters, perhaps understandably given the family's treatment following Culloden, paint a picture of a somewhat sad, perhaps needy, individual. Even in her teens she was bemoaning what had become of the family position and the downsizing that must have been inevitable after the wholesale confiscation that followed the failure of the Jacobite adventure. It would indeed have been a massive shock for such a pre-eminent family, and many Mackenzies were forced to emigrate. Augusta penned the lament:

> Doomed to a prison ere I showed my head
> My father living, yet my father dead
> Dead to his titles, fortune, fame
> And nought remains but slavery and shame

Soon after Murray's birth his father wrote to Lady Arniston, first wife of Henry Dundas, Viscount Melville (Dundas's second wife, following his divorce of his first for adultery, was Lady Jane Hope, sister of Lady Mary Hope who married Patrick.)

> It is pretty singular that one hour should produce both a young George and a young Anthony, considering the connection. Gusty has for these three days past been with

2 Sir William Fraser, *The Earls of Cromartie* (Edinburgh: Tanner Ritchie, 1876), p.231, and *Chambers's Edinburgh Journal* March 18 1832, p 56.

> Powley's leave in the Dining Room and is in perfect health. The young man is also well as could be wished or expected.[3]

The Anthony referred to was Anthony Murray of Dollerie, the home of cousins who lived close by, the other side of Crieff. George and Anthony were, not surprisingly, to remain close in later life.

There is nothing to suggest, at least from the family papers, that his parents' marriage during Murray's formative years was anything other than happy. Further children were born, Helen in 1773, Isabella in 1775 and Augusta in 1777. Helen died in 1783. Two sons were born and died in infancy, in 1779 and 1781. The house where Murray was born was not the current Ochtertyre House but a smaller, and much older, house further up the hill. The old Ochtertyre comprised a parlour, drawing room, schoolroom, housekeeper's room, nine bedrooms, two servants rooms (five beds), three garrets, laundry, kitchen, bottle cellar, and pantry. So not that small, but perhaps not suited to stylish entertaining. During the previous century the family had spent the majority of their time at Fowlis Easter, an estate comprising a castle and an entire parish, with productive farms, just outside Dundee. It had been bought by Sir William, the first Baronet, Murray's three-greats grandfather, in 1667. The family had split their lives between Fowlis and Ochtertyre, the former being the larger of the two houses, using Ochtertyre mainly for sporting purposes.

It is reasonable to assume that when Murray's father inherited in 1764, he made the decision, as so many did at the time, to upgrade the family accommodation to something more comfortable than less peaceful times had permitted. He chose to build a new house at Ochtertyre rather than Fowlis, perhaps because he simply preferred its situation, providing as it did everything a well to do Perthshire family might feel commensurate with their status. It offered a mix of productive farmland, especially following a number of recent purchases nearby, as well as good sport in the hills and lochs behind, all in a magnificent setting. It could be also that William regarded Ochtertyre, correctly, as the true seat of the Murrays.

Certainly all William's children were born at Ochtertyre, so it does look as though a decision had been made, as soon as William inherited, to develop Ochtertyre into the main residence. Building work on the new house, the one that stands proudly overlooking the loch on the road from Crieff to Comrie, commenced in 1784, so Patrick and George would have spent their teenage years watching the Georgian mansion gradually take shape.

From early childhood there seems to have been something quite engaging about Murray. He was described as

> rather delicate, his figure was tall, his countenance handsome and expressive. George had a lively sense of the ridiculous. He did not possess great talent for general conversation but his society was most agreeable and he would relate any anecdote with great effect and when drawn out by circumstances to tell of incidents in which he had taken part, he did so in a most graphic manner, carefully avoiding anything like exaggeration or bringing himself forward.[4]

3 Sir William Murray to Lady Arniston, Ochtertyre, 21 February 1772, Papers of Bonar Mackenzie, National Archives of Scotland GD 235/9/12.

4 Murray Gartshore Papers, Murray Papers, MS 21112.

Ochtertyre House, Near Crieff, Perthshire. (Author's photo)

The two brothers were to spend the year 1789 to 1790 travelling through the Low Countries and studying at Geneva, and Patrick kept a record of their daily progress through Holland.[5] On 5 June 1789, the pair, together with a couple of friends, set off on the London to Harwich stagecoach. On boarding their ship they

> had the honour of a visit from the customs house officers who came to see that we had nothing in our trunks which was prohibited to be carried out of the country.
>
> Upon putting a half a guinea into their hands they took our word that our trunks contained nothing but wearing apparel, and then took their leave with wishing us a pleasant voyage and making several low bows for their bribe.[6]

The crossing was stormy and all suffered from dreadful seasickness, apart from Murray. Given the amount of time that he would be spending on board ships over the next few years, good sea legs were a blessing.

They toured most of the Netherlands and spent some time in The Hague, taking the precaution of wearing orange cockades in their hats to avoid insult or injury as a result of the recent revolution in the country, in support of France's own revolution, before heading for Geneva to concentrate on developing their French.

5 Journal of Sir Patrick on Tour of France and Switzerland 1789, Murray Papers, MS 21105.
6 Journal of Sir Patrick on Tour of France and Switzerland 1789, p.2, Murray Papers, MS 21105.

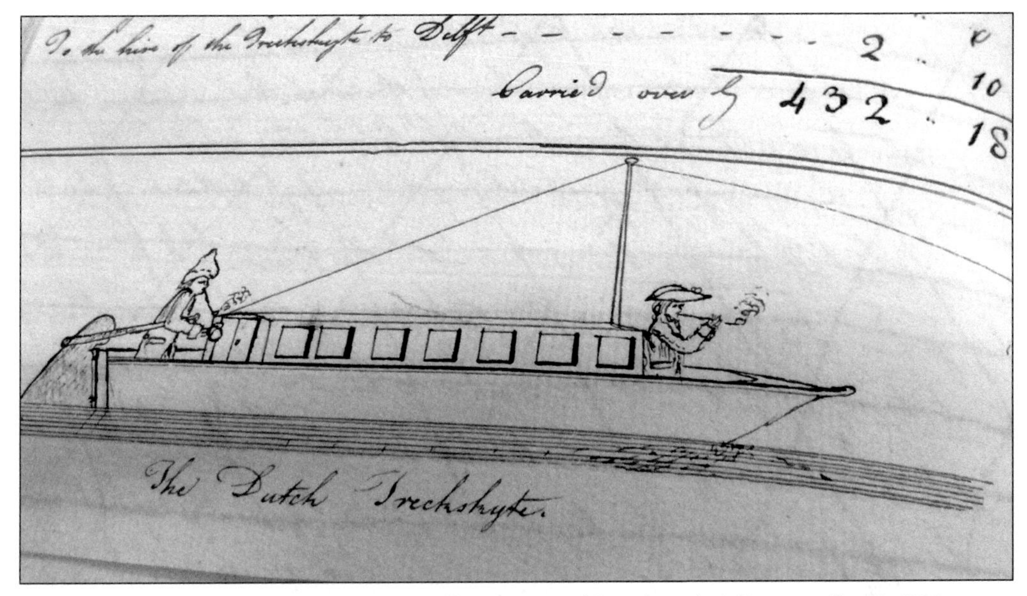

Sketch of typical Dutch transport hired by Murray and Patrick on their European Tour in 1789, presumably by either Patrick or George, in Patrick's Journal. (Author's photo from Murray Papers in The National Library of Scotland)

On leaving a dangerous France, then in revolutionary turmoil, to set sail back to England on 11 June 1790, the pair again persuaded the customs officer to let them pass without searching their trunks in exchange for a small bribe. So the year travelling and studying on the Continent ended very much as it had it had begun, but by this time Murray was completely fluent in French. Patrick's journal, including some deprecating comments on the appearance and dress of the women the two brothers came across on the way, is exactly as one might expect from a young man enjoying a year away from home, and the constraints of Perthshire society.

Life at Ochtertyre was seemingly respectable and comfortable, and Robert Burns, staying with the family in October 1787, wrote at the time: 'Lady Augusta is a most engaging woman, and very happy in her family… a fine looking woman in the maturity of her charms'.[7] However, things went badly awry with the arrival at Ochtertyre in 1790 of Robert Harrup, a doctor, originally from Dumfries and latterly Edinburgh, where it seems he had, a year earlier, lost his wife. He had taken up a position as the local doctor in Crieff. He moved into Ochtertyre and became very much a household fixture, clearly falling for the charms that Burns had described. The result was the birth, in June 1791, to Augusta, of an illegitimate son, William. Even at that point, when the identity of the father must surely have been evident to all and especially, one assumes, Sir William, no action was taken to name and shame Harrup. The family having very recently, indeed in the midst of the affair, moved into the new Ochtertyre House, the servants, as is clear from their evidence at the ensuing

7 Robert Burns, *The Life and Work of Robert Burns* (Edinburgh: W&R Chambers, 1896), Vol II, p.148.

divorce proceedings, knew full well what was going on. They had witnessed all sorts of inappropriate behaviour at both the old and new houses with regular coming and going from Augusta's bedroom. Yet it was not until September that a halt was called, when Harrup, on being discovered in Augusta's room in the early hours of the morning, was unceremoniously thrown out of the house.

It was Patrick who was tasked that night with hammering on his mother's bedroom door, and again it was Patrick who was sent by his father after the divorce to try and persuade Augusta to give up the child and return him to live at Ochtertyre. This attempt failed and it took legal proceedings to achieve Sir William's determination to be reunited with the young William. William was brought up at Ochtertyre as one of the family and went on to serve with some success in India with the East India Company. He died there, unmarried, but seemingly well-off, in 1831.

During the period of the affair there is no mention in any papers or letters of Murray. He had by then started his military career. But when it came to the time where Sir William was seeking advice from family and friends, and outlining his reasoning for trying to get young William back, it is interesting that he ensured that both Patrick and his younger brother were kept in the loop by copying correspondence to them both.

The effect on Murray of all this is impossible to gauge. There does not seem to be any reference to his communicating with his mother following the divorce. She lived, after marrying Harrup, for a while at Chobham in Surrey, and perhaps Murray visited her from time to time when back in London on leave, or between postings. Any effect would have been more marked on Murray's younger sisters, Isabella and Augusta who were 16 and 14 at the time of the divorce. Arrangements needed to be made to complete their education.

Lady Augusta's brother, John, after being forced into exile following his narrow escape from execution alongside his father, had a distinguished military career in Sweden where he was an aide de camp to the King of Sweden, with the title of Count Cromartie, and awarded the Order of the Sword. He had, on his death, left vacant a tenement flat, at the top of Leith Walk in Edinburgh. Following the divorce it became the property of Sir William, even though it had been left to Augusta to enjoy in her lifetime. Conveniently too, Sir William's sister, Joanna Churchill, had quite recently been widowed. Sir William jumped at the chance to bring these two strands together and asked Joanna if she would take responsibility for the completion of the girls' education and all important introduction to Edinburgh Society. Sir William would ensure there was no cost to Joanna. The arrangement brought Joanna, who was always close to Murray, back into the family circle, and relieved Sir William of the awkward task of overseeing the transition of his two teenage girls to adulthood and domestic responsibility.

Augusta and Isabella were thus destined to become young ladies in Edinburgh under the watchful eye of their aunt, so the arrangement suited all. At the time, the Edinburgh social scene was recognizably stratified: A hostess of the time lists the participants as (a) The fashionable set, headed by Lady Grey of Kinfauns (b) within or beyond this was an exclusive set; the Macleods of Macleod, Cumming-Gordons, Shaw Stewarts, Murrays of Ochtertyre etc (c) Card playing set (d) Quiet country gentlemen set (e) Literary set (f) Clever set (g) Law set, (h) strangers and inferiors.[8] The significant number of letters to both his sisters in

8 Ward Notes, Vol I, citing Mrs Smith's Memoire, p.282.

Edinburgh from Murray during his early military career reinforces a feeling of real closeness among the siblings.

Murray's father had inherited an estate in relatively good shape despite the price paid by the family to secure the release of Sir William, 3rd Baronet, Murray's great grandfather, who had fought for the Jacobites at Sheriffmuir in 1715. Captured and imprisoned at Edinburgh and Carlisle Castles, he was fortunate to escape execution, but the estate was burdened with the cost of his pardon and freedom amounting to £25,000. Murray's grandfather Patrick, the Hanoverian 4th Baronet, was captured at the battle of Prestonpans, together with his entire company of Militia, whilst guarding General Cope's baggage train. His penalty was less costly: house arrest at Ochtertyre until released on Cumberland's march north to the decisive battle at Culloden. The estate's finances having to some extent recovered by the time of Murray's father's succession, it seems on the face of it to have been a time of relative prosperity, but there are references in papers and correspondence that contradict this comfortable image, and arrangements with creditors crop up with some regularity.

With concern for his seeming lack of a robust constitution, Murray's parents had been seeking a suitable profession for him which would not place him under too much physical stress, so a military career might not have been their first choice. However, it being entirely normal for the younger son of such a family to look to the Army, Murray was no exception, and he was soon taking the first steps to finding a suitable regiment. Even by the standards of the time he was to subject himself to years of rough military living, on active service for very long periods in difficult conditions, on the Continent, in Egypt and the Mediterranean, Ireland, the West Indies and Canada. He did suffer from at least two major bouts of sickness during his army career, and there are many references to recurring bouts of illness in the Peninsula, but perhaps this was no more than might be expected. He steered clear of major injury, being shot in the leg once, and falling from his horse a few times with resulting broken and dislocated bones, a record which placed him among the fortunate ones.

The family had a long history of military service. Murray's father served in the Coldstream Guards. His Hanoverian paternal grandfather held a commission in Lord Sempill's Highland Regiment of Foot and raised a regiment of militia. His Jacobite paternal great grandfather had narrowly escaped execution following Sheriffmuir. A cousin, Lord George Murray, had famously, and controversially, commanded the Young Pretender's army in the '45 uprising. On his maternal side the Jacobite loyalties could not have been stronger. Earlier ancestors had fought and died in the battles of Flodden and Pinkie. By Murray's time the family's loyalties had gradually shifted, as indeed many had, to support, and benefit from, an established Hanoverian monarchy.

2

1790-1797 – The Young Officer

By the time Murray sought his first commission, continuous military conflict and civil unrest had ebbed and flowed around Europe for generations, with the French Revolution, continuous discontent in Ireland, and the American War of Independence all setting alarm bells ringing in Britain. It was inevitable that a newly commissioned young officer would soon be experiencing serious fighting somewhere abroad, at a time when military successes were rare, and Britain's army poorly resourced. The American experience had exposed how ill equipped the British state was to deal with the growing military, political and financial complexity of major conflict. The embarrassing end to the war had left Britain friendless and isolated. France, Spain, and Holland had all fought against her in the later stages of the war; defeat meant she had lost the respect of Europe's most powerful courts. A period of financial and military consolidation was necessary before Britain could again look any power in Europe in the face. It was war in the Netherlands that would see Britain recommence its military expeditions. French influence was expanding there. The Dutch United Provinces were vital to Britain's interests. The ports along the Dutch coast had to be kept out of hostile French hands to avoid disturbance of trade, and to deny the French bases for any invasion.

France had accumulated vast debts in supporting the American War of Independence and was almost bankrupt. She had no mutual supporting interests between monarchy, aristocracy, and people as had been the case in Britain since the civil war a hundred years earlier. The privilege of the Catholic Church and the Royal Family was deeply resented. The French middle classes were demanding change, and Revolution would soon engulf the nation.

Initially the tumultuous events in France were greeted with some enthusiasm in England. There was a realistic hope that France would be too preoccupied internally to follow an aggressive programme in Europe. Britain went about business as usual. The countries of Europe meanwhile continued with forming alliances and seeking territorial expansion. Britain soon became courted as an ally by most. Prime Minister Pitt saw this as an opportunity to broker peace in Europe. But it was to prove impossible given the numbers of diverging interests.

Events in France were intruding more and more into the British psyche and in July 1791 five days of riots erupted in Birmingham. A nervous establishment became increasingly anxious. Pitt and his ministers were still reluctant to intervene in French affairs. By the spring of 1792 the British economy was in a healthy state and debt reduction over the next 15 years, not military conflict, was a stated priority. How wrong Prime Minister Pitt was when he said: 'unquestionably there never was a time in the history of this country, when, from the situation of Europe, we might more reasonably expect fifteen years of peace, than we may at the present moment'.[1] Europe was in fact on the brink of the greatest conflict it had ever known. However at that point the policy was that Britain would only enter a war if its vital national interests were threatened directly, and at that moment no country seemed likely to threaten them.

The nations of Europe, or perhaps more accurately their monarchies and aristocracies, looked on with increasing horror at events in France. War was declared by France against Austria and Prussia and was unexpectedly successful. Most of the early French military actions had been defensive but there were growing signs of aggressive movements, notably towards Spain. Revolutionary France was in the grip of the mob. The Whig Opposition disputed that there was any cause for alarm. The internal safety of the country could be managed, and there was little appetite for making war against France. Indeed congratulatory messages were sent from some of the Whig Clubs in London to Paris. But the government pushed forward with military preparations and stated an intention to prevent the import of corn, arms, or ammunition into France.

It was at the start of this alarming period that Murray obtained, in March 1789, just before setting out for Geneva, a commission in the 71st Highland Regiment of Foot (Lord Macleod's Highlanders). Murray's maternal uncle had founded the regiment on his return from exile after service in Sweden, the cost of his reprieve from the death sentence in the Tower. Murray moved to 34th Foot soon after, as his constitution was considered too delicate for service in India where the 71st was stationed, before transferring to the 3rd Foot Guards (later to become the Scots Guards), a year later. Until the tradition was abolished towards the end of the 19th century, just about the only way to become an officer in a 'good' regiment was by purchasing a commission. The price varied according to the level of social prestige attached to a given regiment. Commissions in the Guards were the most expensive. As an officer progressed in seniority he would generally be required to pay the difference between the current rank and the more senior rank. On leaving the army the commission could be sold to an incoming officer in the same regiment.

In Murray's case he would have had to pay £900 for his Guards commission, more than twice that of a commission in a 'standard' regiment of foot.[2] He would also have paid a fee for the King to sign his commission, and had to pay for his own uniform. So starting out in the Guards would have set him back the best part of £1,000 (perhaps around £60,000 in 2018 money).[3] As an Ensign he would be paid £106 per annum. After other deductions for rations and other living, dining, and incidental expenses the new officer would only see about 5 pence a day. Sir John Moore reckoned that a junior officer could not be expected to live on his pay and that he would need an outside income of about £100 per year.[4] This would

1 William Hague, *Pitt the Younger* (London: Harper Collins, 2004), p.36.
2 Robert Burnham, and Ron McGuigan, *The British Army Against Napoleon* (Barnsley: Frontline Books, 2010), p 152.
3 Estimates of today's value of an historical sum of money are notoriously divergent and depend on various bases of calculation, all valid in their own way but often of limited application. I have taken the National Archives currency calculator (which does not go beyond 2005) as my guide. Between 1790 and 1830 the approximate multiples on that scale are between 60 and 50, which are likely to be at the lowest end of possible answers.
4 Burnham & McGuigan, *British Army*, p 150.

generally be from his father, or perhaps from an elder brother who had inherited the family estate, and in Murray's case we do see a good deal of financial correspondence between the two brothers, so it is certain that the family would have been funding Murray in the early part of his career. However much the family might have been worried about Murray becoming a young officer at such a threatening time, from Murray's own perspective it was a time when promotion would, in all likelihood, be rapid, as the army expanded and made ready for inevitable conflict.

France declared war on Britain and the United Provinces on 1 February 1793, and began an invasion of the Netherlands. Ministers had been criticised for having delayed too long in sending troops to the Low Countries, but now they were forced to act. The plan was to land forces, push the French back into France, and reinstall the French monarchy. The number of troops in a state of combat readiness was very small, fewer than 14,000 men in Britain, with about twice that number in India and the West Indies. Pitt and Henry Dundas, the Secretary of State for War, decided to send across the Channel what few reserves they had, including a detachment from the Brigade of Guards.

The Guards, with the young Ensign Murray – who had until then been based in London with his regiment – among them, sailed on 25 February 1793 to link up with Hanoverian troops, all under the command of the Duke of York, who was sorely lacking in military experience. A treaty with the Russians was hastily arranged. Alliances were also formed with Austria, Prussia, Spain, Holland, and Portugal. Denmark, Sweden, and Switzerland refused to join. The advancing French army had assembled at Antwerp, entered the Dutch territories and taken Breda. Command of the French army was given to General Dampierre who lost no time in launching more attacks from his fortified camp at Famars in Northern France. The French were to be defeated by the Austrians twice in the course of March, removing the immediate threat to Holland, but Britain was now committed.

On 8 May there was a bitter engagement at St Amand with heavy losses for both the allies and the French. The British troops under the Duke of York played a vital role with particular mention of the Guards' bravery. After the battle Colonel Alexander Campbell of Monzie, (the next door estate to Ochtertyre) a family friend and fellow Guards officer, added a postscript to a letter that Murray was about to send to his father. It read simply: 'George will do'.[5]

The French camp at Famars, which guarded Valenciennes, was soon afterwards captured by the allies and the siege of Valenciennes followed, under the command of the Duke of York. It was during this siege that we have the first reports of Murray in action. Towards the conclusion of the siege Murray was in the trenches during a night attack. When dawn broke he noticed that two soldiers from his regiment were stranded, under the walls, badly wounded. Even had they been able, any attempt by them to regain their lines would have attracted enemy fire. They would never make it. A rescue attempt would be equally risky. Murray took it on himself to move rapidly across a ditch to his right, and climbed the steps of the counterscarp (the side of a defensive ditch) to the traverse, behind which the two wounded men were lying. He called on support, ordering men to come forward by the same route. Together Murray and two guardsmen extracted the wounded men under intense

5 Murray Gartshore Papers, Murray Papers, MS 21112.

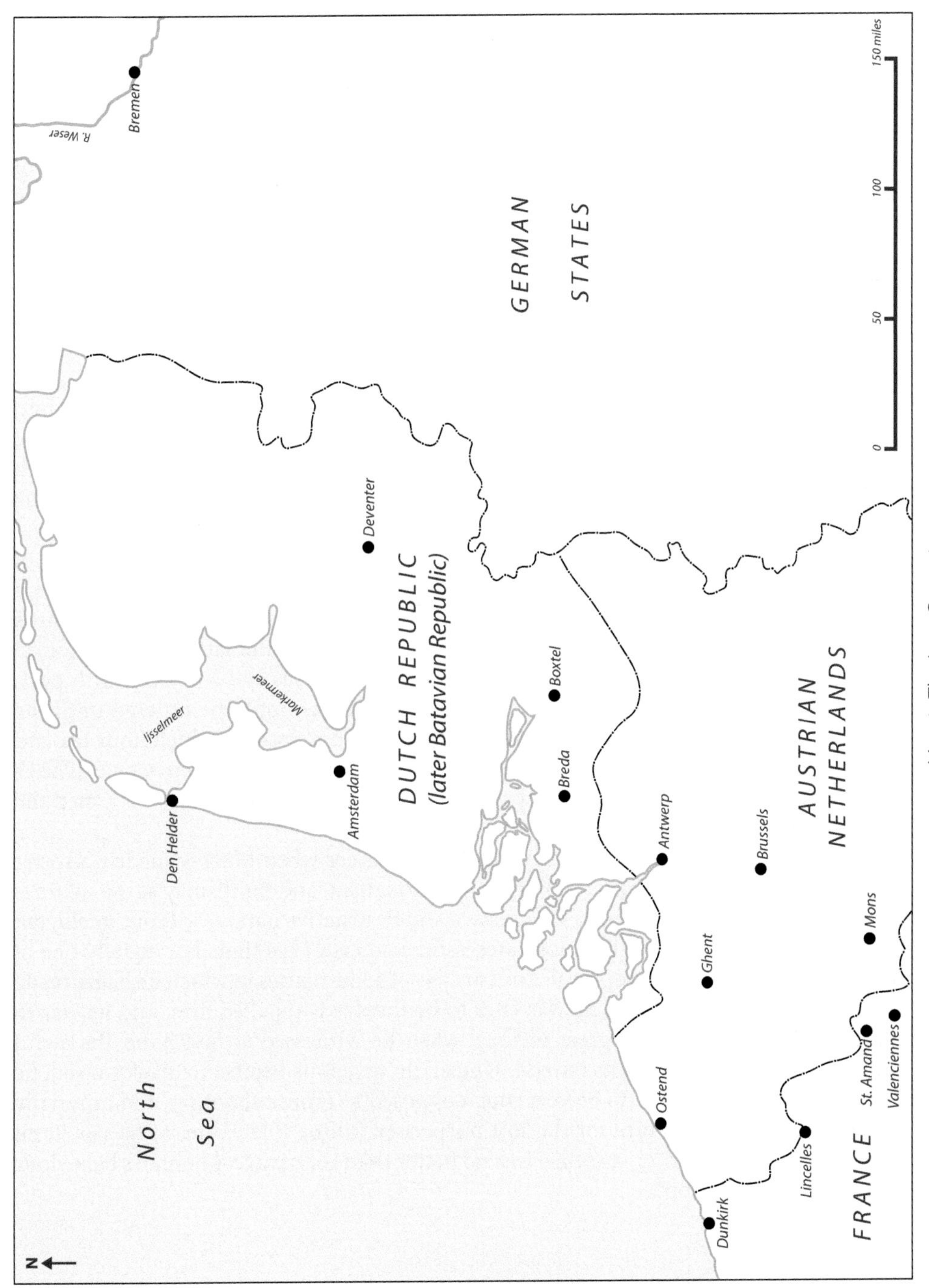

Map 1 The Low Countries.

enemy fire, and delivered them to the regimental surgeon for treatment. The story goes that he gave the two soldiers who had helped in the rescue a dollar each.

On 21 July Valenciennes surrendered to the Duke of York, who took possession of it in the name of the Emperor of Germany. Murray had taken part in all the operations at St Amand, Famars, and Valenciennes, and was about to experience more action.

The Duke turned his attention to Dunkirk, in an attempt to restore it to the British Empire. The French occupied a strongly defended and elevated position in front of the village of Lincelles. Murray's battalion advanced, bayonets fixed, under heavy fire and drove the enemy though the village. An attempted counterattack was defeated. But this early success could not be built on and all efforts to capture Dunkirk failed.

In France itself the capture of Marseilles and Lyons by Republican troops was marked by appalling violence, with the massacre at Lyons surpassing all the horrors of the Revolution thus far. On 26 October 1793 Marie Antoinette was executed, nine months after her husband, Louis XVI. Blood flowed all over the country.

At the end of March 1794, a French army, numbering 200,000 men, marched into Flanders but were defeated, despite more jealousies resurfacing amongst the allies. More actions followed over the course of the next month or so, with the allies proving a much better fighting force than had been the case the previous year. Sustaining heavy losses, the French retreated to Cambrai.

On his promotion to captain, Murray was recalled to London, where, doing his share of guard duty at St James's Palace, he would have found the ceremonial duties comfortable if tedious. The previous year the King had ordered a mess to be established for the Guards regiments at the palace, which provided breakfast and dinner, the latter catering for 13 officers punctually at 7 o'clock, consisting of two regular courses and a dessert, with port, sherry, madeira, wines, ale, porter, and table beer. Claret was not to be ordered until the cloth was removed nor called for, on any account, after ten o'clock, at which hour tea and coffee was served.[6] The officers were expected to be again with their respective guards at 11 o'clock, no doubt fully alert. Such luxury was short lived as Murray quickly re-joined the regiment in the Low Countries.

There are numerous examples in the course of his career when Murray made no secret of his strong dislike of bloodshed and jingoistic nationalism, and his dismay at the willingness of his fellow man to be led by his aggressive and destructive nature, without intelligent reflection. He was to be one of the most successful soldiers of his time, but equally one of the most thoughtful and philosophical. The carnage of some battles in which he had already seen action, and others in which he was later to be involved, appalled him, and he was to take issue with the expression 'great victory' when he witnessed at first hand the awful human suffering occasioned in its pursuit. Unusually, given his Perthshire background, he also seems, at this age at least, to be very much opposed to grouse shooting, and especially the practice of protecting a bird for the sole purpose of killing it later, for, as he saw it, no good reason. Grouse shooting, it seems, was no better than the savagery of man's behaviour on the battlefields of Europe.

6 F. Maurice, *History of the Scots Guards from the Creation of the Regiment to the Great War*, (London: Chatto & Windus, 1934), Vol.I, p 234.

A letter home, to a Reverend Taylor, the new local minister, gives us an idea of how aware Murray was, even at the young age of 22, of social and political matters facing Britain, and the rise of the Reformers at the time, and his clear, but not necessarily standard, Tory leanings:

> I hope you will be able by your Discourses to eradicate those false notions respecting liberty which we find it impossible to overcome by force of arms. It will do honour to the good sense of our countrymen if they can be persuaded by the influence of sound reasoning of the absurdity and wickedness of the projects proposed by mad or interested Reformers…
>
> This being the 12th August I cannot but reflect upon your employment in the north of Scotland and in doing so I must consider with shame and regret the general occupation of a being of so exalted a nature as Man. There we see him destroying his own species and employing to that end all the faculties with which he has been endowed by nature.
>
> With you he appears employing that same means against a harmless race of animals, for whose destruction he does not advance the plea of necessity, not even that of convenience, but whom he openly declares he has protected from their enemies to gratify the savage pleasure of depriving them with his own hands of that existence, the loss of which in himself, he so much dreads, and the enjoyment of which he holds in such high estimation.[7]

The allies and the French continued to engage each other during the coming months with the French tasting victory again. Some of the French success during this period can be attributed to their superiority in numbers, but also the fact that many of the local inhabitants in the Low Countries supported the Revolutionary ideal. The French recruited no fewer than 100,000 supporters and tried to cross the Scheldt to lay siege to the town of Tournai. The allies assembled a large force to face the French at Charleroi, in an attempt to stem the flow of French success. The battle ended in defeat for the allies; a decisive moment, costing 10,000 men. The loss of the Netherlands was now inevitable. Only about half the original allied army of 200,000 remained as a fighting force. The French added to their success by taking Ypres and Bruges. The Duke of York abandoned his position at Oudenarde and retired to Antwerp.

A force was sent to Ostend, but its commander, Lord Moira, on hearing the perilous situation the Duke was in, marched instead to Antwerp. Mons and Brussels fell to the French. Antwerp was the next to fall, on 23 July. The British troops were withdrawn to the borders of the United Provinces and all hopes rested on the success of defensive measures. William, Prince of Orange, prepared to defend Breda and the British took up a position nearby in support. But the French continued to drive forward and the British and Austrian forces were forced to resume their retreat. At Boxtel Murray's 3rd Guards were acting as rearguard when they were forced to retire through the ranks of the 33rd, at that moment under the command of Lieutenant Colonel the Hon. Arthur Wesley (the Wellesley spelling would not

7 Murray to Rev. Taylor, Camp near Breda, 12 August 1794, Murray Papers, ADV MS 46.1.1.

be adopted until 1798), the first recorded instance of Murray and his future commander and friend fighting together.

The French, emboldened by their success, believed they could overwhelm the Netherlands and attacked ports all along the coast. Allied resistance was solid. Nevertheless the French continued to advance steadily and threatened Ostend, but the arrival there of an English fleet carrying reinforcements at least delayed the moment when the Low Countries would fall. The French armies at this time consisted of more than 500,000 men, increasingly swelled by local recruitment. The Dutch eventually capitulated and Amsterdam fell to Revolutionaries sympathetic to the French. The Prince of Orange fled to England, and Dutch Revolutionaries proclaimed the Batavian Republic.

The rigours of the severe winter of 1794-1795 were to test the allied armies to the limit. The troops did all that could be expected from them in the situation in which they were placed. Hopelessly outnumbered, having lost all their stores, they retreated during the exceptionally cold winter. The sick were removed in open wagons, exposed to the intense severity of the weather, to drifting snows, and heavy falls of sleet and rain. The death rate was predictably high. The British army only escaped complete destruction during its retreat from Holland by the masterly manoeuvres of Lieutenant General Sir Ralph Abercromby, who was second-in-command, and Major General David Dundas.

The army reached Deventer on 27 January 1795, but was unable to maintain its position, being relentlessly pursued by a well-equipped French force, upwards of fifty thousand strong. It continued its retreat, alternately fighting and marching, till the end of March, when the main body, now reduced to one-half, reached Bremen, where they were embarked for England. Murray, with the 3rd Guards, had experienced and survived a two year long campaign and retreat which by any standards ranks as one of the most testing in British military history. He was to experience something very similar with Moore in the retreat to Corunna, at the start of the Peninsular War.

The British Army as it then was, part of a fragmented alliance, lacking cohesion and a proper strategy, was no match for the flexibility and efficiency of its French counterpart. York's army had lost more than 20,000 men in the two years of fighting. The size and ability of the French forces had been consistently underestimated. Murray had certainly seen plenty of action, little of it particularly encouraging to a young soldier, though no doubt he had learnt some very important lessons, and had already gained promotion.

The campaign in the Low Countries served to highlight the need for a dramatic reorganisation of the British Army and this would be carried out very successfully, and perhaps surprisingly, by the Duke of York, who was shortly to be removed from active service. The politicians saw him as a weak commander in the field, but there is no doubt that he did possess considerable organisational skills. The army in the coming Peninsular War was a very different organisation, and far better commanded, than that which had met with such little success in the preceding twenty years or so. The Duke would come to hold Murray in very high regard as an effective and resourceful officer, and in return Murray admired the Duke's contribution to the Army, and he was later to be responsible for persuading the government to erect the statue of him in London's Waterloo Place following his death.

Soon after his return from Bremen, Murray was appointed aide de camp to Alexander Campbell, now a major general, who had command of a brigade assembled at Southampton under the Earl of Moira. In the summer of 1795, this brigade embarked on an abortive expedition to Quiberon Bay, in Brittany. Its aim, as with the unsuccessful campaign in the Low Countries, was to raise the whole of western France in revolt, bring an end to the French Revolution, and restore the French Monarchy.

Three thousand French Royalists supplemented by a number of French Republican prisoners from English custody, who were trusted to have seen the error of their ways, were transported by British ships and successfully put ashore at Quiberon. The landings were a failure, according to some reports largely as result of the Republican ex-prisoners re-joining the Revolutionary cause. The invasion force was finally repulsed on 21 July, dealing a disastrous blow to the Royalists. Only a few managed to make it back to the safety of the British fleet. Hundreds were summarily executed, matched by revenge executions of Republican prisoners.

Britain would, after some more poorly executed efforts to reverse the tide of Republicanism in France, then turn its main efforts against the French to military operations in the West Indies, where recently Guadeloupe and St Lucia had fallen to French forces and local insurrection. So, a few months after the Quiberon Expedition Murray, again as aide de camp to Major General Campbell, was on board the expedition to the West Indies under Abercromby, building on his reputation in the Low Countries, and with whom Murray was to work very closely until Abercromby's death in Egypt during the Battle of Alexandria in 1801. The view of the politicians was that the French colonies in the West Indies were an easier target than the French armies in Europe. Pitt wrote to Lord Chatham, his elder brother, who had recently been dismissed from his post as First Lord of the Admiralty: 'I incline to think that our plan must now be changed and that the only great part must be in the West Indies, where I trust enough may yet be gained to counterbalance the French successes in Europe'.[8]

No fewer than 236 vessels conveyed Abercromby's 18,000 troops.[9] Pitt and Dundas, who travelled to Portsmouth to wave them off, believed that if success could be achieved in the West Indies, the resulting interference with trade, when coupled with the dire food shortages that were being suffered in France, might lead to an honourable peace. This hope was supported by the fact that there was still a very unstable internal situation in France. Revolutionary crowds had defeated frequent attempts at control by the succession of French governments. The latest government was much more aggressive in its tactics and authorised the use of grapeshot at close range against protestors. A young artillery officer who was prepared to order his men to carry this out was a Corsican called Napoleon Buonaparte.

Abercromby's expedition sailed on 25 October 1795, was hit by appalling weather in the Channel, and forced back to port. Five ships were wrecked on Chesil Bank with the loss of 250 lives. The next attempt took a month to clear the Channel, then for several weeks the fleet hit more violent storms in the Bay of Biscay and was scattered, with ships forced to return again to Portsmouth on 29 January. Seventy-eight made it to Barbados. The remainder of the fleet again put to sea on 14 February, and this time made landfall on Barbados between 14 March and 21 April 1796.

A list of necessaries written into the front of one of Murray's notebooks at the time illustrates the pretty basic level of creature comfort that a young officer enjoyed:

8 Hague, *Pitt the Younger*, p.371.
9 R. Knight, *Britain Against Napoleon* (London: Penguin Books, 2013), p 74.

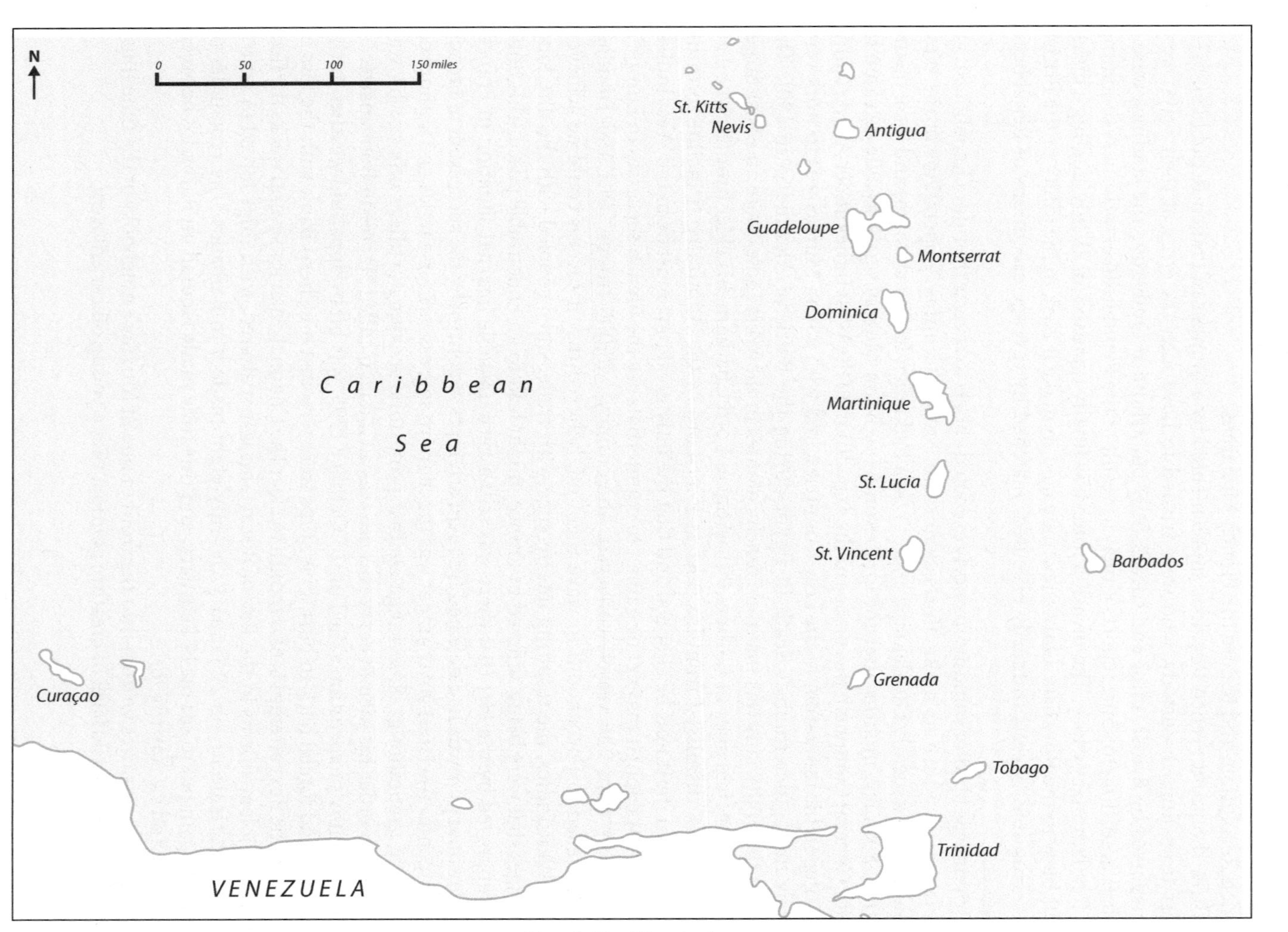

Map 2 The West Indies.

2 Shirts
2 pairs stockings
2 pairs white trousers
2 towels
1 pair boots
2 shoe brushes
1 clothes brush
1 plate brush
1 button brush
1 button stick
1 pair razors
1 pair scissors
1 comb
1 sponge
1 simple fork and spoon
1 blacking box
1 soap box and shaving brush
1 portable case for small articles
1 great coat

Lieutenant General Sir Ralph Abercromby – Mezzotint by SW Reynolds after Hoppner 1801. (Anne S.K. Brown Military Collection)

The events and dates in this expedition provide an insight into the difficulties of moving an army successfully by sea. Success or failure depended to a very large extent on the weather. In this case it took the same time for the fleet to cross from England to Barbados as it had done just to clear the Channel in the earlier attempt. Feeding the troops and keeping them healthy was extraordinarily difficult. There was no way of knowing how long a voyage would take and whether rations would last. The physical conditions must have been almost indescribable. Boredom would have been a major risk to morale and discipline. All this to take into account even before consideration was given to how many ships and men, horses, artillery, and equipment might be lost at sea or, crippled by storms, be forced to return or seek shelter and never arrive at their destination. Even on arrival, on a sometimes hostile shore, it took enormous skill and organisation to disembark troops without significant loss, in such a way as for them to be able to take the fight immediately to a well dug-in enemy.

Large numbers of officers and men died in the stormy voyage across the Atlantic, although Abercromby was credited with having instigated a number of measures, including very strict hygiene, which kept the sickness and mortality to a minimum. Nevertheless Murray became very ill and was in due course to return to Portsmouth. Whether or not he actually served for a short time in the West Indies on this campaign is unclear. There is evidence in the form of three small leather notebooks detailing Abercromby's orders with Murray's name on them. It is quite possible that he arrived in Barbados and turned round almost immediately, having fallen ill on board, or fell ill very soon after landing. Either way Murray missed seeing action on this occasion but would experience the West Indies not long after, as part of another expedition. John Moore, who was also on Abercromby's expedition, returned to England in 1797 suffering from yellow fever.

Many of the problems that beset the ships that set out from Cork on the expedition to the West Indies stemmed from the fact that a number of the troops who were sent had not fully recovered from dysentery and other diseases caught on active service in Ireland. These then flared up again and spread below decks with disastrous consequences. The enormous numbers being lost to sickness and disease (one-eighth of the number assembling at Cork at the end of October 1795 had died or had to be left behind in hospital by the end of February 1796 when they finally left),[10] forced a recognition that the issue needed to be addressed urgently.

Detailed analyses and reports by Army surgeons serving in Ireland at this time came to some conclusions about how to improve health in the military, even in non-tropical countries. Different regiments were analysed and conclusions drawn on a range of issues, from care in the recruiting process, discipline, cleanliness, clothing, diet and, last but not least, the access to both women followers and ladies of the 'dissolute metropolis', which was Dublin. Scottish troops were amongst the least healthy:

> We think it important to remark that the messing of Scotch Regiments in general ought at all times to be watchfully attended to because the men have very universally a strong disposition to save money, and if left to themselves they would willingly sacrifice to this propensity not only the quality but also the quantity of their food, whereas foresight and economy making no part of the Irishman's character he has no objection to live well, let the worst be what it may, any surplus of pay being generally expended at the nearest whiskey shop.[11]

Abercromby was, despite the weakened state of much of his army, successful in capturing Trinidad, St Vincent, and St Lucia and severely limiting France's influence in, and trade with, the region.

Across Europe, and in particular Italy, the French had won a series of brilliant victories, repeatedly defeating the Austrians, and the French authorities were recognising that in Bonaparte they now had one of the greatest military commanders of all time. Spain, encouraged by the seemingly unstoppable French successes, signed an alliance with France, and declared war on Britain on 5 October 1796. In February 1797 twenty seven Spanish ships of the line, over 2,000 guns strong, headed through the Straits of Gibraltar, but were intercepted and defeated off Cape St Vincent, thanks to some daring seamanship by the then Commodore Horatio Nelson, for which he was knighted. The Battle of Cape St Vincent reinforced the supremacy of the Royal Navy, which was for years to prove vital to Britain's defence and the nation's ability to carry the fight to the French in the Iberian Peninsula.

Following his early return from the West Indies, and a lengthy period of recovery, Murray spent 1797 on the staff in England, being appointed again as aide de camp to Major General Campbell, who was no doubt happy to have him again at his side.

10 Observations on the diseases of the Militia and the Fencible Regiments on the Irish Establishment etc. April 1796, Murray Papers, ADV MS 46.1.5.

11 A comparative view of the Disease and Mortality which occurred in the Warwick and First West York Regiments of Militia etc. with observations by the Irish Medical Board in 1800, Murray Papers, ADV MS 46.1.5.

3

1798-1800 – Ireland, Low Countries – A Fear of Invasion

Murray went to Ireland with Campbell, as Assistant Quartermaster General, a new role for him. Moore, recovered from his yellow fever, was also sent there. As far as Murray's qualification for this role, which required a modicum of topographical draughtsmanship, is concerned, we have nothing to prove that Murray ever drew a map. According to one of his officers he 'was most completely ignorant of what a military plan should be and in fact was unacquainted with the nature of military drawing'.[1]

What or who persuaded Murray to join the Quartermaster General's Department, requiring a facility for draughtsmanship for which he had no aptitude, can perhaps be explained by his firm friendship with Lieutenant Colonel Robert Anstruther, a brother officer in the 3rd Guards with whom he had shared lodgings in Leicester Place, in London. Anstruther was to be Quartermaster General to the expeditionary force sent to Holland in 1799, and in Egypt in 1801. Also instrumental in the decision was the Hon. Alexander Hope, half-brother to John, the future Earl of Hopetoun, whose sister Mary had married Murray's brother Patrick in 1794. John was to fight alongside Murray in various campaigns, particularly closely in the Peninsula. Alexander was Deputy Quartermaster General at Horse Guards from 1802 to 1812, was extremely well connected, and was to be Murray's closest confidante for very many years.

The Irish Rebellion of 1798 was perhaps the most concentrated outbreak of violence in Irish history. Since the reign of William and Mary, Ireland had enjoyed very limited independence compared even with other British colonies. France had supported American Independence, and some Irish, seeing the French Revolution as a movement with which they could identify, sought French military support to fight the British. The French saw Ireland as Britain's Achilles' heel. There had been an aborted French invasion of Ireland in December 1796, described by a commentator as Britain's luckiest escape since the Armada. Last-ditch efforts to secure peace with France had failed and at the very moment that the

1 Smith, R.H.P., 'Peninsular War Cartography: A New look at the Military Mapping of General Sir George Murray and the Quartermaster General's Department', *Imago Mundi*, Vol 65, Part 2 (2013), p.237 citing Peaty 'Wellington's surveyors and map makers in the Peninsula'; paper presented at the 35th Internatiomal Congress of Military History in Oporto, 2009 and published in the corresponding Acta (Lisbon:, Commisao Portuguese de Historia Militar, 2012).

final British proposals were being presented in Paris a large French fleet, consisting of seventeen ships of the line and twenty six other vessels carrying 15,000 troops, set sail. This planned invasion failed, disrupted by severe gales, arriving in Bantry Bay severely weakened and lacking effective command. If this force had managed to land it would have outnumbered the militia in Ireland and civil war might well have resulted.

Martial Law was declared in Ireland in March 1797, and the British commenced a policy of divide and rule amongst the various religious groups. Interestingly, because the French had occupied Rome, the Catholic Church in Ireland was opposed to rebellion and supported the British. But Catholics in general and non-Anglican Protestants formed the core of the rebel communities. Closer to home for Murray, the Scottish Militia Act, which permitted Lords Lieutenant to raise militia regiments, by conscription if necessary, as a means of protecting the mainland against invasion, was in some areas met with suspicion and hostility. Some people feared it might be used as a device to remove able bodied men from Scotland into England. Late in August of the same year a mob from Crieff attacked Ochtertyre, protesting against the Act, presumably targeting Patrick and any local attempts at conscription. The whole country was in a state of nervousness about French intentions, and the possibility of local insurrection, with Ireland always the most vulnerable.

On 19 May 1798 Napoleon set sail with an army from Toulon in a fleet of 335 ships, destination unknown, possibly a new invasion force heading for Ireland. Nelson searched in vain for the French fleet, which in fact remained in the Mediterranean and took Malta from the Knights of St John. It looked as though this was not after all an invasion fleet heading for Ireland, but for Egypt. If successful in seizing Egypt, France would deal a major blow to the British Empire and its trade with the East. But the French fleet was eventually trapped in the Bay of Aboukir, and, at the so-called Battle of the Nile, it was annihilated. It took over two months for news of the triumph to reach Britain, as the first despatch was intercepted at sea by the French, and in the meantime a very nervous atmosphere still prevailed at home.

Napoleon had made a decision that he would regret for the rest of his life, ruminating after Waterloo: 'If, instead of the expedition to Egypt I had undertaken that against Ireland, what could England have done now?'[2]

Turkey now joined the war against France, and the Russians too were ready to join with the allies.

On 28 May 1798 a rebel plan to take Dublin on the back of anticipated French support failed, but fighting spread throughout the country. The rebels' greatest successes were in County Wexford. More troops were sent from the mainland. On 21 June 20,000 British troops were victorious at Vinegar Hill, and the rebellion in Wexford was finally snuffed out on 14 July. Appalling atrocities were committed by both sides with numerous and savage summary prisoner executions. An early letter to Augusta reflects an uneasy reliance on military means to subdue the population:

> By the accounts of yesterday from Wexford I look upon the Rebellion as at an end and expect no news of importance. All I wish to do is convince you that there can be no greater mistake than in the horrible idea you have formed to yourself of

2 Hague, *Pitt the Younger*, p.432.

> Ireland and its natives. There being no longer any armed enemy and the Military being supreme the situation of an officer is by no means inconvenient. Our subjects may perhaps feel Martial Law a little irksome, and think unpleasant the hanging shooting and burning sometimes practised on them, but to us rulers of the land and directors of the elements and other instruments of vengeance, there are no inconveniences. Submission and respect are the only features I can see in the Irish Character; and their Hospitality of which you must have heard so much consists in their Houses, horses, provisions and other property, being all ours.[3]

This letter to Augusta is very clear confirmation that the British were carrying out savage reprisals against the rebels and their sympathisers, and its tone is in stark contrast to the letters and reports that a more thoughtful Murray would write as his military career developed. Even if he not actually witnessed them himself, he would have seen reports of some appalling acts committed against British soldiers and Loyalists, while perhaps turning a blind eye or deaf ear to similar atrocities carried out in the name of the King. He clearly wanted to correct any misconceptions Augusta had about the Irish character, but it is an uncharacteristically bitter and triumphalist letter, and leaves one wondering if he was writing in reaction to some raw barbarous act.

On 22 August a French force of 1,000 men landed in County Mayo, but met with limited success. In October another French force, this time 3,000 strong, approached the Donegal coast, but was defeated by the Royal Navy before it could land troops.

Murray left Ireland the following year, this time to join up with Moore, who in June 1799 had been ordered to England to command a brigade, again under Abercromby, with a view to taking the fight to the French. Since the Battle of the Nile, and the snuffing out of the Irish Rebellion (although guerrilla war continued throughout the country until 1803), there seemed to be a much more realistic chance of success on the continent of Europe.

The planned campaign saw Murray appointed senior Assistant Quartermaster General on an expedition to the coast of Holland. He was promoted to lieutenant colonel in command of a company of the 3rd Guards, under the command of Major General Harry Burrard, who was to feature alongside Murray later in a major controversy at the start of the Peninsular campaign. In this period Guards officers held 'dual' rank, that is to say they held a higher rank in the army than that held in the Guards. Thus a Guards captain would rank as, and be referred to in the army generally, as lieutenant colonel.

The expedition to Holland was intended to neutralise the Batavian Navy and to promote a counter-revolution. British and Russian troops, equally matched against Franco-Batavian forces, were involved. Despite a succession of stirring British naval victories, including the Battle of Camperdown in 1797 – where the British fleet was commanded by Admiral Duncan, a distant cousin of Murray – threats to British use of the Channel still remained. The Batavian Navy had been rebuilt and was an important cog in the French Revolutionary war machine, as were Dutch ports. The British, as ever, recognised the importance of denying the French use of the Channel ports, and the necessity of dealing finally with the Batavian fleet.

3 Murray to Augusta, Belfast, 25 June 1798, Murray Papers, MS 21103.

The British force, under the overall command of Abercromby, who had been summoned from Edinburgh on 8 June, assembled in the vicinity of Canterbury, making no secret of their intended invasion. In a scene similar to that played out prior to D Day in 1944, the enemy knew of the plans but not where the landings would actually take place. During August more troops, a large number from local militia, assembled at the camp after being given a bounty of ten guineas to serve in units overseas:

> [T]he militia had been pouring into the appointed camp at Barham Downs in the uproarious condition which, in those days, was invariably produced by a large bounty. Such a sight has rarely been seen in England, even after paying off the fleet. The possession of £10 filled the majority of men with a pride which forbade them to walk to the rendezvous.
>
> They rolled up into the camp, riotously drunk, in post-coaches, post-chaises and six, caravans and every description of vehicle, leaving the officers to plod on foot with such luckless men as had already lost or spent their money.[4]

Several locations were considered for the amphibious landing, and the beaches to the south of Den Helder were eventually chosen. As a lieutenant colonel, Murray became the senior of the assistants in the Quartermaster General's Department, immediately below Anstruther himself. He was detailed to accompany Major General Coote's brigade consisting of 3,500 men, 247 women, and 138 children in fourteen ships. This brigade was the only one to encounter any serious resistance on landing.

A short report on the action formed a letter from Murray to his brother, with a dismissive account of his first campaign wound, a musket ball in the right leg, sustained when the regiment was hemmed in amongst the dunes under heavy fire, after a difficult landing when 20 men drowned. In total 63 were killed with 424 wounded or missing.

> After some unfavourable weather at sea we anchored off this place on 21st, and could we have landed then, might easily have possessed ourselves of the whole Dutch Fleet, as by all accounts the force in the neighbourhood did not at that time exceed 1300 men. The wind however made it impossible for us to land, and on the 22nd forced us again out to sea. On 26th we again took our station along shore about 2 miles south of the Helder, and began to disembark at daybreak on the 27th. The principal force of the enemy was stationed towards the southward, near to the village of Callentsoog, consisting of about 6000 Dutch troops, and they resisted us among the sand hills along shore till dusk with a good deal of obstinacy, but in the night our troops carried the town of Helder and consequently gained command of the passage into the Zuyder Sea. Our ships will go in today and take the Dutch fleet if they are not wise enough to come to terms. I have been lucky enough to get a slight wound which you know at once dubs a man a hero. The ball passed clear through my right leg some way above the ankle, between the bone and the tendon without injuring either and today it feels easy and looks remarkably well.

4 J.W. Fortescue, *History of the British Army*, (London: Macmillan, 1899-1930) Vol.IV Part 2, p.658.

British Troops landing in Holland. View of the second division of the British Army commanded by Sir Ralph Abercromby, landing on the beach near Heik Down on 27 August 1799. (Anne S.K. Brown Military Collection)

> Sir J Pulteney has got a ball in the left arm. To finish to the purpose we have been successful in a very brilliant and important enterprize, which I doubt not will be followed by a Counter-Revolution in Holland.[5]

Having been taken on board the frigate HMS *Circe* with other wounded, Murray was landed a week or so later and transferred to hospital at Huisduinen, where he remained for about six weeks. On 6 October he was reported as 'almost well' and by the 27th was back on duty. The wound left the ankle permanently weak. It was not improved by a fall from his horse in July 1810, and he had trouble with it in 1815 when he had to journey from Fredericton, Nova Scotia to Kingston, in the midst of winter. He had another bad fall in Paris in 1817, dislocating the same ankle, breaking the fibula and cracking the tibia, but made light of all these incidents.

On 30 August the Batavian Fleet surrendered with 632 guns and 3,700 men to Vice Admiral Andrew Mitchell, without a shot being fired. But early successes were not consolidated. Franco-Batavian forces were reinforced, but lost Alkmaar. More British and Russian troops were landed at Den Helder, but despite numerous engagements with the enemy, progress was patchy and sickness was affecting the invasion force. By October and the onset of winter, the Duke of York, perhaps mindful of the savage arctic conditions that had

5 Murray to Patrick, on board the frigate *Circe*, 28 August 1799, Murray Papers, MS 21102.

contributed to the defeat in 1794-1795, proposed an honourable capitulation, the Convention of Alkmaar. Initially at least the Convention was well received by the allies who gained an exchange of prisoners and the surrender of most of the Batavian fleet, but the cost in lives of the campaign gradually sank in at home and there was some criticism of how the allies had failed to press home what looked like a strong position after the initial landings.

Murray returned to Ireland, this time to Bandon, near Cork. With its 3,000-man garrison, Bandon was one of the principal military stations in Ireland, where a renewed rebellion or further attempts at invasion by the French were both still major concerns. Augusta was brought up to date with her brother's activities:

> An Irish Country town you must expect will not offer many subjects worth corresponding about, particularly as I should have to tell you of people whom you will never see, as I hope you will not be obliged to stroll much about at any period of yr life – our only county neighbour is Lord Bandon who has given some of us two dinners – the town people are not of the first fashion and consequently fancy that we quiz them. They have had one Ball, but the ladies were so mightily affronted by our going in boots that they made a rash declaration that they would never come to another, and the Guards with the most unforeseen indifference have made no attempt to procure a reversal of this sad resolve. I continue to amuse myself with riding out and with training the Light Infantry of which I have command. 200 men of my own regiment are given to me for their training and 200 of the Coldstream are put under the orders of a junior officer so that when we are together I command the whole, and whatever I may be to the enemy, I shall certainly be the dread of many old woman in the country who is possessed of a goose or hen which Light infantry always used to be, as General Campbell will tell you. You are all by this time I suppose at Ochtertyre which I hope will be confirmed to me in a few days by a letter dated from there giving me good accounts of you all.
>
> Poor Francis who came lately from England with my horse is in a very bad way. He has a consumptive complaint from which I much fear he will not recover. The doctor has some hope of his getting better as the weather improves, but I hardly expect it.[6]

Anxious to take some leave during the summer, he wrote to Augusta about a delay in Dublin:

> I received a letter from you the day I left Bandon, and was happy to find in it a better account of my father's health. However as I had applied anxiously before to the General for leave of absence and the time was now come when it would be granted, I would not lose the opportunity. I wrote to Peter two or three days ago that I was coming but I have been detained beyond what I then expected by the impossibility of getting a place on the Mail.[7]

6 Murray to Augusta, Bandon, 8 May 1800, Murray Papers, MS 21103.
7 Murray to Augusta, Dublin, 27 July 1800, Murray Papers, MS 21103.

A shared chaise was leaving the next morning and he managed to make it back to Ochtertyre for a short spell in August, the last time he would see his father alive.

Leaving Ochtertyre on 13 August, he set off for Glasgow, where he called on the Glassfords, the wealthy tobacco family, distant cousins, the family Isabella would marry into a few years later, en route to Dublin, arriving too late at Bandon to join the battalion.[8] He re-crossed the Irish Sea to the south coast of England in an effort to link up with his regiment which had been selected to make another attempt at bolstering the Émigré's cause in North West France and arrived at Plymouth without knowing exactly where it was.

> When I left Ochtertyre I remember you gave me a hint about writing to you soon, which I will therefore now comply with. Let it be remembered however that each time I leave home, the letter score begins entirely anew. From Cove I wrote to Peter, dated on board the Phoebe last Wednesday and gave an account of my proceedings up to that time. This morning I was put on shore here and had the satisfaction to find myself as far as ever from my object. My intention was to get out from this place to find Lord St Vincent's fleet where I expected to find the regiment, but a captain of the Navy lately arrived from thence has just told me that the expedition quitted Quiberon Bay before he left the fleet. Here therefore I am almost as well situated for joining my battalion as I should be off Brest. Some of the naval people here think that the expedition is gone against Corunna, where there are five Spanish ships of the line which it is proposed to bring away. Sir James Pulteney commands the troops, and Sir John Moore the naval part of the enterprise in which if their destination be Corunna, I have no chance of partaking. You may continue to direct to me at the orderly room in London for my destination is at present rather uncertain. When I know a little more of my own plans I shall communicate them.[9]

A week later he was still stuck.

> You will be surprised to find what a stationary person I have become of late, still at Plymouth and what is worse likely to remain here a week longer. No opportunity was offered of getting out to the regiment and by letter from London I learn that there are several other officers in the same situation, all of whom have been ordered to Plymouth or Portsmouth to await a conveyance.
>
> In addition to this reason for remaining where I am the accounts in circulation here of the result of the expedition incline one to wish for further intelligence before setting out in search of the regiment. By the Montague, accounts have been received that the troops under Sir James Pulteney landed near Corunna or Ferol and took possession of some batteries; but finding the citadel too strong to be taken except by regular siege, the whole embarked without any loss. This place begins to feel a little dull although perhaps had I a little more society, and more active

8 The Glassfords were a Glasgow family who had amassed a considerable fortune from tobacco. Isabella married James Glassford, an advocate.

9 Murray to Augusta, Plymouth, 30 August 1800, Murray Papers, MS 21103.

> occupation than that of waiting an opportunity to leave it, I might find Plymouth possessed of many advantages which I do not now discover.[10]

In May 1800 Abercromby, by now well used to working with Murray, had been appointed to command the only active British army, comprising 20,000 men, who were to be sent to the Mediterranean. This expedition attempted unsuccessfully to surprise the Spanish naval base at Cadiz, before ending the French occupation of Malta in September. It was Malta where Murray joined up with his regiment again. And it was on opening the despatches that had been conveyed with Murray on the armed brig *Louisa* that the force under Abercromby learned of the planned invasion of Egypt. Since the Battle of the Nile and the resulting British Naval superiority the French army in Egypt had been effectively cut off and was vulnerable.

Murray again found himself in the Quartermaster General's Department, as senior Assistant Quartermaster General under Anstruther, an appointment he surely must have been happy with. He had clearly made an impression on Anstruther on the Helder campaign, and Anstruther, confident in his abilities, swept his friend up on board HMS *Chameleon* to make arrangements for the new base of operations.[11]

10 Murray to Isabella, Plymouth 7 September 1800, Murray Papers, MS 21101.
11 Ward Draft, Ch.III, p.12.

4

1800-1801 – Egypt

In 1798 the French began to recognise the strategic importance of Egypt to protect their trade interests and undermine Britain's access to India. To this end Napoleon led his Armée d'Orient to Egypt, then part of the Ottoman Empire.

The French defeated a Mameluke army at the Battle of the Pyramids. Originally slaves in the Middle East, over the centuries the Mamelukes became noted for their military prowess. Often they gained social status and were appointed to high office. Part of the Ottoman Empire in Egypt, early in the eighteenth century they had fought for independence from the Ottomans. They were non-Muslim and were highly regarded disciplined soldiers, in contrast to the Turkish forces that were now allied to Britain against the French. Despite multiple victories and an initially successful expedition into Syria, mounting conflict in Europe and the earlier defeat of the supporting French fleet at the Battle of the Nile persuaded Napoleon himself to withdraw in late 1799. Command of the Armée d'Orient, after the assassination of his predecessor, eventually fell to Jacques-François Menou. The substantial French army occupied Cairo and Alexandria, Egypt's two major cities.

On 21 November Anstruther received orders from Abercromby to send Murray forward to Jaffa to confer with Brigadier General Koehler, a British artillery officer who had, since 1799, headed up the Military Mission in Turkey. Murray, accompanied by Royal Engineers officer Major Richard Fletcher, who was to become a good friend, and who would work closely with Murray in the Peninsula, was to seek an introduction to the Grand Vizier, whose army, defeated by the French nine months earlier at Heliopolis, was at Jaffa, in a demoralised state. He was to explain to the Vizier that Abercromby was relying on his support to recover Egypt for the Ottoman Empire. Murray was to propose two alternative plans of operation: under the first, the British army would join the Grand Vizier's and march into Egypt along the Syrian coast; the second was a direct march on Cairo. Additionally Murray was to satisfy himself of all matters of supply and transport and to gather all the topographical information he could, as well as assess the reliability of the Turkish troops, and gather any intelligence there might be on the stations and strength of the French army in Egypt.[1] Before setting off he described the situation to Patrick:

1 Ward Draft, Ch.III, p.14.

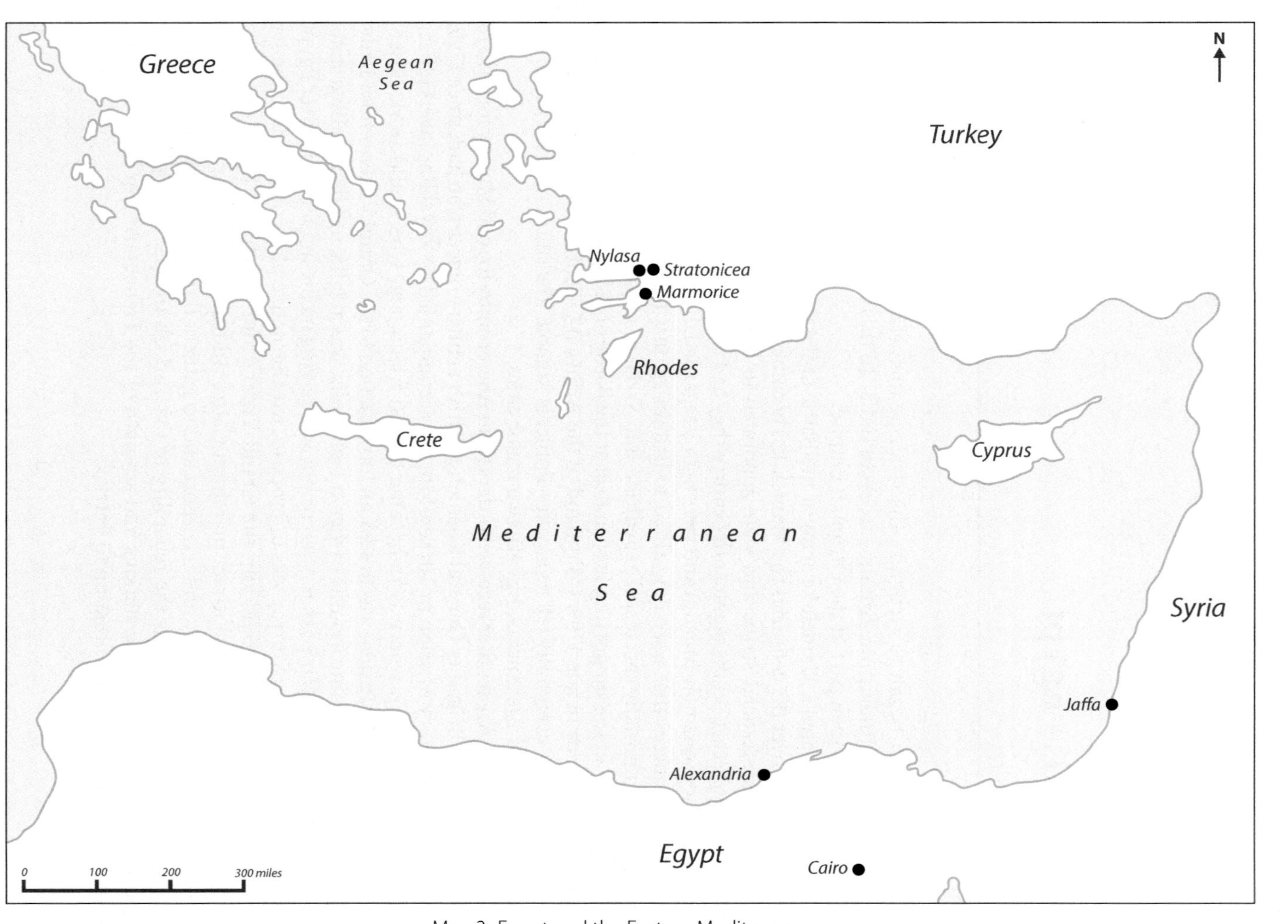

Map 3 Egypt and the Eastern Mediterranean.

I wrote to you from Palermo where the Chameleon touched on our way from Gibraltar, and now take the opportunity of a Tartar going to Constantinople to send you another letter. We arrived a few days ago and found Sir S Smith and some Turkish men of war lying in this bay which with the island of Rhodes will be the rendezvous of the fleet and army. Ld. Keith and Sir Ralph we expect may reach this the middle of Decr and our operations commence about the beginning of Feb. This we hope is making a full allowance for all delays, and what, probably, your impatience in Britain will reckon too ample.

In order to impress you with an idea of our remit, should we succeed in the present enterprize I must give you some notion of the difficulties to be encountered. The Turkish Empire is in fact no longer anything more substantial than a Shadow and of this Shadow the limbs are independent and distrustfull of each other.

Dzezzar Pacha of Acre maintains an Army nearly equal to that of the Vizier, and denies the latter any kind of assistance. The Vizier has from ten to twelve thousand men, and these not good troops. The general is like his troops, without any of the qualities requisite in his situation. The Marmalukes are excellent cavalry, but tired of an unprofitable war, some of them have joined the French, and the greater part remains quiet. Such are our friends. Our enemies were a year ago about 19,000 strong, including 1,800 Greeks etc, whom the French have armed. The soldiers are said to be very tired of their conquest, and perhaps the presence of a British force, sufficient to make a treaty respected will induce them to seek a renewal of the Convention.

Should Menou, however, be able to prevent this, I make no doubt of our being able to succeed 'par la voie des armes'. The Capitana Pacha had left this, before we arrived with 4 ships of the line, it being the practice of the Turks to lay up their vessels in the winter; an express has however been sent to request his return. The Capt Pacha is said to be the man of the greatest energy, and the most attached to European manners, of any of the great personages of the Empire; he was a slave much in favour with the present Sultan before his accession to the throne, and was, upon that, immediately raised to the office of Capt Pacha and has since married the Sultan's Sister. We expect much from his friendship and activity. I was on shore yesterday in Asia Minor at a place where formerly stood a Grecian City of Lycia; there are some remains of antiques. The foundations of an amphitheatre still exist, and several Persian and Grecian tombs. The latter are cut out in the face of the limestone rocks and are, some of them, of the most elegant architecture. I am to go to Jaffa in the Cameleon when Sir Sydney can spare a part of his suit. I shall write you as often as opportunities occur and I beg you will not omit doing as much for me. Send me letters by as many different channels as possible.[2]

Landing at Jaffa on 2 December after a stormy passage, Murray immediately attended a conference arranged by Koehler at which the Grand Vizier, the Kiaya Bey (the second dignitary of the Ottoman state), and Jazzar Pasha, the self-appointed governor of Syria, were

2 Murray to Patrick, Bay of Macri, November 21 1800, Murray Papers, MS 21102.

Egyptian Mamelukes 1800. (Anne S.K. Brown Military Collection)

present. He was invited to a review of 7,500 of the Vizier's 10,000 troops which ended in chaotic scenes of undisciplined shooting. Murray was able to see at close quarters what Ward described as 'the soldiers who had struck terror into Christian Europe for three centuries – helmeted Mamluks, turbaned Arnauts, Anatolians, Timariots, Druses and Janissaries in their strange and exotic costumes.'[3]

On 8 December Murray and some mission officers were invited by the Vizier to dinner, 'a sumptuous if somewhat messy repast of forty dishes served in succession', which he was later to describe in detail to Augusta. On the 11th they dined with the Kiaya Bey, and on the 12th a final conference was held, to give consideration to the plan of operations to be adopted. On the 13th Murray departed for Makri on the *Chameleon* with his report, which was less than encouraging, no doubt feeling fortunate that he had seemingly escaped the plague that was rampant in the camp. The Vizier was not used to being the junior part of an alliance and it was unrealistic to assume his forces would coalesce effectively with a British Army whose modus operandi was inevitably very different. Murray's official report concluded that the Turks were wholly unpredictable, harbouring a deep distrust of the British, although privately he had some hope for them if properly led.[4]

3 Ward Draft, Ch.III, p.15.
4 Ward Draft, Ch.III, pp.15-6

On 20 December Abercromby's army sailed for Marmorice (now known as Marmaris) Bay, on the Turkish mainland, just north of Rhodes, in preparation for the invasion of Egypt. On 29 December the fleet made it through the treacherous narrow entrance to the Bay in a violent thunderstorm, and limited visibility. There was tension on Admiral Keith's flagship HMS *Foudroyant* until the normally tight-lipped Keith shouted out '"God be praised for this great Mercy!"... uncovering and bowing his head with great devotion'.[5]

The troops were to stay at Marmorice for four or five weeks, giving them time to recover from their long confinement on board. Regular exercises were carried out to perfect landing by small boats, a necessary part of the imminent invasion. The forthcoming disembarkation of the troops at Aboukir, in the face of determined opposition, was to be justly ranked among the most daring and brilliant exploits ever carried out by a British army.

The signs from the start were not particularly promising. The local horses that were purchased by the army were in a very poor state. There was a suspicion that the Turks, Britain's new allies in the fight against Napoleon, were not to be relied upon. To some extent this would turn out to be correct, but at least one part of the Turkish army did acquit itself far better than anyone on the British staff believed possible. Although Murray shared his colleagues' views on the poor discipline and order of the Turks, he did manage to build a rapport with them and was less surprised than some when 'his friend' the Vizier's men proved to be at least a match for the French in the battle for Cairo. As he was so often to do on the campaigns that followed, Murray was quite ready to share his views on those allied to the British cause with his brother:

> I wrote to my father from the camp at Jaffa [his father had died on 6 December] and gave him some hints of what I had seen there. All I am afraid of is, that you should think me blinded by prejudice, while I endeavour only to relate the truth. The opinion I had formed of the army under the Vizier, from the reports of others, when I wrote you from Macri have been since, I am very sorry to say, much confirmed by my own observations. The camp is entirely without order or internal police, and having been upon the same spot since the beginning of last April, is well stocked with dead animals and every other nuisance usual in an ill regulated Encampment – pistols and carabiniers are constantly firing, and two shots have passed through the tents of the English Detach/t, and one of the men has been wounded. Parades, drills exercises and manoeuvres, Returns, the Distribution of written orders, and in short all the detail of military arrangements which we find so necessary are here perfectly unknown – outposts, patrols, sentries etc are thought superfluous – there are no magazines but of biscuit, and the country the army moves into is trusted to for everything else. The soldiers find their own arms and ammunition, the former are therefore of all sorts, and of the latter the supply is uncertain. The men come to and go from the camp almost as they please. The Albanians in particular, who are reckoned to be the best infantry, go off sometimes in bands, and a corps of cavalry sent after a parcel of them, upon one occasion, returned without acting – the Turks are under extreme apprehensions of our inter meddling in their Domestic concerns.

5 Knight, *Britain Against Napoleon*, p.200 (citing the Log of HMS *Petrel*, TNA, ADM 51/1364).

> The force of the French from the most authentic accounts does not exceed fourteen thousand effective European troops. The no. of the troops they have armed is very differently stated but is certainly not formidable. They have no places important in point of strength except Alexandria, where the Works are considerable. The Marmalukes in Upper Egypt are not considered as fixed in the French interest. I have nothing further to add, but to wish you and all at home as good health as I enjoy myself.[6]

Shortly after Murray's return, Abercromby sent Moore, now a major general and one of his most trusted officers, to Jaffa, early in January, for a second opinion. His report was if anything even less encouraging than Murray's. Both were appalled by the state of the Vizier's camp and the disease there.

Some time after his meetings with the Grand Vizier, Murray wrote to Augusta from on board Abercromby's ship, HMS *Kent*:

> I take the opportunity of writing to you by a person going to Constantinople.
>
> I promised I think in one of my letters home, to give you an account of a Turkish dinner. In camp I dined with the Vizier, and afterwards with others of the chief officers. We were several English, but the person we dined with was the only Turk at table. On coming to the tent coffee and pipes were served, then basins were brought in and we washed our hands. A cloth was afterwards spread upon the floor, and a small table about 18 inches diameter was placed upon it, upside down – this table was in a red cloth bag. On the feet of the table was placed a silver or plated tray about a yard in diameter, and round the edges of it were laid thin [scones] and 2 spoons to each person there, with a small cushion in the middle, made up all the apparatus of the dinner table. We sat round upon cushions drew the cloth up over our legs and each man having a napkin put upon his knee, and one over his shoulder, we commenced the attack with our fingers, upon each dish as it was brought and placed upon the centre cushion – the spoons, one for hot and the other for cold things were employed only in cases of the greatest necessity where's fingers could not succeed. The Dishes were all excellent & succeeded each other one by one, to the No. of nearly 40. After dinner soap and water is used for the hands and beard and coffees and pipes, the usual occupation of the Turks, are again resorted to.
>
> Since coming here Col. Abercromby [Abercromby's second son] and I have been 75 miles up the country on business with an Aga, the country is mountainous and woody with much picturesque scenery – there are some fine plains of considerable extent but ill cultivated and not peopled as they might be. There are no made roads and in many places the paths are extremely bad. We found the Turks very [paper torn] but not so active as one could have wished either in public in private transactions. The Aga gave us a shelty [i.e a small Shetland Pony] each. In the course of our travels we saw the ruins of Stratonicea and Nylasa, now Eshisass and Melass upon

6 Murray to Patrick, Rhodes, 29 December 1800, Murray Papers, MS 21102.

> which I refer you to the Voyage Pittoresque de de La Grece.[7] We measured some fir trees 14 feet in circumference and some Myrtle 30 feet high. As to public affairs all I can say is that we find our allies rather slow and inefficient. At present they have the fast or feast of the Ramazan which is the change of day into night – from sun rise till it sets they eat nothing and don't even smoke but they stuff themselves during the night. All friends here are well.[8]

On the morning of 7 February 1801 Abercromby assembled his general officers on board the *Kent*, explained his intentions, and gave them their final instructions, based to a large extent on the intelligence gleaned by Murray and Moore in the course of their visits. Information had just been received that two French frigates had made it to Alexandria, evading the British naval blockade, with a large quantity of ammunition and 800 artillerymen. This was a significant blow to the allies, and would make their already difficult landings even more dangerous.

Preparations, with Murray energetically engaged in assembling supplies, horses and equipment, were as complete as they could be, and on 20 February the troops embarked, setting sail two days later. By the 25th gales had split the fleet, comprising some 180 vessels carrying 15,000 troops, forcing some smaller ships to make for the safety of Cyprus.[9]

By 2 March the bulk of the invasion force was off Aboukir near Alexandria but bad weather again struck, interfering with the planned landing. Meantime the French were strengthening their defences, supported by their recently acquired reinforcements. The landing finally commenced in broad daylight on 8 March. The first into the landing craft was the Brigade of Guards. Each flat-bottomed boat could hold fifty men. The plan was to land three thousand in the first fifty eight boats, with a second flotilla of eighty four boats each with thirty men, whilst a third flotilla carried the guns.[10]

For hours the French had been able to watch the landing craft being prepared, loading starting at two in the morning. It was close to eight o'clock before the whole of the flotilla was ready to pull for the shore. Murray boarded his boat with Captain Cochrane, the naval commander of the disembarkation, in the company of John Moore and Brigadier General Hildebrand Oakes, Moore's second in command, with some elite troops of the Reserve. They rowed towards the shore ahead of the line of boats containing the first wave of troops. Captain Thomas Walsh, an aide de camp, relived the scene:

> The moment was awful, and the most solemn silence prevailed, as the boats pulled to the rendezvous, a distance of about five miles. Nothing was heard but the hollow and dismal sound of the oars as they dipped into the water.[11]

7 The *Armchair Travellers Volume of Landscapes and Ruins along the Aegean and Turkish Coasts* compiled by Compte Choiseul-Gouffier in 1776, a copy being among the many volumes in the Ochtertyre Library.

8 Murray to Augusta, Bay of Marmorice, 20 January 1801, Murray Papers, MS 21103.

9 Ward Draft, Ch.III, p.18.

10 Knight, *Britain Against Napoleon*, p.201.

11 T. Walsh, *Journal of the Late Campaign in Egypt* (London: T. Cadell and W. Davies, 1803), p.75.

The landing of the British Troops in Egypt, 8 March 1801. (Anne S.K. Brown Military Collection)

When the signal to advance was given everyone was instantly in motion, pulling eagerly towards the shore:

> When the boats came within range of the enemy's batteries, fifteen pieces of ordnance and the artillery from the opposite hill opened fire upon them, with round and grape shot, and on advancing further musket balls were also showered down. The British soldiers huzzaed occasionally but returned not a shot. Numbers of them were killed and wounded, some boats were sunk and the nearest were turned aside to save the drowning men, while the remainder were rowed steadily onwards.
>
> Sir Ralph Abercromby stood on the deck of a ship looking forward with intense anxiety, and saw with horror the storm of iron and leaded balls descending on his soldiers. He held in his hand the signal for retreat and hardly refrained from raising it.
>
> Captain Cochrane's boat first reached the strand and the officers all stepped out. The boats with the troops then grounded and Moore instantly drew them up in line and gave the word to load.[12]

12 James Carrick Moore, *The Life of Lieutenant General Sir John Moore KB* (London: John Murray, 1833), pp.283-4.

Two boats of the Guards Brigade sank. The French grapeshot inflicted severe damage. Moore and Murray led an attack up a steep sand-hill, driving through two battalions of French infantry with bayonets, capturing four guns. The next two days saw intense fighting with French casualties amounting to about 4,000, while the British losses numbered about 1,300. Senior officers, including Murray, were in the thick of battle, and Murray was lucky to escape uninjured when ordered forward to try and persuade the Aboukir Castle garrison to surrender, to be met by a hail of musket fire, as described by Moore:

> The enemy had eight days to assemble and prepare; the ground was extremely favourable for defence. Our attempt was daring and executed by the troops with the greatest intrepidity and coolness. In the course of the afternoon the rest of the army landed, and the whole moved forward a couple of miles. The castle of Aboukir was blocked. An attempt was made to summon it; but they fired upon Lt Colonel Murray and declined every communication. Sir Ralph directed that some heavy artillery should be landed to fire upon it.[13]

On 12 March the British advanced on Alexandria. Fierce fighting took place over the next few days resulting in the French being blockaded in the city and their lines of communication cut. Menou had lost his last chance of driving the British back to their ships. The cost of this success was high with about ten per cent of the British engaged being killed or wounded.

Murray wrote to Augusta in a very matter of fact, understated, way about the success of the landing at Aboukir Bay, considering what he must just have been through:

> As I understand that duplicates of the Despatches will be sent home, I shall write both to you and Lady Mary. No letters have yet come to me from home; plenty I am certain have been written but two packets having been taken accounts for the fate of some of them. A long detail of our military operations would be little interesting to you. I shall only tell you that we landed at Aboukir in spite of the French on the 8th March, that we advanced upon them the 12th, and beat them the 13th on the ground we now occupy about two miles from Alexandria. Gen Hope is in good health and I find the climate of Egypt agrees with me as well as our own. Remember me to all at home, and though I write you a short letter, I shall not neglect to let you hear of me by every opportunity.[14]

Moore, Hope, and Abercromby were, during the days that followed, all wounded from musket fire, Abercromby fatally. But the landings had been successful and were to be recognised as one of the British army's finest ever actions. The achievement of the landings and the battles of the following few days provided a much needed boost to morale, given the experiences over the last few years. Great credit, rightly so, was heaped on Abercromby

13 J. Maurice, (ed), *The Diary of Sir John Moore*, (London: Edward Arnold, 1904), Vol.II, p.4.

14 Murray to Augusta, Camp near Alexandria, 16 March 1801, Murray Papers, MS 21103.

Death of Sir Ralph Abercromby. Murray can be seen standing next to the horse's head. (Anne S.K. Brown Military Collection)

who had at last provided the sound and inspiring leadership that had so often been lacking. Murray gave Patrick a very positive account of the recent actions.

> The Actions of the 21st gives me another opportunity of sending home good accounts of the Egyptian Expedition. Menou, it appears, had resolved to bring down everything that could be spared from the country of Egypt, in order to secure at once the safety of the colony, by the defeat of this Army. All their troops being assembled on the 20th in the camp before Alexandria, the French attacked before daybreak in the morning of the 21st, with (I think) nine thousand men. The affair was warmest on the right and left of our position, Menou's plan upon paper being to force these points, while our left was occupied by a false attack, and to drive the British Army into the Lake of Aboukir, which is in the rear of our left. Their cavalry which is much superior to ours, made several very bold attacks but were repulsed with great loss.
>
> By comparing some papers taken with the list of the Egyptian Army, I find their whole force mentioned as being here except 2 Demi Brigades and one Regt of Dragoons, if therefore my friend the Vizier the Marmalukes or the people of the Country are to make any effort they have had an opportunity. I make no doubt that

British and Indian soldiers and camp near Alexandria c. 1800. (Anne S.K. Brown Military Collection)

> the enemy lost in this last affair fully 2,500 men. Sir Ralph who goes always where there is the hottest fire received a Ball in the thigh & he was lucky enough to disarm a French Dragoon who made a thrust at him. The surgeons have not found it necessary to extract the Ball and Sir Ralph is doing well. [In fact Abercromby would be dead within three days]. Genl. Hope who was by Sir Ralph had the fore finger of his Right hand shot off, he is on board the Kent and doing well. Egypt agrees very well with me.[15]

Major General John Hely-Hutchinson took over command after Abercromby's death, and on 26 April the advance on Cairo started. By early June the British and the Turks, numbering 36,000 in total, converged on the city, where 8,000 French rapidly came to terms, as Murray had predicted. Murray's French was again put to good use in the negotiations. The French were permitted to leave not only with their arms but also with their personal possessions. Among these were discovered numerous sarcophagi, obelisks, statues, manuscripts, an inscribed granite stone of Rosetta, and other Coptic antiquities. John Moore's biographer (his brother) described these as being wrested from the French 'plunderers' and, without a hint of irony, making their way to the British Museum.

Disease was rife and the British suffered huge losses from dysentery, the plague, and opthalmia. At Rahmaniya some horsemen, who proved to be friendly Arabs 'seized the hands of Col Murray and some officers with him and kissed them, a token of respect and

15 Murray to Patrick, Egypt, 25 March 1801, Murray Papers, MS 21102.

amity which was by no means agreeable, particularly since the plague raged in every town now before the army'.[16]

A letter from home brought news of the death of Elizabeth Hope, John Hope's wife. They had been married for a mere three years. Linked by marriage, Patrick being married to John's sister Lady Mary, the Murray and Hope families moved in the same close-knit social circle in Scotland. Militarily, Murray worked very closely and often confidentially with the two Hope half-brothers, John on campaign and Alexander at Horse Guards, throughout his military career. He wrote at once to Augusta:

> The last letters from England brought us the melancholy accounts of Mrs Hopes Death which I have to regret both from the impression such a loss will make upon her own friends and also from the intimacy which subsisted between you. Occurrences are daily happening which tend to mark the uncertainty of all our views of happiness, and we should prepare our minds therefore, to meet them with firmness and composure neither giving way to thoughtlessness, nor yielding to that timidity or apathy which some falsely take for Virtue, but which leads them from all Society and Usefulness in life. Gen Hope is so far recovered from his wound that he has joined us within these last few days. He is in very low spirits but I am glad he had joined before he received the intelligence of the loss of his wife, as the melancholy impressions it makes upon his mind will be best removed by the employment forced upon him by the duties of his office.[17]

Negotiations for the French evacuation had been concluded and the whole garrison marched back to Rosetta, under escort, to be embarked for France. Murray expressed his hope to Augusta that Alexandria would capitulate as Cairo had.

> Tomorrow we set out for Rosetta in company with our friends the ci-descant garrison of Cairo. It will be a singular thing to see the two armies marching and encamping together in a friendly manner. When those gentlemen are embarked the Country of Egypt is secured to its former owners and I trust Menou will not be so obstinate as to hold out in Alexandria against the good terms he may have from us at present. Tell me sometime what is doing at Ochtertyre and what the neighbours are about. Gen Hope is very well. He has resigned his situation of Adjt. Genl some time ago and now commands a Brigade. I shall be anxious to hear further accounts of Lady Mary.[18]

The French had no more appetite to hold onto Alexandria than they had had for Cairo, and negotiated just as Murray had hoped. The force from India under Major General Baird, just arrived, was not required. The terms of the expulsion of the French from Egypt, as spelled out to Patrick, were to be closely mirrored a few years later in Portugal, where they gave

16 Sir Robert Wilson, *History of the British Expedition to Egypt* (London: Egerton, 1803), Vol.I, pp.128-9.
17 Murray to Augusta, Camp at El Gahm, 30 May 1801, Murray Papers, MS 21103.
18 Murray to Augusta, Camp near Cairo, 14 July 1801, Murray Papers, MS 21103.

rise to a furious reaction at home. But the conclusion of the Egyptian campaign met with nothing but praise from commentators and politicians alike.

> The surrender of Alexandria which terminates the campaign in Egypt will give you considerable satisfaction. Gl Hope has again been our negotiator and tomorrow we take possession of part of the Works of the Place. We have behaved with much moderation, which in the present political prospect is highly proper. The garrison are to sail in ten days, with private property and all the honours of War; they are not being considered as prisoners.
>
> Our further proceedings must be directed from Home, therefore you will not expect I should speculate upon them. Col Abercromby goes home by sea with the Accounts. I send this by a Messenger of the Capt. Pacha going to Constantinople.[19]

In his role as senior Assistant Quartermaster General, Murray was kept busy with the embarkation of the French Army, a massive operation which took many weeks. The campaign had been an outstanding success, and he was happy that the British had behaved with honour and moderation, realistic enough to understand that the British Army's achievements would in any case soon be forgotten by the British public. Egypt seemed very far away: people at home, Augusta among them, were more concerned about the likelihood of a French invasion, and Murray did what he could to reassure his sister:

> I take the opportunity of writing you by Major Honeyman who goes home in the Morgiana. You cannot now expect any intelligence from this country of much public importance, and John Bull has, I dare say, already forgot the Egyptian Army. I do not suspect you however of so much want of recollection and I know that you will be happy to hear of yr friends, although they are no longer occupied in destroying the Human Race.
>
> Various delays have taken place in the embarkation owing to its great extent but a fortnight more will I hope finish the business. I am sorry to say that John Hope is one of the Generals who remain behind, with the troops left in this country, but the arrangement I trust will be only temporary.
>
> No letters have reached me of a long time – Lady Margaret I see by the papers has got a son, but I looked in vain for accounts from home. You are again I perceive alarmed for an invasion, but this is a periodical distemper, which is brought on by long nights and blowing weather every autumn. I hope at Malta I shall find letters.[20]

Major Generals Hely-Hutchison and Craddock, each having taken over in turn as commanders of the British force, and both having succumbed to illness, meant that Moore, despite still suffering badly from his wounded leg, assumed command. By that time the fighting was largely over and Moore's priority was to oversee the final removal of Napoleon's forces from Egypt.

19 Murray to Patrick, Camp near Alexandria, 1 September 1801, Murray Papers, MS 21102.

20 Murray to Augusta, Camp near Alexandria, 21 September 1801, Murray Papers, MS 21103.

The successful Egyptian campaign, under Abercromby, in command of what had been up to that point underachieving troops, became the benchmark against which the British Army's achievements were, for at least a decade, measured. Much credit must be given to Abercromby for his meticulous planning and patient training of his troops, as well as the diplomatic efforts to gain the support of the Turks. Just before leaving the camp near Alexandria for home Murray was awarded, by the Captain Pacha, the diamond studded Order of the Crescent of the Imperial Ottoman Empire, one of many decorations and honours that would be bestowed on him during his military career.

Murray sailed with Anstruther from Aboukir Bay on 7 October in HMS *Astrea*, calling at Malta, Gibraltar (from where he wrote a hasty note to Patrick), and Lisbon before arriving in home waters on 6 December 1801, where the ship was quarantined for ten days.

> I take the opportunity of writing to you by the Minerva Frigate which sails for England the first fair wind. I arrived here with Anstruther in the Astrea, three days ago, and in about a week we hope to proceed on our voyage to England in the same ship.
>
> We sailed from Egypt Octbr 7th when I left John Hope and all our other friends in good health. The Peace, which we heard of at Malta, will bring away all the troops who were to have garrisoned Alexandria, which will give great satisfaction both to them and to their friends.
>
> By the end of the month I hope to be able to write to you from London. Where I shall pass my Christmas I have not yet positively determined.[21]

At the end of this letter there appears in a different hand, identifiable as Patrick's – 'GIBRALTAR!!!!' He must have been glad to get news of his brother's safety.

Throughout the course of the Napoleonic Wars the names of certain generals with whom Murray was particularly friendly, leaving aside Wellington himself of course, arise regularly – Abercromby, Anstruther, Moore, Pulteney, Graham, Cole, Hill and Hope being particularly closely connected. Murray had just witnessed Abercromby's fatal wounding near Alexandria. Moore, Hope, and Pulteney had been wounded too. These were personal friends, well known to the family. Murray had himself been wounded, although not seriously, at Den Helder a year earlier, and had been lucky to survive Egypt unscathed. It must have been a difficult time for a young officer, still only 28. But the familiarity that he had with these senior men suggests that even at this stage in his military career he was trusted and respected. There are clear indications from his letters and other sources that he had already developed useful diplomatic skills, and he was being used more and more in the role of negotiator, evidenced by his being selected to attempt the negotiated surrender of Aboukir Castle, and Cairo, and liaison with difficult allies, as in Jaffa. Much as he might have tried, Murray seemed powerless to avoid diplomatic responsibilities being thrust on him in a variety of extraordinary situations in the years to come.

21 Murray to Patrick, Gibraltar, 9 November 1801, Murray Papers, MS 21102.

5

1802-1806 – West Indies and Ireland – A New Scientific

The Treaty of Amiens was signed in March 1802, on terms that many felt were generous to France. Only months after its signing, mutual suspicion crept back, and the prospect of war again became very real. In fact hostilities between Britain and France would commence again in May 1803. During the short period of peace Murray enjoyed himself at the newly established Royal Military College. He also spent what was obviously a very agreeable time in the West Indies as Adjutant General to the forces there.

The Royal Military College, the precursor of the present Staff College, had been established a couple of years earlier, with support from the Duke of York, to improve the professionalism of staff officers, and particularly the Quartermaster General's Department. Both the Austrian and Prussian armies had evolved a staff of 'military scientists', trained to act as expert consultants to their commanders. The role had developed to such an extent that it was remarked that the deficiencies of a commander were of little consequence provided the Quartermaster General took him firmly in hand. Alexander Hope and Robert Anstruther were keen to replicate this in the British army, and encouraged the Duke to form the school, the Royal Military College, at High Wycombe, in 1799. From now on the Quartermaster General was to take over responsibility for operational movements from the Adjutant General's department. Additionally, the Quartermaster General of a force on active service was no longer to be involved in such matters as hiring of transport, but was to be in the field with auxiliary corps such as guides, artificers, pioneers, draughtsmen, and baggage masters. Add to this a vital role in mapping and intelligence, and the wide-ranging responsibilities that were to fall on Murray during his military career on the continent become apparent. Last, and of great importance in Murray's future relationship with Wellington, was the job of giving effect to the commander's strategy before and during a battle or on a march, a role in which Murray complemented Wellington's tactical skill, with a lawyer-like eye for detail and flair for clear communication.

Murray was among the officers volunteering to be groomed to become the new 'scientifics' at High Wycombe. An unusual step for a Guards lieutenant colonel, fresh from a successful campaign, it demonstrated Murray's intense fascination with the modern approach to the role of the staff, and in particular the opportunities for radically changing the way the Quartermaster General's Department might operate. He willingly subscribed his 30 guineas. On joining, his French was marked at five, his Mathematics at four, and his Drawing at one. He scored nil for Fortification and German. By the time he left four short months later his French was described as 'compleat' while his marks elsewhere were little changed, as he had not progressed from the first two of six classes.[1] However, it should be noted that in 1809 he said he could speak and write French and read German, Italian and Spanish. Murray treasured his brief time at the college and it suited his thoughtful, occasionally academic, and certainly hard working, nature. He enjoyed the stimulation of conversation with others of similar intellect, and valuable relationships were forged. Six of his contemporaries at the College were to serve under him in the Quartermaster General's Department in Ireland, fourteen in the Peninsula. No departmental chief before his time had obtained the insight into the abilities and potential of his subordinates that Murray derived from the schooling he shared with so many.[2]

His letter to Augusta from High Wycombe gives us something of Murray's love of descriptive prose, which, translated into military topographical intelligence, was to become such a feature of his and his department's responsibility. Murray, despite his own shortcomings as a draughtsman, became fascinated by maps and mapping, and one of the most critical duties of the Quartermaster General's Department was to survey the terrain close to any possible area of movement or skirmish and record it for future use.

> [Y]ou desire to know something of the Situation of Wycombe and how I like the place. It is a village in a narrow valley upon the great road from London to Oxford, 29 miles from town. A little rivulet runs through it, and joins the Thames eight or ten miles below.
>
> The country round is formed of an endless variety of Hill and Dales, where all the swells of ground of every different height and extent sweep into each other in curved lines. The cultivated parts are so much intermixed with Wood that the whole has the appearance of having been an immense Forest, portions of which have been selected by nature Herself to remain and beautify that which Her Bounty yielded for the use of man. On one side there still remains a large extent of wood which is intersected in every direction by unmade roads and paths, where in riding along you are every now and then surprised by coming suddenly upon a romantic cottage in the most [secluded] part of the Forest. They have all their little gardens and are almost hid amongst the fruit greens in full bloom.
>
> After this Description you will hardly expect me to say whether or not I like Wycombe. After all however I must tell you, that my chief pleasure arises from having abundance of employment. The more I can force myself to application, the more satisfaction do I feel, and nothing makes me so happy as the thought that were several hours added to the day, I should still find occupations sufficient for them all.
>
> I heard from Lady M from Bath when they were all well.[3]

1 Ward Draft, Ch.III, p.23.
2 Ward Draft, Ch.III, p.25.
3 Murray to Augusta, High Wycombe, 22 April 1802, Murray Papers, MS 21103.

Murray's stay at High Wycombe was, to his regret, cut short in late June 1802. He had, even in the short time spent at the college, made an impression on Colonel John Gaspard Le Marchant, the first commandant there, from whom he departed 'on easy, friendly terms'.[4] It was worth a try to ask for a refund given the shortness of his stay, but this the Commandant firmly declined: 'No; you are a member and may come and take your pennyworth out in science when you have not a better and more profitable thing to detain you'.[5] Murray had been appointed Adjutant General to the British forces in the West Indies, at Lieutenant General William Grinfield's request, and joined him at Portsmouth on 1 July. Grinfield, who had been Murray's commanding officer in the 3rd Guards, was renowned as a brutal, bullying commander, with a violent personality. Murray's calm, measured approach would likely be put under some stress. The ship assigned to the general's party, HM Storeship *Chichester*, must have been one of the worst in the Navy, manned by a mutinous company under a rough seaman of the name of Stephen whom Murray, now accompanied by a new Italian servant, Girolamo Cacamo, described in a letter to Isabella as 'a course specimen even of the salt water productions'.[6]

Murray had dined with Stephen the night before and mentioned to Isabella that the captain had already begun to live on the general's voyage supplies, so that a contrary wind would prove no hardship to him. Impatiently he complained that Isabella's friends in the Navy 'make it a general rule to inconvenience me as much as possible, and in particular by fixing a day for sailing that cannot possibly be met'.[7] This time there was the added issue of the sailors not having been paid, so that the first fair day for sailing would be spent settling with them. After a six-week crossing, punctuated by numerous floggings, Stephen was to die on board at Jamaica, one of a number of deaths on the disease ridden vessel, despite the ship being regularly sprayed with vinegar.

The Peace of Amiens was never going to last. Significant numbers of soldiers would be required to defend the West Indies against French and Dutch interference, as many as 20,000 according to some estimates, recruited locally as well as from friendly European nations, Irish Catholics, and even African slaves.

On arrival, Grinfield and Murray set off on an inspection of the French islands of Martinique, Tobago, and St Lucia, which were to be handed back to France under the peace treaty. He wrote of his contentment with his lot, and, without any pressure of military action, felt relaxed enough to write to Isabella to assure her that he was in good health:

> Hitherto I have found the climate is perfectly congenial to my constitution. To be constantly in a stew, and frequently bit by mosquitos are certainly unpleasant circumstances but they do not amount to very important misfortunes. I hope I shall be consoled in my frying pan with frequent accounts from home.[8]

He followed that next day with a typically descriptive one to Augusta:

4 Ward Draft Ch.III, p.24.

5 Ward Draft Ch.III, p.26.

6 Murray to Isabella Portsmouth, 1 July 1802, Murray Papers, MS 21112.

7 Murray to Isabella, Portsmouth, 1 July 1802, Murray Papers, MS 21112.

8 Murray to Isabella, Port Royal, Martinique, 28 August 1802, Murray Papers, MS 21101.

> In a letter I have written to Isabella by another conveyance I told her that to you only I would attempt to describe this romantic country. Swisserland alone, of all I have hitherto seen, comes near it, in point of the ruggedness and picturesque beauty of the scenery. The mountains are high, rocky, and covered with wood to the very Tops. They are extremely steep and the valleys which fall from them towards the sea are full of romantic situations. To give you a more particular description of Martinique, I have not leisure at present and must refer you therefore to General Campbell who has a taste for the beauties of nature and has often mentioned the West Indian Islands to me with the praise they deserve.
>
> We sail this afternoon for St Lucia, an island which is equally magnificent with Martinique, but in a more rude state. The General means to be at St Lucia only one day, on our way back to Barbados, where we shall be stationary for two or three months.
>
> I do not find any bad effects from the climate, and indeed there is no appearance of sickness in the islands although this is the season at which it used to be most prevalent.
>
> Some of the inhabitants have had colds, attended with a little fever which they call La Maladie des Chapeaux Quarres, because it made its appearance first on the arrival of the French Prefect and suite, who wear cocked hats.[9]

With time on his hands in Barbados, where Grinfield elected to winter, in his 'nice little house (formerly that of [Alexander] Hope when Adjutant General), behind the General's',[10] Murray wrote again to Augusta, with a small reminder of the benefits of good behaviour among the family. By this time the two sisters were in their mid-twenties and presumably still being supported by Patrick and Lady Mary. It is a letter that suggests, as many of his letters do, that he was as close as ever to his siblings and interested always in the latest news and gossip from home. Not that he was above handing out miniature sermons to Augusta from time to time, (and by all accounts she was equally capable of preaching) whether on her relationships or her attitude to misfortune, but the brotherly advice was always offered with genuine affection.

> I am glad to have such good Accts as you send me of all the family and particularly gratified with the happiness yourself and Isabella enjoy through the goodness of my brother and Lady Mary. Happiness very much depends upon the behaviour of those with whom we are nearly connected, and I hope we shall all of us keep this instantly in mind, both in our own conduct towards each other and in the World.
>
> My little friends Mary and Willm,[11] I am glad to find them as we could wish. I expect much pleasure from their company when I return. Children are always pleasant though there is no great pleasure in the recollection that in a few years we

9 Murray to Augusta, Port Royal, Martinique 29 August 1802, Murray Papers, MS 21103.

10 Murray to Isabella, Barbados, 13 November 1802, Murray Papers, MS 21101.

11 Patrick and Lady Mary had lost two children, in 1796 and 1800. Of those who survived, Mary was born in 1800 and William, who was to succeed Patrick as the 7th Baronet, in 1801.

shall be children again ourselves. Give my thanks to Isabella for her Country News of marriages, births etc. I hope our young cousin will not be Dumb.

I am very sorry to find that two of the neighbouring elections have turned out contrary to our wishes. By the last newspapers I see that Lady Ann has got a son and that Wm Hope has resigned his Burghs to the Advocate [Dundas].

I wrote my brother a few days ago, respecting a pipe of Madiera I am to get him here. I propose sending it by the first ship which sails for Glasgow, but shall let him know the details when the final arrangements are made.

The climate continues to agree perfectly well with me.

The French arrived at Martinique on the 15th September

Jack Hope was in good health the 10th Sept

Observe that I am Adjutant General to the Forces (if you will) but not to an individual.[12]

During the stay in Barbados, Grinfield introduced extra parades, including, worst of all, an evening parade of the whole garrison and staff at the unheard of hour of 5 o'clock (after dinner). For a man like Murray, who was no fan of sitting long over dinner, that did not present a problem, but it did interfere with the social intercourse on a hospitable island, and it was not long before the Governor, Henry Bentinck, started to bristle.[13]

Grinfield and Murray wasted no time in reconnoitring the islands, and Murray concentrated on selecting the most favourable points for attack should it be necessary to recapture them on the anticipated resumption of hostilities with France. Similarly in February and March 1803 on the British Islands, particularly Trinidad, time was devoted to their defence, and the assessment of their military value. At least eighteen detailed memoranda were drafted by Murray on these issues including 'the relative importance of the West India Islands'; 'on the defencibility of Grenada, St Vincent, St Kitts, Nevis, Antigua, Trinidad and Dominica'; 'on the principals of the defence of small islands', and above all 'memoranda on the military value of the French Islands of St Lucia and Tobago and Martinique'. In the last case, he deemed St Lucia and Tobago so important in his opinion that he favoured trading Dominica for them.

In each memorandum Murray examined schemes of attack and made recommendations for the points at which landings could best be effected. After hostilities resumed, both St Lucia and Tobago were captured by Grinfield within months of Murray's drafting the schemes for their attack. In each case Grinfield adopted the plans recommended by Murray, under which St Lucia was reduced within 48 hours and Tobago within 24, both at small cost to the force engaged.[14]

Murray also penned some thoughtful reports and views on the efficacy of integrating local inhabitants and slaves into the armed forces charged with defending the British Colonies. The forces comprised a number of differing nationalities already, rather than just British regulars. But the continuing relatively relaxed pace of life allowed for longer thoughtful letters.

12 Murray to Augusta, Barbados, 24 September 1802, Murray Papers, MS 21103.
13 Ward Draft, Ch.III, p.27.
14 Ward Draft, Ch.III, p.28.

I had the pleasure the other day of receiving letters from you and Isabella yours dated 23rd December and 5th Jan and Isabella's the 15th and 31st December.

I arrived in Trinidad a week ago having come with the Genl in Commander Hoods ship. Nothing can be more beautiful than this island. The northern shore which we coasted along for nearly two days presents a bold aspect, being formed by a ridge of rugged hills covered with Wood. Amongst these mountains are many fertile valleys, but as they run in general towards the south they were barred from our view by wider objects. Some places are however discernible where the Woods have begun to be cleared, and we would discern now and then, a solitary hut, built upon the brink of a precipice which overhung the sea. The waves dashed upon the broken fragments which had tumbled headlong from the mountain, and passing onward roared in the hollow caverns at the foot of the cliff. The rock itself seemed shook by the Southern Atlantic Surge, born against it before irascible winds, uninterrupted from the African Shore. Ah could the wretch in bondage dream whence came the gale which fanned him, whilst he toiled beneath a Tyrant Masters Scourge, or could the thought of home bring comfort whilst he stood exposed beneath those beams which beating vertically down upon his head learn him not to fancy even in his own shadow, the thought of Shelter from the Dazzling blaze!

In the evening we passed through the straits into the gulph of Paria. The sun was now retiring beyond the vast continent of South America and sunk by degrees behind the lofty mountains of Cumana, which cast a lengthened gloom far to the east, along the surface of the ocean.

During the night we continued to work up the gulph, and found ourselves at anchor in the morning off the town of Port d'Espagne. The Governor came on board to welcome us to the Island, and we returned onshore with him for a few hours. Next day the General and Commander disembarked in ceremony and the Commander took the Oath as the Commissioner for the administration of the affairs of the Colony.

On the following day I visited the commanding heights to the west of the town which bear the name of Sir Ralph Abercromby, who took the island from the Spaniards – yesterday I rode to St Joseph, the old capital of Trinidad, which is now however but a mere village, the only good buildings being the Barracks and the Hospital for the Troops.

The road to St Joseph passes at the foot of Hills which bound the Island in the North. On this side these hills are less rugged than in that towards the sea – they are however beautifully irregular and are covered with the finest trees. At intervals the Scene opens into the Valleys from which issue little Rivulets of the purest water. The road is bounded with Hedges of lime which send forth the most refreshing odours, and to the left of it are seen the new settlements of the Planters, in the little emminences at the foot of the Hills. These command an extensive prospect over the plain country to the south, part of which has been cleared and is covered with the rich productions of the Climate; part is still concealed by those ancient forests which have not yet yielded their Domain to the Avarice of Man. We dined with Genl Picton at his villa half way between St Joseph and this place and in the morning we returned to Town.

> I have now complemented you my dear Augusta with enough of this Descriptive Jargon. I hope you will be as much delighted in reading it as I have been in the composition – love to all etc Yours most Romantically mad I am.[15]

From time to time the subject of matrimony raised its head, and in his next letter home Murray regretted that he, like most men, was useless at accurately gauging the virtues of a woman. At this point the object of his affection seems to have been Miss Susan Proby, a sister of Lady Seaforth, the Governor's wife, who was visiting.[16]

> I take the opportunity of the Excellent going home to write you a few lines. First I thank you for all the letters I have received since I came to Trinidad. To those by the former Packet I answered by a very beautiful piece of Descriptive Composition, so superior, and so much above the vulgar that I judged it prudent to write a letter to my Brother by the same conveyance, to preserve if possible some claim to Common Sense.
>
> Yours by the last packet bring me accounts of two marriages with comments upon them. I hold myself in no measure responsible, I must tell you for the Matrimonial arrangements of my friends – one of the gentlemen you mention is a man of much Worth, but his last match I did not think altogether suitable – but in this I cannot expect you to agree with me. I hope the present connection though suddenly formed will nevertheless be happy.
>
> What is a poor man to do who is resolved to marry. If he is entirely employed in life he has not time to study the Lady's character, and even if he does it is ten to one but he is mistaken in the opinion he forms. All his tedious courtship therefore with the addition perhaps of a great deal of anxiety, seems in the end but to make his want of discernment the more conspicuous.
>
> For my part I should be inclined to depend more upon the Opinion of a sensible woman, who was my friend, than upon my own, in so far as misguided the character dispositions etc etc.[17]

Although Murray's reports comprised a complete dossier on the defence of all the West Indian Islands, based on comprehensive data assembled by him on his visits to each island, the greatest threat came not from the French, but from sickness.

Great strides were being made to reduce the incidence of serious disease in the Army, but on its continuous expeditions from 1793 to 1801 in the West Indies, according to the historian Martin Howard a total of 44,000 men and NCOs and 1,500 officers died in or en route to the Caribbean. These were deaths from disease, not from the relatively sparse military action, which probably accounted for no more than 10 percent of the overall total. Dysentery, yellow fever, malaria, liver disease, scurvy, and venereal diseases were all common. Nor

15 Murray to Augusta, Port of Spain, Trinidad, 27 February 1803, Murray Papers, MS 21103.

16 Ward Draft, Ch.III, p.30.

17 Murray to Augusta, Trinidad, 13 March 1803, Murray Papers, MS 21103.

were the physicians spared. Of the eleven who accompanied Abercromby to the West Indies six died in the short campaign.[18]

On 18 May 1803, Britain declared war on France. The Treaty of Amiens had lasted less than 14 months and had been constantly undermined by hostility and lack of trust on both sides. One of the earliest moves by the French was to assemble a mighty invasion force across the Channel at Boulogne. Maybe Murray's dismissal of Augusta's invasion concerns in the autumn of 1801 was premature, and her worry was not merely a 'periodical distemper' after all. Murray was urgently summoned back to Horse Guards by Major General Robert Brownrigg, the Quartermaster General of the Forces. His recall in early June was perhaps a lucky escape. After successfully taking St Lucia and Tobago, Grinfield, his wife and another general, Clephane, all fell victim to yellow fever, and were dead by November.[19]

Horse Guards on London's Whitehall was the headquarters of the British Army. It was there that the Commander in Chief, Quartermaster General, Adjutant General, and Military Secretary, aided by a small staff, administered the army's worldwide operations. It was to Horse Guards that Murray would from time to time return from his campaign duties. It was the start of a new era for the Quartermaster General's department. Brownrigg had been instrumental in a root and branch reorganisation of the department. A Military Library, containing detailed accounts of past military events from which lessons might be drawn, and a Drawing Room, containing maps and plans, and draughtsmen and printers for preparing copies, for the guidance of officers 'destined for particular service' were established, together forming the 'Depot for Military Knowledge' in the north pavilion of Horse Guards. The department commanded enhanced prestige, and Murray was selected by Brownrigg to be Assistant Quartermaster General, 'a scientific and intelligent assistant'.[20]

Murray was, from the moment he got back to London, more than fully occupied in making preparations to counter the threat of the imminent invasion. He wrote to Augusta:

> Had I known that you were still with Lady Louden I should have written you a few lines from Liverpool, on my arrival. However although you have heard probably by now from Ochtertyre, and Isabella's letter must have likewise reached Ayrshire, I flatter myself you will yet be well pleased to get a letter from me dated in England.
>
> Excepting the confirmation by signature of my own presence in Europe you can expect little from me, indeed the short time I have been at home has been employed in running about in consequence of some Commissions and Letters I brought from the West Indies, in attending to the Business of my new situation. The preparations for receiving in a suitable manner, the First Consul of France, engross all our time, and the thoughts, I find, of every person in England. If he does us any mischief it must be from our own bad management. Indeed, if we cannot defend ourselves with all the advantages we enjoy, we are extremely unworthy of being any longer an independent nation.

18 Martin R. Howard, *Death Before Glory: The British Soldier in the West Indies in the French Revolutionary and Napoleonic Wars*, (Barnsley: Pen & Sword: 2015), Ch 11.

19 Ward Draft, Ch.III, p.30.

20 Ward Draft, Ch.III, pp.31-2.

> I am sorry to learn that Lady Louden has been unwell. The loss of so good a man as Lord Dumfries must have made a considerable impression on her spirits, but under such misfortunes in life, time and the Reflections which good sense [paper damaged] are the best and indeed the only remedies.
>
> Isabella I suppose has written you whether I look well or ill, or fat or thin, – for my own part I have heard so many different opinions that I dare not presume to state my own poor sentiments upon the subject.[21]

The reference to Isabella and her comments on Murray's health lead to the interesting possibility that Murray caught up with Isabella in Liverpool where he disembarked from the West Indies. If this is so then it raises the question as to why Isabella was in Liverpool. The most likely reason is that she was visiting their mother, Augusta, who lived there in the later stages of her life, though the reasons for that are obscure, and the three of them may well have enjoyed some time together.

The likelihood of invasion by the Boulogne force increased during the course of the year. In England, tens of thousands volunteered during the summer of 1803, and positioned themselves along the Kent coast. Plans were put in place for laying waste to the country to deny an invading force access to livestock and transport. It seemed merely a matter of time before the southern defences would be tested.

John Bull and Bonaparte. An 1803 satirical image depicting John Bull and Napoleon glaring at each other over the English Channel. (Anne S.K. Brown Military Collection)

21 Murray to Augusta, Horse Guards, 16 July 1803, Murray Papers, MS 21103.

Murray played his part alongside Alexander Hope and Robert Brownrigg in preparing the great scheme of national defence.[22] Murray was considered Hope's confidential assistant; his opinions were widely canvassed and his views respected and almost every problem of importance was thrown his way. 'I return to you Colonel Murray's letter' Brownrigg wrote to Hope, 'and I am happy to see how much his general opinions fall in with the system we are acting upon'.[23]

In truth the French ships were continuing to be well contained by the Royal Navy, and Napoleon was not prepared to risk what might have been a massacre at sea. Apart from his earlier attempts to land troops in Ireland, this was the nearest he would get to British soil. Instead the French moved into northern Germany, whilst the British were setting about recovering territories in the East and West Indies that had been evacuated during the short peace. On 18 May 1804 Napoleon was declared hereditary Emperor of France. Britain awaited developments with increasing anxiety.

In September Murray was sent to the south coast, partly to assess the system of Martello Towers, one element of the country's defences. He opposed their use as a system, considering them to have merit as single towers for defending bays or inlets but no more than that. His view was that if the Royal Navy lost control of the Channel for a sufficient period there was nothing to prevent the French army from landing somewhere, and advancing about 20 miles inland. However, they would need to secure a port such as Dover, which would present problems for them. He was concerned about the closeness of London to the coast and emphasised the need to strengthen its defences, to improve lines of communication, and for the construction of field works to delay the enemy's advance. But he was convinced that, given proper preparations, any invasion force could be defeated.[24]

Murray was soon posted to Ireland again, this time as Deputy Quartermaster General, in November 1804. In that role he was to continue the work of other generals of the time including Alexander Hope, readying Ireland against possible invasion. His experience in preparing the south of England was to be put to good use and his arrival gave rise to some encouraging comments:

> You will have seen by the gazette that George Murray is appointed DQMG here, to my great satisfaction, as with him I shall be able to communicate freely. If you see GM before he comes to Ireland, you may have the opportunity of talking over matters with him and give him some insight into Clinton's character, who told me that he not only knew him as a brother-Guardsman, but that he had heard that he was clever. I fear between ourselves that he is a little jealous of him… If George Murray plays his cards well he may contrive to get the management and entire superintendence of our part of the staff to himself.[25]

22 TNA, WO 80/7, 'Defence of London and South East Coast'. This was to come up again in 1845 when Wellington asked for Murray's recollections on how best to defend London.

23 Ward Draft, Ch.III, p.33.

24 Ward Draft, Ch.III, pp.33-4.

25 Major Pine-Coffin to Major General John Le Marchant (promoted since his time at High Wycombe) Dublin, 11 November 1804, Ward Draft Ch III, p.34 citing Le Marchant Mss.

If that were to be the case then science would reign supreme in Ireland.

Colonel William Clinton, Quartermaster General in Ireland since April 1804, 'solitary, diffident, and awkward in company',[26] seemed to have an innate suspicion of the inhabitants of North Britain, so Murray, arriving in Dublin on 23 January 1805, must have turned on his charm to win Clinton's plaudits:

> 24 January 1805 'I like the appearance of my deputy. I hope I shall never find anything of the Scot in him, and I shall be much disposed to take to him if I do not'.
> 26 January 1805 'A sound hearted man... I can easily perceive that he is a Scot, but I hope he is a fair one'.
> 31 January 1805 'I like Murray the more I see of him'.[27]

By March Murray had got his feet well under the desk, fully aware of his allotted task which was to reorganise the department along modern lines, and was clearly taking advantage of Clinton's absence on leave to get things done, as reported by Pine-Coffin: 'Our friend GM is now conducting the department in the absence of General C and with ability you may be assured'[28] A matter of days later, Pine-Coffin wrote again: 'An excellent fellow and very intelligent... GM has made more progress in arranging the department during the short time that General Clinton has been absent than has been done during the whole time I have been in Ireland...every day serves to convince me what a valuable acquisition he is to us in this country'.[29]

There are volumes of military memoranda and reports by Murray and his predecessors on how best to garrison Ireland against the real prospect of a French invasion, supported by local revolutionaries.[30] In Murray's view, and certainly others shared the fear, Ireland was still the most likely choice for Napoleon to commence any invasion of Britain. The Irish had already demonstrated their support for France's Revolutionary ideas. In any case, it suited Napoleon to force Britain to station a very substantial number of troops there, thus depriving the British forces fighting on the Continent and in the West Indies of much needed support. Ireland still remained an unstable country and detailed attention was constantly paid to its defence.

Murray made it clear that, in his view, any army landing would encourage local insurrection and would also seek to take Dublin and install a new government, as well as try and cut off supply from the mainland with a big naval presence. He advocated building and improving a number of fortifications – including, despite his caution as to their use on England's south coast, the numerous Martello Towers that are still evident around Dublin – and fortifying the Pidgeon House at the entrance to Dublin Bay. On Clinton's return he

26 Ward Draft, Ch.III, p.35.
27 Ward Draft, Ch.III, p 38, citing W. Clinton Ms Diary pp.44-5.
28 Major Pine-Coffin to Le Marchant, Dublin, 17 March 1805, Ward Draft, Ch.III, p.38, citing Le Marchant Mss.
29 Major Pine-Coffin to Le Marchant, Dublin, 9 April 1805, Ward Draft, Ch.III, p.38, citing Le Marchant Mss.
30 Murray Papers, ADV MS 46.1.7 – 1805 military reports; defence of Cork etc.

bade Murray to dine 'en famille' and repeated his earlier compliments 'The more I see of this young man the more estimable his character appears'.[31]

In the summer of 1805, Murray visited over 30 towns including Johnstown, Waterford, Cork, Limerick, Killarney, Bantry, Kilkenny, Bandon and other military bases to assess their readiness to withstand attack. His very detailed plans anticipated possible landing points and the necessity of moving forces quickly to counter any invading force before it could get a secure foothold. The reports prepared by him demonstrate his growing skill in interpreting the advantages and disadvantages of the particular terrain in given localities and how defences might be best arranged, as well as how the enemy would behave in the same countryside.[32]

About this time Murray was charged by the Government with preparing a report on the idea of introducing limited service in the Army, which had been experimented with in a preparatory way already. His draft memorandum was, as ever, a thoughtful and carefully argued piece of work, compiled only after taking the views of a dozen senior military men including Sir David Dundas, the Earl of Moira, Sir James Pulteney, Marquess Cornwallis and Lieutenant General Fox. He considered, amongst other things, discipline (Murray felt 'temporary soldiers' might become insubordinate), recruitment (he could see families would be more inclined to encourage men to join) and risk of desertion. His Report concluded:

> I have now stated the principal arguments which have been advanced upon both sides in regard to this question and after considering these with the greatest attention and receiving the pleas which have at different times presented themselves to my own mind upon the subject, I cannot but come to the conclusion unfavourable to the plan of enlisting men into the regular army for a limited period of service.
>
> When I look to the high character which the British Army has hitherto borne throughout every period of history, I feel naturally averse to the idea of an alteration; at best of a very doubtful tendency, in a most important point of the constitution, especially do I deprecate the introduction of so essential a change, at a moment when all the energies of our military system are requisite for the Security of the Country.
>
> We have recently added to our establishment a body of regular forces engaged under limitations both as to place and time of Service. Let us preserve at the same time in the original stock of our Army the system to which it has so long been accustomed – and let us rest for the present upon the hope, in my opinion well founded, that we have adopted an arrangement, which will put us in possession of all the benefits which can result from the Plan of Establishment for a limited period, at the same time that we have not deprived ourselves of the advantages and tried excellence, inherent in an Army comprised of men attached for their whole life to the military profession.[33]

31 Ward Draft, Ch,III, p,39, citing W. Clinton Ms. Diary, p.66.

32 Murray's papers of his time in Dublin are in Murray Papers, ADV MS 46.1.5-46.1.11.

33 Undated report, Murray Papers, ADV MS 46.1.21.

In fact a form of limited service was actually introduced in 1806, with minimum service of seven years for infantry and ten for cavalry and artillery.

Late in 1805 Murray was recalled from Ireland by Brownrigg, to act at the head of the Quartermaster General's Department with the advanced division of the army destined for Northern Germany, which was preparing for embarkation at Deal and Ramsgate. He had hoped to call on Le Marchant at Wycombe on his way, but missed him narrowly at the Inn, only to gallop past him soon after. Arriving in London on 1 November, he had instead to write to Le Marchant seeking his views on how to establish the Department on foreign service. Le Marchant replied enthusiastically with some useful advice.

Murray was not unduly depressed by the defeat of the Austrians at Ulm. Of Nelson's success at Trafalgar he commented in a letter to Isabella: 'The navy have given us a noble example and if we do not attempt to imitate them as far as circumstances will permit, I shall be ashamed of the service'.[34]Arriving on the South Coast, Murray came first under the command of Lieutenant General George Don and latterly Lieutenant General Lord Cathcart, who had been Commander in Chief in Ireland when Murray had been serving there. The force of 14,000 occupied Hanover in December, having combined with Prussian forces. Murray carried with him the names of all the former officers of the Hanoverian Engineers which had been disbanded by Napoleon, with a view, no doubt, of tapping into this valuable source of scientific talent.[35] He embarked at Harwich, landing at Cuxhaven on 19 November. After some skirmishes with the French, the expedition ceased to have much relevance after a Franco-Prussian agreement handed Hanover to the Prussians, and the British returned to England in February 1806, rather than risk resistance against combined Prussian and French forces.

The Hanover expedition is variously described as 'luckless' and 'useless'. It certainly fell victim to the extraordinary fluidity of alliances in Europe, and was affected by Napoleon's stunning victory at the Battle of Austerlitz. Sometimes it must have been very difficult to ascertain just who was supposed to be fighting with, or against, whom, and certainly alliances were formed and dismantled with great gusto in a constant attempt to promote self-interest or to deny advantage to another country.

In his few weeks as Quartermaster General on the Continent, Murray had no opportunity to display his abilities or put into operation any part of the plan which Le Marchant had provided for him. His main occupations were the cantonment of troops, the arrangement of one or two marches, and reconnaissance of routes to the crossing places of the Elbe in case the army was squeezed in that direction. His concerns also seem to have included feeding the army, notable as one of the last instances where this was still considered the responsibility of the Quartermaster General's department, rather than the Commissariat which would soon take over that role.

On his return from what must have been a disappointing campaign for him, Murray resumed his appointment in Ireland. There is evidence in 1806 of some discussion around his being sent to South America, in particular Chile, with the local rank of brigadier, but this came to nothing. It was a time when the politicians were becoming increasingly

34 Murray to Isabella, London, 7 November 1805, Murray Papers, MS 21101.
35 Ward Draft, Ch.IV, p.2.

excited about the possibility of exploiting the wealth and untapped markets of that continent, bolstered by the recent successful capture of Buenos Aires, a result welcomed by the British public who were becoming sickened by the endless war in Europe. Wellesley too was sounded out about command of a force there to take Mexico, but this plan foundered, as the success at Buenos Aires was soon overturned by the local inhabitants.

During his time in Dublin, an immense amount of work flowed from Murray's pen – his handwriting deteriorating as a result – and he successfully remodelled the department, so that by 1807, when Wellesley was taking over as Chief Secretary in Ireland, it needed no further reorganisation.[36] The two must have briefly worked together on all aspects of the defence of Ireland, with detailed reports being sent to London about the vulnerability of the Irish coastline and the likely support of the Irish people for any French landing, all based on work which Murray had prepared two years earlier. If the rest of the country was overrun it was essential that Cork and Dublin remained in British hands to maintain vital links with Britain, and they thus needed to be fortified. Here was more of Murray's work, on its way to London, now strengthened with the Wellesley stamp of approval.

Life for the bachelor Murray in Dublin was 'like being in a barracks'. Social life was badly affected by the two recent Irish Rebellions. Army headquarters were in the Royal Hospital at Kilmainham.[37] The officers commonly lodged elsewhere in the city. There is no record of where Murray actually stayed, but Clinton wrote, on 19 September 1807, when he was on his own, of taking up quarters 'at Murray's old shop' which appears to have been in or near Dame Street.[38] But there were plenty of social occasions among a relatively small group of acquaintances and fellow officers, and no doubt Murray and Wellesley would have mixed in the same Dublin society. There were some grand occasions at the Castle and informal parties at the Royal Hospital. At one of the latter Murray met Julia, daughter of Lieutenant General Sir John Floyd, acting Commander in Chief in Ireland during Cathcart's absence. Julia was to reappear later in Murray's life as Lady Peel, wife of the Prime Minister. Anstruther, in Ireland as Adjutant General, was an excellent host. His dinners were elaborate affairs where his guests would be entertained by the attractive, and musically accomplished, Mrs Anstruther, after they had left the table, often as late as eleven o'clock.[39]

Murray was still finding it difficult to warm to Ireland, although this antipathy seemed to soften somewhat in his later years. He struggled with the political and religious situations. He advocated the government to remain firm in its treatment of the Irish; he saw no possibility of successful concessions owing to the degree of bitterness and religious bigotry that was ever present. He had done his bit to ensure the country was amply prepared against invasion. His situation was more that of an official in a conquered province than a staff officer on a home establishment. If he did not much care for Ireland or the Irish, his time there provided Murray with rapidly increasing confidence in his own abilities. He was starting to feel he could handle anything that came his way. Imposing his will more by quiet insistence rather than outbursts of irritability, he recognised that arguments between departments only led to the service as a whole suffering. Unassuming, modest, with a strong Presbyterian

36 Ward Draft, Ch.III, pp.39-40.
37 Ward Draft, Ch.III, p.40.
38 Ward Draft, Ch.III, p.40.
39 Ward Draft, Ch.III, pp.40-1.

upbringing, he was aware of his own strengths and weaknesses, and was confident enough not to wait for opportunities merely to arise. Seemingly unconstrained by formal methods, he was happy to remind others of his expectations by quiet words in the right place at the best time. He had very useful allies in senior positions, whom he had impressed with his diligence and skills, and he was not too shy in using them to his advantage. Alexander Hope was, of course, his number one target for such requests, and support. Clinton was driven to distraction as Murray sought excitement after excitement, and increased exposure to front line soldiering. As Ward noted: 'Well-bred man did not strive so: he accepted what he was offered, unless it were a nuisance, and then he declined… His colleagues were now treated to the spectacle of Murray forcing his way remorselessly up the ladder, and a formidable spectacle it was'.[40]

40 Ward Draft, Ch.III, p.43.

6

1807 – Denmark – Bombardment of Copenhagen

In the summer of 1807 the French were perceived as being about to treat with Denmark in an effort to assume control of the substantial Danish fleet. The Danes had remained neutral during the ongoing war against France, and their navy's continued neutrality was seen as critical to avoid disruption to Britain's trade in the Baltic. Not only that, but were the fleet to fall into French hands, it could be used in an invasion of Britain, possibly via Ireland. Somehow this threat needed to be neutralised and discussions took place to try to persuade the Danes to place their fleet beyond French reach, under British protection, to be returned at the cessation of hostilities. The Danes would have none of it and the decision was made to despatch an expedition to Copenhagen to place the Danes under more pressure.

The British had, a little earlier, sent a force under Lieutenant General Lord Cathcart to assist the King of Sweden, Gustav IV Adolf, who was under attack from the French at Stralsund. Cathcart and his staff landed and were quartered on the island of Rügen. Murray, as the expedition's Deputy Quartermaster General, was quartered in the small village of Swantow. A period of relatively comfortable inactivity followed while events elsewhere unravelled. Soon the British Government heard of the secret articles of the Treaty of Tilsit, signed between France, Russia, and Prussia under the terms of which, inter alia, it was planned to force Denmark, Sweden, and Portugal to close their ports to the British, and to declare war, if by 1 November Britain had refused to come to terms with Napoleon. This would give Napoleon almost unlimited naval power, 180 ships of the line, with which to challenge British naval supremacy and renew the threat of invasion.

It was simply too dangerous for Britain to allow this to happen. An additional force, in total about 25,000 men, originally destined for Rügen, carried in 38 warships with 400 transports, was hastily rerouted to Copenhagen to join up with Cathcart's force, which, abandoning its original mission, sailed from Rügen on 10 August. Murray sailed with Cathcart on the frigate HMS *Africaine* arriving off Elsinore on 12 August, thence to Copenhagen on 15 August, where he boarded another frigate, HMS *Surveillante*.

The plan was to continue to pressurise the Danes into handing over their fleet, to keep it out of French hands, but if all diplomatic means failed, Copenhagen, where the Danish fleet was berthed, was to be besieged or bombarded. Among the vessels that formed the British force were numerous bomb ships. Poorly conducted negotiations had humiliated the Danes, the negotiators seemingly having failed to clearly offer various subsidies and omitted to stress the British naval assistance that would have been made available to provide protection, if the Danes had concurred with the British suggestion.

Several meetings of general officers were held on Admiral James Gambier's flagship, HMS *Prince of Wales*, off Elsinore, to discuss possible plans of attack, culminating at a council of War on 14 August, at which four alternative plans were discussed. Murray, demonstrating substantial confidence, insisted that none of the plans was practicable for a number of sound military reasons. He put forward his own proposals in a memorandum when the council of war adjourned to consider the first four, delicately avoiding demolishing the more senior officers' various proposals. According to Murray's intelligence summary, Zealand was almost denuded of regular troops, whilst the Copenhagen garrison consisted of about 13,000 infantry, 200 cavalry and about 400 artillerymen. Cathcart seemed to be relying on others to propose ways of forcing the garrison to capitulate. A regular siege was cautioned against by his engineers, as the city's defences were too strong for the equipment at their disposal.[1] Aware that the stated aim of the campaign was the capture of, not the destruction of or partial damage to, the Danish fleet, the options were limited. One plan, to attempt to take the Three Crowns Battery which guarded the harbour, was deemed too risky in terms of likely damage to the Danish fleet. Cathcart, in any case, was less than happy with the orders he had been given.[2]

Murray's plan involved a landing by the army in Zealand, away from Copenhagen, movement towards Amager, and laying siege to the city from two sides. Further Danish resistance would invite bombardment. Murray acknowledged that there was serious disquiet among the senior British officers, including Wellesley, commanding the Reserve, at the prospect of subjecting the civilian inhabitants of one of Europe's neutral capitals to such treatment, but he argued that given the time of year, there was no time for delay, and that the other options all had flaws. Despite reservations on the part of some of the senior officers the logic of Murray's proposals won them over, his plan being adopted by Cathcart in preference to any other of those proposed, a reflection perhaps of the confidence Murray had inspired in his commander in Ireland.

Wellesley stood with him as an early ally. As Ward put it:

> At this critical moment in a delicate operation, it is clear that Murray already discerned in the General those transcendent abilities by which the nation itself was soon to recognize the Duke of Wellington, and that Wellesley detected in the cautious Scot with the intelligent eye a man who possessed as lively a comprehension as his own and as steady a nerve. In the careers of both it was a moment of profound significance. For Murray it was decisive.[3]

1 See Wellesley to Hawkesbury, on board *Goliath* off Elsinor, 14 August 1807, Wellington, 2nd Duke of (ed.) *Supplementary Despatches, Correspondence, and Memoranda, of Field Marshal Arthur, Duke of Wellington* (London: John Murray, 1858-62), Vol.VI p. 2; Muir, online commentary for *Wellington: The Path to Victory*, Chapter 13, at www.lifeofwellington.co.uk/commentary/chapter-thirteen-copenhagen-july-september-1807/.

2 Muir, online commentary for *Wellington: The Path to Victory*, Chapter 13.

3 Ward Draft, Ch.IV, p.21.

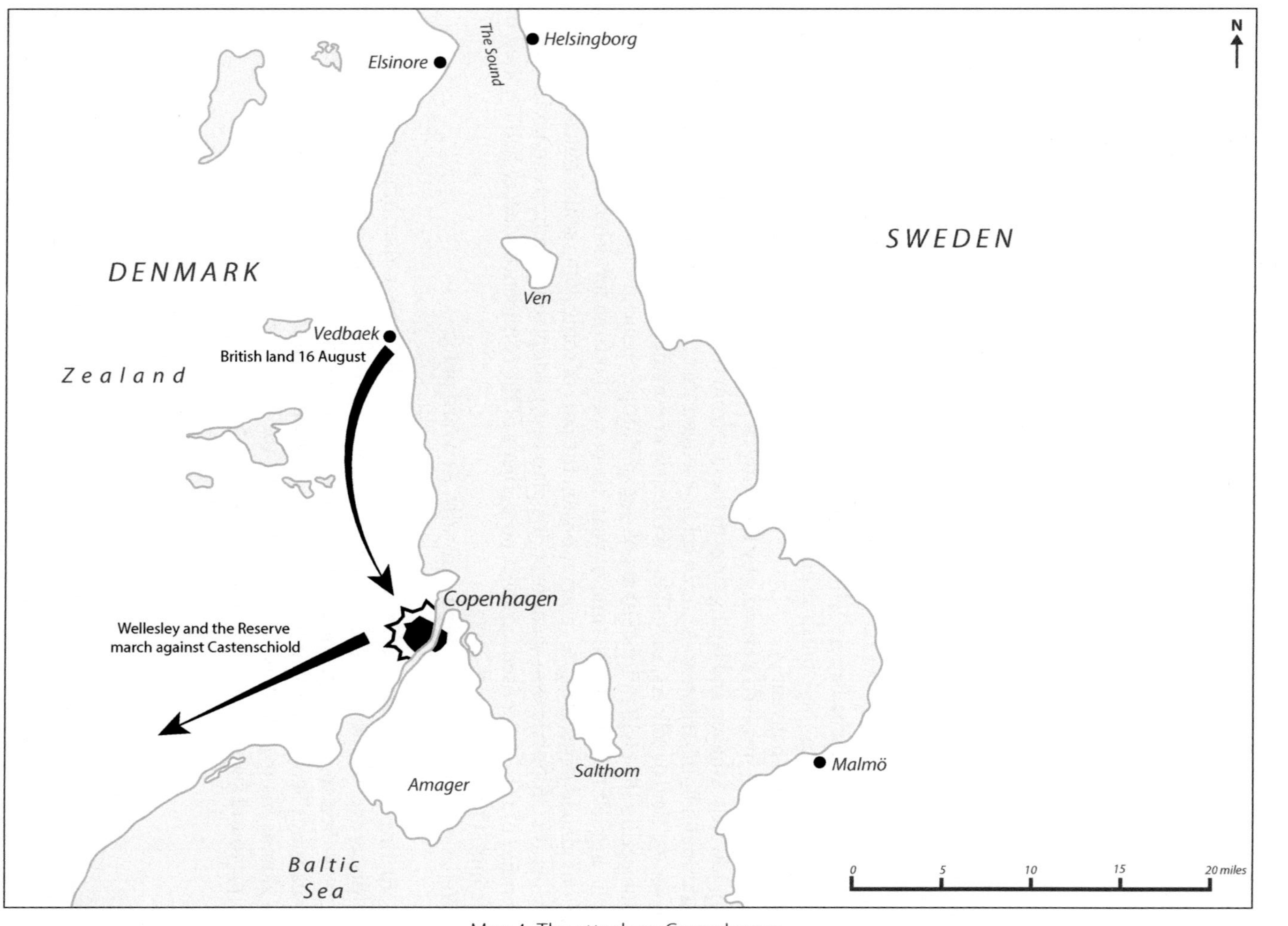

Map 4 The attack on Copenhagen.

Wellesley agreed that the Three Crowns Battery idea would not deliver the required result either militarily or politically. However, he baulked at the idea of bombardment and advocated a last attempt at close investment, cutting off supplies of water and food to try to bring the campaign to a satisfactory end with as little loss of life as possible. At the same time, he also realised that this was unlikely to deliver the required results and reluctantly agreed to support Murray's plan – indeed, perhaps even had a hand in drafting it – if the city continued to hold out.

Murray, whist recognizing the reservations which many of his fellow officers held, namely that 'the bombardment of the town itself was generally held to be improper', stuck firmly to the necessity of such an attack:

> The lateness of the season and the possibility of our operations being interrupted in spite of all our exertions to guard the Belt, render it very probable that any attempt to reduce Copenhagen by a regular siege might prove unsuccessful… It appears therefore that our principal reliance must be upon the effect of a bombardment, and that we must endeavour by that means to destroy the Danish fleet or force the government to surrender it into our hands.
>
> Different opinions are entertained as to the efficacy of a bombardment towards destroying the fleet… If it is found by experience that the destruction of the fleet is actually not within the power of our mortar batteries, we must then of necessity resort to the harsh measure of forcing the town into our terms, by the sufferings of the inhabitants themselves. But to give this mode of attack its fullest effect, it is necessary completely to invest the place, and oblige by that means, all persons of whatever description, to undergo the same hardships and dangers – and from the nature of the force which composes the principal part of the garrison, it is not improbable but that the bombardment of the town itself may be found the speediest means of bringing the governor to accede to the conditions which it is understood we are disposed to offer.[4]

Murray, in his proposal, referred to the nature of the force composing most of the garrison of the city. Francis Jackson, a diplomat sent secretly to negotiate with the Danes, wrote on 15 August that, contrary to the intelligence that Murray had received earlier, 'The garrison of Copenhagen does not amount to more than four thousand regular troops. The landwehr is a mere rabble… The people are said to be anxious to capitulate before a conflagration takes place, which must happen soon after a bombardment begins'. In the same letter he noted the limited preparations being made for a sustained defence of the town.[5]

On 16 August Christian Bernstorff, the Danish foreign minister, wrote:

> There is no room for hiding from ourselves that the inequality of the forces engaged will be such that we hardly dare indulge in the hope of retaining Zealand for any length of time. The island was taken off guard, practically denuded of troops, and is

4 Plan of attack on Copenhagen submitted by Murray to Cathcart, 14 August 1807, Murray Papers, ADV MS 46.1.12.

5 Muir, online commentary for *Wellington: The Path to Victory*, Chapter 13, citing Francis Jackson to George Jackson, 15 August 1807, *Diaries and Letters of Sir George Jackson*, Vol.2, pp.194-8.

The Bombardment of Copenhagen. (Anne S.K. Brown Military Collection)

> so surrounded by the English, that it is virtually impossible to elude their vigilance and pass reinforcements to it.[6]

Murray's preparations for this part of the overall operation were clear and detailed, and he worked with Wellesley in preparing and positioning his troops, ensuring they had back up supplies of food and spare ammunition in accordance with his Quartermaster's role. It was the start of a close working relationship with Wellesley, which was to form such a successful team in Portugal and Spain.

Lieutenant General Castenschiold, the Danish Commander in Zealand faced a stark choice: an ultimately fruitless and costly attempt to interfere with the siege, or sitting back and watching the city fall. The number under his command was small but on 23 August he was encouraged by the addition of troops from Mon, a small island next to Zealand, bringing his active total to about 8,000. However, these were largely inexperienced militia. Castenschiold moved south to Kioge, linking up with the Mon force there.[7]

Cathcart despatched Wellesley to Roskilde too late to prevent the Danish general from moving towards Kioge. The plan was to turn the Danes with a flanking movement and force them to move north after their anticipated defeat by the main force under Wellesley. The plan was sound, but neutralized by Castenschiolds's earlier move south. Wellesley followed

6 Muir, online commentary for *Wellington: The Path to Victory*, Chapter 13, citing Munch-Petersen, *Defying Napoleon*, p.109.

7 Muir, online commentary for *Wellington: The Path to Victory*, Chapter 13, citing Ryan 'The Copenhagen Expedition, 1807' (MA thesis), pp.148-151.

the Danes south and attacked them on the 29th. The same type of flanking movement was put in place to cut off any possible retreat. This time the plan worked, and following a number of engagements over the next few days, the Danish militia was finished.

The landing at Amager, which had been promoted by Murray, and supported by Wellesley as increasing the pressure on the city, never took place, partly as a result of Cathcart's inertia, and partly owing to the activity of Danish gunboats. These were smaller and nimbler than the British vessels and were capable of inflicting a good deal of damage, sitting very low in the water and able to get close in under the British naval guns, although they suffered badly from British shore based batteries when they returned to their bases. Full attention was now directed at Copenhagen itself, which was invited to surrender. The British forces moved closer to the edges of the city than was originally anticipated. By 31 August the British guns were in place. The next day the Danish commander, Major General Peymann, was called on to surrender, but refused.

When it became apparent that the Danes, even in their weak situation, would not budge in the negotiations concerning the fate of the capital, and despite Cathcart's preference to allow time to play out, other opinions prevailed, specifically Murray's, and the order was given for the start of the bombardment.

For three days and nights, over 2 to 5 September, artillery, mortars and rockets, three times the amount of gunpowder and shot that was to be deployed at Waterloo, rained down on the defenceless city,[8] and by the morning of the 5th the whole of the western quarter was ablaze. Numerous civilians, inevitably including many women and children, became casualties, with estimates of exact numbers fluctuating wildly (the latest Danish research suggests that initial estimates of around 2,000 were grossly inflated and the actual number killed in the city was around 200).[9] Thirty per cent of the city's buildings were destroyed, including the Vor Frue Kirke; much of the damage caused by Congreve's rockets, a new weapon, designed as much as anything to spread fire. It was a terrifying experience for the citizens, made all the worse in the knowledge that the women and children could have been spared the dreadful horror had they been evacuated by their own commander, who had spurned the opportunity granted by the British before the bombardment began.

A realisation of the futility of his stance forced Peymann to propose a 24-hour armistice for the settlement of preliminaries to a capitulation. Murray was instructed by Cathcart to cross the lines and receive Peymann's proposal. He returned next morning with the Governor's proposal to deliver up the Danish Fleet, and an armistice was declared. Cathcart's report from the citadel of Copenhagen to Castlereagh, the British Secretary of State for War and the Colonies, on the bombardment and surrender included the following:

> On the evening of 5 September, a letter was sent by a Danish General to propose an armistice of 24 hours, for preparing an agreement on which Articles of Capitulation might be founded. The armistice was declined, as tending towards unnecessary delay, and the works were continued, but the firing was countermanded and Lt. Col

8 Knight, *Britain Against Napoleon*, p.372.

9 Rasmus Glenthoj and Morten Nordhagen Ottosen, *Experiences of War and Nationality in Denmark and Norway 1807-1815*, (Basingstoke: Palgrave Macmillan, 2014).

> Murray was sent to explain that no proposal of capitulation could be listened to unless accompanied by agreement for surrender of the fleet.[10]

Yet again it was Murray, whose military plan had proved successful, if not wholly embraced by others, who was selected as the man to negotiate terms of surrender. On this occasion, faced with the possibility of the virtual obliteration of their capital city, the Danes had little choice. The resultant Articles of Capitulation, with Murray's as one of the signatures next to Wellesley's, proved enormously beneficial to Britain.

On 6 September Wellesley, Rear Admiral Sir Home Riggs Popham and Murray were appointed to prepare and sign the Articles. With no time wasted, the Articles were drawn up during the night between the 6th and 7th. Article III of the final document stated:

> The ships and vessels of war of every description, with all the naval stores belonging to His Danish Majesty, shall be delivered into the charge of such persons as shall be appointed by the commanders in Chief of His Britannic Majesty's forces; and they are to be put into immediate possession in the dockyards, and all the buildings and storehouses belonging thereto.[11]

At 4 pm the next day Lieutenant General Burrard took possession of the 71-strong Danish Fleet. It included 17 ships of the line, 11 frigates, and a number of smaller vessels. Many were to be declared later, on arrival in England, as unseaworthy. If the ships had been surrendered in accordance with the original British proposals they would have been effectively quarantined and left idle. Some ships of the line were subsumed into the British Navy with minor name changes and used in the continuing war against the French. Two million pounds' worth of naval stores as well as a number of Danish merchant ships, and the Danish colonies in the West Indies were also taken.[12] On the more commercial aspects Wellesley was resolute: on attempting to haggle over naval stores a Danish admiral was firmly told 'Now Admiral, mind every stick, every stick'.[13]

Murray's diplomatic talents were required to placate the Danes when preparations for sail took longer than the six weeks allowed for in the Articles, despite the 2,000-strong working parties that were sent daily into the dockyard to make the vessels seaworthy. Murray was the last to embark when the huge fleet of ships sailed for England on the morning of 21 October. Murray's share of the prize money from the capture of so many ships amounted to £742, less than half Wellesley's, who outranked him and whose prize of £1,700 might be worth about £80,000 in today's money. From a total pot of about £1 million, Cathcart received £18,000.[14]

The news of the successful expedition, and the large numbers of Danish naval vessels brought back to England, was initially greeted with enthusiasm. However, when the details

10 Gurwood, Lieut. Colonel (ed.), *The Dispatches of Field Marshal the Duke of Wellington, During his Various Campaigns in India, Denmark, Portugal, Spain, The Low Countries, and France* (London: John Murray, 1837-1839),Vol. IV, p.5.

11 Gurwood (ed.), Dispatches, Vol.II, p.621.

12 Muir, online commentary for *Wellington: The Path to Victory*, Chapter 13, citing James *Naval History*, Vol.4, pp.209, 212.

13 Murray Gartshore Papers, Murray Papers, MS 21112.

14 Ward Draft, Ch.V, p,1, citing the ledgers of Messrs Greenwood, Cox & Co, Regimental Agents.

British forces under the command of Sir Home Popham and Murray taking possession of Copenhagen. (National Maritime Museum)

of the bombardment became more widely known the mood changed, and there was a lengthy and passionate debate in the House of Commons. Many felt the action was dishonourable. George III privately described the attack as 'a very immoral act'. Defenders of it regarded it as necessary in view of Danish intransigence, the Danes having been given plenty of honourable opportunities to allow the women and children to leave, and to surrender the city and the fleet, which would then have been kept out of reach of the French. Some regarded the whole expedition and its aims as wrong. Peymann was blamed by the Danish authorities for not capitulating sooner. He was put on trial for dereliction of duty in connection with the Articles of Capitulation and condemned to death, the sentence being ultimately reversed.

There are numerous interesting theories about false intelligence being placed by the French regarding their plans for an invasion of Ireland, and certainly the British decisions seem to have been made to guard against an event that the establishment considered to be a very real likelihood. The Danish fleet had to be kept out of the hands of the French at all costs and, given its safe harbour in Copenhagen, it was necessary, in the absence of Danish co-operation, to take the city by force. A bombardment was seen as a quicker and more effective way of ensuring capitulation than a traditional siege.

There are many accounts of the bravery, and good nature, of the defending forces who in many cases were nothing more than students or poorly trained militia. One story, recorded in the journal of Captain Thomas Henry Browne, describes how the British, in making preparations for the siege, advanced into the suburbs, forcing the locals back inside the city fortifications. One evening a house that some British Officers from the 23rd Regiment were occupying, caught fire. Noticed by a Dane on the city wall, the Copenhagen fire brigade volunteered to come out under a white flag and help fight the fire. This was agreed, and 'a beautiful corps made its appearance, with six engines capitally well appointed who began operations without delay'.[15]

15 Buckley, R. (ed.), *The Napoleonic War Journal Of Captain Thomas Henry Browne 1807-1816* (London: Army Records Society, 1987), p.55.

The fire was eventually extinguished. During the exercise there must have been a good deal of friendly chat as Browne notes not just the varying items of equipment, (he describes 'contrivances of pulleys, baskets and ropes' for extricating people) and their uses, but also details of the brigade's regular training – including placing colleagues in burning houses before attempting to rescue them. The job done, the firefighters bade the British officers farewell, and returned inside the city walls, to face whatever the British might throw at them.

Copenhagen Fireman 1810.
(Anne S.K. Brown Military Collection)

> I never saw so complete a security against the effects of fire, and we could not help bestowing our warmest applause on this Danish fire corps when it returned to the city. We regretted afterwards to learn that by far the greater part of them perished in the great conflagration produced by our subsequent bombardment.[16]

The same journal describes the atmosphere when British officers were permitted to visit the city after the capitulation:

> The utmost gloom and surliness was depicted on every Danish countenance, and walking through the streets was anything but a pleasurable sensation. He did not observe much beauty in the women, but much taste and elegance in dress and good figures. The female fashions were principally French.

And again, not surprisingly:

> The Traiteurs of Copenhagen soon began to charge exorbitantly for refreshments taken at their coffee houses by the English officers, and the same sort of attention

16 Buckley (ed.), *Browne*, p.56.

> was quickly shewn us in all the shops of the place, for any little purchases we might have to make for friends at home.[17]

Part of the deal with the Danes was to recognise the Danish desire that as few British soldiers as possible should enter the city, and only officers with specially issued passes were permitted. Their unpopularity was understandable. During the hostilities and even before, British soldiers had been guilty of indiscipline and plundering on a large scale, were likened to a band of Cossacks, and only in a few instances were the perpetrators suitably punished.

The whole campaign had cost fewer than 300 British casualties – it was an unequal fight and there were genuine feelings of pity for the Danes. One officer reflected the views of many of his fellow soldiers, remarking: 'it requires all the assurance we can muster to look the poor Danes in the face'.[18]

Cathcart had succeeded. Following Murray's plan the Danish Fleet was more than neutralised – it had been gained as a prize – and Cathcart was well rewarded on his return home. Nevertheless his indecision and lacklustre performance generally attracted a lot of criticism from many differing, and well-placed, sources. He seemed to have been regarded, at least by a number of those serving under him, including Cathcart's own military secretary, as incapable of effective command. Murray was one of these officers who seemed to have contemplated resignation:

> Things have been altogether conducted in such a way and so completely divested of everything bearing the shadow of system or punctuality (and this ever since we left England) that Colonel Murray and myself had it frequently in contemplation to resign our situations rather than be parties to so discreditable scene.[19]

The Assistant Quartermaster General John Pine-Coffin, who had been such a supporter of Murray's appointment in Ireland, and one of the new 'scientifics', was on Murray's staff at Copenhagen and made his views on Cathcart known to fellow scientific, Major General John Le Marchant. They were less than complimentary:

> However I might have heretofore disliked the conduct of Lord C as a man, I have always given him credit for being one of the best officers in our service, but I am now convinced that there is scarcely one that is worse, and I believe I am correct in saying that there is hardly a general officer that has served with him on this expedition would consent to do so on another.[20]

A new breed of professional officer was developing, of which Murray was one, Wellesley another, and Moore a third, who were to stem the tide of muddle and incompetence that had

17 Buckley (ed.), *Browne*, pp.61-2.

18 Rory Muir, *Wellington – The Path to Victory 1769-1814* (New Haven: Yale University Press 2013), p.219, citing Freer, *Letters from the Peninsula, The Freer Family Correspondence 1807-1814*, p.50.

19 Major John Macdonald (Cathcart's Military Secretary) to Sir John Hope, Headquarters, 5 [?] September 1807, quoted in Ward Draft, Ch.IV, p.19, citing Linlithgow Mss 6 1-20.

20 Pine-Coffin to Le Marchant, Bath, 9 November 1807, quoted in Muir, *Path to Victory*, p.216.

been all too evident in commanders – with some notable exceptions such as Abercromby – pitched against Napoleon to date, and who were to command the respect of the politicians at home, as well as the enemy generals they were confronting, in marked contrast to what had gone before. It seems too, in this particular case at least, that subordinates such as Wellesley and Murray were confident enough to take responsibility on their own shoulders in the event that rapid action was needed and coherent orders from above were lacking. The two men began to recognize in each other their particular qualities, different characters though they certainly were. Copenhagen was the start of an extraordinary relationship that was to last well beyond the defeat of Napoleon, through the turbulent political years that followed, right up to Murray's death in 1846.

The expedition to Copenhagen is the first time that Murray and Wellesley actually worked together on campaign. In fact they must have known each other personally by this stage, if only as a result of Murray's appointment as Deputy Quartermaster General in Ireland and Wellesley's as Chief Secretary there, where they overlapped for a very short spell earlier in the year. They may have even known each other as young officers fighting in the Low Countries in 1795/96, where Murray had cause to be thankful to Wellesley for the rear-guard action which allowed Murray, with a company of the 3rd Guards, to escape from the French through Wellesley's 33rd Regiment lines. They may too have come across each other in Hanover in 1806, when Wellesley commanded a brigade.

Murray had, alongside what was evidently considerable military ability in the Quartermaster role, already gained experience in the diplomatic skills required in seeking cooperation, and negotiating, with foreign combatants. In the expedition to Egypt he had been involved in agreeing plans with the Turks for an alliance against the French, spending time gaining the confidence of the Grand Vizier at Jaffa. He had been fired on at Aboukir while attempting to arrange a surrender of the castle. He had helped negotiate the surrender of Cairo by the French. In Copenhagen he was clearly used, not just as a go between whilst hostilities were ongoing, but also as a negotiator and draftsman in framing the necessary Articles of Capitulation. His diplomatic experience would be called upon in two more politically contentious and historically important situations in the following eighteen months, one involving Sir John Moore, the British Government, and the King of Sweden, and the other, again in close cooperation with Wellesley, and involving Sir Harry Burrard, at the outset of the Peninsular War. Murray was becoming recognised as not just an accomplished officer, with a flair for organisation and planning, but much more than that – a man who could be trusted with responsibility, and capable of bringing effective resolution to situations at the highest level off the battlefield.

A few days after the siege Murray found time to write to Isabella:

> If we bring away all that is due to us under the capitulation we shall have made a very handsome contribution for the Naval Establishment. As it happened your sea friends could do little more than look on till the prize was won.

> I am sorry that Mary is unwell and I am glad that last accounts make her recovering. I make no doubt that by sufficient application of salads, Corstorphine Creams etc she has now been restored to Perfect health.[21]

The Scottish recipe was nothing more than a cooling drink, a sort of milk shake, made by mixing equal quantities of milk obtained on two succeeding days, letting it stand for 12 hours, then adding a little new milk, and beating all well together with sugar. There is no clue in the family correspondence as to its effectiveness, but it can certainly have done no harm.

Following the successful action against Denmark, Britain's only remaining ally in Europe, other than Portugal, was Sweden. It was hardly a close or friendly alliance, but maintaining good relations with Sweden was seen as essential in the continuing effort to keep Napoleon from controlling the Baltic. Foreign Secretary Canning, in direct contravention of the terms of the Danish Articles of Capitulation, initially proposed an Anglo Swedish occupation of Zealand to reduce the threat of French invasion. Sweden was reluctant to be seen as too closely allied to Britain as it was felt this could be regarded as implication in Canning's 'crime' at Copenhagen. Moore was to be critical of the failure to build on the success at Copenhagen, when the following year he was placed in an impossible situation in Sweden by Canning and Castlereagh. Plans were being discussed for ways to support the Swedes who were under mounting pressure on a number of fronts against a variety of enemies. These plans required a trusted senior officer for a special assignment. Murray, perhaps building on their close alliance formed in Denmark, had already been corresponding with Wellesley on possible actions in Sweden.

21 Murray to Isabella, Copenhagen, 12 September 1807, Murray Papers, MS 21101.

7

1808 – Sweden – A Mad King

Amongst other things, Murray's experience at Copenhagen had shown him how a staff officer could 'run' his commander, in line with the model adopted by some continental armies. In the absence of an effective plan he had, with Wellesley, drafted a workable scheme, overcome Cathcart's doubts so he was happy to adopt it, and executed it. This was precisely what scientifics were trained to do.[1] There were still plenty of mediocre generals who could benefit from such all-round support. Two notable exceptions to that mediocrity were Moore and Wellesley, and Wellesley was now moving swiftly up the ranking to overtake Moore in the estimation of a number of his colleagues, perhaps based on Murray's own reports of the events in Denmark.

Early in 1808 Murray wrote to Wellesley enclosing a long, detailed, memorandum with his views on possible action in Sweden, where Russian forces were threatening. Denmark was about to declare war on both Sweden and Britain, and, jointly with the French, threaten from the south, and Norway, a dominion of Denmark, was ready to move against Gothenburg from the west.[2] It is unclear if Wellesley had asked for this report or whether Murray prepared it on his own initiative. It could not have made it clearer that Murray already had misgivings about the likely success of assisting the Swedes, and the memorandum highlighted the issues that were to be so confrontational in the months ahead, namely the competence of the Swedish king as a military man, the question of command, and the lack of enthusiasm of the nation itself in confronting the French and their allies.

Wellesley agreed with Murray's analysis:

> I received your letter and its enclosure this morning for which I am very much obliged to you. I agree entirely in your opinions about Sweden. We must not pass the Gulf of Finland with our army and we must secure our right flank by the possession of Norway and by a naval blockade of the Categat &c &c &c.
>
> Tom Burgh has offered me for the Government some maps particularly a remarkably good one of Cork which he values at 200 and others of other counties at 100 each. I intended to buy them for the Quartermaster General's department and I

1 Ward Draft, Ch.V, p.2.

2 Memorandum dated 13 March 1808, Murray Papers, ADV MS 46.12.12.

> wish you and General Clinton to look at them and see and let me know whether they are worth having.[3]

Discussions took place in London on how best to handle the necessary co-operation with the difficult King Gustav IV Adolf. Murray was, clearly on the recommendation of Wellesley, by this time Castlereagh's close military advisor, chosen to go to Sweden in advance of a force under Sir John Moore, now a lieutenant general, to discuss the situation with the Swedish King, and report back on the situation there. Wellesley, acting as a go-between, injected a sense of urgency:

> The government are very desirous to send an officer of rank in whom they can confide to Sweden, in order to see how matters are going on there and to make certain arrangements in case there should be any military cooperation from this country. Lord Castlereagh with whom I conversed upon this subject this morning has desired me to tell you that he wishes to employ you upon this service and wishes that you would come over here as soon as possible after you will have received this letter. He will mention the subject to the Duke of York this afternoon but he wishes you to lose no time as he expects that before you will have arrived he will have settled his plan with the Cabinet.
>
> You will do well therefore to make haste and I am particularly anxious that you should do so as I may then see you even if I should go to Ireland next week.[4]

Plans were well developed to send an army of 10,000 men under Moore, with Sir John Hope as second in command, with a view to supporting the Swedish forces against the growing threat from Russia – which had abandoned its alliance with Sweden – and Denmark. The Swedish armies were vastly outnumbered and facing danger on a number of fronts. But the shortage of European allies rendered Sweden of prime importance to Britain, however difficult her monarch might be.

Murray arrived in London and received his instructions in a letter from Castlereagh on 20 April, marked 'Secret'.[5] He was required to travel quickly to Stockholm to establish the position on eighteen separate and clearly expressed points, covering the state of Sweden's defences against possible attack, and the existence of any Swedish plans for military action, as well as to report on the appetite of the Swedes for resistance to Napoleon and his allies. He was requested to report his findings to Moore when the latter arrived in Sweden with the army.

The force under Moore's command consisted of British and King's German Legion infantry, one regiment of light cavalry, and artillery, a body of nearly 12,000 men in 180 ships. This was a force capable of serious action, not just of moral support. At this stage there seemed to be a genuine intention to assist the Swedes and build on the success at Copenhagen. The force sailed from Portsmouth on 11 May, arriving off Gothenburg six days later. The troops did not disembark from their cramped vessels, awaiting permission from

3 Wellesley to Murray, London, 19 March 1808, Murray Papers, ADV MS 46.1.12.
4 Wellesley to Murray, London, 8 April 1808, Wellington (ed.), *Supplementary Despatches*, Vol.V, pp.399-400.
5 Castlereagh to Murray, Downing Street, 20 April 1808, Murray Papers, ADV MS 46.1.12.

the Swedish King. Moore was, like many people, suspicious of the sanity of the King and was quite content to have his forces on board in the event that a swift reversal was required.

Murray had written to Isabella from Sheerness on 22 April that 'There is a good deal of reason to suppose that we shall have no other trouble than that of going out and of coming back again in the autumn. I arrived here today to embark on the Victory with Sir James Saumarez whose captain is your friend George Hope'.[6]

The lengthy instructions given by Castlereagh demonstrate a lack of understanding of the Swedish situation, and both the political and military establishments must have harboured reservations. The eighteen points in the Castlereagh letter suggest distinct uncertainty of a successful outcome, unless the position that Murray found was to be more optimistic than it seemed in London. After travelling by land from Gothenburg, Murray arrived in Stockholm on the day that Moore left Portsmouth. As soon as Moore's fleet arrived off Gothenburg, news of what Murray had discovered in early audiences with the King evidenced what many privately had feared, both in connection with the lack of strength of the Swedish army and navy, and the state of mind of their royal commander. It was to be the start of a month of extremely delicate negotiations and royal audiences during which Moore's patience was to be tested beyond what he was capable of handling. Murray's role was to act as a facilitator and broker between the unstable monarch and occasionally hot-headed British general, and as a shuttle diplomat between Stockholm and London. It was a task that must have tested Murray to the full. He recorded each day's conversations, written up daily, as the convoluted and circuitous discussions continued.

The notebooks and drafts kept by Murray during this episode, including a 46 page report, illustrate the bizarre nature of the discussions and the difficulties of dealing with a monarch who apparently had full command of the Swedish forces, but who clearly had no military skill or experience, and who seemed never to be prepared to take on board the opinions of his generals or admirals, who seemed powerless in his presence.[7]

On the evening of his arrival in Stockholm Murray met the King in the state apartments of the palace, in the presence only of Edward Thornton, the British Ambassador. Despite an unflattering countenance, with thick lips, a small moustache, bad teeth, and receding forehead and chin, the King could display great charm, and his reception of Murray was gracious and flattering. No business was discussed, and Murray was invited to attend a parade next morning. He then embarked on a series of daily audiences with the King, conducted on foot, up and down the palace's gleaming parquet floor for hour after hour, all in French, which Murray took in his stride. He was able to recall every detail of the discussions, noting down occasional sentences in a tiny pocket book as he left in his coach. Murray gradually established an unusual rapport with this unpredictable man, some of the initial goodwill quite possibly being due to the service that his maternal uncle had given to the Swedish Crown for many years, after his banishment from Britain in 1747.[8]

There was initially a good understanding between the 30-year-old King and the British Guards officer, six years his senior. Murray was made welcome at the palace and introduced to the Royal Family. Following the audiences Murray would report back in the evenings

6 Murray to Isabella, Sheerness, 22 April 1808, Murray Papers, MS 21101.
7 The full accounts of Murray's Swedish mission are in Murray Papers, ADV MS 46.1.12 – 46.1.20.
8 Ward Draft, Ch.V, p.10.

to Thornton, and General Tibell, Sweden's Minister for War, who had served with the French Army in Italy where he had risen to the rank of brigadier general, on what the King was suggesting in the way of military action. It is quite evident that not only did the Swedish military command feel that the King had ambitions far in excess of Sweden's capability, but at the same time they had little control over the King's actions and were compelled to support the royal ideas.

Gustav IV Adolf, King of Sweden. (Anne S.K. Brown Military Collection)

At one point Murray argued against the King's plans, especially his idea for an invasion of Zealand, as the British had not the equipment or heavy artillery for a siege of Copenhagen which would probably be necessary, but seemed to give tacit approval to the plan to attack Norway, in support of Sweden's operations there which had commenced without adequate means.

Late in the evening of 17 May, after a full day at the palace in Stockholm and at the King's mansion at Haga, the initial negotiations, during the course of which only Murray was present, reached their unsatisfactory conclusion. Yet the conversations had remained cordial, and wide-ranging. Murray set off for Gothenburg to report to Moore, arriving there on the morning of 21 May. He had already written to Moore from Stockholm forewarning him of the difficulties.[9] Moore had been sent with some difficult orders, no doubt framed in the knowledge that the Swedish King was well known for eccentricity, if not worse. A particular condition of the British troops being made available to Sweden was that on disembarkation, contrary to what was customary at the time, they were to remain under British command.

Murray was immediately despatched by Moore back to London that evening, on board the fast brig HMS *Protector*, to report to the Duke of York and Castlereagh, arriving in London on the 29th. It was clear to Murray on his arrival at Horse Guards that, during his absence, there had been a major shift in opinion towards an expedition to the Peninsula, on the back of a popular uprising in Spain. The Baltic was no longer top of the agenda. Murray himself might have been tempted to think that, even if he were not to go to Spain, then perhaps his days in Dublin might be numbered, with a chance of his becoming Deputy to Alexander Hope in the Quartermaster General's Department in London.

Murray wrote to Moore from Horse Guards on 31 May. He had made his view of the situation and the danger of further involvement on the King's terms very clear in his meetings with ministers. There was to be a cabinet meeting in the morning and he would be heading

9 Ward Draft, Ch.V, p.18.

back to Sweden immediately thereafter. 'It will be impossible for those most willing to look at things in a wrong light to do so for more than a couple of days. I have stated facts, and shall repeat those which leave no question as to what remained to be done'[10]

The next day the Military Secretary, Lieutenant Colonel James Willoughby Gordon, gave Murray a letter to be delivered to Moore, stating the Commander in Chief's view: 'You could not have acted safely otherwise under the most embarrassing circumstances in which you found yourself placed. An error has been made in sending the force'.[11]

Having thus reported personally to Castlereagh as to the seriousness of the problems he and Moore had encountered in Sweden, and having had it acknowledged that the whole plan was moving dangerously close to farce, Murray left London on 2 June, embarking on HMS *Africa* to return to Gothenburg, which he reached on the morning of the 11th. He brought sealed orders and numerous letters for various parties, delicately drafted to accommodate as many contrasting views and positions as possible. Moore talked to Murray, and read the various letters and orders from London, among them a letter from Brownrigg:

> I sincerely hope that Murray who left town yesterday will take to you such instructions as will prove satisfactory. He appears to have acted with a great deal of judgement and good sense, and I do not think you could have a better negotiator.[12]

In fact the Cabinet had relented on the vexed issue of who should be in command of the British troops were they to land on Swedish soil. However, this was conditional on their only being used for limited objectives and if Moore was conscious of any departure from the principles outlined he was permitted to stall and seek further instructions from home.

Moore decided to travel to Stockholm immediately, taking with him only Murray and his Military Secretary, Major John Colborne, who was, twenty years later, to be appointed Lieutenant Governor of Upper Canada by Murray when the latter was serving as Colonial Secretary. Hope, left at Gothenburg, still reckoned on a solution, relying on 'Moore's sound judgement' and the

> necessity of doing everything in the most gentle and engaging manner. He will derive from Murray's excellent understanding and temper, as well as from his previous knowledge of the actual situation and character of the person, with whom they have to treat and from the confidence which he appears already to have established in that quarter, the most material assistance.[13]

They checked into an hotel, and the King was made aware of their arrival. Instead of inviting Moore to meet with him, it was Murray alone who was summoned to an audience at the palace at three o'clock on the 15th. This was a breach of etiquette, and embarrassing, as Murray was no longer a representative of his sovereign but a staff officer of Moore's. Murray would have been aware that he was now involved at the centre of a major historical episode

10 Murray to Moore, Horse Guards, 31 May 1808, Moore Papers, British Library ADD MS 57543.
11 Gordon to Moore, Horse Guards 1 June 1808, Moore Papers, British Library ADD MS 57543.
12 Maurice (ed.), *Moore Diary*, Vol.II, p.216.
13 John Hope to Alexander Hope, Confidential, Gothenburg, 13 June 1808, Luffness Mss, GD 364/1/1179.

requiring every ounce of his diplomatic skills and quiet temperament. Still no progress was made. Even though Murray was received with the same graciousness as in the past, the meeting was unprofitable.[14]

The next day Moore was invited too. The talking continued. The basic issue remained – under whose command would the troops be, on disembarkation?

There was stalemate. Moore's and Murray's views were consistent.

On a notable occasion variously reported by Moore, in his diaries, and by Murray years later in the *Quarterly Review*, Moore and Murray were discussing the deteriorating atmosphere one evening with General Tibell, and solemnly rehearsing the Swedish King's fatuous plans. Tibell yet again was detailing how the King saw things working. Moore, his patience stretched beyond breaking exclaimed 'we have all three played our parts quite long enough in this farce, so for God's sake let us throw off the mask and indulge in the laugh we are all longing for'[15] Tibell readily concurred; they sat back and, no doubt partaking of some much needed alcohol, talked until bedtime of Gustav and of Tibell's campaigns in Italy under Bonaparte.

Moore felt he had no option but to withdraw the troops, and requested an audience to take his leave of the King. Murray attended as an observer. The King insisted on the presence of three chief dignitaries of his bureaucracy. The King did not trust Moore to take back a true account of the discussions and the three were to act as witnesses, and take minutes to be sent to his British counterpart. Moore was incensed at this attack on his honour, and responded very robustly. The atmosphere was icy.

The talks then returned yet again to the various military options and the command of the British force. The records of the conversation show clearly the Swedish King overstepping the mark in his hostility to Moore, and his suggestions that Moore was a liar. To Murray's concern, instead of standing on his dignity, secure in the knowledge that he was carrying out his orders from London and his sovereign, Moore started to wobble, in an effort perhaps not to appear inexorable, and offered to postpone withdrawal.

No doubt muddled with a cold he had caught, a re-read of his instructions on return to his hotel made clear the extent to which any detaining of the troops would be a clear breach of his orders.[16] News of this reached the King, in a letter delivered on Moore's behalf by Thornton. For him it was the final straw and an insult. By now Murray must have been acutely aware of any useful role as broker being at an end. However, he still had a part to play in what had become a major drama involving two Royal Houses, military allies, now in the midst of a serious breakdown of trust and cooperation. Sweden was, apart from Portugal, the only European country which might side with Britain against Napoleon, and this friendship was now shattered.

Murray was in bed at the hotel, at quarter past eleven that night, when the Swedish Adjutant General arrived, demanding to see Moore. Murray asked the officer to wait and went into Moore's room to explain. Moore asked if the message could be delivered in writing, as he was in bed, still nursing his heavy cold, but the officer insisted his orders were

14 Ward Draft, Ch.V, p.21.

15 Ward Draft, Ch.V, p.22. The story is repeated in Moore's diary, and by Murray in his account in the *Quarterly Review*, Vol 56, p 208.

16 Ward Draft, Ch.V, p.26.

to speak direct to Moore, which he did, in French. The orders were clear. Moore was not to leave Stockholm without the Kings permission.

Murray was at the palace again next day at noon, having been asked to attend the King. Gustav listed what seemed to him to be the true reasons behind the British volte face, based on what he felt was an urge to commit large numbers to the Peninsula, and Moore's own ambitions to command there. Murray denied all of this and gradually drew the conversation back to Moore's predicament. He succeeded in eliciting an acknowledgment that there was a difference between being under arrest, and being required not to leave Stockholm without permission. A small victory perhaps, but indicative of Murray's ability to think clearly about the smaller detail in the midst of a bigger crisis, and not insignificant when one considers the possible options facing Moore at that moment.

The King asked if Murray would kindly carry to London for him a transcript of the minutes of the 23rd and deliver them to King George? Murray declined. As a staff officer of Moore's, he could do nothing without his orders. 'I came here' he said, aware no doubt that he was living dangerously, 'with the General, who is now placed in a situation certainly little looked for, and I am not at all disposed to leave him'.[17]

Murray agreed to attend the King at Haga that evening, but when Moore and Thornton conferred together on his return from the palace, it was decided that the next communication should be through diplomatic channels and that permission should be asked for Murray to be excused attendance. The next day Murray received a note asking if it was a mistake that he had not attended the evening before, and asking him to come at 2 that afternoon.[18] Murray's polite explanation met with a second note requiring him to attend at 5, after dinner. Murray was inclined to decline again, but Count Piper, the King's Officer in Waiting, who had delivered the notes, replied that the King would force Murray to attend if necessary. Murray attended, clearly having no option. Tedious old ground was covered, but openly and without rancour. The King asked for a further audience next morning, and in a display intended to demonstrate that, despite all, Murray was a man he trusted, invited him to drink tea with him in an adjoining room, before leaving.

The next day's meeting followed the same depressing, repetitive pattern. Murray tried and failed to get the restrictions on Moore lifted. He warned that he feared that the matters were now likely to take a public turn, alluding to the anxiety that must have been being felt by Vice Admiral Saumarez and Lieutenant General Hope now that they were aware of their commander's 'arrest', and asked leave to withdraw, leaving Gustav to ponder the possible consequences. On taking his leave of the King for the final time Murray recorded on the last page of a comprehensive 80-page report on the mission: 'At the close of the conversation HM expressed Himself in terms of particular regard and friendship towards the King and as I was taking leave HM was pleased to repeat some of the same obliging expressions towards myself when I left'.[19]

Moore made a hasty escape from Stockholm, helped by Thornton, travelling part of the way with the British Secretary of Legation, and thereafter with an English messenger carrying

17 Ward Draft, Ch.V, p.27.

18 Capt Count Piper to Murray, Haga, 26 June 1808; two draft notes Murray to Piper, 26 June 1808, Murray Papers, ADV MS 46.1.12.

19 Draft Report to Brownrigg, Stockholm 18 June 1808, Murray Papers, ADV MS 46.1.12.

despatches to Gothenburg, while Murray was still in discussion with the King. Murray himself left Stockholm quietly, without fuss or the need for any clandestine methods, early on the 28th, carrying a passport signed by the Swedish foreign secretary, complete with its impressive black seal, dated 27 June. Reaching Gothenburg on the 30th he was immediately sent ahead to London with the despatches, arriving on 7 July. Moore followed with the fleet on the morning of Sunday 3 July.

The episode, although a tragi-comedy with little in the way of discernible military consequence, reinforced Horse Guards' belief that in Murray they had a man with enviable talent for diplomacy, demonstrably loyal, politically aware, and strategically sound. Between Murray and Moore, in severe fighting in Egypt and now in dealing with a King's delicate ego, a mutual trust had grown, notwithstanding the different characters that they were. It would not be long before the partnership was to be seen again, in very difficult circumstances.

Murray submitted his expenses claim on his return. He had received £500 ahead of his trip. His expenses for his journeys from Dublin to London, the sea journey to Gothenburg, thence to Stockholm, Stockholm to Gothenburg, then London and back to Gothenburg, and finally from Stockholm to London via Gothenburg amounted to £211.14.0 and so he repaid the £288.6.0 balance to the Government.[20] The Establishment might have felt the price of Murray's role in containing a situation which looked from the start to be less than promising, and which had the makings of severe embarrassment for the British establishment, to be money well spent. King Gustav was dethroned in March the following year, declared physically and mentally unfit to rule.

20 'Account of Expenses incurred by Lt. Col. G. Murray in the Public Service', 1808, Murray Papers, ADV MS 46.1.12.

8

1808 – Peninsula – Convention of Cintra

The Government had indeed decided to add Moore's army to the planned expedition to face the French in Portugal and Spain, clearly abandoning any idea that military operations in Scandinavia in alliance with Sweden could ever be countenanced while Gustav was in power. The Swedish King's suspicions surrounding the alternative destination for the troops originally sent to Sweden were well founded. All efforts were now directed to assembling a large enough force to land in the Peninsula in support of recent uprisings there, and confront the French. British sentiment was strongly in favour of assisting the Spanish and Portuguese. Napoleon had forced the abdication of the Spanish king and installed his brother Joseph on the throne. The Portuguese Royal Court had gone into exile and General Junot was in control of Lisbon. But Spanish resistance was widespread, and was meeting with unexpected successes throughout the country. The British Admiral Cotton reported that Junot had barely 4,000 men in Lisbon and the Russian fleet, moored in the Tagus in support of the French, could be dealt with if a decent sized force were despatched. There was an assumption that were Spain and Portugal to be subjugated the French influence would extend to their colonies in South America.

The initial intention was that the British expedition be commanded by Wellesley, recently promoted to lieutenant general, who was in fact preparing to sail to take on the Spanish colonies in Central America. Wellesley's lack of seniority became an issue when it became apparent that the force required in Portugal would need to be larger owing to new intelligence on the countrywide strength of the French there. That meant that Moore was the clear favourite to take command, except that he had now made enough enemies in the Cabinet to ensure that this would not happen. Moore was minded not to be easily side-lined and was given command of a separate force, comprising his Baltic army straight from Sweden. The Cabinet felt that it was necessary to appoint a more senior figure to Moore to avoid his taking overall command and settled on Lieutenant General Sir Hew Dalrymple. However, Dalrymple was in Gibraltar, as acting Governor, where he had gained some credence as a result of his involvement in a rising in Andalucia, but no experience of command in the field, so they hastily asked Lieutenant General Harry Burrard, 'a portly, amiable man, with no claims, whether in his own estimation or anyone else's, to being a "warrior"',[1] to step

1 Ward Draft, Ch.VI, p.4.

in as a temporary measure until Dalrymple could take effective command. Different fleets were assembled and set off, with Wellesley's, the only one with a clear mandate, in advance of the rest.

Murray wrote, at the end of the campaign, of the Government's role: 'There is total incapacity to conduct the army either before the enemy or even without an enemy. This incapacity was brought forward, and doubled, at the head of the Army by the Government with their eyes open'.[2] Castlereagh had written to Dalrymple exhorting him to make the most use possible of Wellesley, perhaps contemplating an arrangement, to be attempted later by Murray in the field, to allow Wellesley free rein, and to stand back, much as Cathcart had done at Copenhagen, allowing the junior, more 'modern' officers to take the decisions in the field. Murray's role might therefore become critical. He was the essential link between Wellesley and the executive power of the Commander. Murray might be able to repeat his performance at Copenhagen and in this instance promote Wellesley's plans, or at least act as mediator between Wellesley and Dalrymple, if the latter found it impossible to surrender any authority.[3]

So the expedition, now comprising no fewer than seven separate military forces from various embarkation points, under different generals, was to be commanded by Lieutenant General Dalrymple. Second in command was Lieutenant General Burrard, with Lieutenant Generals Moore and Hope ranking thereafter, with Lieutenant General Wellesley further down the order of seniority.

Lieutenant Colonel Murray, 3rd Foot Guards, was appointed Acting Quartermaster General 'the appointment in the army I like the best'. His views on Spaniards and their resistance were:

> That Buonaparte will give them time to learn to make war is very improbable… If the war can be protracted we may hope for much but unless Buonaparte's attention and his forces, are withheld in a great means from Spain… I apprehend the balance will soon begin to incline in favour of the French… Do not mention these as my sentiments for some people will imagine that a man can be no soldier who does not always talk big – and others will think that when the Government of the Country undertake an Enterprize one ought never to see it but on the most flattering side.[4]

Wellesley set sail for Portugal from Cork on 11 July, having embarked his troops on board much earlier, between 15 and 17 June. He arrived in Portugal on 26 July, landing his force on 1 August. His orders were to engage with the enemy in whatever manner he felt right, having assessed the military situation on the ground. Intelligence on the strength of the French forces was sketchy, and discretion had to be given to the commander to act as he saw fit – a responsibility that Wellesley would have been entirely happy with, although he was mightily unhappy with the lack of tools which had been provided for him to carry out the task.

2 Murray to Patrick, Confidential, 20 September 1808, Murray Papers, ADV MS 46.1.22.
3 Ward Draft, Ch.VI, p.6.
4 Murray to Patrick, Portsmouth 25 July 1808, Murray Papers, MS 21102.

Murray, having stayed in London since his return from Sweden on 7 July, witnessing at first hand the preparations for this new campaign, left at two in the afternoon on the 23rd, and headed for Portsmouth. Burrard joined the force there on the 27th. He boarded HMS *Audacious* at noon, accompanied by his staff and Murray, and moved off under a favourable easterly breeze. The wind then veered to the south-west and remained that way for the next fortnight. After understandably slow progress *Audacious* hove-to off Cape Finisterre on 16 August to allow Burrard and some of his staff, including Murray, to board the faster HMS *Brazen*, in which they were to go ahead. *Brazen* arrived off Maceira, on the coast of Portugal, north of Lisbon, on 20 August.[5]

The timings of the arrival in Portugal of Wellesley and the other British Generals are an important element in what was to follow. Damaged egos and contrasting characters also played a part in the drama that unfolded over the next few days. One general's seniority over another was determined by the date each became a major general, and was fixed for all time vis-a-vis each other. No 'senior' general was expected, except in very rare circumstances, to serve under the command of a 'junior'. Wellesley was the most junior lieutenant general on the expedition and Dalrymple the most senior. Each recognised his position and played his part accordingly. To his credit, during initial actions in Portugal, Wellesley had kept Burrard as fully briefed as would have been possible in all the circumstances, Burrard still being at sea, knowing that he was going to have to hand over command as soon as Burrard landed. Similarly, if Moore had arrived earlier than Burrard he would have taken temporary command from Wellesley. It was always going to be the case that Dalrymple would assume overall command as soon as he arrived.

The effect of such strict adherence to hierarchy was very clearly demonstrated in this new initiative in Portugal, and made any coherent military planning very difficult. Murray must have felt his loyalties horribly stretched as he acted as a go between, and confidante, among the generals who sought his support for their decisions in the confusion of a fast moving military engagement. The best knowledge of the unravelling situation lay with the most junior general, to whom Murray had already become very close, whilst Murray's immediate commander, Burrard, sought his support for views which were totally contrary to Wellesley's. Murray's short time at Horse Guards had allowed him to witness the extraordinary machinations of the selection process, after a very demanding time in Sweden trying to keep another general, to whom he was also close, from destroying his country's alliance with a somewhat deranged King. By this stage in his career he was trusted by the political and military establishment in London, including the Duke of York and Castlereagh. He was equally well known to, and admired by, the various generals involved in this expedition. He was about to become embroiled in another major international incident, with senior military men following differing agendas, relying on him for a workable solution.

It is worth at this point considering the actual events as they unfolded on the coast of Portugal, on an hour by hour basis, before settling on the extent to which responsibility should be attached to any individual for what was regarded by many as a lost opportunity, and by many more as a humiliation. An examination of Wellesley's thoughts and actions, as described in his and Murray's despatches and letters, demonstrates clearly the situation

5 Ward Draft, Ch.VI, pp.6-7.

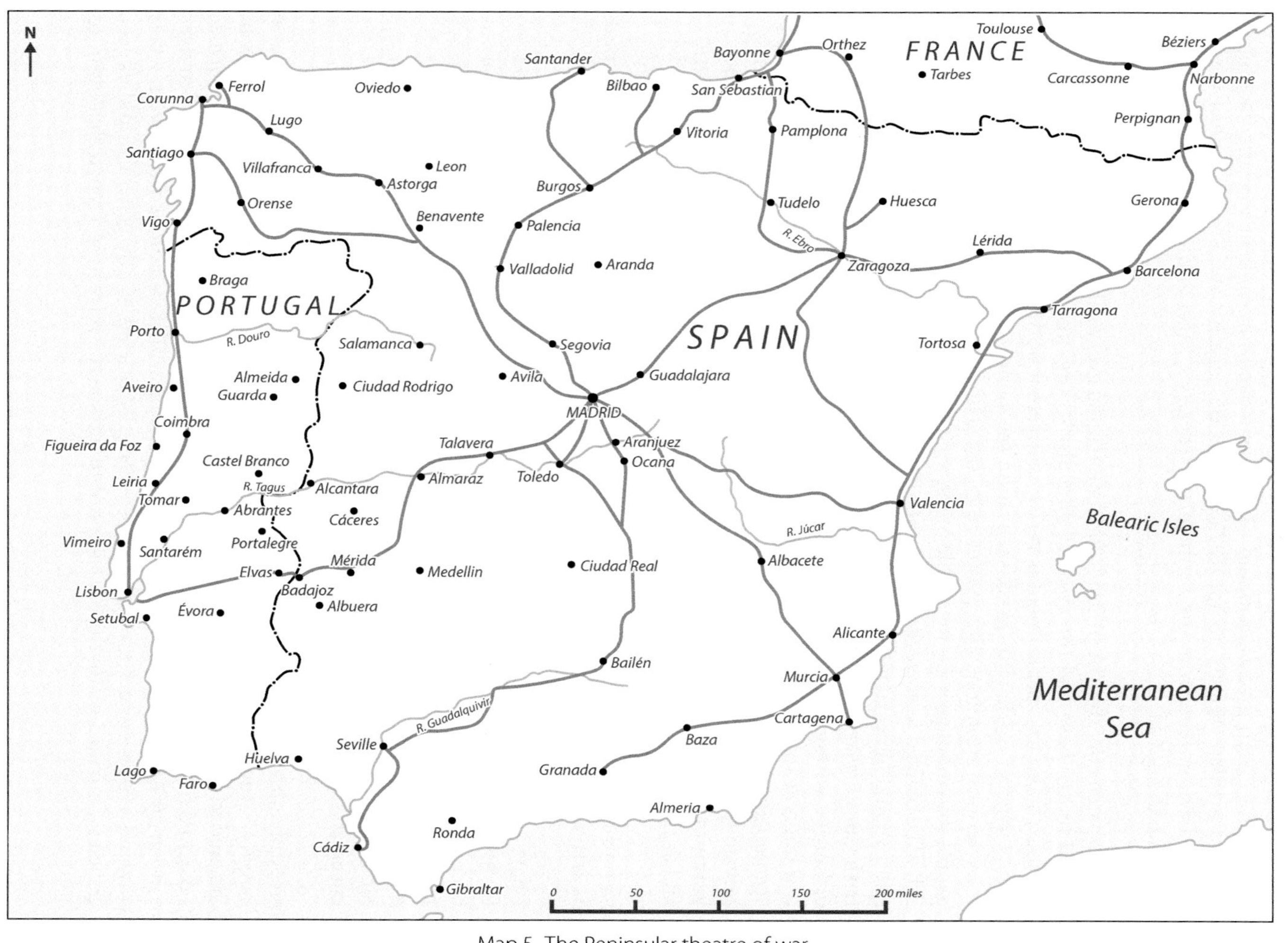

Map 5 The Peninsular theatre of war.

the British found themselves in, and the results of a rapid double transition of power, from Wellesley to Burrard and almost immediately thereafter to Dalrymple.

Wellesley had been given command of a decent sized force, albeit woefully lacking in cavalry and artillery horses, to spearhead operations against the French with a view to ultimately driving them from the Peninsula. Wellesley's anger at the lack of planning was evident from the outset:

> My despatch contains the fullest information upon every subject and I have nothing to add to it. I have had the greatest difficulty in organising my commissariat for the march and that department is very incompetent notwithstanding the arrangements which I made with Huskisson upon the subject. This department deserves your serious attention. The existence of the army depends upon it and yet the people who manage it are incapable of managing anything out of a counting house. I shall be obliged to leave Spencer's guns behind for want of means of moving them and I should have been obliged to leave my own if it were not for the horses of the Irish Commissariat. Let nobody ever prevail upon you to send a corps to any part of Europe without horses to draw their guns. It is not true that horses lose their condition at sea. I have just heard that Joseph Buonaparte left Madrid for France accompanied by all the French on the 29th of last month. I have received your private letter of the 21st July for which I am much obliged to you. I shall be the junior of the Lieut Generals however I am ready to serve the government wherever and as they please.[6]

He acknowledged (without much enthusiasm) that he would be subordinate to Dalrymple on his arrival, to whom he wrote, briefing him fully, as was entirely correct:

> I have been appraised by the Secretary of State that His Majesty has been pleased to appoint you to command his troops employed in this part of Europe, and it becomes my duty to make you acquainted with the situation of affairs in Portugal. In order to perform this duty in the best manner in my power I have the honor to enclose the copy of a letter and of its enclosures which I have written to Lieut Gen Sir H Burrard who is expected to arrive on the coast of Portugal to command a corps of troops.[7]

Despite difficulties of supply and lack of horses, Wellesley defeated a small French force at Rolica on 17 August. He was confident that Moore would provide support as soon as he arrived, and kept Burrard, in the same fleet as Moore and as his senior general, informed from day to day with situation reports of activities on land. So by the time Burrard arrived offshore on 20 August, taking command that evening whilst still on board *Brazen*, where Murray and Wellesley met up again, he was as fully briefed as any general could expect. Nevertheless, Burrard made the decision not to pursue the retreating French that evening,

6 Wellesley to Castlereagh, Lavos, 8 August 1808, Gurwood (ed.) *Dispatches*, Vol.IV, p.72.
7 Wellesley to Dalrymple, Lavos, 8 August 1808, Gurwood (ed.) *Dispatches*, Vol.IV, p.73.

much to Wellesley's disappointment, who was convinced that he had the chance to rout the French and take Lisbon within a matter of days. His frustration was immediately, and clearly, expressed to Castlereagh:

> Sir H Burrard will probably acquaint your Lordship with the reasons which have induced him to call Sir J Moore's corps to the assistance of our army which consists of 20,000 men including the Portuguese army which was to join this morning notwithstanding former determinations to the contrary and is opposed by I am convinced not more than 12,000 or 14,000 Frenchmen and to halt here till Sir John's corps shall join. You will readily believe however that this determination is not in conformity with my opinion and I only wish that Sir Harry had landed and seen things with his own eyes before he had made it. Gen Acland's brigade landed last night. The French are in and about Torres Vedras. Junot's corps which arrived last is the advanced guard and the others are in the rear nearly on the ground to which Laborde retreated after the battle of the 17th.[8]

That morning, the 21st, Burrard, Brigadier General Henry Clinton, and Murray were rowed ashore. Hearing that the French were advancing on Wellesley in large numbers, they made it to Vimeiro by 10 o'clock, by which time a battle was well under way, and Wellesley master of the situation. All French attacks being successfully repulsed, Burrard wisely allowed Wellesley authority to conduct the final stages of the battle as he saw fit. The British lost a significant proportion of their very small cavalry force after a typically undisciplined charge, but otherwise suffered only 700 casualties that day. The French, having lost perhaps as many as 3,000 men, retreated towards Torres Vedras in disarray. Coming so soon after the engagement at Rolica a few days earlier, also an emphatic Wellesley success, the French were recognising this young British general as a more accomplished opponent than perhaps they had anticipated.

Wellesley begged Burrard to let him advance. Burrard refused. Wellesley raged, incoherent with anger. Burrard seemed more interested in satisfying his mid-day hunger. Wellesley 'turned his horse's head, and with a cold and contemptuous bitterness, said aloud to his aid-de-camp [sic] "you may think about dinner, for there is nothing more for soldiers to do today"'.[9]

Murray did not, at this point, take the opportunity to intervene, perhaps reflecting the rules of the service that precluded him from offering advice at variance with the commander's decision in the presence of others. It is possible that he genuinely felt Wellesley's plans to be impracticable or overly risky.[10] Murray possessed a natural caution, which occasionally led him to doubt where Wellington, often himself labelled as a cautious commander, would weigh matters more positively. Murray stated later, to Patrick, that he felt that the fate of the army was about to be staked on the result of one battle, against an enemy force of perhaps equal strength. What is clear is that Wellesley did not blame Murray for withholding his

8 Wellesley to Castlereagh, Vimeiro, 21 August 1808, 6 a.m, Gurwood (ed.) *Dispatches*, Vol.IV, p.107.

9 Moyle Sherer, *Recollections of the Peninsula* (London: Longman, Rees, Orme, Brown and Green, 1827), p.43. Other equally caustic asides are recorded by other commentators.

10 Ward Draft, Ch.VI, p.11.

support at this critical moment, and continued to treat him as his closest ally throughout the remainder of his time in the campaign.

Murray, on 21 August, was confident of ultimately defeating the French, while still conscious of the need for the reinforcements, especially cavalry, that Moore's force would provide, as he said to Patrick in his letter of that day, penned presumably after the successful Vimeiro action: 'It is perhaps not being too sanguine to say that we have it in our power to be masters of Lisbon in a few days. We have as yet on shore however little more than half our force, for none of Gen Moore's troops have yet got so far as to be landed'.[11]

Wellesley's force was ordered by Burrard to wait in the position they were in. Burrard was nervous that the French cavalry, far superior in numbers to the British, could still be the deciding factor. He, like Murray, wanted to be up to full strength by the addition of Moore's troops. He was concerned too with the fragility of the supplies available to the force, given the fact that the men were reliant on being supplied by ships offshore, where weather and the Atlantic surf had already made disembarking hazardous. He thought that Brigadier General Acland's brigade at least should be fully operational before the army advanced. There seems to be an inconsistency between Burrard's and Wellesley's belief as to the readiness of Acland's force, although it disembarked early on the 21st and took part in the battle.

Murray concurred with Burrard's views. Maybe he attributed more weight than did Wellesley to the potential problems of supplies, the relative superiority of the French cavalry – which could have caused havoc, although it was some way off – and the fact that the French were still in possession of most of the forts in the area, seen as a major issue. Interestingly Wellesley was later to acknowledge the difficulties which would have faced the British if the French had had to be dislodged from their strongholds in the course of the autumn and winter.

The decision made, *Brazen* was sent off with orders to Moore to bring his convoy south with all speed. Wellesley's plan had been for Moore, when disembarked, to move inland to Santarem to cut off the obvious escape route for the French. This was now countermanded by Burrard, and Moore re-embarked those of his force that had already come ashore. Burrard, Murray and the other staff officers transferred to HMS *Alfred* for the night.[12]

Burrard surrendered his command to Dalrymple on the latter's arrival on the 22nd. Murray recognized that the rapid changes of command were only hindering the British effort, and attempted to find a solution. Murray's idea was put to Dalrymple when he, in the company of Clinton, met Dalrymple at his landing point on the beach at Porto Novo. Asked by Dalrymple to brief him on the situation, Murray floated the plan, possibly hatched in conversations the night before with Anstruther and Wellesley, of allowing Wellesley temporary operational command of Burrard's and Dalrymple's forces, with Moore maintaining command of his own force until Junot was finally dealt with. Later, after meeting up with Burrard and Wellesley, Dalrymple asked Murray to repeat his views, at which point Dalrymple agreed to follow the Murray line.[13]

11 Murray to Patrick, no location given, 21 August 1808, Murray Papers, MS 21102.

12 Ward Draft, Ch.VI, p.9.

13 Muir, online commentary for *Wellington: The Path to Victory*, Chapter 15, at www.lifeofwellington.co.uk/commentary/chapter-fifteen-vimeiro-and-cintra-july-september-1808/, describes the situation in detail.

Lieutenant General Sir Hew Dalrymple.
(Public Domain)

Somewhere around this time, Murray implies, Wellesley overplayed his hand, and in so doing caused a marked change in Dalrymple's attitude: probably insufficiently sensitive to Dalrymple's pride, Wellesley 'assumed a decided lead, or at least sought to do it'.[14] Despite his apparent earlier agreement to Murray's radical plan, Dalrymple refused to agree to set the army in motion as Wellesley demanded. To Wellesley's relief, Murray now stepped in, 'took him [Dalrymple] aside & settled in a few words that we should march'.[15] So Murray's conciliatory skills again allowed momentum to be resumed, at least for a fleeting moment.

Dalrymple was preparing to ride to Vimeiro to dine with Wellesley when a report arrived that the French were attacking again. This was in fact the arrival of the French *Général de Division* Kellermann with two squadrons of cavalry under a flag of truce. Wellesley offered to go and meet with Kellermann. Dalrymple had had enough of this assertive junior general who seemed to want to be everywhere, doing everything. He denied the request, saying he would send a staff officer instead, anxious to retain as much authority as he still could.

Murray was, from the first moment of arrival in Portugal, involved in acting as an intermediary, first between Wellesley and Burrard, and then between Wellesley and Dalrymple. Wellesley was still, understandably and perfectly correctly, determined to have his voice heard. He was conscious of Dalrymple's apparent lack of confidence in him and, aware of Murray's skills of persuasion, was more than happy to allow him to intervene with Dalrymple on his behalf. Murray, as a more junior officer, presented no threat to Dalrymple and was certainly less confrontational than Wellesley. Not only had his suggested operational command structure been considered sensible by Dalrymple, but he was, significantly, persuasive enough to have Dalrymple agree to allow Wellesley to march his army against Junot, minutes before the arrival of Kellermann with the French proposals for an armistice. However, from the moment that Kellermann arrived at Vimeiro, Dalrymple was, as the senior general, responsible for the negotiations. All ideas of an advance against the French were abandoned to allow talks, conducted in French, to commence, which they did, early in the afternoon, lasting for about seven hours, with only a break for dinner. Kellermann

14 Ward Draft Ch VI, p 13 (quoting Murray's words – uncited).

15 Wellesley to William Wellesley-Pole, Ramalhal, 24 August 1808. Duke of Wellington, *Some Letters of the Duke of Wellington to his Brother, William Wellesley-Pole* (Camden Miscellany Vol. XVIII), (London: Royal Historical Society, 1948), pp.5-6.

dined with the British generals. He would have enjoyed himself. The French timing had been immaculate.

Murray hovered in the next door room while the meeting took place to discuss the terms of an armistice, not directly involved in its negotiation, and was ignorant of the details until it was signed, except as to the position with the Russians with their fleet in the Tagus, to which he offered a suggestion, not adopted by the senior officers that evening, but which was afterwards acted upon. Murray's account of the Armistice proceedings is a masterly précis of the opening scene of a complex affair, right from the moment Kellermann commenced discussions:

> After they had been a very considerable time together, these three officers came out and having called Gen Clinton and myself into the room, they told us that after a great deal of argument that they had come to this point: that everything turned upon what was to be done towards the Russians; that Kellerman had declared that their being included was a sine qua non of all negotiations; and that we must either admit some stipulation in their favour on the ground of the neutrality of the port, or that their force, consisting of 10,000 men, would not act against us. It appeared to me that if all other points were settled (which the generals, all three, stated to be the case), the only thing to be taken care of was that, in regards to the Russians, whatever was granted should be made to come as a boon to them direct from ourselves and not as an advantage extracted from us by the friendly interference of France. The generals then returned to the conference and with the intention, as I conceived, of adhering to every principle I had mentioned. The terms, however, showed it was not so, or that they thought they could not carry it. The precise point however about which the generals asked Clinton and myself was what was the maritime law in regards to the time ships could leave a neutral port before they were to be pursued, and that in order to have a distinct notion of the amount of what they were to concede about the Russian fleet. The principal reason of their coming out of the room, however, was, I believe, to give the French officers the same opportunity they wished for themselves: of considering a little amongst them the points in discussion and also time to write out the terms that had been assented to on both sides.
>
> It was proposed that a British officer should go with Gen Kellerman to Lisbon as the shortest way to communicate with the Admiral [Cotton], and I think the generals concurred in fixing upon me. I had not seen the terms, but Sir Arthur asked me privately in my opinion generally as to entering into a convention for the evacuation of the country by the French. I said there ought not to be much doubt of our being able to force the French to a surrender if they remained at Lisbon, since it might perhaps not contain more than one thousand or twelve hundred men; That, on the other hand, it was uncertain how far it might be in their power to retreat toward Spain, and we did not know whether affairs there were in a state to make that anything to be apprehended as likely to affect, materially or not, the turn of the war in the part of Spain they might get to; that at all events we could not follow the enemy from the coast with any degree of rapidity nor any distance; and that, finally, the fortresses might continue to hold out. Sir Arthur said that he did not feel altogether satisfied about the business but that upon the whole he thought it is an

> important object to get the French out of the country, and above all, to get hold of the fortresses, which might otherwise cost us a winters campaign and a great deal of difficulty; and on these grounds that he thought the views of government would be fulfilled by such an arrangement as was proposed.[16]

Général de Division Francois Etienne Kellermann, the French negotiator opposite Murray for the Convention of Cintra. (Musees de Senlis)

Murray, on leaving for Lisbon with Kellermann, initially saw himself as little more than a go-between in connection with the Convention, and indeed had no instructions but to communicate the initial treaty to Admiral Sir Charles Cotton for his concurrence, and to settle with him and Junot the place for the conference they were to hold together with Dalrymple. So at an early stage, post-armistice, Murray did not anticipate any role in completing negotiations, as was ultimately to be his responsibility, rather than just facilitating a 'summit' at Mafra, the venue which had been agreed by Junot at Murray's suggestion, knowing Dalrymple was happy with it

> I got a copy of the Preliminaries that night and in the morning [23rd] set out for Lisbon. I could consider myself in no other light, almost, then as a messenger, and I had no instructions but communicate the treaty to the Admiral for his concurrence and to settle with him and General Junot the place for the conference they were to hold together with the generals. Sir Arthur enjoined me to lose no time as everything turned upon the business being quickly carried through.
>
> I saw Junot at Lisbon on the night of the 23rd and fixed upon Maffra with him as the place of the conference, which had also been named by Sir H Dalrymple. When I got to the Admiral next morning I found him not disposed to be satisfied with the Treaty and that he was very widely mistaken as to the enemy's force, which he rated I think at about seven or from that to nine, thousand, at the utmost. After talking over the matter with the captain of the fleet, Sir Charles Cotton said he could never admit the Articles respecting the Russian fleet; that as to the rest of the treaty he did not pretend to be so good a judge of it as the generals, who must know better the situation of things on shore then he could be supposed to do, although he was satisfied his opinion respecting the enemy's numbers was pretty correct. The Admiral stated strong difficulties, however, to going to a conference at Maffra, as being at too

16 Murray to Patrick, Lisbon, 30 October 1808, Murray Papers, ADV MS 46.1.22.

> great a distance from his fleet at that season of the year and at a time when it was possible the enemies ships might make an attempt to escape.[17]

While Murray was in Lisbon involved with the preliminary discussions, Wellesley went to some length to detail what he felt were important issues that needed fixing in any final Convention, and requested Dalrymple to ensure Murray was aware of them, suggesting that Wellesley was, from the outset, supporting the idea of Murray as the man to front the negotiating of any Convention. They demonstrate Wellesley's constant attention to detail, his lack of confidence in Dalrymple's abilities, and his distrust of the French. They included neutralising the Russian Fleet in the Tagus, setting timescales for the surrender of various forts, fixing details of the transportation of the French troops and choosing destinations as far as possible from the Spanish and Austrian borders, to delay their re-joining the armies ranged against the allies. Security was to be taken for the safe return of the British ships provided as transport, as after the French were expelled from Egypt they had refused to release 50 of the vessels that had been provided. There were to be no vessels supplied for the French cavalry horses, and an exchange of prisoners should be arranged. He also made it clear that 'the French Generals [should] disgorge the church plate which they have stolen'.[18]

Armed with Cotton's forthright views on the Russian fleet, Murray returned to headquarters at Ramalhal late on the 24th, by way of Mafra, a detour that added about ten miles to the forty mile ride, but which enabled him to assess the state of the two principal roads which might yet play a part in any necessary action.

> The next morning Sir H Dalrymple sent for Sir H Burrard and Sir Arthur Wellesley and had a good deal of conversation about the state the negotiation was in. I mentioned the conversation I had had with the Admiral and that he had positively excluded the seventh article [about the Russian Squadron]; That he was willing, however, to treat separately with the Russians upon the basis of an instruction he had received from England when there was supposed to have been a famine in Lisbon; And that he concurred in the principle I had originally stated at Vimeiro, that whatever was given to the Russians should be made to appear as a concession from us to former friendship which we wished to renew, and not as a concession we made to the French. After some discussion it was determined to propose to the French to proceed with the Treaty excluding the seventh article, and, to do away the difficulties of a conference of the commanders in chief, it was resolved to give me the authority to negotiate the definitive convention at Lisbon provided the French still accepted the basis with the alteration above mentioned. There was no difficulty in regards to this on the part of the Navy, because the Admiral had said it was quite sufficient for him to be informed of the business and to have the power, of course, of objecting when it came to the ratification. I felt of course much reluctance at undertaking the task proposed, more especially of undertaking it at French headquarters, and therefore proposed that some other person should be sent along with me or

17 Murray to Patrick, (confidential) 30 September 1808, Murray Papers, ADV MS 46.1.22.

18 'Memorandum to Sir H Dalrymple by Sir A Wellesley for Lieut. Col. Murray charged with the negotiation for a Convention', Ramalhal, 23 August 1808, Murray Papers, ADV MS 46.1.22.

> that the negotiations should be transferred to Torres Vedras after I had ascertained merely whether Junot would go on or not without the Russians. Sir Hew Dalrymple and Sir Arthur, however, both encouraged me and pressed it as much the best way of proceeding.
>
> I set out therefore to return to Lisbon upon the 25th and got there the following morning. After much discussion and some very absurd scenes, the Convention was finally settled on the 30th. The delay arose principally from the distance of our headquarters from Lisbon and the badness of the roads, as also from the necessity of communicating with the Admiral.[19]

Dalrymple had provided Murray with his orders:

> I have the honor to enclose a letter which you will deliver to the French Commander in Chief and you will apprise his Excellency that as Gen Kellermann appeared to attach much importance to the article respecting the Russians, and as it is exceedingly inconvenient and disadvantageous to the British army to be liable to the agreement for an unlimited suspension of hostilities, you will inform his Excellency that I shall consider that to which I have agreed to be at an end at 12 o' clock at noon on the 28th. In case his Excellency should manifest a desire to continue the negotiations for a Convention on the basis of the remaining articles of the agreement I authorise you to enter upon and conclude it with such officer as shall be appointed by the Commander in Chief of the French army upon the terms specified in the enclosed memoranda subject to the ratification of the Admiral and myself and in case you should find this disposition to exist in his Excellency's mind and if you should enter upon the negotiation under these powers, you are authorised to apprise the Commander in Chief of the French army that I shall have no objection to a renewal of the agreement for the suspension of hostilities for a definite period to enable the officers employed to bring the negotiations to their result.[20]

So Murray prepared to confront Kellermann, saddled with a weight of responsibility which he had reluctantly accepted, after persuasive encouragement from both Wellesley and Dalrymple. The Russian fleet was a major issue in the negotiations. Without agreement on the Russians, Dalrymple was ready to move and resume hostilities. Troop movements continued on the ground, just in case. Much depended on the outcome of Murray's discussions, and he was left in no doubt that he had very limited time to reach agreement with Kellermann. Dalrymple wrote to him from Ramalhal on 29 August stressing the need for securing the Tagus for British ships, putting him firmly on the spot, but demonstrating a very human concern for his safety in the event that hostilities were resumed.

> It grieves me to place you in so embarrassing a situation, but I cannot help it. I am so confident that you will set out to join me before the hour that I have named for

19 Murray to Patrick, Confidential, 30 September 1808, Murray Papers, ADV MS 46.1.22.
20 Dalrymple to Murray, Ramalhal, 25 August 1808, Murray Papers, ADV MS 46.1.22.

> our advance that if I hear nothing from you I shall be uneasy for you. If therefore, for any reason you should be induced to remain, notwithstanding our advance, take care to send me in time one of the officers with you.[21]

The British insisted on treating separately with the Russians along the lines Murray had previously suggested. The French succumbed to the British demands, and the Russian fleet was surrendered to the British, to be returned when hostilities between the two nations were at an end, and the crews meanwhile to be transported to the Baltic in British ships.

Murray was aware that the British objectives had changed from those which he had been party to on landing with Burrard. He was with the other generals in accepting a situation that should perhaps have never arisen but for the crazy command carousel that was played out during a critical period in the game, and which probably spared the French in Portugal from a humiliating defeat. His views of Dalrymple were similar to those expressed by others. Murray was now a professional soldier of the 'scientific' era. He and Wellesley were in each other's confidence and itching to challenge old military traditions.

Wellesley too, even as early as the evening of the 22nd, had accepted the situation as it was. Destruction of the French in the field was not going to happen. The next best thing was a negotiated expulsion of the French from Portugal. Critically, both Wellesley and Murray had identified the need to prevent any possibility of the French leaving Portugal with looted prizes. To provide transport was not unusual; it had been provided to the defeated French in Egypt. The space on board was rationed to exclude French cavalry horses. But it would be careless and an insult to the Portuguese, who were at no point involved or consulted, to allow the French to take their Portuguese booty with them. Wellesley's views on the principles behind the terms of the armistice at this point were quite clear:

> I wrote to you after the battle of the 21st. On the 22nd in the morning Sir H Dalrymple arrived and on that evening Gen Kellermann came in to ask for a suspension of hostilities to give time for the negotiation of a Convention for the evacuation of Portugal by the French by sea. Sir Hew consented to this and desired me to sign it notwithstanding that I neither negotiated nor approved of it. This agreement contained many improper stipulations – among others it gave the French 48 hours notice of an intention to put an end to it. It likewise contained a stipulation in respect to the Russians which ought never to have been admitted and it was in other respects objectionable on account of its French verbiage. I have not got a copy of it. The objections to it have however since been considerably removed by the refusal of the Admiral to consent to the stipulation respecting the Russians and by the determination of the suspension of hostilities tomorrow at 12 o'clock unless Murray who is negotiating the Convention should be of opinion that an additional period of 24 hours is necessary to enable him to perform his work. I am ready to march in the evening and Sir J Moore next day and whether there is a Convention or not I hope to be in Lisbon by the beginning of September.

21 Dalrymple to Murray, Ramalhal, 29 August 1808, Wellington (ed.) *Supplementary Despatches*, Vol.XIII, p.306.

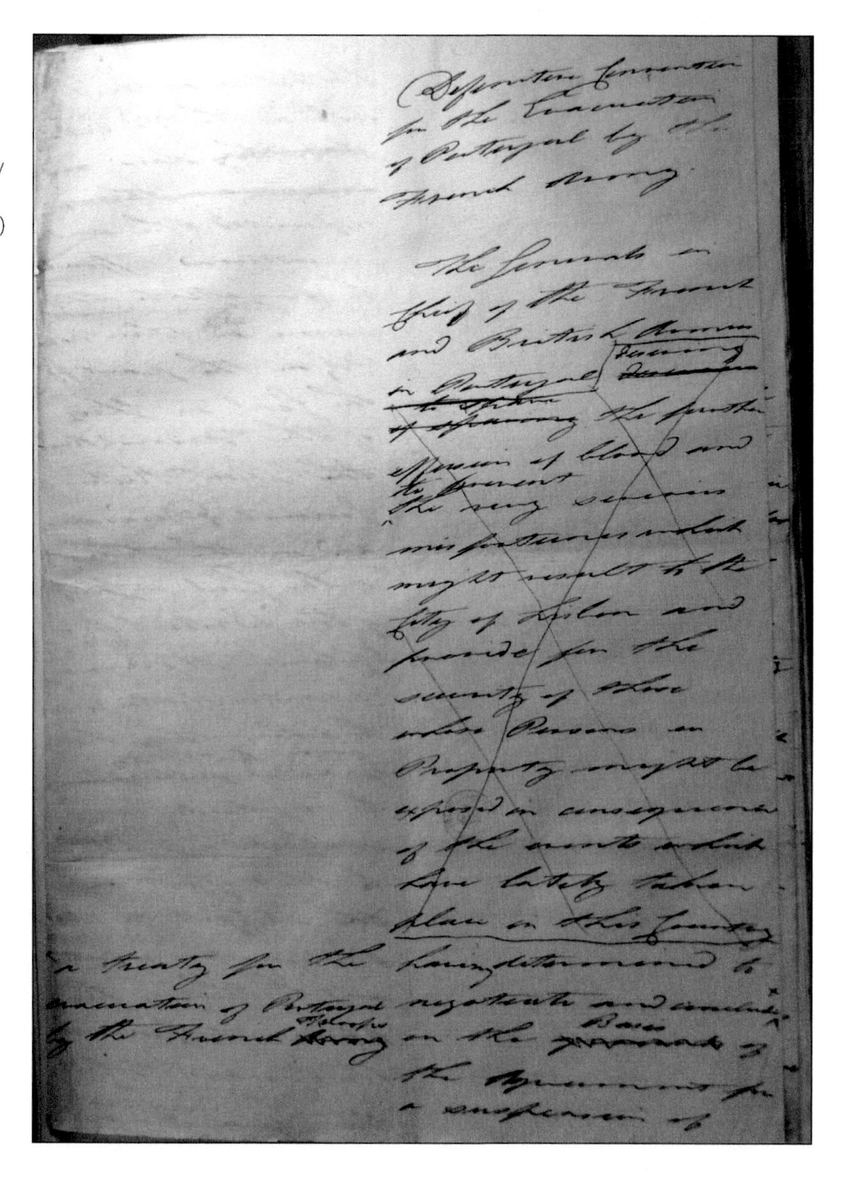

One of Murray's early drafts of the Convention of Cintra. (Author's photo from Murray Papers in National Library of Scotland)

I approve of allowing the French to evacuate the country for I [am] convinced that if we did not we should be obliged to attack Elvas, Fort Lippe, Almeida and Peniche regularly or blockade them and thus autumn would pass away and it is better to have 10,000 or 12,000 additional Frenchmen on the northern frontier of Spain and the army in Spain than the Frenchmen in Portugal and the English blockading them in strong places. This necessity would have been avoided if Sir H Burrard would or could have carried on with Sir J corps the operations upon Santarem which I recommended to him which the French would certainly have been cut off from Elvas and Almeida. The French got a terrible beating on the 21st.

> They did not lose less I believe than 4,000 men and they would have been entirely destroyed if Sir H Burrard had not prevented me from pursuing them. Indeed since the arrival of the great generals we appear to have been palsied. Everything has gone on wrong.

He continued, clearly anticipating an early exit from what he regarded as a shambles:

> I am not very well pleased between ourselves with the way in which things in this country are likely to go on and I shall not be sorry to go home if I can do so with propriety in which case I shall soon see you. But I don't like to desire to go lest it should be imputed to me that I am unwilling to serve where I don't command.[22]

When the result of Murray's negotiations with Kellermann and Junot was relayed to British headquarters a number of the British senior officers were unhappy with it, among them Wellesley. Amendments were agreed and sent by Dalrymple to Murray for insertion into the final document. Significantly the vexed issue of baggage was still being negotiated although Dalrymple's amendments were hardly examples of great forcefulness: Article V, he drafted,

> is understood to apply to the baggage usually possessed by military officers and persons attached to the Army as explained by General Kellerman in the negotiation for the agreement for the suspension of hostilities, property belonging to churches, monasteries, and galleries of painting etc cannot be carried away.

He also added an additional clause prohibiting the removal of any Portuguese property that had been confiscated by the French.

The commissioners later charged with effecting the evacuation apparently turned a blind eye to the copious quantities of plundered artworks and valuables taken from the Portuguese. There seemed to be little effort made at the point of embarkation towards relieving the French of their booty, surely something that could have been achieved. Perhaps all such items were well hidden in the vast amounts of baggage and equipment that the French were allowed to hold onto. Maybe it was not gentlemanly or honourable to search for such things in such circumstances. The French certainly took advantage at every opportunity. They were transported back to France on British vessels and not regarded as prisoners of war.

In contrast to some similar treaties, there was an acceptance that the French army was not regarded as being neutralized. On the contrary, it was openly acknowledged in the Convention that soldiers could still serve in the French army after repatriation. It was recognized that before very long the same men would be despatched to fight again wherever needed, probably Spain, and sooner rather than later. There was some military logic to this, it being felt preferable to have them well away in the north of Spain, than tying up British forces closer to hand. Murray had already witnessed the French habit of ignoring military conventions of the time, as had clearly happened following the siege of Valenciennes in

22 Wellesley to Duke of Richmond, Ramalhal, 27 August 1808, Wellington (ed.) *Supplementary Despatches*, Vol.VI, pp.126-7.

1793, an action that Murray (and Burrard) had witnessed. Following that defeat, French troops returned to action despite agreeing terms that had them neutralized. So perhaps there was a recognition of reality and an acceptance that there was no way of successfully preventing a return to campaigning by Junot's army.

Murray's private view of the preliminary armistice on which he was required to base his negotiations was that the articles were drawn with too little consideration. He told his brother that he felt there were two choices: either to agree a treaty, or to play for time pretending to negotiate, while Moore arrived with his army, and then hit the French. He was in favour of the second, but it was the first that Dalrymple and others determined to pursue. Given Junot's reputation as a practised rogue, and Dalrymple not seemingly knowing what he wanted from the treaty, Murray's task was more than usually difficult. Thiébault, Junot's chief of staff, wrote afterwards that Murray – although seemingly confusing him with Marshal Beresford – was a man of polished manners but very firm character, who showed great obstinacy in the negotiations.[23]

If it had to be a treaty then better, Murray considered, army to army, rather than involving the Portuguese, who had played no military part and would only complicate matters. He also felt it better not to humiliate the French as had happened in similar situations in the recent past. He was also aware of the necessity of dealing with one of the most potentially controversial issues: 'as to their carrying away plunder it was clearly understood that they should not and that understanding has been acted upon'.[24] He drew up, on 5 September, a statement clarifying his understanding of the provisions agreed on plunder. A clause initially in the draft Convention specifically forbidding the French from taking it with them had been dropped, on Junot mischievously claiming that such a clause appearing in a public document 'would be a standing reproach on the honour of the French army'. Murray agreed to its omission, but only when Junot had pledged his word that nothing of the kind would be removed from Portugal.[25] In a modern context this seems naïve and weak; against the military traditions of the day, less so. Murray made the point in a letter to Patrick immediately on leaving Lisbon with the Convention, signed on 30 August by him and Kellermann, and ratified by Junot, that he felt there was merit in sparing the honour of the French Army. Nevertheless, given the concerns which had already been expressed, and particularly addressed, about the importance of relieving the French of their ill-gotten gains, British reliance on good faith certainly did not help when it came to enforcement. It may reflect well on Murray's standards of honour, but hardly demonstrates 'the great obstinacy' that Thiébault credited him with.

The French so completely disregarded the 'understanding', and Junot's word of honour, that they included in their baggage church plate, valuable manuscripts, books from the royal library and silver ingots from the Portuguese treasury. This was despite letters from French headquarters insisting on the restoration of private property, and a proclamation by British and French Commissioners, working together in Lisbon, which specifically stated 'property of every kind confiscated or seized from the subjects or other persons residing in Portugal, whether of the royal palace, royal and public libraries and museums and from individuals

23 Paul Charles Thiébault, *Mémoires du Généeral Baron de Thiébault* (Paris: E.Plon, Nourrit et Cie., 1895), Vol.IV, p.196.
24 Murray to Patrick, Confidential, 30 September 1808, Murray Papers, ADV MS 46.1.22.
25 Ward Draft, Ch.VI, p.19.

that are still existing in Portugal should be restored'.[26] Plenty of other sums levied from the inhabitants of Lisbon were used to discharge the army's debts. Junot's private effects on embarkation contained, among other articles of value, 53 boxes of Indigo worth £5,000.[27] There was outrage in Oporto when the French garrison from Almeida, having been escorted all the way by British troops, was discovered on embarkation to have quantities of church linen hidden in their baggage. The local population forced the French off the ships, stripping them of their arms and possessions, an act which, according to British interpretation, was in contravention of the articles of the Convention. The confiscation was reversed and the French re-embarked, presumably with all their spoils.

So the French success in taking with them vast quantities of plunder was not as a result of the negotiated terms, but rather their lack of implementation and/or the seemingly habitual French tendency to not quite play the game as the British liked to think it should be played. Much was left to honour between armies or at least their commanders, but here was an instance where the British clearly should have been far more robust. However, there does seem to have been a tendency, faced with a Convention that was avoiding the likelihood of a drawn out bloody conflict, not to be seen as being unreasonable, and to ensure that evacuation took place as swiftly as possible, while the French were set on taking every possible inch from a situation that had been handed to them by British muddle and lack of cohesion. There was some justification for the military decisions that were made at Vimeiro. There was equally an argument to be made for a sensibly negotiated Convention. The implementation of the Convention, itself weighted too much towards the easy terms agreed in the initial armistice, seems to have gone embarrassingly wrong.

Murray, in his lengthy letters home to Patrick, repeated his view that the whole episode would have ended better if Dalrymple had let Wellesley get on with temporary command, the idea promoted by him immediately on Dalrymple's arrival. He also blamed the government for appointing Dalrymple with their eyes open, knowing he was not well qualified for the job. Finally he, not surprisingly, begged Patrick to keep his comments confidential.

There was great rejoicing when the news first reached Britain of the military success at Vimeiro. This quickly turned to disbelief and outrage when the details of the Convention became apparent. In London there was a determination that the embarrassing outcome should not be seen as a political affair but a military one. As Canning wrote to Lord Castlereagh: 'This Convention must be distinctly ours, or our Commanders. We must judge them…or the public will judge us… I shall not be prepared to consent to take an atom of the responsibility for this work'.[28] Wellesley had already made clear his disapproval of the decisions of Burrard and Dalrymple only days after he surrendered command, and returned home, bitterly disappointed, ready, if need be, to return to politics or private life, but not before throwing his support behind Moore as the man best equipped to carry on the campaign in his place.

The Convention of Cintra, so labelled probably as a result of the delay in it being finally despatched to London, by which time British headquarters had moved there, became the

26 Appendix 9 to Anon., *Minutes of Proceedings of the Court of Inquiry upon the Treaty of Armistice and The Convention of Cintra* (London: Samuel Tipper and John Booth, 1808), p.11.
27 Ward Draft, Ch.VI, p.18.
28 Canning to Perceval, 17 September 1808, Canning Papers, 32/1.

subject of intense discussion and analysis. Allowing the French to be spared total defeat and instead to quit Portugal, in British ships, only to fight again, was regarded by most of the British public, and, inevitably, by Whig politicians and newspapers, as a disgraceful waste of a golden opportunity to finally destroy French ambitions in the Peninsula.

It was more than unfortunate that the official report of the armistice and negotiations were only transmitted to London upon the army reaching Cintra on 3 September. News had gradually been filtering out through interested Portuguese sources, while the government, owing to what Murray stigmatised as 'a most culpable degree of dilatoriness on Dalrymple's part', lacked any authentic information with which to resist the outcry until it had spun out of control.[29] *The Times*, on 19 September, hoped that 'a curse, a deep curse might wring the heart and wither the hand that were base enough to devise and execute this cruel injury on their country's peace and honour' and demanded a condemnation of all concerned. The pressure on the government was intense and, soon after the details of the Convention were made public, an inquiry was set up. Burrard and Dalrymple were summoned back to London to attend. Wellesley had already quit the army with a view to returning to his post in Ireland and was back in London, the subject of considerable personal abuse. Seen as sharing responsibility for letting the chance of a French humiliation slip away, he was also required to attend and give evidence.

As in Sweden and Denmark, Murray had again been at the centre of one of the most important and controversial episodes of the war against Napoleon. A lieutenant colonel, now the army's acting Quartermaster General, he had, on arrival in Portugal, immediately been thrown into the melee, being present at the Battle of Vimeiro alongside Wellesley and Burrard, but, more importantly, being closely involved in the handovers of power that followed that British victory, and the negotiating and drafting of the Convention of Cintra itself. He had found himself caught in the crossfire between the competing ambitions and demands of more senior military officers. Throughout this extraordinary period he sought to clarify and give effect to conflicting orders, to act as a conduit for the dissemination of differing strategies between commanders whose characters and ambitions were vastly different, and, last but not least, to sit for days with a senior French general negotiating and signing a treaty of enormous importance, on a brief which was certainly less than forceful. All in the knowledge that it was certain that whatever he might put his name to was likely to meet with the disapproval of at least one of his senior officers, and certainly enrage the British public, whose appetite for a French humiliation had been whetted. The fact that he was charged with the task clearly demonstrates that by this time his skills as a negotiator and facilitator were well recognised.

At the inquiry into Cintra, there was evidence of mutual respect between Burrard and Wellesley and little evidence of anything other than anger on the part of Wellesley at what he saw as the incompetent bungling in the handling of the whole affair by Dalrymple. Wellesley's relationship with Murray was strengthened as an ally and confidante. The inquiry, perhaps surprisingly, did not recall Murray to London, although Murray did see that as a distinct possibility. His evidence would have made compelling reading as he was perhaps in the best position of all to know the thinking and intentions of the three main British players. He was

29 Ward Draft, Ch,VI, p,19, citing *Quarterly Review*, April 1836, p 205.

of course the one person who could, with authority, throw light on the strengths and weaknesses on the French side, as he, Kellermann, and Junot hammered out the final terms and signed them. It could well be that the politicians in London felt that having one general leave Portugal in a rage, and recalling two more, all to attend the inquiry, was enough of a demonstration to the public that they were taking the idea of a full investigation seriously, but that denuding the Peninsular army of its Quartermaster General at a time when it was advancing into Spain, would serve no useful purpose and only weaken the campaign.

Maybe Murray's hatred of unnecessary bloodshed played a part in how he conducted the negotiations. The overriding principle of getting the French out of Portugal seemed by this stage to have broad support, significantly even from Wellesley himself. Events on the ground, particularly the double handover of command, played wonderfully into the hands of the French. Had Burrard been even 24 hours later in arriving then undoubtedly Wellesley would have continued to advance in an attempt to crush the French, who, until 22 August, were in disarray. Burrard's decision, quite openly acknowledged later by Wellesley as a perfectly reasonable military one, was designed to avoid any possibility of being defeated by a French counter attack, with particular concern over the superiority of the French cavalry, and the damage it could cause. Supplies from the ships anchored offshore were being badly disrupted by the weather and the surf, and Burrard wanted to ensure a greater superiority in numbers by giving time for Moore and his considerable force to supplement operations. Murray's letter of 30 August, written to Patrick from Lisbon, immediately following his signing of the Convention, gives us a personal view of the situation, and is interesting in its lack of belligerence.

> Since the action of the 21st, I have been chiefly at the French Headquarters in Lisbon negotiating a convention for the evacuation of Portugal by the Enemy. I have at length signed the terms and shall set out tonight for our camp to submit them for ratification. I suppose it will be thought in England that after a victory we should have imposed harder conditions. Such is generally the view of the public in the like cases and it is only those who are acquainted with all the circumstances who can support the contrary argument.
>
> The original proposal was made on the 22nd, upon the part of the French, and the Basis of the Negotiation was signed that evening by Sir Arthur Wellesley and Gen Kellerman. During the time which has since lapsed we have had the advantage of moving reinforcements but as we were fully aware of the approach of these reinforcements when the Basis was established I leave it to you to judge whether in strict honour, we should have been justified in changing our ground on that account.
>
> The following argument may be used in favour of the suspension of hostilities and subsequent Convention.
>
> We were still forty miles from Lisbon having before us difficult country with the worst possible roads, and some strong passes.
>
> Our communications with our shipping was extremely precarious, being sometimes entirely cut off by the surf. Our means of conveyance limited as well as for our supplies as for our Artillery and ammunition. Our cavalry in comparison to that of the enemy, nothing. Our infantry excellent in a fixed position but not yet much in the habit of acting in the field in considerable corps, in fighting in individual situations in which this enemy might have been sent on a march. The command fluctuating

from the arrival of different generals. The arrival of Reinforcements uncertain as to days at least if not more. On the other hand there was also the prospect getting the French out of the country at once without further risk or loss to ourselves and without further injury to Portugal. There was the advantage of putting an end to Military Operations here, and being at liberty to act elsewhere with certainty in a definite time. The chance of the Enemy embarrassing us by holding out the Fortresses was guarded against as also that of his attempting a Retreat towards Spain, in which we could not have followed him, and by which it might have happened that his March would have embarrassed the operations of the Spaniards.

I don't know whether it ought to enter at all into consideration that from the nature of the Wars and Expeditions we carry on, we are exposed more than any other nation to have occasion to look towards such arrangements for ourselves. Perhaps it would be refining too much to say it may be politic to spare the honour of the French Army, and prefer sending them back without personal animosity, to tell we have beat them, than to press matters to the utmost in the risk of making them prisoners of war.[30]

After Vimeiro it was entirely likely that Burrard saw every chance of continuing where Wellesley had left off, but only when reinforcements and supplies were properly in place. Next day saw apparent agreement by Dalrymple, persuaded by Murray, that the army should be prepared to march, as Wellesley wanted. It was Kellermann's surprise arrival at Wellesley's headquarters on the 22nd and his proposals for an armistice that halted the momentum. From that moment it was Dalrymple who was solely in command. His agreement to the Convention, based closely on the armistice's disastrously easy terms, which largely mirrored French suggestions, is the act for which he was held responsible.

Wellesley was increasingly unhappy and bitter, and forewarned Murray of the likelihood of his return home, writing to Murray on 5 September:

I believe your experience of the zeal with which I served Lord Cathcart would convince you that I would not decline performing any duty which the government would require from me. I shall not conceal from you, however, that I consider myself in a very different situation in this army from that in which Lord Cathcart placed me; and I acknowledge that I cannot venture to do many things which I did for him, because it is evident that there exists a want of confidence which never existed in respect to me in any former instance.[31]

Murray wrote back soothingly:

As far as I can judge there is no want of confidence in the head to you. There may be something in a man being placed in a situation so new to him and in regard

30 Murray to Patrick, Lisbon, 30 August 1808, Murray Papers, MS 21102. See also Murray's later opinion on the Convention in the *Quarterly Review* where he deplored the lack of communication with London until 3 September.

31 Wellesley to Murray, Zambujal, 5 September 1808, Guwood (ed.) *Dispatches*, Vol.IV.p.139; also Murray Papers, ADV MS 46.1.22.

> to whose appointment so many other circumstances and considerations than that of selecting a good general had weight. There may at first be an apprehension of appearing to yield too much, which, if nothing is pressed, will soon wear off.[32]

All Murray's attempts to keep Wellesley in Portugal were to no avail, and Murray saw, for the first time, a frailty in Wellesley.

On 13 September Wellesley again wrote to Murray that he could not march as requested as he had to await supplies of new shoes for the troops. Wellesley also exchanged views on how unfolding matters should now be dealt with, aware that such military operations would not involve him. He thought the maximum size of an army to march into Spain was 25,000-30,000, including 5,000 cavalry. Wellesley also maintained that he did not understand Dalrymple's latest instruction – was he to go to Madrid? It is a letter of a demoralised General at the end of his tether. Wellesley's penultimate letter to Murray was on 19 September from Lisbon telling him he would leave next day for London and that he was sorry to have missed him. He had not concealed from him that he was less than satisfied with the situation. Interestingly, he said that he intended to return as soon as he could, and asked Murray 'to command me, if I can do anything for you'.[33]

The two men had clearly developed a mutual trust and respect and freely shared their personal misgivings. Wellesley felt that Dalrymple had not given him credit for what he had achieved. Murray might well have felt concern at this point that he was losing a close ally, but equally was more than fully occupied in dealing with the aftermath of the Convention on many fronts. He was being bombarded with issues concerning the transportation of the French back to France – not least the tendency of the French to push the boundaries on the arrangements especially as regards their 'personal property'.

British forces were now pushing inland, and, as agreed in the Convention, taking control of substantial French garrisons at Elvas and Almeida. Lieutenant General John Hope was in Lisbon trying to put together a Regency, in the absence of the Portuguese Court in Brazil, and was writing to Murray on the problems he was facing, seeking his support. Murray's concurrence in this role was less than enthusiastic – he described the added responsibility as 'inconvenient'. The onslaught of letters from Hope, occasionally two per day, all needed consideration and reply, and it must certainly have given Murray an immense amount of additional work, not to mention hard thinking. What was a young British officer supposed to know about the relative merits of Portuguese politicians or administrators, or indeed the intricacies of the Constitution of this foreign country? Nevertheless the exchanges of letters between the two soldiers are quite extraordinary in the level of detail, and apparent understanding of Portuguese national affairs. Hope's despair at Dalrymple's inability to make decisions was as strong as any, and he pleaded with Murray: 'I dislike this job… If I could be certain that you were always consulted when such decisions became necessary, or if the correspondence was suffered to be carried on between you and me, much of my anxiety would be removed'.[34]

32 Murray to Wellesley, Oeiras, 6 September 1808, Wellington (ed.), *Supplementary Despatches*, Vol.VI, pp.130-1.

33 Wellesley to Murray, Lisbon, 19 September 1808, Gurwood (ed.), *Dispatches*, Vol.IV, p.159; also Murray Papers, ADV MS 46.1.22.

34 Hope to Murray, Lisbon, 11 September 1808, Murray Papers, ADV MS 46.1.22.

Here again Murray was being employed in a diplomatic role at the highest level, and taking responsibility off the shoulders of an ineffective commander. His and Hope's efforts were rewarded when the new Regency was officially sworn in on 23 September. Portuguese sovereignty and sensitivities were uppermost in Murray's mind when he reiterated the importance of hoisting the Portuguese flag wherever British forces took over from the French. The British, he maintained, were there as an auxiliary force for the establishment of the Portuguese Government.

It is clear that much of this fluid situation was being handled by Murray himself albeit, no doubt, with an awareness of his relatively junior rank. Dalrymple was summoned back to London by a letter received by him on 28 September, formally surrendering command back to Burrard on 2 October. Burrard was in turn summoned back shortly after, and Moore took over command. So Murray, and indeed Hope and Anstruther with whom he was working closely, had, since landing on the Portuguese shore barely four weeks earlier, been reporting to Burrard then Dalrymple then Burrard again and, lastly, Moore. It would not be surprising if Murray and his fellow senior officers felt the only way to get things done sensibly was to sort them out among themselves, although Dalrymple was clearly aware of both Hope's and Anstruther's activities, and approved the appointment of the Bishop of Oporto to head the Regency, an appointment made after that intense diplomatic work by Hope and Murray.

Murray was also conscious of the likelihood that soon there would be a move to advance out of Portugal into Spain and to seek to confront the French there. To do this it was essential that as much intelligence as possible could be gathered, not just on the possible strength of the enemy, but also the position and readiness of Spanish forces, with whom now it would be necessary to co-operate, as well as the state of the roads, their ability to support the movement of cavalry and artillery, and difficulties of maintaining supplies, bearing in mind that, before long, the weather would be deteriorating. All classic Quartermaster General duties.

Murray still found the time to write a letter from Lisbon, firmly marked 'Confidential' to Patrick, on 30 September, covering more than 20 large pages, expanding on his letter, written in haste immediately after signing the Convention exactly a month earlier, and explaining in much greater detail the background to the uneasy relations between the three generals and the events leading to the Convention. It was becoming clear to him by then that the Convention was giving rise to even more consternation at home than he had anticipated, and he had previously acknowledged that it would not be popular. He commented on Burrard:

> verifying what I had indeed never doubted, his total incapacity for such a command. It was distressing to see a man so much out of his place, and it was doubly so from knowing him to be a brave, amicable and worthy man in private, and from knowing the secret causes which had brought him forward to a situation for which he was so unfit.[35]

Given the close cooperation between Wellesley and Murray at Copenhagen a year earlier and their willingness to combine to drive forward as they saw best, in the absence of forceful

35 Murray to Patrick, Confidential, 30 September 1808, Murray Papers, ADV MS 46.1.22.

leadership from a more senior officer, it is perhaps surprising that between them Wellesley and Murray did not take closer control of the negotiations with the French. Wellesley did attempt to ensure that Murray would not negotiate away certain elements which he highlighted as important, and which he seemingly did not trust Dalrymple to cover effectively, but such was his disappointment in the immediate aftermath of Vimeiro, and his anger towards the senior command, that he had perhaps lost the appetite to interfere further. Without direct support from Wellesley, Murray had little choice but to follow through the heads of terms agreed by Dalrymple, weak as they were. Murray's view was that the arrival of Moore's force altered the situation, and there was no need for the generals to agree to terms which were ignoring the significant effect on the balance of power that the additional numbers provided.

There is an interesting postscript to the dramas surrounding the Convention. In Murray's papers there lies a document carefully written by Murray marked 'Private', in amongst some exchanges of correspondence with Hope, but with the instructions 'You may open and peruse the accompanying letter before forwarding it. You will see that it is altogether private though not in the first person'. At the foot is written: 'To be sent to Liverpool'. It is a summary of events leading to the signing of the Armistice in the style of a formal affidavit. Included in it is the following:

> When General Kellerman came into British Headquarters to make proposals for a suspension of hostilities, Sir Hew Dalrymple, Sir Harry Burrard and Sir Arthur Wellesley were the persons with whom the discussion of the terms took place, and amongst these people Sir Arthur took the greatest share if not the entire lead in the conversation, which his having had the command till two days before, gave him some right to do, and which is natural to the eagerness of his temper.

It went on:

> If the Preliminaries were an improper Basis the real responsibility rests not with Sir Hew Dalrymple, but the blame is equally with Sir Harry Burrard, and Sir Arthur Wellesley.[36]

The position adopted by Wellesley as to his role in the negotiations and drafting of the armistice on which the Convention, both privately and to the Inquiry, was that he had little input into, and took no responsibility for, the terms that were agreed that evening with Kellermann, and only signed as a matter of protocol. This document of Murray's does more than suggest otherwise. It is as strong a statement as he could make that Wellesley in fact led the negotiations, something that Murray knew was entirely in keeping with his temperament, especially given the characters of the two generals he was working alongside.

Murray's statement is in direct contradiction of Wellesley's oft-repeated assertion that nothing in the Armistice terms had anything to do with him. Wellesley had written to Castlereagh on the day after its signing: 'Although my name is affixed to this instrument, I

36 Undated document inside a letter from Hope to Murray of 14 September 1808, Murray Papers, ADV MS 46.1.22.

beg that you will not believe that I negotiated it, that I approve of it or that I had any hand in wording it'.[37] He followed this up with another letter to Castlereagh when back in London:

> I beg leave to inform your Lordship that I did not negotiate the agreement; that it was negotiated and settled by his Excellency [Dalrymple] in person, with Gen. Kellerman, in the presence of Lt. Gen. Sir H Burrard and myself and that I signed it by his Excellency's desire. But I could not consider myself responsible in any degree for the terms in which it was framed, or for any of its provisions.[38]

The denials could not have been stronger and Wellesley relied on them for his defence in the inquiry. Murray and Clinton, according to Murray's own account, were not in the same room as the negotiators and were only called upon to give advice on the issue of the Russian fleet. It is therefore a little difficult to understand Murray's apparently clear impression that Wellesley took the lead. Murray was already held in high regard in Whitehall after the Swedish debacle, and was known to be loyal to Wellesley. If he maintained that Wellesley was not only closely involved in, but actually led, the armistice discussions, this would surely have impacted on Wellesley's case.

At the top of the document, in what looks like Patrick's hand are the words: 'Supposed to be written Lisbon, 3 October 1808'. Yet it seems to have been sent back from Hope to Murray under cover of a letter dated 14 September. Here was Murray putting pen to paper in a considered way, very soon after the final signing of the Convention, as if he knew his statement might end up in a formal court. That he sent it to Hope to peruse before it being sent on, seemingly to his brother, was typical. The two men were already working closely together on political and military issues in the aftermath of the French expulsion. They knew each other well on a personal basis, being connected by marriage, and relied on each other for support and advice. It is a reasonable assumption that the reference to Liverpool is to Lord Liverpool – Home Secretary at the time, later to be Prime Minister – in London, and the frequent future recipient of much correspondence from the Peninsula, including, naturally, from Wellesley, yet the slight mystery is compounded by the fact that Liverpool only acceded to the title on the death of his father in December that year. There is no evidence that the document ever reached him. Yet it also sits, in full, in Wellington's *Supplementary Despatches*, without any signature, merely headed: 'A Memorandum respecting the Convention of Cintra'. So it did surface eventually, if not at the inquiry itself.

Murray played no active part at all in the inquiry. Although his conversations and actions during the fraught week between landing and the signing of the Convention were referred to in sworn statements, he was never called to give evidence. He had more than enough to occupy his days as Moore took command and planned a rapid advance into Spain to confront the French.

37 Wellesley to Castlereagh, Camp at Ramalhal, 23 August 1808, Wellington (ed.), *Supplementary Despatches*, Vol.VI, p.122.

38 Wellesley to Castlereagh, London, 6 October 1808, Gurwood (ed.), *Dispatches*, Vol.IV, p.161.

9

1808 – Peninsula – Moore – Advance and Retreat

Dalrymple and Wellesley having departed for London, with Burrard soon to follow, the command of the British Forces in Portugal moved to Moore. On 8 October 1808, the day Moore's command began, Murray was confirmed as Quartermaster General to the Army in the Peninsula. He was still only 36, but a figure who had often been at the forefront of major events. Moore, thankful no doubt for all the preliminary work put in by Murray while Dalrymple was still hanging onto command, now planned his march into Spain, as agreed with Castlereagh. A relatively small garrison would be left in Portugal. Murray told Patrick that he was happy with his new commander:

> It must have given you satisfaction to find that amidst all the changes I still retain my situation, and you will be aware that the retaining it under Sir John Moore does not render it the less acceptable to me. The only thing I have ever apprehended was that circumstances might force an enquiry in which my presence would be thought necessary, as having been in situations to know every thing that has passed in this country.[1]

Murray was relieved not to have had to return to London to give evidence at the Cintra inquiry, although the danger of this did not pass until late November, in part as a result of a letter written by Moore to Castlereagh from Salamanca, begging that neither Clinton nor Murray 'the two officers upon whom hinges the whole business of the army' be recalled to London. Moore suggested that if their evidence was required perhaps they could give it under oath before the Judge Advocate of the Army in the Peninsula, or if that were not possible, then perhaps the inquiry could be postponed 'until quieter times'.[2] When Moore's retreat commenced a few weeks later, another inquiry on that score seemed entirely possible, and Colonel Rufane Donkin, described by Ward as 'an ugly, busy, contentious man, a talker

1 Murray to Patrick, Lisbon, 26 October 1808, Murray Papers, MS 21102.

2 James Carrick Moore, *A Narrative of the Campaign of the British Army in Spain commanded by His Excellency Sir John Moore* (London: Joseph Johnson, 1809), p.31.

and a mischief maker',[3] who had been on Burrard's staff, told Murray, with more than a hint of malice 'you already have (do you feel it?) a polarity towards Chelsea'.[4]

Moore was acutely aware of the responsibility on his shoulders. Circumstances had placed the best of the British Army in his hands, when only a few months earlier he had been pressed to resign. Almost all the infantry were the first battalions of their regiments. Not even Marlborough had commanded so many high-calibre British troops. Murray of course knew his new commander well, both from Egypt, and, more recently, Sweden. Murray's admiration of Moore as a man remained profound. Perhaps he was less enthusiastic about his capacities as a commander. He appeared to have some reservations. Murray was admitted to Moore's confidence partly at least as a reflection of Moore's recognition of Murray's reputation as a scientific. Moore's strategic planning has been questioned, not least by Ward:

> In the forty nine days between 28 November and 16 January his original design was subjected to no fewer than seven major alterations, one of them involving a change of base and two of them a reversal of a previous order… It cannot be dignified as a plan of campaign.[5]

Questions about his operational plan certainly seem justified, never mind the difficulties it presented for his Quartermaster General.

The problems facing the British were daunting. Moore's army was dispersed over large distances, partly to ease the burden on the countryside, partly as a result of a woeful lack of accurate intelligence as to passable roads. The vast bulk of the artillery was attached to Hope's division, which was to take a southern route towards Salamanca, running close to Madrid, leaving Moore's main force dangerously weakened, which was to have a profound effect on events as they unravelled over the next two months. The decision to allow Hope to take the Madrid route dismayed Murray. George Scovell, at that point a captain and mere deputy assistant quartermaster general, recorded Murray's view, expressed to him two years later: 'in all military movements every precaution should be taken but that after all something must be left to accident, for as with every occurrence in life there is no one thing to be found perfect'.[6]

News had reached Lisbon that that an additional British force of 10,000 men was being sent to the northern coast of Spain, under Lieutenant General Sir David Baird, with which the southern force was required to unite. This gave definite focus to the plan, which Murray favoured, of marching to Almeida, Burgos, and thence the Pyrenees, with the possibility of falling back on Portugal or the coast if necessary. Indeed he felt it very likely that the campaign would wither, as a result of lack of Spanish support, a view expressed clearly to Brownrigg:

3 Ward Draft, Ch.VI, p.33.
4 Donkin to Murray, 13 January 1809, Murray Papers, ADV MS 46.2.2 (The Cintra inquiry was held at Chelsea Hospital).
5 Ward Draft Ch.VI, p.36.
6 TNA, WO37/7a, Scovell Diary. Report of a conversation with Murray, Santo-Quintino, 10 October 1810.

> We shall have great difficulty I apprehend in moving forward our stores from this side, partly owing to the extremely bad roads of Portugal, partly to the Rainy Season which must be expected to come on, and perhaps still more than all, to the want either of energy – of intelligence or of good will in the Government of this country. Were we enemies we could force the authorities of the country to act, and by vigorous measures, and a good system, much might be done; but all now is in a kind of neutral or inert state, the most adverse possible to military exertions such as the present crisis merits and requires.[7]

He would indeed be writing to Anstruther, (now a brigadier general) within a month on the necessary supplies and troop movements involved in any planned retreat, with the view that they should present as brave a face as possible to the Portuguese, and only let such plans for what would be an unpopular withdrawal into the public domain by degrees.[8] Anstruther had been sent ahead to take the frontier fortress of Almeida from the French, as well as report on the state of the roads to the frontier.

A long tedious march separated the British from the enemy in Spain. Work needed to be done and plans drafted to combine Baird – who had landed at Corunna in command of the northern force, after a disembarkation delayed by slow Spanish permission – Hope – who had entered Spain via Badajoz – and Moore's force. Murray said he would shortly set out for Almeida, bemoaning the lack of supplies and ammunition, and foreseeing clearly the difficulties in uniting the three forces. He left Lisbon with Moore, the ultimate aim being a convergence of the scattered British forces, and arrived at Salamanca on 13 November.

On it being discovered that his writing case had been packed up by mistake with Murray's belongings and carried from Almeida on to Salamanca, Anstruther entreated Murray: 'pray do not let it fall into Boney's hands; the blackguard would publish any private correspondence'.[9] Clearly Murray felt no threat of that, as his reply to Anstruther contained, in amongst an update on the positions of the fragmented army, a request for 'a small supply of Port out of the Wine Country'.[10] Yes, there were substantial difficulties to be overcome, but perhaps the problems might seem less daunting after a glass or two. In fact the difficulties were about to multiply rapidly over the course of the next week.

Hope's contingent, having marched very close to French forces and Madrid, arrived later at Salamanca. There was a ten day gap between the first artillery brigade and the last squadron of dragoons in the Hope column. Murray had sent officers ahead from Lisbon to produce maps and reports on road conditions but their findings, that the direct route taken by Moore was in fact possible for artillery, contrary to what they had been told by the locals, did not reach Moore in time to avoid sending Hope on the longer march. It was an early example of over-reliance on local misinformation.[11] As a result Moore was left without any cavalry and almost all his artillery for two critical weeks in which he could do nothing.

7 Murray to Brownrigg, Lisbon, 18 October 1808, Luffness Mss, GD 364/1/1179.
8 Murray to Anstruther, Salamanca, 29 November 1808, Murray Papers, ADV MS 46.1.23.
9 Anstruther to Murray, Almeida, 20 November 1808, Murray Papers, ADV MS 46.1 23.
10 Murray to Anstruther, Salamanca, 22 November 1808, Murray Papers, ADV MS 46.1.23.
11 See Anstruther letters in Murray Papers, ADV MS 46.1.22, where he attempted to inform Murray of the best way to move an army across the poor Portuguese and Spanish roads.

Courtyard of Moore's Salamanca headquarters in Plaza San Boal, now the Cultural Centre for Hispanic-Japanese Relations, University of Salamanca. (Author's Photo)

Murray penned a downbeat letter to Patrick on 27 November from Salamanca, following a string of depressing reports on French successes over the Spanish, and the inability of Baird's force to meet up with Moore in view of French movements. He expressed exasperation at the Spanish forces, their lack of equipment and the resultant need for England to supply them with ammunition and other necessaries. Baird in fact had commenced a withdrawal after receiving information that a French force was assembling to prevent him joining Moore. Hope was still some way away from joining up. The options open to Moore were limited by the absence of Hope's force and the difficulties Baird was experiencing. Nevertheless Murray and Anstruther had together been exploring a variety of options, rather than settling for a retreat into Portugal, which Moore kept contemplating. As ever there seemed to be a lack of money, and the news relayed by Anstruther that a convoy with 40,000 dollars was on its way from Almeida to Salamanca must have been very welcome. A further 60,000 dollars was awaiting collection at Oporto, which would be picked up by an escort accompanying 60 women and 100 children to the coast for embarkation for England.[12] As each piece of new intelligence presented itself to Murray, he would send his fresh ideas to Anstruther, his erstwhile mentor. He, after puzzling for hours over 'Lopez's

12 Anstruther to Murray, Almeida, 26 November 1808, Murray Papers, ADV MS 46.1.23.

abominable maps',[13] would respond with his considered advice. Only if the Spanish gave up completely would such 'a desperate extremity as retreat' be necessary.[14] Murray tried again and again to persuade Moore of the viable alternatives, specifically an advance to the Douro. Moore eventually yielded to the combined arguments of the two scientifics, and on the morning of 28 November the order was given to advance.[15]

Everything changed that afternoon with the arrival of Sir Charles Vaughan, a British diplomat, later to become Secretary to the British Legation, who had been accompanying the Spanish army of Castanos in Aragon, after a ride of 476 miles in six days, with shocking news of the fate of the last and most powerful of the Spanish armies at Tudela on the 23rd. A postscript to Murray's letter of the 27th to his brother adds: 'I am sorry to say accts have arrived of Castanos' defeat'.[16] The plans had to change, and later that night (the 28th) Murray relayed to Hope, Baird, and Anstruther Moore's new determination to retreat.[17]

Moore's decision was based on the likely timings of any link up with Baird, and Hope's distance from him. The French might execute a pincer movement which would be fatal. His decision nevertheless was greeted with dismay. Murray and Anstruther both thought it a mistake. Murray remained convinced that a junction with Baird was still quite possible and confessed he 'never saw very strongly the necessity for retiring on the information we had of the enemy's force and movements'.[18] Whilst there was no real difficulty in a retreat back along the supply lines what was unclear was what that might lead to. Murray's view was that the French could probably be held for a time, but the most palatable plan would be for the army to be embarked and then landed later in southern Spain, probably at Cadiz. Arrangements for the retreat were completed by Murray and the orders to the fighting formations were issued early on 5 December. Then Moore changed his mind again that evening.

By this time the French strength in Spain totalled over 200,000 men. Nevertheless, it seemed there had been spirited resistance to the French attempt to take Madrid, and this, together with more encouraging news on the performance of Spanish forces elsewhere, persuaded Moore to reverse his planned retreat, and go on the offensive, persuaded by letters from the Supreme Junta, urging him to join with La Romana's Galician army and march on Madrid. Moore seemingly never had an accurate picture of the total French strength. He thus appreciated that he was taking a calculated risk, but those calculations were not based on reliable information. Though by no means sanguine about the future, suspecting rightly a wild underestimation of French numbers, Murray thought it possible the popular spirit of Spanish resistance might 'effect a very important change' and that 'I still count upon this country being the hardest morsel Buonaparte has to chew'.[19]

'Why', he wrote to Anstruther, in a slightly more optimistic vein than his letter a week earlier:

13 Anstruther to Murray, Almeida, 28 November 1808, Murray Papers, ADV MS 46.1.23.

14 Anstruther to Murray, Almeida, 28 November 1808, Murray Papers, ADV MS 46.1.23.

15 Ward Draft, Ch.VII, p.41.

16 Murray to Patrick, Salamanca, 27 November 1808, Murray Papers, MS 21102.

17 Murray to Hope, Salamanca, 28 November 1808, Murray Papers, ADV MS 46.1.23.

18 Ward Draft, Ch,VII, p.42 (citing Murray to Bathurst, Salamanca, 2 December 1808, Murray Papers, ADV MS 46.2.1).

19 Murray to Patrick, Salamanca, 5 December 1808, Murray Papers, MS 21102.

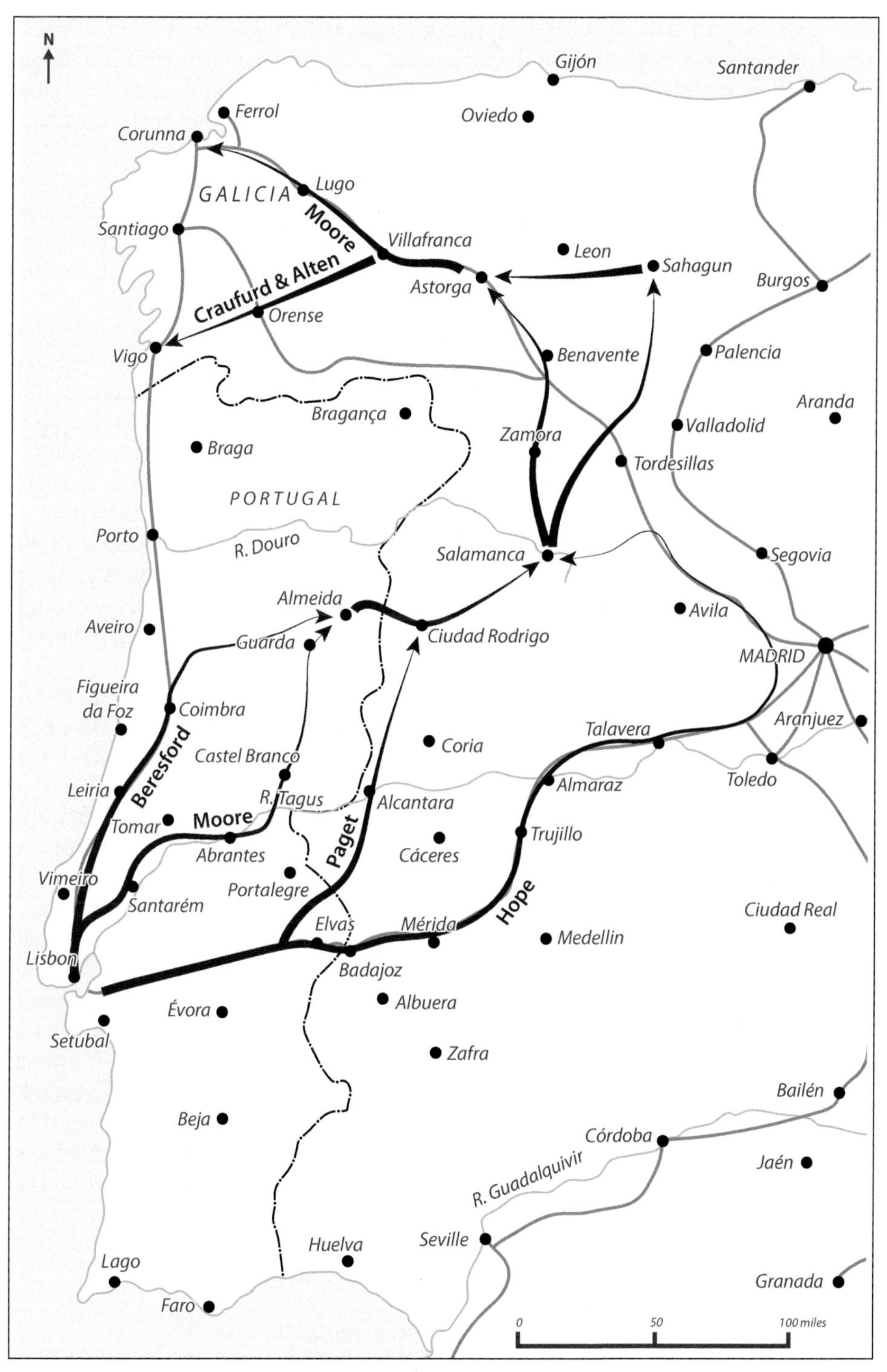

Map 6 Moore's Corunna campaign.

> may not the Spaniards do at Madrid what they did at Saragossa or at Buenos Aires, or what the Turks have done in many places? ... If the Spaniards continue to go down hill as rapidly as they began, to withdraw from this country may be highly necessary and perfectly justifiable. But if, on the contrary, they yet make a gallant struggle our going back can neither be the one nor the other.[20]

Moore was unaware that Napoleon himself planned to go on the offensive, with superior forces, which Murray estimated to Anstruther might number at least 50,000, advancing through the Guadarrama Pass between Madrid and Salamanca. Winter was now setting in and conditions were deteriorating rapidly.

Murray presented Moore with two alternative plans, Moore choosing the one that called for an amalgamation of Moore's, Baird's and La Romana's forces, with an initial advance to Valladolid in an attempt to destroy French communications in the neighbourhood of Burgos. Such advance northward called for a radical reorganisation of the army's lines of supply and retreat, originally based round a more southerly line through Almeida into Portugal. The possibility of the Army falling back through Galicia, in the north, had in fact occurred to Murray before leaving Lisbon and while dealing with the new arrangements he now reiterated his former plans to Lieutenant Colonel Bathurst, his assistant embedded with Baird's corps.[21] There were plenty of supply depots, all adequately stocked. Suitable arrangements would also need to be made for the re-routing of all ammunition that was being brought up from the rear. Bathurst had collected opinions on the port that was the preferred option in the case of a forced embarkation, all clearly in favour of Vigo over Corunna.

Having made the difficult decision to move forward, rather than retreat, Moore's whole demeanour altered and he was ready to chance his luck; 'Things are very bad. If I can make them better I shall think myself a clever fellow. In short, I am going to place myself in Fortune's way. If she jilts me, God damn her'.[22]

Murray had found himself a new horse, described proudly by his Spanish acquirer as being very handsome, strong, young, and sound. It cost him 230 dollars and was on its way from Ciudad Rodrigo. It would need all its stamina over the coming weeks.

A letter from Napoleon's chief of staff to Marshal Soult, intercepted four days after Moore's decision to advance on Valladolid, illustrated the lack of intelligence available to the French as well as the complete isolation of Soult's corps, which was heavily outnumbered by the combined forces of Moore, Baird, and La Romana. Moore showed the letter to Murray who stressed that whatever might happen later, it was now essential to move to link with Baird rather than waiting for him to catch up at Valladolid. Moore agreed Murray's plan, and the army was left-wheeled, joining with Baird on the 20th. The men were rested and re-provisioned over the next two days, during which Lieutenant General Henry Paget's hussars destroyed a French cavalry brigade outside Sahagun, where headquarters were then established.[23] On the 23rd the united British army, totalling 27,000 infantry and

20 Murray to Anstruther, Salamanca, 6 December 1808, Murray Papers, ADV MS 46.2.1.

21 Murray to Bathurst, Salamanca 10 December 1808, Murray Papers, ADV MS 46.2.1.

22 Moore to Willoughby Gordon, Salamanca, 10 December 1808, quoted in Ward Draft, Ch.VII, p.48.

23 Henry Paget, later the second Earl of Uxbridge and subsequently created Marquess of Anglesey, commanded Moore's cavalry with distinction. He did not serve further in the Peninsula owing to his affair with Charlotte Wellesley,

2,700 cavalry, was poised to attack Soult, in a three pronged advance. Moore was leaving his Headquarters at Sahagun at dusk to follow the troops, when a messenger from La Romana arrived with a letter informing him that Napoleon had already crossed the Guadarrama pass heading their way. Murray, on reading the letter, concluded that the halt at Sahagun had denied them the chance of a surprise attack on Soult who was now likely to fall back. In the meantime he thought that Napoleon would have time to cut the British line of retreat. Napoleon was indeed moving to attack Moore's rear with every element of his 40,000-strong force. Consequently there was no alternative but to abandon the advance and fall back at once. Moore agreed and ordered Murray to countermand the movement against Soult and draw up orders for the retreat to the north-west.[24]

Napoleon never in fact made enough progress, fast enough, to engage Moore in battle. Frustrated, and having urgent political issues to deal with in Paris, he left the pursuit of Moore to Soult, and headed back across the Pyrenees.

Moore's army felt cheated and the mood of the troops became ugly. In addition to the difficulty of maintaining morale, the weather was now becoming an issue. Snow and frost gave way to a thaw and heavy rain, causing the rivers to swell. Logistics became a nightmare, one problem being the 330 carts carrying stores and equipment that needed to make crossings at suitable places. The bulk of the army had to make a detour of fifty miles to cross the Esla. Soult was now closing on the army's rearguard. Paget's cavalry was in action frequently protecting the straggling infantry and artillery.[25]

It was very clear to Moore by now that he could not rely on anything more than isolated pockets of support from the Spanish people. This was to become even more obvious during the long march back to the coast in the most appalling conditions. There was a growing enmity between the British, who saw themselves as there to liberate the Spanish from the clutches of Napoleon and his brother Joseph, who had in August 1808 been inserted as Spanish King, and the Spanish population, who, for the most part, provided singularly little support to the British soldiers. There was also a growing feeling in the British ranks that the promises and efforts of the Spanish Juntas and military were worse than useless and had played a large part in bringing the military situation to the dangerous point it was now at. Henry Paget had clear views on Spain and the Spanish:

> Tis not worth saving. Such ignorance, such deceit, such apathy, such pusillanimity, such cruelty, was never more united. There is not one army that has fought at all. There is not one general who has exerted himself. There is not one province that has made any sacrifice whatever… We are treated like enemies. The houses are shut against us. The resources of the country are withheld from us.[26]

Wellington's sister-in-law. He was to become Murray's brother-in-law after Murray married Lady Louisa Erskine (nee Paget), Henry's sister. Paget lost a leg at Waterloo.

24 Ward Draft, Ch.VII, pp.49-50.

25 Ward Draft, Ch.VII, p.51.

26 Paget to Lord Holland, Sahagun, 20 December 1808, cited in Ian Robertson, *A Commanding Presence – Wellington in the Peninsula 1808-1814* (Stroud: Spellmount, 2008), p.75.

In the event of any relaxation on the part of the French, Murray felt it might still be possible to maintain a foothold in the Peninsula, which was his preferred option at this point, but the enemy did not relax. Rather than attempt to stop Soult at Astorga, Moore decided to continue the retreat. La Romana had been defeated at Mansilla, and his disordered men soon arrived at Astorga and in the villages behind, upsetting the British army's billeting – carefully parcelled out on the morning of the 30th between the two armies by Murray and La Romana – depriving them of any rest. They compensated themselves by descending on Astorga's well stocked wine cellars, in a disgusting display. Murray ascribed many of the subsequent misfortunes of the retreat to this early disturbance of his carefully regulated routes. The roads were, apart from one, in an appalling state, exacerbated by the cold wet winter. There were no sizeable towns or villages between Astorga and Lugo, a distance of about 110 miles. Billeting was non almost existent. In any event there was a hostile reception awaiting them from the native Gallegos, who had a well-known dislike of foreigners. All they saw was a rabble of an army, abandoning them. What in September had been the pick of the British military had degenerated into a mob of desperate men concerned only with keeping alive.[27] The lack of respect by British soldiers for property and fine antiques was painfully evident. Every town and village that lay on the army's route probably suffered the commonplace burning and looting. Drunken soldiers were frequently out of control.

August Schaumann, a deputy assistant commissary in the King's German Legion, one of the British Army's best corps, who kept a diary, much of it describing his amorous exploits during the campaign, recorded:

> The English soldier who was now quite aware that he had been lured to this country and into a parlous position by the Spaniards under false pretences, and that they had been left in the lurch... set about burning everything out of revenge. It was a good thing, though, that he wreaked his vengeance on inanimate objects and not on the inhabitants... the officers, enraged by their men's lust of destruction and desecration, seemed crushed with grief, and did all in their power to limit the damage... but the numbers were too much for them and the hidden corners too numerous. Besides, insubordination was already apparent... and in spite of all the discipline, it was impossible to stop it in an army which already felt it was retreating from a country it hated.[28]

Schaumann had earlier reported that the Portuguese had been declaring with one voice:

> Do not trust the Spaniards and their promises; for all they tell you about ample stores and large armies are sheer lies; all they wish you to do is lure you into their country, claim your victories as their own, hardly mention the help you have given them, and not even thank you. If things go wrong they will vanish in a twinkling, and return to their homes, and leave you to your fate in the heart of Spain, surrounded by your enemies and exposed to every possible privation. Furthermore

27 Ward Draft, Ch.VII, p.55.

28 A.L.F. Schaumann, *On the Road with Wellington.* (London: Greenhill Books 1999), p.93.

> the year is too far advanced and the rainy season will hurry you on too much and do you a lot of damage.[29]

Thus the mutual distrust must have ramped up, incident by incident, with disgust for the fraud, indifference, and backstabbing of the Spanish being relieved by British vandalism and drunkenness which in turn alienated the local population even more. The Spanish population suffered at the hands of both armies.

Moore himself, possibly feeling vulnerable for having so readily trusted various promises of the Spanish Junta of substantial military support, and recognising that his forces were hopelessly outnumbered, fixed on as rapid a retreat to the coast as possible. Those who could not keep up were abandoned and either died of exposure in the freezing conditions, or at the hands of the French who were never far behind. Many of the women and children who were with the army perished. The French continued to harass the rear of the army, kept at bay by some commendable actions by Paget's cavalry. The discovery that the Lugo to Vigo road was so bad that it risked the loss of all the artillery, led to the decision to alter the route of retreat to Corunna, with the exception of Craufurd's and Alten's brigades which were to continue to Vigo and board such transports that remained there.

At Lugo Moore kept the army drawn up for battle for 3 days from 6 to 8 January. Stragglers caught up, and the appearance of the army improved dramatically. Although the opposing armies were drawn up close to each other on adjacent hills Moore declined to give battle, on the basis of a less than helpful position with the river Minho behind him, and lack of supplies, and gave the order yet again to continue the retreat.[30] The army left Lugo under cover of darkness, continuing all night and through the following day in an attempt to gain 24 hours on the French. In the darkness there was near chaos. Sleet pelted the men who sought shelter wherever they could. What little rest that was permitted was in the open, exposed to the relentless freezing storms. The retreat continued the next night too. On the morning of the 10th the first troops staggered into Betanzos, almost within sight of Corunna, with some regiments down to their last fifty men behind the colours.[31]

George Scovell, who had been sent ahead by Murray to make preparations for the embarkation at Corunna, noted in his journal the arrival of the army:

> I went to Betanzos to see Colonel Murray, and on my way met what I once thought the most perfect and best disciplined army that could be brought into the field on its march. Never did so sudden an alteration take place in men, they were now a mere rabble, marching in groups of 20 or 30 each, looking quite broken hearted, and worn out, many without shoes or stockings.[32]

The locals, to the surprise of many, given the generally accepted surliness of the Galician population, greeted the soldiers almost as heroes, and provided food and physical support in preparing the city to defend itself against the imminent arrival of the pursuing French.

29 Schaumann, *On the Road*, p.42.
30 Ward Draft, Ch.IX, p.56.
31 J. Macdonald, *Sir John Moore, The Making of a Controversial Hero* (Barnsley: Pen & Sword, 2016), p.234.
32 TNA, WO 37/4, Scovell Diary, 7 January 1809.

It only took a couple of days enjoyment of this unexpected welcome for the soldiers to put behind them the ghastly deprivations and horrors of the last month, and become a force ready to protect its own embarkation with great spirit. The French had been weakened by their own march in pursuit, along a route already stripped bare, and were not in good shape. The British were rearmed, fed, and buoyed up by a local population who at last seemed to recognise the value of the British presence, or at least its advantages over French occupation.

The British plan was for Moore's army to be loaded onto the troopships which had sailed north from Vigo, but only a handful of the 250 or so transports were at Corunna when the army arrived, expecting to embark. There was an anxious wait for the ships. Murray wrote to Alexander Hope, on 13 January from Corunna:

> the situation is now very precarious, particularly if we are forced from our position into the town before the fleet arrives. However the weather is favourable. It is a state of uncertainty and suspense. Yet we have no cause to despair. I am greatly fatigued.[33]

Robert Anstruther had caught a cold during the march which had turned to what was almost certainly pneumonia, and his condition, already dire when he arrived at Corunna, was worsening hourly. Murray, his close companion in so many ventures, sat with him all day, helped him prepare his will, and wrote to Anstruther's father, Sir Robert Anstruther, warning him of his son's condition. He wrote a last sympathetic letter in the early hours of the morning to the old man, just after his son's death.[34] Anstruther was the closest among many senior officers who were friends and confidantes of Murray. The two scientifics had worked together alongside Moore in the campaign, in the same way that Murray and Wellesley had combined at Copenhagen. Murray and Anstruther had corresponded tirelessly, day by day, against a background of a serious lack of all forms of intelligence, maps, and logistical support, in an effort to bring some order to a confused, deteriorating situation.

Murray helped bury Anstruther in the flat bastion of the Citadel, on the morning of the 14th. It was later that day that the first transports from Vigo were spotted, and the embarkation of the sick and wounded hastily began, continuing with some cavalry, women, and the commissariat over the next 36 hours. The afternoon of the 16th saw Moore setting out to the anxious troops, with Murray, to issue orders for completing the withdrawal. On their reaching the front line the French attacked behind an artillery bombardment in a number of places. Pugnacious resistance dealt with the immediate danger, with stories of extraordinary bravery and determination. However, during the action Moore was hit in the shoulder by a cannon ball, almost severing his arm from his body. Murray, to his intense regret, was not at Moore's side at the moment when he was hit, though shortly beforehand he had witnessed the boost in morale his presence among the troops provided. He was simply too busy to visit him before he was carried from the field and he never saw him again, writing 'I shall ever consider it as a misfortune that I did not see Sir John after his fall'.[35] Moore died soon after and was buried the following morning next to Anstruther.

33 Murray to Hope, Corunna, 13 January 1809, Luffness Mss, GD 364/1/1182.

34 Murray to Sir Robert Anstruther, 13-14 January 1809, quoted in Ward Draft, Ch.VII, p.59.

35 Murray to Brownrigg, on board *Audacious* at sea off Corunna, 18 January 1809, Luffness Mss, GD 364/1/1182.

The Battle of Corunna 16 January 1809. (Anne S.K. Brown Military Collection)

With no time to dwell on the death of his two closest colleagues, Murray's immediate task was to complete the embarkation before a further French attack. The sick, who had been placed on board earlier, awaiting the main body of the army, had been taken off and hospitalised locally to allow for fumigating and cleaning of the ships, as the mortality rate on board was devastating. The last brigade, some 2,300 men, boarded in confusion owing to the difficulty in the dark of recognising ships that still had capacity, in the early hours of 18 January.

The last act in the retreat involved dreadful scenes where almost all the army's horses – Oman gives a figure of 2,000 – had to be slaughtered, to prevent them falling into enemy hands, as there was no room on the ships. Even if there had been space, it would have been impossible to load them on board in the time available, given the tides at that time of year. Eight thousand of Moore's army, out of its original strength of 35,000, failed to make it home. Very few of those actually lost their lives in the Battle of Corunna itself. Most died or were made prisoner during the retreat. Six thousand were listed sick on arrival back in England, four or five days after embarkation. The boats of the now familiar *Audacious* destroyed the beached transports and took off 308 men, Hope and his staff, and stragglers, including 13 wives and children and 33 French prisoners.[36] Although there are a number of others who wrote that they were the last to leave, Murray later told his nephew that he was the very last man to embark, close to exhaustion, handing over to his French cook his two chargers as he boarded. The cook gathered together another ten horses. His ownership of

36 Knight, *Britain Against Napoleon*, p.204.

the horses was short-lived, as Murray witnessed the advancing French soldiers take the lot from him.

Praising Moore's qualities as a soldier – 'no one could surpass him' – he apologised to Brownrigg for writing hastily 'at a time when I am in part perhaps exhausted by the fatigues I have undergone, and certainly much affected by the misfortunes and the private losses I have lately had to lament'[37] Many officers were highly critical of Moore's handling of the attempt to confront Napoleon's forces in Spain, although the retreat and rescue of the army were generally well regarded compared with what might have befallen the relatively small British force. Whether the campaign was a military debacle, involving disgraceful behaviour among ill-disciplined troops, or a well-executed retreat, has been the subject of long debate. It has sometimes been overlooked that Moore's campaign had successfully disrupted Napoleon's plans for the Peninsula; certainly Oman asserts as much,[38] and Moore's actions ensured that Wellesley was shortly afterwards able to return to a supportive Portugal and commence operations with fresh troops. As so often in the years to come, much blame was attached to the Spanish and their lack of credibility and willingness to provide support when and where it was needed, in contrast to the Portuguese.

Murray was privy to all Moore's decisions, disagreed with a number of them, but had little to find fault with in retrospect. He thought Moore was wrong to send his artillery and cavalry round by the Madrid route, thereby causing a potentially dangerous delay at Salamanca; and he thought Moore ought not to have paused at as he did during the early part of the retreat.[39] Subject to those qualifications he considered, he later told Hope, the army's movements to have been 'judicious'. Much has been written about the campaign and particularly the retreat. Could it have been better handled to avoid the terrible losses? Was the campaign itself misguided? The latter point has been debated long and hard and the balance of considered opinion, including Oman's, seems to be that the French were delayed just long enough for the spirit of resistance to be harnessed and profitably exploited. Soult's army had been seriously weakened during the pursuit. In a later letter to Hope, Murray described a conversation he had had with General Alava about Moore's campaign. Alava's view was that all the British operations after leaving Salamanca gave the Spanish valuable time in which to recover and occupy the vastly superior French who would otherwise have overwhelmed the 12,000-strong Spanish army in the southern provinces.[40] The Tory politicians in London, perhaps inevitably, came under fire from the opposition. Canning initially blamed Moore for an unnecessary retreat, though softened his views later. A motion for an inquiry, embarrassingly soon after Cintra, was narrowly defeated in the Commons.

On the retreat itself and its management, it is certainly true that it was not as closely controlled and executed as movements of the army were to be in the years to come, when Murray's undoubted talents were put to such good use. Murray's staff officers were, at the time of Moore's campaign, very inexperienced, most being straight out of High Wycombe, and Murray had no say in their choice. Greater effort could perhaps have been made to

37 Murray to Brownrigg, on board *Audacious*, 18 January 1809, Luffness Mss, GD364/1/1182,

38 Oman, Sir Charles, *A History of the Peninsular War* (Oxford: Oxford University Press, 1902-1930), Vol.I, p.598. This work has been long regarded as the most comprehensive and accurate account of the war.

39 Ward Draft, Ch,VII, p.63.

40 Murray to Hope, Abrantes, 15 June 1809, Luffness Mss, GD 364/1/1192.

prepare the eventual line of retreat, although the frequent changes of plan made this extremely difficult. Murray certainly was crying out for information on which to base his plans, begging Bathurst on 28 December: 'I am much at a loss for want of the information you possess about everything behind us'.[41]

As Ward put it:

> Murray can at least take credit for foreseeing the shape the campaign might assume at its very outset and for providing against some of the consequences. It is impossible to single out one aspect of the retreat for which he was to blame. Yet at the same time, in comparing this with his other campaigns, there is no denying that one does miss that minute examination of all contingencies and possibilities, that firm unemotional application of all the means at his disposal and the prompt resolution of difficulties which were later to distinguish his method of working. This is only one way of saying that he still had to learn by experience that it is one thing to foresee, quite another to forestall.[42]

It was a bitterly sad campaign for Murray. He lost not only Moore, who had become a close friend, and for whose personal qualities he had a profound admiration, but also Anstruther, his closest brother officer in the 3rd Guards, who had previously fought alongside him in Egypt, the West Indies, and Ireland, and other senior colleagues too.

Murray arrived back in Portsmouth in the evening of 23 January, after gales had driven the ships in all sorts of directions, before each one made it to whichever was the safest port on the south coast. Brownrigg himself left Horse Guards to meet the ships. For a few days Murray remained at Portsmouth assisting him in the accommodation and re-equipping of the men. He applied to Brownrigg on the 30th for leave, which was granted: 'Murray is very anxious to go away and I do not like to oppose his wishes'.[43] What he did during his few precious days leave is not clear, and he was back at Horse Guards by 7 February writing letters from there on Quartermaster General matters. Anstruther's death at Corunna caused a problem in Ireland and Wellesley put Murray's name forward for the post of Adjutant General there, preferring him to Henry Clinton who he did not think of 'sufficient calibre', perhaps still smarting from Clinton's lack of support at Vimiero. Murray was 'in every way the best qualified for the situation'.[44] No visit to Ochtertyre was possible in the time frame; in any case Murray no doubt wanted to stop travelling for a short period. He would have missed another sad event, the funeral of his mother, who had died just days earlier, on 20 January, in Liverpool.

41 Murray to Bathurst, Benavente, 28 December, 1808, Murray Papers, ADV MS 46.2.2.

42 Ward Draft, Ch.VII, p.67.

43 Brownrigg to Alexander Hope, Portsmouth, 30 January 1809, Luffness Mss, GD364/1/1182.

44 Wellesley to Major Geneneral Hugh Mackay Gordon, Military Secretary in Ireland, London, 22 January 1809, Wellington (ed.) *Supplementary Despatches*, Vol.V, pp.537-8.

10

1809 – Peninsula – Oporto, Talavera, and Retreat

Murray had made it back to England with the remains of Moore's army, commanded in its final hours by John Hope. He had been on the move for 12 months, in Sweden, travelling between Gothenburg and Stockholm, completing four North Sea crossings between Gothenburg and London, sailing to Portugal, riding, often overnight, around Lisbon during the Cintra negotiations, marching through Portugal and advancing into Spain, fighting rearguard actions during the horrendous retreat to Corunna, and making the perilous voyage in January, with the remnants of the army, back to England. He was exhausted.

Another rapid turnaround confronted him soon after arriving back in late January. Promoted colonel on 9 March, Murray was delighted to be chosen by Wellesley to be Quartermaster General to the army posted to Portugal under his command, and was on board ship again in April, heading back to a country that, notwithstanding the exciting new challenge, must have held many unpleasant memories. Wellesley had been exonerated at the Cintra inquiry, and in fact honoured for his victories at Rolica and Vimeiro. His views on the effectiveness of his senior generals, Burrard and Dalrymple, particularly the latter, had been taken on board by the inquiry, and neither was to be given command in the field again.

Murray's commander in Ireland, Major General William Clinton, brother of Henry who had worked closely with him in Portugal and in earlier times a slightly reluctant supporter, was now losing patience at Murray's continued absence, and felt he was stretching a friendship, though it was hardly Murray's fault that he had been selected for the roles that he had. Clinton's diary entry of 30 March 1809 records his realisation that Murray was about to go on active service again, which clearly annoyed him: 'I am much mistaken if he be not a false man of whom nothing can be made as a friend, although he may be an excellent officer'.[1] Perhaps Murray had been guilty of not keeping him fully informed of his latest appointment, but Clinton was clearly not happy, perhaps even a little jealous.

Murray's exciting news of his appointment to Wellesley's staff was shared with both Isabella and Augusta, now both happily married, from 8 St Albans Street, London on 5 April 1809. Augusta had married Lieutenant General Duncan Campbell of Lochnell who, in 1794, had raised the 91st (Argyllshire Highlanders) Regiment of Foot, later to become the Argyll and Sutherland Highlanders. Isabella was by now married to James Glassford, of

1 Ward Draft, Ch.III, p.44, (citing W. Clinton Ms Diary, 30 March 1809, p.163).

the wealthy Glasgow tobacco family, an Advocate in Edinburgh. All the family were now in Scotland. Sadly there was no time for Murray to make a visit, during the very short spell of leave he had, although it is clear from his letters how happy his two sisters' marriages made him, especially perhaps in the case of the affectionate Isabella who had always been in delicate health. So instead of being able to say his farewells personally, letters would have to do:

> I am again upon the wing, not to take a flight towards Edinburgh, but to fly after Fame, Wealth, Honours etc, etc, etc and all those fine things which you know is so becoming to desire…
>
> My present situation is to be QM General to Sir Arthur Wellesley.
>
> I suppose you are now under a Political Regimen; taking strong purgatives to drive out all the Ministerial Nutriment you may have heretofore fed upon, and swallowing large portions of some new Opposition diet [Duncan Campbell was a committed Whig].
>
> I should like to see the food you eat; but if it be at all strong you must have a plain dish for me when I come to dine with my friend the General, for high seasoned viands, of either one sort or the other, do not suit my palate. However I must not pursue this graphic any further or you will begin to think I am serious.[2]

Murray's knowledge of Peninsular realities and the small likelihood of a rapid return home, had persuaded him to appoint his brother to manage his affairs in Scotland, particularly his properties, listed as 'Strathgartney and others in Perthshire' lately purchased from the trustee of the late James, Lord Perth.

Murray boarded the same ship as Wellesley, the frigate HMS *Surveillante*, which sailed on 15 April, and which had, according to a number of reports, the narrowest of escapes from shipwreck on the first night of the voyage. These tell of significant damage being sustained in a severe storm off the Isle of Wight and the captain ordering all passengers on deck as the ship narrowly avoided being driven onto rocks by a timely change in the wind direction. There were certainly an uncomfortable few hours of very squally conditions but probably no seriously life-threatening emergency on board that night.[3]

The closeness that would develop between Murray and Wellesley was not especially apparent at the outset, although there was a large measure of mutual respect on military issues, as well as genuine friendship. The two had shared a number of experiences, including at Copenhagen, where they had very successfully worked closely together in the face of ineffective command. By the time of Wellesley's initial successes in the Peninsula the two men had developed a professional rapport and it was to Murray that Wellesley had written as he made his preparations to leave the Peninsula, explaining his decision, not in any way hiding his anger and disappointment at the turn of events, being openly critical of senior officers, and ending with an offer to do anything he could on a personal level for Murray when he, Wellesley, got back to London. He was probably aware of the lack of opportunity that Murray would have had to attend to anything given the rush in his posting from Sweden to

2 Murray to Augusta, St Albans Street, London, 5 April 1809, Murray Papers, MS 21103.

3 Muir, *Path to Glory*, p.297, citing various versions of the story including John Sweetman, *Raglan: From the Peninsula to the Crimea*, p.26, which quotes the ship's logs to discredit the story.

Portugal. Wellesley, in his active promotion of Murray's qualification for the Irish Adjutant General's role, demonstrated a confidence in, and loyalty to, a brother officer, with whom he had already worked closely in two campaigns.

Wellesley had always kept much operational control to himself. That was the man's character; it had worked for him in India, and this reticence to delegate was in part the result of a past lack of support from good quality staff officers. He knew what each department was for and applied himself in the role of head of it. Nor, perhaps surprisingly, did he readily appreciate the new scientific approach, and the skills and knowledge such officers possessed. Both Murray and Wellesley's Adjutant General Charles Stewart (Castlereagh's half brother) were initially, after arrival in Portugal, kept somewhat at arm's length. Wellesley was happy enough for Murray to do the donkey-work, when he had not the time to attend to something himself. This must initially have come as a great disappointment to Murray who had been used to recent involvement in strategy, and operational decisions with Moore.

Nevertheless this was the point at which the Quartermaster General's role and the responsibilities of the department started to expand and assume significant new powers, based to a large degree on the lessons taught at the new Royal Military College at High Wycombe. Now the constant companion of Wellesley, Murray was generally regarded as:

> very clever, an officer who may be relied on in all emergencies, and familiar to the army at large from the 'Geo. Murray Q.M.Gl.' which appeared at the foot of all routes and requisitions, and magically opened the doors of houses to soldiers on the march.[4]

The Quartermaster General of the Army was responsible for three broad areas: provision of certain stores and equipment, quartering, and movements. In fact the first of these duties was more a supervisory and control role as the Commissariat, a department of the Treasury, provided food, forage and transport. Arms and ammunition were seen to by the Board of Ordnance, pay by the Paymaster-General, and clothing and equipment by the Adjutant General. The Quartermaster General was the link in the chain between the demands of the army and the response of these supplying departments.

The normal marches of any army were organized with an eye to the quarters available at the end of each day. As elsewhere in Europe at the time, the year was divided into the campaigning season and winter quartering, the latter being generally spent billeted in towns and villages, although this pattern was soon to be broken in the Peninsula. The soldiers on the move in the fighting months might camp, bivouac, or occasionally be billeted, depending on where they were, the time of year and current operational requirements.

The third responsibility, movements, was readily apparent in the constant issuance of 'routes'. To make a route was bread and butter to any officer in the department. Wellington was delighted when, in a fit of impatience, on suggesting a certain officer may go to hell, the latter's friend was heard to mutter 'I'll go Sir, to the Quartermaster General for a Route'.[5] The route was the authority without which no body of men could move. It could be simple or

4 Ward Draft, Ch.VIII, p.1.

5 Sir George Larpent (ed.), *The Private Journal of Judge Advocate Larpent* (Staplehurst, Spellmount, 2000), p.96.

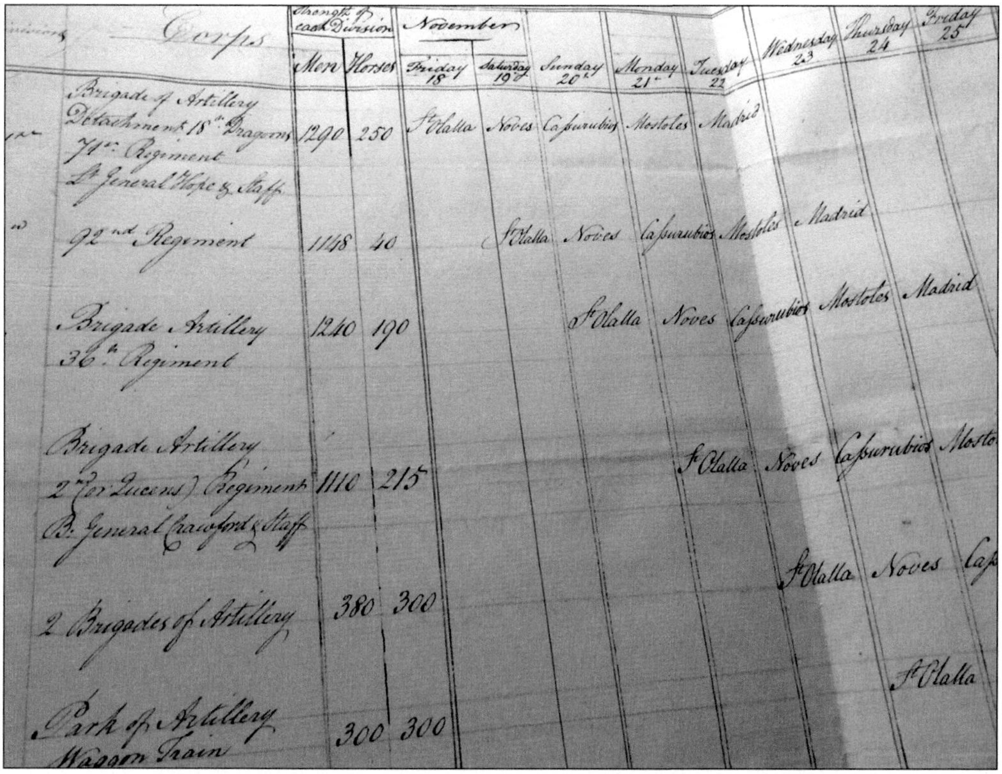

Corps	Strength of each Division: Men	Horses	November Friday 18	Saturday 19	Sunday 20	Monday 21	Tuesday 22	Wednesday 23	Thursday 24	Friday 25
Brigade of Artillery Detachment 18th Dragoons 71st Regiment Lt General Hope & Staff	1290	250	St Olalla	Noves	Casarubios	Mostoles	Madrid			
92nd Regiment	1148	40		St Olalla	Noves	Casarubios	Mostoles	Madrid		
Brigade Artillery 36th Regiment	1240	190			St Olalla	Noves	Casarubios	Mostoles	Madrid	
Brigade Artillery 2nd (or Queens) Regiment B. General Crawford & Staff	1110	215				St Olalla	Noves	Casarubios	Mosto	
2 Brigades of Artillery	380	300					St Olalla	Noves	Cas	
Park of Artillery Waggon Train	300	300						St Olalla		

A typical Route. (Author's photo from Murray Papers in The National Library of Scotland)

incredibly elaborate, depending on whether it was a small detachment being repositioned, or a number of divisions comprising the bulk of an army, in a co-ordinated advance on parallel routes over many weeks. It encompassed staggered marches between points, rest days, and arrangements for provisioning and forage for horses. It became a simple and straightforward solution to a difficult problem; a clerical tour de force. It was the elegantly handwritten equivalent of the computer-era spreadsheet. A successful route or order of march required knowledge of widths and inclines of roads, few of which were paved, and their suitability for artillery and wagons. Fords and ferries might be needed if bridges had been blown up by the retreating enemy. It was essential to know the depth and flow of the rivers at differing times of year. Information on the ability of an area to feed men, horses, and oxen, as well as the location of bread ovens and forges was crucial. Spain and Portugal were predominantly rural, accommodation and food supplies accordingly thinly spread, and as a result moving large bodies of troops often required a number of parallel marches, or at least an element of staggering over a number of days.[6]

6 R.H.P. Smith, "Getting Lost and Finding the Way: the Use, Misuse and Nonuse of Maps and Reconnaissance for Route Planning in the Peninsular War (1807-1814)", *Napoleon Series*, at www.napoleon-series.org/military/battles/Peninsula/GettingLost.pdf (Paper adapted from a talk in May 2015 at the Warburg Institute of London University).

The march of a working party, the approach to the battlefield, and even the movement of the different corps during battle itself were all equally in the province of the Quartermaster General. From this broad base, Murray was to expand the responsibilities and reach of the department dramatically. Reconnaissance, escorting convoys, secret intelligence gathering, positions of defence, in general everything that related to movements of the army and its parts and the great operations of the campaign would pass through Murray's hands. Mark Urban in his biography of Scovell describes Murray's role in the retreat to Corunna:

> His job was to translate General Moore's orders into reality; to choose the routes of march, find the fodder, chart unknown countryside, locate the billets and to gather information. The QMG's labour was vast and unending, for, like some burden of Sisyphus, it began all over again each time the Army marched into some new place.[7]

Wellesley had experienced revolutionary uprisings in Ireland and was wary of encouraging the rise of a new professional class of soldier, conscious of the emergence of Napoleon himself from an artillery academy. He felt that officers who did not have a stake in property or society could be easily tempted to challenge a country's institutions, particularly if discontented and soured by an inability to live on inadequate pay when they had no private means. Murray was entirely acceptable as a new breed of officer as he came from long established landowning stock. De Lancey, Murray's deputy, although American born, was from the same sort of background,[8] but George Scovell, the code breaker, and at the time a junior officer in the Quartermaster General's department, another scientific from High Wycombe, was from a humbler background. It was Murray, with his considerable charm, and ability to get on with most men, who, initially at least, bridged the considerable social gap between Scovell and his commander, in order to ensure that his extraordinary talents did not go to waste.

Why was Wellesley so reluctant to allow Murray a greater degree of responsibility? Was he intimidated in some way by this new scientific soldier? There was undoubtedly a sensitive side to Wellesley's character and pride that took hurt easily. Ward was alert to this element and its effect on the men's relationship in the early days:

> It is one thing to keep at arm's length a man who will be seen only two or three times a week; quite another to keep in indefinite subjection a staff officer who is in daily consultation, who shares one's innermost thoughts as a wife, in a position, if he choses, to ridicule one's most cherished ambitions. No one was more conscious than Wellesley that he was a self-taught general, and that he had the touchiness of the non-university man in the presence of the academic.[9]

7 Mark Urban, *The Man who Broke Napoleon's Codes* (London: Faber and Faber 2001), p.9.

8 William Howe De Lancey was an American born officer who had served for some time with Murray as his deputy, and who was well thought of and trusted by both Murray and Wellington. He was at Waterloo as acting Quartermaster General owing to Murray's absence in Canada, when, mounted beside Wellington, he was struck by a ricocheting canon ball. He died a few days later, nursed by his wife Magdalene, of Dunglass near Dunbar, whom he had married only two months earlier, and who had gone to Brussels with him.

9 Ward Draft, Ch.VIII, p.10.

Additionally, Wellesley was aware that Murray was under instructions to report periodically on operations to his departmental chiefs at Horse Guards, a job that Murray fulfilled with extraordinary energy and in great detail. Others were to write less formally. Here was scope for a good deal of secretive opinion sharing, should Murray or any of his scientific colleagues wish it, and it would have been entirely human for Wellesley to have concerns that such letters might have a bearing on how his political masters viewed the whole campaign, and its funding, regardless of some authors' limited access to the whole picture. In Murray's case he was as fully informed as anyone, but others were certainly less so.

If Wellesley was initially reluctant to delegate, his trust in Murray's abilities grew, and he came to allow Murray considerable latitude in writing orders on his behalf, certainly evident from 1813 onwards. At the very least it was more often than not a joint effort: '*Je vous ecrirai moi-meme, ou je vous ferai ecrire par le General Murray, avec qui j'arrange toujours le detail des mouvements*', he wrote to a Spanish general.[10]

There is evidence of Murray, on many occasions, controlling certain actions himself, as in the pursuit of Massena from Torres Vedras in March 1811. In 1813, on the advance into Spain, and again in the Pyrenees, when separated from his commander, he certainly issued movement orders for parts of the army on his own. None of this might seem particularly unusual except that Wellesley simply did not readily delegate. He was not accustomed to being surrounded by much other than inexperienced British officers, and felt the need at all times to control everything that he possibly could. His ability to immerse himself in work, and to shrug off physical hardships, meant he was able to do far more than could ever be imagined in one commander. In many cases his somewhat brow-beaten officers were perhaps happy to let this continue rather than take to themselves any great initiative, fearing a dreadful dressing down were they to instigate an unsuccessful departure from the Wellesley plan.

Transport was provided by the commissary department, but its quantity and distribution was overseen by the Quartermaster General. This was a major challenge in the Peninsula, particularly in the early stages. For the relatively small field force assembled at Lisbon in November 1808, when Murray was appointed Quartermaster General to Moore, there were 322 mules and 40 carts. These numbers would increase enormously in the course of the campaign – a couple of years later there was, attached to the army, a permanent force of 800 bullock carts and some 12,000 mules carrying equipment, ammunition, medical supplies, portable forges, and officers' baggage.[11] An infantry division complete with artillery (typically 6 guns) would possess a train of between 400 and 600 mules. An additional transport service operated by the Royal Wagon Train was reserved for the sick. The speed of the army's advance was dependent on the ability of supplies and artillery to keep up. The infantry generally marched at a rate of no more than 12-15 miles a day. Anything more than that resulted in an overstretched supply system, leading to the need for troops to resort to

10 That is to say, 'I will write to you myself, or will write to you by General Murray, with whom I always arrange the details of the movements'. Wellington to the Conde de la Bispal, San Estevan, 1 August 1813, Gurwood (ed.), *Dispatches*, Vol.X, p.575.

11 Robertson, *Commanding Presence*, p.234, and S.G.P. Ward, *Wellington's Headquarters* (Barnsley: Pen & Sword, 2017), p.87.

living off the country. The most a pack mule could manage in a day was about 12 miles. Everything depended on the state of the roads.

Under Murray, collection of intelligence, initially of the physical geographical kind, was becoming an important part of the Quartermaster General's responsibilities, a role recognised as even more vital and valuable as the war went on. Very few reliable maps of the Peninsula, especially Spain, existed at the start of the 19th century. In late 1809 Murray gave orders for a number of officers to start compiling appropriate topographical information, from which skeleton maps of large areas could be prepared, on a scale of four English miles to one inch. At the conclusion of significant battles, officers in the Quartermaster General's Department were to send a sketch of their area of action which would be joined up into a plan of the whole.

The prime duty of officers of the department was to acquire a knowledge of the country in which the theatre of operations lay, its natural and political divisions including, as set out in Murray's own instructions issued in 1810, précised below:

a. The nature of each district – i.e if mountainous; if the hills are steep or gradual, in what direction the ridges run etc; whether the country is barren or cultivated, if it produces olives or corn; whether open or closed, and if the latter, whether with hedges or stone walls; the nature of the soil; what parts are favourable to the acting of cavalry and what for infantry only.
b. the rivers, the lesser streams and canals; what direction they take and whether rapid; the nature of their banks; where they are bridged; whether they are navigable; what types of traffic the canals take; whether tracked by men or whether by horses; where the boats are to be found and their dimensions.
c. the towns, their population and the resources and accommodation for troops; the size of the towns; if well supplied; if the houses are commodious and how many troops they will take, with plans and sketches of all walled towns defensible villages and detached buildings; whether the towns are healthy or not.
d. the roads 'in the description of which it is impossible to be too minute'; for the variations in them from one milestone to the next; whether favourable for certain types of traffic; if a new line for the road could be adopted, or if there is a possibility of obstructing or breaking up the surface; care must be taken that the names of towns, villages, rivers etc are spelt in the same manner as by the natives of the country, and, when the spelling and pronunciation differ very much, the name should also be written (in a parenthesis) as it is pronounced.
e. possible sites for camps and positions; all strong passes posts or more extensive positions which present themselves, 'as also places favourable for encamping. Sketches should never be made upon a smaller scale than four inches to an English mile'.
f. such information should be extended or verified at every available opportunity, and always put into such shape that the head of the department or the general officer may read it. 'It should also be said what parts are based on personal observation and what on the authority of others' and the Quartermaster General is to be informed whenever reconnaissance is made, whether on the officers own initiative or whether on the orders of the general officer he is attached to. The results of his labours are, as already has been said, to be regarded as belonging to the department and the property of the public.

Murray also made it clear that

> The troops must never be kept waiting for their quarters or their ground of encampment, at the end of a march, as all arrangements that depend upon the officers of the QMG Department ought (except in extraordinary cases) be completed before the troops arrive.
>
> An AQMG will always go with the advance guard and get rid of obstacles etc. using Pioneer Corps if necessary.[12]

These instructions of Murray's were in themselves the Quartermaster General's charter, and would have been drummed into each officer joining the department. Most of this work was targeted towards obtaining intelligence to assist marching and quartering. This steadily expanded towards obtaining intelligence of the enemy's strength and movements. The Quartermaster General also extended his tentacles to the repair and maintenance of roads and positions and their fortification. Murray entrusted to the Staff Corps the solution of any issue involving bridging, road making, map making, even convoying – any problem that was not the clear preserve of another branch.

In the later stages of the Peninsular War there was no aspect of a military operation, other than personal or disciplinary, that the Quartermaster General's department was not equipped to deal with. It had to handle all the unforeseen contingencies and emergencies that confront an army engaged in a mobile war. No longer was Murray limited to the large scale movements of divisions, an overwhelming task in itself; one of his greatest skills was to translate Wellington's ideas on the conduct of a battle into the movement and advance positioning of troops in readiness for the imminent action, and thereafter to make the necessary adjustments as the battle unfolded, sometimes on Wellington's instructions, but often, at least in the latter part of the war, on his own initiative. By the end of the war, under Murray's command, apart from a short period in 1812, the Quartermaster General's Department had become the most vital and enterprising of all the departments in the British army in the Peninsula, benefitting hugely from Murray's imperturbability and pleasant manners, his administrative efficiency, and his keen understanding of topography and logistics.[13]

The situation that confronted Wellesley and Murray on arrival in Lisbon on 22 April was hardly promising. Soult, after refreshing his troops and re-equipping them with, amongst other things, 20,000 muskets which had been stockpiled by the British and left behind after Corunna, had turned his attention to an invasion of Portugal, and soon reached Oporto in the north, which fell after the Portuguese army had sustained devastating losses. Early in May he received reports of Wellesley's landing at Lisbon with British reinforcements, having taken over from Lieutenant General Sir John Cradock who had been left in command of the residual forces in Portugal. Wellesley's strategy was to pin down parts of the French forces in the Peninsula while hitting the others hard. He had insufficient numbers under his command for any other approach. Marshal Victor's army was poised to invade Portugal

12 Instructions to Officers of the Quartermaster General's Department, Murray Papers, ADV MS 46.5.2.
13 Muir, *Path to Victory*, p.308.

from Badajoz; *Général de Division* Lapisse was moving towards Almeida on the Portuguese border further north; Soult had halted at Oporto and was Wellesley's first target.

He headed north, in what Ward describes as a typical Wellesley offensive, combining a straightforward thrust with a long, concealed flanking movement.[14] The principal force reached Coimbra on 28 April, where the army was very warmly welcomed after their 140-mile march. Major General Hill's brigade made for Aviero where it embarked on shallow-draught vessels for Ovar, successfully turning Soult's advance position. On 6 May Wellesley reviewed his army, including the new addition of about 8,500 Portuguese. His march north continued over the 80 remaining miles to Oporto, where he was to take on Soult, having made plans to avoid any possible retreat eastwards by the French. Many in the army had their first taste of the dreadful savagery between the French and the local population that marked the Peninsular War, when they passed the decomposed bodies of three priests hanging from trees having been murdered by the French; certainly not an isolated incident. Spanish wounded and sick prisoners, who could not keep up, had been shot by the wayside; Napoleon himself advocated regular executions to keep local populations in line – hangings and shootings that led to revenge assassinations of French soldiers.

Murray was busy making the necessary arrangements for available units to be moved north from Lisbon, including much needed cavalry, and was kept even more occupied by the speed of advance, bearing in mind his and his staff's lack of knowledge of the countryside through which they were moving, having only been in the country a matter of days. Marshal Beresford was hurriedly sent forward to cross the Douro upstream from Oporto near Amarante in order to be in position to prevent Soult from moving east to unite with Lapisse. The main force continued north towards Portugal's second city. It was a major test for Murray to manage such a large scale and rapid multi-pronged movement of British and Portuguese forces over unfamiliar territory, so soon after landing, with supplies struggling to keep up. It seems to have been accomplished with great competence, a start that must have impressed Wellesley.

Owing to some lax French preparations around Oporto, which allowed Wellesley to exploit the lack of defence in the eastern suburbs, the British were able to cross the Douro on the 12th by commandeering local boats at two points, one close to the town, to occupy a deserted seminary. Men were shuttled across the river, thirty at a time, and six hundred had crossed and established a substantial foothold at the seminary before the French were aware of it. French resistance to the surprise attacks was shattered by Wellesley's artillery firing from the south bank, and musket fire from the seminary walls and roof. More troops crossed in the course of the fighting and made advances into the upper town. Soult made frantic preparations for an immediate evacuation. He was forced to retreat northwards to Galicia, abandoning his heavy baggage, artillery and sick. That evening Wellesley dined at The Lodge, the English club of wine merchants, where Soult had ordered his dinner.[15]

So rapid was Soult's flight from Oporto that the British lost touch with him for a number of days. It was not until 15 May that contact was made. At two o'clock that afternoon Murray, at Braga, learnt from his deputy De Lancey that there was a body of French troops

14 Ward Draft, Ch,VIII, p,14,

15 Maurice, *History of the Scots Guards*, Vol.I, p.302.

only a few miles ahead. Although this conflicted with other intelligence that Soult had doubled back to Amarante, he issued orders to all the brigades, by now dispersed quite widely, to converge on Braga. 'If we can subsist' Murray said 'I trust we shall come up with the enemy and perhaps force him to surrender'.[16] At dusk on the 16th contact was made with the French rearguard, but dawn the next day evidenced Soult's narrow escape overnight via a small bridge over the Rabagao that had not been destroyed as planned by the Portuguese. Murray accelerated in an effort to catch up, but despite further attempts over the next few days to cut off Soult's escape, the French eluded the pursuit and by the 19th the chase was given up.

The taking of Oporto so quickly and cheaply was a remarkable achievement, and, building on his successes at Rolica and Vimeiro, reinforced Wellesley's reputation as a commander. When news reached London it was welcomed, but there was still solid Whig opposition to the renewed campaign in Portugal, many believing Portugal indefensible. The criticism of Wellesley and government policy by the Whigs was to continue more or less unabated during the whole course of the war. In some ways this was understandable, if inexcusable, as Wellesley was himself a politician as well as a soldier and was inevitably targeted as a political tool. Early on Wellesley bristled at the constant carping and failure to recognise his notable military achievements, his critics frequently accusing him of exaggerating his successes, but in time learnt to ignore it.

Murray was becoming increasingly aware of the need to improve the army's knowledge of what awaited them in their operations in the Peninsula. Spain and Portugal were both poorly mapped, except for the grossly inadequate provincial maps by Tomas Lopez issued after 1765, which Anstruther had wrestled with before the retreat to Corunna. These were mainly office compilations based on replies to circulars to local dignitaries, especially clerics, requesting information and sketches. As such they were of little use for military activity.[17] There were a few others by the time Wellesley arrived, but nothing that could be confidently relied upon, most of the country's military archive having gone to Brazil with the royal family. The few maps that remained were taken by the French army when it reached Lisbon in December 1807. Murray ordered officers forward to sketch the areas likely to be of importance to an advancing army, noting bridges, distances between villages and local resources. His request to Brownrigg to be sent more staff for his department met with partial success – he could have five more to add to his current eighteen – beyond that he would have to look to fill places from the army already in the Peninsula.[18]

Murray chose Scovell to take charge of the formation of a Corps of Guides, mounted men, to be responsible for intelligence gathering of all kinds. Scovell set off to Lisbon to start recruiting his Guides, comprising initially an officer and 18 men, a headcount that increased later to 12 officers and 200 troops, used, amongst their other duties, as flag men to indicate routes to the marching armies. His raw material was a group of individuals with language skills, from good Spanish and Portuguese families, but lacking any knowledge of soldiering. Selected Guides were to be entrusted with tasks involving highly sensitive information. It was made very clear at the outset that 'the officers are to be very particular as to

16 Quoted in Ward Draft, Ch,VIII, p.15.
17 Smith, 'Peninsular War Cartography', p.235.
18 TNA, WO 133/13, Brownrigg to Murray, Horse Guards, 16 June 1809.

the character of the men'.[19] On the uniform to be adopted for the Guides, Murray took the view that 'I am inclined to think that it might be scarlet in order to avoid the inconveniences experienced last year from their dress being mistaken for that of French dragoons'.[20]

At the moment of abandoning the pursuit of Soult, Wellesley heard of Victor's move towards Portugal. He turned at once and marched south via Coimbra, which Murray described to Augusta as beautiful, with a climate to match.

> Were you here you would think it quite impossible that anyone could be otherwise than well, in a climate so delightful and amidst scenery so beautiful as this part of Portugal offers. We have the Mondego, a beautiful river running close to the Town with a clear stream and a bed of fine gravel washed down from the mountains by the winter torrents. The banks are formed of unequal heights, varied with woods vineyards, Houses & Cultivated grounds, and the Town itself rises on the north side of the Mondego, upon a steep slope, which shows to the best advantage the Colleges, Churches, Convents and other stately buildings of which it is chiefly comprised. A long bridge unites it to the southern bank, which rises very abrubtly and is covered with Olive trees, amongst which the Lisbon Road winds in a zig zad [sic] direction with a very abrupt ascent. I shall say nothing to you about our Military Operations, for even a soldier can hardly think that war has a right to intrude into such places as this.[21]

It now appeared that Victor's advance was not an intended invasion, and on reflection his movements presented an attractive target for attack, particularly if the British were able to combine with Spanish forces under General Cuesta.

Already Wellesley was coming face to face with issues that were to be a continuing headache – the absence of decent footwear and ready money, never mind the lack of horses, bullock carts, mules, and numerous other tedious but important elements that make up a successful army. He sent for 20,000 pairs of shoes on 28 May and a couple of days later wrote that the army was desperately short of funds. Wellesley estimated that to keep his army, currently around 30,000 men, would cost about £200,000 a month. By the end of May he owed money in all directions. He urgently required £300,000 cash.[22]

Plundering by the troops was already emerging as a problem. Wellesley wrote from Coimbra on 31 May to John Villiers, British envoy to the Portuguese Court:

> I have long been of the opinion that a British Army could bear neither success nor failure and I have had manifest proof of the truth of this opinion in the first of its branches in the recent conduct of the soldiers of this army. They have plundered the country most terribly, which has given me the greatest concern.[23]

19 TNA, WO 37/10/5, Scovell Papers.

20 Murray to Scovell, Abrantes, 8 June 1809, Murray Papers, ADV MS 46.5.6.

21 Murray to Augusta, Coimbra, 4 May 1809, Murray Papers, MS 21103.

22 Muir, *Path to Victory*, p.323.

23 Wellesley to Villiers, Coimbra, 31 May 1809, Gurwood (ed.) *Dispatches*, Vol.IV, p.374.

From the beginning there was a recognition that it would be essential to win the trust of the local population and things had not got off to a particularly promising start. Wellesley attempted to deal with it by, amongst other measures, ensuring that there were far more regular inspections of the men by officers and NCOs – occasionally, where there had been persistent bad behaviour, hourly day and night – when attendance was made compulsory for both officers and men. Many officers and NCOs were new to campaigning and incapable of controlling the soldiers. Both Wellesley and Murray were very sensitive to the fact that they were in Portugal with an army to assist in ridding it and, hopefully, Spain, of a tyrant. It was essential, they knew, not to behave in the manner of a conquering force in the event of winning battles or occupying territory. On chasing the French from Oporto, 3,000 tons of wine fell into British hands. Most would have regarded it as a fair prize of war, wrested from the enemy. Wellesley saw it differently and insisted on its return to the Portuguese who were the rightful owners, notwithstanding the existing rules of war. This exemplified Wellesley's attitude to even more valuable prizes, especially after the capture of Joseph's baggage train after the Battle of Vitoria, when a good number of plundered works of art came under his control. In many ways this reflected the unpretentious nature of the man – no gaudy uniforms or, except on special occasions such as anniversaries of victories, extravagant dinners, were on show at headquarters. Wellington lived very simply, although he was well rewarded during his career, as well as benefitting from occasional prize money, as awarded after Copenhagen. There is no trace of prizes taken from the battlefield by Murray. Given Wellesley's lack of interest in such things, his attempts to prevent any sort of plundering, and not least the proximity in which the two men existed, it would have been well-nigh impossible for Murray to have helped himself to what most soldiers regarded as their right after victory in battle.

Wellesley was already becoming concerned at the general level of unacceptable behaviour of his officers towards the Portuguese, and recommended officers of the Quartermaster General's Department as the only ones who could be relied upon to deal professionally with Iberian allies. If things needed to get done it was the organization that Wellesley turned to.[24] Ward suggests that Wellesley was impressed enough, even at this early stage in their relationship, to follow Murray's suggestion to transform the army from a force of nine infantry brigades into one of four infantry divisions.[25]

Advancing east and halting at Abrantes, Wellesley's force, now totalling about 25,000, was delayed for a while by the shortage of ready money, but crossed the frontier into Spain on 3 July. At this point Murray, whilst advocating the use of Spanish troops to undertake harassment rather than pitched battles, nevertheless was in agreement with Wellesley that an offensive in Spain was the proper course to adopt. He said:

> I think if we drive back a discouraged and discontented army to the Pyrenees we may gain as much by that as by any other operation we can undertake. I would rather indeed that the French army continued to waste itself by endeavouring to maintain all the country it now occupies in Spain, and that it should train the

24 Urban, *Man Who Broke Napoleon's Codes*, pp.67, 73.
25 Ward Draft, Ch.VIII, p.20.

> whole Peninsula to war by that attempt. But things will return to that if Buonaparte subdues the Germans, and in the meantime we should not repose too much but push our advantage where we are and where it appears likely that we can do it.[26]

Plasencia was to be British Headquarters for a short time – described enthusiastically in a letter to Murray from Colonel Robert Wilson as 'a good city, excellent accommodation for all Ranks, the best chocolate manufactory in Spain with all kinds of Refreshment for Man and Horse'.[27]

After a preliminary meeting at the bridge at Bazagona, near Plasencia, on 11 July Wellesley, with Murray by his side, met again with General Cuesta to discuss a plan of campaign involving both armies, at the 'wretched hovel' Casas del Puerto, where the Spanish were headquartered. Cuesta was singularly unforthcoming, having recently suffered a stroke, and Wellesley was unimpressed by what he saw of the Spanish army, which struck him as more like bold peasantry than trained soldiers. Wellesley's plan to unite both armies and march on Madrid, following the river Tagus, was the one eventually agreed.

Wellesley confided to Murray after the meeting that he did not know what was to be done with the Spanish, suggesting the answer might be to put them behind stone walls in any battle. Scathing though this sounds in fact it was probably a metaphor for using the Spanish troops to garrison the numerous fortified towns rather than having them fight the French in major actions. Despite a reasonably cordial start, relations were to become increasingly damaged. A constant issue was the failure of the Spanish to carry out their promises of supplying the British troops, and providing the necessary transport. The British suspected that the Spanish authorities were unwilling to compel the locals to provide the mules and bullock carts which the army relied on. Wellesley threatened to cut short the campaign if this major problem was not fixed.

A few days later, after continuing the advance, Murray wrote to Patrick detailing the position and strength of the various French armies in Spain, suggesting that the British strategy should be to avoid pitched battles in favour of harassing the enemy, given the nature of the ground and the quality of the Spanish forces. This was the centrepiece of Murray's theory on the conduct of the war.[28] It seemed likely that this was the letter that Patrick later forwarded to his political ally, Lord Melville at Dunira, just along the road from Ochtertyre, who replied on 18 August saying he agreed with everything in the letter, and from the accounts received that morning (perhaps, by that time, reports on the Battle of Talavera), 'if Sir Arthur Wellesley does not act a manly part and retire from the mischief impending over him, we can look for nothing else but some very serious disaster'.[29]

Still, the joint British and Spanish force of 50,000 men was an awesome spectacle as it closed on Talavera, across the open plain. On 22 July there was an opportunity to defeat Marshal Victor close to the town, but it was squandered, leading to further ill feeling. A midnight meeting between Wellesley and Cuesta had agreed a Spanish dawn attack. It failed to materialize. Nevertheless when Victor's French army retreated on the night of the 23rd,

26 Quoted in Ward Draft, Ch.VIII, p.27.
27 Robert Wilson to Murray, Plasencia, 2 July 1809, Murray Papers, ADV MS 46.2.3.
28 Murray to Patrick, Plasencia, 15 July 1809, Murray Papers, MS 21102.
29 Melville to Patrick, Dunira, 18 August 1809, Murray Papers, MP MS 21102.

Cuesta headed off in pursuit. Wellesley refused to move any further until the supply issue was sorted. He was finding the completely unreliable Cuesta impossible to deal with. In fact he would have liked to see him replaced. He was also aware that Cuesta, in pursuit of Victor without British support, was heading for disaster. The Spaniard learned of a concentration of French forces at Toledo and sensibly withdrew back towards Talavera on the 26th, where preparations were under way to make a stand against the French.

Murray wrote to Hope on 25 July:

> I am still very little desirous of seeing matters brought to the issue of a General Action in this quarter. It may appear a strong expression, but it is but too true that the Spaniards have neither an army nor a General. It is a very extraordinary thing that a great people engaged in the most interesting contest possible now for above a year should be still as far behind hand. One would think that there must be either the most gross mismanagement at Seville, or something more to keep things in the state they are.[30]

Despite his misgivings as to the wisdom of engaging in major battles, Murray set to preparing some preparatory orders, based on Wellesley's plan.

It was imperative that commanders were aware of the positions that had been taken up by various British units as they were thinly spread on the 25th, some quite far forward, partially owing to the location of provisions. It was also recognised that there might well be a need for a rapid withdrawal in the face on an enemy advance, which would mean identifying usable crossing places over the river Alberche. Murray gave orders to Lieutenant General Payne accordingly:

> Lieut General Payne will proceed with cavalry before day break tomorrow morning the ford of the river Alberche where the troops under Lieut General Sherbrooke crossed on morning of the 24th. This ford is opposite the foot of the slope on which the right of the enemy was placed when he occupied the position of Cazalegas. Lieut General Payne will report his arrival at the above point to General Sherbrooke at Cazalegas and he will cross the river with the cavalry should General Sherbrooke require his assistance. If General Sherbrooke does not find it necessary to call for the support of the cavalry Lieut General Payne will remain on the right bank of the Alberche at the ford already mentioned and will send to head quarters for further orders. It is not intended that either the troops at Cazalegas or the cavalry under General Payne if the latter pass by the river should return by the ford to which Lieut General Payne has been directed to proceed tomorrow morning. And in the event of falling back before the enemy the whole are to re cross the Alberche at a ford there which is about a mile above the bridge.[31]

30 Murray to Hope, Talavera, 25 July 1809, Luffness Mss, GD 364/1/1193.
31 Murray's orders for the cavalry as detailed in the *Quarterly Review*, Article Fourth, Vol LXI January-April 1838, p.74.

On the morning of the 27th Cuesta made it back to Talavera and Sherbrooke's First Division withdrew to open ground north of the town, leaving Major General Mackenzie's Third Division as the most advanced British unit. The following were Wellesley's instructions to Sherbrooke, dated at Talavera 27 July 1809, 'past 9 am'.

> As soon as you receive this you may withdraw across the river. Leave Mackenzie's division and the cavalry [Anson's brigade] at their old positions in the wood and come yourself with the Germans to this town. If you have no enemy near you it does not much signify where you cross river, if you have an enemy near you I recommend you to cross at a ford nearer the bridge and at a greater distance from the heights than the ford is at which you first crossed.
>
> PS I have desired Murray to look this morning for such a ford as I have above described and to have it shown you.[32]

Wellesley and Murray were working together to ensure all angles in the movement and positioning of the troops were covered in the lead up to the major battle that was about to unfold. Murray had gone out during the night with Payne's cavalry and positioned them in a situation where they would be at hand if required. He then joined Sherbrooke at Cazalegas, towards where the French were rapidly advancing. Wellesley, in the course of the same morning, looking out over the river Alberche from the tower of Casa de Salinas, a large house in the trees, initially failed to spot the fast French approach. He scrambled out of the house with his staff and rode off, denying the French a prize they could only dream of.

The British fell back to a line north of Talavera, to the small steep hill of the Cerro de Medellin two and a half miles from the Tagus. From the summit of the hill Wellesley could see the whole French force of 45,000 including 5,000 cavalry and 80 guns arrayed beneath him. Muir describes them as 'the finest French army Wellesley would face during the entire war in the Peninsula'.[33] It was clear that a very major battle was underway.

An early advance by the French saw the Spanish under Cuesta fail to offer any resistance, which pretty well sealed Wellesley's pessimistic view of their fighting abilities. As evening drew in Victor saw an opportunity to take the Cerro de Medellin during the night, and was only pushed back by some heroic infantry fighting. The initial fighting ended with 800 British casualties. An uneasy night followed. Wellesley slept with his staff, including Murray, on the open ground behind the centre of the British lines. An hour before daybreak he directed Murray to ride around and ascertain whether the several divisions were in the places originally allotted to them. On his return Murray reported that the left of the First Division was not sufficiently thrown back, which exposed it to be taken in flank, as had been the case in the attack of the previous evening, and orders were given for this slight change of position of the troops. No sooner had this adjustment been made than the French opened fire.

32 Gurwood (ed.) *Dispatches*, Vol.IV, pp.531-2; see also *Quarterly Review*, Vol LXI, Article Fourth, January-April 1838, p.74.

33 Muir, *Path to Victory* p.333.

The Battle of Talavera 27-8 July 1809. (Anne S.K. Brown Military Collection)

Following their initial artillery barrage, the French repeated their attempt on the Cerro de Medellin. The fighting was fierce and involved large numbers of troops on both sides. Murray's letter, written three days later, described the very strong French attack on the hill:

> The progress of this formidable column was not checked until it got within a few yards of the summit of the hill, when our men succeeded in driving it back in the utmost confusion.[34]

French losses totalled about 1,200, British casualties slightly fewer. An informal truce followed, during which men from both armies slaked their thirst from the Portina brook. However, elsewhere, other events were moving in favour of the British. Spanish forces were threatening Madrid; Soult, marching south to join the French forces in the Tagus valley, had been delayed and would not reach Plasencia for another week. So, for the French, a swift conclusion to Talavera was essential.

Wellesley and Cuesta met mid-morning, Cuesta agreeing generously (for once) to Wellesley's requests for reinforcements for his rear, and for heavy artillery. Around midday the French artillery opened up again, raining down on Sherbrooke's division. Attack and counter attack went on for most of the day with very high casualty rates among the Guards and other infantry battalions. British casualties ran at around thirty per cent, with as much

34 Murray to Alexander Hope, 'Private' Talavera 31 July 1809, Luffness Mss, GD 364/1/ 1193.

as fifty per cent in some brigades. French casualties were extremely high too. Before both sides had fought themselves to a standstill, there was the familiar undisciplined cavalry charge, resulting in huge numbers of killed, missing and captured.

Wellesley told his brother William after the battle: 'ever was there such a murderous Battle. Two days of the hardest fighting I have ever been party to'![35] Murray, who had a horse shot from under him on the second day of the battle, described the action, in an interesting contrast to his commander's style, as 'the most interesting, most critical, and most costly I think that I have ever witnessed'.[36] Descriptions of the battle and its aftermath are full of the scenes of the bodies of the soldiers and the horses burning in the grass fires ignited by the guns, of plundering by the Spanish from both their allies and the French, and of desperate attempts to find food and clean water, amongst the flies and filth. Murray's surviving letters remain remarkably detached and factual, despite the awfulness of the scenes in his midst.

Exhausted, he could, at last, after two horrific days, look forward to some rest. One of the first things he did was open a letter from home, from Patrick. It brought news of the death of their sister Isabella. It must have been devastating for him after so much death and destruction on the battlefield. Murray now composed himself to write immediately to his brother in an effort to have his reply catch the despatches heading back to London.

> It is at the moment of returning from an action the most obstinate and critical that I have seen, that I have received your letter with the accounts of poor Isabella's death. Poor Isabella has had many trials and she has borne them all with the same resignation with which you mention that she met this last trial of all.

He expressed his sincere sorrow for James Glassford, Isabella's advocate husband, recognizing his devotion to Isabella and his own excellent qualities. He went on:

> I cannot write more to you at present. I am almost exhausted with the fatigue I have undergone for several days past, and interruptions of some kind or other are every moment occurring. I shall endeavour to give you an account of the Battle we have gained before the departure of despatches to England.[37]

Not finished yet, he wrote also to Augusta, at her London house, 76 Sloane Street, the same evening: 'I shall bear up against it after the first shock, with perfect calmness, and I intreat of you my dear Augusta to do likewise'. He hoped that

> the loss of one individual so dear to us out of our family will serve to draw still closer if possible the ties that have ever united us all so closely together, and I am sure I shall find in your heart feelings consonant to this. We must remember to include poor James Glassford in this little circle of family attachment. He has ever been well deserving of it and his tried attachment to Isabella establishes for him with us all a claim to the place of a Brother.

35 Wellington to William Wellesley-Pole, 1 August 1809, Wellington, *Some Letters*, pp.17-18.

36 Murray to Alexander Hope, Talavera, 31 July 1809, Luffness Mss, GD 364/1/1193.

37 Murray to Patrick, Talavera, 29 July 1809, Murray Papers, MS 21102.

Typically, although clearly affected by Isabella's death, he took a robust approach to the sad news: 'We must not encourage the indulgence of unending sorrow'. The day's battle had been:

> a severe and lasting action. The troops behaved with the most distinguished gallantry, and defeated the enemy in every attempt he made against us. Many have fallen, and I regret that at this moment I cannot give you any particulars of those respecting whom either yourself or the General might take particular interest. If I have an opportunity of informing myself further before the despatches are closed for England I shall not omit to write again, as I know how much anxiety will exist at home when the first intelligence of the Battle is received.[38]

Despite his exhaustion and the necessary preparations to move the army, Murray wrote another of his long reports to the colonel of the 3rd Guards, Prince William, Duke of Gloucester the next day, to which the Prince later replied; 'I do not think I ever read any letter that gave me so clear an account of an action as the one you sent to me on 30 July. It is a most able letter'.[39] Not only was Murray reporting in detail on the battle to Prince William, with whom he had exchanged regular letters, but also, fighting off fatigue, to Alexander Hope at Horse Guards – a full 26 pages of, again, remarkably coherent handwriting.

The French retired from the field of Talavera after 24 hours. Losses had been horrific. The British lost 5,365 killed wounded and missing; nearly a quarter of the army. Two generals lost their lives. The French lost 7,263, almost one sixth of their army. Notwithstanding Wellington's 'murderous battle' tag, it was regarded as a British victory, if a very costly one. On the night of 28 July the French withdrew behind the Alberche, defeated, but not broken.

The French in Spain were likely to remain too strong for Wellesley to gain the really decisive victories that the British at home were impatient for, unless Napoleon was forced to withdraw men to assist elsewhere in Europe. The allied advance into Spain had been halted and the Spanish attempt to capture Madrid had failed, but it had been a risk worth taking.

A few months later Prince William took the trouble again to write a private letter to Murray

> to express to you the sincere respect I feel at learning that at the time of the Battle of Talavera you experienced a severe family misfortune and that your health has suffered during the late periods of the campaign. I hope that it is now entirely re-established and that you do not find any ill-effects from the great fatigue you have undergone.

He went on to agree with what Murray had written, on making better use of the Spanish in harassing the enemy, interfering with supplies and so on. He disapproved of Moore's advance into Spain, as well as the British Army being sent to the Peninsula after the events of 1808. He was also critical of Wellesley's latest advance,

38 Murray to Augusta, Talavera, 29 July 1809, Murray Papers, MS 21103.

39 Prince William to Murray, Cowes, 28 August 1809, Murray Papers, ADV MS 46.2. 3.

HRH Prince William Frederick, Duke of Gloucester. (Anne S.K. Brown Military Collection)

> which I was convinced could only be followed by the unfortunate consequences that have occurred. You can see that I write to you very openly and confidentially... it affords me the greatest satisfaction to hear from you and to hear your sentiments upon the different occurrences that take place.[40]

Murray too was having difficulty in agreeing with some of Wellesley's decisions and was looking to a likely exit from Portugal, whether or not on the back of a political settlement, as he could see no immediate likelihood of success against the huge French war machine, especially if the Spanish failed to provide more support. This line was distinctly Whig, although Murray, more instinctively a Tory, never in his military career considered himself politically driven.

Cuesta was to remain at Talavera while Wellesley set off to march against another French force under Marshal Mortier, who was threatening to cut off his line of retreat into Portugal. Cuesta withdrew the next day, to lend assistance to Wellesley, leaving the wounded under the control of the French, who could be relied on to look after enemy soldiers, but whose own troops were rarely spared by the Spanish. Meanwhile the British back home revelled in the news of victory at Talavera, unaware of, or unwilling to accept, except perhaps in the case of some Whigs, the gloomier aspects of the bigger picture. Wellesley was elevated to the Peerage as Baron Douro of Wellesley and Viscount Wellington of Talavera. An annuity of £2,000 was more tangible proof of the country's admiration and gratitude. There was considerable opposition to the honours bestowed on Wellesley, when the scale of the casualties and the subsequent retreat sank in. The British government had now to consider the future of its commitment in the Peninsula.

The vanguard of Wellington's ravenous army reached Oropesa, en route to face the combined corps of Ney, Mortier, and Soult, who had just taken Plasencia. On 4 August Cuesta, Wellington and Murray conferred again. Cuesta wanted to continue operations against Soult but Wellington had had enough of the Spanish and their broken promises and elected to continue his march west. It had been a difficult meeting with Cuesta when Wellington declined to fight Soult, as intercepted despatches showed the true strength of Soult's force, which until then had been underestimated. He was not prepared to ask his men to undergo a repeat of Talavera, particularly as there was only one narrow road to retreat by if needed. To have continued the march against Soult or to have stood and fought at Oropesa would have been, as Murray wrote, 'to disregard everything like prudence'.[41] Wellesley marched south towards the bridge on the Tagus at El Puento del Arzobispo, which he crossed that evening, followed shortly by Cuesta.

Diaries record discomfort and deprivation almost as bad as the retreat to Corunna, but this time the main cause was heat. Fever and dysentery were everywhere. Organised food was still virtually non-existent. The horses were in a shocking state. The Spanish allies were proving hopeless combatants, running away at the sound of their own guns and the first sight of the enemy, who gratefully received abandoned artillery to add to what had been captured at Talavera. The Spanish officers were described as miserable, and worse than

40 Prince William to Murray, Foley, 14 November 1809, Murray Papers, ADV MS 46.2.3.
41 Quoted in Ward Draft, Ch.VIII, p.24.

the men. British morale, following the costly victory of Talavera, and subsequent retreat, was low. Many, including Murray, continued to question the wisdom of committing large numbers of troops in Portugal and Spain, and had serious concerns too about the level of support they had received so far, and might continue to expect from the Spanish military and civilian population. They not only faced superior numbers, but their own effectiveness was being terribly reduced by disease. Spanish promises of food supplies were still hollow. Even after reaching relatively comfortable camps near Badajoz, nearly one third of their number were hospitalized and thousands died. Elsewhere in Europe, Napoleon had triumphed over the Austrians, and would soon be able to turn his full attention, and his vast forces, to the Peninsula. There was a feeling that continuing the fight in the Peninsula would only lead to yet another retreat and evacuation from Portugal.

Wellington must have felt isolated at times in his decision, in part influenced by factors outside his control, to continue the fight. Murray's private letters certainly do not share his commander's stubborn optimism. Whether he hid his grave doubts from Wellington is unclear. Certainly Wellington was aware that many of his senior officers did not understand his determination to continue the Iberian campaign, particularly given the complete lack of support from the Spanish. Support at home ran pretty much along political lines. It is clear, though, that Wellington still commanded strong loyalty from his men, who were prepared to trust in his judgement, however hard they found it.

Murray kept writing during the retreat:

> We have unfortunately not been able to draw any of the consequences from the victory at Talavera to which so gallant an action entitled the Army. The enemy has deprived us of those by a manoeuvre in our rear upon our line of communication with Portugal which has thrown us into considerable embarrassments or perhaps I might properly say, has deprived us of the power of any longer neglecting those which had been growing round us for some time.[42]

Perhaps there is there a hint of criticism here that Wellesley had failed to take some factors into account. Was this a reference to the now unarguable truth that the Spanish were not to be relied on? Murray repeated his view to Hope that 'Spain is miserably managed. I have always been of the opinion however that a harassing warfare, a warfare of detail was the one to pursue and not a warfare of great battles'.[43]

Murray's lack of enthusiasm for set piece actions at this stage in the campaign looked well founded. In a further letter to Hope, he still regarded embarkation as the only outcome of the campaign, and remarked on the very low level of supplies. A week later in another gloomy letter he advocated a staged withdrawal as the only sensible option, as 'I fear the only question is how it can be done with the least discredit, not whether or not it must be done at all'.[44]

Murray reflected to Augusta not just on the low morale amongst his countrymen but also the local population's disenchantment with its rulers:

42 Murray to Alexander Hope, Delaytosa, 8 August 1809, Luffness Mss, GD 364/1/1193.
43 Murray to Alexander Hope, Delaytosa, 8 August 1809, Luffness Mss, GD 364/1/1193.
44 Murray to Alexander Hope, Merida, 27 August 1809, Luffness Mss, GD 364/1/1193.

> the Junta are in great consternation – they have plans for their country, but still greater plans for themselves. They apprehend that if we leave Spain it will be the signal for some populous commotion that may very immediately affect both their plans and their necks.

His letter also commented, as Murray usually did, when passing through an interesting place however difficult the circumstances, on Merida, which he described as being 'one of the most interesting towns in Spain for an Antiquarian… the remains of Roman Grandeur are very considerable'.[45]

Murray knew that the future of the Peninsular campaign was closely tied to the events in Northern Europe and was constantly asking for intelligence on developments there. If Napoleon continued with successes elsewhere in Europe then he would be in a position to apply ever more troops in the Peninsula which would render the British effort even more futile. On hearing the news of the then-ongoing Walcheren expedition – an unsuccessful campaign, with the British force decimated by disease – he wrote, from Badajoz, on 4 September: 'I cannot but feel a good deal of anxiety about the Dutch Expedition'.[46]

He followed up a few weeks later with a very detailed list of reasons why the Walcheren expedition would not be a success. His concerns were to be proved right. More immediately, all the Spanish seemed to be capable of were more dispiriting defeats: 'about twenty defeats in all of which they have appeared more as a Rabble than an army, and yet they are ready apparently to go on under the same mismanagement in the same hopeless system'.[47]

To make matters worse, illness had simultaneously struck the three most important figures in the army – its commander, its Quartermaster General and its Adjutant General. Murray wrote first in late September of Charles Stewart's illness. Stewart was clearly not well but, more worryingly, very depressed:

> Dr Franks who attends him has been very anxious on account of the impression that his illness makes upon his own mind than from the actual strength of the disease…
>
> The first day I got out, which was yesterday, I called and sat with him for half an hour. He was very low when I first went into the room. Today when I called the Doctor was there and asked him to be left quiet and therefore I did not see him. Lord Wellington however went into his room and I think it probable that he will write Lord Castlereagh what he thinks of him.[48]

Murray went into great detail to ensure that Alexander Hope was fully aware of the exact issues involved in Stewart's condition as he wanted to neutralize any exaggerated accounts that might reach England, given Stewart's seniority and position. He reported too on the fact that Wellington had been in a very indifferent state of health, and had recently had one of his a regular attacks of the ague. Murray wanted to reassure those back in London that

45 Murray to Augusta, Merida, 27 August 1809, Murray Papers, MS 21103.
46 Murray to Alexander Hope, Badajoz, 4 September 1809, Luffness Mss, GD 364/1/1194.
47 Murray to Alexander Hope, Badajoz, 23 September 1809, Luffness Mss, GD 364/1/1194.
48 Murray to Alexander Hope, Badajoz, 23 September 1809, Luffness Mss, GD 364/1/1194.

despite such illness among the staff, on the whole, given the season and the general circumstances, the state of the army was not as sickly as some might think.

By the 24th Murray reported a great improvement in Stewart's health 'and he is satisfied of that himself which is a material point'.[49]

Wellington would have preferred to base his army in Portugal but was persuaded against this by, amongst other factors, the appointment of his brother as Ambassador to Spain. So Badajoz, on the Spanish side of the border, became the headquarters of the British Army during the months of September to December 1809. Wellington had written scathingly to Castlereagh of the Spanish: 'I feel no inclination to join in co-operation with them again on my own responsibility… and I do not recommend you have anything to do with them in their present state'.[50] The Spanish armies were, he said, insubordinate and ill disciplined. He predicted a French attempt to rid Portugal of the English, and requested the return of transports which had been used elsewhere in Europe, as a precaution against the possibility of being driven out. However he still retained some small hope of managing to defend Portugal even if Spain were overrun.

In London, Castlereagh had challenged Foreign Secretary Canning to a duel during the Government's paralysis owing to continuing disputes between the two men, after becoming aware that Canning had been plotting for some time to have him moved from the War Department. Both men resigned following the duel. Lord Liverpool replaced Castlereagh, as Secretary of State for War and the Colonies in a new Tory administration under Perceval, which many thought would be short-lived. Wellington's first communications with the new War Office Minister reflected the gloomy prospects of success in the Peninsula, and dealt with the need to ensure the safe return of the army in the event of a serious French attack.

This was on top of the bad news from the Walcheren expedition. Many of the soldiers who served on the ill-fated campaign were ordered to Portugal to reinforce Wellington, but a good number had not recovered from their fevers and increased the Peninsular sick lists enormously.

Murray now took the opportunity to moan to Alexander Hope about the quality of the men he had been given to work with in the Quartermaster General's Department. Of the 21 men on his staff, apart from De Lancey and Scovell, there was not one that seemed to pass muster. The majority were seconded to various regiments or with the Portuguese army, providing regular reports and intelligence. Three on the list as serving officers had never even appeared. His comments on others were scathing: 'his health is so bad that one day's exertion is all that he can stand' and 'can't even relay verbal messages in the field' and 'quite a joke his belonging to the department – a matter of charity keeping him. He has long been an officer, and he now remains without health, without advancement and without money' and 'worthy but not naturally quick and has the double misfortune of having very bad health and of being extremely short sighted'. He concluded that 'Exclusive De Lancey I cannot muster at the utmost more than four officers whom I can pretend to entrust with the business of a Division'.[51] Eye problems seemed to be very common among officers on the Quartermaster General's staff, who were performing jobs which would naturally call for

49 Murray to Alexander Hope, Badajoz, 24 September 1809, Luffness Mss, GD 364/1/1194.

50 Wellington to Castlereagh, Merida, 25 August 1809, Gurwood (ed.) *Dispatches*, Vol.V, p.86.

51 Murray to Alexander Hope, Badajoz, 6 October 1809, Luffness Mss, GD 364/1/1194.

close detail, particularly in the preparation of maps and routes, much of the work being completed in difficult conditions, often under candlelight.

Murray and Wellington now turned their attention to the arrangements required in case embarkation from Portugal should become necessary, though this was still, so far as Wellington was concerned, a last resort. Nevertheless, it would have been a departure from his customary attendance to detail, and recognition that circumstances could change rapidly, were he not to ensure that adequate capacity could be called upon in such an event. At Wellington's request Murray ordered and received, in early December 1809, a comprehensive list of the ships at Lisbon with the number of troops they could accommodate – each ship being categorized by tonnage, which translated into numbers of men that could be safely carried. This detailed analysis, followed by updates on a regular basis over the following six months as more vessels arrived, shows how seriously the idea was being entertained that evacuation by sea was a very likely outcome. At this time there was capacity to move a total of 24,290 men in 65 ships, plus a number of horse ships and vessels to transport supplies and equipment. By April the following year, in a document headed 'Return of the army in Portugal for Embarkation' this capacity had expanded to 35,304 men, 1,712 Officers, 963 women and 361 children.[52]

Col. Sir William Howe De Lancey c.1813. De Lancey was one of Murray's deputies and was appointed Quartermaster General in the lead-up to the Battle of Waterloo, where he was killed. (Public Domain)

Wellington now seemed to becoming prey to serious doubts that Portugal could be successfully defended. Murray's view was at least as pessimistic as his commander's. He saw no likelihood of a good outcome in the Peninsula, or at least none unless events in the north of Europe came to the rescue by forcing on Napoleon a significant reduction in his troop numbers in Spain. Nor did he hold out any chance of success in fighting pitched battles against an enemy who, by weight of numbers, could afford the odd defeat. Whilst all remained loyal to Wellington, other generals, amongst the most experienced and able in the army, undoubtedly shared Murray's assessment. The strategy that most appealed to him, so long as the army were able to quit Portugal in an honourable way, was to provide ongoing support to a guerrilla campaign, which would be possible owing to Britain's mastery of the seas between England and the Peninsula, thus providing an unbroken supply chain. But Wellington had been buoyed up by a visit to Lisbon in October where he was received with great enthusiasm, in marked contrast to Spanish disdain. During this visit, with Murray

52 'Return of the army in Portugal for Embarkation', Murray Papers, ADV MS 46.2.5.

present, he issued orders for the construction of what would become known as the Lines of Torres Vedras. These massive fortifications surrounding Lisbon would, he calculated, halt any French advance on the city; or in the event that they did not hold, at least allow time for the embarkation of the entire British Army should such be necessary. Murray had in fact, on Wellington's resignation after Cintra, drawn his attention to a memorandum by Junot's chief engineer which stressed the strength of the natural defences surrounding Lisbon, their existence having been noticed by both men after Vimeiro.

On arrival in Lisbon Murray wrote to Hope, with only the vaguest of hints that they had embarked on the construction of the extensive Lines: 'our object in coming to Lisbon was to examine the country in its neighbourhood and come to some determination as to the possibility of maintaining ourselves in Portugal in the event of the Enemy attempting the conquest of it'.[53] The Lines would comprise three lines of fortifications, not in themselves a complete barrier but mutually supporting elements in rugged countryside. The principal line consisted of 59 redoubts and forts containing 232 guns, garrisoned by 17,500 men, along a 22 mile front.[54] They were not intended to be impenetrable but any French attempt at a given point would be laborious and bloody and give the defenders plenty of time to position support behind the front line of second tier troops.

Historian David Gates describes the strength of the Lines:

> Wherever nature's barriers left a loophole the Allied engineers obliterated it; large areas were flooded, ravines blocked, all trace of cover removed and thousands of yards of steep escarpment converted into sheer cliffs by blasting. Semaphore systems linked every command post and an elaborate road network allowed for the easy passage of reinforcements to any threatened sector. Supported by the Royal Navy and with unassailable flanks, this Maginot line of the Napoleonic era was impregnable by the standards of the day.[55]

The Lines were not just an extraordinary feat of engineering, carried out under the command of Lieutenant Colonel Richard Fletcher, Royal Engineers, with the manpower largely provided by 6,000 Portuguese militia, Ordenanza and peasants, but for so enormous a project it was still carried out in total secrecy. Wellington even left London in the dark; most of his officers and staff seemed ignorant of it, and certainly the French had no clue that massive fortified lines were being constructed to provide protection for Lisbon and to give time for an army to embark if required. Murray was one of the few who did know, but again there was no mention of the works in any of his letters home. He accompanied Wellington on his regular inspections of the construction during the winter of 1809. The majority of the Lines were completed by mid-summer of 1810.

More detailed information on the current situation was carried in a letter Murray sent to Hope on 27 October,[56] but there was still no direct reference to the Lines, and Murray, still sufficiently unimpressed by their ability to hold against sustained French assault, again put

53 Murray to Alexander Hope, Lisbon, 14 October 1809, Luffness Mss, GD 364/1/1194,
54 Muir, *Path to Glory*, p 368; Wellington (ed.), *Supplementary Despatches*, Vol.VI, pp.538-47.
55 D. Gates, *The Spanish Ulcer*, (Cambridge Mass.: Da Capo Press, 1986), p.223.
56 Murray to Alexander Hope, Lisbon, 27 October 1809, Luffness Mss, GD 364/1/1194.

the case for a staged withdrawal. But if the army was to stay, which was certainly Wellington's strategy, then Murray advocated a fresh advance towards Salamanca, if possible avoiding big set-piece battles.

On returning from Lisbon Murray went with Wellington to Seville, and thence to Cadiz.

> I had the honour of seeing the Supreme Junta when Wellington took his leave of them and did not, from a nearer inspection of these gentlemen form any more favourable opinion of them than I had before entertained. They are to be superseded next year by the Cortez who are to be summoned on the first of January to meet on the first of March. I wish this had taken place a year sooner, as I have always looked towards some such change as the most likely means of identifying the government with the people. They may view some risk indeed of Revolutionary scenes but if that is not better than French Dominion for the Spanish themselves it is at least better for the rest of the world that they should hazard that than that they should be united to the Empire of Buonaparte without the most desperate struggle that they are capable of making.[57]

However, Wellington also needed reinforcements and money if any planned defence was to be a success. Horse Guards provided them both, despite facing enormous shortages. It was a vote of confidence in a commander who warned the politicians that it was unlikely there would be any 'brilliant events'.[58]

In Badajoz the army passed the autumn not quite knowing how to fully occupy and entertain itself. It was more used to Wellington's constant activity. In the meantime the much larger Spanish armies were being systematically destroyed by the French. Murray wrote to Patrick on the defeat of the Spanish forces in central Spain: 'The business was as complete as it could be. All the troops dispersed, all their arms thrown away, all their artillery, baggage etc lost'.

This was the common theme of most of the battles that Spanish were forced to fight. These were the armies that Britain had assumed would take the lead in confronting the French in their own country, with British troops in support. Events had shown beyond any doubt that the Spanish were a lost cause as far as a successful military alliance was concerned, and were not to be relied on. The British army was also, Murray wrote, in poor shape, emphasizing the gravity of the situation:

> the army is sickly and out of spirits – the Portuguese will not certainly behave better than the Spaniards and the Port of Lisbon as a plan of embarkation in case of misfortune is in some respects less advantageous even than Corunna... as to the French I think it very probable that they are not yet prepared to push their advantages and bring matters to a crisis; however there can be little doubt but that they are bringing forward the means of doing it.[59]

57 Murray to Alexander Hope, Badajoz, 16 November 1809, Luffness Mss, GD 364/1/1194.

58 Wellington to Lord Liverpool, Badajoz, 28 November 1809, Gurwood (ed.) *Dispatches*, Vol.III, pp.610-1.

59 Murray to Patrick, Badajoz, 7 December 1809, Murray Papers, MS 21102.

Murray was dismissive of the Portuguese troops, in his view lacking spirit and often coerced into serving. Their equipment was so woeful that much had to be supplied from England. The troops were badly led by their officers. Of the British officers that had become part of the Portuguese service, many saw it as an easy way to accelerate promotion over their colleagues in British regiments, and were not great quality.

Murray's final letter to the family, at the end of yet another testing year, was to Augusta from Badajoz to wish her a happy Christmas and New Year: 'You will not think that I pass my Xmases in a very merry way, when I tell you that last year I began my march from Sahagun that day and this year I shall begin it from Badajoz. The same good wishes to all the party in Sloane Street as to yourself'.[60] Murray's relative pessimism, shared by a number of Wellington's senior generals, including Rowland Hill, as well as a number at Horse Guards, had not subsided, although he was careful to whom he expressed his views to avoid any suggestion that he was not fully supportive of his commander, whose role was, of necessity, to project confidence. One of those who he trusted with his most private musings was, of course, Hope:

> There are some people who seem to fancy we can defend Portugal but upon what solid grounds their expectations are founded I do not know. For my own part I do not see any reason to alter the sentiments contained in the letters I wrote you between our leaving Talavera and our arrival at this place.[61]

And later that month:

> I do not consider our prospects at all mended of late, consequently I entertain the same opinion I have always expressed respecting this country. The cause in my mind is hopeless.[62]

In Murray's view at least, a positive outcome of the British campaign in the Peninsula was increasingly unlikely.

60 Murray to Augusta, Badajoz, 24 December 1809, Murray Papers, MS 21103.

61 Murray to Alexander Hope, Badajoz, 6 December 1809, Luffness Mss, GD 364/1/1197.

62 Murray to Alexander Hope, 31 December 1809, Luffness Mss, GD 364/1/1197.

11

1810 – Peninsula – Bussaco and the Lines of Torres Vedras

With a better flow of supplies, the army's morale gradually recovered, and with it came a marked improvement in discipline. It moved back across the border into Portugal and based itself near Coimbra. The Portuguese proved much more tolerant hosts than the Spanish. Murray was clearly in possession of some intelligence from London on the possibility of peace negotiations. He wrote to Patrick of 'some symptoms of an opening for negotiations and I suspect that our ministers are not without some inclination to nibble at that bait if held out to them. Let me hear when you are in town something of what is going on'.[1]

The collection of intelligence, both physical and military, had by this time become a significant part of the department's responsibilities and Murray busied himself making preparations for any required positioning of the army behind the Lines of Torres Vedras. He wrote from Coimbra to his assistant in Lisbon early in January asking him to arrange for a map, one mile to an inch, of the environs of Lisbon, showing all roads, villages, and other places where troops could be accommodated, and the rivulets. The officers of the department on leave in Lisbon were required to come back and assist.

The spy network was also becoming well established, both Wellington and Murray being closely involved. Early in January Wellington wrote to Murray, referring to an earlier letter from him, and said he was prepared to pay one Don Felippe Leno Chamingo 100 dollars a month for all information on the enemy, as long as the information was all founded in fact or useful, plus a bit more for specially important information, 'in proportion to the value of the information'.[2] Other letters from generals closer to the French armies dealt with intelligence gathering and paying for it. Brigadier General Cox wrote to Murray on 9 February, from Almeida, thanking him for the £400 he had been sent and asking for the remaining £400 which was to his credit. He had recruited an intelligent man, a native of Salamanca, to return there and continue the feeding of information.

Intelligence gathering was now a recognized, and invaluable, part of the British armoury. After Talavera Wellington had complained that he had no intelligence whatsoever, as a direct

1 Murray to Patrick, Coimbra, 6 January 1810, Murray Papers, MS 21102.
2 Wellington to Murray, Coimbra, 9 January 1810, Murray Papers, ADV MS 46.2.4.

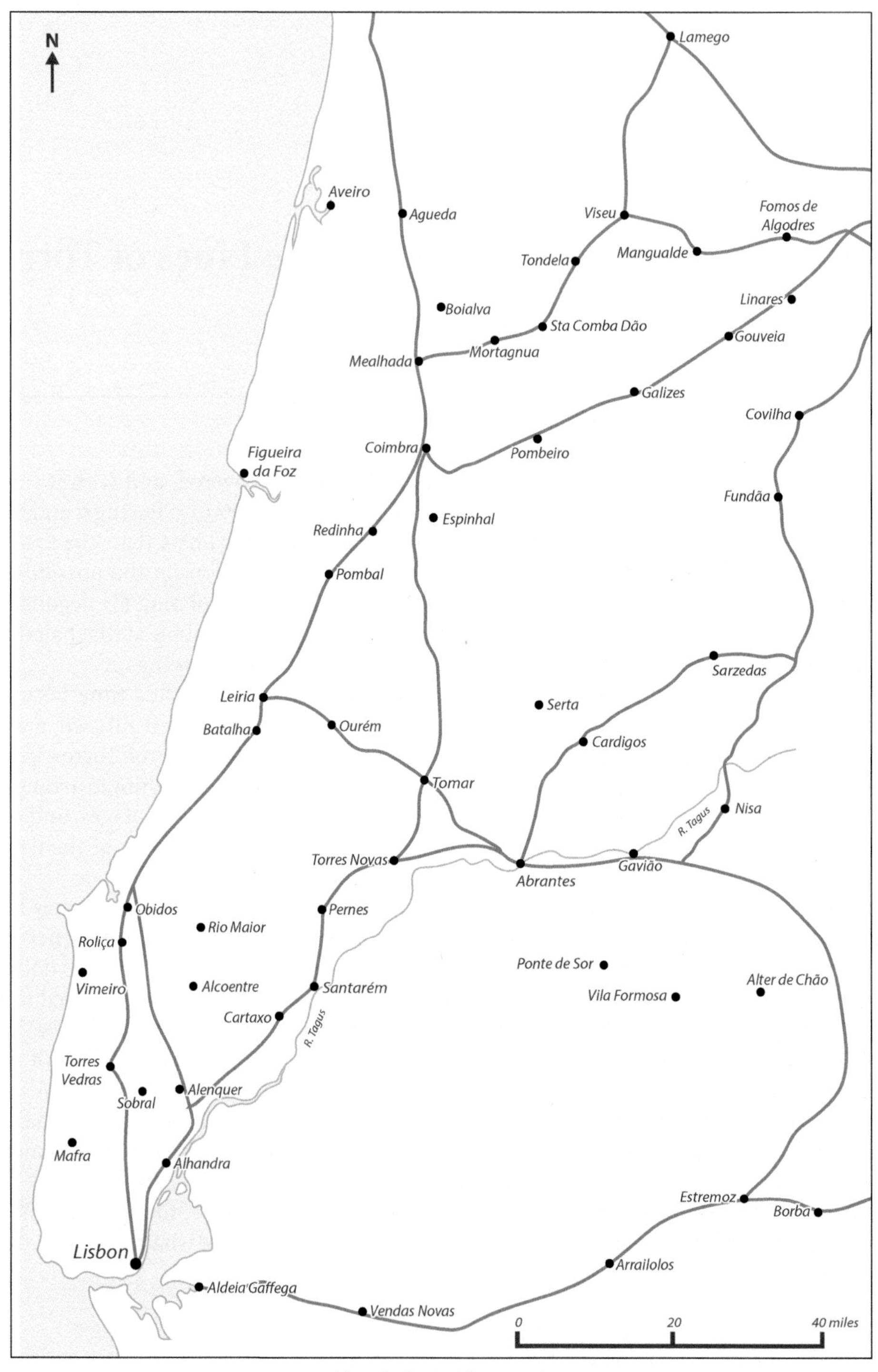

Map 7 Central Portugal.

result of Spanish interference. This was now changing. Captured French despatches proved to be an accurate source of information, and better than waiting for other forms of information on enemy movements. Now the British could plan their moves even before the French had started theirs. Guerrillas were bribed to hand over their reports direct to the British rather than to the Spanish army. Combined with intelligence from Scovell's Guides, the flow of accurate, reliable, information was increasing rapidly, and was to continue throughout the war to be of enormous value.

Another source of intelligence gathering took place at an altogether different level, as described by Lieutenant Colonel Alexander Gordon, one of Wellington's aides de camp, in a letter to his brother Lord Aberdeen from Celorico on 1 August 1810.

> Lord Wellington sent me in to the French with a flag of truce yesterday concerning an exchange of some officer prisoners. I went into Pinhel and remained some time with General La Motte; they have a brigade there and I imagine the greatest part of their force can not be far off, as at first they said they would conduct me to Massena whom I insisted upon seeing; however after a consultation they make an excuse, and would not let me go, they were uncommonly polite. Indeed you can have no idea how gallant we are to one another, Lord W send his compliments to the Duc D'Abrantes [General Junot] and in return he sends his, and all sorts of civilities are shown by both nations when opportunities offer. The Enemy are far from being well off, with respect to provisions etc. They complain amazingly of the whole country being deserted through which they come, I did not see a single inhabitant in the French lines. If this system continues they will find great difficulty in getting on in this Country.[3]

Gordon was regularly chosen for this task – in late December he had been sent to the French army,

> for the purpose of deceiving them with respect to our movement, gaining intelligence, and with some letters respecting our prisoners and money for them. I hope I shall be able to penetrate further this time as I believe they have not returned to Talavera or at least not further.[4]

He reported a few days later, on his return, confirming low French morale, and that they had about 10,000 men near Talavera watching the British. The corps of Soult, Victor, Sébastiani and Mortier were moving towards Seville. 'The French all told me that next month they would probably begin their operations against us, about the end of which they expect their reinforcements, they say 10,000 men have already arrived at Burgos'.[5]

In other areas the intelligence operation was also rapidly improving. Officers were frequently sent ahead to sketch areas to assess their suitability for marching, halting, or giving battle. They would move behind and around enemy lines mounted on fast horses,

3 Muir (ed.) *Wellington's Right Hand*, p.102.
4 Muir (ed.) *Wellington's Right Hand*, p.77.
5 Muir (ed.) *Wellington's Right Hand*, p.78.

reporting back to Murray and Wellington on enemy troop movements. Correctly uniformed so, if captured, they would not be shot as spies but become prisoners of war, they relied on speed to keep ahead of any enemy when spotted, and were happy to taunt the French from a visible distance, who knew that their activities would soon be analysed by Murray and his staff at British headquarters. Many of these exploring officers had been trained at High Wycombe and were skilled draughtsmen; some of the small maps produced by them are miniature works of art, often far prettier than was entirely necessary in the circumstances, but immensely detailed. Other maps were speedily drawn sketches on scraps of paper, showing the relative location at a given time of a number of regiments, artillery brigades, and the divisional commander.

Scovell, with encouragement from Murray, was making rapid progress on training his intelligence officers, as a result of which numerous French communications were intercepted and, if encoded, broken.

Later in January Murray was headquartered at Viseu, just north of Coimbra, where despite his commenting on his luxurious quarters as 'superb', he could not escape the snow brought in on a biting north wind. He had time to write at length to Patrick covering all sorts of personal and political topics. He dealt first with the career of 'our young friend' – his illegitimate half-brother William. Wellington had pointed out in his conversation with Murray the great advantages if young William were to learn Hindustani and Persian

> I took an opportunity of asking Lord Wellington's opinion about the eligibility of the military branch of the [East India] Company's service in India, and he tells me that for a young man without money and with little interest (the case I put) the service alluded to is as good a line as can be chosen.[6]

Murray wrote to Augusta from Thomar in mid-February, after what almost certainly included another tour of the Lines of Torres Vedras, still a heavily guarded secret.

> You will think that I do nothing but ride about the country for my amusement. Since writing to you from Viseu at the end of last month I have been at Coimbra, Pombal, Leiria, Batalha, Alcobaca, Obidos, Peniche, Vimiero, Torres Vedras and Maffra. At Lisbon for one day and thence to Villa Franca, Alenquer, Santarem, Golega, Thomar. We set out from this place tomorrow for Viseu.

He praised Batalha as being 'one of the most beautiful pieces of Gothic architecture I ever saw', before sharing his thoughts on political events at home

> I shall say but little on Public matters. At home things seem to be in a very unsettled state, and I think Mr Perceval appears to be in fully as bad a situation as I predicted he would be in a former letter.

6 Murray to Patrick, Viseu, 28 January 1810, Murray Papers, MS 21102.

He signed off with a gloomy reference to the 'fresh disasters that have befallen our friends the Spaniards'.[7]

Murray, by now familiar with Wellington's physical strength, and ability to travel great distances in the saddle, on occasion up to 70 miles a day, was well able to match his commander's stamina. They seemed to agree the necessity for such exertions; both knew that to keep control of, and in contact with, the allied forces in Spain they could not expect to sit at headquarters, but needed to be constantly moving among the various allied corps. Murray put such journeys to good use in gaining his own intelligence on the state of roads, river crossing points, and potential obstacles which might face a moving army, as well as intelligence on the level of local support, and enemy intentions. One moment Murray was with Wellington making preparations for the defence of Lisbon and the next, such was the scope of the Quartermaster General's duties, Murray's attention turned to the necessary detail of clothing for one of the regiments. He attached to a letter to Major General Lowry Cole a small square sample of linen – still, in 2018, in pristine condition – 'which might be purchased at the rate of two dollars per shirt. If the Regiment would prefer calico it may be had for about 850 Reals per shirt'.[8] He worried about the importance of not letting Cadiz fall to the French and wrote a long letter to Captain Whittingham there in which he outlined his ideas for fortifying the city, as he had heard unfavourable accounts of the Spanish preparations, and thus was very pleased to hear that Lieutenant General Sir Thomas Graham had been ordered there with a British contribution to the garrison, which he considered would be welcomed by the Spanish as a demonstration of support, and important in keeping the hopes of their cause alive.[9]

Murray sent congratulations to his brother on his appointment as Secretary to the Commissioners for the Affairs of India in Whitehall, on top of his role as MP for Edinburgh, which he had held since 1806, but warned that the new job might not last long owing to the political upheavals. Patrick owed his political career to Lord Melville, his cousin and Lady Mary's brother in law, the eminent and powerful Scottish lawyer and Tory politician. Patrick had made it clear to the electorate, at the time of his candidacy, that his political allegiance was to Melville, although he later attempted to serve as an independent. Perceval had become Prime Minister the previous October in succession to Lord Portland, but his Tory administration was riven with internal squabbling, not helped by the antagonism between Canning and Castlereagh, and was hanging onto the slimmest of majorities in the House of Commons. His Government was not expected to survive long, although it did, in fact, until Perceval's assassination in 1812. Murray teased his brother about the £1,500 salary he was hoping to soon have increased to £2,000, in case it never happened. There is a strong political slant to all Murray's correspondence with his brother, and Murray was frequently critical of the way things were being run in London. In particular there was, over the next few months, a growing criticism of the politicians in London and their apparent determination to prolong the campaign without adequate resources, when Murray could see no good coming out of it, an approach again more Whig than Tory. 'I do not feel very sanguine about your friends [the current administration] keeping their places', he wrote.

7 Murray to Augusta, Thomar, 14 February 1810, Murray Papers, ADV MS 46.2.4.

8 Murray to Cole, Viseu, 23 February 1810, Murray Papers, ADV MS 46.2.4

9 Murray to Capt. Whittingham, Viseu, 9 March 1810, Murray Papers, ADV MS 46.2.4.

He hoped that Patrick would not have to put himself to expense in London, acknowledging that 'You will think this bit of advice smells too much of the Finance Committee of former days of our poor father',[10] which suggests that their father, Sir William, the 5th Baronet, had significant money troubles during his life. The thread that runs through much of the correspondence is that the family was still struggling financially, hence the need for Patrick to pursue his more remunerative legal and Parliamentary careers, away from Ochtertyre. Whenever there was a letter there was a comment that reflected Murray's conviction that Portugal would be given up, either as a result of some negotiation with Napoleon or of the continuing military imbalance in the Peninsula, leading to an early return home. His mind too was turning to the possibility of a spell of leave, although he was conscious of Wellington's irritation when faced with such requests from his senior officers: 'But if you keep your place I shall be very happy to hear of the whole family being in London, but you must make it a real emigration and not continue to live in both London and Scotland. The London residence will, I think, very probably be our general rendezvous before many months are over'

In fact Patrick's appointment as Secretary to the Commissioners for the Affairs of India ran from January 1810 till March 1812.

As to Drumlandrick, the small estate that Murray had purchased in 1810 on the shores of Loch Venachar, near Loch Katrine in Perthshire, Murray was entirely happy to leave decisions with Patrick if he felt another estate might be better in a different neighbourhood, but he was quite content with things as they were. Regardless of Iberian fortunes, his uncertain army life might prevent an early return to residence in Scotland. Lanric Mead, as Murray often referred to it, was an investment at least and qualified Murray for the franchise in Scotland, which would be important in the event of any future political life. His share of the prize money from Copenhagen had been his deposit, but he still required to take out a large mortgage. Even after payments of £800 a year there was still almost £3,500 outstanding in 1811, and full repayment was not achieved until 1816. He looked forward to another fall of timber in the spring and hoped Patrick would advertise it with the same success as the previous season. As it turned out, the farms and slate quarries of Drumlandrick were retained and were still providing an income in 1825 when new tenants were being sought for the 1,200 acre estate.

Murray's letter then intriguingly turned to domestic issues, and Patrick's observations:

> If I come home in Spring I shall take your remarks into consideration, but in the meantime I beg to turn your attention to Bonaparte who proposes at 40 to get children and to bring them up to Man's estate, imbued with his own principles and confirmed by his own example. If an Emperor looks to finding time for all these things I do not see that I should need yet despair.

Murray was now 38 and Patrick seemed to be nudging him towards matrimony. We do not know if there was a particular lady in mind or whether this was just a brotherly bit of general encouragement. Apart from anything else it is very difficult to see when Murray could have

10 Murray to Patrick, Viseu, 28 January 1810, Murray Papers, MS 21102.

had any time for developing a relationship owing to his almost continuous campaigning. Was there too a chance of the command in India? 'I say nothing about India, though I do not at all like the prospect at present in that quarter. If it mends I shall hear from you'.[11]

So in the spring of 1810 a number of factors were in play that might possibly have a bearing on Murray's future. There were the present military concerns that holding onto Portugal was looking very difficult. There was a change of Government at home and hints at a possible political solution to the war. There were Murray's own concerns on the wisdom of making more sacrifices on behalf of the Spanish and Portuguese. There would be a natural tiredness from constant campaigning – Murray had not had a break from extremely taxing military operations and diplomatic crises since Copenhagen in September 1807. He was being encouraged to put down roots by his family and he had acquired property in Scotland. Perhaps, too, there was a hint that he was looking for more than the post of Quartermaster General, important and influential as it was, which was not providing the satisfaction or the recognition that he felt it merited.

He had lost a number of close friends; fellow Scots Abercromby, Moore, and Anstruther had all died during battles alongside him. His younger sister Isabella had recently died, soon after she had married and set up home in Edinburgh. He had clearly been quite sick for some time around the time of Talavera. He had served in military campaigns, with few exceptions, generally greatly outnumbered, against better organized armies. He had suffered appalling privations during three major retreats – in the Low Countries and to Corunna in Arctic conditions, the one just completed from Talavera in extreme heat. He was certainly, at this point at least, not convinced that the local population in any way appreciated or welcomed the British presence, and was angry with the Spanish and Portuguese leadership, although, significantly, less so with the soldiers themselves.

The overwhelming weight of the French military machine seemed more than a small British army, and badly trained and led Spanish and Portuguese forces, would ever be able to defeat. There was continual criticism by the Whig opposition at home of the performance of the army, much of it personal against the army's commander with whom Murray was now working so closely. The highlights of his career, leaving Aboukir aside, had all ended in significant unease between the military and Britain's politicians. The siege of Copenhagen, at his instigation, had been much debated by politicians and public as to its questionable morality, despite its strategic and financial success. The episode with the Swedish King had ended in a major debacle, and Moore's growing distrust of his political masters. The Convention of Cintra was perhaps the most hotly debated episode of all and might have even ended Wellington's career, and potentially Murray's with it. The period since Talavera had seen no real action between the French and British and there had been time for reflection – and Murray was a thoughtful individual, who never ceased to be deeply affected by the tragedies of war.

Murray used the lull to deal with the outstanding question of his position and pay as Quartermaster General in Ireland. On leaving the post to serve in Sweden he had agreed with William Clinton that he would accept whatever arrangement he, Clinton, felt right while he was away serving overseas. Nothing had happened. Murray had talked to Wellington

11 Murray to Patrick, Viseu, 28 January 1810, Murray Papers, MS 21102.

about it. Wellington thought it ridiculous that a man should have his pay reduced, and good officers should be encouraged to seek to serve overseas. He would write to Dundas. Then, however, the change in government intervened. Perhaps Patrick could find out from Dundas where things stood? Back in Lisbon on 10 February with Wellington, after the latest inspection of the Lines of Torres Vedras, Murray wrote to his brother:

> For my own part I hardly expect that matters will ever come to our fighting on the ground we have been looking at. I have no idea that your friends the present government have nerves to stake the Army on so precarious a risk as the issue of a battle within one march of our place of embarkation, although I am very nearly to believe that want of Nerves will equally delay the decision of withdrawing it from Portugal before it is forced out.[12]

He was still occupied with the reinforcement of Cadiz against a French threat and said that he had ordered three battalions of infantry to Cadiz, with two artillery companies.

Murray and Wellington then set out back to Viseu from where he wrote again to Patrick: 'I enclose you a bill of fare of what we and the Spaniards must eat up in order to keep your administration upon their legs. As for the Portuguese I much mistake them if they have any taste for such diet'. He enclosed a statement of the strength of the French Armies in the major provinces of Spain, excluding a further six provinces:

Andalucia	44,000
Estremadura	36,000
Leon	24,500
Asturias	6,000
Old Castile	22,000
Biscay	24,000
Bayonne	15,000
	172,500[13]

The extent of the task still facing the allies was enormous and, in pure military terms and the weight of French numbers, it looked impossible for there to be a victorious outcome in the Peninsula. Gloomy letters from officers of all ranks in the army were reaching London. Murray himself, as part of his duties, sent very regular and lengthy letters – at important moments every 48 hours or so – to Brownrigg at Horse Guards, each one a detailed report on everything that was going on, including actions the Portuguese and Spanish had been involved in, as well as intelligence received. Nor did Murray omit to express his own reasoning on the likely outcome of the campaign, and, as Muir recognizes, Horse Guards must from time to time have taken Murray's opinions into account in forming strategy: 'Among the correspondents men like Murray and Hill were highly respected at Horse

12 Murray to Patrick, Lisbon, 10 February 1810, Murray Papers, MS 21102.
13 Murray to Patrick, Viseu, 21 February 1810, Murray Papers, MS 21102.

Guards, and their views were taken all the more seriously because they were known to be well disposed towards Wellington'.[14]

Next to Wellington's, Murray's opinions would probably have carried the greatest weight. Murray had the most comprehensive view of all that was happening at the time. Brownrigg would have been able to offset Murray's more pessimistic views against those of his commander. In one of these letters to Brownrigg Murray expressed his relief at the arrival of three British battalions from Lisbon, grudgingly despatched by Wellington, to strengthen the force holding Cadiz:

> If we can keep hold of Cadiz, of Minorca, and the other Islands in the Mediterranean, and of Peniche (and Corunna might also be one) so as to enable us to maintain a constant communication with the Spaniards – I am persuaded we should be able to keep alive a spirit of discontent and rebellion in Spain that would employ more of Buonaparte's troops and give him more uneasiness than any other war he has yet waged in other countries – I don't think our government has ever looked sufficiently towards the prospect of our having no other hold in the Peninsula, but such as is above mentioned, nor to the important service we could derive for the Spanish cause when reduced even to that apparently low ebb.
>
> If we ever reaped instruction from experience we should learn from what has occurred in Spain, the necessity of having some point of strength in Ireland – we want a place there such as Cadiz is, by which to keep a hold of the country, even though driven out of the field; and through which to introduce the whole force of Great Britain again (if necessary) to drive the enemy out – that has always appeared to me the basis of the true system of defence for Ireland, and that which would secure the possession of it until we shall have lost our Naval Superiority.

He wrote of

> the fallacy of expecting that people who have never seen war will be able in any country, where armies can move, to keep the field against regular troops – whether they are patriots or volunteers or militia or yeomanry – the observations will I am persuaded be proved equally just when they come to be tried under similar circumstances, and I hope we shall not continue under a contrary impression in England till it is too late.[15]

Throughout his years in the Peninsula Murray would continue to argue the case for using the Spanish in a different way. Evidence at this time certainly supported Murray's theory that it was pointless to expect the Spaniards to stand up to the well trained and equipped French armies in organized action. A far better plan was to use them in small mobile units, in various forms of guerrilla warfare, to harass the enemy constantly and to tie down large numbers of French troops in different parts of the country, if possible avoiding pitched

14 Muir, *Path to Victory*, p.374.

15 Murray to Brownrigg, Viseu, 28 February 1810 and 9 March 1810, Luffness Mss, GD 364/1/1196.

battle. This approach was to prove successful, if never implemented to the full. Despite occasionally writing dismissively of their lack of courage and discipline, Murray laid most of the blame on their officers, and gradually came to respect their doggedness, and the independent spirit that ran through the general population, which grew as the war progressed, manifesting itself in stubborn resistance to any form of oppression.

There is an interesting contrast here. Wellington could never bring himself to trust the Spanish. He did though, with ultimate success, place his confidence in the Portuguese. Murray seemed to admire the pride of the Spaniard over the more compliant Portuguese.[16] Nevertheless he shared Wellington's anger at the Spanish duplicitousness and ill-discipline that was so prevalent particularly in the early stages of the campaign.

Wellington and Murray held very differing views on the likelihood of success in holding onto Portugal in the event of a renewed concentrated French onslaught. Murray's was, understandably, the calculated opinion. Wellington's was less scientific. He was one of those few commanders able to seize on the element of the irrational, and for such men there is a point at which analysis ceases to be profitable. Ward makes the interesting point that:

> In Murray's military papers, however, there is not a hint that his appreciation differed in any respect from Wellington's. All his arrangements were made either in accordance with Wellington's orders or in anticipation of his wishes within the framework of his design. So completely and so loyally were his own views subordinated to those of his chief, that, but for his private letters to Patrick, to Alexander Hope, and the colonel of his regiment, Prince William, it would be impossible to guess that his and Wellington's strategies were not identical.[17]

Murray repeated to Patrick his relief concerning Cadiz, that if the French had been able to take the city it would have been a death blow to the Spanish cause, but equally if they were to give up on Cadiz, they would turn their attention to Portugal, and Patrick knew what his views were on the ability of the British to hold on in such an event:

> Unless there is an insurrection in France (which has been so much talked of) or there is a new coalition, which is to spring up like a mushroom, or Buonaparte is to die upon the road from Paris, our being driven out of this country is a matter of certainty, and it will be with disgrace at all events, and if we push matters too far it will be with a loss which there is no probability of success in the business to warrant our incurring. One must be blind, willingly or naturally, to expect any other result, unless the common course of events is changed in our favour.
>
> I shall not however despair of the Spaniards when our army is driven out of the Peninsula. When they have no longer an army in the field to play the fool with, nor me either, they will begin to carry on the kind of warfare which they ought always to have done, and by having the command at seas, and a hold of the strong points along the coast, we shall be able to support them in it.[18]

16 Ward Draft, Ch.IX, p.21.

17 Ward Draft, Ch.IX, pp.22-3.

18 Murray to Patrick, Viseu, 28 February 1810, Murray Papers, MS 21102.

On family matters, there was more talk of what could be done to help young William on his career path. Murray said he was going to ask Wellington if he would give him some letters of recommendation for William on his way to India, but with a familiar caveat:

> [I]t is advisable to impress as strongly as possible upon the young man's mind that it is by his own exertions he must look to getting forward, and not any interest that can be made for him. From the account you give of him I trust he will do well although he may not rise to a very high sphere.
>
> You will see that I have anticipated in my letter of yesterday the possibility of your not remaining with the present ministry and that I shall not lament your leaving them.

The more cautious of the two brothers, Murray felt he had said enough previously about Patrick's financial management.

> I approve of your Double Speculation in the Lottery and I hope we shall meet with more success than usual. I never calculate however on these windfalls, which I fear you sometimes do, but I gave you enough of solemn advice in the letter I wrote you about a month ago.[19]

After unusually dry weather the rain arrived, welcomed by Murray. He remained busy ensuring the army was ready for whatever came next. He wrote to Graham from Viseu on 8 April congratulating him on his appointment as Wellington's second in command – although Graham was unable to take up his appointment immediately owing to his responsibilities in defending Cadiz – but was still taking a pessimistic line:

> We have no immediate prospect I think of doing anything in this quarter, and as I have already observed, unless something favourable turns up in the north of Europe I doubt our being able to effect anything beyond a considerable defensive operation.[20]

Preparations continued with an eye on evacuation, with updated returns being regularly produced. Murray issued a series of instructions to Captain Mackenzie, his assistant at Lisbon, to report to him on the readiness of the Navy to embark the army should it become necessary to evacuate Portugal: 'I now transmit to you a corrected return of the army with a view to its eventual embarkation which has been furnished to me by the Deputy Adjutant-General'.[21] Shortly after he again updated his orders to Mackenzie – more transports had arrived – changes were necessary 'so as to have a scheme of embarkation always in readiness'. By 9 May the available transports would be able to handle a total of 40,470 men.

19 Murray to Patrick, Viseu, 1 March 1810, Murray Papers, MS 21102.
20 Murray to Graham, Viseu, 8 April 1810, Murray Papers, ADV MS 46.2.5.
21 Murray to Capt. Mackenzie, Viseu, 13 April 1810, Murray Papers, ADV MS 46.2.5.

Murray's assessment of the chances of Peninsular success was constant, and always against the background of the progress of the struggle in Northern Europe. He now turned his mind to the possibility of a negotiated peace and an inevitable political carve up

> I am prepared to expect some thing like Negotiation if there is no war in the North of Europe. The arrangement of this Peninsula must however be a matter of great difficulty. The best way would be that B should give Italy to his Brother Joseph, and that some Prince should have Spain who is neither a Bourbon nor a Buonaparte. If Napoleon has moderation enough to listen to an arrangement on that basis we ought to be satisfied.
>
> Augusta writes me that our young friend is at length ready to set out on his voyage and that Gen Campbell has been good enough to take some charge in regard to his equipment etc. From all the accounts I have had, I am inclined to hope he will do well though he may never make a great figure in life, which is not at all necessary.
>
> You have not mentioned in what light I should mention his connection with us in case I should ask any of my friends for letters in his favour.[22]

A month or so later he returned to this theme repeating his belief that there would be a political settlement, and suggesting, maybe with some mischief, giving the Spanish dominions in America to the Bourbons, getting them out of Europe altogether. Bonaparte should give up his claim to Spain, and the Spanish Crown should be given to a 'Prince of the House of Austria or some other German Family'. Sicily might be given to the House of Brunswick and Bonaparte might have Portugal for one of his friends.[23]

During this spell of relative inactivity Murray kept up a very regular weekly correspondence with his brother. Many of these letters are of a political nature, illustrative of just how well informed he was on the ongoing crises at home. It is sometimes hard to fathom exactly where Murray placed himself on the political spectrum during this period, but he had always had doubts about the ability of Perceval's administration, of which Patrick was a member, to long survive. As to the likely outcome of the campaign, Murray's views were, at this stage at least, close to the prevailing Whig position, that it could only end one way, and that was with another embarkation from Portugal with little to show for it. Murray was taking a military line as to what Wellington faced in the way of seemingly overwhelming French force, but at the same time expressed the view more than once, that, whatever happened, Britain needed a strong incorrupt government, and hinted at his suspicion of both the political parties, somewhat in line with his brother's independent stance.

Plans for his own advancement were never far beneath the surface, and he had received Alexander Hope's advice that he should not chase after another regimental position but should remain with 3rd Foot Guards. Whilst this was part of the answer, Murray was still concerned that if peace were to be negotiated, it was inevitable that there would be considerable disbanding of regiments and retirement of officers, never mind the certainty that opportunities for advancement would be under threat.

22 Murray to Patrick, Viseu, 19 April 1810, Murray Papers, MS 21102.
23 Murray to Patrick, Celorico, 15 May 1810, Murray Papers, MS 21102.

Despite a lull in apparent action, the work of the Quartermaster General went on remorselessly. Corps were constantly being repositioned with all the detailed work that that entailed. In his instructions to the various generals as to their movements and positioning, Murray made a point of telling each recipient where headquarters would be the next day, as, when the army moved, so generally did headquarters. Advance parties were sent ahead to seek out suitable lodgings for Wellington and the staff at least a day in advance. In particular there was developing a regular mail between elements of Wellington's forces and headquarters, with new orders given daily and intelligence being sent back from all directions.

On 4 May Murray wrote to Lieutenant General Graham taking the same view as Wellington, viz, that Graham should remain at Cadiz for the time being rather than joining Wellington in Portugal. He gave a detailed summary of the strength of the French armies, the challenge they presented, and the continuing worries about the abilities of the Spanish – they were untried and

> therefore those who chose to call it good have a plan for doing so until proof forces an acknowledgement of the contrary. I cannot see a prospect of any good coming out of it or of the business of this country as far as we are personally concerned lasting much longer, unless upon other than mere military calculations, and on that view of things I think your command at Cadiz should not be relinquished for a situation so precarious as I think you would exchange it for in this country.[24]

Two letters were written on 9 May to Patrick from Celorico, the first on personal matters including his determination to reduce the debt on Lanric Mead; he had heard from Sir Stapleton Cotton that the price of bark in Cheshire had been good and hoped the same can be said of Perthshire. He also asked for 'two spy glasses with leather cases and straps' from Berge in Picadilly, opposite Sackville Street. He wanted them to be 'of the middle size, which I think is about 30 inches or three feet in length'. He finished with a postscript: 'unless you are bullying and negotiating, I cannot fathom your policy in wishing the Army in this Country'. The second letter dealt with the possibility of looking for a regiment and the apparent opportunity of moving back to Ireland. He seemed as certain as ever that there was no future for the campaign in the Peninsula. The choice was to stick with the Guards, as Hope had advised, and which was perhaps the safer option, or look for something different: 'I have pretensions already to one of those floating corps in the service which officers of higher rank might not think it worth their while to aim at'.[25]

In part this was prompted by his growing belief that there was a real likelihood of a negotiated peace and the concern that some regiments risked being disbanded. This was perhaps not too fanciful given that, in his eyes a military victory in the Peninsula was looking increasingly unlikely. He reckoned the Portuguese army 'quite unworthy of the name of an army' serving a 'pitiful, weak, and despised Regency which is only propped upon its legs by the countenance of Great Britain'. He was depressed by the knowledge that England supplied everything except the food for the Portuguese troops, which was extorted from the peasants

24 Murray to Graham, Celorico, 4 May 1810, Murray Papers, ADV MS 46.2.5.
25 Murray to Patrick, Celorico, 9 May 1810, Murray Papers, MS 21102

without payment. The Portuguese army, he felt, had no character and was led by the most unpopular commander in Beresford. In his gloomy assessment of the future Portuguese contribution Murray was ultimately to be proved quite wrong, and even at this point his comments made to Patrick six months earlier were looking out of date. Better officers had instilled improved discipline and morale and the quality of the recruits had grown. Still, at this point, abject pessimism prevailed. 'I have said enough I think, to convince you of the futility of our expectations to defend this country if it is seriously attacked'.[26]

On 17 May, the same day that 2,596 men, mainly sick and wounded, were on transports heading home, he reiterated to Graham that it seemed

> quite impossible to believe that [the French] will delay much longer. The Spanish seem to be the same at Cadiz as they have been all along every where. It is a great pity for I maintain still as I have ever done that they are a fine people and capable of far better things. I am inclined to think that the pot was not stirred enough at first but on this subject I shall say no more.[27]

Murray himself had succumbed to another bout of illness, probably malaria or dysentery, something that was almost inevitable on a long campaign in such a climate, and perhaps explains his gloomy letters around this time. There was concern among fellow officers as to his likely recovery and a recognition that his loss to the army would be keenly felt. He did later make it clear to Augusta that despite various reports of illnesses he had, in particular 'the Ague', a malaria-like fever, he reckoned he had never had malaria itself. By mid-June he was able to tell Patrick that he was now quite well and getting stronger every day, making light of his problems. That same day he wrote one of his regular reports to Brownrigg in which he apologised for not having written for some time, explaining that his illness had been a bit more drawn out than usual and had left him quite weak. He followed that up with a letter to Patrick on 20 June:

> I am getting stout by degrees. Today I go a few miles from hence to live in the Vale of Mondego, which some compare to Scotland, others to Wales. I expect by changing the air to make a more rapid progress than I do here.[28]

Murray would need to be fit, as, after months of relative quiet, the pace of life was about to quicken with the French planning to push the British westwards to the sea and expulsion from the Peninsula. Murray confided in Lowry Cole, his close friend, who could be relied upon not to betray that trust, his feelings on Wellington's plans:

> I am clear myself that we should not quit hold of Portugal before it is necessary to do so, but I should not, had I the command, keep the bulk of the army so far in advance. If the whole were a Portuguese army, which was to sink or swim with the country, the case would be different. If the French besiege Ciudad Rodrigo and

26 Murray to Patrick, Celorico, 15 May 1810, Murray Papers, MS 21102.

27 Murray to Graham, Celorico, 11 May 1810, Murray Papers, ADV MS 46.2.5.

28 Murray to Patrick, Celorico, 20 June 1810, Murray Papers, MS 21102.

Murray's father, Sir William Murray, 5th Baronet of Ochtertyre. (Private Collection)

Murray's mother, Augusta, wearing the veil that hid the strange marks on her neck. (Private Collection)

Sir Patrick Murray, Murray's brother, by Watson Gordon c.1801. (Private Collection)

John Murray Gartshore, Murray's nephew who inherited Gartshore. (Private Collection)

Murray, probably on appointment as Adjutant General in West Indies, by Hoppner, c.1802. (By kind permission of Sotheby's)

Lieutenant General Sir John Moore. (Anne S.K. Brown Military Collection)

General Sir Alexander Hope, Murray's close confidante at Horse Guards. (Sandhurst Collection)

General Sir John Hope, half-brother of Alexander Hope, related to Murray by marriage, who worked closely with him in the Peninsula. (Anne S.K. Brown Military Collection)

General Sir Lowry Cole, one of Murray's closest friends. (Anne S.K. Brown Military Collection)

General Duncan Campbell, Augusta's husband. He raised the 91st Regiment of Foot. (By kind permission of The Argyll and Sutherland Highlanders Museum)

Wellington, by Heaphy 1813. (National Portrait Gallery)

Murray, by Heaphy 1813. (National Portrait Gallery)

Murray's quarters before the Battle of Bussaco, September 1810. (Author's Photo).

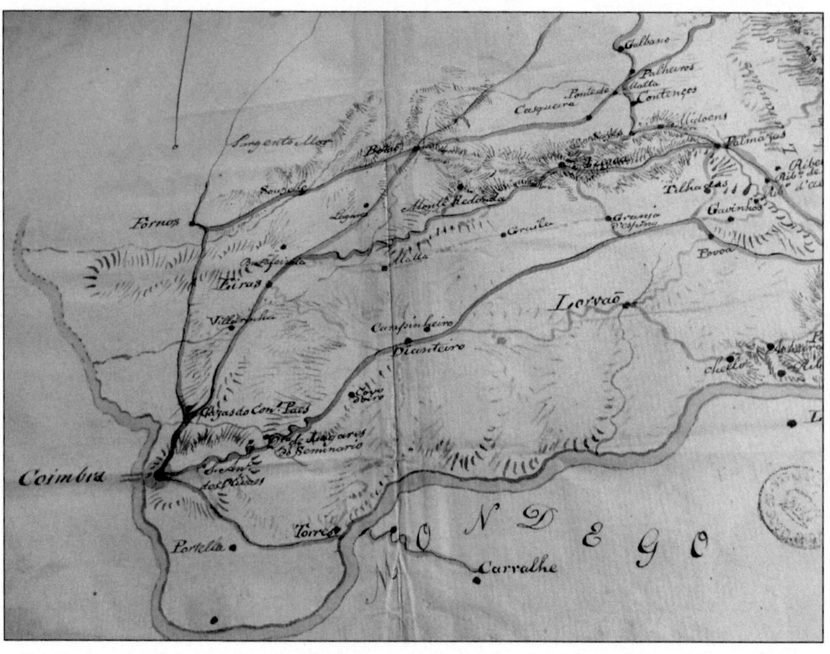

Map illustrating the routes earmarked for the withdrawal to Coimbra after the Battle of Bussaco, September 1810. (Author's Photo from Murray Papers in The National Library of Scotland)

Fort Sao Vicente, part of the Lines of Torres Vedras. (Author's Photo)

Freineda, near the Portuguese/Spanish border – Wellington's headquarters over two winters, 1811-12 and 1812-13. (Author's Photo)

Murray's daughter Louisa, painted by Sir Thomas Lawrence c.1824; the familiar image seen on biscuit tins, jigsaws and playing cards. (Frick Collection)

Murray by Sir Thomas Lawrence, commissioned by the city of Perth in honour of their MP. Completed by Henry Pickersgill c.1830. (By Kind Permission of the City of Perth, Western Australia)

Unfinished portrait of Murray by Sir Thomas Lawrence c.1829. (Philip Mould & Company)

Sir James Erskine of Torrie, Lady Louisa's first husband. (Painting by Sir Thomas Lawrence. By kind permission of the Trustees of the Mrs M. Sharpe Erskine Trust – photo by Chris Park)

Murray by John Linell, 1836.
(National Portrait Gallery)

Murray by John Prescott Knight c.1842, acquired by Wellington to hang at Apsley House.
(English Heritage)

The snuff box presented to Murray by, the evidence suggests, Prince William Frederick. The lid of the watch is decorated with a crown, the Order of the Garter insignia, and the initials W.F.
(Private Collection)

Murray's medals and decorations. Murray was the most decorated soldier of his generation after Wellington. (By kind permission of the Regimental Trustees of the Scots Guards)

Badajoz we shall probably have time enough to take what measures we please. But if they do not besiege these places – and I confess to me it does not appear necessary they should with a force so superior as they have in Spain – we are likely to be more hurried than will be either for our interest or our pleasure.[29]

The questioning of the army's role in the Peninsula continued, this time directed to Patrick:

I have often before told you that I could not comprehend the policy of our government in regard to the management of matters here. The proof is drawing near and means what might have been foreseen, that we are not able to defend Portugal. But we shall do more than lose Portugal; we shall numb the spirit of the whole Peninsula. Highly as I may be supposed to estimate the merits of a Regular Army, I value much higher, in a case like the present, the enthusiasm of a whole Nation; and I have been therefore always inclined to think that our thirty thousand men in Spain is but a drop in the ocean in comparison of the fury, I may almost call it, of the whole Spanish people. But how must it chill the spirit of these people and how much must it alienate them from us, to see that when dangers and misfortunes press upon them, we continuously hold back and finally withdraw altogether from their support. But we must act thus or commit ourselves, and perhaps incur many serious losses in the vain attempt to maintain what is altogether untenable.[30]

In a letter to Augusta on 8 July from Alverca, on the road between Almeida and Celorico, he talked of the French actions against Ciudad Rodrigo, 'And my friends the Spaniards are as usual desporting themselves much better than the strength of the place gave any reason to expect'.[31] Despite the Spanish resistance the town capitulated the very next day.

A few days later he expressed his concerns over Augusta's health:

I hope your illness is not a return of the complaint that has been so long troublesome to you.

I hope either my aunt or James Glassford will be good enough to give me some further account by the next post which you give me to expect will be the case. I could not read your description of what you saw on the road without thinking you had sometimes indulged your curiosity a little too much at the expense of fatigue. The visit to the Cave at Matlock I did not approve of.

I received the other day by Major Gordon the Lady of the Lake, and I have read it with much pleasure on its own account as well as much interest on mine. You see what good taste I had in selecting the spot to make my future residence. As a military man could I have fixed upon anything better than the Gathering Place chosen by so great a captain as Sir Roderick Dhu. Or as a man of taste could I have

29 Quoted in Ward Draft Ch.IX, p.15.

30 Murray to Patrick, Alverca, 3 July 1810, Murray Papers, MS 21102.

31 Murray to Augusta, Alverca, 8 July 1810, Murray Papers, ADV MS 46.2.5.

> set myself down anywhere better than amidst the scenery that has so aroused the imagination of the poet?[32]

Convalescence allowed Murray's own mind to stray from the landscape of the Peninsula to the highlands of Scotland, in particular his spot on the banks of Loch Venachar, as a place for him to put down roots on his return, which he clearly saw as likely. However, he was conscious of the debt that needed attention – and showed a very clearheaded approach to it in the coming months. He needed concise information on the financial position at Lanric Mead which Patrick had been slow in delivering:

> If I hold my present situation another year, I hope to come down with about another £600 at least, and that, together with the wood cutting of next Spring ought to bring the debt very low, according to my calculations. However I want data to go upon for I neither know the actual amount of the debt at present nor the Rent of the Estate.[33]

There was more time than usual for writing and receiving letters during this lull in operations, and Murray's correspondence with Prince William was regular and detailed. The Prince appreciated the first-hand accounts of the campaign, and Murray received in return some nuggets of confidential information on broader European politics, and the military ambitions of the French in northern Europe.

Although Murray was making a good recovery, this was not a happy time for him, and he wrote on 18 July that he had had a fall from his horse 'on the same leg that was so unlucky before. The mischief however is not great. I have been on horseback since, but I am making myself a sort of invalid for a few days on account of it'.[34]

At the end of the month, Murray described to Patrick details of 'the affair' at the river Coa near Almeida where Brigadier General Craufurd had risked his small force unnecessarily when outnumbered, and made a comparison with the campaign as a whole.

> [O]ur troops had to retire by this bridge and the enemy, much superior in force pressed upon them. The British infantry engaged were the 43rd, 52nd and 95th all of which behaved with the greatest gallantry. There were some of our cavalry also, and a troop of Horse Artillery, but the business rested chiefly with the infantry. There were also two Portuguese battalions, the one of which made off without loss of time on the approach of the enemy, and the other is said to have behaved in part tolerably well.
>
> The question asked is, why the Troops were not moved across the Coa on the approach of so superior a force as was seen to be advancing, and against which there was no prospect of competing with any success. To compare small things with great, the same question will perhaps be hereafter asked in reference to the whole

32 Murray to Augusta, Alverca, 11 July 1810, Murray Papers, ADV MS 46.2.5 (Sir Walter Scott's poem (Canto III, Stanza xii) refers to Lanric Mead as a mustering place).

33 Murray to Patrick, Alverca, 11 July 1810, Murray Papers, MS 21102.

34 Murray to Patrick, Alverca, 18 July 1810, Murray Papers, MS 21102.

> of the Army, that is now started in regard General Robert Crauford's Brigade. I am inclined to think Massena is going to besiege Almeida'.
>
> PS – my spy glasses arrived today which is very a propos.[35]

Murray's views of the performance of the Cacadores (the Portuguese light infantry) at the Coa proved, fortunately, to be overly-critical. If these elite Portuguese troops had proved incapable of fighting then Wellington's entire strategy for the defence of Portugal would be shredded.

To Graham, Murray now repeated his familiar line that there was only one realistic end to the campaign – ultimately having to give up Portugal in the face of a 'great machine' of a French army. More immediately, the fate of the Portuguese border fortress of Almeida, an imposing stronghold in joint British and Portuguese hands, was now concerning Murray. Almeida lay in the path of the French army's westward advance.

> The enemy have been a long time before Almeida in seeming idleness and it was only yesterday that we heard of them breaking ground. I do not know what stand Cox [The governor – a brigadier in the Portuguese Army and brother-in-law of Beresford] will be able to make in Almeida but if one allows a week to the enemy to make their approach, a week of open batteries and a day or two for the adjustment of terms I think it is nearly as much as we can safely reckon upon. What may follow after that I shall not pretend to conjecture.[36]

A couple of days later he added the assurance:

> I am now quite well. My confinement was protracted further than it would otherwise have been in consequence of my horse falling with me and bruising my leg and (as the surgeons think) breaking the small bone; but that is now six weeks ago and I am stout enough for anything I have to do as Moorfowl shooting forms no part of it.[37]

Murray's expectation of the start of the Almeida siege was pretty accurate. But he could not have foreseen the rapid outcome.

The French opened fire on Almeida on 26 August. A matter of hours after the start of the bombardment there was a massive explosion caused by a shell landing near the main magazine and igniting a trail of gunpowder leading from it, which sheared off the roofs of buildings throughout the town. Few structures escaped and hardly anything remained undamaged except the outer fortifications. 500 men were reportedly killed in the explosion. Cox had no choice but to surrender. Almost the entire Portuguese garrison agreed to serve the French. Cox and five British officers were made prisoners of war. Almeida had

35 Murray to Patrick, Alverca, 25 July 1810, Murray Papers, MS 21102.

36 Murray to Graham, Celorico, 17 August 1810, Murray Papers, ADV MS 46.2.5.

37 Murray to Graham, Celorico, 19 August 1810, Murray Papers, ADV MS 46.2.5.

fallen, adding to Murray's gloom: 'The dreams of defending Portugal will begin to dissipate I suppose even in Downing Street'.[38]

The fall of Almeida reinforced the feelings of many of those at home, and indeed the army itself, that the defence of Portugal was now a lost cause. Following his success at Almeida, Marshal Massena was now free to turn his force of 65,000 men, including 8,400 cavalry and 114 guns against the much smaller British force. Wellington had no option but to order a retreat and Celorico was evacuated.[39] Massena's advance was mercifully slow, caused in part by a serious lack of transport, as well as harassment by the Portuguese Ordenanza, a sort of home guard, allowing Wellington more time to complete his preparations for the fall-back defence of the country, which was to be based on the Lines of Torres Vedras. The waiting for the French affected all, and for some it was unclear just what the plan was. Wellington became more and more reserved and was angry at the 'croaking' of many of his officers, especially those directed at headquarters. Ward nevertheless defends Murray's constant flow of correspondence to London:

> His letters home might to some extent have influenced opinion in certain quarters in England, but they were written, not with any view of creating mischief, but for the purpose of divining the probable course of future events. They did not break the rules of correspondence laid down by Wellington in a General Order issued at the height of the 'croaking campaign' to check the spread of despondency and prevent the enemy from acquiring valuable military intelligence, and cannot be compared with those sent home by Willoughby Gordon, Murray's successor as QMG in 1812, which were designed to be leaked to the opposition press before the originals reached the Secretary of State.[40]

Not surprisingly, Wellington felt isolated.

> I have always been accustomed to have the confidence and support of the officers of the armies which I have commanded; for the first time whether owing to the opposition in England or whether the magnitude of the concern is too much for their nerves, or whether I am mistaken and they are right I cannot tell.[41]

Charles Stewart, the Adjutant General, had already warned London of Wellington becoming

> more and more reserved and buried in himself – Neither Spencer nor Murray are confided in or communicated with more intimately than myself so I have no grounds particularly to complain. I can tell you little of future intentions or resolutions, and nothing of the communications to and from the Government. We are all in the dark.[42]

38 Murray to Patrick, Celorico, 29 August 1810, Murray Papers, MS 21102.

39 Robertson, *Commanding Presence*, p.162.

40 Ward Draft, Ch.IX, p.32.

41 Wellington to Charles Stewart, Gouveia, 11 September 1810, Gurwood (ed.), *Dispatches*, Vol.VI, p.403.

42 PRONI, D3030/P/22, Charles Stewart to Castlereagh, 4 September 1810.

Wellington's extensive defensive plan was to strip the countryside north of Lisbon bare of people, livestock, and provisions – indeed, anything that might be of use to the enemy – and move the entire population in the path of any French advance behind the Lines of Torres Vedras. He issued a proclamation, in the name of the Portuguese Prince Regent, warning of the appalling treatment by the French of inhabitants of villages near the frontier and the need for the people to deny the enemy any resources whatsoever. Any provision of assistance to the enemy would be considered traitorous behaviour and be punished accordingly. Many British officers were shocked at the human misery the policy caused. The countryside south of Coimbra filled with refugees packed on donkeys and bullock carts, desperate to avoid being overtaken and probably slaughtered by the advancing French, but equally unsure what lay ahead of them. The Peninsula was experiencing unbounded brutality and depravity. Massena now refused to recognize the legitimacy of the Ordenanza. No quarter would be given by the French to anyone who was caught carrying arms but not wearing a uniform. Wellington protested to Massena that the Ordenanza was an ancient institution of the Kingdom of Portugal and that its members were entitled to the protection of the laws of war. He predicted grisly retaliation and he was right – French stragglers were shown no mercy and throat slitting of wounded and sick French soldiers by Portuguese peasants was commonplace.[43]

There was to be no let-up in the constant movement of the army, immersing Murray daily in those precise and intricate plans necessary to preserve Wellington's men as a cohesive and effective fighting force in the face of constant French threats. One of Murray's recognised skills was his remarkable topographical memory, as admired by a young officer sent out from High Wycombe, Captain Nathaniel Still:

> As soon as he knows the intentions of Lord Wellington, everything is set in motion with the utmost precision and facility. This is certainly his forte, and it is impossible for anyone to regulate the marches of an army with greater adroitness. He has likewise a wonderful talent of recollecting the features of a country, so that, I am told, he will several months after describe what he has perhaps seen in an accidental ride, and he is most completely capable of taking advantage of ground and occupying it accordingly. He is indefatigable and he disregards everything like fatigue, hard living or constant exertion.[44]

On 25 September Massena reached Bussaco, just north of Coimbra, where the entire combined Anglo-Portuguese army had halted. Even as a combined force the allies could not match the French strength, but their position on a ridge had been carefully chosen and Wellington was happy to give battle. His troops were in good order, and that included the Portuguese.

Wellington had chosen as his headquarters the Convent of Bussaco, where Murray had already been installed for three days, fully occupied with moving the allied forces into

43 Muir, *Path to Victory* pp.383-4.
44 Ward Draft, Ch.IX, p.34, source not cited.

position. The months from January to September had been spent establishing his mastery over the geography of Portugal by constant surveying and reconnaissance. As Ward put it:

> It was during this period that he fashioned the 'magic wand' with which he wafted divisions and brigades, with every appearance of ease and assurance, down roads that had never been trodden by soldiers shoes and into villages that had never seen the red coat of the British infantry. By the end of that time it was he who, except at critical moments, suggested, and it was Wellington who concurred. The pace at which the operational department of the army moved was Murray's. It moved, of course, in response to the direction of Wellington; but the impulse, the initiative, was Murray's, not Wellington's.[45]

'I propose to move my Headquarters to Cea' wrote Wellington to Beresford from Gouveia in the morning of 16 September, shortly before Bussaco 'Murray wishes me to go to Villa Doce, which is a league further back, but I shall not determine upon that till I see how things turn out in the course of the day'. They moved to Villa Doce.[46]

Murray had become aware of the defensive importance of the Bussaco ridge years earlier when campaigning with Moore, and reckoned Bussaco and the ridge opposite were almost impossible to overcome by direct attack. Although the position occupied by the British and Portuguese was strong, there was no complacency, indeed an awareness that, even were the French to launch an attack and be driven back, the options open to Wellington were limited, and a fall back to Lisbon was likely. The French army, described as 'a magnificent scene' by one officer, took up position opposite. Massena was equally confident – reckoning that the Portuguese troops were still unreliable and that the position held by the allies was too extensive for the relatively small numbers. He is reported in a number of accounts of the battle to have boasted 'Tomorrow we will finish the conquest of Portugal, and in a few days I will drown the leopard'.

Amazingly Murray spent quite some time on 25 September, when one would imagine there were so many things calling for his attention, penning a letter to Augusta describing the convent and its surroundings:

> We are here in one of the most singular places I have ever been in. It is a convent of monks of a very rigid order, who debar themselves not only the use of Meat and wine, but even from exercising the faculty of speech and who discipline themselves into the bargain with cords every four and twenty hours. But it is not the unspeakable follies of Mankind that please me here, it is the beauties of nature which the place presents. There is a very lofty ridge of mountains which at the southern extremity touches the River Mondego a few leagues above Coimbra, and which stretches directly for the River to the Northward for several miles. This ridge looks at a distance like an immense wall, separating the Country upon the east from that along the right bank of the Mondego towards Viseu etc; and the latter though very unclear looks from its top like an extended plain.

45 Ward Draft, Ch.IX, p.29.

46 Wellington to Beresford, Gouveia, 16 September 1810, Gurwood (ed.), *Dispatches*, Vol.VI, p.423.

It is at the northern extremity of this mountain where it falls by a very rapid descent, that the Convent of Bussaco is situated. It stands in an extensive park which is surrounded by a high wall – if indeed that can be called a park which is every where a thick wood, except where it is intersected by the Roads and walks made through it. The wood has a great variety of trees. That part which includes the top of the mountain is fringed with Pines and through the rest of it are scattered the largest cedars I ever saw. The underwood which is every where almost impenetrable is formed of the arbutus myrtle and an endless variety of other shrubs and plants of a lesser growth.

Besides the convent itself there are numerous small buildings scattered up and down the Wood. Some are little Hermitages for single individuals to retire to, others are small chapels situated upon the projecting rocks that jut out in some places and ambush the trees, and others are small shrines with figures of our Saviour and others personages contained in scripture or of the saints most revered by the Order.

I have taken up my quarters in one of the little Hermitages. My dwelling consists of a little cell, with a still smaller apartment off it, to serve as a kitchen. The remainder of the house consists of a chapel upon the same diminutive scale with my cell, and a little apartment behind it, of the same size with the kitchen. In front of the house is a little court surrounded by a wall, and lined by bricks set in with four very small Plots which if they produced flowers are now overgrown only with moss. On each side of the little gate on another side of the court is a remarkable myrtle, dropping lower through age, and want of care. Opposite to each corner of this little establishment is a large and lofty cedar, and the branches of these stretch over to meet each other above my roof. The top of the building is adorned with a little bell, which I believe has long been silent.

If I were now to take you out of the Park Wall my dear Augusta, I should show you the extensive country to the Eastward of this mountain, stretching toward Celorico, Trancoso – and other places which you already know, with the Sierra D'Estrella bordering it upon the Right, and the source of Coa upon the left, and the river Mondego flowing through the middle of it. I should show you the French army in the plain below the mountain and the British and Portuguese upon the summit. But these are not scenes that would give to you half the pleasure that my little Hermitage does, and therefore I shall not take you to look at them.

I shall now close my letter my Dear Augusta, by assuring you that to me our situation is full of interest, and that it does not give rise to any anxiety. What more can one desire than to have such feelings. My only wish is, that I could infuse them into your mind, and make them take place of that anxiety and apprehension which often exists there, but which if you cannot conquer, I imagine you at least to combat, and never to indulge.[47]

The convent formed part of what is now a luxury hotel – the woods and walled estate have probably changed little although the ridge was far less wooded than it is today. Murray's

47 Murray to Augusta, Bussaco, 25 September 1810, Murray Papers, ADV MS 46.2.6.

One of the shrines described by Murray close to his 'Hermitage' at Bussaco. (Author's Photo)

'hermitage' is still standing and exactly as he described it, and in 2015 was in the process of being restored. The small shrines leading from it along a steep path are also mostly intact and contain the beautifully carved biblical figures he refers to. If he had walked to a vantage point to paint a picture for Augusta of the French army as seen from the ridge, Murray might have bumped into Schaumann who, peering down from the ridge in the afternoon of the 26th could see:

> three dark columns of a colossal army – advancing under clouds of dust and gleaming with the glint of arms. Below, at the foot of the Sera [sic] and beyond a ravine, enemy pickets were already stationed. At last the huge mass seemed to break up into small regular clumps as the army went to bivouac. At some distance beyond… one could see the huge bivouacs of their cavalry, and still further away a black mass, consisting of wagons, carts, mules, ambulances and the commissariat could be divined.[48]

48 Schaumann, *On the Road*, p.246.

William Tomkinson of 16th Light Dragoons was also brimming with confidence: 'The army is in most beautiful order, and the Portuguese as fine-looking men and as steady under arms as any in the world'.[49]

Overnight and next day Murray planned the routes that the various allied corps would take in the event that they were forced to retire. His department had done its homework well and the roads chosen for each corps were capable of moving cavalry, artillery, and baggage carts as might be required. Immaculate and intricate maps had been drawn, in colour, clearly showing the degree of difficulty for artillery movement.[50]

The full orders for the retreat were set out as follows:

> In the event of the army being ordered to retire from the position which it occupies on the Siera de Busaco the following are the roads by which the several divisions are to move:
>
> 1st The troops under the orders of Lieutenant General Sir Brent Spencer will move by the great road through Mealhada to Fornos, and thence into the large plain below Coimbra; and will cross the river Mondego at the ford near Casas Novas. Sir Brent Spencer is already aware how his column is to avoid interfering with any other troops in passing through Fornos; and he will be pleased to give orders that an officer, who knows the turn that the column is to take in the village of Fornos, may be placed there, (with a guard), in due time to prevent any part of the baggage that precedes the troops from taking a wrong direction. The whole of this route is practicable for artillery. Sir Brent Spencer will receive further orders how to proceed after crossing the Mondego.
>
> 2nd The 4th Division will retire by the road which leads direct from Busaco to Fornos, through the village of Marmeleira. This road has been reconnaitred by Lieutenant Westmacott, of the Royal Staff Corps, and reported fit for British Artillery. Lieutenant Westmacott will be sent to conduct the column. After reaching Fornos the 4th Division is to continue its march by the great Coimbra road. It will cross the Mondego by the bridge at Coimbra, and ascend the hill upon the other side of the river. Major General Cole will not discontinue his march along the great road, after passing the Mondego, until he receives orders to that effect; it being necessary that he should move on sufficiently to give room for the divisions following in the rear of the 4th.
>
> 3rd The Light Division will retire by the road which passes through the village of Paul to Botao and then to Fornos. From Fornos the Light Division will take the great road to Coimbra; but it will halt before reaching the house called Cazas do Corigo Paes, at which point the troops under Major General Picton are to enter the great road, and these troops are to be allowed to move into the great road before the Light Division resumes its march. The road through Paul and Botao to Fornos has been reconnaitred by officers of the Light Division and also by Captain Scovell, of the Quartermaster General's Department, who will be attached to the Light Division during the march as far as Fornos. The whole of this road is reported

49 James Tomkinson (ed.), *Diary of a Cavalry Officer in the Peninsular War and Waterloo Campaigns* (London: Swan Sonnenschein & Co, 1895), p 42; see also Robertson, *Commanding Presence* p.164.

50 See numerous maps in Murray Papers, ADV MS 46.2.6.

practicable for British Artillery. Brigadier General Crauford will receive further orders during the halt of his division between Fornos and Cazas do Corigo Paes.

4th The troops under Major General Picton will retire by the road which runs through Alagoa and Eiras and join the Coimbra road at Cazas do Corigo Paes. This road has been reconnaitred and reported fit for Portuguese artillery by Lieutenant Shanahan of the Royal Staff Corps, who will be sent to conduct the column. The troops under Major General Picton will enter the great road at Cazas do Corigo Paes, after the 4th Division has passed that point, taking their place in the column of march between the 4th Division and the Light Division. After coming into the great road, Major General Picton will continue to follow the 4th Division, until he receives further orders.

5th Major General Leith's division will retire by the road which leads through the village of Poroa to Dientiero, and thence by the Quinta dos Lagares do Seminario to the Convent of S. Antonio dos Olivaes above the town of Coimbra, where Major General Leith will halt and wait for further orders. This road has been reconnaitred and reported practicable for light artillery (aided by men at some steep ascents), by Lieutenant Shanahan of the Royal Staff Corps; as that officer is however to be attached to the 3rd Division during the march to Coimbra, Major General Leith will lose no time in having the road reconnaitred by officers of his own division. The 9 pounder brigade which was with Major General Leith having been attached for the present to the corps under the orders of Lieutenant General Hill, it will conform to the movements of that corps.

6th The troops under Lieutenant General Hill which are in the position of Busaco will (in the event of the Army retiring) recross the Mondego at the ford near Penacova, and will be placed between that part and the village of San Miguel de Poyares. A separate instruction will be given to Lieutenant General Hill respecting the further operation of the above part of his corps, and also of the other troops belonging to it which are still on the left of the Mondego, in the neighbourhood of Ponte de Murcella.

7th Lieutenant General Hill's corps on retiring will march by its right. All the other divisions above mentioned will move by their left.

8th The cavalry will retire by the great road through Mealhada and Fornos, and thence into the large plain below Coimbra, following Lieutenant General Sir Brent Spencer's corps.

Lieutenant General Sir Stapleton Cotton will forward a small party of dragoons to Fornos to take post at the point where the road turns in that village to lead into the great plain. This officer is to prevent any part of the cavalry from taking a wrong direction, or from interfering with any of the other troops that are to move from Fornos by the great road to Coimbra. The officer and guard directed to be stationed at this point by Sir Brent Spencer is not to quit it until relieved by the party of dragoons above mentioned. Lieutenant General Sir Stapleton Cotton will form the cavalry into the great plain below Coimbra, and will there wait for further orders.

9th It is clearly to be understood that no movement under this instruction is to take place, unless in the case of orders being received for the army to retire.[51]

51 Reproduced in Wellington (ed.), *Supplementary Despatches*, Vol.XII, p.254.

Murray spent the early evening issuing arrangements for feeding and positioning the army overnight. He ordered the whole army to be under arms awaiting the French attack. The Quartermaster General's restless activity did not end there. Just before he retired to bed, Murray warned Wellington to move additional forces to cover a small track which ran through the village of San Antonio do Cantara, parallel to the main Coimbra road. Earlier in the day Murray had noticed Massena and his staff, conspicuous in their gorgeous uniforms, making a detailed examination of this route. He correctly assumed that at least one of the French columns would follow this track, and Wellington adjusted his dispositions accordingly.[52] Murray was proved entirely right when the next day a French corps advanced against the British line exactly as predicted. Almost certainly this was not the first time that Murray had felt confident enough to make or suggest alterations to the battle plan set upon by Wellington. The mutual confidence had grown to a level that was very rarely demonstrated in Wellington's relationships with his senior officers. Wellington had always found it difficult to delegate much authority and had the stamina, expertise, and intellect to manage matters personally to an extraordinary degree. In Murray he had discovered an individual who had an uncanny ability to read his own mind, and he was to become more and more comfortable in allowing Murray a good deal of headroom to interpret and carry out his large scale plans, in a way that Murray felt the most effective. Murray's ability to relate to people, his calmness, diplomacy and organizational abilities made him the ideal conduit between Wellington and many of his more headstrong generals.

The Battle of Bussaco started early on the 27th. As the thick mist gradually lifted the first French attack began up the slope, and was repelled. The French plan was to hit the British lines hard close to the centre then to turn right along the ridge to link up with other troops that were making their way along the road on the British left flank – already recognized by Wellington as the weakness in his position. Solid resistance however proved too much for three French attempts, which were repulsed with heavy losses. The Portuguese troops, for the first time, gave a very good account of themselves. By midday no more attacks were attempted and despite some skirmishing during the afternoon, a truce was agreed which allowed both armies time to collect their dead and wounded, and provided opportunities for both officers and men to fraternize with the enemy in a now familiar manner. Drinking from the same stream, men leant over to shake hands, and in one case to exchange forage caps.[53]

Massena had been comprehensively defeated but not broken. Next day Wellington noticed Massena gradually shifting his forces backwards. The possibility of Massena being able to turn the British flank still remained. Wellington gave orders, through Murray, for the bulk of the army to withdraw on the evening of 28 September, the start of a withdrawal all the way to the Lines of Torres Vedras.

Murray issued a lengthy order that started: 'The army will retire from its present position this night'. The first draft is in Murray's own hand, copied many times, as of course it had to be, so that each subordinate commander would know not only what he was to be doing, but would also be aware of the movement and position of every other part of the army. Such

52 L. James, *The Iron Duke* (London: Pimlico, 1992), p.153.
53 Robertson, *Commanding Presence*, p 166.

The Battle of Bussaco 27 September 1810. (Anne S.K. Brown Military Collection)

orders were typically lengthy and were extraordinarily detailed. It was normal for orders to move to be issued between the afternoon of one day and three o'clock the next morning, with the troops marching before dawn to escape the heat. However, to move an entire army, quietly, in good order, from a mountainous battlefield, at the dead of night, was no easy job. The speed at which Wellington's broad plan was committed to paper and rolled out to tens of thousands of men was impressive. Murray ordered that 'the fires in the lines are to be kept up – all the arrangements and movements, particularly of the Artillery, are to be made with as much silence as possible, and no torches or other lights of that sort are to be shown until the troops are behind the Sierra when lights may be made use of to assist in finding the road and in conducting the Artillery'. He finished by announcing that headquarters would be at Coimbra next morning.[54]

Many more orders were drafted when headquarters arrived at Coimbra, keeping the army moving in an orderly fashion. Constant intelligence was also delivered to Murray on the movement of the French army. Reports on the state of roads from officers in the department came in regularly, many with detailed sketches. Yet, again on the 30th he had the urge to write to Augusta from Coimbra, even if it was short and to the point: 'I wrote you a long letter the day before the battle of Bussaco. I have now only time for a very short one. All I can tell you is that, as usual, we have beat the French, and that there is nothing in the world

54 Murray Papers, ADV MS 46.2.6.

that can give me more pleasure'.[55] Augusta must by now have been in great demand in the drawing rooms of Chelsea and Argyll, as she would often have been one of the very earliest recipients of the result of actions in the Peninsula. The victory at Bussaco gave the allies' confidence an enormous boost. The question of whether the Portuguese army would fight or give way when facing a French battering had been conclusively answered. They had emerged from Bussaco with great credit. Many officers who previously were sceptical were fulsome in their praise in their letters home. Wellington's faith in them had been vindicated. Suddenly it seemed that it was no longer inevitable, as it had seemed only a few weeks earlier, that the end result would be withdrawal and the evacuation of the country from behind the Lines.

News of the success reached London in the middle of October. The Whig Opposition again found reason to criticize – another Talavera; a retreat after an initial success – but the Bussaco result was certainly enough for the government to boast of a glorious victory, and gave cause for optimism that Perceval's government could survive, and arguably Patrick's political ambitions with it. Wellington's despatch of the battle, published in the London *Gazette* of 15 October states: 'I am particularly indebted to the Adjutant and the Quartermaster General and the officers of their departments'. Wellington also made special mention of Marshal Beresford: 'to him exclusively, under the Portuguese Government, is due the Merit of having raised, formed, disciplined, and equipped the Portuguese army which has now shown itself capable of engaging and defeating the Enemy'.

A well-organized march from Coimbra, again orchestrated with meticulous planning by Murray, saw the allied armies in position behind the first line of Torres Vedras, just before the autumn rains started in mid-October. Another letter to Augusta evidenced a man at the peak of his game, thoroughly confident, clearly enjoying the challenges of moving Wellington's forces around the country, and drafting and implementing battle plans. Murray was never happier than when under pressure, but in control of events.

> We are moving to a strong position between this and Lisbon, where I hope we shall again beat the French, when they come to it. Do not give yourself any anxiousness about the matter, for I told you in my letter from Bussaco before that Action, I feel none. Whatever the aspect of affairs may seem to be, we always somehow or other beat the French.
>
> When the Army is in a state of Activity as it has been for some time back, I have a good deal to do, and I am always then most interested, and always stout and well... What would appear fatigue or hardship at other times, is then no more than amusement. And you may be assured that however horrible war may be imagined to be by those who hear of it, to those who are engaged in it, and have any considerable part to act, an occupation of extraordinary interest.[56]

Nevertheless, he was still, despite his detailed knowledge of their construction, not totally convinced that the Lines would hold, and if they did not then Brownrigg should be aware

55 Murray to Augusta, Coimbra, 30 September 1810, Murray Papers, ADV MS 46.2.6.
56 Murray to Augusta, Convent of Alcobaca, 5 October 1810, Murray Papers, ADV MS 46.2.7.

that getting the army out of Lisbon without catastrophic loss was going to be an immense challenge. Murray's regular reports to Brownrigg at Horse Guards continued.

> All I shall say about our intended Position is that as a general line it presents throughout advantageous features, and the main points of it as likewise the principal approaches to it are fortified by substantial Field Works – it has against it its great extent and I may add (notwithstanding their good conduct at Bussaco) the disadvantage of raw troops. As to Lines in general, experience has made it proverbial with Military Men that little reliance is to be placed upon them. In spite of all this however, matters may turn out well.
>
> Whatever may happen the question of our risking every thing in front of Lisbon, is one that it belongs to the Government to judge of, not to Military Men, It has been decided upon I suppose, in the affirmative, and all that remains for us to do is to act our part in such a manner, that whether successful or otherwise, we may preserve our credit as soldiers.[57]

Four days later he commented that 'The crisis is important and critical for both parties. If we are beat it is very problematical, whether the remainder of the army will be able in any manner to extricate itself.[58]

Despite clearly suffering from yet another bout of illness, perhaps having never fully recovered from his earlier attack, Murray provided Brownrigg with a further update of the Lines: 'Excuse my not entering into greater detail, as I am not very well today, and writing on business requires rather an effort'.[59] Sketches were included in the correspondence, including one of the Battle of Bussaco, which led Murray to think that the one of Corunna that he remembered was at Horse Guards was less than perfect, an extraordinary demonstration of the level of detail that Murray applied to all the aspects of his department's responsibilities, regardless of what else might have been more pressing. He recommended that Brownrigg should send a young officer called Wellermine back to Corunna to do it properly, if he was not too busy. Having an eye on detail, he was not going to have any application of the 'Wycombe style'. Murray subsequently complained to Colonel Lewis Lindenthal, one of Brownrigg's Assistant Deputy Quartermaster Generals at Horse Guards, that the Wycombe style of drawing was in general very bad and few of them had any knowledge of surveying.[60]

Now the weather really turned and the armies were facing gales and rain, which Murray knew would be worse for the French. He wrote a private letter to Graham, apologising for not writing earlier but he had been busy with 'many occurrences':

> The Enemy have followed us up to the out works of our intrenched positions here, and we are now looking at each other... it looks very much as if the French had acted upon the belief that we should at once go to our Ships, and not show the bold and strong front we do here. If that is the case, and they are obliged to come

57 Murray to Brownrigg, Leiria, 5 October 1810, Luffness Mss, GD 364/1/1196.

58 Murray to Brownrigg, Aruda, 9 October 1810, Luffness Mss, GD 364/1/1196.

59 Murray to Brownrigg, Near Bucellar, 13 October 1810, Luffness Mss, GD 364/1/1196.

60 Murray to Lindenthal, Cartaxo, 8 December 1810, Luffness Mss, GD 364/1/1196.

> forward I am sanguine in my hope of their having got themselves into a scrape. But if Massena has foreseen that he might be obliged to draw up here, and has made his arrangements for having his communications opened for him from the side of Spain by fresh arrivals of troops, our situation may perhaps now be at its best.[61]

The troops were in good spirits. Morale was high after Bussaco. The first view of the Lines for most of the soldiers must have filled them with a great sense of security. They were a truly massive defensive obstacle.

Wellington also felt that Massena was in a scrape but was still not sure of the wholehearted support of his own officers and political masters. 'Nothing can equal the conduct of Lord Wellington' wrote Alexander Gordon, his aide-de-camp 'but I am sorry to say that he is not well supported & has to trust to himself alone'.[62] Massena had advanced steadily through a completely deserted Coimbra, his army plundering what little was left, and turned south, expecting their next sight of the British army to be its embarkation on troopships in the Tagus. He had no intelligence of the existence of the massive fortifications that lay in their path. He left Coimbra under-garrisoned, which was promptly retaken by Brigadier General Trant and his Portuguese militia. Four thousand French prisoners were taken and conveyed to Oporto.

The French learned of the capture of so many of their colleagues the moment they saw for the first time the great defensive works that awaited them. They had not remotely imagined the existence of anything on this scale. Massena knew after a couple of probing attempts that any attempt to storm the Lines would result in heavy defeat. Wellington commented to his brother Henry that he had 'no idea what the French will, or rather can, do. I think it is certain that they can do us no mischief, and that they will lose the greatest part of their army if they attack us. They will starve if they stay much longer; and they will experience great difficulty in their retreat'.[63] Wellington was certainly tempted to move against Massena, inflict a defeat, and force the French to endure a ghastly winter in countryside and mountains stripped of any provisions by his scorched earth policy. But it was still risky; 'I could lick these fellows any day, but it would cost me 10,000 men, and as this is the last army England has here we must take care of it'.[64]

Settling in behind the Lines, Murray wrote to Augusta on 27 October, talking of her journey to Argyll and his longing to see the places she mentioned – Loch Lomond, Dumbarton, and to get to the top of Rest and Be Thankful

> for all these places interest me much more than all those I have written to you about from this country. Massena is I suppose waiting for reinforcements that I hope are not upon their way to join him, and if the stories of the Deserters are true he and his men have in the meantime very empty stomachs.[65]

61 Murray to Graham, Enxara des Cavalleras between Montelevar and Torres Vedras, 16 October 1810, Murray Papers, ADV MS 46.2.7.

62 Muir (ed.), *Wellington's Right Hand*, p.119.

63 Wellington to Henry Wellesley, Pero Negro, 21 October 1810, Gurwood (ed.) *Dispatches*, Vol.VI, p.502.

64 Comment to Colonel James Stanhope, Muir, *Path to Victory*, p.398, quoting papers of James Stanhope, journal entry for 23 June 1812 recalling the incident.

65 Murray to Augusta, Peronegro, 27 October 1810, Murray Papers, ADV MS 46.2.7.

By the same post he wrote to Patrick on the growing success of the department's intelligence operations:

> We have this great advantage that by means of our friends the Guerrillas, we get at, not only all the secrets of the French Etat Major, but now at those of Buonaparte's Cabinet, whilst Massena is cut off from all communication with any of the French Army, as well as with France.[66]

He knew what the talk was in Massena's camp about various corps coming to reinforce him, but Murray's intelligence-gathering was vastly superior to the French. He was aware exactly what the movements were of the units Massena was hoping for, and that they had actually fallen back. Intercepted letters provide evidence of Napoleon's anger at the dead end at Torres Vedras. Murray went on:

> All this proves is that Buonaparte had underestimated our means of defending this country, and the style of reproach used seems to imply that Massena had made representations on the inadequacy of his force to the Enterprize. This I consider of great importance.
>
> I suppose I shall soon hear of your living again in London. If matters turn out well here it will go a great way towards making your Campaign in Parliament more easy than it would otherwise have been. However, though our prospects are fair at present, it is impossible yet to say that they may not change.[67]

After a few weeks in relative safety behind the Lines, the British felt free to indulge themselves with amusements to occupy the approaching winter. Murray was invited with other senior officers and dignitaries from Lisbon to a fete at the palace at Mafra, described by Murray in one of his regular letters to Augusta as an immense building, uniting under one roof a palace and a convent and 'acceding at once the foolish vanity of the Portuguese Princes by the vastness of the place'.[68] It was chosen by Wellington as the venue for the ceremony of investing Beresford, in recognition of his achievements in commanding the Portuguese forces, with the Order of the Bath. Beresford had, in a short space of time, transformed them into a recognisable fighting force in the British military tradition, who had, if only recently, proved that, with the right leadership and discipline, they were as capable as most of the British troops.

Two hundred of Lisbon's best, Murray among them, were invited to attend the ceremony and afterwards a dinner. Dinner was to be followed by a ball, which part of the evening was open to British officers and Lisbon's fashionable set, and the festivities were to finish with supper. Owing to the vastness of the palace and the ambitiousness of the undertaking generally, dinner for the select two hundred was not ready when the ceremony finished – indeed there was to be a delay of two hours. By that time the less important guests, who had not been invited to the dinner, had arrived. Seeing

66 Murray to Patrick, Peronegro, 27 October 1810, Murray Papers, MS 21102.

67 Murray to Patrick, Peronegro, 27 October 1810, Murray Papers, MS 21102.

68 Murray to Augusta, Portugal, 10 November 1810, Murray Papers, ADV MS 46.2.8.

Mafra Palace. (Author's Photo)

the magnificent spread when dinner was announced, they all, at least three times the number intended, scrambled for places. There was chaos. The assembled company made light work of the food and drink, and then tried to squeeze back into the drawing room and to make room for a few people to dance. Murray, unsurprisingly, made his exit at this point, and went home, but he learnt that the supper scene surpassed the competition for dinner, with the gentlemen who had been least successful at dinner making sure they were in prime position before most of the dishes had even been laid out. Shockingly they began their attack on the food without waiting for grace or any other signal or authority.

By the end of November it was clear enough to Massena that without substantial reinforcement he was never going to break the Lines. He was caught in unforgiving terrain, stripped bare as a result of Wellington's policy, with winter upon him. His only option was to withdraw.

Murray wrote to Patrick from Alenquer, just in front of the most northern line, indicating that he was with the forward British force, hard on the retreating Massena's heels, confident that this was a moment when it was safe to move outside the protection of the Lines:

> The French have fallen back... If Massena quits the hold he has of Portugal for this year Lord Wellington will have had a great triumph, even as it is he has had a considerable one over French Arrogance.

> The Enemy fall back upon Santarem. Their rearguard was yesterday 10 miles on this side of Santarem and our most advanced parties exchanged a few shots with them.[69]

Murray was being forced to recognize, along with many others, that Wellington's strategy had worked, against all the odds, and that the elaborate evacuation preparations might not be required after all. In the course of the following months Massena did indeed retreat, the first stage in what would be a gradual shift in the odds in Wellington's favour, but Murray held to the view that the French had been let down by their generals' blunders as much as by any superiority of the British and their allies.

By mid-December British headquarters had moved forward to Cartaxo, very close to Santarem, but no major actions were planned and thus Murray had less to do than in the recent few months.

> We are without any intelligence from England by the Packet later than to the 31st Octr and begin now to be very impatient for another mail. Some Merchant Ships have come in later than the Packet which bring very unfavourable accounts of the King, which of course lead our politicians to various speculations according to their fears or hopes from a change taking place.
>
> Massena has been reinforced by the arrival of five or six thousand men which will make no great difference for the present in the state of things here. These reinforcements are part of Massena's army left sick in a garrison when he first moved forward.[70]

Bearing in mind the political situation at home:

> I confess I approve entirely of your determination in regard to your own future plans of life, but I think the present state of things must occasion a little doubt as to your having it at your option to fulfil them. But no matter, we should be prepared for times of good and bad, and you have a sheet anchor put in the ground, although those you endeavour to cast into the Political Stream should not hold.[71]

Murray hoped that any changes that did come about would not be made from a narrow party political viewpoint. He felt Britain urgently needed a strong, efficient and respectable government.

He also had time to write to Lindenthal from Cartaxo on the latest copying device:

> Thank you for the sketches of the country round Lisbon. The stone may be very useful in striking off copies in that way for the use of the General Officers of an

69 Murray to Patrick, Alenquer, 17 November 1810, Murray Papers, MS 21102.

70 Murray to Patrick, Cartaxo, 1 December 1810, Murray Papers, MS 21102.

71 Murray to Patrick, Cartaxo, 8 December 1810, Murray Papers, MS 21102.

> army, and if I had an apparatus of the kind at Lisbon much time and trouble would be saved in the Department here.[72]

He had promised Augusta that he would write regularly and kept his word, but he felt he had little to write about compared with the life that he imagined Augusta must be living back in London, where she can describe the 'gaieties of the capital, deaths and marriages, scandal'.[73] By the end of December he was complaining that he could not think how some husbands and wives he had heard of can write every day – what did they have to say to each other?

He had started to plan the best moment for a short spell of leave, which he was realistic enough to recognize would only work if there were to be a total shutdown in hostilities for the winter, leaving the British safe behind the Lines. He was certainly bored with the current stand-off where there was not enough to occupy his restless nature. In his quarters at Cartaxo he complained to Augusta he had

> no windows but board windows for some time which I at least improved by putting in a few glass panes and also a few paper panes into the boards and now I have the pleasure of having some light in my room and of seeing the village church without sitting in the open air for it. If I go out of the village there are some fir trees (delightful objects) and a little further a great heath. This last object is the most agreeable of all (for the church you know is a Roman Catholic one) for it affords us capital galloping ground which, having been confined within our Lines, and obliged to ride over hard causeways or dead mud, it is a great luxury both for ourselves and for our horses.
>
> I am glad you have a room to offer me in your flat. I should certainly endeavour to come to it if Massena… would only be gentlemanlike enough to go back to Spain for the winter. But can one hope for anything so gentlemanlike from such an upstart and such a Bandetti as he is at the head of ?[74]

Murray would not have to suffer the relative idleness for long. Intelligence was soon filtering through that additional reinforcements were moving up to support Massena, and that it appeared likely that offensive operations were about to be resumed, so there would be no prospect of leave in London for some time to come.

72 Murray to Lindenthal, Cartaxo, 8 December 1810, Luffness Mss, GD364/1/1196.

73 Murray to Augusta, Cartaxo, 15 December 1810, Murray Papers, ADV MS 46.2.8.

74 Murray to Augusta, Cartaxo, 15 December 1810, Murray Papers, ADV MS 46.2.8.

12

1811 – Peninsula – On Massena's Heels

The New Year correspondence opened with a letter to Patrick, mildly complaining that the communication between them was rather one-sided, as indeed it was. Over the previous few months Murray had written weekly to both Augusta and Patrick. Since Bussaco the quietness had not agreed with him and it is easy to see from his letters that he was becoming a bit scratchy, still worrying about his future in the army

> You write now and then, but I write, like a machine, any time that Packet day comes round – today indeed I anticipate a little, for our Bag is not made up till tomorrow, but as I shall have a good many letters to write.

He also had little time for his brother's uncertain political future

> a matter seemingly of a good deal of indifference to yourself… you may be sure it will not break my heart. If you entered decidedly into Politics, took an active part, and were likely to be an important aid to me in the world by that means, perhaps I should then regret your relinquishing the pursuit.

He thought it mistaken to assume the French would give up on Portugal just because their latest narrow attempt had hit problems. His deep seated pessimism seemed to have returned: 'I shall be very glad if I prove to have been mistaken, at present however I do not perceive any grounds for seeing matters in a different light from what I did'.[1]

Murray's fears seem to have been substantiated when on 15 January he wrote again from Cartaxo on the advance of reinforcements for Massena's army. Information showed Massena as being:

> [I]n the utmost distress for want of supplies… a spy of ours writes that they actually eat Apes, Cats, etc in Santarem. For my own part I do not believe this story, but at the same time it is impossible not to wonder at their being able to feed their army so long as they have done in the small extent of country that it occupies.

1 Murray to Patrick, Cartaxo, 11 January 1811, Murray Papers, MS 21102.

Despite that 'At all accounts it appears pretty certain I think that the enemy is about to resume Offensive Operations in this country'.[2]

Bad news was also filtering through of another Spanish defeat:

> From the sick at Estremadura we hear that Olivenza has fallen. The Spaniards were foolish enough to put a garrison into it without provisions, Artillery, or ammunition, and on hearing of it being blockaded by the enemy, we heard at the same time that it contained but four days provisions. It is not a place of great strength but it may be useful to the Enemy as a secure depot.
>
> We have lost the Marquis of Romana. His death was very sudden and occasioned by an aneurism in the heart... certainly a great loss as he was a most useful link between the British and Spaniards, satisfied of our sincerity in the Cause, and not insensible of the defects of his countrymen.[3]

La Romana's death was a major blow. Probably the best of the Spanish generals, he had been happy to answer Wellington's request for 8,000 troops for Bussaco, and was one of the few Spaniards that the British found easy to work with.

The regular weekly correspondence continued, with Murray returning to a theme of his – namely that he considered most of the blame for the dismal performance of Spanish and Portuguese troops to lie with their officers. Among the correspondence at this time is a letter to Alexander Hope asking for his support for Scovell's request for promotion to major, 'an intelligent and deserving officer'.[4] As so often seemed to happen, Scovell's application had got held up in the bureaucracy at Horse Guards, as well as the usual army procedures.

It was not only the advancement of deserving officers in his department that was exercising minds – behind the scenes there was a push to secure Murray's promotion to brigadier general, supported in London by Hope, who received a letter from the Duke of York's private secretary early in January; 'our friend Murray's interests and speculations cannot be committed to a more friendly mind or one which contains a higher regard for him than the Duke's'.[5] It looks as though news of this support from the highest level was relayed to Murray, as on 9 February he was able to write to Hope:

> The rank of Brigadier General begins to approach me. Lord Wellington expects the appointment of the colonels in this country as low down as Colonel Stoppard who is to be included. There will then remain above me here only Col De Lancey and Col Hawkes and if any thing should lead to their being appointed Brigadiers, I conceive it is a matter of course that I should have the rank also.
>
> My being Quartermaster General, in place of being an obstacle, can be considered only I think, as an additional reason for the rank of Brigadier General being given me.[6]

2 Murray to Patrick, Cartaxo, 15 January 1811, Murray Papers, MS 21102.
3 Murray to Patrick, Cartaxo, 26 January 1811, Murray Papers, MS 21102.
4 Murray to Alexander Hope, Cartaxo, 2 February 1811, Luffness Mss, GD 364/1/1216.
5 Taylor to Alexander Hope, Windsor Castle, 6 January 1811, Luffness Mss, GD 364/1/1216.
6 Murray to Alexander Hope, Cartaxo, 9 February 1811, Luffness Mss, GD 364/1/1216.

The Quartermaster General's Department in Wellington's army, by this time with a staff of almost 30, had flourished under Murray's command, one obvious success story being Scovell, who had been backed by Murray in the face, initially anyway, of a lack of support from Wellington. Scovell's Guides had become a very important part of the army, and the intelligence apparatus built by the department was vastly superior to anything the French had. Wellington had been in the habit of running what limited intelligence operations there were himself, but was confident enough in Murray's industry and administrative talent to allow him to take charge of, at least, all the army's topographical intelligence.[7] Large amounts of information would also appear on Murray's desk from spies in the pay of the British, as well as from local guerrillas and peasants who might be well disposed to the British, or, just as likely, determined to inflict as much harm on a French army that had entered into a shameful phase of murder, rape, burning, and looting.

The French had commenced operations against the Spanish near Badajoz. Murray reported on the Spanish defeat: It 'passed like most of their other battles that is to say they have been beat, killed, wounded, taken or dispersed with loss of artillery, arms, baggage etc. etc.' and yet he refused to write off the Spanish completely as many of his fellow officers had. He said he had always tried to persuade them against battles, but in this case they were surprised. He was still amazed at their perseverance: 'I am persuaded they want only a Wallace or a Bruce to render them successful'.[8]

Murray's correspondence was, as he pointedly mentioned to his brother and sister, meticulously regular. A weekly post left for England and Murray never seemed to miss it, generally with letters to both, sometimes no more than a couple of sides of small writing paper, often covering five or six larger sides. In Augusta's case he frequently included descriptive passages of places he had visited, or musings on life and its tribulations. Patrick simultaneously received a full blown account of actions, intelligence operations, and political news and views. Murray frequently chided his siblings for the paucity of their writing effort compared with his – and had another go at Patrick.

> You have a very easy way of carrying on a correspondence by enclosing other peoples letters, or scraps of letters with a few additions in a Blank form. However I excuse this in a Politician in these doubtful times.[9]

As one of the new breed of senior officer, Murray was set on limiting the reliance on the letter of recommendation, at that time much used as a helping hand into positions in the army. There is no question but that he himself had benefitted from the practice in his earlier years, but he was now one of the professional officers who were determined to see personal advancement based on merit rather than family connection. The bulk of Wellington's officers at this time still came from the old mould, having originally purchased their commissions, and the method of promotion thereafter was still very rigid, as Murray himself was discovering. He was extremely cautious about opening doors for individuals where such individual's own

7 James, *The Iron Duke*, p.190.
8 Murray to Augusta, Cartaxo, 23 February 1811, Murray Papers, MS 21103.
9 Murray to Patrick, Cartaxo, 25 February 1811, Murray Papers, MS 21102.

talents would not have been able to achieve the same result, and gave the cold shoulder to a letter of recommendation forwarded from Patrick:

> I shall keep your Recommendation and shall be very happy to be useful to the person concerned if any opportunity of my being so offers. People in general have a very erroneous idea however of the advantages to be derived from Recommendations to Military Men in official Situations such as mine. In my Department there are particular acquirements and a particular kind of intelligence which are requisite, and it affords openings for such officers only as possess these. I seek out these wherever I can find them, and if I acted upon any other principle I should never get through my business at all. This I am sure you will very well understand but perhaps you may not be able to make it quite as intelligible to others who have friends whom they wish to see in Staff Situations.[10]

At home the King had again fallen ill with a recurrence of his 'madness' (a number of differing illnesses have been suggested) and Perceval's hold on power was accordingly looking shaky once more. If a renewed Regency was to be inevitable there was an assumption that the Prince Regent would dismiss Perceval and invite the Whig opposition to form a government, with serious consequences not just for the conduct of the Peninsular campaign but also for Patrick's career. The political developments were followed closely both by Wellington and Murray. Wellington was constantly at loggerheads with the government and never related particularly well to Liverpool or Perceval. He was always complaining of the shortages he had to endure. That was to be expected. But a Whig administration might undermine his strategy completely. In the event the King's health improved and it looked as though the Regency would be brief. There was no change in Government. Patrick's position was safe for the time being, and political support for the war continued.

Massena's withdrawal to Santarem, the countryside around which was better able to feed his troops, had marginally improved the comfort of his men. Still, his losses were substantial, through sickness and lack of food and clothing. Napoleon still had 350,000 men strung across Portugal and Spain at the beginning of 1811, but the armies were overstretched and resources increasingly limited. In contrast the health of the British improved greatly, and the numbers of active fit men rose substantially. But Wellington was not very sympathetic towards senior officers, who like Murray, wanted to go home for business reasons or just to see family and friends.

On 2 March Murray provided an update on the situation at Badajoz and again put his case to Patrick for what he saw as an overdue promotion to brigadier general:

> In a letter which I wrote to Alexr Hope some time ago, I adverted to the approach of the rank of Brigadier General to me. I believe by this time all the colonels who above me who have any sort of pretensions must have been appointed Br. Generals except perhaps two. I begin to think therefore that I may put forward some pretensions to

10 Murray to Patrick, Cartaxo, 25 February 1811, Murray Papers, MS 21102.

> obtaining that Rank without having to reproach myself with being too hasty in my expectations of advancement.
>
> I wish you to speak with Alxr Hope upon this subject and to unite in urging the point. Without forgetting what is due to modesty, I think I may fairly submit that my endeavours in the service have been as constant as I could make them, and that they have been sufficiently frequent and called upon in situations of sufficient importance, to intitle me to some slight deviation from common routine, when a fair opening offers for such a favour.
>
> I might mention the number of General Officers in Command whose confidence I have in a particular manner enjoyed and other points of that nature which make the course of my service a little different from that of some others of perhaps equal, or a little more standing in the army, but I do not think it necessary to dwell upon those points. And other considerations such as that my situation makes me stand clear of any interference in point of command with others, that in point of the little distinctions that result from Service the circumstance of being a general officer or not makes a most important difference; that the being employed in an Allied Army, in a permanent situation makes rank more desirable as well as of more real utility; that there are in this army when considered as one whole (which it is in all my dealings with it) many Officers of junior rank in our own Service, who are General Officers; all those considerations Alexr Hope will perfectly understand and explain to you without my going into any detail upon them.
>
> I assure you this is a matter which has for some time back occupied my thoughts very seriously, and I cannot help feeling that it will be fully as satisfactory to me to content myself with the station that has been allotted to me at home, as to continue here, only to show that until my turn in the Army List slowly comes round, I have no chance of any more distinction than if I had never filled a situation of the smallest importance, nor seen an hours service since I got my commission.
>
> You may of course show this letter to Alxr Hope and I leave it entirely to him and you to act on it as you think best. You have my ideas and my feelings on the subject.[11]

By the next packet he was reporting on the enemy falling back but it was unclear if a full-scale retreat into Spain was underway. A letter to Augusta from near Condeixa on 14 March talked of the French leaving Portugal, by Almeida and Ciudad Rodrigo: 'We see each other every day' he wrote. The British were harassing the French, the operation having more the appearance of 'Reivers and sham fights rather than of real war'.[12]

As soon as it became clear that the French were indeed in full retreat no time was lost in mounting the pursuit, and Murray, taking advantage of a short break in the advance to allow supplies to catch up, wrote to Patrick with his views on the French incompetence:

11 Murray to Patrick, Cartaxo, 2 March 1811, Murray Papers, MS 21102.

12 Murray to Augusta, near Condeixa, 14 March 1811, Murray Papers, MS 21103.

> I cannot myself reconcile to my military reasoning, the French going out of Portugal at this time. When they came in they neglected to throw a force into the Alentjo, which I have always considered as the ground work of their failure; and now that Soult is carrying every thing before him in the frontier of that province, Massena goes back. I can compare the conduct to nothing else than that of a man who should first tie up his Left hand when he was going to execute a difficult work that required both, and who finding the Right did not succeed, tied it up next, and let loose the Left. Have such blunderers been allowed to be the conquerors of Europe![13]

Retreat through a barren country at the end of winter resulted in now familiar ill-discipline. The British were appalled by the scenes they encountered as they hounded the French. Many of the local half-starved inhabitants were murdered, raped, and mutilated. The Portuguese retaliated with unconstrained brutality, taking out their rage on French sick who had been left behind. Many towns and villages were burnt to the ground as the French marched through. Wellington said that the French conduct 'has been marked by a barbarity seldom equalled and never surpassed'.[14]

Murray's regular letter to Augusta, this time on 21 March from Arganil (another pretty village devastated by the French) contained scenes of butchery carried out by them. He described the village as one of the most beautiful in Portugal or anywhere. He was captivated by the view of two little white chapels which could be seen from the surrounding countryside, accessed by two winding steep paths. 'One reflection I can not help making at every stop which is that it would be better to die fifty deaths than ever to suffer such miscreants to set foot in Britain'.[15] A few days later, from Olivenza d'Hospital, he wrote another of his full reports to Brownrigg at Horse Guards:

> The enemy is continuing his retreat towards Celorico. I need not detain you long with an account of the horrors which the French every where commit, Burnings and Destructions, Violations, and Murders are their daily occupation in every place through which they pass; and all I regret is that many more of them have not fallen, a sacrifice to the just indignation which every one must feel towards so infamous a Banditti.[16]

The unrelenting brutality of war took its toll on Murray's normal calm demeanour. In response to Hope's suggestion that he should be patient until his turn comes up for promotion to brigadier general, he snapped:

> I should hope there will never be a matter of doubt or hesitation, but if it is made so, I have but one line to take, and that is to beg leave to resign my situation here and live at home. For as I have always shown every inclination to serve, I shall certainly show that I have the spirit also to decline serving when I cannot do it with that

13 Murray to Patrick, Lousao, 16 March 1811, Murray Papers, MS 21102.
14 Wellington to Liverpool, Villa Seca, 14 March 1811, Gurwood (ed.), *Dispatches*, Vol.VII, p.358.
15 Murray to Augusta, Arganil, 21 March 1811, Murray Papers, MS 21103.
16 Murray to Brownrigg, Olivenza d'Hospital, 21 March 1811, Luffness Mss, GD 364/1/1216.

> distinction which I feel myself entitled to. With all this I am confident that in your hands my interests are well placed, and I hope that I shall not meet with disappointment in my expectations of the rank I have mentioned, but at all events I think it right to prepare my mind against the possibility of such an event, and to tell you the line of conduct which I will adopt.[17]

The pursuit soon slowed, hampered by want of supplies. A few hundred of Massena's stragglers had been rounded up and Murray's feeling was that Massena would probably fall back behind the River Coa. He was anxious to hear from Patrick how the reports of the turnaround had been received in London, and what John Bull's expectations were. Graham's recent success at Cadiz was singled out for praise, where the allies had held out against all French attempts to take it. He argued that it might not make a lot of difference in overall terms, but it was of great benefit to morale.

Weekly letters during this period continued, as ever, to deal with domestic, as well as military, matters. Murray consented to the partial sale of Fowlis Wester, a small estate the other side of Crieff from Ochtertyre, by Patrick, necessitated by a deteriorating financial position.

> The business has my most hearty concurrence, as being I think a most rational arrangement, and more especially as it will rid you of a load of debt, the greatest bar I believe to any man's comfort, and more especially to a man with a family who will in a short time have claims to be the occasion of many very considerable outlays.

Murray must have been told of the death of Charles Churchill's wife and hoped 'the prudence which I have understood she introduced into the family will not be lost with her'.[18] Charles was Murray's first cousin, son of Joanna, his Aunt. Joanna herself had been widowed in 1786 when her husband, also Charles, died in India. As a result of his wife's death Charles would soon be making his way back to Britain.

His view on life's slings and arrows was that everybody should just make the best of what might be thrown at them. For his part he was glad he chose a soldier's career, but acknowledged to Augusta that 'nine tenths of the fathers and mothers in Britain would rather see their sons adopt any other than it. If I had gone to India perhaps it might have turned out just as well. I might have been as contented, probably much richer, and you perhaps as well pleased'.[19]

His previous ideas about coming home for a month or two had come to nought, which he did not regret 'but I felt I could not, with propriety, think of such a thing. I am well pleased now that I judged so, and I am sure that your man would have been sorry had I not been in Portugal since the French began their retreat'.[20]

His mood was becoming more upbeat.

17 Murray to Hope, Santa Marinha, 23 March 1811, Luffness Mss, GD 364/1/1216.
18 Murray to Patrick, Santa Marinha, 25 March 1811, Murray Papers, MS 21102.
19 Murray to Augusta, Celorico, 28 March 1811, Murray Papers, MS 21103.
20 Murray to Augusta, Celorico, 28 March 1811, Murray Papers, MS 21103.

> If our information about Almeida is correct, Massena will not fight a Battle for it, and if it is not correct we shall probably not fight a Battle either unless we see a certainty of giving His Serene Highness a Coup de Grace at the close of his Retreat. If it comes to this we have the satisfaction of knowing that our troops (better at all times than the French) are now highly elated and full of confidence, and that theirs, beat at Busaco, disappointed and fooled before our Lines, ennuied at Santorem, have been hunted and hunted for this month past... At least in the management of the war in the Peninsula since the Battle of Ocana, they seem to me to have committed as many blunders as we could desire.[21]

Patrick had obviously briefed Murray on developments at Horse Guards. Changes were likely. Murray saw no future in his current role if things were to turn out as seemed to be suggested. Back in November Henry Clinton, the Peninsular general, had been writing to Alexander Hope putting in a claim on behalf of his brother, William, Quartermaster General in Ireland, to step into Hope's role as Deputy Quartermaster General at Horse Guards, on Hope's likely promotion to Quartermaster General there, in place of Brownrigg. He did temper his suggestion by saying that he was aware that Murray's name had been in the frame as a possibility for the position, and he would not want to do anything that might cut across Murray's ambitions. It was certainly less than clear at that point whether Murray knew anything about this – one suspects not. It is interesting that Clinton reminded Hope that the pay of the Quartermaster General in Ireland was a lot higher than Hope's as Deputy Quartermaster General at Horse Guards – a factor that might have had some bearing on Murray's anxious deliberations that were to occupy him for so much of the next year, which was to lead ultimately to his choosing the Quartermaster General position in Ireland, made vacant when William Clinton was posted to the Mediterranean. In fact Hope did not succeed Brownrigg, moving instead to become Governor of the Royal Military College, shortly to relocate to Sandhurst.

> As to the arrangements with Brownrigg etc etc, all I have to say is, that I should have been better pleased had our old views been carried into effect. A year however is a great way to look forward, and much beyond what a Soldier as I am without a family should give himself any trouble about. If I were to speculate however upon the Arrangement you mention, I should calculate upon my giving up my situation here when the Department gets into new hands at home. The new chief will be busy, interfering, and probably overbearing towards the branches of the Department abroad, which it is quite out of my line either to compeat with as to induce. But by the time these changes take place I shall have Rank enough to have some command of troops, and I shall adopt that line. Or if I have not Rank I will, (as I have already told you and Alxr) retire from business until other opportunities and other times arrive.[22]

21 Murray to Patrick, Celorico, 1 April 1811, Murray Papers, MS 21102.

22 Murray to Patrick, Villa Maior, between Almeida and Alfiantes, 8 April 1811, Murray Papers, MS 21102.

Murray wrote by the same mail to Hope again asking to be considered for

> Quartermaster General in Ireland if Clinton moved from there, or if he didn't get that, then something 'in consolation', and repeated his long held complaint: As to my situation here it has many attractions, but I am resolved not to keep it unless I am made Brigadier General. I have seen enough of service, as much and probably more than any of my contemporaries, certainly in situations of higher trust, responsibility and real utility than some who nominally have held higher rank.[23]

In amongst the military matters, Murray acknowledged that he was glad to see the advertisement for the sale of the wood at Lanric, although at less profit than anticipated, but it would help clear the debt.

> Things continue to go on well here. Except the garrison of Almeida the French are all out of Portugal that day month after their retreat from Santorem. Wherever we come up with them we beat them. Perhaps we might have beat them more heartily once or twice, but to have beat them always, and that without comparatively any loss, ought to satisfy us.
>
> It seems yet a little doubtful what we may be able to do with Almeida. If it requires a regular Siege we shall probably not have any thing to say for it. It is not worth the labour, expense and delay of such an operation.[24]

When writing about Almeida to Augusta and it being not worth having, he felt she 'will smile and say 'sour grapes'. He remarked that instead of her 'preaching' in her last letter – there is a reference to her having subscribed to the idea that all soldiers were reprobates – her latest letter

> has no preaching in it however, and a great deal about my acquaintances and other people which is what I like.
>
> I am very happy that your husband has resolved to give up Parliament and the concerns of the State. Some ladies would have their poor husbands always upon the stage and the world applauding, whilst others would willingly convert them into a piece of household furniture. You shall see what order I will keep my wife in. How I shall indulge in retirement when I have a fancy for it, and how I shall dash out into public life when the fit comes upon me to do so. You may think this very bold language; and I suppose out of friendship to me you will never whisper a word of it amongst your female acquaintances.[25]

The rather sudden reference to a possible married state may well have been an off the cuff remark, but may also be an admission that he was ready to look beyond the military life, which seemed to hold no guarantee of long term satisfaction. Significantly, having only

23 Murray to Alexander Hope, Villa Maior, 8 April 1811 Luffness Mss, GD 364/1/1216.

24 Murray to Patrick, Villa Maior, 8 April 1811, Murray Papers, MS 21102.

25 Murray to Augusta, Villa Formosa, 9 April 1811, Murray Papers MS 21103.

weeks earlier decided that he was not pushing for home leave, up pops the idea again. He had been speaking to Wellington about 'his interests at home'.

> I begin to think it very possible that I may see you in England in the course of this Spring. Since I wrote to you last I have mentioned to Lord Wellington my wish to attend a little to my interests at home, and I hope that in the interval of active service which is likely to follow Massena's Retreat out of Portugal, I may be allowed to go home without much inconvenience.[26]

Murray had now decided that he has waited long enough for promotion – he had seen others move up the ladder controlled by the men at Horse Guards, operating a system that he saw as outdated, and based on seniority dependent on the order in which individuals attained the rank of major general, with seemingly no credit being given for active performance in the field. There had long been an issue with officers agreeing to go on overseas campaigns and the effect on pay and rank. Murray had given his situation a great deal of thought, and was now prepared to leave his military career behind if he failed to achieve what he considered to be the promotion that he had earned.

> I mentioned at the same time to Lord Wellington the fair claim I think I have to the Rank of Brigadier General, both in consideration of the station which I hold in this army, and of the course of Service which I have gone through here and in other places.
>
> I have expressed to you of late something of what my feelings are upon the above point, and in making my application to Lord Wellington, for leave to go to England as soon as circumstances permit, I do it with the firm resolution of not returning to the Army, if the Rank of BR General is not given me.
>
> I have for many years been endeavouring to lay a foundation for some claim to notice in the service, and though I have not been [puffed] in Gazettes, nor cared to be so, and do not mean to lower myself by making a public boast of my Services, I know very well what the value of them has been on many occasions, to the several Commanders under whom I have been employed.
>
> I have held, it is true, important and very desirable situations in the Service, and such as, perhaps I may be told, carry with them their own reward, That I think is the case when these Situations are filled by Officers who go through the routine of ordinary and minor duties belonging to them in the way it is commonly done. But if such Situations are filled with views somewhat more enlarged of the nature of Duties belonging to them and a little wider range both of thought and activity, it appears to me that in that case they do not carry their own reward with them.
>
> Perhaps my holding a Staff Situation in Ireland may be made a plea for not giving me the Rank I ask for. Should that be the case I shall be sorry for it. I shall not however attempt to argue the matter, or to refer to the precedent of what has been allowed to others under similar circumstances. If the alternative is put to me of

26 Murray to Patrick, Villa Formosa, 12 April 1811, Murray Papers, MS 21102.

> giving up my situation in Ireland, or of being contented to remain without the rank of Brigadier General, I will return to Ireland and plant myself there. For if my seeking Foreign Service, instead of being thought laudable is to be made the ground of undermining my more permanent interests in my Profession, I will not bind myself to such a transaction. I have served enough for my own credit, and if my Services are not valued, and I am to continue to drudge in an unnoticed and subordinate way, I do not feel that either inclination or duty oblige me to exert myself any longer; and I will not throw away unprofitably all the views and wishes I may have towards pursuing a more settled establishment in life.
>
> I have thought it right to enter into this explanation to you of the line of conduct I propose to follow, but have avoided going into any details that would lengthen my letter too much, and which I can give you at another time. What I have said will be sufficient I hope to give my plans your entire concurrence, and I do not despair of it being sufficient also to satisfy any other of my friends who may take the trouble to enquire into my motives for abandoning the active part which I have hitherto sought to take in the Service.[27]

Meanwhile the British continued to harass Massena's army as it made its retreat from Portugal, often coming across scenes of French atrocities within hours of their being committed. It was rare for a village to escape, and Murray expressed some of his relief on entering a scene of relative normality.

> You can not imagine how much pleasure it gives me to hear the noise of a smith's Forge at work under my window after the dismal and silent desolation that pervades the tract of the country through which the French passed in their Retreat.[28]

Murray was incensed by the French actions, but was able to see a distinct contrast in the behaviour of the French towards the Spanish villages through which Massena was now marching, compared with those on the Portuguese side of the border. It was perhaps indicative of a more general support that each country provided to the competing armies – the Portuguese had demonstrated a willingness to provide support to the British at most levels, and there was a definite clarity of purpose in their joint determination to be rid of Napoleon, whereas the British never achieved anything like the same level of support from the Spanish population – a fact which angered Wellington from his very first meeting with Cuesta.

Near Penamacor, where Murray dallied for an hour or so on the way through, with its hilltop fortification and panoramic views of the Estrella Mountains, the hills towards Abrantes, the Tagus and beyond, Spain, provided Murray with a brief moment of solitude.

> [S]uch places set afloat a thousand varied ideas in ones imagination and occasion a pleasing Reverie of times past that contrasts very agreeably with the reality and intensive bustle of the present that one has escaped from.[29]

27 Murray to Patrick, Villa Formosa, 12 April 1811, Murray Papers, MS 21102.

28 Murray to Augusta, Pedrogao, 16 April 1811, Murray Papers, MS 21103.

29 Murray to Augusta, Pedrogao, 16 April 1811, Murray Papers, MS 21103.

From time to time Murray's sister-in-law would receive letters from him. He by now had reluctantly accepted that his brother was not a natural letter writer and Lady Mary would be a better source of home news, and a more appreciative recipient of his own although the numbers of letters Murray wrote to Patrick during the war never flagged, and almost matched those to Augusta.

> In our last march after Massena we had an opportunity of witnessing a very remarkable contrast. As soon as he and his Bandette passed the Spanish Frontier their conduct was intirely changed. The inhabitants were no longer ill treated, nor their property destroyed and plundered. It was most singular to see, within the distance of a mile, in one village nothing but dismay, desolation and distress, and to find in the next every thing meaning the face of peace and contentment – to see the sheep and cattle grazing in the fields, the plough going, the women washing their linens in the stream and the little Spanish brats playing about upon the green. Nothing could mark more strongly how much policy and injustice go and in hand with these French Scoundrels and how much discipline there is amongst their troops, and how much barbarity amongst their Generals. Pray let them be painted in their true colours to your children, and let the detestation of them be handed down in Britain to the latest posterity.[30]

The rain was incessant, and the resulting rise of the Guadiana posed a considerable obstacle to the proposed operations against Badajoz, to which several divisions had been detached. The army was not well prepared for sieges anyway and the allies seemingly incapable of supplying what was needed. He was sanguine about their being able to take the town.

Murray retired with Wellington to Villa Formosa, in response to signs of Massena preparing to give battle; he hoped if it were so that, as he wrote to Patrick, 'our old habit of beating he French will not fail us'[31] Almeida still held out, and starving the French out would not be easy, or quick. Although he thought that Massena was about to attack imminently, at daybreak Massena withdrew, but not that far as to allow Murray to say that he had given up altogether on the idea of relieving Almeida. He described the major actions of 3 and 5 May in which, the French attempting to force the village of Fuentes de Onoro, 'but our men beat them back very handsomely'.[32]

This was a fierce battle over three days which had stretched the allies to the full, and they had been within a whisker of defeat. Wellington said, at dinner after the battle, that he had never been in a worse scrape 'and if Boney had been there we should have been beaten'.[33]

The highland regiments, the 71st, 79th, and 42nd, were at the heart of the combat in the village. This was street fighting at its most violent. Fuentes de Onoro was a victory in as much as Wellington had prevented Massena in achieving what he wanted, the French suffering large losses, but the British had little to show for it.

30 Murray to Patrick, Castel Branco, 17 April 1811, Murray Papers, MS 21102.
31 Murray to Patrick, Villa Formosa, 1 May 1811, Murray Papers, MS 21102.
32 Murray to Patrick, Villa Formosa, 8 May 1811, Murray Papers, MS 21102.
33 Wellington to William Wellesley-Pole, Quinta de S. Joao, 2 July 1811, Wellington (ed.), *Supplementary Despatches*, Vol.VII, pp175-7.

> Since the 5th we have been looking at each other till this morning, when the French began to retire. It is not our object to follow them, and I am pretty confident they will not think it for their interest to attack us again.
>
> Massena had scraped together all the force he could collect from Castille, having added the Duke of Istria with part of the Imperial Guard, to his own army. The ruin which the Expedition into Portugal has brought upon this army of Massena may be guessed of from our beating it with little more than half of ours.[34]

Massena had failed to relieve the siege of Almeida. However, despite the British returning to their siege positions on the night of 10/11 May, the French garrison, in a daring escapade, slipped out of the town unnoticed, leaving slow fuses burning to destroy much of the fortress. Wellington was understandably furious, particularly as it was surely ammunition to his critics back home. As Wellington wrote to Liverpool: 'I have never been so much distressed by any military event as by the escape of even a man of them' describing it to Beresford as'the most disgraceful military event that has yet occurred to us'.[35] Although no officer was directly blamed by Wellington for this appalling lapse, there was a fall-out. One senior officer returned to England and another committed suicide at Portalegre two months later. The 'mad' Major General Sir William Erskine was also held partly responsible.[36] Wellington commented in a letter to his brother on the garrison's escape: 'I begin to be of the opinion, with you, that there is nothing on earth so stupid as a gallant officer… They allowed the garrison to slip through their fingers and escape… There they were all sleeping in their spurs even; but the French got off'.[37]

Some commentators have blamed Wellington for having a heartless approach on occasions. Certainly he was unsparing in his treatment of underperforming officers, and would not tolerate any feuding among them, to the extent of occasionally, as in this case, making an example of them in front of their men. Equally there were plenty in his army who had little but good to say of their commander. There are many instances, particularly in Wellington's private correspondence, that demonstrate a more sensitive and caring side. Wellington was probably no more a bully than many, handling responsibilities that would crush lesser men, and in the Peninsula he was up against the most challenging and unending difficulties. He certainly had a tendency to think that he was always right, again typical of his type, and he was intolerant of incompetent officers, of which he had been handed plenty by Horse Guards, but the majority of his senior officers, Murray included, found he appreciated the application of intelligent hard work, which he received in full measure from Murray, hence

34 Murray to Patrick, Villa Formosa, 8 May 1811, Murray Papers, MS 21102.

35 Wellington to Liverpool, Villa Formosa, 15 May 1811, Gurwood (ed.) *Dispatches*, Vol.VII, p.563, and to Beresford, Villa Formosa, 12 May 1811, ibid., p.547

36 When it came to incompetent officers, one of the worst was Sir William Erskine, whose actions or inactions at Sabugal cost large numbers of lives, and he was partially responsible for the escape of the garrison from Almeida. Horse Guards, on sending him out to Portugal, commented: 'no doubt he is sometimes a little mad, but in his lucid intervals he is an uncommonly clever fellow; and I trust he will have no fit during the campaign, though he looked a little wild as he embarked'. He died in 1813 and his younger brother James inherited the baronetcy and would play an important role in Murray's later life.

37 Wellington to William Wellesley-Pole, Villa Formosa, 15 May 1811, Wellington (ed.), *Supplementary Despatches*, Vol. VII, p.123.

ensuring a good, and highly productive, working relationship, which had developed into a close personal friendship.

Murray's report of the Almeida debacle was, as usual, less emotional than Wellington's, concentrating on the success in forcing Massena back into Spain, and again refusing to succumb to the prevailing pessimistic view of the Spanish.

> The fortress of Almeida was blown up last night and the garrison I am sorry to say constrained to effect its escape without much loss. This ends our operations here. [Massena being no longer in Portugal] is a glorious termination of the labours of our Commander.
>
> I hope we shall now try once more what aid we can give to the Spaniards for as far as I am concerned I am not yet alienated from their cause and not even from themselves in spite of all their misconduct.[38]

The Lines of Torres Vedras had proved everything Wellington could have hoped for, and proved Murray, and many others, to have been overly pessimistic. Portugal had been denied to the French. Murray's earlier gloom had given way to cautious optimism on the worth of the Spanish and their abilities. The cause was still alive.

38 Murray to Augusta, Villa Formosa, 11 May 1811, Murray Papers, MS 21103.

13

1811 – Peninsula – A Push for Promotion

With Massena driven out of Portugal, a period of relative inactivity followed, allowing Murray to think more about his own future. There was ample time for letter writing and he was more regular than ever in his correspondence with the family, as well as those at Horse Guards, particularly Alexander Hope, who held the key to his prospects in the Army.

Augusta had given him an account of her recent travels, including her

> march towards the Highlands and your sojournings with your friends on the way. What a different march yours is from those we make in this country…
>
> Although at the moment of bustle and action there is nothing that can exceed the interest of a military life, yet at other times the thought comes across one that to witness scenes of Domestic enjoyment, and to behold mankind engaged in pursuits of peace and industry, is far more gratifying than to see him straining his powers both of mind and body to lay waste the earth and destroy his fellow creatures. You must not imagine however that I am insensible to the glory that accompanies successful war.
>
> You give me great credit for writing so often, but when I consider that it can seldom make any other difference to me than a quarter of an hour, or somewhat more occasionally, whether I let you hear from me or not, it would be strange if I were to neglect it. It would be very odd too if I could not be composed when I write to you, which I have never done but in a house of one sort or another, whereas almost all the arrangements and orders which I have to make out for marches or manoeuvres of the army are written in the field, upon a stone, or under a tree, in the midst generally of what you would think much more than enough bustle and interruptions. The most complicated arrangements are those in general which must be made most when there is the least time and the least tranquillity.[1]

The promotion issue rumbled on, and on 14 May Murray wrote to Hope making his case, citing a number of factors that he felt that were needed to be understood, as the role in which he had been acting was a very different one to what he thought may be imagined by those back home. First, nobody had held such a position in the British Army on so permanent a basis;

1 Murray to Augusta, Villa Formosa, 13 May 1811, Murray Papers, MS 21103.

secondly, his duties embraced some of the most important branches of the service and they were completely different to anything required in a home posting. He had been responsible for countless marches and manoeuvres of the army, and suggested that his role, if less glamourous than those mentioned in despatches for being fortunate enough to pick off a few enemy stragglers, was actually far more important and influential. He could understand the likelihood that in the coffee houses and newspapers his job was misunderstood, but if the head of the army was still labouring under such misconception then 'the profession is low indeed'.

He wrote to Hope:

> The old notions, I suppose, of an issue of Camp Equipage, shoes and blankets, of lining out the streets of an encampment or billeting soldiers in a village, hang about those who have seen the QMG's Department conducted in another manner. And if these were indeed my duties I should think the drudgery more than sufficiently rewarded by the pay I receive.
>
> But I need not describe to you how different my avocations are. You know well enough that they embrace some of the most important branches of the service; and you know also that I am the first officer who has held that situation in the British army upon such an enlarged and permanent scale of service as makes it what I have described.
>
> It is always most disagreeable, I should suppose, to a man who has any pretensions to honourable feelings to allude to his own deserts, but I will not omit to mention to you something at least of the nature of those services on which I rest my claims to notice. I shall not go back to old dates, because I don't wish to write a catalogue of whatever services I can sum together. I shall refer only to the late retreat of Massena's Army, and I will assure you that if any subordinate officer has a right to be supposed to have had an important share in conducting the marches and manoeuvres of our Army during that operation that right is exclusively mine. If there was no merit in suggesting those manoeuvres, there would have been some even in drawing out every instruction relating to them and in watching day and night even, their just execution. And I might add too that where any slight deviations took place from those instructions, or from the suggestions on which they were founded, the ill consequences of that deviation were uniformly apparent.
>
> But if those services were ill executed (although I flatter myself to the contrary), or of they are in fact of trivial importance, or if the above is the only period in which I have had to act a part of equal trust and of equal anxiety and exertion, I am willing to relinquish at once every pretension to the notice of those who manage the concerns of the army. I know very well that if an officer is fortunate enough to surprise an enemy picquet...what sort of notice is sometimes bestowed upon him. But I feel that a long series of services, of far more general importance, are reckoned as nothing.
>
> The request I make of having the rank of Brigadier General is no very exorbitant one and hardly deserves the name of a favour... If it is to be received therefore with coldness and indifference I shall feel that I have already served too long.[2]

2 Murray to Alexander Hope, Villa Formosa, 14 May 1811, Luffness Mss, GD 364/1/1217.

Through all runs the thread that Murray was raising such issues reluctantly, only after a great deal of thought, and in the full belief in the value of his contribution and the justness of his request. Here is clarity on the importance of Murray's role in the campaign – he plainly had been given his head in planning and executing the expulsion of Massena from Portugal. This had largely been Murray's show and he wanted those at headquarters to take notice.

During yet another lull in operations, Murray wrote again to Patrick placing orders for firstly a 'cocked hat'. He had bought the last at Bucknell at the corner of Bond Street, Piccadilly, 'and if you please you may do the same. I wish it to be of the smallest pattern worn by Gentlemen who do not however seek to be singular'. His second request was for

> one of these leather cases (black or blue that roll up and hold combs, Razors etc), and I should wish to have it furnished with those articles. A circular silver box also to hold soap for shaving would be an addition, as I have only a pewter one, which is not elegant. This box should have my initials, or crest upon it. I like to have the above articles in the form I have mentioned rather than in a Dressing Box, which is less portable.
>
> This is a very unimportant letter to receive from the army, but I have nothing else to write about. The siege of Badajoz is too far off for me to enter into any details about it, and we have nothing going forward here.
>
> I hope to hear soon from you about my wood, and also about your proposed sale of land at Fowlis Wester. I should wish to know what my debts will amount to after this years Wood Cutting, that I may make a great effort to clear myself if possible in another season.
>
> This is not a proper time of year to mention it but I should like to have you plant for me some Sweet Chestnuts, Beeches, and what we call Planes, and any other trees of that sort that will make a pleasing variety, for I suppose there is nothing now but Oak and perhaps a few birches at Lanric Mead.[3]

The next morning Murray set off with Wellington on the long ride south back to Estremadura, unaware of the battle being fought that day at Albuera.

The British siege of Badajoz had been making little progress and it had been called off when Beresford heard of Soult's threatening approach. Soult's and Beresford's armies clashed at Albuera on 16 May. The battle was fiercely contested and both armies were left stunned by its severity. Each side suffered huge casualties. The combined allied loss was 6,000 killed, wounded or missing, the French probably losing even more. Beresford on this occasion seemed to lack confidence in many parts of his allied force and many officers and men had correspondingly little faith in their commander.

Murray, with Wellington and the rest of the staff, reached Elvas, close to Albuera, on the afternoon of 19 May, three days after the battle, and inspected the battle site on the 21st. Wellington was generous to Beresford and helped him rewrite the official despatch of the battle in a more flattering light than had been presented to him, seemingly instructing his

3 Murray to Patrick, Villa Formosa, 15 May 1811, Murray Papers, MS 21102.

staff to frame the report as a victory.[4] Nevertheless, the escape of the garrison at Almeida in the North and the lack of clear command at Albuera in the south reinforced Wellington's conviction that he still could not rely on his subordinates, and needed to be everywhere himself, with the immediate task seen as the resumption of the siege of Badajoz. Murray continued to juggle his official duties with his pre-occupation with his personal advancement, about which he again acknowledged the efforts being made by his brother and Hope on his behalf back in London.

> I have received this afternoon your letter of the 1st of May in which you give me an account of your interview at Chelsea, and your management of my affairs in that quarter. I am quite satisfied of Alexr Hope and you having acted with the greatest prudence, and the greatest friendship towards me in that business. I will do what I can to square my conduct to your joint advice, but I can not go on as long. I am quite clear with you that there is no need for arguing the matter, and I am very glad that you did not at your visit at Chelsea. I am satisfied that on that occasion you put matters into as good a train as it was possible you could, considering the character of the person you had to deal with. However, my resolutions remain the same as before. I shall not act upon them hastily and in a manner that might tend to injure my Military Reputation, but when an opportunity offers of resigning my situation here without that disadvantage, I shall be upon the watch to seize it. Whatever may be thought at Chelsea I am certain that my conduct will excite no astonishment in this Army when I do so. Do not allow yourself to be under any apprehension however on this head, but be assured that although the patience that I have so long practiced is quite exhausted, and I believe most justly so, yet I have prudence enough left to not to act with precipitation although I shall with firmness.
>
> Perhaps I shall write to you before the next Post goes, some account of the Battle of Albuera. I had not the good fortune to be at it, as Lord Wellington had not yet quitted the Army in the north of the Tagus when it occurred.[5]

In a letter the same day to Augusta he tried to allay her fears of reports she will have heard about a severe action, but assured her too that he was not at Albuera. He could not add anything about casualties that she would not get from the *Gazette*.

If the French were to have sufficient men to raise the siege at Badajoz then they might have to take them from Cadiz which would help the British there, but it looked as though the alternative of moving troops from the north and Salamanca may have already started. Despite this Murray still remained confident. On the morning of 3 June, 34 allied guns opened fire against the San Cristobal Fort, part of Badajoz' defences. Over the next three days progress was much slower than had been hoped and time was pressing – unless success was achieved in the next three or four days the siege would have to be lifted again in the light of news of a fresh French advance.

4 Wellington to William Wellesley-Pole, Quinta de S. Joao, 2 July 1811, Wellington (ed.), *Supplementary Despatches*, Vol.VII, p.175; see also C.M. Woolgar, 'Writing the Despatch: Wellington and Official Communication', *Wellington Studies II* (Southampton: Hartley Institute, University of Southampton 1999), pp.12-16.

5 Murray to Patrick, Elvas, 22 May 1811, Murray Papers, MS 21102.

News then arrived from London. Horse Guards had rejected Murray's request for promotion. He mocked the reasons behind the decision, and did not hide from his brother his sarcastic feelings about the man who was blocking his progress:

> Let me know what sort of grouse shooting you expect this year that I may consider of amusing myself in that way for the Gentlemen at the Head Quarters decline making me a Brigadier, in very pretty phrases, because they have not a brigade of cavalry to give to Colonel Hawker. This is quite a joke of Office. Besides it is rather hard to be kept down by a man who had sufficient merit some years ago to be made a Kings Aide de Camp, and who has added to that the merit of having married one of Mrs. Jordan's daughters, and having been wounded (by his own account) at Talavera.[6]

Murray wrote to Augusta the same day:

> I live at present in a little Farm House between Elvas and Badajoz, in the most rural way you can imagine. One room (the farmers best parlour) serves me for Dining Room, Bed Room, Business Room, etc etc etc. besides which there are half a dozen Swallows with their families who share the room with me. They make a great noise and sometimes dirty my brick floor very much, but you will easily believe I am far too sentimental to think of dispossessing them – besides which they were in fact here first, and I know no right I have to turn them out, any better than Buonaparte's right to the Government of Spain, which I for one I trust will never admit. As we are all self interested I will confess privately to you however, that I would gladly count the swallows into an alliance against the flies, towards whom I have no sentimental feelings, and who have intruded themselves upon my Empire worse than the Northern Hive.
>
> Do you know I should like to have it established by your Chief, that the name of your County should be always written Argyle and not Argyll unless you Campbells can show cause to the contrary as old as least as Ossian.[7]

That night an unsuccessful attempt was made to storm San Cristobal. A second attempt was made on 9 June. Again it failed, and orders were given to raise the siege. In the face of an advancing Army of Portugal under Marshal Marmont – who had replaced Massena – which was to join up with Soult, thus outnumbering a tired and bloodied allied force, Wellington ordered a withdrawal to a strong position between Elvas and Campo Maior. It was a disappointing end to a mixed few months. The battles had been successes, if costly, but the sieges had not. The French armies still survived in huge numbers. However, the tide of war had turned with Massena's withdrawal from Portugal, and the increasing strength and efficiency of the allies. Portugal looked safe for now, even if Spain remained firmly in French hands. At

6 Murray to Patrick, Elvas, 13 June 1811, Murray Papers, MS 21102. The officer Murray is referring to seems to be Colonel Samuel Hawker, 14th Light Dragoons, who was promoted major general in June 1811. He was married to Lucy, one of Mrs Jordan's illegitimate daughters by the Duke of Clarence (the future King William IV).

7 Murray to Augusta, Elvas, 6 June 1811, Murray Papers, MS 21103.

home the critics were less vocal and the Tory supporters positively delighted at the hard won victories at Albuera and Fuentes de Onoro, although Badajoz remained a hard nut.

The usual updates for the family continued.

> We could not succeed in taking Badajoz, and as the French came from the North and came from the South, both at the same time we thought it most prudent not to wait for them. I am sure you will think we did right, whatever the people may say of us.
>
> I have just got into an excellent house as to walls and roof, but doors or windows it has none, neither had it any furniture till six chairs and one table were brought out yesterday evening to me from Elvas. The floors are of Brick and the ceilings of the rooms are arched which makes it very cool. I can see from my window Elvas, Badajoz, Campo Maior, and at a distance upon a rocky hill, the castle of Albuquerque. Immediately beneath the Window is a little garden, which has a grove of fig trees and another of orange trees, a few fruit trees of other sorts, a small vineyard and a fountain with a stream of fresh clear water running from it. All this is perfect luxury, and well it may be to me for but the other day we were living amidst the ruins of Albuera, amongst all the disgusting remains of that battle, watching the progress of the two French armies and calculating whether or not it would be possible for us to beat Marshall Soult before Marmont came near enough to assist him, but as I before said prudence prevailed in our councils.[8]

Despite the previous denial of Murray's request for promotion by Horse Guards, some behind the scenes activity, including the Duke of York, had resulted in Murray's immediate promotion to brigadier general. The lobbying by Hope had succeeded. He wrote to Hope on 26 June, by way of thanks, recording his satisfaction with that rank and agreeing that it may, as Hope had suggested, be better at that stage than getting the bigger step up to major general.[9]

On 27 June he asked Patrick to do two things: to order a newspaper 'I should give preference to a well written intelligent paper, and one not seriously bound to either party' and to purchase a sabre and belt, and send them out by the first opportunity. 'I wish both to be neat and plain, not gaudy, and the sword to be of rather a small size and light, not such a Machine as William [Patrick's 10 year old son] would recommend for hacking off French Mens heads, three or four at a blow'.[10]

Murray's letter the following week to Augusta relayed the news of his promotion, a smaller step than he had hoped for, which left him dissatisfied. 'You will hear that I have been made about the oldest Brigadier General when I ought to have been the <u>very youngest</u> Major General in the Army'.[11]

8 Murray to Augusta, San Vincente Nr Elvas, 20 June 1811, Murray Papers, MS 21103.
9 Murray to Alexander Hope, San Vincente, 26 June 1811, Luffness Mss, GD/364/1/1217.
10 Murray to Patrick, San Vincente, 27 June 1811, Murray Papers, MS 21102.
11 Murray to Augusta, San Vincente, 4 July 1811, Murray Papers, MS 21103.

Quinta Das Longas, San Vincente. Murray's spacious, if sparsely furnished and windowless, quarters in June, July 1811. (Author's Photo, by kind permission of Maria Joao and Margarida Catarino)

His disenchantment with developments, and the lack of understanding back home of just what the Peninsular army was experiencing, had tested Murray's patience to the limit and he did not hold back in his next letter to his sister:

> You fancy Albuera was the finest battle in the world because there were so many people killed. An English Officer is very foolish therefore who endeavours to carry on War with Skill and not by main force. The true way to gain the favour of his countrymen and countrywomen also is to set about his business as awkwardly as he can, only remembering to follow Falstaff's rule of putting his fellows where they may be well peppered.
>
> I am sorry to hear bad accounts of the General's Rents. Peter speaks in the same unfavourable manner of mine but I was in hopes it would turn out to be only the old trick of managers who deceive their masters, when they are about, that they may put half the profits into their own Pockets. By the bye your husband may also have an interest in checking your extravagance, by telling you the rents are ill paid. I recommend you to believe him no more than I believe Sir Peter.[12]

12 Murray to Augusta, San Vincente, 11 July 1811, Murray Papers, MS 21103.

In London, the Prince Regent had decided to reappoint the Duke of York as Commander in Chief, pressure for which had also come from Horse Guards. The appointment was generally welcomed by the Army, including Wellington, and, somewhat more cautiously, by Murray, unclear as to the possible effect on his own career.

During the week between 18 July and 25 July there was stalemate in the Peninsula with neither side willing to risk offensive actions.

In his regular communications with Augusta, Murray went to some length to set his news in a context that would be easy for Augusta to follow at home. She was equipped with published travel journals and maps and could easily visualize the sort of distances between towns and villages, and the descriptions of the places he visited or where he was billeted, and sometimes the places the army was occupying. The right of the army was now dispersed over seven locations, the centre in more than ten places and the left in more than half a dozen, a number of miles separating them all. It is evidence of a confident Quartermaster General, in complete control of the positioning of several divisions, each ready for immediate action.

> You will think no doubt that we take matters very easily in scattering ourselves all over the Country in this way. However by a touch of my wand the whole can be got together again in a shorter time than it will take you to find out the places upon the map.
>
> Of course you will consider this Distribution of the Army as a great secret, and not to be published in the County Newspaper in case you have such a thing in Argyle.[13]

Wellington now turned his attention, as part of a limited strategy, to Ciudad Rodrigo, with a view to blockading it.

> The army has been put in motion. We had some hope of coming upon Ciudad Rodrigo in an unprepared state in regard to supplies but I believe we shall lose this hope, and probably stop our march before the troops get much further.[14]

Murray had, in July, coincident with his promotion to brigadier general, been appointed Lieutenant Governor of Edinburgh Castle in succession to Alexander Hope – perhaps as part of a package to deal with Murray's disappointment at his lack of promotion to major general. He held the post till 1818, before leaving to take on the Governorship of Sandhurst, in succession to Hope again. The Edinburgh position was a sinecure, but no doubt a welcome addition to Murray's income. Wellington had been briefed by the Military Secretary, Major General Henry Torrens, 'knowing the interest that you take in the welfare of Colonel Murray' telling him that the Duke of York had recommended him to the Prince. It would give him £3-£4,000 a year and an excellent house, to use when convenient. Torrens expressed his happiness that it might make up for Murray's disappointment in Colonel

13 Murray to Augusta, Portalegre, 25 July 1811, Murray Papers, MS 21103.

14 Murray to Patrick, Castelo Branco, 1 August 1811, Murray Papers, MS 21102.

Gordon becoming Quartermaster General at Horse Guards in place of Brownrigg who had been appointed Commander in Chief in Ceylon.

> I suppose you will be delighted to hear of my being made Lt Governor of Edinburgh Castle. I expect to be called upon by you for a salute when you come to the Metropolis, and that Peter will give a hint to open a battery upon the Baillies if they should get any new fangled ideas about the Representation of their City. For my own part I have thought of no use for the Artillery of the Fortress yet but to raise a Contribution upon the Grass Market once a week.[15]

Murray's correspondence with Hope during the remainder of the campaign increased in intensity and frequency following Brownrigg's appointment to Ceylon. He reminded Hope to keep an eye on Ireland for him, in case Clinton should be on the move, while now pressing his case for further promotion to major general. He was also in close communication with Brownrigg who was optimistic about Murray's chances of replacing Clinton in Ireland:

> I sincerely hope that your views on Ireland may not be disappointed. I do not think that they will – every possible consideration is due to your merit and particularly for the distinguished part you have acted in the Allied Army in Portugal.[16]

Never forgetting his scientific bent, he urged Hope, on his move to Sandhurst, to take with him the books that had been accumulated at Horse Guards, as he felt that the Military Academy was the place where they would be most use.[17]

In the meantime, Murray hoped that Patrick would have time to sit down with Mr. Duncan to work out his financial affairs. In particular, he was anxious

> about getting rid of this abominable debt that disfigures Lanric Mead, and as the prospect of extinguishing it comes nearer, I become the more anxious to have exact information how much still remains to be paid. I mentioned in a previous letter that I should make a Remittance before long.

He then mentioned, as he had to Augusta, his recent appointment:

> You would be glad to see the Lt Governorship of Edinburgh Castle put into such safe hands as mine in these times. It is a pleasant thing to have got this appointment amidst all the changes taking place in the arrangements and prospects at the Horse Guards.
>
> However I must keep my friends in mind that no man has better claims than I have upon the QM Generals department and at some future period there may be an

15 Murray to Augusta, Penamacor, 6 August 1811, Murray Papers, MS 21103.

16 TNA, WO 133/13, Brownrigg to Murray, Horse Guards, 30 August 1811.

17 Murray to Alexander Hope, Sabugal, 7 August 1811, Luffness Mss, GD 364/1/1218A.

> opportunity of attending to them in Ireland, in case of any thing moving Clinton into any other situation.[18]

He finished by reporting that the army was still moving towards Ciudad Rodrigo, where they arrived to commence their blockade on 10 August. Early success was very unlikely as the town had two months supplies, and the transporting of siege equipment from Oporto was slow.

The heavy equipment was extremely difficult to move into place. For this siege 194 boats were required to carry the guns, ammunition and equipment up the Douro. To haul it over the final 130 miles by road took no fewer than 384 pairs of oxen, over 1,000 country carts making two journeys for shot and powder, and 200 carts for engineer stores.[19] One thousand five hundred Portuguese militia were employed to improve the road and guard the guns. Murray, although not directly responsible, it being an artillery operation, would certainly been involved in much of the logistical processes that were involved. He had doubts about the likely success for the siege, which he expressed openly to Hope.[20] Throughout the war the British army in the Peninsula was supplied by a sophisticated lifeline, relying on the Royal Navy, which had almost complete freedom of the seas. In 1811 alone no fewer than 98 convoys of merchantmen, six of them containing over one hundred vessels, sailed from British ports. Delivering this from the coast, or as far up the rivers as the ships could navigate, was also an immense operation. There was a permanent force of 800 bullock carts. In addition the Commissariat employed more than 9,000 mules with muleteers carrying biscuit, rum, rice and corn. Meat moved on its own hooves.[21] All this was supplemented by the purchase locally of fresh supplies.

Over the next few weeks little was happening to prevent Murray again turning his attention to matters in Scotland. To Augusta he expressed his doubts about Charles Churchill, now back from India, being able to settle back into life in England:

> I believe I said something about my not being very well, which now would not be true. In your letter (28) you make a very true confession I daresay, but a very unguarded one for a Highland Lady. You confess that the Bag Pipes give you a Head-ache. I think right to appraise you that your pen has run away with you. ... take good care that your tongue does not play you the same trick and get you for ever into disgrace with all the legitimate Descendants of that Great Irishman who founded the Clan you belong to.
>
> As to our friend Charles coming back from India, all I can say is that I shall be very glad to see him. As to his being very happy at home however I have my doubts. No one I think would go to India but to make a fortune and if he has not succeeded in doing so after a stay of 22 years, he will be apt to repine and consider this period of his life as so much time lost. He will have acquired habits too and become accustomed to modes of life that will make our style of living appear very insipid. All this

18 Murray to Patrick, Sabugal, 7 August 1811, Murray Papers, MS 21102.

19 Knight, *Britain Against Napoleon*, p.427.

20 Murray to Alexander Hope, Fuente Guinaldo, 21 August 1811, Luffness Mss, GD 364/1/1218A.

21 Muir, *The Path to Victory*, pp.438-9.

> I fear – say nothing of the kind however to our Aunt, and let us hope that I shall prove to be mistaken.[22]

His letter to Patrick expressed his support for the continuation of the Dundas dynasty.

> Nothing has occurred for a long time that has given me more satisfaction than Robert's [Dundas] appointment to succeed his father in the situation of Lord Privy Seal of Scotland. It is a most just and proper Nomination, and one that must have the approval of every person in Scotland who is not a Desperado of Party, or who had no selfish expectations of the place for himself.

The appointment of Robert Dundas, a close friend of the family, was presumably welcomed by Patrick whose own career had started to look very shaky. He went on to say there was nothing much happening and no immediate likelihood of an advance into Spain.

> I dare say after all our triumphs over Massena this will be thought very odd in England, especially as we have been considerably reinforced. However, it is one thing to have been able to maintain Portugal against an ill managed Invasion and another to be able to invade Spain.[23]

Whenever there was a bit of a lull, and a chance for reflection, Murray tended to indulge his talent for descriptive prose, and so, of the massive grass fires that burnt in autumn all over the country, he explained that some were intentional, some not, and in a lighter note, he could not resist describing the playground antics of the officers and men, enjoying themselves away from immediate engagement with the enemy, at headquarters.

> We have witnessed scenes of this sort in various situations. We beheld the fire sweeping along the field of Battle of Talavera, whilst it was yet covered with the dead, and with the wounded unable to extricate themselves from it. We saw it afterwards raging before the wind at different times during our march through Estremadura and sometimes it made its way into our camps, before the soldiers had time to move their Arms and other Equipment out of its way. This year we had some grand scenes of this sort when the armies were opposite to each other in the plains of Badajoz, and the fire caught in the extensive tracts of land where the Corn fields join onto one another without fences or any other interruptions.
>
> In the day time, the volumes of smoke that roll along from these burnings of the Country are sometimes truly sublime; but it is in the night that the spectacle is the most brilliant, as well as the most impressive. I do not know how to describe the scene to you, but perhaps the most just idea will be found of it by conceiving to yourself a vast range of fire as regular and as bright as the row of lamps on front of the stage at the Playhouse, of the extent and brilliancy of which however, you

22 Murray to Augusta, Fuente Guinaldo, 21 August 1811, Murray Papers, MS 21103.

23 Murray to Patrick, Fuente Guinaldo, 21 August 1811, Murray Papers, MS 21102.

can only judge by recollecting that it is seen sometimes at the distance of fifteen or twenty miles. If you do not like this comparison you may represent to yourself a Host of Flame in one extended and continued front, marching in steady progression over the country and leaving behind it nothing but a black and smoking waste. When you have fixed your imagination firmly upon this picture fancy to yourself that you are looking upon an emblem of France inflamed by Buonaparte and raging under his guidance among the fairest regions of Europe.[24]

A few days later Murray described a carefree scene played beneath his window at headquarters

There is nothing going on here at present but some of our soldiers and some also of the young officers playing at foot ball in the Market place and spreading confusion and disarray in all directions. The whole Market is in an uproar. Melons, grapes, Cheeses, Corn sacks, pigs and eggs share by turns in the kicks aimed at the foot ball. The Market stands are overturned, and the modesty of the old ladies who preside at them is not a little discomposed by the awkward pastimes they are jostled into in the crowd. These are part of the labours and dangers of War that you do not find an account of in our gazettes.[25]

The peaceful interlude gave Murray the time to think of his creature comforts, and after giving Patrick a report on the latest French movements, he continued:

You must be in London I think by this time and I therefore send you some Commissions;

The first is to get me a pair of saddle bags from Gibson & Peat (Coventry Street, I believe) such as those mentioned in the enclosed extract of a letter from Col Offeney. [*Extract* – I believe called 'the improved Spanish saddle bags – although I am of the opinion that they still admit of a further improvement, by having the flaps on each side made sufficiently long to cover the whole of the bags when full']

The next is to get me a Portugal Cloak from Parlsford & Searjeant (Tavistock Street I believe). They make their cloaks as they say 'water proof'.

You may send me also a Simsons Euclid for my winter studies. The one, I mean, which we used at Edinr. I ordered some thing a good while ago of Messrs Williams & Armour Tailors, Conduit Street. I wish you would send to ask if they have anything for me. I have not yet got any account of the box with my hat, dressing case etc.[26]

Never one for complaining about the discomforts of campaigning, Murray had obviously been suffering from the heat of the Portuguese summer.

I feel much recovered by the coolness of the weather and can gallop about in the forenoon and eat a hearty dinner at six o'clock, which is more suitable to a British

24 Murray to Augusta, Fuente Guinaldo, 28 August 1811, Murray Papers, MS 21103.
25 Murray to Augusta, Fuente Guinaldo, 2 September 1811, Murray Papers, MS 21103.
26 Murray to Patrick, Fuente Guinaldo, 10 September 1811, Murray Papers, MS 21102.

The market square at Fuente Guinaldo, scene of the football game with melons. (Author's Photo)

> Constitution than hiding all day from the sun, eating some dinner at 3 and taking the air on horseback in the evening.[27]

A combined French force of 58,000 men had arrived to relieve Ciudad Rodrigo and Wellington had no option but to withdraw southwards to Fuente Guinaldo on 25 September, in the course of which there was a difficult moment at El Bodon with Wellington in the thick of the action, and fortunate to escape unhurt. Murray's relaxed demeanour, at least in his correspondence home, continued despite serious French efforts:

> I received your letter of the 30th August, No 31, two or three days ago in front of Fuente Guinaldo when the French and we were looking at each other in expectation of no very civil treatment on either side. They had brought together their army of Portugal (as they are pleased to call it) and their Army of the North, which were rather too strong for us; however we fell back very leisurely. The first day of their advance a few columns passed at El Bodon about 5 or 6 miles from our Head Quarters at Fuente Guinaldo. The 2nd day we put on a good countenance and stood

27 Murray to Augusta, Fuente Guinaldo, 18 September 1811, Murray Papers, MS 21103.

> in front of Fuente Guinaldo with less than half our army and obliged them to bring up all theirs. In the night we walked off, and left them to display all their fine dispositions of Attack next morning against nothing.
>
> On the afternoon of the 3rd day their Advanced Guard was again with us at Aldeia da Ponte, but they were received in a way they did not much relish. In the night we again moved back a few miles to the neighbourhood of this place (between Alfaiates and Sabugal) and thus the Operations ended.
>
> You will be much affronted no doubt when I tell you that during all this time I carried your letter about without reading it till this morning, after I came in from my early ride to the front of the Army. This was certainly most impolite treatment, but I hope you will lay all the blame of it upon those rude Frenchmen of modern days.[28]

Operations were over, Murray was well, and learnt that Patrick was on his way to London with his two boys, it being the start of the school year. This was the exact moment when Patrick had to face the fact that his hopes that the additional income from his place at the India Office would enable him to bring his family to London had evaporated, and that his private affairs were so much 'embarrassed' that he would have to curtail his attendance. The sale of Fowlis Wester had seemingly failed to shore up Ochtertyre's ailing finances. He offered to resign his place at the India Office, but meanwhile he would be absent until February owing to Mary's confinement, pregnant with Peter, their ninth child. Mary went on to have two more sons, the last being born 22 years after her first.

The summer's heat and actions in Portugal had resulted in very large numbers of sick and injured. After Albuera and Fuentes de Onoro there were nearly 13,000 sick and fewer than 30,000 fit for duty. Some reinforcements had been sent from home. Sir Thomas Graham had joined the army from Cadiz in August, and, despite a significant age difference, he and Wellington were to work harmoniously together. Alexander Campbell left for a command on Mauritius, and Cole was forced home by illness at the end of the year. Wellington himself was almost unique among senior officers in serving the whole five years of the Peninsular War from 1809 to 1814 without a break. It is interesting to ponder whether Murray might have equalled his commander's record if he had not been so concerned about the apparent lack of recognition and appreciation, not so much from Wellington, but from Horse Guards. Even then, despite his constant wish to be able to go home to attend to his affairs, Murray was very conscious of Wellington's feelings on the incessant requests for home leave from his senior officers, and tried hard to choose a moment where there was likely to be a pause in hostilities. He had already come close, but drawn back from pursuing the issue, in the light of imminent military activity.

28 Murray to Augusta, Quadrazais, 29 September 1811, Murray Papers, MS 21103.

14

1811 – Peninsula – Winter Quarters

The latest pause in hostilities gave Murray another chance to concentrate on personal matters. The increased income from his promotion would allow him to provide a little more by way of support for his old nanny, as he noted in a letter to Augusta:

> You tell me in your last that you still stew yourself, which I am sorry for. However you cannot do better than persevere in whatever you find benefits your health.
>
> For my part nothing benefits my health as much as beating the French, and upon the last occasion, I maintain we did beat them, although we did it walking backwards at the same time.
>
> I have intended for some time to mention to you that I think I should make a little addition to Nurses Pension. Having become a Gnl and a Lt Governor since the original grant I think Nurse should profit a little by the addition to my honours – be good enough to manage this and let me know you have done so. Give me notice when you are to be at Bath.[1]

As a brigadier general, one step below major general, Murray's ambitions had been only partially satisfied. Yet it is a nice reflection on his character that he should at once think of his slightly increased income as providing an opportunity to bolster his childhood nanny's pension. At the same time he grasped the opportunity to make further inroads into extinguishing his debts over Lanric Mead.

> I have this day written to Mr. Duncan desiring him to draw upon Messrs Greenwood & Fox for £600 on my account to be employed towards extinction of Debt. We must get rid of this Monster at last, even though Fortune should continue to refuse us any assistance from her Wheel.[2]

If his debt was to be extinguished (and evidently there had been no success in the Lottery), that could only be achieved by getting the promotion he felt was due. Having exhausted his

1 Murray to Augusta, Freineda, 2 October 1811, Murray Papers, MS 21103.
2 Murray to Patrick, Freineda, 5 October 1811, Murray Papers, MS 21102.

London options, Murray turned to his most obvious and influential ally, his commander. No one was better placed to appreciate the contribution he had made to the campaign, and no one carried more influence. Murray calculated that the blockage at Horse Guards would melt away in the face of a quiet word from Wellington.

> I spoke to Lord Wellington the other day about my having the local rank of Major General, which he said he thought was a very reasonable request, and offered to write home about it. This he will probably do by today's mail and I wish you to speak with Alxr Hope upon the subject, and get him to make some little movement in the business at the Horse Guards. It would be a desirable distinction for me, and I am not aware that a single objection of any might can be made to it.
>
> I have some thoughts of trying to make out a trip to England in the course of this winter, if there should be an interval when nothing is doing, and nothing likely to be undertaken.
>
> It is very pleasant to be floating amongst those who are high up in the World, and to be, as it were, in the Cabinet in Military Affairs of the first importance, but I must look about me a little to see what may be my lot when things take a turn, and this war comes perhaps to a sudden conclusion.[3]

In fact Wellington had, perhaps surprisingly, and certainly frustratingly, little control over the appointment and promotion of his officers. Dundas and his successor, the Duke of York, were unwilling to let Wellington have an overriding say in who received advancement, and Horse Guards always had an eye on the effect that elevation of a Wellington favourite might have politically, where the opposition might make major issues out of such patronage. Torrens, as Military Secretary, did what he could to accommodate Wellington's wishes, but Murray would have been aware that, even with Wellington's backing, further promotion was not guaranteed.

He was still impatiently waiting for the newspapers he had asked his brother to arrange, softening his earlier demand that he wanted a paper that was politically independent.

> I do not much care what paper it is or of what party provided it be not a particularly stupid one.
>
> I mentioned to you by last mail my wish to have the local rank of Major General in the Peninsula. I have several reasons for thinking this a very desirable object and I hope it will be obtained.[4]

His consistent views on what was admirable in the Spanish character are interesting, as spelled out in letters the same day to Hope, and Augusta. Their actions reinforced Murray's long held views that the Spanish suffered most of all from poor leadership, but in other respects were not as bad as others might believe:

3 Murray to Patrick, Freineda, 9 October 1811, Murray Papers, MS 21102.
4 Murray to Patrick, Freineda, 16 October 1811, Murray Papers, MS 21102.

> Having always upheld the Spaniards and their cause, under all their faults, and almost all their numberless blunders, it gives me such delight when they do any thing well. Their perseverance, their hatred of the French and their attachment to us (of all the lower orders I mean), are unbounded. Half our people have quarrelled with them because they are as proud as ourselves which is the very quality we ought to prize and to cherish in them. A Spanish peasant is as blunt a fellow and thinks himself just as much entitled to be master in his own house as John Bull does, and for my part although I should have been glad now and then to have a little more attention shown me in my billet, I could never but consider that a fellow who put himself by no means out of his own way on my account was much less likely to be tamed and trampled upon by the French than if he had shown five times more obsequiousness. Some people, I believe, imagined this coldness of manner to proceed from an indifference, if not a dislike, to the English; but the fact is that it proceeds from a characteristic independence of sentiment which pervades all the lower orders of the Spaniards and which holds them up against their oppressors in so wonderful a way. This trait in the Spanish character, together with the neatness and comfort one finds in every cottage throughout the country, convinces me that whatever may have been the defects of the old Spanish government in a general point of view, the lower orders of the state were very far from being unhappy under it or from being debased by it.[5]

He therefore delighted in being able to tell Augusta:

> In a small way Don Julian performed the exploit yesterday of catching the French Governor of Ciudad Rodrigo at his ride, with his two Aide de Camps. He drew off also 200 cattle which the garrison had sent to graze a little way outside the Gates. You see in what hot water my friends the Spaniards keep these Scoundrels.[6]

While writing to Patrick about the likely income and expenses of his Edinburgh Castle position, he also made arrangements for his groom who needed to send money back to his father:

> The enclosed is a letter from my groom to his father, which I beg you will have conveyed to him. I wish you to have £10 paid to him, which my Groom sends him out of his wages, and let me know when it has been paid. I conclude that you have some agent at Perth who can easily manage this matter.
>
> I should mention also that I have told my Groom that he may direct his father to send his letters to you to be forwarded to me. I suppose they will not be very numerous.

He had been asked to lend his backing to yet another request to look favourably on a young officer, a relation of his mother's, and his views on such patronage again are clearly expressed:

5 Murray to Hope, Freineda, 16 October 1811, Luffness Mss, GD 364/1/1218A.
6 Murray to Augusta, Freineda, 16 October 1811, Murray Papers, MS 21103.

> I had a letter from Mrs. Mackenzie lately about her son Roderick who is in the 77th Regiment now in this country. He was with Lord Forbes in Sicily, but as Lord Forbes is gone home Roderick will have to come and join his regiment. If you should see him pray write me what sort of a young man he appears to be. If he is intelligent and can write a good hand and possesses such ordinary accomplishments I shall be able to do something for him; and perhaps may make him my Aide de Camp. However I cannot afford to have any but useful men about me, be they cousins or not.
>
> I have written already to Mrs Mackenzie much to the above prospect.[7]

He quickly satisfied himself as to the young Mackenzie's worth:

> Since I wrote to you about Roderick Mackenzie I have heard of his arrival at Lisbon and he has sent me from there a letter from Lord Forbes who speaks so favourably of him that I have at once appointed him my Aide de Camp.
>
> My Portmanteaus are become so bad that I wish you would send me a couple to replace them. I shall put a memorandum about them on the opposite page. If you should quit London be so good as to send the Portmanteaus to Mrs Kell, 18 Leicester Square. I will endeavour to prevail upon some of my friends to bring them out in case no previous opportunity of forwarding them has offered itself to you.
>
> You will think this looks like my not coming home this winter, however upon that point I am not at all decided and still incline towards trying to get away for a couple of months.

The Memorandum is headed 'Two Portmanteaus for Br. Gl Murray'.

> The size to be about 2 foot long, I foot wide and 7 or 8 inches deep inside measure. The Portmanteaus to have Tops opening from the inside. Each to have a Brass Plate marked G Murray and each a canvas painted cover with the letters GM painted upon the top of the cover. The covers to be numbered No 1 and No 2 – as also the Brass Plates.[8]

Freineda, described by Murray as in a letter the same day to Augusta as 'a miserable half ruined village' near the Spanish border, was the place chosen by Wellington as the British winter headquarters. Murray had a wretched room which was not weather proof. The accompaniments to his letter-writing included the noisy conversation of his English and Portuguese grooms downstairs; another officer carrying on business, assisted where required by Murray; and a man nailing a board over a large hole in the floor. Another man was fitting a latch to his door and the masons were mixing mortar in the court, preparing, as soon as the carpenters were finished, to fit a papered window. With all this going on he meant 'to finish my English correspondence as usual, to take a good ride, and finish by eating a hearty dinner with my friend the Adjutant General'.[9]

7 Murray to Patrick, Freineda, 16 October 1811, Murray Papers, MS 21102.
8 Murray to Patrick, Freineda, 30 October 1811, Murray Papers, MS 21102.
9 Murray to Augusta, Freineda, 30 October 1811, Murray Papers, MS 21103.

Out fox hunting a week later he fell from his horse and broke his collar bone. He assured Augusta that it was nothing serious, it gave him no pain at the time and he made it home over a distance of about six miles leading his horse. Now and then it was painful if the broken bone moved. He urged Augusta not to attribute any blame to either the horse or his horsemanship:

> We were galloping downhill in the middle of a very capital chase when my horses fore legs came suddenly into a piece of soft ground so that he necessarily fell forward and I pitched over his head upon my left shoulder.
>
> The only remedy, my surgeon frequently reminds me, is holding up my head and lock my shoulders like a Boarding School Miss, so that I appear very much upon my grand behaviour. I think however in about eight days I shall be released from my boarding school attitudes.[10]

A week later the injury seemed to be healing well and

> I already consider it to be cured, but I must continue to nurse it for some time longer. It was broke in two places but after all it is far from being a serious accident.
>
> In the meantime I have had my apartment made quite comfortable. I have a paper window, a fire place in one corner and a portable bed in another. The latter is a luxury I have not had since I was an Ensign; in which high character I took the field with a much larger stack of Equipment than I have ever since had.[11]

Another medical bulletin, making light of the issue, was issued by the next mail:

> The long awaited mail arrived two days ago.
>
> I keep my arm in a black silk handkerchief still, for show, and to please my surgeon; to gain whose good will I also refrain from Riding. However were it necessary to run away from the Enemy, I think that I could gallop off with the foremost. I have taken my walk every day regularly (except One) since the accident happened, so that the breaking of a Collar Bone is no very serious matter you see, although I make no doubt you have been endeavouring for some time back to view it through the largest magnifying glass you could find.
>
> You mention Peter having quitted his Official situation in Town which I have not heard from any other quarter; but indeed he never writes himself, and I rather imagine Lady Mary supposes that I should receive that intelligence as bad news.[12]

Patrick, who had held office as an independent MP for Edinburgh since 1806, largely owing to the support of the Melville family, now faced a bleak political future at a time when he could least afford it. He had been informed that he would be discarded by the Melville Junta in favour of Sir William Dundas at the next election, and was unsuccessful in being

10 Murray to Augusta, Freineda, 6 November 1811, Murray Papers, MS 21103.
11 Murray to Augusta, Freineda, 12 November 1811, Murray Papers, MS 21103.
12 Murray to Augusta, Freineda, 20 November 1811, Murray Papers, MS 21103.

supported in the Perthshire seat, which was in the gift of the Duke of Atholl, who was giving that opportunity to his son-in-law. The last alternative might have been to do a deal with Sir Thomas Graham, who was absent in the Peninsula – now second in command to Wellington and close to Murray – to take his seat, but Patrick had always pursued a staunchly independent line. He felt uncomfortable with any close alliance with either party and as a result his independent political career was brought to an unhappy end.

On hearing of the sudden death of Charles Churchill simultaneously from Patrick and Augusta, Murray wrote to Augusta:

> We have every year something to remind us of the uncertainty of all our hopes and enjoyments, and to point out to us how very necessary it is to strengthen our minds against the losses we must sooner or later all sustain, and to prepare ourselves for misfortunes, and the disappointment of our most anxious wishes. I am glad my Aunt and Mary were at Ochtertyre when this [labour] came upon them, and that you are likely soon to meet them there. If they go to Edinburgh I hope you will be able to be with them there also for some time.

After updating her on some minor military events he closed: 'I had almost forgotten to tell you I am quite well. I rode from Freineda here (about 18 miles) without any inconvenience that day three weeks after my accident so that you see my bones heal easily'.[13]

The topic of Charles' sudden death was naturally still uppermost in the family's mind. As in the case of Isabella's, Murray was keen that no one should fall apart, sad though a death in the family might be. He of course had seen so much death, much of it in horrific circumstances and involving close friends, that he was naturally perhaps more impervious to its effects than the womenfolk back home, but there was scarcely concealed impatience in his comments when he compared the lot of many at the bottom of the social tree who had no time to grieve, and must of necessity get on with their daily lives after the death of a loved one. He seemed to be directing his comments, not at Augusta herself, but rather at Lady Mary or his Aunt Joanna.

> I am happy to have such good accounts of our Aunt as your last letter brings. On this subject however, I felt a half inclination on reading one of your letters, to administer a little sort of a lecture to you. You may say it was more than you dared to hope that neither the health of my Aunt nor of Mary would suffer by the shock, but thank God it has not. Now you must really not suffer yourself to imagine, that peoples health or peoples minds are so weak as not to bear up against the misfortunes of this life, if they prepare themselves properly for them.
>
> People may, by effeminacy and by ill judged imaginary refinement, fritter away either their minds or their bodies, but Nature has found us capable of performing our parts with more dignity if we will but attempt to do so. Remember my dear Augusta how many poor Beings there are who are doomed to see perhaps an Only Child, their sole hope and comfort, perish before their eyes, and are yet themselves

13 Murray to Augusta, Fuente Guinaldo, 27 November 1811, Murray Papers, MS 21103.

> obliged to shake off at once their heavy weights of affliction, and repair at early dawn the very next day to their usual labours and occupations. I am willing to make considerable allowances for difference of habits and of education, but I am not willing that people in any sphere of life should allow the vigour of their minds to dwindle away under bad habits voluntarily indulged.
>
> You must not take this as a lecture to yourself, my Dear Augusta, for I have said a great deal more than I should have done had I meant my observations for you. But however I cannot now write a new letter upon the subject, and I am not afraid of your taking blame from me that is not meant.
>
> I still retain thoughts of getting home this winter. It will only be for a short time however and I fear I shall be under the necessity of spending most of it in London. I hope by next mail I may be able to speak more positively.[14]

Wellington's attitude to the vexed issue of leave for officers was well known. Many went home to recover from illness and returned as soon as they had regained their strength. Others wanted time to attend to business affairs, and, not unnaturally, to visit families. Murray had been agonizing about the best time to raise the subject, knowing that he might be labelled along with others as less than fully committed. He was not acutely ill – broken bones were certainly not enough to merit leave – and at this moment Cole had jumped in with a request. Erskine had already gone, probably much to Wellington's relief, and there would no doubt be others who sought to take the opportunity that the Spanish winter allowed. Wellington remarked that 'Murray also I am sorry to say is desirous of going for a short time. All that I am afraid of is that on some fine day I shall be found with this large army without the assistance which is necessary to conduct it'.[15]

Having raised the matter with Wellington, Murray would have to curb his impatience for a few days while Wellington considered if he could let him go without major inconvenience. So he could only put Patrick in the picture and repeat that he was still hopeful of making it to London at least.

> I cannot yet say anything positive about my coming home. For my own part I think the present time the best, because, although we may be teased by expectations, it is pretty clear that neither party can now, or for some time to come, undertake any important operations. Lord Wellington however rather discourages my going yet and I wish of course to consult his inclinations more than my own but I do not by any means give up my plan of getting home this winter. I doubt much however being able to get to Scotland. I reckon it will take me a month to get home from here, and a month to return from London to the Headquarters of the army. If I stay a month in England it is all I can well propose to do and were I to give a fortnight out of that to travelling in Mail Coaches or Post Chaises there would be nothing left but a few hurried days of Shopping, Paying Court, and paying Bills in London.

14 Murray to Augusta, Freineda, 4 December 1811, Murray Papers, MS 21103.

15 Wellington to Torrens, Freineda, 7 December 1811, Gurwood (ed.) *Dispatches*, Vol.VIII, p.443.

> Such a calculation is almost enough to make me abandon the thought of going home, however there are many things that incline me to it.
>
> Stragarth seems to have made rather a Persecuting sort of a will. As to his Place I was never so anxious about becoming the Purchaser of it as you were, because the prospect of my ever settling in the Country is so uncertain that I never set my heart upon any plan connected with that idea.
>
> I am much obliged to you for the statement of my affairs that you have sent. I see now clearly what I am about. The price of the Enemy amounts to £3,496 and I am determined to subdue him whatever the cost may be. If you can make a stronger Division than £900 through the Oak Wood in the spring it will be so much the better, for if I can make out my trip home there will be no remittance.
>
> It is no part of my plan to save money after having paid my debts. If an accidental hundred pounds is ever mine now and then, of course it will go to the Heap, but I do not mean to grow rich by saving. I think I have done right to get a little before the World, but as a Single Man and a Soldier, I do not want more.
>
> I have received your statement about Edinburgh Castle and by it and Alexr Hope together I make out about £440 a year. Of course whatever liberality Alexr showed towards Old Tenants I wish Mr Duncan to do the like.
>
> I signed the Deed of Consent to the Sale you wish to make [the sale of Fowlis Wester] and sent it home by last mail under Cover to Colonel Gordon
>
> I propose addressing your letters always to Edinr – of course you will give me notice when I am to leave out the MP.[16]

A letter next day to Hope, acknowledging what must have been the involvement of the Duke of York in his promotion to brigadier general, also referred to Hope's new position as Governor at Sandhurst.

> I have no doubt of your finding your new situation interesting and of its appearing more engaging and important the more you enter into it... Viewed as a source of general improvement to the army, the institution is great and important, and its beneficial effects on the Service will become every day more evident.[17]

Murray certainly seemed to be putting the best spin on a position that had perhaps come to Hope as a disappointment given that he had been confident of getting the role of Quartermaster General at Horse Guards, which had gone to Willoughby Gordon, an appointment that must have disappointed Murray as much as it did Hope. If Hope had got it, then Murray would probably have succeeded as his deputy.

Freineda was Wellington's headquarters for some time – a welcome respite from the constant movement earlier in the year. While being stationary might be welcome, the conditions in which headquarters staff lived were Spartan, and the villages often decayed and dirty. Instead of coming across a smart centre full of 'gallant men on stately steeds' a young

16 Murray to Patrick, Freineda, 10 December 1811, Murray Papers, MS 21102.

17 Murray to Hope, Freineda, 11 December 1811, Luffness Mss. GD 364/1/1216.

commissary out from England found at Fuente Guinaldo, headquarters before the move to Freineda,

> half a dozen Spanish women sitting in a row, selling eggs and cabbages, and half a dozen soldiers in their undress were their buyers. Now and then an officer in a plain blue coat would cross the plaza, on foot or on horseback; and that was all that met the eye.[18]

Oman shared the same view:

> Nothing could be less showy than its headquarters staff – a small group of blue coated officers, with an orderly dragoon or two, riding in the wake of the dark cape and low glazed cocked hat of the most unpretentious of chiefs. It contrasted in the strangest way with the plumes and gold lace of the French Marshals and their elaborately ornate staffs.[19]

Freineda was not much to write home about – maybe that explains why Murray never did, apart from complaining about his quarters. Others described it in less than glowing terms: 'it is about the size of Ashted without the three gentlemen's houses in it… a village much in decay; in the streets are immense masses of stones and holes, and dung all about, houses like a farm kitchen, with this difference that there are the stables underneath'.[20]

The accommodation of the junior officers was generally wretched, and these young men survived on meagre rations, whilst

> the Officers of the Adjutant & Quartermaster General's staff were however invited to dine very frequently with Ld Wellington & at his table drank the best of French wines, which were from time to time sent him as presents by the different Guerrilla chiefs, who had been successful in capturing French convoys. The cheerfulness or gloom of our Commanders table depended much on news which he received from England, or reports from the different divisions of his army. I have dined there at times when scarce anyone dare open his mouth except to take in his dinner, & at other times when the conversation was constant and general & Ld Wellington himself the most playful of the party. He would sit after dinner a long or a short time according to circumstances, & when he wished us to retire would call for coffee. After finishing his cup which gave us sufficient time to drink our own he would leave the room & it was then expected that we should all go to our quarters.[21]

There was no lack of pricey food at Freineda, where three women suttlers had cornered the market, among whom was one Antonia, 'a stout lusty creature of rather a jolly countenance,

18 E.W Buckham, *Personal Narrative of Adventures in the Peninsula during the War in 1812-1813*, (London: John Murray, 1827), p.43.

19 Oman, *Peninsular War*, Vol.II, p.296.

20 Michael Glover, *Wellington's Peninsular Victories* (London: Windrush, 2001), p.85.

21 Muir (ed.) *Wellington's Right Hand*, p.229.

dirty enough' who 'amassed a considerable fortune by her attendance at Headquarters, to which she was attached for several years, her goods becoming worse and her prices more exorbitant each succeeding campaign'.[22]

The numbers at headquarters amounted to some 400 men, of which about one third belonged to Wellington's personal household; his military secretary, a dozen aides de camp, two Spanish liaison officers, a Portuguese interpreter and about 100 servants, orderly dragoons, and muleteers. The departments of the army – the Adjutant General, Quartermaster General, Artillery, Engineers, Medical, Commissary, Paymaster and others – all had a handful of officers and some clerks, but the need for servants, grooms and orderlies swelled the numbers.[23]

Wellington's habits were, when settled in a headquarters for any length of time, fairly consistent, rising at six, and working on papers till breakfast at nine. After that he would see the heads of departments including Murray, which would take much of the day. A ride was followed by dinner.[24] Wellington would read or write letters till he retired, and Murray clearly was busy doing the same. Murray's daily timetable was similar, except that he would generally go for a ride first thing in the morning to allow his servant time to tidy his lodgings and make his breakfast of toast and marmalade, and tea. As well as a daily meeting with Wellington, Murray would meet regularly with the Commissary General, vital to ensure coordination of supply with any movement of troops, and important enough when the army was stationary. Any shortcomings in this area would be reported very quickly to the Quartermaster General's Department and action expected to effect a rapid improvement.

Fitzroy Somerset had arranged for his brother the Duke of Beaufort to send out a pack of hounds. Murray claimed that on hunting days he could get almost anything done as Wellington despatched all business standing, whip in hand, eager to mount and be off.[25] Dinner-time at Freineda was somewhere between 5 and 7 o'clock and the officers generally retired to bed around nine. One of Wellington's cooks was 26-year-old James Thornton, who was engaged by Colin Campbell, the Headquarters Commandant, responsible for Wellington's household, servants and baggage. At the end of the war he became cook to Patrick at Ochtertyre, a position arranged for him by Murray. By April 1815 he was engaged again by Campbell to go to Brussels and, it is said, cooked Wellington's dinner after Waterloo. Although an invitation to dine with the commander was no doubt highly prized, Cole was reputed to host the best dinners in the Peninsula. To keep this up, he had travelling with him a cow, ten or twelve goats for milk, three dozen sheep with their own shepherd, barrels of wine and all the necessary pots and pans and dishes, tables and chairs, all carried on mules.

With no actions or troop movements to mastermind Murray had little to do and could not even participate in the hunting

> I never had less to say. As to my own health… It is very good, and I have been out again with the Hounds rather as a looker on however rather than a Sportsman, a

22 Buckley (ed.) *Browne*, p.200.
23 Muir, *Path to Victory*, p.495.
24 Muir, *Path to Victory*, p.497.
25 Larpent (ed.), *Private Journal*, p.96.

> change of Character which you will much approve. I have left off carrying my arm in a sling however as there is no use in looking interesting here.
>
> I am still unsettled about the time of getting away, but I will reckon upon paying you a visit before next spring. Let me know all your plans, but do not allow the General to advert to me at all in making his arrangements. I am too uncertain a being for sober family folks like you to calculate upon. We have no news and bad weather.[26]

At last, it happened – Wellington relented and gave Murray the permission for leave that he had been seeking, and he was able to tell Augusta that he was on his way imminently:

> Human life is full of uncertainties and a soldier of all others should be the best prepared at all times to take things as they come. This is my preface to telling you that I have got Lord Wellington's Leave to pay you a visit. I propose setting out from here the day after tomorrow, on my way to Lisbon. The journey to Lisbon is a matter of 10 or 12 days however. The voyage to England is no one can say how long and the Post Chaise from Portsmouth or Plymouth or Falmouth you may reckon.
>
> I shall say nothing about the possibility of the French inducing me to change my plans before I get to Lisbon because I see no great prospect of that, or I would not have asked Leave at all, neither do I include in my calculations the distance round by Verdun [the prisoner of war camp used by the French] because I propose getting home in a Man of War.
>
> Now you have all my History for the next six weeks. I shall very likely not write to you now by the next packet, as I shall be on the road to Lisbon when the Mail is made up.[27]

He made good time to Lisbon where was looking forward to a comfortable berth, and a quick voyage home. However he was not to be so lucky:

> I am very sorry at having to write you another letter from Lisbon, however having made all my arrangements with a view to going in a Man of War I do not like changing to the Packet although the delays we have experienced have almost induced me to do so. Our expectation is now that we embark on board the Leopard Troopship on Tuesday and sail the day after. We can not reckon upon being at Portsmouth before the end of the month. Be so good as send a letter to lie in the Post Office at Portsmouth for me that I may know where to find you, and what you are about.
>
> I wish you many happy New Years but not a thousand as my friends the Spaniards would.[28]

26 Murray to Augusta, Freineda, 17 December 1811, Murray Papers, MS 21103.

27 Murray to Augusta, Freineda, 18 December 1811, Murray Papers, MS 21103.

28 Murray to Augusta, Lisbon, 4 January 1812, Murray Papers, MS 21103.

15

1812 – Peninsula – Resignation, Engagement, Return

There is nothing in Murray's final letters from the Peninsula in 1811 to Augusta, or indeed elsewhere, to suggest he had any intention other than to return quickly to Wellington's side after a short break in London; indeed he had only chosen this moment, and received Wellington's permission to go on leave, in light of little anticipated action over the winter months. Exactly what Murray did when he first arrived back in London is not clear, but it can safely be assumed that he called at Horse Guards and paid his compliments to Willoughby Gordon, the new Quartermaster General there.

His late correspondence from Freineda suggests that his worries had settled down a bit – he had been promoted to brigadier general and was clearly relishing the successes the army was having in the field – successes in which Murray himself had played a not insignificant part. There was always the possibility of a negotiated peace, and it was reasonable to think that it was worthwhile hanging on to see the war brought to a good conclusion. Yet it was that very conclusion that worried him. As he saw it, a lasting peace might easily spell the end of his career as a full time army officer, and, unlike many of his contemporaries, he did not have the luxury of a decent income at home to fall back on. Typically he saw the need to think ahead and secure for himself a position that did not depend directly on war in Europe with Napoleon. A return to Ireland, in a more senior role that he had left, would achieve this, even though it might not promise the personal satisfaction of his successful service in Portugal and Spain. Underlying this was his continued feeling that his contribution in the Peninsula had been overlooked, and the army's career structure did not recognize the importance of foreign service and raw talent in the field when it came to rewards and promotions.

It does look as though there was some sort of deal done to get Murray to agree to quietly relinquish the Quartermaster General's role in Wellington's army to take on a position in Ireland – perhaps the offer of the major generalship, after which Murray had hankered, played a part. There have always been theories about political pressure to have Colonel Willoughby Gordon, formerly Military Secretary and more recently Commissary in Chief, take Murray's place. There had been references in Murray's letters, a few months earlier, that he thought Clinton might be relinquishing the Irish Quartermaster General's role, so perhaps there had been some correspondence meantime suggesting this for him and whetting his appetite. Perhaps there was too a natural inclination when home at last, to see the attractions of a more measured and ordered existence – Murray had suffered bouts of serious illness, a few broken bones, and had endured a hard life on the move, sometimes in appalling conditions, for the last four years, without any home leave. Yet the interesting thing about one of his more significant letters to Patrick is his well-expressed view that the Quartermaster General's role had, as far as he was concerned, significant limitations – too much administration and theory and not enough direct contact with ordinary soldiering. His brother had perhaps also said one or two things which led him to think about his future life.

He did not see any prospect of getting to Scotland. Nor did he want to inconvenience his brother who he had heard might be standing for Parliament representing Perthshire. There was, also, Lady Mary's confinement to take into account and he certainly did not wish Patrick to leave her until he was happy with her progress. But now news of unexpected action in the Peninsula led him to stress that 'the important operations that Lord Wellington has since been engaged in make me unwilling to think of prolonging my stay far in the Spring'. So at this point at least Murray still planned a return to Wellington's side. He told Patrick that he felt he was 'as well at the Horse Guards as heretofore but at the present crisis I still believe I judged right in coming to the spot myself'.[1]

In a further letter to Patrick he said that to follow any change in plan for his life as suggested by Patrick (and we can only guess whether or not this might have been matrimony) it would be necessary to be in England for some time, and he could not do that without giving up his position in Portugal. To do this against a speculative matter was a delicate question and Murray preferred to discuss it with Patrick in conversation. However he saw a real prospect of Clinton quitting Ireland and it is probable that he would be his successor, a pretty comfortable situation as regards money.

> All this however involves very serious questions as to my future prospects in the World, and I cannot make up my mind suddenly on the subject. Perhaps I may write you more about these matters soon but in the mean time the best thing you can do is burn this letter which has been written in a hurry, and with the interruption of several visitors but I was resolved to let you know what has been passing in my mind on the main subject of which your letter of the 7th refers.
>
> I cannot make any decision at present upon what you propose about my coming down immediately to Scotland.[2]

Mystery surrounds exactly what was in Patrick's letter of 7 February, to which Murray was responding, that seems so confidential. Whatever it was, it was clearly central to Murray's plans for his own future. The front-runner in those plans was to take the offer, which seems to have been made, of Quartermaster General in Ireland, which would certainly help financially. It would buy him time to sort himself out, now clearly of a mind that if he were to continue in the military he wanted a position that gave him direct command and contact

1 Murray to Patrick, St Albans Street, 10 February 1812, Murray Papers, MS 21102.

2 Murray to Patrick, London, 11 February 1812, Murray Papers, MS 21102.

with troops. His promotion to major general would certainly help in this aim. What, though, of the alternative that Patrick was seemingly suggesting? It is reasonable to speculate that this might have been some political position – possibly something in India, which Patrick would be aware of through his position as Secretary to the India Office. Or might Patrick have been keen to tempt Murray back to Perthshire and a life as a country squire, perhaps with local political involvement as an MP? Then there are the hints that the two brothers had discussed Murray's settling down to comfortable married life. Was his brother trying to match-make? Had Patrick a suitable young lady in mind, with a good dowry, who might be happy to be courted by a very successful and engaging army officer with access to the very top of society? Whatever the reasons, they were occupying Murray's thoughts completely, and another long letter to his brother followed next day.

> I do not think of coming down immediately to Scotland. It would be very gratifying to me to be at Ochtertyre, but I cannot at present make up my mind positively upon the disposal of my time. I mentioned in my last that I am somewhat disposed to see matters in the same light you do in regard to my action plan for life, and on that ground, as also upon other considerations I entertain thoughts at times of giving up my situation in Lord Wellington's army, and confining myself for a time to home service. It would require too much both of time and purpose for me to explain to you all the pros and cons of a military nature, that occur to me on this head, but I shall mention a few. In the first place the situation of QMG as it is arranged in our service is not sufficiently extended in the sphere of its duties. It embraces indeed all the great and important parts of the operations of our army in the field, but then it does not connect one sufficiently with the troops and the details of the service. These fall under the Adjutant General chiefly and although they are troublesome and often minute and unimportant compared with the employment of the QMG yet I am persuaded that it is very prejudicial to an officer to be thrown out of the way of all acquaintance with them. The fact is I think that the two situations should be visited on the same person, for at present the QMG has in a manner only the theory of war, which is grand and interesting, but he wants the details of the service, which though often vexatious, and of little general importance, are yet very necessary to be known.
>
> Under this view of the matter I am rather inclined to seek the Command of troops in preference to returning to the Staff. Although I am disposed to quit the Staff Appointment I hold in Portugal however, it should very wrong were I to abandon the claims I have to the Quartermaster Generalship of Ireland, and therefore I must use some management and caution in regard to the disclosure of my inclinations and the forming any final determination upon them. I have thoughts of opening myself to Alexr Hope next time we meet upon the military part of my plans, as also upon the views of life that you have touched upon.
>
> My own idea at present is to leave Lord Wellington's Staff, and step into the situation of Quartermaster General in Ireland. I should thus have time to look about me, and consider at leisure whether I am to devote the remainder of my life to being a mere soldier, or if I shall become attached to Society likewise by other ties, and even if the former should be my final determination, I think I might take the Field

> again a year or two hence without much diminution of Professional character or prospects.
>
> As to quitting my Staff Appointment under Lord Wellington perhaps I can now do it better. My late promotion gives an opening to my changing my plan of service, and I part from the situation of QMG of Lord Wellington's army with full credit as to the discharge of the duties of that Appointment and with the satisfaction of having been at all times upon the very best and most confidential footing with Lord Wellington himself, and on terms of good understanding and cordiality with all the other Officers of Rank that I have had to do with; which is not always the case with those who hold high Official Situations.
>
> This letter argues perhaps too much upon one side of the question; but however it is as well that you should know the substance of what I can say on that side – we may discuss the subject more fully hereafter. I the meantime I beg you will keep the contents wholly to yourself.[3]

As far back as November 1810 there had been talk of the suitability of the Quartermaster General's role in Ireland for Murray. Henry Clinton had written to Alexander Hope, assuming that on Brownrigg's moving from being Quartermaster General at Horse Guards that role would go to Hope. Would Hope then consider having William Clinton, Henry's brother, as his deputy? If that could be arranged then the Ireland position, currently occupied by William Clinton, would be vacant and ready for Murray. It was an important position and attracted a good salary, all of which might suit Murray. Clinton did go to some length to stress that he did not wish to come between Murray and the position of Hope's deputy, if that was what Hope had in mind, and Murray wished it, but still put a strong case for his brother to move to Horse Guards as Hope's deputy, which would suit him as he had reasons to be in London, and Murray to the Irish position.

At Freineda, De Lancey had stepped up to fill the gap left by Murray's departure. Murray seems to have given instructions that he was to receive regular updates on the campaign during his absence and the first of these is a report from De Lancey dated 19 February addressed to Murray, in London. During the following month, he was brought fully up to date on the sieges of Cuidad Rodrigo and Badajoz. By mid-March news reached the front line in Portugal that the machinations at Horse Guards were going to impact on Murray's anticipated early return. De Lancey wrote to Murray:

> Lt Col Campbell who joined headquarters on the 12th inst led us to hope that you would have left London for this country on the 1st but your letter of the 3rd has convinced me that we must not look forward quite so soon to the pleasure of seeing you again.
>
> I feel most sincerely obliged to you for the steps you have taken to obtain permanent Rank for me – it has completely revived my hope of ultimate success.[4]

3 Murray to Patrick, London, 13 February 1812, Murray Papers, MS 21102.

4 De Lancey to Murray, Merida, 25 March 1812, Murray Papers, ADV MS 46.2.15.

Nothing was yet clear on Murray's new plans, and the full address on the letter seems, perhaps unconsciously, to reflect De Lancey's wish that Murray's absence as his superior would not too long be delayed. His letter was marked 'Private – Major General Murray, Quarter Master General, British Army under command of Earl Wellington'.

Despite all the activity at Horse Guards dealing with Hope, Clinton, and Willoughby Gordon, Murray's idea of a move to Ireland was taking time to become reality, and in the meantime he adhered to the original plan of a return to the Peninsula. He wrote to Hope on his preparations for his departure, arrangements that would take about three weeks, enough time he hoped for Sir Thomas Lawrence, who was working on his portrait, to finish the work. This had probably been commissioned by Augusta, in whose possession it was at the time of her death. The plan was to change with dramatic suddenness within those three weeks. He confirmed to Hope that he would burn the enclosures received with a letter from him, all of which adds to the mystery of what was going on. Certainly it was something major and something delicate, or which might turn out, if discovered, to be embarrassing to somebody.

Murray, still in London, wrote to his old friend and confidante Graham on 10 May, with the first piece of real intelligence as to what had been going on behind the scenes and explaining why he was not returning to Wellington's side. There were a number of reasons which, taken together, as well as the timing of the offer he had received, were enough to convince Murray that it was time for a change. Running through this is the suggestion, made before, that he felt his contribution to the war in the Peninsula had been too little recognised and too late – even though he had gained the promotion to major general that not so long earlier seemed to have been less than likely.

> I do not know whether it will be altogether an unexpected piece of information when I tell you that I am not to return to the Peninsula. When I came home, besides some private affairs I have to arrange, one of my objects was to ascertain what my services were likely to lead to. On the voyage a letter passed me (from Torrens) holding out to me the prospect of succeeding to William Clinton, as it was understood that he was to resign the QMG situation in Ireland, after being fully established in the appointment he was going to fill in the Mediterranean. Had I got this letter before leaving Portugal it would probably have decided me to defer my visit to England. Having got here however, the case appeared to me somewhat altered, and I thought it necessary to consider it as my first object to put myself out of all reach of uncertainly in regard to my Irish Appointment.
>
> Besides the above considerations you know that my mind has had a bias for some time towards giving up the situation of QMG in the field. I think that the Appointment has too little connection with the troops to be long pursued, after one has attained a Rank that gives claims to Command. As to the importance of the Duties attached to the Situation there are probably different opinions, as there must be also in regard to the manner in which those duties are executed by me. However this may be, a pretty long experience had at least forced me to perceive that I was not on a road that led to any particular notice.
>
> My object is in future to serve with the troops, and I think I cannot break my connection with staff employment in the field better than in the mode which has

> at present offered itself by my appointment in Ireland, which will be notified in a few days.
>
> It has been offered to Lord Wellington that Colonel Gordon should be my successor in the Peninsula, which of course will be accepted. The arrangement is to be kept secret however until Lord Wellington's sanction to it has been obtained.
>
> Since I have come home I have been sharing (for the first time) in Perthshire Politics. Had it not been for the exertions of Government, which were latterly very eagerly pushed, I am inclined to think the result would have been different from what it was. There has hardly been time yet for receiving any positive decision from you as to your future intentions in this head, although I infer from what I have heard, that you will certainly be a candidate at the next General Election. If you should decline it however, I trust my Brother will have the full benefit of your support, and in either case we have very fair prospects I believe of success.
>
> I do not propose going to Ireland for some time and if I can be of any use to you here, pray address your commands to me under cover to the QMG at the Horse Guards.[5]

Wellington was deeply dismayed on hearing of Murray's decision.

> I rec'd this day your letter of 2nd and I can't express to you how much concerned I am that you have relinquished your situation with this army.
>
> In answer to your letter I can only express hope that you relinquish your situation with as much regret as I feel upon losing your assistance; and I assure you that I shall always be happy to receive it again when you feel disposed to give it.[6]

He wrote to Torrens the same day: 'I very much regret the loss of General Murray's assistance, to whom I have so long been accustomed, and who has been of so much service to me'.[7]

As the new plans fell into place, correspondence was also kept up from Ochtertyre with Alexander Hope, to whom Murray wrote about the defeat of his brother in the candidacy battle at Perth. He was loyal to his brother and maintained that he was the most fit and proper candidate to serve the county, even though the electorate had other ideas.

By early August Murray had taken up his position in Dublin and received more military reports from De Lancey, bringing him news on the Battle of Salamanca. De Lancey added a few caustic lines on his new boss, Willoughby Gordon:

> Col Gordon is arrived and is placed at the Head of all the Departments of the Army without the name of the Head of the Staff.
>
> It appears to me that he will place everything in admirable order, soon, but I think in some instances that he is endeavouring to apply a remedy before he has ascertained the nature of the disease.[8]

5 Murray to Graham, London, 10 May 1812, Murray Papers, ADV MS 46.2.15,

6 Wellington to Murray, Fuente Guinaldo, 28 May 1812, Gurwood (ed.) *Dispatches*, Vol.IX, p.181.

7 Wellington to Torrens, Fuente Guinaldo, 28 May 1812, Gurwood (ed.) *Dispatches*, Vol.IX, p.182.

8 De Lancey to Murray, Headquarters, 4 August 1812, Murray Papers, ADV MS 46.2.15.

Alexander Gordon, one of Wellington's aides de camp, and next to Murray and Stewart probably the man who knew most about Wellington's views and plans, wrote of his new Quartermaster General; 'Colonel Gordon is arrived and is likely to become a great man here. However I think him a very improper person to be in Lord W's confidence & the greatest Intriguant in the world'.[9] A few weeks later the aide's opinion had hardened: 'Remember me to Murray & Woodford; tell M that Everybody wishes him back here, that Gordon knows nothing about the matter, is quite a child out of his office, and I think altogether a damned heavy fellow'.[10]

Wellington was suspicious that the loss of the efficient and dependable Murray had been orchestrated as part of a manoeuvre to allow Gordon, a favourite of the Duke of York, to succeed him. Gordon's idea was to create the position of chief of staff, but this was vetoed at Horse Guards as risking a weakening of the authority of the general in command. Gordon's position was damaged further when Wellington discovered that he was writing behind his back to the Duke of York and to Earl Grey, the Whig politician and future Prime Minister, and that the contents of his letters were finding their way into the Whig-leaning *Morning Chronicle*.[11] Wellington wrote to the Earl of Bathurst on 23 September. 'It would be no great loss to the army however if he were recalled to England'.[12]

Certainly, on leaving Wellington in Freineda, Murray would have promised to call from time to time on Kitty, Wellington's wife, whilst in London. It is touching that on receiving the news of the great British success at Salamanca, and of her husband's resultant elevation to the rank of marquess, she should immediately write of her joy and relief to Murray, very much aware of the closeness that existed between the two men:

> My Dear General Murray
> I know you would enjoy the glory of my husband, that you would rejoice in his safety and in that of my excellent Edward [Pakenham].
> Edward led the attack and in Lord Wellington's <u>own</u> words behaved admirably. Never, no never in my life was as I so happy as when I read those few words written by Lord Wellington. My life my dear sir, has been for these last 6 years one of extreme, almost perpetual anxiety. But these are moments, procured for me by Lord Wellington's <u>matchless</u> worth, which repay me for all my sufferings....
> As well earned honours are always gratifying, I tell with pleasure that Lord Wellington will be gazetted a marquis this evening.[13]

Pakenham himself wrote to Murray at St Albans Street, London, perhaps unaware that he was already in Dublin, with some distinctly uncomplimentary remarks about Gordon's

9 Alexander Gordon to Charles Gordon, Cuellar, 4 August 1812, Tomes Mss (Correspondence of Alexander Charles and Alicia Gordon, in the possession of Mrs J.N. Tomes) per Muir (ed.) *Wellington's Right Hand*, p.307.

10 Alexander Gordon to Charles Gordon, Madrid, 25th August 1812, Tomes Mss, per Muir (ed.) *Wellington's Right Hand*, p.308.

11 Compare with Murray's correspondence to Hope and Prince William which Wellington must have been aware of as he merely regarded those letters as 'not very regular'.

12 Wellington (ed.), *Supplementary Despatches*, Vol,VII, p.427.

13 Kitty Wellington to Murray, 11 Harley Street, 18 August 1812, Murray Papers, ADV MS 46.2.15.

attempts at reorganisation and suggested Gordon's inexperience was pathetically obvious to even the most junior officers. Not only did Murray continue to receive letters on the progress of the war from British officers but he also was in communication with at least one Spanish general, Miguel de Alava, with whom he corresponded, in French, in a degree of rapport which not every senior British officer might have had with their peers in the Spanish army.

Murray's support of Patrick in his attempts to remain an MP continued, with letters to and from Graham, who wrote from Perth on 29 September on political matters. Graham had had to quit the Peninsula owing to severe problems with his eyesight: he did return for a period, at the same time as Murray, before his eyes again let him down.

When Murray was installed in Dublin, comments from his Peninsular colleagues about his impending marriage are tantalizing. An engagement seems to have been official enough for news to have reached Spain, and his fellow officers impatiently awaited news as to who the fortunate young lady might be. But then, silence. Historians have wondered whether Murray's wanting to return to England on leave was, at least in part, because there was a young lady waiting for him. This is the evidence that he was now, at least informally, engaged, yet it is hard to believe that during all the time that Murray had been away on campaigns he would have had any opportunity to court a suitable candidate. He had been on the go without a break since early in 1808 when he had accompanied Moore to negotiate with the King of Sweden. For a solid four years he had not stopped and certainly had not had any leave, apart from a very few days on his return, exhausted, from Corunna in early 1809. There is no suggestion in any of the letters between him and Patrick and Augusta up to this time that there was any particular lady who might have been the object of his affection. Certainly there were hints from time to time from Patrick that he should consider settling down but these were met with dismissive comments and there was nothing obvious to suggest that matrimony was on the cards. Perhaps on return from the Peninsula he had more time on his hands and looked up an old flame or met someone completely new in London. There is also the possibility that, spending time at Ochtertyre supporting Patrick in Perthshire politics, he was introduced to someone suitable from the county aristocracy. We will probably never know. Maybe the idea of domestic bliss played a part in Murray's decision to opt for service in Ireland rather than a return to the horrors of the Peninsula. There is no further mention of the matter, and what seemed a certain event strangely never materialised. In the way of such things there would have been plenty of time for a wedding to have taken place before Murray made his eventual return to the Peninsula, so the reasons for the original announcement followed by silence remain a mystery. Somebody's mind changed abruptly; of that there is no doubt.

Murray wrote to Wellington from Tunbridge Wells on 18 August to congratulate him on his victory at Salamanca, and received back a reply from Valadolid on 7 September carrying an admission of the gap that Wellington was now having to cover, with Murray absent: 'every day I have fresh reason to regret your departure'.[14] By the end of October Wellington had lost patience with Gordon, who on one occasion, when Wellington needed to open a line of supply through Corunna, took five days to produce a partial answer, pleading the need for more time to examine the 'profiles' of the country, a job which Murray might

14 Wellington to Murray, Valladolid, 7 September 1812, Gurwood (ed.), *Dispatches*, Vol.IX, p.398.

have completed in half an hour with no references to contours or any other difficulties.[15] Wellington accused him of having no talent 'except those of a clerk at his desk… He is no more fit to be QMG of the Army than he is to be King of England'. De Lancey, who is the idlest fellow I ever saw, did the business much better'.[16]

Murray was by this time in Edinburgh, perhaps carrying out some duties at Edinburgh Castle, en route to Ochtertyre.

De Lancey kept up his regular correspondence. As usual it was full of detail on the various actions that had taken place recently. Then he made it clear how much of a problem Murray's absence had become – but was not prepared to put his concerns on paper:

> I hope you will see Sydenham and Cadogan who are so good as to take charge of this and other letters of mine. They will explain to you many occurrences which I do not think right to place in a letter and which I think ought to be made known to you, as they concern yourself and the welfare of the army. I hear that I shall have soon to congratulate you upon your marriage. Can you get me the medal for Corunna. It is plain sailing, the statement of Sir John Hope that I served with his division on the day of that battle and that I didn't run away will be sufficient.[17]

Many others shared Wellington's views of Murray's replacement, and hankered for his early return: 'I must now tell you that frequently during this retreat I was much pleased to hear your absence from the Army greatly lamented'.[18] Even the Spaniard Alava joined in with his sentiments of regret.

Murray's close friend, Lowry Cole, wrote to him a twenty-page letter on 28 December, with a full account of recent operations. Whilst he thought that under the present set-up it would be unlikely that Murray would find himself in command of a division, nevertheless he felt that Wellington would be extremely pleased if he wanted to return to his old position. He too has heard the happy news: 'I am told that you are going to take a wife but I cannot find out who she is'.[19]

The Willoughby Gordon issue resolved itself neatly when he had to return to England at the very end of 1812, apparently suffering badly from piles, leaving the way open for Murray to resume his former post. Torrens – who had expressed his concerns about Murray's initial decision, concluding that the only reason he would have made such a choice, given his skills and prospects, was Murray's 'intended change of situation in life' – noted, when writing to Murray on 26 December that nothing in that quarter had occurred and perhaps nothing but its approach would prevent his return to Lord Wellington. Not being entirely sure where Murray was, he addressed the letter to Edinburgh but sent copies to Ochtertyre, where Murray had been staying, and to Dublin, underlining the determination not to let him off the hook and to ensure there was no delay in bringing him back into Wellington's fold.

15 Ward Draft, Ch.IX, p.41.
16 Wellington to Torrens, Rueda, 31 October 1812, Wellington Papers, WP1/351.
17 De Lancey to Murray, Salamanca, 14 November 1812, Murray Papers, ADV MS 46.2.15.
18 Lieutenant Colonel Maclean to Murray, Villa de Ciervo, 22 November 1812, Murray Papers ADV MS 46.2.15.
19 Cole to Murray, S. Joao de Pesquiera, 28 December 1812, Murray Papers, ADV MS 46.2.15.

> His Lordship expresses an earnest wish, coupled with the regret he has never ceased to experience for the loss of your services, that you should return to your old situation upon the Peninsula; and as the Commander in Chief feels that the good of the public service is intimately connected with your decision, His Royal Highness cannot fail to indulge a hope that your own private convenience and inclinations may not be prejudiced by a compliance with Lord Wellington's wishes.
>
> Your return to the army is of such importance – such magnitude that HRH must look to you for your acquiescence with considerable interest and solicitude. You stand too high in the estimation of the military world to sanction your retirement from that active course of your profession which will undoubtably lead to any elevation as a soldier which your ambition might suggest to you.[20]

There was no intrigue, he said, on Gordon's earlier appointment. It had only been decided upon after Murray's resignation. He was aware that Wellington had grave suspicions and asked that Murray provide him with some words that he could forward to Wellington to convince him that his suspicions were groundless. Major General Herbert Taylor, the King's Private Secretary, wrote from Windsor expressing much the same sentiments, acknowledging how essential Murray's presence with Wellington's army was.

There was total silence on the matrimonial front, but no more fretting about the future. Murray was, after twelve months away from active service, in a much more comfortable position, with a significant increase in pay and elevated status, happy to return to the role he had left behind, although with a much greater recognition on the part of those senior to him of the importance and scope of the Quartermaster General's role and his particular talents. Perhaps he had not given up hope of taking command of a division when he got back to Wellington's side – whether as a temporary measure as a result of stepping into a dead man's shoes (always a distinct possibility) or by more discussion with Horse Guards, although simply on seniority grounds any permanent appointment was unlikely. Maybe he just missed being an important part of the most exciting action currently taking place in Europe, or maybe he needed to get away following his broken engagement.

Kitty could hardly contain her excitement at the news that he was to return to her husband's side:

> I have just heard what has given me more pleasure than I have felt for a long time, more than the Regt of Royal Horse Guards Blue had given me, and that was a great deal. It is that you are returning to Lord Wellington. Pray write me a line to say it is true! Indeed I delighted at the thoughts of his again having the advantage of so able an assistant, the comfort and pleasure of the society of so valuable a friend.
>
> I will give you as many pr of pulse – covers as you chose and my blessing into the bargain, my best wishes and hope for your future success.[21]

20 TNA WO 3/604, Murray Papers, Torrens to Murray, London, 26 December 1812, pp.9-11.

21 Kitty Wellington to Murray, Tunbridge Wells, 24 January 1813, Murray Papers, MS 21104.

On Murray's return to the Peninsula in March 1813, Wellington welcomed him back with a heightened appreciation of his worth, and placed much more confidence in him than previously. His position in fact, if not in name, was very little short of that of chief of staff –that which Willoughby Gordon had sought for himself and so comprehensively failed to achieve – and arguably the second most important man in the army, in practice if not by strict seniority.

16

1813 – Peninsula – Advance Through Spain

During his absence Murray kept in touch with all that was going on in the Peninsula. Wellington had successfully besieged Ciudad Rodrigo in January 1812, the aftermath of which was the depressingly familiar scene of looting and destruction. From there the army marched south to the Spanish frontier fortress of Badajoz, a much more formidable obstacle. It took a lengthy operation in which the allies suffered appalling casualties; 3,700 in the storming alone, 744 of them fatal. When the allies did eventually succeed in taking the town in early April, more atrocious acts of undisciplined vengeance were committed against the inhabitants and property. For all the outrage that Murray had expressed about French behaviour it would have been interesting to read his comments on the orgy of violence that British officers were seemingly unable to control. Wellington wrote to Murray of his reluctant belief that 'We had brought matters to that state where we could do no more, and it was necessary to storm or raise the siege'.[1]

Wellington's major triumph by way of staged battles in the Peninsula was probably at Salamanca in July 1812. The French *Général de Division* Foy regarded it as his most brilliant offensive battle to date. This success left open the road for an advance on Madrid which Wellington entered, and proceeded to occupy, on 12 August. It was then essential for Wellington to take the citadel at Burgos, north west of Madrid, in order to continue his advance. Hampered again by lack of siege equipment, the attempt failed, and in the face of a combined French force, the siege was lifted and yet another retreat faced the allies. French overall strength was again the critical factor. The army suffered significant losses both during the siege and the subsequent retreat. In mid-October the army took itself back to winter cantonments just over the Portuguese border, and for the second winter in succession Freineda was the choice of headquarters. Madrid was given up and reoccupied by King Joseph in November. The year had been a punishing one in terms of losses and the numbers were, as ever, swelled by the sick, at this stage numbering no less than 18,000. But reequipping and better food saw the numbers of effective fighting men increase rapidly during the winter.

So Murray had missed some very significant actions during his year of absence. He was returning to familiar quarters, to an army that had tasted success, bolstered by the news

1 Wellington to Murray, Fuente Guinaldo, 28 May 1812, Gurwood (ed.) *Dispatches*, Vol.IX, p.181.

of Napoleon's disastrous Russian campaign, but which yet again had been unable to drive home its advantage in the face of superior French strength.

Murray arrived back in Freineda on 18 March after a high speed journey from London, on HMS *Favourite*, which, to the roar of the thirteen-gun salute to which his new rank entitled him, had put him ashore at Oporto on the 15th. Larpent records his arrival:

> The day before yesterday we had a most extraordinary arrival here in Gen Murray, the quartermaster general of the army. He left Plymouth late on the 10th instant and was here at Freineda on the 18th in the morning in about seven days and a half. He got to Oporto from Plymouth in less than five days, And here in three, travelling post on horses, ponies, mules, and anything he could get: he brought London papers of the eighth. His baggage went round by Lisbon. He was to have come out with General Graham and General Stuart, but was sent off here express with Despatches in a sloop of war. No one knows what the important news is which made it advisable to send out a quartermaster general as a messenger.[2]

The despatches that Murray carried at such speed were from Lord Bathurst, the Secretary of State for War and the Colonies, to Wellington, opening a discussion as to who would command the army were Wellington to become a casualty, the possibility of Russian troops being sent to the Peninsula, and, manna from heaven, an increase in the Peninsular army's budget from £100,000 a month to £150,000, made possible by new banking arrangements that Murray was instructed to explain.

He immediately picked up his old habit of a regular letter to Augusta. He had already written from Oporto on landing, filling her in on an exciting chase they had had after a French schooner. On the very day he arrived in Freineda, back in his draughty quarters and tired from what had been a record breaking journey, he somehow again found the time and energy to write to her: 'However now the journey is over I am pleased with it and all my old friends here high and low seem pleased to see me again. I am in my old quarters here with which you are already acquainted'.[3]

His return was indeed widely welcomed, including by Alexander Gordon: 'I am very glad Genl. Murray is coming back to us'.[4] With his new rank of major general and the clear messages that had been given, that Royalty, the army and Wellington really wanted him back, Murray, credited as being the only individual of the army who enjoyed the unlimited confidence of Wellington, seemed happy to adopt a role that placed him squarely alongside his commander with significant delegated authority. Judge Advocate Larpent was among those close to Wellington who recognised a shift in his attitude 'Gen Murray is apparently very clever and clearheaded. In my opinion he comes next to Lord Wellington, as far as I have seen'.[5] Augusta must have teased Murray about his new braid on his major general's

2 Larpent (ed.), *Private Journal*, 19 March 1813, p.76.
3 Murray to Augusta, Freineda, 18 March 1813, *Murray Papers*, MS 21103.
4 Alexander Gordon to Lord Aberdeen, Freineda, 24 March 1813, Muir (ed.) *Wellington's Right Hand*, p.371.
5 Larpent (ed.), *Private Journal*, 4 April 1813, p.86.

uniform and Murray replied: 'Your meditations upon my Gold Beads amused me a good deal. I am quite satisfied that they are very well placed where they are'.[6]

Possible negotiations with Napoleon were still on the agenda, but planning was well under way for yet another move into Spain. Whatever discussions had taken place during the time he was back home, Murray was most insistent that the momentum on his career plans should not be lost, and wrote to Hope on the longstanding debate on the question of retaining pay for a role in Ireland while on active service in the Peninsula. In the event of peace Murray wanted to ensure he was at the head of the queue for an appointment with a decent income attached.

> As to Ireland you already know what I mentioned to the Duke. I wish nothing less than to appear grasping or to be bargain maker about Public Service. I shall be very well placed however if arrangements admit of my retaining my hold of the Home Staff, more especially if matters assume at all a peaceable aspect, which is to be apprehended I think this summer.[7]

Although Murray was certainly busy preparing for the planned offensive, most days seemed to have a routine to them which he went to some length to describe:

> I must tell you how I pass my time here in general. I get up early and go out to walk as soon as I am dressed. I commonly stay out about an hour, which gives time to my servant to clean out the room and prepare breakfast. At present I breakfast alone, for I have no Aide de Camp yet, and the officer who does that business of the office does not breakfast with me although he comes to dinner. My breakfast consists of tea, Toast, Butter and Marmalade of which last a supply has been sent me by a friend at Lisbon.
>
> There is generally a packet of letters and papers arrives early in the morning. Then I open and read and sort those that are to be answered or attended to by my assistant before going to breakfast. I set to work upon my own share of business. Between 10 and 11 o'clock generally I go to Lord Wellington, and after seeing him I return to complete the business of the day. After that is over, I mount my horse and ride till sunset. Dinner is about 7 o'clock, and that concludes the day, for the people have an abominable habit of sitting so long at table that nothing more interesting or amusing can be done in the evening.
>
> I forgot to mention one very essential part of my business, which is that I see my cook and order dinner every day as my servant is taking away the breakfast things. I have got a very good cook who lived with Sir W Erskine. His only fault is giving me so many dishes that I shall be in great luck if I escape the gout.
>
> My establishment is far from complete yet. About my own person I have only the lad I hired in London, and in my stables I have Mrs Churchill's groom. Gordon

6 Murray to Augusta, Freineda, 5 April 1813, Murray Papers, MS 21103.
7 Murray to Alexander Hope, Freineda, 4 April 1813, Luffness Mss, GD364/1/1250.

> Monroe is still at Lisbon, and my groom Andrew has not yet made his appearance with my horses and baggage from Ireland.
>
> You must not suppose from the sketch I have given you about that my life is always so regular. Tomorrow for instance I am going from home to dine with Major General Kempt. Afterwards to go to a play (performed by officers of the Light Division) and then to a supper. However if I can I will cut the latter part of the entertainment and ride home.[8]

Then, after the event, he could not resist a description of the evening's entertainment:

> I don't suppose you are acquainted with any of the players either men or women, And all I can tell you of them is that one (Capt. Beckwith) is an assistant in my department, and manager of the theatre, and another (Lt. Pemberton) is the brother of Sir Alex Campbell's wife, and is as classy a performer upon the stage as I have seen anywhere.
>
> What will shock you most of all in our theatricals however, is that the play house is a church. At almost every village in this country besides the Church of the place (which is generally in the middle of the village) there is also a small chapel at the distance of about two or three hundred yards in the country. It is a small chapel of this sort at Gallegos that has been fitted up as a theatre. There is a sufficient stage, and very good scenery. That Pit is spacious and the rows of benches are raised as they retire from the front. There are no boxes, but there is a good large gallery, which is the seat of honour, and the great ascend to it by a narrow winding stair leading to the Belfry. The whole playhouse is about as large as the Kirk of Monzievaird but much handsomer.
>
> We dined with Genl. Kempt, who gave us a supper also after the play and I got home to Freineda which is 10 miles from Gallegos – at three the next morning. You may see from this that it is not a very <u>triste</u> thing to be a soldier.[9]

A few months later Larpent was commenting on Murray who was again worryingly noted as 'not quite well' as being 'the life and soul of the army next to Lord Wellington, … he appears to me to be decidedly the second man, and it is thought that without him and perhaps Kennedy and the Commissary in Chief we could never have done what we have'.[10] The relationship between Wellington and his Quartermaster General was now very close and probably enabled Murray, more than the other generals, to challenge Wellington's views, to stand up to him while all the time remaining loyal – he certainly had not forgotten Wellington's ability to dismember those who did not measure up. One officer, flustered in an interview with the commander of the forces, was the subject of a remark from Wellington: 'I took care to let him feel that I thought him very stupid'. Upon which Murray commented in an aside: 'That must have been by telling him so in plain terms, I have no doubt'.[11]

8 Murray to Augusta, Freineda, 14 April 1813, Murray Papers, MS 21103.
9 Murray to Augusta, Freineda, 18 April 1813, Murray Papers, MS 21103.
10 Larpent (ed.), *Private Journal*, 16 July 1813, p.188.
11 Larpent (ed.), *Private Journal*, 24 April 1813, p.96.

Murray set about immersing himself in accumulating first hand topographical information and mapping the extensive territory through which Wellington's planned advance northwards would move, in a concerted effort to drive the French back across the Pyrenees. The army, significantly enlarged by the addition of Portuguese and Spanish troops, the latter now under Wellington's direct command, was in as good shape, both in terms of morale and physically, as it had ever been. The winter months in cantonments had improved its health immeasurably, and fresh troops had been sent from England. Reequipping took place, including the arrival of lightweight camp kettles and of tents, thus far in the campaign not generally used by the army and enthusiastically welcomed by the soldiers. Arrangements had to be made to carry the tents, and experiments took place involving submerging a tent in a river then hanging it out to dry for half an hour before weighing it to calculate how many tents a mule could carry, they having been freed up by the lighter camp kettles now to be carried by the men themselves. More attention was paid to areas suitable for encampment. Plans on large sheets of tracing paper detailing the exact layout of tents for various numbers in a camp were sent from Horse Guards by the recently-returned Gordon, precise in the scale and measurements, tent by tent, line by line, even down to the dimensions of the trench for horse dung, and the months in such an environment saw levels of training and preparedness for campaigning taken to a higher level.[12]

Each soldier was to be equipped with a lighter billhook used for cutting brush and firewood. This, along with the instructions for the layout of camps, and issue of the lighter camp kettles, was to be organised by Murray's department and he took direct control of all such issues. 'As it will be impossible to complete the army with bill hooks we must find a substitute for them. I believe the best things to be had are the pruning knives used by the people of the country for pruning the Vines'.[13]

Murray was now pretty settled with all that a major general required.

> I have at last got all my establishment united, and I have the pleasure of thinking there are few people better served, or better mounted than I am. Indeed in respect to Horses I ought to be pretty well off, for those I have here, (eight in number) have cost me £658, exclusive of all collateral expenses attaching them.
>
> I shall be in much need of a rise of rents at Lanric Mead.[14]

Lieutenant Generals Graham and Picton had also returned to the army. On 12 May there was activity at Freineda, including the packing of Wellington's claret.[15] Rowland Hill had already made a start towards Spain with his corps. One final grand occasion was staged – an anniversary dinner on 16 May commemorating the Battle of Albuera, in honour of Beresford's victory, at which 'Full medals were worn to provide a "glittering array" by the assembly of high ranking British and Portuguese officers, their staffs, Wellington's personal staff and his heads of department'.[16]

12 20 April 1813, Murray Papers, ADV MS 46.2.16.

13 Murray to Sir K.H. Kennedy, Freineda, 5 May 1813, Murray Papers, ADV MS 46.2.17.

14 Murray to Augusta, Freineda, 12 May 1813, Murray Papers, MS 21103.

15 Larpent (ed.), *Private Journal*, p.112.

16 John Sweetman, *Raglan. From the Peninsula to the Crimea* (Barnsley: Pen & Sword, 2010), p.40.

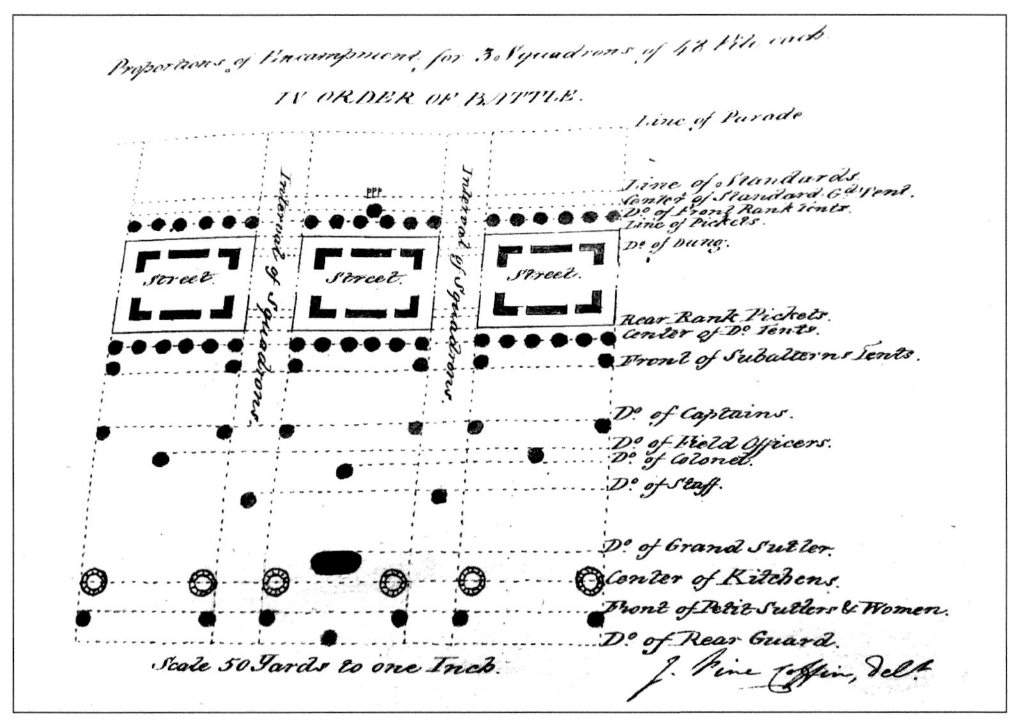

A typical plan of a camp prepared by Horse Guards. 'To find the front required for a battalion of infantry – multiply the number of files by 22 and divide that product by 36 which will give the answer in yards. From this product deduct 5 times the number of companies of which the corps consists for the standing of the tents and the remainder will be the total breadth of all the tents'. (Author's photo from Murray Papers in The National Library of Scotland)

The final push to expel the French from the Peninsula was under way within hours of the last revolution of the port. Murray left Freineda on the 22nd, reaching Matilla on the 25th which he described with his usual eye for detail to Augusta, finishing:

> Add to this view that I have described, a dusty ride from Tamares – a hot sun – and best of all a tolerable dinner, actually upon my table, and my friends waiting until I finish the note and you may be able to persuade yourself that I have some enjoyments and also to find a good apology for finishing this letter.[17]

Wellington had negotiated well with the Spanish authorities at Cadiz in January, in the face of much disgruntlement among senior figures, providing him with command of a less top-heavy force. The defeat of Napoleon's army in Russia had resulted in the withdrawal of some French troops from Spain, and the armies that remained in various parts of the country were being very effectively pinned down by Spanish guerrillas. Intelligence was flowing at

17 Murray to Augusta, Matilla, 25 May 1813, Murray Papers, MS 21103.

an increased rate and local Spanish were reassessing their loyalties in the face of what was looking like a turning of the tide in Wellington's favour.

The army, with Hill's corps in the van, always in close communication with Murray, crossed the Douro, and marched rapidly over the mostly well mapped and planned routes, although there were times when it was impossible to move men and equipment at more than a snail's pace over almost impassable tracks. Murray orchestrated the flanking movement through the rugged terrain of Portugal's north-west province, Tras-os-Montes, which required immensely detailed planning and co-ordination and a constant flow of maps, from officers of his department sent ahead. The army was divided into three parts, each with its own route, and Murray's skills in planning and coordinating the advance is evident from the mass of orders and reports of progress, including up to date reports on the state of various roads, that flowed to and from him, including the impressive exercise in crossing the Douro. The Quartermaster General's Department, now numbering 32, was at full stretch. The success of this massive movement by which over 50,000 men, with artillery, countless horses, baggage animals, and bullocks were moved over 150 miles of roads, upon none of which Wellington nor any of his principal staff officers had ever set eyes, and crossed two large rivers, without losing a day of the time allowed was as much a tribute to Murray's skills and to his officers' maps as it was to Wellington's audacity in proposing it.[18]

Wellington, Murray, and most of the staff took the central route, re-entered Salamanca, but did not halt, moving swiftly in pursuit of the retreating French, past Burgos, which the French blew up, much to British relief.

> I have seldom had more occupation than since the army was put in motion, but all goes on well and I have seldom had greater satisfaction. We are manoeuvring the enemy out of the Country. They have blown up Burgos. The left of our army will cross the Ebro tomorrow and the whole I trust will be over that river on the 16th.[19]

By the 18th Wellington's corps had caught up with the French. 'We are in the presence of the enemy but cannot ascertain his force on account of the hills'.[20]

Messages and orders flowed incessantly on an hourly basis – Murray, Graham, and Hill were in constant communication with each other and shared information about what they could see on front of them or what intelligence was being brought to them by locals. As always there was the possibility of orders going astray, as happened with one to Rowland Hill:

> I wrote to you at 2 pm today to request you would halt your troops, but I understand the letter was lost on the way by a sergeant of Dragoons who was the bearer of it. I fear this accident left you for some time in suspense, and would give you the appearance of my having forgotten you.[21]

18 Smith, 'Peninsular War Cartography', p 241; Ward, *Wellingtons Headquarters*, p.111.

19 Murray to Augusta, Villadiego, 13 June 1813, Murray Papers, MS 21103.

20 Murray to Hill, Benavente, 18 June 1813, Murray Papers, ADV MS 46.2.18.

21 Murrsay to Hill, Benavente, 18 June 1813, Murray Papers, ADV MS 46.2.18.

The next day Murray was able to report to Graham that he was in sight of Vitoria, where the next major battle would be fought. 'We can see from the ground of the 4th Division Vitoria and I suppose the whole army of the Enemy'.[22]

On the 20th Murray asked Cole for an update on the enemy's situation overnight, and on the 21st he started to disseminate orders to the various generals for placing their troops for battle.

The French had retreated towards the town where they were brought to a halt by vast numbers of vehicles, camp followers, and civilians making their slow way back on the main road towards France. They would have to make a stand. Approximately 57,000 French were to take the field against 75,000 allies.[23] A hard fought battle resulted in the continuation of the French retreat but this time without much of the booty that they had carried with them this far. Almost all of this fell into the grateful hands of the allied soldiers, everything from masses of gold and silver coins, to watches, spyglasses, and jewellery as well as more useful items such as new shoes, and not a few women, described as '*un bordel ambulant*', who abandoned the French and now sought the protection of the British soldiers. Succumbing to the temptation of such valuable plunder interfered badly with the pursuit that the allies should have been making after the French. Wellington was incensed by the behaviour of his men, including some officers whom he stripped of command.

Huge quantities of guns, stores and artillery wagons were captured after the one-sided battle, although there was still criticism that more should have been made of the rout and the French should have been cut off from their retreat. King Joseph lost all his private baggage at Vitoria, including his silver chamber pot (which became the regimental souvenir of the 14th Light Dragoons), and, of perhaps more military relevance, the French Army's code book, the Grand Paris Cipher, pounced on eagerly by Scovell. Wellington cast an eye over a mass of artworks from Joseph's baggage, and sent them home for safekeeping. Included in the collection were paintings by Titian, Velazquez, and Murillo, from the Royal Collection in Madrid. Later he offered to return them but Spain's King Ferdinand insisted they be treated as a gift and they now hang at Apsley House.

In the chaotic aftermath of the battle there were still some clear heads at work, and Murray hurriedly suggested to Wellington that it might be possible to cut off a large part of the retreating French army:

> It appears to me from the map, that by moving a part of the left column of the army upon Villa Franca we might be enabled to cut in upon the Bayonne road, and intercept perhaps some part of the Enemy's force, or of his Artillery or other convoys. I have sent to procure information here respecting the roads by which such a movement could be made, and I shall go myself by the Route marked out for the Left Column to gain further information and also to prepare Sir Thomas Graham for acting upon any order your Lordship may think proper to send him upon this subject.

22 Murray to Graham, Subijana nr Morillas, 19 1813, Murray Papers, ADV MS 46.2.18.

23 For details of the battle orders see Sir George Murray, *Memoir annexed to an Atlas, containing plans of the principle battles, sieges, and affairs, in which the British Troops were engaged during the War in the Spanish Peninsular and in the south of France from 1808 to 1814* (London: James Wyld, 1841), pp.98-100.

> I should suppose that it might be sufficient to send the 5th Division (or the 1st) and Regiment of Cavalry if the thing should appear expedient, and without artillery if the roads are bad. The 6th Division would replace if requisite the Division sent from the Left Column.
>
> I have just learned that there is a road leading upon Villafranca which shortens the distance 12 leagues from this to Villafranca and only 8 or so by the direct road to Villafranca. The Light column of the Army is now about a league nearer that direction. I should think that I have got the names of the places through which the Road passes and I am told that the Country Carts go by it but that part of it called the Puerto de St Adrian is very steep and difficult.[24]

Wellington scribbled his approval of the plan at the foot of Murray's confident letter, but it has a hint of exasperation at the lost opportunities of the previous day: 'I approve of this if it is not now too late'. The plan went ahead but Wellington's doubts were justified. Critical time had been lost and the French eventually slipped the net.

As ever, even in the thick of action, the regular letter was penned to Augusta on the 24th, now from Irurtzun on the road to Pamplona. 'We have gained a great victory and I think we are only beginning to gather the fruits of it, although the Harvest has already been pretty abundant' – he was clearly referring to the capture of the French Baggage train – 'As to myself I shall only tell you that I am satisfied with the share I have had in the operations of the campaign'.[25] Murray seemed to be hinting that he has not enjoyed the spoils of war which so many of his fellow soldiers had. This would not be surprising as Wellington was furious at the surrender to temptation that overcame almost all of the soldiers, which badly affected the chance of pursuit and a much more decisive victory. It would presumably not have been seemly, or even possible, for his senior staff to be seen helping themselves to the gold, silver, and trinkets that were hoovered up by those on the road out of Vitoria. Murray instead took his reward from the very significant contribution he had made to the army's success over the last few days. He would not have known it at this point, but in recognition of his contribution to the victory at Vitoria he, along with a number of other generals, was to be awarded the Order of the Bath.

In London there were great celebrations. Wellington was promoted to field marshal. This enabled generals who had previously been senior to Wellington, including John Hope, to serve under him, and Hope took Graham's place when again the latter's eye problems forced his retirement a few months later.

Despite the clear victory at Vitoria, and the French being in full retreat, there were still lingering concerns that some parts of the French army might launch counter attacks. The allies were now in the foothills of the Pyrenees, spread out through the various mountain passes. Communications between the separate elements were becoming very difficult. Supplies and equipment were having trouble keeping up with the rapid advance. Murray was now at his busiest, keeping track of progress and threats. Intelligence flowed in, some

24 Murray to Wellington, Vitoria, 22 June 1813, Murray Papers, ADV MS 46.2.18,

25 Murray to Augusta, Irurtzun, 24 June 1813, Murray Papers, MS 21103.

bits of it more reliable than others. The next few days were to be a very testing time as the French turned and took the battle to the British, pass by pass.

On 25 and 26 June Murray exchanged numerous letters with Graham as a clearer picture of the movements of *Général de Division* Clausel, commanding a French force that had missed the fighting at Vitoria, emerged. This was a game of chess and it was not easy keeping tabs on what the enemy was up to. From Olague, near Pamplona, Murray was hot on Clausel's heels and trying to trap him. Murray suspected the French general might even turn back to Vitoria if he thought the bulk of the allied forces had moved away from there. The familiar problems of unforgiving terrain, dire weather and lack of supplies made life miserable for both armies, more so the French, who still managed to evade the pursuing Wellington:

> [A]fter we had followed the enemy's army till yesterday through the worst roads, and in the worst weather possible we were obliged to give up the pursuit on account of the exhausted state of the men and the want of supplies. The French army (in the state I should think of beggars) are gone off through the pass of Roncesvalles.
>
> You will see by my other letter in what state matters stand in regard to Clausel. I trust we shall have him. Foy has to thank some accidental circumstances, I believe for getting off so well as he has done.[26]

Reports also reached Murray on the 26th that large numbers of the fearful population were leaving Pamplona, where the French garrison had been ordered to defend the town 'to the last extremity'.

Daily orders for the army, at this point spread out over 30 or 40 miles from edge to edge, continued to be drafted and issued by Murray: an extraordinarily difficult job, orchestrating a fragmented force where, without him necessarily knowing, each formation may have moved, or been forced to retreat, before the next day's orders were issued. Each commander was provided with a copy – and needed to be able to rely on others carrying out their orders, perhaps in an operation to join two forces. Murray did not stop at issuing the day's orders –often seven or eight pages long with detailed instructions for each division or group of divisions dovetailing into some other part – but followed them up with personal letters to the generals he was working closely with – Cole, Graham and Hill in particular – explaining his reasons behind various orders. Murray could well expect one or two letters back from a distance perhaps of ten or twenty miles, to assist him in forming the picture on which the next day's orders would be based. The situation was fluid in the extreme and each part of the army was to a very large extent working blind from the others which prevented any useful panorama.

Many of the letters received by Murray during these hectic few days were from Hill and others asking for new orders. The battle-hardened and vastly experienced generals were finding it difficult to operate when they were cut off from each other and headquarters by the terrain, and hampered by the unseasonable and incessant cold and wet weather – made worse by intermittent violent storms of wind, hail, and thunder. Headquarters were often only operational in a particular location for 24 hours before moving on to keep pace with

26 Murray to Graham, Irurtzun, 26 June 1813, Murray Papers, ADV MS 46.2.18.

the action. An additional burden stemmed from the fact that Wellington now commanded the Spanish armies directly. As a consequence orders and reports from a number of Spanish generals hurtled backwards and forwards in French, which did not slow Murray down, given his command of the language, but no doubt more tact had to be shown and a different approach adopted, than was perhaps the case with British counterparts.

Murray had still not given up on catching Clausel: 'We go today to Tudela. I fear we shall have two or three hard marches to catch Clausel. He appears to be moving down the Ebro. If he marches out decidedly he may perhaps escape with a few scratches only. If he hesitates I think he will certainly fall into our hands'.[27] His orders to Hill were to keep up the pursuit of Clausel even though there seemed no hope of intercepting him at Tudela. Murray received a report from one of his officers in his department to the effect that Clausel was now heading for Zaragoza by Mallen. His rear guard had been harassed by the Portuguese but lack of cavalry had prevented them from inflicting significant damage. A bridge blown up by Clausel across the Ebro was repaired within two hours. Stores were destroyed and a howitzer flung into the river but recovered by the allies.

Augusta would have been following her brother's progress as usual on maps she had, and Murray made sure she was fully informed as to his recent movements covering the six weeks since moving out from Freineda. He listed 33 towns and villages he had been at, many of which would have served as temporary headquarters. It demonstrated the speed of the allied advance and it takes little imagination to appreciate the significant scale of the operation to move the armies under Wellington's command through sometimes difficult country with the everyday issues of supplying and feeding troops and horses. A day short of Lanz, Murray finished by saying: 'What would you give to behold the snowy tips of the Pyrenees'.[28]

Graham, alert to Murray's appetite for good maps, told him in early July that he knew of excellent large scale maps of the Pyrenees at Cadiz – issued for setting the frontier and showing every house, which no doubt Murray followed up, even though they seemed for some reason to be on a man-of-war in the hands of a Spanish geographer.

On 9 July he declared, in philosophical mood, to Augusta,

> We have walked the French out of Spain upon this side and we did so with great ease. Experience had taught them that it was not prudent to show much resistance. Yesterday morning our troops stood upon the top of the pass (the Puerto de Maya) which leads from the valley into France, the plains of which we saw extending below us to a great distance. It looked very tempting.
>
> If I were not too idle to write a long letter, I would give you a picture of this valley, which could not fail to delight you if it all resembled the original. It unites everything that can be required to make a country beautiful and happy. All it wants is to get rid of us, as it has already got rid of the French, for armies can never contribute to the happiness of any country whatever.

27 Murray to Graham, Irurtzun, 27 June 1813, Murray Papers, ADV MS 46.2.18.
28 Murray to Augusta, Oskotz, 3 July 1813, Murray Papers, MS 21103.

The valley of Baztan, he told her,

> possesses the most romantic scenery, the most fertile fields, the finest peasantry, in short, I have before said, anything that could be wished. It is studied with the finest villages, and as we drew the French out of it on the Saints day of Navarre it was quite a Jubilee. All people, men, women and children accompanied our troops. Amongst the men every one who could find a musket joined in the pursuit of the enemy. The women stood at the doors offering cyder to our troops as they passed, and all who were not employed in either war or the offers of hospitality were busily ringing the bells of every village the moment the French troops were out of it, so that it was an unceasing peal for many miles as far as the continuity of the valley.
>
> Is it possible that I should have left it to the postscript to tell you that the men here wear blue bonnets, speak a jargon of that nobody understands and have high cheekbones![29]

By 13 July, Graham had been left by Wellington with orders to take San Sebastian, and Murray wrote to him saying he would speak to him further tomorrow about the siege. Wellington himself rode over to reconnoitre. The siege started on the 25th following the arrival of heavy equipment by sea from England at nearby Pasajes.

Although Murray was effectively chief of staff, and entrusted with significant authority by Wellington, he still had the 'old' responsibilities of the Quartermaster General which required attention to detail, often at times when his mind must have been more than fully occupied with urgent operational matters. On 13 July he was dealing with the location and capacity of the 22 hospital stations throughout the Peninsula treating tens of thousands of British, Spanish, Portuguese, and French sick and wounded, and wrote a long memorandum on their organisation. On 20 July he was writing to Commissary General Kennedy, ordering the distribution of 5,000 pairs of shoes to the 2nd, 7th and Light Divisions. All the while he was instructing frequent patrols, with instructions to keep out of the enemy's sight to avoid alerting them. On 22 July, the anniversary of the Battle of Salamanca, celebrated by Wellington with a grand dinner, he wrote to Lieutenant Colonel the Hon. Alexander Abercromby, Sir Ralph's youngest son and one of his assistant quartermaster generals, to ask him for his views on the various officers who had been seconded to the department for sketching, as he as he would like to recruit the good ones for permanent positions; this suggests that Wellington must have been prepared to allow Murray considerable freedom in strengthening his department. Looking at their sketches was not enough; he needed to know 'something more of their manners and characters'.[30]

Larpent noticed the degree to which Wellington felt he now had a man he could trust and who could take responsibility from his shoulders: 'Lord Wellington is not so easily roused from his bed as he used to be. This is the only change in him; and it is said that he has been in part encouraged to this by having such confidence in General Murray'. He also recognised

29 Murray to Augusta, Irurita, 9 July 1813, Murray Papers, MS 21103.

30 Murray to Abercromby, Lezaca 22 Jul 1813, Murray Papers, ADV MS 46.2.20.

the limitations elsewhere in the senior ranks: 'things do not seem to go on well when Lord Wellington or General Murray are not on the spot'.[31]

A junior officer in the Quartermaster General's Department, Captain Nathaniel Still, a Wycombite, was also in admiration of Murray's skills;

> As soon as he knows the intention of Lord Wellington, everything is set in motion with the utmost precision and facility. It is impossible for anyone to regulate the marches of an army with greater adroitness. He has likewise a wonderful talent of recollecting the features of a country, so that, I am told, he will several months after describe what he has perhaps seen in an accidental ride, and he is most completely capable of taking advantage of ground and occupying it accordingly. He is indefatigable and disregards everything like fatigue hard living or constant exertion.[32]

Torrens wrote to Murray from Horse Guards in unconstrained acclamation of Wellington's recent glories, thanking Murray for having written to him on 22 June immediately following the Battle of Vitoria, and for thinking of him 'during the bustle of such a moment', as well as making sure Murray knew how much his contribution was appreciated.

> Without going out of my way to pay you any compliment, I must say that it is a fortunate circumstance that the Army has had the advantage of your services during the brilliant campaign. It should be an injustice to such a man as Lord Wellington to be allowed to work with even indifferent tools, and I am certain that it is needless to say how much gratified I have been with the well earned credit you have gained from Lord Wellington.[33]

He went on to refer to 'a friend' (which must surely be Willoughby Gordon) being mortified at missing out on such a success.

Wellington and Murray together controlled the campaign, and between them were closely involved in all important actions, but even the two of them could not be everywhere at once. The period between the Battle of Vitoria and the end of July was so fast moving and disjointed that, despite every effort made by both the commander and his chief of staff to be where they were most needed, it was impossible to cover every likely spot where the French might strike. The nine days of 25 July to 2 August were of frantic movement, rapid decisions, and little sleep, with Murray sprinting from Lesaca to Olague, Almandoz, Lanz, Villaba, Lizaso, Osacain, Villaba, Ostiz, Lizaso, Lanz, and back to Lesaca. The final week of July saw Wellington riding from Lesaca to San Sebastian and back again on a number of occasions, about fifteen miles over difficult roads – he heard the news of the failure of the first attempt at storming San Sebastian, in the churchyard at Lesaca, within earshot of the siege guns. Wellington immediately rode over to see for himself, leaving Murray in command at Lesaca. He was reckoning that if Soult, now in command of the combined French forces

31 Larpent (ed.), *Private Journal*, 23 July 1813, p.199.

32 General Sir James Marshall-Cornwall 'Our First Soldier President', *The Journal of the Royal Geographical Society*, Vol.151 Part 1 (March 1985).

33 Torrens to Murray, Horse Guards, 22 July 1813, Murray Papers, ADV MS 46.2.20.

Map 8 The Western Pyrenees.

that had escaped from Vitoria, were he to make a move, would attack on the western end of the allies' position near San Sebastian. That morning, Soult surprised the allies by moving against the passes at the eastern end, away from San Sebastian. Murray now had effective command of the allied forces during a critical day until Wellington arrived back that evening from San Sebastian.

On hearing that the French were looking to attack, Murray sent orders to the commanders of the 7th and Light Divisions to let them know that they might have to move at short notice. A little later he instructed a troop of horse artillery to move to Sunbilla.

Lowry Cole had been given orders to maintain his position in the pass of Roncesvalles 'to the utmost'. This order only arrived on the morning of the 25th when Cole had already been under attack for several hours. The French were also threatening the pass at Maya, occupied by Hill. Cole retreated that night despite having held the pass successfully. Hill too surrendered Maya to the French after heavy fighting. Cole failed to keep Wellington and Murray fully informed which made subsequent planning more difficult. All of this reinforced Wellington's own view that he need to be everywhere at once directing operations personally – he hated extended operations where he was not in direct control. That said, Wellington relied greatly on Murray during the anxious days that were to follow, and the tone of Murray's orders and letters demonstrate that he was in sole control of the army and its operations at any moment that Wellington was not personally present to direct proceedings. In truth there was no alternative – events moved with extraordinary speed hour by hour and Murray was inundated with reports and requests for fresh orders. Unless Wellington was at his elbow there was no question of any possible discussion. Murray took control and maintained constant contact with the generals in the forward positions most vulnerable to French attack. He briefed Hill as follows:

> It looks very much as if Soult were going to make an effort against Byng and Cole upon the Roncesvalles road. If he does so he will probably make some Demonstration at least in other points and be prepared to follow these up if he has any success in his principal attack.
>
> In the latter case I should think Campbell would be obliged to fall back from Los Aldendes, and that happening, you would have to evacuate your most advance dispositions probably in the valley of Bastan. The Enemy would of course follow up these Retrograde Movements, and the result I should think would be our having to draw back also the 7th and Light Divisions, and to take up, for the moment, a more retired line.
>
> If the accounts from the right continue to threaten active operations on the part of the Enemy in that Quarter, Headquarters will probably move that way.
>
> Lord Wellington is gone towards San Sebastian. An assault was made upon the breach there this morning but it failed. I do not understand that our loss has been very considerable.[34]

34 Murray to Hill, Lezaca, 25 July 1813, Murray Papers, ADV MS 46.2.21.

Picton, who was nearby, offered his support to Cole who was under attack at the pass of Roncesvalles. But if he did move, he asked Murray, what should he do with the two brigades of artillery he had?

By 6.00 pm Hill had retreated from the pass of Maya suffering considerable loss. He scribbled a note to this effect to Wellington, but it would be a while before Murray would receive confirmation of this. Murray wrote to Hill at 7.00 pm from Lesaca informing him of Cole's difficulties and his falling back to a new position. He ordered Picton to move to Elizondo.

> When Brigadier General Campbell finds himself obliged to abandon the valley of Los Aldendes he will maintain himself in the pass in front of the foundry of Elizondo and dispute the ground as long as possible there…
>
> If still obliged to retire BG Campbell will retreat successively from post to post towards Eugi where he will be supported by Sir Thomas Picton and enabled to maintain his ground. The 6th Division will in the meantime move from St Esteban to Olague as a further support to the right of the Army.[35]

So 25 July 1813 was a day of confused action, rapid movements, severe casualties, urgent communications, and ultimate retreat in the face of determined French attacks. The volume of letters and reports and orders, each noting the precise time of writing, spanning a few hours, gives a taste of the urgency and pressure which must have affected everyone. This was not a battle fought on undulating farmland or framed by natural boundaries as so many were, where a good vantage point allowed the commander and his staff to direct operations with a degree of certainty and relatively little time between order and action. This was blindfold decision-making for much of the time – with the added problem of leapfrogging orders and reports, carried by dragoons in hostile and unfamiliar terrain, and inevitable lack of awareness in many parts of what others were suffering or planning. The confusion is neatly illustrated by a letter from Cole, clearly dated the 27th, reporting being faced by a vastly superior French force and asking for orders. He had had no sleep for two nights, writing that he was 'somewhat fagged and cannot be as particular as I could be'.[36] Indeed – evidence suggests the letter must have been written on the 25th or perhaps the 26th but certainly not the 27th. Cole seems to have been overwhelmed by the responsibility, and the state of his mind is evidenced by his willingness to cede control to Picton and to make arrangements for an unnecessary retreat beyond Pamplona towards Vitoria.

On Wellington's return on the night of the 25th from San Sebastian he was briefed by Murray on the day's developments, and fully approved of Murray's handling of the actions. Hill's despatch received at 10.00 pm confirmed his falling back to Elizondo.

Confused fighting and continuing reversals filled the few days between the 25th and 28th. On the 28th Hill reported he was still in retreat and had lost two artillery pieces and four waggons over a cliff in the dark. At Lanz, on the 27th, Larpent found 'General Murray and several officers, all looking very serious and gloomy, and orders given for everything to be turned off the road to the right and not to go to Ulague, as Cole had been pressed'.[37]

35 Murray to Hill, Lezaca, 25 July 1813, Murray Papers, ADV MS 46.2.21.

36 Cole to Murray, Linzoain, 27 July 1813, Murray Papers, ADV MS 46.2.21.

37 Larpent (ed.), *Private Journal*, p.205.

Despite the difficulties imposed by the two of them being separated for hours or days at a time, the collaboration between the commander and his Quartermaster General was exemplary. Wellington seemed to be comfortable with the necessary delegation and Murray confident that he could read his commander's mind. He had, in turn, the respect of the experienced generals to whom he was giving orders. On the 27th Wellington was at the bridge at Sorauren, face to face with the advancing French, and narrowly escaped capture by them, sending Fitzroy Somerset, who also just eluded the French, back to Murray who was at Olague with instructions to re-route Major General Pack's 6th Division by a safe route to support him. The 2nd and 6th Divisions were to move towards Lanz and Lizaso respectively.

Soon after Pack's arrival the next morning the French, under Marshal Soult, attacked what was a strong position on 'Cole's Ridge' held by Wellington. The day ended in another British success; the French suffered as many as 4,000 casualties, the allies a not insignificant 2,500. The next morning, as Soult, his army yet again going hungry, made his move to retreat in various directions, Wellington's artillery opened fire, followed up with actions by Dalhousie, Cole, Picton, and Pakenham – the last-named having replaced the wounded Pack – further demoralising a defeated French force. Meanwhile Murray's own activities continued apace, as reported to Graham:

> We pressed the enemy yesterday on the Roncesvalles and Lanz Roads and have made about 3,000 of them prisoners. We are going back immediately against a column which is retiring by the Dona Maria road. We have plenty of troops in the proper directions and if we can overtake the column I hope its rear will suffer considerably.[38]

At the same time he instructed Hill on his operations, only to have Wellington make an arm's length amendment: 'I have just received yours of 11 am. Things cannot be better than as settled last night with the alteration of the situation of Sir Rowland Hill's corps. It will be strong enough without Campbell. Let Murillo attend him'.[39] So Murray added another short note to Hill following Wellington's intervention: 'If you can still do it therefore I think Murillo had better be sent by the Road to the left of the Dona Maria Road… And some other part of your force may go by the Route he was destined for'.[40] Then Wellington brought Murray up to date on what was happening in his quarter. Over the nine days of the so-called Battles of the Pyrenees, allied losses totalled about 7,000, the French losses perhaps almost double.

Extraordinarily, in amongst all the action, and one assumes with little ceremony, Murray was, on 27 July, invested with the Order of the Bath at Lesaca. On 9th August he was appointed colonel commandant of the newly raised 7/60th Regiment of Foot. Only a few weeks earlier, in May, the Prince Regent had granted permission for Murray to accept the honour of Knight Commander of the Portuguese Military Order of the Tower and the Sword, conferred by the Prince Regent of Portugal. His major contribution to the success of the campaign was being recognised at the highest levels.

38 Murray to Graham, Lizasso, 31 July 1813, Murray Papers, ADV MS 46.2.21.
39 Wellington to Murray, Heights at Arista, 31 July 1813, Murray Papers, ADV MS 46.2.21.
40 Murray to Hill, Lanz, 1 August 1813, Murray Papers, ADV MS 46.2.22.

The Battle of the Pyrenees. (Anne S.K. Brown Military Collection)

Losing no time, Murray now concerned himself with the need to protect the gains that had been made against future French attack, and relayed his cautious instructions to Hill.

> It may appear over cautious but I still feel a little anxiety in regard to so large a force of the Enemy standing towards the left of our Army. If you have no objection, I should be glad you would remain yourself a little while after your troops march and that you should keep back the baggage a little and have it in your power to recall the troops or suspend their march in case of it becoming at all advisable to do so. I have just written to Lord Wellington at Berroeta to say I should take so much precaution because it does no harm at least and does not interfere with the arrangement already ordered.[41]

With the immediate threat diminished, Wellington, back with Murray at Lesaca, turned his attention again to the siege of San Sebastian. There would be no advance into France until it had fallen. Lesaca, where 'nothing is safe at all from their [Spanish soldiers'] fingers – from a horse or mule down to a bit of biscuit',[42] remained as headquarters until 10 October, when headquarters moved to Vera, closer to the border.

41 Murray to Hill, Lanz, 1 August 1813, Murray Papers, ADV MS 46.2.22.
42 Larpent (ed.), *Private Journal*, p.225.

Murray's instincts, and the recent French counter attacks, forced him to consider some defensive measures:

> It has always appeared to me a very essential point that we should strengthen the positions in front of Oiartzun. Under whatever circumstances we are placed, whether acting offensively or defensively, this appears to me equally important. I believe you have had some conversation with Lord Wellington upon the subject, but I do not know whether any thing has been determined upon, or when anything is likely to be done.
>
> I have but a very imperfect knowledge of the ground, having merely taken a general look at it from a point upon the Pena de Agua.

He went on for a number of pages giving details of his suggested deployment, with a self-effacing reference to his penchant for caution, order, and forethought.

> I give you the above as the general outline of the ideas I have formed about the position to cover the left of the army. I am not at all satisfied that they were correct but I am very anxious that attention should be given to the subject. We get on wonderfully well without the precautions, and with the method that most other armies think indispensable, but as I wrote you once before, I have some Quarter Master General like prejudices about me and my mind is not quite satisfied unless certain forms are attended to in making our arrangements, whether offensive or defensive. I wish to see us act upon a basis that may secure ourselves against the sudden alterations that now and then arise in military matters, at the same time that we were prepared to profit operations by any advantage that good fortune flows in our way.

Having dealt with what he saw as gaps in the British position:

> In addition to all this, we must recollect that the enemy is close to his resources, and that there is a power to call them forth which nothing can resist. And that on the contrary our resources are both distant and limited, and that we cannot yet tell for how long or how arduous the contest they must be made to suffice.[43]

From Lesaca he outlined his concerns to Alexander Hope:

> In England I suppose it has been long ago expected that we should invade France. Nothing would have been more easy, but it could only be to come out again without any object gained. You cannot examine into our late operations without seeing how near we were to learning a lesson on account of that the forward situation of part of our line in that quarter. We have as yet no solid hold of our conquests of this campaign and until we have, we cannot undertake to make any serious impression on France.[44]

43 Murray to Graham, Lezaca, 7 August 1813, Murray Papers, ADV MS 46.2.22.

44 Murray to Alexander Hope, Lezaca, 18 August 1813, Luffness Mss, GD 364/1/1250.

Throughout the successes, and challenges, of the days following Vitoria, the eyes of the senior officers were on events in northern Europe and the real possibility of an armistice. Success was tantalisingly close, and Murray was happy with the part he continued to play.

> Speaking selfishly I ought to wish the war to go on. At least short of the command of an army (a precarious honour Tarragona shows)[a reference to the incompetence of Lieutenant General Sir John Murray, no relation] I could not be placed in a situation more honourable or gratifying than the one I now hold.[45]

So Murray's deep concerns from 18 months earlier had dissipated – he was well satisfied in his role – no doubt greatly bolstered by the additional responsibilities entrusted to him by Wellington as well as the tangible benefits of his rapid promotion to major general. It was still, though, his ambition to command an army, or at least a division, and to get back to a closer connection with the men.

San Sebastian had eventually been taken by the allies, with Wellington again taking a close interest and happy to leave Murray temporarily in control of all other operations. 'We remain here much in the dark of course while he is away; General Murray stays here to protect us with the Light Division in our front'.[46] Much of the success of the siege, after an inauspicious start, was down to Graham who, when the assault looked again to be faltering, ordered his artillery to open fire at the breach straight over the heads of the front ranks of the British attackers – a high risk action but one which paid off and allowed the British to take the town. The appalling scenes that had debased the British at Badajoz, and which had so incensed Wellington and left his officers apparently powerless, occurred yet again, with looting burning and raping in a drink fuelled orgy of violence. Official complaints were lodged by the Spanish authorities, and Wellington was drawn into a series of communications where he strongly denied the accusations made of burning the town – he said the town was burned by the French, and many British men lost their lives and were wounded in efforts to put out fires while under fire, from not only the French in the castle, but also the Spanish townspeople themselves – whilst admitting that plundering had taken place.

Murray described the siege as 'a very severe encounter' and he was saddened by the death of Sir Richard Fletcher, the engineer who had been close to him since they were together in Jaffa in 1800, and who had overseen the construction of the Lines of Torres Vedras. Murray admired him as a man and a fellow officer; 'but military men must have their minds every day prepared for such losses'.[47] The siege proved very costly and once again there was to be some criticism of the way it was handled by Wellington, although much of the blame for the high casualties was pinned on his Engineers and their impatience.

San Sebastian was to be the last Peninsular action that Graham was to be involved in, as his eyesight had deteriorated to such an extent that he could no longer continue. Murray commiserated with him but told him that he should not push himself beyond the limit. He wanted to pay him a visit to say farewell and invited himself to dine, hoping that dining at three would be acceptable as his time was very short. He encouraged Graham, on his return

45 Murray to Augusta, Lezaca, 10 August 1813, Murray Papers, MS 21103.

46 Larpent (ed.) *Private Journal*, p.249.

47 Murray to Augusta, Lezaca, 3 September 1813, Murray Papers, MS 21103.

to Scotland, to work closely with his brother, suggesting that the uncommunicative Patrick would benefit from Graham's public support in Perthshire politics.

> As to my Brother's concern in this matter, if I were to advise him, I should recommend that the Address to the County come in the first instance from you as soon as your change of situation takes place. An address from you under such circumstances in his favour would have a very great effect.
>
> One should think that my Brother must be wholly absorbed in his politics, for although you have heard from him, upon that head he has not had the grace to write a single letter since my return to the Peninsula.[48]

As had always been the case, the fate of the campaign in the Peninsula was dependant on events in northern Europe, and matters were now coming to a head there. The vast scale of the recent battles east of the Rhine, and Napoleon's costly defeats, were soon to lead to an end to the war. Whilst the Peninsular campaign was crucially important, the numbers involved never matched those in the northern European theatre with its attendant huge losses. Wellington, and to a sometimes underappreciated extent the Spanish and Portuguese guerrillas, had kept significant numbers of French troops occupied, and had rallied two nations that were on the brink of capitulating, which required Napoleon always to keep an eye on this other front. Politically, however, the Prussians and Austrians were going to be the first to negotiate with the Emperor, and it was something of a worry to Wellington, and those back in London, that the northern forces might agree peace terms with Napoleon that would leave him exposed in the Peninsula, continuing the fight alone. Murray voiced his concerns to Hill:

> We have nothing positive from Germany as to whether the war is to be resumed or not, but the rumours latterly among the French are that Hostilities would recommence. If so the 16th instant would be the last day of the truce. Up to the latest date the allies seem to pursue a firm line, and to be confident of the support of Austria.[49]

Regardless of events in the north the French were certainly not finished yet in Spain; Murray made his views clearly known to Hope that the Spaniards, now anticipating an advance into France, had been performing increasingly well. By contrast the French had been unable to take advantage, on their own doorstep, of the allies' dangerously extended line of defence. Despite that, there was plenty of fight still left in them. On 31 August Murray wrote to Hill, enclosing 'an arrangement for strengthening the left of the army in the consequence of it appearing to be threatened by the recent movements of the enemy'.[50] The following day he reported that:

> The enemy attacked us yesterday. On his right he passed the Bidassoa by the fords above Irun, and endeavoured at the same time to establish a bridge of boats. The

48 Murray to Graham, Lezaca, 24 August 1813, Murray Papers, ADV MS 46.2.22.

49 Murray to Hill, Lezaca, 26 August 1813, Murray Papers, ADV MS 46.2.22.

50 Murray to Hill, Lezaca, 31 August 1813, Murray Papers, ADV MS 46.2.22.

> Spanish Army of Galicia alone however, drove him back over the river in a very successful and gallant style, and the British and Portuguese troops in that quarter had no reason to act.[51]

In fact Wellington had been keeping an eye on the progress of the battle, declining to lend support in order to give the Spaniards the full glory of the day.

Murray asked Hill to let him know immediately if there was any sign of the enemy towards his left and repeated his orders to the other generals to be on their guard as French movement had been observed. By 3 September news had reached headquartrers that hostilities were to recommence in the north of Europe. Heightened readiness had Murray reconnoitring the surrounding countryside and estimating the strength of the enemy. By the 6th he had intelligence that they had returned to the neighbourhood of St Jean Pied de Port.

Murray received a letter from Lieutenant Colonel Abercromby about a French attack around 5 o'clock in the morning on 7 September, and prepared to reinforce him. He asked Hill to hold his position on the right as long as possible but if forced to retire, to go towards Pamplona, slowly, to give time for support to arrive. Later in the day he also advised Hill of reports that Soult was receiving reinforcements from Catalonia. Later again that day he enclosed an intercepted letter from Soult to the Governor of Pamplona, and issued additional instructions to Hill. The next day he was still communicating with Hill on strengthening an adjacent valley.

Meanwhile in the midst of these actions the usual requests that so irked Murray continued to flow. The latest concerned a young Moore. Murray had agreed to ask Wellington to let him be appointed to the Quartermaster General's Department 'as it is understood to be his father's wish to have him in a staff situation'. Murray was inclined to place him with the Light Division, which owed so much to his father, Sir John. In the same letter that he wrote to Graham he also said he was dealing with a request from a young man by the name of Stirling of the 42nd (Black Watch) who was looking for a commission in the 60th.[52] There were many requests of this nature, an increasing number now that Murray was a general, and all required his attention despite the enormous pressure he was under.

Correspondence, still dominated by urgent communications with Hill and others as to French movements, nevertheless included the release valve of domestic matters back home. Augusta and the general seemed keen on acquiring a farm, presumably in Scotland, and had also had the offer of Joanna Churchill's house in Sunninghill.

> I am delighted with the idea of my Aunt's villa. [The Oaks, Sunninghill, a Churchill house, now a Country House Hotel] It seems to be very cheap and I hope is good. Being near Windsor I expect to hear of Dejeuners and little parties with the Royal neighbours. However in the intervals of more quiet amusements I promise myself a pleasant trip occasionally to the Villa when I happen to be in Town.[53]

51 Murray to Hill, Lezaca, 1 September 1813, Murray Papers, ADV MS 46.2.22.

52 Murray to Graham, Lesaca, 14 September 1813, Murray Papers, ADV MS 46.2.22.

53 Murray to Augusta, Lezaca, 15 September 1813, Murray Papers, MS 21103.

He finished by returning to his long held belief on the continuing hostilities, that it was in the north of Europe and not in Spain that the final outcome of the war would be decided.

Murray equated soldiers to actors – they sometimes got pelted if they failed to please the galleries. That said, he cautioned against drawing room gossip about military affairs, and could not resist an aside at political interference.

> We must take these things as they come. A man may have a Ribbon today [a reference to his KB] and may be abused next week as more deserving of a Halter. As to the Ribbon, the pleasure intirely is in the earning of it, for once it is got, it seems a very indifferent matter...
>
> You write me about the affairs of the North which is pardonable enough when you are shut up in Argyleshire but when you come Perthshire beware of such humdrum concerns. It may be very well of me to talk of Buonaparte and his battles, and fancy the subject may have some interest, till I perceive my friends all asleep, but if you do so when you get into a civilised county, I shall send you back to your dreary wastes and frightful climate.
>
> I confess however I have a cold fit now and then, when I recollect how few men know anything of war and how signal the punishment sometimes is when those who do not, presume to intermeddle in it.[54]

Thomas Heaphy, the society portrait painter, had arrived at headquarters with a view to recording the activities of the generals at the heart of the latest allied successes. His sitters included, of course, Wellington and Murray, in preparation for a large composite work including most of the Peninsular generals. Heaphy had at one point strayed a little too close to the action, which understandably shook him, and resulted in his immediately increasing his price for a half-length water colour portrait from 40 to 50 guineas. Even so, his collection of head and shoulders portraits of individual generals, now in the National Portrait Gallery, is testament to his skill, in what must have been testing circumstances.

Over the next month or so the regular letters to Augusta dealt with such varied topics as the arrival of Sir John Hope to take over from Graham, to a gentle criticism of a grandmother who wanted a good word put in for her grandson. Murray thought the war would end in the next few months, but that negotiations would drag on, requiring the armies to remain in position for some time to come. Early October saw more rapid movement of the army and a resultant day-by-day increase in orders to Hill, with Murray struggling with yet another bout of feverish illness, which lasted two or three weeks and forced him to take to his bed for a few days.

Murray issued orders for the forward movement of the army – 13 pages of tightly packed orchestration, as well as another 11 pages written by Murray in French to the Spanish forces who were to provide support to the Light Division in assaulting the French position on the heights of the Grande Rhune. Ward describes the arrangements for the crossing of the Bidassoa as 'one of the most, if not the most, comprehensive movement orders for a

54 Murray to Augusta, Lezaca, 25 September 1813, Murray Papers, MS 21103.

Wellington's Generals by Heaphy, Murray seated with map.
(Crown Copyright UK Government Art Collection)

successful "set piece" operation ever issued by a staff officer'.[55] The plan was to cross the river at low tide early in the morning of the 7th, which the 5th Division did, although the water was up to their chins, taking the French almost totally by surprise.

> Our operations went on very well in this quarter yesterday and the French yielded up some very strong ground without obliging our people to make extraordinary efforts…
>
> The enemy still hold the summit of the mountain of La Rhune which is like a castle formed of bricks. I think however we shall turn him out of it…
>
> The Spaniards have conducted themselves admirably well.[56]

The operation to cross the Bidassoa behind them, Wellington and Murray began collecting intelligence in preparation for the next assault. A long and very detailed plan for a possible retreat, should that prove necessary, was drafted by Murray and sent to Hope, concluding: 'Spain is a very strong country to defend if its military means were placed upon any tolerable footing of respectability. I need hardly tell you that they are very, very, far indeed from that at present'.[57] By 25 October preparations for the surrender of Pamplona were completed,

55 Ward, *Wellington's Headquarters*, p.139.
56 Murray to Hill, Lezaca, 8 October 1813, Murray Papers, ADV MS 46.2.23.
57 Murray to Hope, Vera, 17 October 1813, Luffness Mss, GD 364/1/1250.

which was finally given up to the Spanish on the 31st. Vera became the new headquarters, where, from a hill nearby, Murray had a clear view of the plains of France and the River Nivelle falling to the sea at St Jean de Luz, as ever described in his letters home:

> And all along its banks the French troops busily employed in preparing works of defences and seemingly with as much timidity as we were fortifying our shores against the Boulogne flotilla in 1803.

And rising from Bayonne was

> [T]he abundant smoke of the French kitchens, bespeaking hospitality and luxury, or comfort. Above the town, to the right, are the windings of the Ardour flowing through the country in broad and stately majesty, and below the town to the left is the meeting of the River with the Ocean, and the contest which has continued for ages of the stream with the swell of the Bay of Biscay. After heavy rains the Dominion of the river is extended, and the dark brown colour of the water marks the spread of his conquests till bounded at a distance in a wide semicircle by the blue waves of the sea. Far to the eastward are the peaks of the higher Pyrenees tipped with ice on their summits and having the lustre of their sides covered with fresh snows.
>
> Behind is Spain, a country whether we consider its fame in ancient Times, its renown in the age of chivalry, its elevations and depressions in Modern History, its connections with the New World, the Dotage of its Slavery, or the Infancy of its Liberty, most deserving of the contemplation of man.[58]

At the start of November news reached headquarters of Napoleon's defeat at the Battle of Leipzig, a massive affair lasting three days and involving more than half a million men. This was excellent news for Wellington, as he planned his further assault on Soult. It would add to the increasing confidence of the allies and the growing despair of the demoralised French. Wellington surveyed his area of intended operations from the top of the Grande Rhune, a nine hundred metre high ridge dominating the western end of the Pyrenees.

The hills that stretch from the coast to the steep foothills of the Pyrenees, combined with the anchorage of the River Nivelle on the French left, provided an apparently strong defensive line which Soult chose to occupy. Having been surprised on his right, at the coast, on 7 October, Soult paid most attention to this area, but in general occupied every hilltop and fortress which existed on the border west of the Pyrenean mountain range; a defensive line which stretched seventeen miles in total. On reconnaissance, Wellington rode with Murray to observe the entire French line from the summit of La Rhune. The conversation that followed appears to be the moment at which Wellington firmed up his plans for the attack on the French positions.

An eyewitness described the scene:

58 Murray to Augusta, Vera, 24 October 1813, Murray Papers, MS 21103.

> [T]he Duke was lying down, and begun a very earnest conversation. Gen Alton, Kempt, Colborne, I, and other staff officers were preparing to leave the Duke when he says 'Oh lie still'. After he had conversed for some time with Sir G Murray, Murray took out of his sabretache his writing materials, and began to write a plan of attack for the whole army. When it was finished, so clearly had he understood the Duke, I don't think he erased one word. He says 'my Lord is this your desire?' It was one of the most interesting scenes I have ever witnessed. As Murray read the Duke's eye was directed with his telescope to the spot in question. He never asked Sir G Murray one question, but the muscles of his face evinced lines of the deepest thought. When Sir G Murray had finished, the Duke smiled and said 'Ah Murray, this will put us in possession of the fellows lines. Shall we be ready tomorrow?
>
> I fear not, my Lord, but next day.[59]

In cold, clear conditions, with little left to chance, the Battle of the Nivelle, one of Wellington's last major battles, was fought on 10 November 1813, recognized as a significant milestone in Wellington's career:

> From La Rhune, the highest point of the seventeen-mile wide battlefield, Wellington commanded a force of approximately 80,000 allied troops, 40,000 of whom were British, the rest Portuguese and Spanish. In opposition, Marshal Soult had dispersed his force of nearly 70,000 in defensive fortresses, redoubts and entrenchments on nearly every hilltop from the coast to the River Nivelle... Barely a year and a half before Wellington fought at Nivelle, he had commanded at the battle of Salamanca, in a space barely three miles wide. In the space of little more than a year, Wellington was able to conceive a battle nearly six times the size of Salamanca, in terrain that was physically brutal and near impossible for nineteenth century infantry to negotiate, on a scale that resembled battles of the Second World War. In short, in the fifteen months between Salamanca and the Nivelle, Wellington and Murray had overseen a transformation in warfare of incredibly significant proportions. Quite possibly, but for the intervention of Waterloo, the Nivelle might have been Wellington's greatest victory.[60]

The allies succeeded in overrunning the enemy's extensive defensive earthworks, and forced the French to retreat towards Bayonne, leaving most of their artillery. The day ended with a comprehensive allied victory although again casualties were high, between three and four thousand on each side. In the allies' case about one quarter of them were Spanish. The battle, if not generally accorded the same praise as Salamanca and Vitoria, nevertheless was one of the most brilliantly conceived operations of the Peninsular War, much of the credit for which must lie with Murray's ability to interpret Wellington's thoughts on how he envisaged the best plan of attack. Soult had been comprehensively outgeneralled, and the allies had broken through the mountain barrier.

59 G.C. Moore Smith (ed.), *The Autobiography of Lt. General Sir Harry Smith* (London: John Murray, 1903), pp.142-3.

60 Huw J. Davies, 'Moving Forward in the Old Style; Revisiting Wellington's Greatest Battles from Assaye to Waterloo', *British Journal for Military History*, Vol I, Issue 3 (June 2015), p.11.

Thus, with his back to Spain, Murray was able to tell Augusta, on 13 November 1813, 'Nous sommes enfin dans la Belle France'.[61]

In France indeed they were, but the problem that faced Wellington now was the anticipated Spanish orgies of plundering and violence, brought on to some extent by the lack of pay and food. As Wellington wrote, 'The superiority of numbers which I can take into France will consist in about 25,000 Spaniards, neither paid nor fed, and who must plunder, and will set the whole country against us'.[62] Most were sent back to Spain.

The winter headquarters would be at St Jean de Luz, on the coast near Bayonne, where the locals soon started supplying the allies with food and other necessities, all paid for in accordance with Wellington's strict instructions. Dinners, soirees, and balls were enjoyed by the officers, just reward for the successful but rigorous six months since leaving Freineda. An (informal) regulation was enforced: dinner guests might only leave when the two ends of the table were joined by an uninterrupted line of empty champagne bottles along the centre. The two armies were very close to each other and, as was now almost commonplace, they conversed freely and exchanged rations. Murray, able to relax a little, continued to write from here to Augusta, in the run up to Christmas, a moment in earlier years that had seen the start of difficult retreats. This year was very different, and even the cautious Murray could start looking forward to being back in Scotland:

> Many good Christmases and Good New Years to yourself and to the General.
>
> I begin to think you are quite right in having a place upon the Coast. I walk by the sea side here every day, and every day the scene is interesting. There is something in the grandeur and ceaseless motion of the sea that occupies and interests me at all times. Thus the Western Sea is much the finest. Its magnificence is far beyond that of the fishpond which lies between England and Holland, and the western gales have a Salubrity in them that seems to bring fresh life to everything upon which they blow.
>
> However I won't go on to flatter your county any more that I may reserve some fine things to say of it when I come there.[63]

Since re-joining the army in the spring, Murray had firmly established himself as Wellington's chief of staff, applying his skills with an energy that matched his commander's, orchestrating a complex offensive through extraordinarily difficult terrain, and playing a commanding role in some of the hard won clashes in the Pyrenees. He could take credit for much of the success over the summer and autumn of 1813. He would not have had any time to regret his broken engagement. He had received many encouraging comments, from so many quarters, about his performance and his indispensability that his confidence brimmed. Nothing suited him better than being busy – and the satisfaction of not only executing his duties in exemplary fashion, but receiving the recognition of the enlarged role of Quartermaster General, fully justified his actions a year or so earlier. Well-planned victories had been achieved in the mountains of northern Spain; so too had Murray won his personal battle.

61 Murray to Augusta, St Pe, 13 November 1813, Murray Papers, MS 21103.

62 Wellington to Bathurst, 19 September 1813, Gurwood (ed.), *Dispatches*, Vol.XI, pp.123-4.

63 Murray to Augusta, St Jean de Luz, 26 December 1813, Murray Papers, MS 21103.

17

1814 – France, Napoleon's Abdication

Murray's first letters of the New Year were to Augusta, written in cautiously optimistic tone, with the usual element of political teasing : 'Your first wish, I have no doubt, is that it may prove a year of restoration to peace and Tranquillity in which I heartily join, although that is not my trade. I distrust Buonaparte however, and doubt his being contented to sit down by his fire-side'.[1] But Murray thought the war would soon be over. 'for if the allies have the good sense to give Buonaparte no rest he must make peace, or be got rid of altogether'.[2] In a later letter he remarked that he was

> [A]mused to hear you reading Caesar. However I think it would interest you and if you mean to be a Great Commander, you could not I think, read a better book. I admire the man, but I have a prejudice in favour of the other side in Roman Politicks.[3]

Alongside the usual familial banter, detailed orders continued to flow from Murray's pen. Preparations were under way for a further push into France. The order below is typical of hundreds that are in the Murray Papers in the National Library of Scotland, if much shorter than most. It gives an idea of the need for good intelligence on the state of the roads in front of the army's current position, as well as clear identification of places on the intended advance, if disasters are not to occur in the midst of concerted action by complimentary units along differing routes. Typically drafted by Murray's hand and in this instance copied three times – to Lieutenant Generals Sir Stapleton Cotton and Sir Thomas Picton and to Major General Walker, who had taken over from the Earl of Dalhousie commanding the 7th Division, while the latter had gone home on leave:

> It is intended to dislodge the enemy tomorrow from the Ridge of La Coste which he occupies upon the left bank of the Jayeusen (or Arran/Benalit) near La Bastide.

1 Murray to Augusta, St Jean de Luz, 3 January 1814, Murray Papers, MS 21103.
2 Murray to Augusta, St Jean de Luz, 10 January 1814, Murray Papers, MS 21103.
3 Murray to Augusta, St Jean de Luz, 23 January 1814, Murray Papers, MS 21103.

> The attack on the left of the enemy's posts will be made by the 3rd Division which will move for that purpose from the side of the Hasparen by the road which leads by the ridge of La Coste towards La Bastide.
>
> Sir Stapleton Cotton will be so good as order a detachment of cavalry to co-operate with the 3rd Division and direct half of Major Gardiners troop of Horse Artillery to move with it (if the roads are practicable) as it is not intended that the division should be accompanied by its own Artillery.
>
> The 7th Division, and such part of the cavalry in the neighbourhood of Hasparen as is not employed towards La Coste and La Bastide will cover Macaye and Hasparen and protect the right against any attack by the enemy from the side of Montdiande Boulac or any where Sir Stapleton Cotton will be so good as take the direction of the troops in observation upon the right during the operation against the ridge of La Coste.
>
> The 4th Division with the Brigade of Mountain Guns will move by the Moulin d'au Haut, and will act against the centre of the enemy posts.
>
> And a part of the troops under the orders of Sir Rowland Hill will act against the right of the enemy, according to the instruction which Sir Rowland Hill has already received.
>
> All the three attacks above-mentioned to commence at 11 am. The general officers commanding them will be so good as to make their previous arrangements therefore accordingly.
>
> It is not meant to push the operation of the troops beyond the river Hayeuse which runs between La Coste and La Bastide.[4]

The weather had been dreadful for weeks and Wellington's plans for advancing had been delayed, as the roads were quagmires. Shortage of cash was again a problem; debts had mounted and many men had not been paid. The government authorised the London banker Nathan Rothschild to purchase French and foreign coin in the Low Countries and Germany for use in France, and more was sent from England. Wellington was determined that the local French population were to be paid for anything that the allies required from them, in an effort to avoid the same alienation that marked the relationship of the Spanish and Portuguese population with the French in the Peninsula.

The recent successes in Northern Europe encouraged Wellington to make preparations to move further into the country as soon as the weather permitted. Murray would have heard of the allies' advance from Germany into eastern France. By the end of January he was even more convinced that Napoleon would be forced to call for quarter very soon upon any terms. 'It is delightful to see him in such straits. The Russians I dare say are full of the thoughts of burning Paris'.[5]

He had received news from home of his nephew John's succession to the Gartshore estate, which had come into the family recently. This was a consequence of the 4th Ochtertyre Baronet marrying a Gartshore daughter a few generations earlier, followed by a lack of

4 Ustaritz, 5 January 1814, Murray Papers, ADV MS 46.3.1.

5 Murray to Augusta, St Jean de Luz, 30 January 1814, Murray Papers, MS 21103.

Gartshore House. (Private Collection)

Gartshore offspring thereafter. With his mind naturally on more pressing matters, he gave the impression at least that the life of a Scottish laird was not something he hankered after, although, as events turned out a few years later, it might have played a central role in his life after military service: 'when I was John's age the Gartshore succession was talked of for me. I am quite satisfied that I have been better without it, and I hope John on the contrary will be better with it'.[6] He had other more pressing things to attend to.

A few days at the end of February saw an extraordinary feat in the construction of a pontoon of boats, local fishing vessels lashed together, forming a bridge almost 500 yards long across the River Adour at Bayonne, within reach of the French garrison, which enabled thousands of men to cross and provided a new supply route. The town was invested but not besieged. Wellington was happy to contain the garrison, although this occupied over 20,000 men under John Hope, which Murray for one felt was not a good use of British troops, reckoning that Spanish should have been used for the purpose. He felt strongly enough to argue his case with Wellington, to no avail, as he explained to Alexander Hope.

> I have always been of the opinion that the thing to do was to leave the Spanish force there to blockade the place, and to enable ourselves by that means to carry forward a commanding and efficient force into the country...

6 Murray to Alexander Hope, St Jean de Luz, 6 February 1814. Luffness Mss, GD 364/1/1256.

> Locking up such a large proportion of that part of our force which is best adapted for the field, appear to me inconsistent with the object in view...
>
> I have not failed to submit my ideas on this subject to Lord Wellington, but he appears not to have taken the same view of the matter, and has only observed in reply that he could not depend on the Spaniards and that he regretted it had fallen to you to have the charge of the operation before Bayonne.[7]

Murray repeated this strong opinion to Graham with whom he was still regularly corresponding, Graham having been posted to the Low Countries, in a singularly unsuccessful expedition with badly trained troops, many of whom were taken prisoner at Burgen-op-Zoom, for which Graham was not blamed, although he was clearly deeply affected by the experience and had to be consoled by Murray. 'Hope is before Bayonne which I am very sorry for. I should have liked that that job had been given to the Spaniards and that he had been with us in the field'.[8]

Meanwhile the allied advance had been checked by Soult's remaining divisions at Orthez. Only temporarily slowed, and with a numerical superiority of about 7,000 men, Wellington broke through the strong French position just as Hill's column arrived to turn their left flank, and the day's fighting ended when the French gave way. Wellington was slightly injured during the fighting, hit in the thigh by a spent bullet. Murray's report on the recent operations and the Battle of Orthez to Augusta was typically to the point: 'We have always beat the French and on the 27th at Orthez the beating they got was pretty serious. At the close of the day it was a complete rout, and had not the large ditches saved the enemy from our cavalry they would have lost the greater part of their army'.[9]

Many French soldiers, now back on home soil, took the chance of slipping off home, and Wellington made it clear that they would be left in peace if they caused no trouble.[10] As the British advanced they were well received. The treatment the French population in the south received from their own soldiers was appalling and did nothing to help Bonaparte's cause. Nor were Wellington's soldiers perfect in the country of their sworn enemy, any more than they had been in the Peninsula, and there were many instances of pillaging and plunder, but the difference seems to have been that complaints were followed up, the offenders flogged and compensation paid. Soult left St Sever and moved southeast in a bold move – back towards the Pyrenees, hoping to draw Wellington with him. Wellington resisted the temptation and entered St Sever on 1 March.[11]

Peace talks among the Russians, Austrians, and Bonaparte were under way at Chatillon but were faltering. The dilemma for the British was the extent to which they should support a return of the Bourbons over a negotiated settlement with Bonaparte. Differing views existed amongst the allies. Locally, however, it was becoming increasingly clear that there was precious little support for Bonaparte in southwest France and this encouraged Wellington to move to occupy strongly royalist Bordeaux. However, Wellington was

7 Murray to Alexander Hope, St Sever, 5 March 1814, Murray Papers, ADV MS 46.3.2.
8 Murray to Graham, St Sever, 5 March 1814, Murray Papers, ADV MS 46.3.2.
9 Murray to Augusta, St Sever, 3 March 1814, Murray Papers, MS 21103.
10 Muir, *Path to Victory*, p.572.
11 Muir, *Path to Victory*, p.573.

Thomas Graham, Lord Lynedoch. (Anne S.K. Brown Military Collection)

cautious in openly supporting the Bourbons, although sentiment at home was swinging in their favour. Disgraceful behaviour by the remaining Spanish troops in France was an enormous concern, and in an act that demonstrated a high degree of confidence in the French population's relationship with the British, he issued a proclamation that villages should arm themselves against plunderers.

Napoleon refused the terms offered by the northern allies on 10 March, their expiry date. The pendulum swung further towards the Bourbon option. French 'hosts', no doubt sensing that Napoleon's reign was nearly at an end, made their new guests welcome, as Murray was delighted to report to his brother:

> You will perhaps be glad to hear, however, from a tolerably impartial person, how we have found the minds of the people of this Country disposed. I cannot give you a stronger or a more true idea upon that head, than by telling you that in that part of the Country through which we passed previous to the battle of Orthez, you might have supposed that our army was that of the country and the French army that of the Enemy. The Peasantry came about us every where with the most perfect confidence, and seeming feelings of friendship, and there was evident exultation in their countenances upon every discomfiture of their own troops. They went forward to show us the best roads, to point out the fords in the rivers; in short to contribute in any way, but by arms, to our success. I had to cross the country one day, going from one of our columns to another and nothing could be more gratifying than the reception I every where met with.[12]

This view he repeated to Augusta:

> The people all over this Country seem very well pleased to see us, and are very civil. They are agreeably disappointed too at finding us not quite such monsters as Buonaparte has endeavoured to represent us to be.[13]

Leaving a force at Bordeaux, Wellington advanced on Toulouse, a major arsenal and military depot, to where Soult had retired, hoping to re-equip and refresh his troops. Wellington arrived on 27 March, three days after Soult, and set about planning to cross the river Garonne, the attempt failing as a result of the pontoon bridge being too short, much to Wellington's fury, and in stark contrast to the success of Hope's crossing of the Adour at Bayonne only a few weeks earlier. A crossing at a different point was attempted a few days later – this time a rapid rise in the level of the river left three divisions and three brigades of cavalry stranded on the far side. In the event Soult did not dare risk his now poorer-quality troops in attacking and concentrated on improving his defensive position near the town.

During these preparations Murray was billeted comfortably close by with a family loyal to the Bourbons, from where he wrote reflectively to Augusta:

12 Murray to Patrick, Aire, 11 March 1814, Murray Papers, MS 21102.
13 Murray to Augusta, L'Isle en Dodon, 24 March 1814, Murray Papers, MS 21103.

> If war is ever hideous and disgusting it is in Spring. All nature seems then striving to give to the world and every living thing, and even indeed to everything inanimate in it, peace, happiness and enjoyment, and War, like an evil spirit, seems active in counteracting nature's plan, and in blasting all her work.
>
> I am lodged in the house of a poor old gentleman who had emigrated during the Revolution, and served under the Princes. He lost all his Property, but a younger brother [whom] bad health obtained from emigration, was fortunate enough to preserve his little share of the family inheritance, and they now live together, and make the most of the remnant of the wreck of their fortune. And though the eldest lost all, he still continues to be looked upon as the head of the house.
>
> My room has still a few portraits of the ancestors of the family. Under these are portraits of Louis 16th and the Queen and beneath them is a list of the First National Assembly and profiles of one or two of the principal members of it. There is on that wall food for reflection. And if there is enough without to disgust me with war, there is enough within to warn me against political ambition…
>
> I will stop here however lest this train of Reflections should lead me to relinquish the world, and retire to a Hermitage. And I have paper enough I believe to bring me to such a conclusion were I not to stop my pen.[14]

Notwithstanding Murray's suspicion of politics generally, his genuine and thoughtful interest, not to mention his direct experience of power in differing countries, would lead inevitably to an evening or two of philosophical and political discussion, no doubt sharing the local wine with his hosts, about the nature of monarchy and the rights of the people. Yet again his total fluency in the language must have made his life immeasurably easier.

Despite encouraging reports from Paris about the imminent end of Napoleon's reign, it was too early for both sides to do anything but continue operations. After a careful examination of the French positions Wellington launched a series of attacks on Soult on Easter day, 10 April. Hill, Picton, and Alten were to advance against the western and northern fronts of the city but would not press their attacks home. The main thrust would be by Beresford to the east. To get into position Beresford's flank would be exposed to French attack, but Wellington was confident that the risk was less than it might have been given the greater experience of the British troops. Soult was not taken in by Wellington's plan and moved the majority of his force to face Beresford, now supported by Spanish divisions. Beresford's force suffered during its slow, muddy, progress. There was some debate later about Beresford acting on his own initiative rather than in accordance with Wellington's orders. The Spanish, strangely unsupported, perhaps too from moving without orders, failed to take a strong French position, and scattered. All depended on Beresford, who wheeled west towards the well defended city. Wellington joined him and the battle entered its most intense phase. After both sides had sustained severe casualties, it became something of a stalemate. Soult, however, recognised that his position was untenable and, late the following day, abandoned Toulouse, unmolested.

14 Murray to Augusta, Sysses, near Toulouse, 2 April 1814, Murray Papers, MS 21103.

At dawn on 12 April Wellington was invited into the city amidst great celebrations, his forces welcomed as 'liberateurs'. Napoleon had abdicated unconditionally on 4 April, the news only reaching the city in the afternoon eight days later. The battle had been a wasteful loss of many lives. The allied army suffered 4,558 casualties – 2,103 of them British, around an equal number of Spanish, and 500 or so Portuguese. French losses were fewer at just over 3,000.[15] It had been a messy victory, won by courage and dogged determination rather than tactical brilliance.

Murray was quick to relay his feelings on the abdication in a congratulatory letter to Alexander Hope :

> I congratulate you upon this great political event, more than I should upon twenty victories; but as a military man I cannot help adding an additional congratulation that the closing scene of so many struggles should be the victory of a British Army at this place. It ends all in a manner worthy of the high character which Britain has upheld during so many years of trial.[16]

The celebrations really kicked in now, and Wellington basked in the adoration of the people. Bayonne continued to hold out and refused to recognise Napoleon's abdication without additional hard documentary evidence. The French broke out in strength during the early hours of 14 April, surprising the investing forces, who lost 400 men, with a number of senior officers killed and John Hope injured, probably by 'friendly fire', and captured. On his eventual release Murray used his considerable influence to secure him, leg broken, a comfortable passage back to England.

Unsurprisingly it was Murray whom Wellington asked to negotiate and draft the convention for the cessation of hostilities at Toulouse. Certainly a simpler task than at Cintra five years earlier. The convention, dated 18 April 1814, was signed by Murray and Major General Don Luis Wimpffen for the allies and by *Général de Division* Count Gazan for the French. It was later duly ratified by Wellington, Suchet, and Soult.

Hostilities at an end, all that remained, albeit a huge logistical exercise, was to effect the safe embarkation of the entire British army – the allied numbers around Toulouse at this point comprising about 90,000 men – together with officers, all its equipment, artillery and horses. This was of course the responsibility of the Quartermaster General. Murray was left in control of the operation, while Wellington headed for Madrid 'to endeavour to keep the Spaniards from cutting each others throats'.[17] Murray's role included ensuring that the remaining Spanish forces returned peacefully to Spain without taking reprisals on the French, a risk that had been recognised as soon as the Pyrenees were crossed and which had resulted in relatively few Spanish actually being in France. The Spanish relationship with the British was worse than ever, following the appalling scenes at San Sebastian.

Despite almost half of the British cavalry horses being sold or gifted to the Spanish and Portuguese, transport had to be found for the 9,000 or so that still remained in France. Special approval was sought to move the huge numbers right across France to embark at

15 Muir, *Path to Victory*, p.582.

16 Murray to Alexander Hope, Toulouse, 13 April 1814, Luffness Mss, GD 364/1/1256.

17 Murray to Alexander Hope, Toulouse, 15 May 1814, Luffness Mss, GD 364/1/1256.

Calais and Boulogne. One convoy of 1,500 of them was placed under Scovell's command. They made their way in two columns each of four groups, accompanied by the horse artillery batteries. There were occasional disputes on the crowded roads, some with French troops and conscripts making their way home, and some with immense numbers of French prisoners of war just landed from England, where many of them had been confined for years.

Some infantry battalions were despatched straight to America to fight in the war that had been occupying increasing numbers of British forces there since 1812. Admiral Lord Keith had been requested by Wellington to keep Murray fully informed as to the availability of transport, and the two were to liaise closely on the arrangements for repatriation to England and the simultaneous mounting of the expedition to America, no small task. Murray was invited by Torrens to take command of a division in America, conscious of the desire Murray had expressed previously to command troops, and also hinting that there might not be many opportunities for active service coming up. Strangely, perhaps, Murray declined, wary of the likely overall command, although the identity of the chosen commander was at this point unclear – Wellington had been offered the command of the army in America by Liverpool, but had refused, critical of the arrangements there.

Murray would, he said, have viewed the case in a different light if he had been offered overall command. In any event Wellington had asked him to continue in France for some time to oversee the repatriation of the army. 'Under all the circumstances... it does not appear to me that the offer is very tempting, and I think the main point for me to consider is how far duty obliges me to accept it'.[18] He regarded the proffered opportunity as sinking considerably from the 'spoiled situation' he had under Wellington, although he was to take up a potentially more senior role in America at the end of the year. Before long he had instead accepted yet another position in Ireland.

Kitty Wellington had persuaded her husband to send their sons to Temple Grove school, where Patrick's sons were, having elicited Murray's support in an attempt to win Wellington over. In her letter of thanks to Murray for his successful efforts, she referred to her brother Edward Pakenham's appointment as Adjutant General to Wellington's army, and the pleasure it gave her recognising that her three heroes now probably lived much of their lives alongside each other: 'I wish I could join your party once a week and we might have a few glasses of ginger wine together', she wrote.[19]

Wellington soon returned from Madrid, after discussing the return of a number of looted artworks, and dealing with a number of delicate political matters, and left France in mid-June, arriving back in England to a well-deserved hero's welcome on the 23rd. Murray himself was still in Bordeaux overseeing the departure of the remaining troops and the sick. He wrote to Hope on 7 June that the American business had 'got itself into another shape' and he could not in any case have left France given the complexity and numbers of interests involved in the peaceful extraction of the British forces, where he was known to all the parties. His message to Hope was that an appointment on the home staff would be acceptable, but preferably in England rather than Scotland or Ireland.[20]

18 Murray to Wellington, Toulouse, 1 May 1814, Wellington (ed.), *Supplementary Despatches*, Vol.IX, p.57.

19 Kitty Wellington to Murray (no location), 18 May 1814, Murray Papers, MS 21104.

20 Murray to Alexander Hope, Bordeaux, 7 June 1814, Luffness Mss, GD 364/1/1256.

By 17 July the repatriation exercise was almost complete and he was getting bored. In his last surviving letter to Augusta from France he said:

> There is nothing makes me so idle as having nothing to do, and I suppose even Buonaparte himself has become indolent since he was dethroned. The mail from England of last night brings me the unlooked for intelligence of my appointment to be Adjutant General in Ireland.
>
> I know you are not very partial to appointments in that country; however they are very good and being wholly unsolicited on my part there is a greater gratification when they are bestowed.[21]

So Hope's magical powers had not worked this time and Murray was forced to put a brave face on his appointment to Ireland, in his eyes the least attractive location, aware that the options for officers of his rank in peacetime were limited and he had taken something of a gamble in turning down an American command. He said he would journey to Dublin via Scotland and hoped to embark in about ten days.

Despite the demands on his time, Murray's fascination with maps and the accurate sketching of military actions was not far from the surface, and he started to plan the recording of the great events that had shaped his life and so many others for the past six years. His idea was to get funding from the Treasury for the drawing of accurate maps of the major actions the British Army had been involved in and to this end he earmarked the talented and industrious Captain Thomas Mitchell, who had already spent some time in the Quartermaster General's Department, as the man he considered best able to produce the accurate detail he required. Treasury approved the plan and Mitchell commenced a spell of four years in Portugal and Spain carrying out Murray's instructions. Initially the Spanish refused permission for a British officer to carry out the work, in contrast to the Portuguese who provided every assistance. Henry Wellesley, Wellington's brother and British Ambassador in Madrid, tried unsuccessfully to get the Spanish to agree to Murray's request and it took a later, direct approach from Mitchell himself to obtain the necessary passport. It is not surprising that Murray's lively topographical memory demanded a high standard as well as a copious supply of maps and plans to add to his growing collection. The reserve store in Lisbon in 1810 contained 51 printed maps of Spain and Portugal, some in separate parts, and 37 manuscript sketches and plans; Murray's library in France in 1818 contained at least 61 printed maps over and above the manuscript sketches drawn for departmental use.[22]

The result of Mitchell's extraordinary work is Wyld's Atlas, published eventually in 1841, containing a series of beautifully executed plans and sketches of the Peninsular War. Murray wrote a 200-page memoir by way of preface to the publication. This comprised his written orders for moving the army during the significant battles in the campaign, which are reproduced in full. There is no better way to understand this element of Murray's duties. Whether Murray intended to write his complete memoirs is open to speculation; this is the

21 Murray to Augusta, Bordeaux, 17 July 1814, Murray Papers, MS 21103.

22 Ward Draft, Ch.IX, p.36.

closest we have and is certainly not in any way what Murray would have produced had he had the time, which he never had, to devote to such a task.

Following the end of the occupation of France in 1818 the army was in large part disbanded and Mitchell was placed on half pay. In recognition of his work he was rewarded, in 1827, with promotion as Assistant Surveyor General in New South Wales, which was to build on the relationship that he and Murray had as a result of the Peninsular War, and which was to become the focus of Mitchell's life. There was considerable communication between the two men as Australia was opening up, and rampant jealousies arose among the small community in Sydney. Many issues that no doubt Murray would have preferred not to have to deal with landed on his desk during his tenure as Secretary of State for the Colonies between 1828 and 1830, as Mitchell was not short of an ability to take offence from every quarter.

Murray arrived back in Portsmouth on 3 August 1814, planning to be in London for a spell before heading, via Ochtertyre and Lochnell, to Dublin, where his stay was destined, yet again, to be short.

18

1815 – Canada, Command

The task of defeating Napoleon apparently behind him, Murray immediately wrote to Augusta telling her of his safe arrival back in London, at Mellor's Hotel in Jermyn Street. He was intending to be there for about three weeks before heading north to visit the family before crossing the Irish Sea again, to take up his new position as Adjutant General in Dublin.

Not for the first time, however, persuasive elements at Horse Guards homed in on Murray for yet another delicate task combining military responsibility with diplomatic skills and a possible taste of civil government. He was very soon busily engaged with typical thoroughness in gathering as much information as he could on the present situation, both political and military, in North America, where the War of 1812 was still dragging on. The Treaty of Ghent, to bring an end to the war, was not to be signed until 24 December 1814, although negotiations had been ongoing since August, following Napoleon's abdication. In the meantime full-scale military operations in America continued, including the attack on Washington and the burning of the White House. A long and detailed memorandum lies in the Murray Papers describing every step of the secret attack on Washington.[1] On 2 June the 4th, 44th, and 85th Regiments, two brigades of artillery, four 9-pounders, 2 howitzers, four 3-pounders, some rockets, and a company of Sappers and Miners, all under Major General Robert Ross, had sailed out of the Garonne with sealed orders, details of which must certainly have been known to Murray. The treaty was eventually ratified in mid-February 1815 by the US Senate, with fighting continuing up till the last moment.

As a result it seems that Murray never made it to Dublin, indeed perhaps never left London. The lack of his appearance in Scotland persuaded Augusta to plan a trip to London to catch up with him. He wrote to Augusta on 2 December warning her and the general not to make any plans to come to London to meet up with him referring to 'much uncertainty' on all his matters, and that he might have to leave London soon. Even if he were still there he would be so occupied with business that 'you would hardly ever see me and that always in a hurried and unsatisfactory manner'.[2] Murray had been chosen to head across the Atlantic to Canada, armed with letters from Horse Guards in terms of which he was

1 'Memorandum of Operations on the shores of the Chesapeake in 1814', Murray Papers, ADV MS 46.6.6.

2 Murray to Augusta, London, 2 December 1814, Murray Papers, MS 21103.

to relieve Lieutenant General George Prevost, the Governor General of Upper Canada – broadly today's Ontario – of his civil and military authority. Murray was instructed by Lord Bathurst to inform Prevost of the decision of the Prince Regent to recall him to explain his conduct at the defeat of the British forces by the Americans at Plattsburgh in September. Prevost was to surrender authority for civil affairs to Lieutenant General Drummond, the senior officer on the staff in Canada, until permanent arrangements were put in place.[3]

Not only was Prevost being blamed for mismanagement of the battle of Plattsburgh but he had certainly alienated many of the best troops that had been sent out from the Peninsula. His petty concerns about correctness of dress and behaviour were in marked contrast to the priorities they had grown used to under Wellington, leaving no doubt in Wellington's mind about the action that was required.

> It is very obvious to me that you must remove Sir George Prevost. I see he has gone to war about trifles with the general officers I sent him, which are certainly the best of their rank in the army; and his subsequent failure and distresses will be aggravated by that circumstance; and will probably with the usual fairness of the public be attributed to it.[4]

Prince William was quick with his congratulations to Murray:

> I have learnt with very great satisfaction your appointment to America. It would afford me very sincere pleasure to see you here on Saturday next at 12 o'clock should it not be inconvenient to you.
>
> I would greatly regret not having an opportunity of taking my leave of you before your departure and of assuring you in person that my best wishes will ever accompany you and that with perfect truth, regard and esteem.[5]

On 22 December Murray sailed from Spithead, on a strong easterly wind which promised a rapid Atlantic crossing, along with Commodore Sir Edward Owen, who was to succeed Sir James Yeo as naval commander in Canada, writing a final rushed letter to Augusta with some instructions regarding his possessions in London:

> We have got a fair wind this morning and are preparing to go on board. The Niobe is reckoned a very good ship for our purposes, and we have an abundant crew, as we take out both officers and seamen for other ships besides our own compliment.
>
> I left two keys with Mrs Churchill for you. One is the key of a writing desk I left in the Drawing room in N. Burlington Street, and the other is the key of one of the Drawers in your Drawing Room table. In that Drawer is the key of a closet upstairs containing my trunks and also the key of the cellar where I have left some of my Bordeaux Wine for the General's drinking.

3 Bathurst to Murray, Horse Guards, 13 December 1814, Murray Papers, ADV MS 46.6.5.

4 Anon., *Report of the Manuscripts of Earl Bathurst* (London: HM Stationery Office, 1923), p.302, quoting Wellington's letter to Bathurst of 30 October 1814, from Paris.

5 Prince William to Murray, Gloucester House, 15 December 1814, Murray Papers, MS 21104.

Lieutenant General Sir George Prevost. (Anne S.K. Brown Military Collection)

> In the drawer are some books belonging to Lady Mary and some seeds for necklaces which I brought home from the West Indies. You may do with them what you please. Perhaps you may find some person who will wear them.[6]

The *Bristol Mirror* of 24 December suggested that Murray's appointment was not properly understood by the public – he had been ordered to implement a complete review and overhaul of the army in North America, in preparation for the opening of a new campaign, after a number of setbacks. The newspaper did not suspect that Murray's first job was to be to deliver the dismissal notice to Prevost. However, the reporter did seem to have knowledge of the winter journey, some of it on foot, that awaited Murray and Owen on their arrival in Halifax, but reassured readers by pointing out that the pair were 'veteran officers', and that they would probably reach the army's headquarters inland after about a fortnight's freezing progress.

On arrival, after an event-free Atlantic crossing, Murray lost no time in writing again to Augusta:

> I wrote to you or the General, I forget which, from Spithead I believe on 21st or 22nd of December.
>
> We sailed from thence the next day and for the season of the year we have had a short and by no means disagreeable passage. We came to anchor last Sunday morning and I landed yesterday morning.
>
> Had we known the coast better our passage would probably have been still shorter for we were a week upon the coast before getting in. The weather is severe, but I do not find it unpleasant, for it is at present a dry cold, against which Clothing and Exercise are sufficient protection.
>
> Sir John Sherbrooke [commander of the British forces in the Atlantic Provinces] has received me very kindly and lodged me most comfortably.
>
> I left my star [Murray's Order of the Bath] at Mr Lawrences. When you come to town you may get it and put it by for me. It need not be sent out here as I have another with me.[7]

He wrote to Lord Bathurst next day:

> The Niobe came to anchor here on the evening of 29th January.
>
> The weather has set in with unusual severity since our arrival here and the harbour is at present covered with ice.
>
> Commodore Owen and myself have made arrangements for our conveyance by sleigh as far as Frederickton and we propose setting out upon Monday next.[8]

Murray must have taken Sherbrooke into his confidence about the intended recall of Prevost as he also mentioned Sherbrooke's concerns about what might be expected of him as second

6 Murray to Augusta, Portsmouth, 21 December 1814, Murray Papers, MS 21103.
7 Murray to Augusta, Halifax, 31 January 1815, Murray Papers, MS 21103.
8 Murray to Bathurst, Halifax, 1 February 1815, Murray Papers, ADV MS 46.6.5.

in command, about which Sherbrooke was less than enthusiastic. Murray heard for the first time of the ratification of the Treaty of Ghent by the Americans. From this moment Murray started to consider his options, none of which were at all clear, now that there was no military role for him, or at least no role that he had written authority for. For the next two months he repeatedly asked London, and appealed to Alexander Hope at Horse Guards, to let him at least have written authority as to his appointment on the staff in Canada.

The first section of the journey, from Halifax to Frederickton, a distance of 302 miles, was covered in 10 days. After a two day halt, Owen and Murray covered the next 372 miles to Quebec in 13 days, where they rested for five days. The Quebec-Montreal leg, a distance of 188 miles, took three days. The final part of the journey, Montreal to Kingston, 189 miles, where they arrived on 19 March, took five days. The whole journey was 1,051 miles, the longest single day covering 75 miles.[9] This was by a mixture of toboggan and on foot, in the depth of a Canadian winter. At least this time there was no harassment from French cavalry as there had been in his earlier winter retreats, and the pair were comfortably billeted at inns along the way, but it was impressive progress nonetheless.

Murray described the toboggan as a thin plank, 18 feet by six, turned up at the front in such a way as to flick off the snow, drawn by three dogs. Progress was faster on frozen lakes and rivers at more than five miles per hour, compared with three miles per hour over land. If the conditions were not right for this more comfortable mode of transport, the small party was forced to don snowshoes and walk, for a total of 62 miles. This caused Murray a good deal of pain, probably made worse as a result of his injury sustained at Den Helder. The constant lifting of his foot to a level about 15 inches above the snow caused his Achilles tendon to act up. This was, it seems, a common complaint when walking with snowshoes and was known as 'mal de racquette'. To add to their problems Murray's aide-de-camp suffered from frostbite from the very first day.

On reaching Montreal, with still no news as to what exactly Horse Guards planned for him, Murray turned yet again to his old friend Alexander Hope with a few requests for domestic items, seemingly preparing to hunker down for a spell in Canada, in a role which required a degree of style and entertaining. 'I am strongly recommended to get every thing out from England and I apprehend I shall require a great many things if I stay here'. He asked if Hope would try and track down some plate to match some he had already sourced from a shop in New Bond Street as well as asking for 'some stoneware from English Manufactories, both Dinner and Tea'. At the same time he made it quite clear to Hope that he was not interested in America unless he got the Government of Canada.[10]

From Kingston he wrote to Augusta describing his journey and the weather, going on to tell her that he regarded himself as a bit of a tourist with no pressing duties:

> As I have no military duties to attend to I look upon myself in the light of a traveller and mean to amuse myself accordingly.
>
> I calculate upon not knowing till May whether I am to remain in this country or not, and therefore consider myself as a free man till then.

9 Murray Papers, ADV MS 46.6.6.

10 Murray to Alexander Hope, Montreal, 14 March 1815, Luffness Mss, GD364/1/1267.

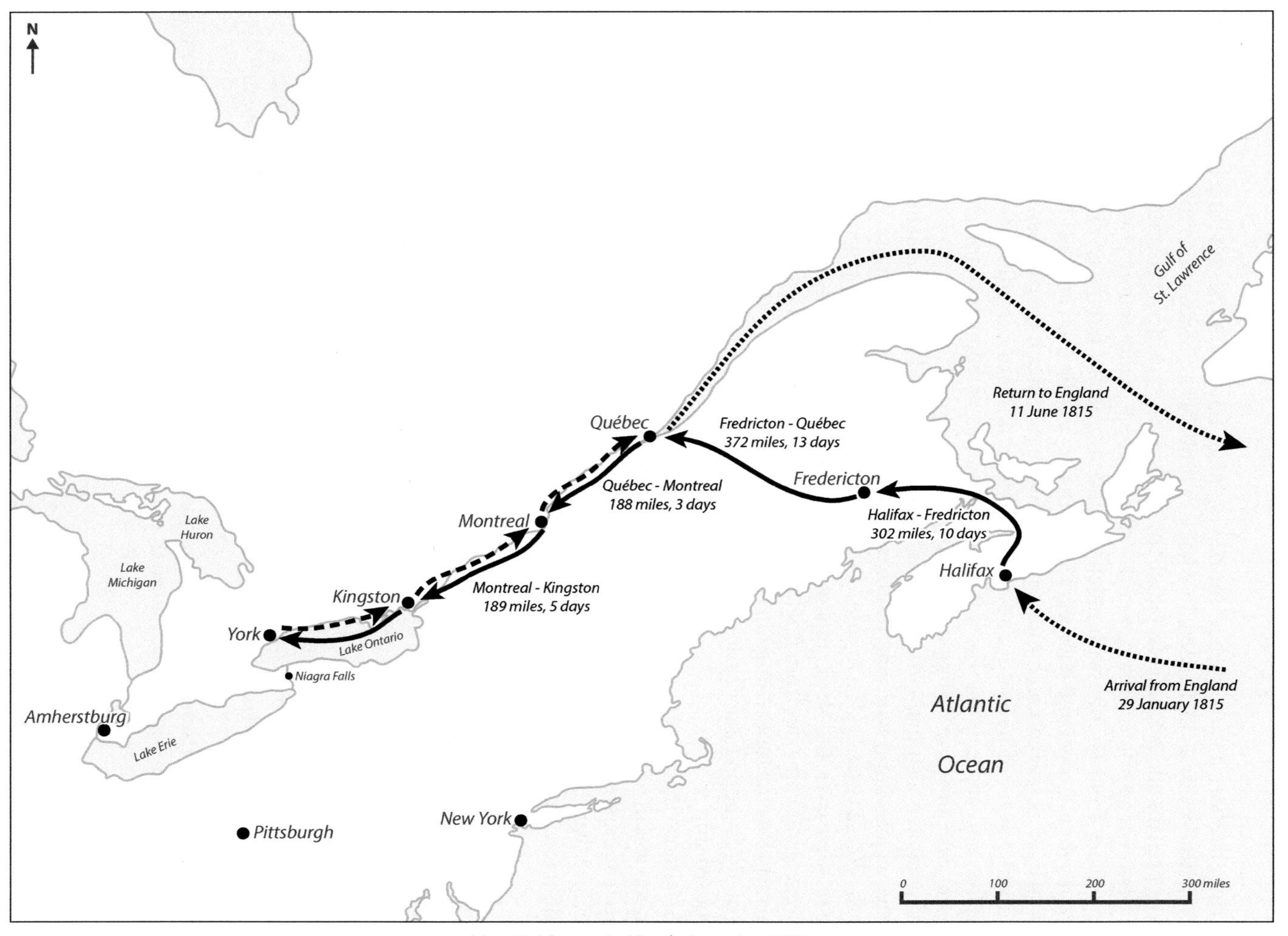

Map 9 Murray in North America, 1815.

> I am very comfortably situated here in Gl Drummond's House. He returned yesterday from the upper part of the Province.[11]

During the short stay in Quebec, Murray wrote to Lord Bathurst, advising him that he had dealt with Prevost as instructed, in what was probably an awkward conversation – Prevost, being, perhaps understandably, put out by the way his sacking was communicated to him in the person of an officer junior in rank – and went on: 'Commodore Owen and myself made our journey from Halifax with much less inconvenience, fatigue or difficulty that we had been taught to expect and it appears to me that by a little exertion, that line of communication may be rendered much more practicable than it has hitherto been'.[12] So Murray's old Peninsular habit of never squandering an opportunity to consider movement of men and supplies, and appreciating the potential difficulties or opportunities certain routes might present, was alive and being put to good use.

Murray had also had conversations with Drummond about the latter's wish to return home, which, along with Sherbrooke's reluctance to take on a more senior military role left the Horse Guards plan in some disarray. 'I propose going on towards Upper Canada in two or three days and shall employ myself in seeing as much of the country as I can, until arrangements come out from England to give me a fixed destination'.[13]Arriving at Kingston, Murray wrote to Hope telling him that he meant to get as far west as Amherstburg, 'making use of my canoe on Lake Erie for which purpose I shall have it conveyed at present to Niagara on board ship'.[14]

At almost the same moment, Bathurst was writing to Murray from Downing Street. London was in turmoil following Napoleon's escape from Elba at the end of February. On 20 March he entered Paris having already gathered significant military support. It was clear to the allies that they would have to regroup for a final attempt to rid Europe of him. Bathurst dealt first with the situation in Canada:

> I am very much puzzled as to how to act towards you. If I understand you right, you at parting told me that if war should take place in Europe, you were anxious to return.

But if there was to be peace;

> in that case on Drummond's return you were to be left in possession of the government of Canada (in the same manner for the present) as he holds it. If war breaks out, I shall counsel for Alexr Hope what he thinks you would wish to have decided for you.[15]

Torrens also wrote from Horse Guards a few days later when the seriousness of the situation in France must have made itself more than clear:

11 Murray to Augusta, Kingston, 23 March 1815, Murray Papers, MS 21103.

12 Murray to Bathurst, Quebec, 2 March 1815, Murray Papers, ADV MS 46.6.5.

13 Murray to Bathurst, Quebec, 2 March 1815, Murray Papers, ADV MS 46.6.5.

14 Murray to Hope, Kingston, 6 April 1815, Luffness Mss, GD 364/1/1264.

15 Bathurst to Murray, Downing Street, 20 March 1815, Murray Papers, ADV MS 46.6.5.

> The extraordinary events in Europe have suggested to the Duke and Lord Bathurst the desire of having the advantage of your able services once more in the field of Europe. Desirable however as this object must be in the public point of view nothing can be further from the wish of HRH and His Lordship than to force you to a step contrary either to your instincts or inclination and it was not until an encouragement was received from your friend Alexr Hope that a decision was formed upon sending for you at all.
>
> My official letter leaves the matter entirely to your option.
>
> Who could have supposed that Bonaparte could have taken back possession of the French Throne without firing a shot!! Fatal Event![16]

While the exchanges of correspondence were making their inevitably slow progress across the Atlantic and inland from Halifax, Murray was not idle. He assumed de facto command of the troops in Upper Canada and involved himself in their relocation after the ratification of the Treaty of Ghent. He produced a long memorandum on the proposed naval establishment on Lake Huron, and published his views on the best way to handle new settlers and where to locate them. The system at the time allowed for field officers in the army to be granted 5,000 acres, with reduced acreage for more junior officers and those from the ranks. A corporal would be granted 400 acres. All these grants of land were free. Common settlers, those not from the armed forces, would be allowed between 200 and 1,200 acres each, but they had to pay for them.

Murray also had something to say about where to relocate the people of the aboriginal first nations who had fought with the British, to ensure they were settled in areas where they could live easily and productively. The British military recommendation that the area surrounding Chenail Ecarte, a river running into Lake St Clair, Ontario, be used as a settlement for aboriginal warriors who had fought for the crown was correct he felt, rather than the prevailing view that they should be settled around Detroit. His feeling was that they would be much better situated at Chenail Ecarte where they could plant and benefit by hunting and fishing during the summer. However the military recommendations failed to materialize and the land Murray had wanted to see them settled on was instead subdivided and sold, or given to settlers and speculators or to non-aboriginal soldiers as their reward for services in the war just ended.

By 22 April 1815 Murray's latest instructions from London had caught up with him, by now at Burlington. He wrote to Commodore Owen that he had received instructions on addressing the Civil Administration of the Province, and intended to return to York immediately. On arrival there on 25 April, he sent word to Drummond, with a fuller letter to Bathurst the same day: 'I have the honour to acquaint you that I have this day taken upon me the Civil Government of the Province of Upper Canada, as senior officer of the troops serving within the Province'.[17]

Murray assumed the title of Provisional Lieutenant Governor, but was still anxious not to be seen to have assumed authority, where it was not correctly granted, and wrote to

16 Torrens to Murray, Horse Guards, 30 March 1815, Murray Papers, ADV MS 46.6.5.

17 Murray to Drummond, and Murray to Bathurst, York, 25 April 1815, Murray Papers, ADV MS 46.6.5.

Lord Bathurst the same day hoping that he had acted in accordance with His Majesty's Government's intentions. He left it to Bathurst to correct any mistakes he might have made 'in case the opinion which has guided me on this occasion should appear to your Lordship to be erroneous'. From this moment he would be addressed as 'Your Excellency'. No doubt he would have been on the receiving end of a good deal of teasing by Augusta were it not for the rapidly unfolding events in France, which were to cut his tenure of office short. He did write to her on 24 April with his faint praise of Niagara, and a hint of the interest he was taking in the treatment of the native population:

> I must say it is stupendous but it hardly gives pleasure. A picturesque fall in Switzerland or in the Highlands is a far more pleasing object and one to which you would go much oftener and stay much longer.
>
> Amongst the other sights I have seen several of the Indians. It is a sad sight to see them brutalized to the degree that they have by their acquaintance with us. I have been working in my mind various schemes for an attempt to improve them, but I can hardly hope that my plan would succeed. It struck me amongst other things that it would be desirable that they had a translation of Ossian that they might see the virtues of the savage (begging your ancestors pardon) without his vices. I will let you know more of these people when I have been more amongst them.[18]

Events conspired to deny him the chance to settle into his new role in Canada, with its trappings of power, and prestige. He was being given a clear choice by Horse Guards. He could stay – and in fact there was a feeling that any new war in Europe against Napoleon would inevitably mean a renewal of the hostilities in America, so there would be military command for Murray on this side of the Atlantic – or he could return to the old team and help Wellington despatch Napoleon finally. In reply to Bathurst's options he wrote: 'I shall not hesitate to comply with the latter alternative'.[19]

He wrote to Torrens from Kingston on 20 May thanking him for allowing him to choose, and to notify him that 'a couple of days will suffice. I hope to wind up my business here and I shall then proceed to Quebec to take my passage home by the first opportunity that offers'.[20] At the same time he was happy to admit that were it not for the renewal of hostilities in Europe, 'I would have no objection to be placed for a time on this side of the Atlantic'.[21]

He wrote to Owen on 31 May, looking for the fastest vessel possible to speed him back to join his old commander.

> [T]he letters for me, saved from the wreck of the Penelope, have induced me to decide upon getting to the coast and I shall probably be desirous of the first opportunity that offers for passage to Europe.

18 Murray to Augusta, York, 24 April 1815, Murray Papers, MS 21103.

19 Murray to Bathurst, (Draft letter) Kingston, 30 May 1815, Murray Papers, ADV MS 46.6.5.

20 Murray to Torrens, Kingston, 30 May 1815, Murray Papers, ADV MS 46.6.5.

21 Murray to Lord Melville, Kingston, 30 May 1815, Murray Papers, ADV MS 46.6.5.

> I shall have to request a favour of your good office towards obtaining me a passage in a Man of War to Europe, if any means of that kind is possible.[22]

Murray penned one final letter to Augusta before leaving Kingston, telling her that he was on his way back: 'It is high time I should hasten back there now that my old friend has again got into power'.[23]

Meticulous as ever in attending to his expenses, before leaving York on 3 June Murray repaid the £150 advanced as travelling expenses for him and Owen at Halifax. His entire expense account covering the four months he was in Canada and the pay he received is recorded in fine detail. It shows that his pay was 84 shillings a day, on top of which he was allowed lodging money of 10 shillings a day. Bat and Forage allowance, allowable expenses for servants, was 21 shillings a day. The hire of the sleighs from Halifax to Kingston cost £91 14s 9 1/2d.[24]

Murray embarked at Quebec, bound for a Europe that was again on a war footing, on 11 June, ignorant of the events that culminated exactly a week later at the Battle of Waterloo. In Murray's absence, Wellington was to rely on De Lancey, Murray's longstanding loyal assistant in the Peninsula, in the role of Quartermaster General. He was to die, in his wife's arms, two days after the battle, after being shot at the height of the action while sitting on his horse alongside Wellington.

Given the time it took for correspondence to make its way across the Atlantic and the loss and delay of critical correspondence on board HMS *Penelope* which had been shipwrecked on 27 April in the St Lawrence, with the loss of forty of her crew, London had no idea what Murray had decided; was he still in Canada or on his way home? As late as 3 July Lord Bathurst was seeking assurance from Hope that, as his own letter must have gone down with the *Penelope*, he could rely on Hope's letter of around the same time as having outlined the same alternatives. He was keen to discuss the whole matter at his house in Putney over dinner the following week, as now the situation had changed since Waterloo. What on earth was he to do with Murray if and when he did appear?[25] Hope had left Sandhurst, where he was now Governor, for Scotland, and Bathurst's letter followed him there. Hope replied that he had never sent his letter. Nevertheless, perhaps fortunately, Murray in fact was acting on the basis of Torrens' letter. Hope stated that he was entirely confident, knowing his brother-in-law as he did, that Murray would not pass up an opportunity to come back to Wellington's side, especially in the light of Murray's earlier comments on his reluctance to stay in America unless as Governor General, which was certainly far from being decided. That said, he expressed the view that if there was nothing for him in Europe, Murray should be offered the Canada Governorship. Hope considered him well qualified for the Canadian role, with his knowledge of mankind, calmness and judgement. His military skills would also be useful in the event of any war with America, and he would be good at negotiating boundaries if it came to that. It certainly seemed that a return to Canada would make the

22 Murray to Owen, Kingston, 31 May 1815, Murray Papers, ADV MS 46.6.5.
23 Murray to Augusta, Kingston, 31 May 1815, Murray Papers, MS 21103.
24 For meticulous details of all Murray's Canadian expenses, see Murray Papers, ADV MS 46.6.5.
25 Bathurst to Alexander Hope, Downing Street, 3 July 1815, Luffness Mss, GD 364/1/1267.

most of Murray's talents and reinforced his reputation as a fixer where a variety of skills, both military and diplomatic, were likely to be required in a difficult arena.

Murray arrived in Portsmouth on 13 July. His arrival coincided with the disembarkation of 12,800 troops from Canada off 52 transports. He hastened to London with despatches for the government and to establish what was intended as the ultimate destination for the soldiers. As far as his own movements were concerned, he renewed his habit of contacting Kitty, who wrote back about the death of her adored brother, Edward Pakenham, who had been killed at the Battle of New Orleans in January, after the Treaty of Ghent had been signed.

> We have indeed suffered my Dear General Murray and often have we felt for you whom he so affectionately loved, so true a friend, so true a character is hardly to be found and the loss of such a companion will be long and sharply felt.[26]

There were to be no more dreams of ginger wine in the company of her three favourite men.

After alerting Wellington to his arrival, and receiving a letter by return, he let Hope know that he had agreed with Bathurst to go at once to Paris, to join Wellington. Perhaps the ammunition of a summons from Wellington in Murray's pocket was enough to let Bathurst see that there was an immediate solution to the question of Murray's employment, but it still seemed that options were being floated in front of Murray. 'Confidentially' he said to Hope, 'there seems some idea of my returning to Canada'.[27] Hope's persuasive voice had yet again been heeded. Murray was still holding out firmly for the Governor's post or nothing, if he was to be persuaded to return across the Atlantic.

Wellington was growing impatient. He had missed Murray's proven ability to work alongside him effectively in times of crisis. There was a good deal of catching up to be done.

> I have received your letter of the 17th for which I am very much obliged to you. I regretted much that you went to America at the moment you did and I think that if you had received a letter which I wrote to you from hence immediately previous to your departure before you had sailed you would not have gone. I regretted it still more since. I conclude you will come out here immediately and by the direct road and I defer till I see you to advert to our loss of many friends &c.[28]

Wellington's letter was clear in tone as regards the past, and forceful about the present. It was another example of how lives and their journeys could be affected by the occasional delays in getting mail to the addressee, especially when on the move. No doubt if Wellington's letter had arrived, Murray would have taken up whatever Wellington was offering, would have been at the centre of planning from the moment Bonaparte landed in southern France from Elba, and perhaps put in place better contingencies prior to the Emperor's arrival on the Belgian border. He might well have gratefully taken the alarm as an excuse to cut short his evening at the Duchess of Richmond's Ball, to use every scrap of time to move the army into

26 Kitty Wellington to Murray, London, (undated), Murray Papers, ADV MS 46.6.5.

27 Murray to Alexander Hope, London, 20 July 1815, Luffness Mss, GD 364/1/1268.

28 Wellington to Murray, Paris, 23 July 1815, Murray Papers, ADV MS 46.6.5.

better defensive positions. He would certainly have worked very closely with Wellington over the three crucial days which saw such bitter fighting. He, not De Lancey, would have been mounted next to his commander in the thick of the day's fighting at Waterloo, and perhaps he would have paid for his loyalty with his life.

Having absorbed Hope's advice Bathurst considered Murray's position, which was somewhat altered since Wellington's intervention. Murray was able to write to Hope from Paris in August that he had been offered temporary Governor Generalship in Canada, but in the interim he had been persuaded by Wellington that he was required for some time yet in Paris and he intended to carry on there for the time being. His first impressions of Paris were that it was not for him. Noting that Augusta had failed to source some cloth for him, he said:

> [I]t is of no sort of consequence. When I mean to be incognito I put on my blue Great Coat which answers the purpose in most cases very well. As to yourself, though all who see your wish to be at Paris will tell you that nothing is so pleasant, yet I apprehend that you would not like it long. For my part I have seen most of the sights and would not be sorry now to get away. However I am still in the dark as to my plans, but I propose bringing things to an issue soon.[29]

While familiarizing himself with his new duties, Murray started to weigh up the two options that were now both seemingly on offer; Canada or peacetime Europe? At this point the role that seemed to be the most likely one for him was that of Quartermaster General to the British Army in France. That gave Murray some concern. The responsibilities would be limited, despite the closeness to Wellington, and certainly less demanding of his battle-hardened skills gained as Wellington's number two in the Peninsula. So, ever aware of the maxim that if one does not ask one does not get, with the confidence gained from knowing that he now was held in great esteem at the very highest levels in London, and aware of Wellington's profound confidence in him, he floated the idea that he might be appointed chief of staff of all the allied armies. He acknowledged that such a situation was not one that was recognized in the British Army, but did exist elsewhere and would be an ideal solution for the current circumstances, where there were so many differing national forces occupying France. He was always conscious of the money on offer for any position that he might be considered for, but in this instance he was happy that 'neither emoluments nor the comforts of Society' should get in the way and his 'main object was to follow up whatever branch of useful public employment circumstances render it most proper to lean to, and to trust to that course bringing ultimately such rewards fortune may put in the way'.[30]

By September Murray was in London again, and wrote to Wellington on the 26th confirming the conversation that he had had with Bathurst, who was happy to leave things in Murray's hands, so he planned to return to France as chief of staff, a position 'which seemed to accord perfectly to your views'.[31]

29 Murray to Augusta, Paris, 21 August 1815, Murray Papers, MS 21103.
30 Murray to Alexander Hope, Paris, 21 August 1815, Luffness Mss, GD 364/1/1268.
31 Murray to Wellington, London, 26 September 1815, Murray Papers, MS ADV 46.6.7.

British officer in blue great coat c.1810. (Anne S.K. Brown Military Collection)

Having had a riding accident on arrival in London he was still on crutches but was hopeful of regaining the use of his leg in a few days. From his familiar quarters at 16 New Burlington Street he wrote to Hope, referring to the accident he had had on arriving which had prevented him seeing Bathurst, but he had sent him notice that he would take whatever job was allotted to him. Bathurst had called on him and it had been finally, he thought, determined that Murray was to return to Wellington, who was soon impatiently urging Murray to get back to him, writing from Paris on 27 October:

> I desired your ADC to write to you the day before yesterday, and tell you how anxious I was for your early arrival, and lest he should have omitted to do so, I now write to beg you will come without loss of time.[32]

32 Wellington to Murray, Paris, 27 October 1815, Gurwood (ed.), *Dispatches*, Vol.XII, p.672.

19

1815-1818 – France, Army of Occupation

On arrival back in Paris Murray did not take long to assume authority over the numerous and varied issues that were to be his lot for the next three years. The copious quantities of correspondence with allies and the French War Ministry, as well as French customs, were conducted largely in French. The problems and disputes that arose, or threatened to break the uneasy peace, landed on Murray's desk without let up. English society, now gleefully embarking on the short Channel crossing, made determined attempts to circumvent French customs controls, leaving Murray to decide on whether to intervene on their behalf with the authorities. Some had resorted to suitcases with false bottoms to bring in goods for their ladies. In delicate matters of interpretation referral was made to the Treaty of 20 November 1815, which covered such matters; for example importing gunpowder and shot was prohibited, and snuff was dutiable.

There were a number of issues concerning the Prussians in particular, when arrangements had to be made to replace French garrisons in numerous forts around the country with allied troops. One of the more mundane tasks required of the British officers sent to oversee each handover was the making of full inventories in every case, so that after the occupation the assets seized could be accounted for and handed back to the French. In a number of cases the Prussians claimed arms, horses, and artillery pieces as belonging to them, on the basis that they had taken control of a particular fort prior to the signing of the peace treaty and as such they were fairly the spoils of war. Murray cautioned his officers not to get caught in the crossfire:

> Any questions that arise between the French Government and that of a separate power where troops were already in possession of any fortress before the signing of the Treaty and Convention of 20th November is foreign to the business on which you are specially employed.[1]

Some fortresses remained blockaded by the Prussians and it was proving difficult to arrange a flow of meal and flour to keep the garrisons alive. In the case of Charlemont the Prussians refused to leave the fort, still with French military in it, until the Russian replacement

1 Murray to Lieutenant Colonel Adye, Paris, 17 December 1815, Murray Papers, ADV MS 46.6.7.

garrison was actually at the gates. The British officer insisted on having a couple of days to clean the barracks and whitewash the buildings. An appeal went back to Murray in Paris asking him to send the necessary stiff letter to his Prussian counterpart. The handover went off smoothly a week later, the French leaving at 9 o'clock the morning after the Russians had arrived. The French National Guard marched off to their several villages and the regular French troops marched to Verdun, to be disbanded. Such scenes were repeated all over France. The French, for their part, regularly disputed the accuracy of the paperwork on which British authority relied.

Wellington was, as ever, conscious of costs and sought Murray's assistance in finding ways to reduce the numbers of backroom staff, particularly in areas such as commissaries, storekeepers, and paymasters as well as the Royal Artillery and Royal Engineers. Some of these functions might, he felt, just as well be carried out from England. There was a constant need to be alert to ill-discipline of troops. There were the usual complaints to be dealt with of troops subsisting on putrid meat and poor quality bread, without salt or candles. Murray's role, responsible for the management of 150,000 victorious troops, of many differing nationalities, was a huge one.

Paris was the fashionable place to be in the years after Waterloo, and British society flocked there to mix with their European counterparts at the glittering dinners, balls and military displays. Cambrai, 60 or so miles north, was headquarters to the 30,000 British troops that remained in France, under the command of Lieutenant General Sir Lowry Cole, the Irishman, one of Murray's closest friends from the Peninsula. He lived at No 1 in the Rue de Poissonier near the Cathedral and close to Wellington's house, and, one assumes, to Murray's. On one trip to Paris, Murray was asked by Cole's wife to buy a hat for her, she being clearly delighted with the result of the last joint shopping expedition carried out on her behalf by the two generals. He replied:

> I shall go about your commission this morning and shall do my best to equal Sir Lowry in taste. As to price however you must expect me to pay at least double, for I have no chance single-handed against a Marchande de Modes! Indeed I think Sir Lowry owed half his success to my modesty, for I was so much ashamed of his bargaining that I was forced to go out of the shop, from which the woman supposed we were going off altogether and instantly came down in her demands! My manoeuvre will probably turn to my own confusion, however when I am without a well practiced second capable of turning it to account.
>
> You were extremely welcome to make the use you did of my house for your aunt and cousins. As there seems such a want of other accommodation I shall offer the same use of it to the Erskines, who talk of setting out for Brussels on Monday. Although indeed if we make a general move about that time I shall be at a loss how to give up my house, but as I propose dining with an Irish friend I may possibly find a night's lodging under the table![2]

2 Murray to Cole, 6 April 1816, Maud Lowry Cole and Stephen Gwynn (eds.), *Memoirs of Sir Lowry Cole* (London: Macmillan, 1934), p.185.

Murray opened an account with Messrs Perrigaux Lafitte & Co in Paris, which was used frequently to arrange payment for the very large quantities of wine that his household and guests consumed. On 9 September he paid £120 to Mr Payon, having already made a large payment at the end of August. On 27 January 1816 he ordered 26 bottles of Bordeaux and 12 of Madiera, with an identical order three weeks later, supplemented by good numbers of Port and Champagne. The next month he placed an order with Messrs Martell for no less than 430 bottles of Bordeaux, 300 of Madiera, and 80 Port, to be sent to his house in Cambrai. Total wine consumption between 1815 and 1818 amounted to no less than 3,232 bottles, or about 3 bottles a day at home.[3] The entertaining must have been intense. His pay at this point was £2,400per annum, plus an allowance for Table Money of £1,500.

His letters to Augusta are, as might be expected, full of his and her social engagements. She was enjoying London social life as she always had; he was doing his best to keep up in Paris and Cambrai. Her 'long catalogues of the names of the people you give dinners to' were matched by his tongue in cheek name dropping, including dining with Lord Charles Murray, Mr Playfair, and the Breadalbanes.[4]

Life in Edinburgh and Perthshire was not perhaps being carried on on such a grand scale for brother Patrick, although he had settled back into his legal career and held the positions of Lord Chief Baron and Lord Justice Clerk, but was probably still spending more than his income. Throughout the country dinners were being held to celebrate the victory at Waterloo, and Patrick attended the Edinburgh function at the Assembly Rooms with 400 others. The toasts went on and on but two were notable. One was to Sir William De Lancey, replacement Quartermaster General for Murray at the battle, who had died of his wounds. The other was to then-Sergeant Ewart of the Scots Greys, now commissioned as an ensign, who had captured a French Eagle. When begged to speak Ewart politely declined saying he would rather fight the battle all over again than speak before such a gathering.

Murray moved frequently between Paris, where he often stayed at Hotel des Americains, and Cambrai, where the house he had taken seemed to be in a state of disrepair. In July 1816 a requisition was sent for kitchen and chamber grates for the house and a stove for the servants' room. This was accompanied by a request to have the oven fitted up and a kitchen table supplied. There were payments on a regular basis for wood for fitting up the house, iron for the stoves in the kitchen, and materials for doing up the chapel. Carpenters' and masons' bills came in regularly. Nor was the garden neglected, where more expenses were incurred. The alcohol must have helped alleviate the relative discomfort – 100 bottles of Champagne in September 1816 followed by 250 bottles of various wines and a barrel of Sauternes in December. Murray did not neglect his mind though, and paid a six month subscription to the Cambrai Book Society in December. He had *Gazette de France* delivered regularly. He was a subscriber to the theatre in Cambrai as well as the Guards Club.[5]

Certainly good reports flowed from Cambrai – Captain George Bowles of the Guards, encamped with his regiment, wrote of the 'incessant round of parties by day and night', and 'impossible to imagine any schoolboy in higher spirits or up to any sort of fun than the

3 Murray Papers, ADV MS 46.8.5.

4 Murray to Augusta, Paris, 4 July 1816, Murray Papers, MS 21103.

5 Murray Papers, ADV MS 46.8.5, small green leather notebook stamped 'Comptes du General Murray du 1 Janvier 1815'. This account book also gives details of the wine consumption.

Duke of Wellington' who had just sent for a pack of hounds.[6] During his time there Murray again fell from his horse, early in 1817, although on a Paris street rather than in a chase, but by the end of February his right leg – which was broken and dislocated – was mending well and Murray was again mobile, on crutches. His rapid recovery was put down to 'that tranquillity which never abandons him on any occasion', as well as the speed at which passers-by lent a hand and called for medical assistance.[7]

It is difficult to gauge accurately what level of staff Murray had at Cambrai and Paris. Ward records about a dozen, including three French cooks, a butler (Gordon Monro), a groom (Andrew Blyth), both of whom had been with him in the Peninsula, a batman (John Hill), a coachman, a valet, housemaid and kitchenmaid. By the middle of 1817 work on the house at Cambrai was still not complete, but they had at least reached the painting stage.

Rumours circulated towards the end of January 1818 that an attempt was to be made on Wellington's life. Lord Kinnaird, who had received the information from a leading French exile in Brussels, passed on the intelligence to Murray in Paris who replied that, having in turn communicated the plot to Wellington, the latter was unconcerned and planned to continue his business as before. Then, however, a shot was fired at the Duke in his carriage, just outside his Paris mansion on the Champs Elysees, on his way home from an evening's amusement. The shot went wide. It was a strange affair with Kinnaird himself being arrested at one point and nobody being convicted. Wellington refused to increase his personal protection, but, aware of possible attempts on his life, he became careful where he went unless in the presence of crowds or police. He used a plain carriage at night whose doors had been altered to frustrate attack, with some arms inside and an armed guard on the box.[8] However, neither this plot not any other political pressures would move Wellington from his determination to end the occupation at the earliest possible moment. The Congress of Aix la Chapelle opened on 1 October 1818 and negotiations commenced for the future shape of Europe. Murray left France for the last time in December 1818 taking with him, it seems, John Hill, Auguste (one of his cooks), Monro, and a housemaid.

Murray's return from Paris followed soon after the attempt of Sir Walter Scott – who was later to stage manage the elaborate visit of George IV to Scotland in 1822 – to unearth the long 'lost' Scottish Crown Jewels. The Prince Regent had given his support to an initiative to try and find them, thought to be secured in Edinburgh Castle's Crown Room. On 4 February 1818 they were discovered in a huge chest wrapped in linen, exactly as they had been for over 100 years, since being secreted away from public view lest they acted as a magnet for Jacobite Scots following the Union in 1707. The scene was depicted by Edinburgh artist Andrew Geddes in a large painting, showing the Commissioners, Murray amongst them, who were given the responsibility for their safekeeping, gathered round the chest as it was opened. Murray was certainly appointed as one of those Commissioners, and the date of 4 February is not in dispute, as it is recorded at the time by Scott. There was, however, no way that Murray could have been present as he was still in France.

Throughout the three years of the allied occupation, Murray's relationship with the French authorities was professional and cordial. Given Murray's recognized diplomatic skill

6 Cole and Gwynn (eds.), *Sir Lowry Cole*, pp.186-7.
7 Captain Eckersley to General Campbell, Paris, 24 February 1817, Murray Papers, MS 21101.
8 Muir, *Waterloo and the Fortunes of Peace*, p.112.

and the respect in which he was held by both the victorious allies and the French, there were no doubt many occasions where the inevitable tensions involving so many nations in the aftermath of a long and bloody war were relieved by his calm, measured approach and natural charm, but equally he seemed more than ready to leave when the time came. Reading between the lines of one of his final letters from Cambrai, in this case to Hill, his peacetime role seems to have been less than totally fulfilling:

> I shall set out from Paris the day after tomorrow and I shall not regret it myself though it should prove to be my last visit there in our present situation. It will be interesting to see next year how the French go on when left to themselves.[9]

9 Murray to Hill, Cambrai, 19 June 1818, Hill Papers, MS 49508.

20

Love and Marriage

Murray may not have regretted leaving France, but personal events that had taken place there during his time as chief of staff were to alter his life completely.[1] In the aftermath of Napoleon's defeat, British society made for Paris. After, in some cases – including Murray's – twenty years of intense military service, it was inevitable that army officers, no doubt smartened up in new uniforms, would find themselves the centre of attraction for the young ladies who had made the short crossing. After the long years of austerity and fear the young and not-so-young enjoyed the peace, and allowed themselves to be absorbed into the rounds of parties and receptions that were thrown, especially by those anxious to demonstrate their Bourbon loyalties.

One such couple welcoming the incomers were the Craufurds, Quintin and Anna. They were an unusual couple, Madame Craufurd in particular having had a varied life in India and on the Continent, as mistress to different men, eventually marrying Craufurd, an uncle of the Peninsular general. They occupied a grand house with large garden standing on the Rue d'Anjou.[2] Madame Craufurd was not to everyone's taste but that did not prevent her generous and regular hospitality being freely accepted and enjoyed. An afternoon at 'Craw's' was socially just within the bounds of propriety but there is no doubt that it was a venue for a good deal of flirtatious behaviour, if not anything more serious, and both sexes felt free to enjoy themselves, whether married and visiting with spouses, or unattached.

Sir James Erskine, younger brother of Major General Sir William Erskine, the Peninsular general whose fragile mental state had resulted in many unnecessary Peninsular casualties, including his own death below a Lisbon balcony, was one of those establishment figures persuaded that Paris was the place to be and be seen. He was less interested in the

1 The sources consulted by the author for this chapter are from the evidence contained in the Libel and Exhibits of the case of Erskine v Erskine in the Lambeth Palace Library, including a series of letters from Louisa to Erskine, (Arches H 340/1-9, Arches Aaa 42 (Film 108); the reports of the Sheriff's Court case of 23 July 1824, in the *Morning Chronicle*, and other newspapers, and the Murray Papers, MS 21192 which contain some legal papers. Some correspondence, referred to by Ward as being in the possession of the Marquess of Anglesey (Anglesey Mss), has not been examined by the author.

2 Ward Draft, Ch.XVII, pp.1-2. As pointed out by Ward in a footnote, the identity of the owners was kept from the court, but the house was in the Rue d'Anjou where the Hotel de Craufurd was situated, and Louisa refers to 'Craw's'). Ward, opposite p.2 of Ch XVII, cites numerous sources for his background on the Craufurds.

socializing, more in the opportunity for acquiring substantial works of art, for which he had an extraordinary eye.

Sir James' military career was less than heroic. He had made rapid progress up the promotions ladder owing largely to his and his wife's connections at court. He had met Louisa Paget, daughter of the 1st Earl of Uxbridge, whilst on duty at Windsor. After carrying on a romantic courtship against the wishes of both sets of parents, he succeeded in tipping the balance in his favour on the back of the promise of an annual pension of £509 for Louisa from the State; this was at the instigation of the King, who appointed Erskine one of his aides de camp.[3] Louisa's parents relented and also granted her money from a trust fund, so, despite being a younger son, James was relatively well set up, and following their marriage in 1801 he continued with a comfortable, undemanding and quite well paid military career at home, where promotion was unusually rapid, to the rank of lieutenant general in 1814. His limited overseas service was a short spell in the Peninsula in 1809 when he travelled to join Wellington shortly before the Battle of Talavera. He was in command of a cavalry brigade, but never had the chance to demonstrate whether he had the qualities necessary for such a demanding role, as he was taken ill at Plasencia and transported back to Lisbon, thence to England. He inherited the Torrie estate in Fife, after his elder brother's suicide in 1813, which significantly improved his finances, although, in common with so many Scottish estates at the time, including Ochtertyre, it was heavily indebted.

What looks on the face of it to have been something of a charmed life, with easy promotion based on royal patronage, a decent income, a large estate, a charming, pretty, and well-connected wife, was less than happy, or at least gradually became so. Louisa had expensive tastes and loved all things new. Erskine's income was good but certainly not capable of being stretched to the extent that Louisa might have felt was requisite for her comfort. The debts started to mount. There was perhaps too an element of sexual disharmony. It seems that Erskine was less highly sexed than Louisa, who had perhaps inherited the Paget appetite. During Erskine's absences from home, Louisa would often go and stay with the Wemyss family, not far from Torrie. General William Wemyss was colonel of the 93rd Regiment of Foot, and related to Erskine by marriage. There were rumours of an affair. Erskine knew of the rumours and it had a devastating effect on him.

> I knew not how to act. I had seen the thing long myself… and knowing how delicate the knot is which really binds the married state, I delayed speaking perhaps too long, unwilling to show any want of confidence… I saw with an undescribable pain that she did not feel it as I did, but her natural irritation of disposition was augmented to a degree that, day after day, I left the house to seek quiet out of doors… My whole frame eventually began to sink.[4]

There are a few clues to the reasons why such an apparently well matched couple should, from quite early in their marriage, have hit problems, apart from the sexual mismatch. Clinton, who had known Erskine at Horse Guards disliked him intensely: 'Among the characters',

3 Ward Draft, Ch.XVII, p.3.

4 Ward Draft, Ch.XVII, pp.4-5 (including citing draft letter Erskine to Lord Harcourt undated but about November 1819, from the Anglesey Mss).

he recorded, 'I mostly dislike that I now and then meet with at the office is a certain Jemmy Erskine. I never liked him much, but there is something in his manner exceedingly offensive. I am sure he is a proud unfeeling fellow, and though he may be pushed by friends he will never shine as a great man'.[5]

Incapable of confronting Louisa, or dealing with the causes of the stresses in the marriage, Erskine soldiered on. For some people in such a situation the solution might have been to settle on the continent, and to start afresh away from the stultifying house parties of London or Scotland. Napoleon, however, had put paid to any such thoughts. By the time of the allied occupation of France in 1815 the marriage had reached an unhappy stage of tolerance and lack of interest. If the idea was that a tour of France and the Low Countries might provide a cure then such a dream was to be rudely shattered. Irreparable damage would be done in the temptingly decadent surroundings of 'Craw's'.

The tour included Paris, at the Hotel Irlande, and Brussels where they stayed with Caroline Capel, Louisa's sister. By December 1816 they were back in Paris where they were based until they headed back to Britain in March 1817. While in Paris they were in the habit of sampling Madame Craufurd's hospitality. Wellington and Murray were also regulars. Some suggested that such a place was perhaps not in keeping with the dignity of a commander in chief, and arguably by the same measure the chief of staff, but it was bound to be the case that the military men of all nations would find amusement and feel at home there. Surely, too, nobody would dare to question the right of such men, the saviours of Europe, to enjoy each other's company and the flattery of Paris's most charming ladies.

The Erskines it seems would often arrive together, occasionally accompanied by Caroline. James, perhaps feeling less a hero than those in whose company he now found himself, frequently left to scour the shops and galleries of the city in search of paintings and sculptures. He had an excellent eye for antiques and seemed to find the money to indulge his passion, with the result that his acquisitions during his time in France form the bulk of the valuable Torrie Collection at the University of Edinburgh, a substantial part of which is now on permanent loan to the National Galleries of Scotland. Louisa was left in the company of some attractive men, men like Wellington and Murray with glittering military backgrounds, whose company was no doubt keenly sought. Given the state of her marriage, and the hothouse atmosphere of the French capital, it is not surprising that flirtatious activity flourished. To Louisa, Murray was successful, handsome, educated, mature; a man at the peak of an illustrious military career. He had access to the senior French military and political figures who were trying to rebuild France. She was smitten. That she still loved her husband is probable, but here was excitement and glamour at the very top of society, where she felt she belonged. Although sharing with James a love of art, and perhaps his satisfaction of a day's successful bargaining, the laughter, gossip and political manoeuvring amongst lively minds in glamorous surroundings would prove too much of a temptation, as Louisa came to realise that, although now in her early forties, she was still attractive and could turn men's heads. She captivated Murray.

What actually happened at 'Craw's' between the two of them is unclear – even from the testimonies of those involved in later divorce proceedings. That they spent time alone in

5 Ward Draft, Ch.XVII, p.6 (citing W. Clinton Ms Diary, 14 October 1800, p.35).

bedrooms does not in itself prove there was any sexual relationship. This was not considered abnormal behaviour in France at the time. They were described as holding hands and laughing together when Erskine was on his buying expeditions. That they were behaving immoderately, given that one of them was married, was a fact, but that was almost expected at such a place. There was much coming and going, and slamming of doors, when Erskine once returned unexpectedly early, and he had to wait for a while until his wife appeared. He must certainly have felt that same sinking feeling he had felt when the rumours surfaced of the affair with Wemyss.

Murray and Louisa continued to meet regularly at 'Craw's', most afternoons, and would pass messages to each other via their servants should one or other of them be unable to be there. Even after breaking his ankle in 1817, and barely able to walk, he would try and meet Louisa there, often entering from the garden, which added a clandestine air to the meetings.

Murray had, in April 1816, lent the couple his Cambrai house. There was evidence given that Murray and Erskine dined together in Paris and Cambrai, which suggests that Erskine at this time did not consider Louisa's and Murray's behaviour to be particularly objectionable. However, Murray privately acknowledged to his sister that 'Paris notions' had wrought a change in his outlook which made him 'almost doubt whether I be really a sound Presbyterian'.[6] On one occasion he suggested:

> It would be folly to take offence at folly…We are all a little foolish in our own turns perhaps… If great offences are taken every time that little offences are given such breaks would occur that society would very soon fall to pieces altogether.[7]

Perhaps there was a niggling worry that the carefree meetings with Louisa were starting to be viewed in a much more serious light by her husband. He mentioned Louisa in one of his letters to Augusta, when commenting on Augusta's friends: 'I have heard Lady Louisa Erskine speak of her [the Duchess of Argyll] with great partiality'.[8] These are the only hints we have of his possibly being smitten by her.

By March 1817 Erskine and Louisa were back in Britain; she mainly at Torrie, while he found business to occupy himself in Edinburgh and London. The relationship, already fragile when they arrived in France, was now beyond saving. There must have been times when in the safety of Torrie they found enough common interest, perhaps in the further pursuit of art works with which to furnish the house, to enable a reasonably harmonious front to be maintained. However, lasting damage had been done by Louisa's adventurous behaviour in Paris. Once again Erskine seemed unable to deal with the situation and so, publicly at least, their troubles remained buried. But for the absence of children, things might have been unremarkable, and moderately bearable.

The delivery of the post one afternoon in late November 1818 was to end any further pretence of normality. One of the servants had been sent to Dunblane it seems, to fetch, from the post office there, mail that had probably arrived there after Louisa had returned from taking the waters. The servant returned to Torrie with the contents in a locked bag.

6 Murray to Augusta, Paris 15 July 1816, Murray Papers, MS 21103.

7 Murray to Augusta, Paris 11 June 1816, Murray Papers, MS 21103.

8 Murray to Augusta, Paris, 11 June 1816, Murray Papers, MS 21103.

Louisa was reading to her husband in the autumnal gloom when Mrs Anderson, the housekeeper, came in and handed the bag to Louisa. Louisa left the room to fetch the key. Erskine, perhaps suspicious of any correspondence that might be addressed to his wife, took the bag and on Louisa's return demanded she open it in his presence and show him the contents. Open it she did but turned away and refused to show Erskine a thick packet, franked 'Quartermaster General'.

On being pressed further Louisa hastily left the room. A short while later she sent down a letter from Murray to Lady Mary Murray and one from Madame Craufurd to herself, insisting that that was all there was in the package.

Erskine refused to believe her and left Torrie the very next morning. Louisa, he said, could remain at Torrie for as long as she liked, but he was leaving her. There followed a series of pleading letters from Louisa to Erskine, seven heartbroken appeals.[9] The only desire, she said, was for her husband's happiness; she bitterly regretted that her careless behaviour had caused him anguish, and stressed over and over that she remained devoted to him, hating having made him unhappy, signing a letter 'Ever, very Dearest Jamie, your devoted and truly affectionate and very wretched Lou', and another: 'Farewell my Dearest James. Little do you know how sincerely I love you; and: 'God Almighty bless you my dearest Jamie – if I could but ensure your being happy and contented, every misfortune and calamity in life I could then bear with resignation. Believe me it is from the bottom of my heart'. The tone moved gradually from heartbroken to explanation to justification for her behaviour. She begged his forgiveness. It was all a misunderstanding. She was mortified that her unthinking behaviour had caused him so much unhappiness. All she wanted was to be able to turn the clock back. He was the only one she had ever loved. The pleas and arguments were those of a desperate woman who realized that she had gone too far, had behaved badly, and would always regret the damage she had caused. Erskine was unmoved. The episode with the letters was one episode too far. His mind was set.

What else was in that suspect package we shall probably never know. If indeed it was an innocent covering letter from Murray asking her to forward the letter to his sister-in-law and politely enquiring after life at Torrie, then why did not Louisa just show it to Erskine and be done? Even if it went a bit further than that and included some expressions of affection then she could have promised to reply to Murray asking to be left alone and demanding that whatever had happened in Paris between them should stay in Paris. Yet instead she chose the worst possible course of action – one that could only fan the flames of Erskine's smouldering suspicion.

Murray returned from Paris a few weeks after the incident with the post bag. He went to stay with Augusta at Lochnell. Whether Louisa had written to him about the new crisis in her marriage we do not know. In the circumstances it seems probable. But he certainly was left in no doubt as to the seriousness of affairs when he received a letter from Erskine.

> Sir, From an occurrence which has lately taken place, I am imperiously called upon to demand of you to declare upon your honor whether you have ever carried on a

9 These are part of a series of nine letters appended to the Libel of Erskine v Erskine as exhibits, in Lambeth Palace Library, Arches H 340 /1-9.

> secret or clandestine correspondence with Lady Louisa Erskine with a view to its being concealed from me, or if you have ever introduced into any letter you may have written to her sentiments or expressions derogatory to my honor. I am, Sir, your obedient humble Servant, James Erskine.[10]

Murray wasted no time in penning his forthright response:

> Sir, I have received this afternoon your letter of the 18th Instant. It is written in a style which appears to me to preclude my making any other answer to it, insofar as it concerns myself only, than my merely acknowledging the receipt of it.
>
> That I may not leave for a moment, however, any opening for surmises which might be prejudicial to another person and which would be wholly groundless, I take this opportunity to declare that in any intercourse which may have taken place between Lady Louisa and myself nothing has ever occurred injurious to your honor or which ought in the slightest degree to affect that of Lady Louisa herself. I am, Sir, your obedient humble Servant, G. Murray.[11]

Erskine seems to have pondered his next move for a while, before arranging, three months later, for Sir Robert Wilson, a Peninsular general known to both him and Murray, to act as an emissary. Wilson was charged with confronting Murray with a view to establishing whether he was telling the truth. Murray, well aware of the seriousness of the situation, must have hoped that Wilson's assurances, given in a letter to Erskine after the meeting, would have been enough to put an end to the matter. 'No conversation could be more satisfactory' Wilson reported. 'I feel authorized to require that you henceforth dismiss the subject of the correspondence from your mind'. It could, he added, be buried totally 'in the tomb of oblivion'.[12]

Wilson was to be disappointed: for whatever reason Erskine ignored his advice. Murray was now faced with deciding where his heart lay and where his duty lay. What were his true feelings for Louisa? How much of the blame for what had happened lay at his feet? What could be done in practical ways to deal with the situation now confronting Louisa? Should he go to her, support her, offer marriage if that were possible? Could he possibly hope to provide the sort of lifestyle which Louisa craved? His wealth was simply insufficient to meet those sort of costs. While his income was more than adequate for a single man, comprising as it did his military appointments, including his Lieutenant Governorship of Edinburgh Castle, about £440, and the colonelcy of 72nd Highlanders, to which he had been appointed in 1817, about £520, altogether his military income probably did not exceed £1,500. His Drumlandrick estate produced perhaps another £300. Her tastes ran to something substantial in London, from where she might partake in London society, not a suburban villa.[13]

10 Erskine to Murray, Edinburgh, 18 January 1819, reproduced in *Bell's London and Sporting Chronicle*, 1 August 1824.

11 Murray to Erskine, Lochnell, 25 January 1819, reproduced in *Bell's London and Sporting Chronicle*, 1 August 1824.

12 Letter appended to the Libel of Erskine v Erskine as an exhibit; Wilson to Erskine, 11 Charles Street, 11 April 1819, reproduced in full in *Bell's London and Sporting Chronicle*, 1 August 1824

13 Ward Draft, Ch.XVII, p.13.

Sir Robert Wilson. (Anne S.K. Brown Military Collection)

Perhaps a governor's residence overseas might satisfy, but he had already turned down the government of Ceylon and such opportunities did not arise at convenient times.

Not only would Murray's lack of income and a country house be a constant issue and concern, but were events to take their inevitable course, he would have to face the crippling costs of divorce. He was 47, had no doubt enjoyed his dalliance in Paris, but living for months or years in the mire of adultery and divorce courts, newspaper revelations and drawing room gossip was everything Murray abhorred. Yet he felt it right to offer himself, and his support, to Louisa, to rescue her from her miserable marriage and to stand together against the opprobrium that adultery and failed marriage inevitably attracted.

His mind made up, he went to her. The alternatives that faced the couple were all unattractive. Scots Law provided an easier route to divorce than England. His parents had benefitted from that. However, it would mean contriving an adulterous situation, which had to be acted upon by Erskine. Should he ignore the humiliation, then the next best solution was for Murray and Louisa to bring an action against Erskine for desertion, but that could not be brought for at least four years from the desertion itself, and if Erskine were minded he could use stalling tactics to make the wait even longer. It was also open to Erskine to bring an action of divorce in the English courts, a lengthy and complicated process, vastly expensive, and involving interminable hearings in differing courts, including the ecclesiastical courts, the so called Court of Arches. To gain the right to remarry an Act of Parliament was required.

This, however, was not the half of it. The husband would generally bring an action against the co-respondent for damages in what were known as Criminal Conversation proceedings in the civil courts. Such damages commonly ran into tens of thousands of pounds.

If all this dented Murray's passion for Louisa it was not for long and, having made up his mind that his future lay with her, he set about preparing the ground for the least damaging and quickest way to engineer the necessary break from Erskine, namely clear adultery, which could be used by Erskine to complete the divorce in Scotland. In June 1819, soon after Murray returned from giving evidence at the trial of Marinet and Carillon, who were accused of trying to assassinate Wellington in Paris, Louisa took rooms in Dunblane at the house of a Mrs Rob. Some weeks later Murray joined her there. Murray's name was kept secret from Mrs Rob's servants. Cutler, Louisa's servant who had gone with her, was under instruction to refer to Murray as Mr Thingammy, pretending to have forgotten his name if she was asked. This was a device to circumvent the rule that under Scots Law a divorcee was prohibited from marrying the person with whom they had committed adultery.

The carefully constructed plan was a failure. Erskine did not react, leaving the country soon afterwards to live in Berlin. Murray was thus thrown onto the next option of taking the initiative and having Louisa sue Erskine for desertion, but nothing could be done for four years. Events in Murray's professional life did not take heed of his domestic difficulties, and in August 1819 he was appointed Governor of the Royal Military College at Sandhurst, with an annual income of £1,500. Obviously that required relocating south. The appointment was the result of suggestion made by Alexander Hope to the Duke of York.[14] He was aware of Murray's predicament and applied his influence to secure as good an income and

14 Ward Draft Ch.XVII, p.16.

as interesting situation as he could for Murray. The deal suited both Murray and Hope, who wanted to move to live in Dresden. Murray would have to give up his sinecure at Edinburgh Castle in Hope's favour, but the net effect was an increase in Murray's income of about £1,000. Besides which, Murray was well qualified to carry out the role successfully.

Thus Murray and Louisa were to be parted for the best part of a year with no immediately-apparent solution to their difficulties. Honours continued to be bestowed on Murray including an honorary degree of Doctor of Laws from Oxford University. Wellington was kind to him and invited him regularly to stay at Stratfield Saye, where a room was kept for him. As a Peninsular hero, and having such close connections with Wellington, Murray was in great demand in army circles. A dinner at Hythe in Kent in his honour, was perhaps not untypical. It was attended by officers of the Rifle Brigade, the Tipperary Militia and the South Devon Militia, some fifty diners in all. In many regiments it was normal to allow a bottle of port a head, and sometimes two or three would be drunk. No one was allowed to escape a 'bumper' toast without a certificate from a doctor. The dinner got under way at 6 o'clock in the evening and did not finish until seven o'clock next morning. The Tipperary boys were noisy and full of obscene and indecent toasts, while the general himself three times appeared to fall asleep. While Murray was in one of these slumbers the President gave the toast 'To the immortal memory of the late lamented Sir John Moore, to be drunk in silence'. Whether the word silence or a jog of Murray's elbow roused him is not clear, but he attempted to rise from the chair and said 'Mr President, I rise', but instead of rising, fell to his knees and then continued 'Mr President, this is a toast I always drink kneeling'. Tremendous applause followed from everyone present sober enough to witness this drama. A few remnants of this extraordinary banquet remained until breakfast time when Murray washed himself, had his boots cleaned, and, apparently sober, appeared on parade at ten o'clock, when as a joke he put an officer under arrest for being drunk.[15]

In the middle of 1820 Murray joined Louisa for two months at Matlock where she had taken rooms. In September they rented a furnished house in Earls Court, at that time on the very edge of the country and convenient for Sandhurst. Here they lived for eighteen months, trying desperately to avoid recognition as a pair. When visitors called unexpectedly Murray hid in his room or ensured he was out if they were there by prior invitation.

By March 1822 Louisa was seven months pregnant. That prompted a move to Finchley where they rented a substantial house, Brent Lodge. They were now calling themselves Mr and Mrs Evans. Louisa was now 45, and Mr and Mrs Evans must have been concerned about the imminent birth, so they arranged for a resident midwife, who was present when Louisa gave birth to a girl on 22 April 1822. She was a pretty little thing, with her father's blue eyes and her mother's colouring.[16] She was baptized at Finchley Parish Church on 11 May with the names Louisa Georgiana Augusta Anne, daughter of George Evans, gentleman, and Louisa Evans, his wife.

It being necessary to live nearer Sandhurst, the family moved, via a coaching inn on the Basingstoke road, the Wellesley Arms at Murrell Green, to a house in Odiham belonging to a Mrs Cole, where they lived, with the bare minimum of staff, until May 1823, when the

15 Extract based on Max Hastings (ed), *The Oxford Book of Military Anecdotes* (Oxford: Oxford University Press, 1986), p 250

16 Ward Draft, Ch.XVII, p.18.

Brent Lodge, Finchley where Murray's daughter Louisa was born in 1822.
(By kind permission of the University of Southampton)

two Louisas moved to a cottage at Sunninghill, close to Joanna Churchill, which had been bought for Louisa by her Trustees under her original marriage settlement.

Louisa had become pregnant again in the autumn of 1822 but miscarried, and from that time she seemed to suffer from problems with her health. No doubt, happy as she might have been with her 'husband' and daughter, the continuing worries over the possible outcomes of the separation from Erskine must have taken their toll. Four years had elapsed since the original 'desertion' and Louisa was now entitled to take the first steps in an action known as a Suit of Adherence. Erskine, now back from the continent, responded by offering Louisa the chance to live with him at 31 St Andrew Square, in Edinburgh. After an initial refusal, presumably on legal advice, Louisa did accept an offer, in November 1823, to live with him at 1 Albany Street.[17] She stayed for a month before leaving, insisting that during the time of cohabitation Erskine had never communicated with her and that no intercourse, sexual or otherwise, had taken place.

17 Ward Draft Ch.XVII, p.19, highlights a potential clerical mistake as to the address in the Libel in Erskine v Erskine. There was no Albany Place, as per the Libel transcript. Ward concludes it must have been 1 Albyn Place, a newly built street at the other end of Edinburgh's New Town. It is perhaps more likely to have been the address used here, being close to the previously-offered accommodation.

The scene was now set for the lawyers to take up the case. In a strange move, James Moray of Abercairney, who was a brother of Murray's former aide de camp and a close Ochtertyre neighbour, took it upon himself to make a formal statement regarding the whole series of events that had happened between the pair over the last four years, although Erskine must have been pretty well aware of most of the story. He supposedly sought an undertaking before making the statement that Erskine would not seek personal satisfaction from Murray, something which was clearly ignored later.[18] Erskine now had all the evidence he needed to pursue an action for divorce in the English courts, and to counter any accusations of desertion. The action for damages under Crim. Con. was first off, heard before a jury at the Sheriff Court in London on 23 July 1824. The lawyers lining up on both sides were an impressive array; on Murray's team were the Attorney General, later Lord Lyndhurst, Lord Chancellor in Wellington's and Peel's administrations, and James Scarlett, later Lord Abinger, Attorney General in Wellington's administration. There was a chance that Wellington would be called as a witness but he heard from Murray's legal team at Lincoln's Inn a week before that he would not be required.[19]

The jury was left unconvinced of Erskine's case. The Attorney General seems to have persuaded them in his summing up that the real damage to the marriage had been done prior to the Erskines' journey to France. The shenanigans at 'Craw's' did not amount to proof of anything. The principle of Crim. Con. was that damages should be awarded for stealing a wife's affections which were rightly owed to the husband. Louisa's due affections were already diminished by the time the pair arrived in Paris. After a short deliberation they reduced the damages claimed from £20,000 to £2,500, a figure that Murray's lawyer in London was to describe as much less than had been anticipated.[20]

Legal opinions were sought on the status of young Louisa in the event of Erskine's death. First, was she regarded as illegitimate under Scots Law? Whereas it seems pretty much a clear-cut case, the law of the time regarded any child born to a married woman as being the legitimate offspring of the husband, regardless of any abandonment, unless it could be proved that there was no possible opportunity of connection between husband and wife during the period commencing one month before conception and ending mid pregnancy. One of the few factors that might contradict such assumption was if the husband was overseas. Murray was concerned that there should be clarity on this as it would have a bearing on Louisa's right to inherit from Erskine. Not only that, but he wanted clarity on a supplementary point, that being Louisa's position vis a vis any claims of later offspring, if, for example, Erskine should marry again and have children, or whether brothers, and any other relations might have claims too. It does seem that Louisa's claim to Erskine's estate was unarguable unless Erskine was able to persuade a judge of the complete impossibility of any sexual congress.[21] In the event, she was left nothing in his will, and there is no evidence that this was ever challenged.

Murray no doubt felt that the legal fees he was incurring had been worth every penny and was happy to settle his Edinburgh lawyer Francis Wilson's £200 bill in October, under

18 Ward Draft, Ch.XVII, p.19.
19 J. Parkinson to Wellington, Lincoln's Inn Fields, 18 July 1824, Wellington Papers, WP1/796/10.
20 J. Parkinson to Murray, Lincoln's Inn Fields, 24 July 1824, Murray Papers, MS 21192.
21 The two legal opinions are in Murray Papers MS 21192.

cover of a letter expressing grateful thanks: 'Those in whose cause you acted with so much zeal and ability are all well and retain the same sense which I have myself of your contribution to their affairs'.[22] During 1824 it seems that Louisa had sold a property for £6,000 and advice was sought regarding an alternative destination of the proceeds. The advice was that it ought to be done 'by deed in the Scotch form' which suggests something in Scotland rather than Sunninghill. Perhaps she was transferring the proceeds to Murray to cover the costs of the damages and legal costs.

Meanwhile the main action for divorce continued, and was heard on 27 January 1825. Difficulties in assembling witnesses caused a delay. Erskine started to fret. He had been advised that another child born to Murray and Louisa might be a son, who, given the peculiarities of the system, would be Erskine's lawful heir. Frantic efforts were made to get the action under way again and the whole unhappy affair completed. There was a flurry of correspondence in February. A month later Erskine was dead, having collapsed in his chambers at 19 Dover Street on 3 March at the age of 52.[23]

Murray had been alerted to Erskine's fatal illness the day before and had passed on a hurried, and no doubt somewhat relieved, message to his lawyer in Edinburgh: 'Life is not likely to be prolonged many hours'.[24] Wasting no time, Murray procured a special marriage licence. Three days later, on 28 April 1825, he and Lady Louisa were finally united at the Parish Church of Sunninghill by the Curate, the Reverend James Hitchings.[25]

22 Murray to Francis Wilson, London 15 October 1824, Murray Papers, MS 21192.
23 Ward Draft, Ch.XVII, p.21.
24 Murray to Francis Wilson, London, 2 March 1825, Murray Papers, MS 21192.
25 Ward Draft, Ch.XVII, p.21.

21

Marriage and Military Life

The various newspaper reports of the events in Paris, at Torrie, and of the clumsy attempts at recordable adultery, placed the whole affair squarely, and in some detail, in front of the public, or at least those who read the relevant columns. It was impossible to hide the story. The Murrays would have to live with the consequences.

The tone of the reports were, perhaps unsurprisingly, predominantly suggestive that Murray had been led into an impossible position by Louisa, and had, out of a deep sense of duty, refused to abandon her. Old friends and colleagues were supportive. When it came to judging Murray's performance in public life there were those who spoke of 'poor Sir George'. One colleague referred to 'particular circumstances' which made him 'unhappy and unfortunate' and added that it was 'wrong to comment with harshness on his struggles for success amidst great difficulties'.[1] Certainly he was losing his confident ability to take on any task he might be asked to undertake and see it through with practiced ease.

Murray must have been concerned about the effect of the affair on his military career. After Waterloo the army was naturally reduced and good officer positions were scarce. Yet Murray's reputation ensured that, whenever an interesting job came up, his name was firmly in the frame. He had, after all, the support of Wellington and the Duke of York, neither of whom were likely to judge Murray's, or Louisa's, behaviour, given their own relationships with women. Thus, dovetailing neatly with Alexander Hope at Horse Guards, with whom he swopped Edinburgh Castle, Murray found himself Governor of Sandhurst from 1819 to 1824.

By the time of Murray's tenure as Governor of Sandhurst the college had expanded. The Senior Department from High Wycombe joined the Junior Department at Sandhurst, eventually being split off and becoming the Staff College. The Senior Department remained, as it had been in Murray's time there, the centre for scientific skills, based on the continental model. Ever conscious of value for money, Wellington, focusing on what looks like possible overstaffing at Sandhurst, wrote to Murray comparing the numbers and costs of their respective establishments – Wellington's was the Military Academy, Woolwich, which came under his authority (and later Murray's) as Master General of the Ordnance. Murray

1 Sir James Graham to Charles Arbuthnot, 12 September 1839, A. Aspinall (ed.) *The Correspondence of Charles Arbuthnot* (London: Royal Historical Society, 1941), p.208.

was employing one master to ten scholars, which Wellington pointed out looked rather high by comparison with Woolwich.

Murray relinquished his Sandhurst role early in 1824, in favour of Alexander Hope, who had, in 1819, vacated to allow Murray to the command. Hope was to have another two years in the post, before being succeeded by Scovell. On Wellington's recommendation, Murray succeeded Beresford as Lieutenant General of the Ordnance, a political office for which he became qualified by being elected as the Member of Parliament for the County of Perth. He was also destined for the Privy Council. These positions he considered himself more than equipped for without a trace of false modesty:

> The importance of the situation which I held with the army in the Peninsula should not be measured merely by the name of the appointment I filled in the British Army, but by the might the Duke of Wellington himself gave it by allowing it to be generally understood, both by the British and the foreign part of the army under him, that whatever communication came from me either had already, or would most certainly attain his intire approval...
>
> I found myself [after Toulouse, and in the absence of Wellington at Paris and Madrid] the only person left at Headquarters who could be understood to be in possession of all the Duke's intentions, and who could be referred to respecting them.[2]

At the end of January 1825, Murray was offered command of the British forces in Ireland in succession to Lord Combermere (previously Sir Stapleton Cotton, latterly in command of Wellington's cavalry during the Peninsular War), who had been sent to India as commander in chief.[3] Apart from the fact that this offer was made at an embarrassing time for Murray, with Erskine still alive and divorce proceedings still very much ongoing, there was the ever present need, more pressing than ever now, to consider the pay and conditions of any role to which he might aspire. Combermere, he learnt, had spent £3,000 a year beyond his pay; John Hope's expenditure as Commander in Chief in Ireland in 1812-1813 had been at the rate of £5,356 a year. 'That could not happen to me,' wrote Murray, 'for the Royal Highlanders (in Ireland) and my picturesque estates in Scotland will scarcely make up more than £1,000 when put together'.[4] There seemed to have been an understanding that any shortfall would be dealt with by the Treasury, which provided Murray with enough comfort to enable him to accept the position, and he moved to Kilmainham in Dublin early in August: initially without Louisa, who followed some months later.[5]

His life in Ireland was, as commander in chief, inevitably a combination of government and military business, and official and social functions, of which there were an immense number. Monthly reports were sent to London, which, at least during 1825-26, suggested 'general tranquility', punctuated by 'outrages'.[6] He was later to be described around this

2 Murray to Lord Fitzroy Somerset, [Sandhurst?], 28 February 1824, Wellington Papers WP1/785/17.
3 Ward Draft, Ch.XVII, p.23.
4 Murray to Hope, 11 Old Burlington Street, 1 February 1825, Luffness Mss, GD/364/1286.
5 Ward Draft, Ch.XVII, p.23.
6 Various reports by Murray are in TNA, WO 80/6.

time as possessing a face notable for 'a pleasing and happy combination of intelligence, sweetness and spirit, with regularity, beauty and a noble cast of features'.[7] The Irish took to this model of apparent perfection and the invitations rolled in.

Newspaper reports abound with descriptions of military reviews, theatre visits, levees, dinners (often for more than 500 guests), at which there were endless toasts and the requirement for speeches. Given Murray's comments some years earlier about the dreariness of sitting too long at dinner he must often have longed for an excuse to escape, unless the sociability of the Irish had rubbed off on him. Certainly everything from his official residence to his transport arrangements was stylish, and, according to one report, 'a very elegant carriage upon a new principle has been built for General Sir George Murray'.[8]

Despite the grand social occasions military readiness was still a priority. A new emergency in Portugal, in effect a civil war between constitutionalists and absolute monarchists, resulted in Canning, the Foreign Secretary, asking Murray in December 1826 to select two regiments to sail at once from Cork to Lisbon, under the command of Sir William Clinton.

Louisa was by his side on certain occasions, but by no means all, during his spell in Ireland. Murray was, on 24 November 1826 granted the freedom of the City of Cork and presented with a small 'freedom casket'. He had arrived there on the 9th and inspected the garrison next day, to be treated to a full military display on a field 'full of rank, beauty and fashion'.[9] But the rank, beauty and fashion on show that day did not include Lady Louisa.

There is no record of her with him at many of his trips to the theatre. The Theatre Royal was honoured to secure his patronage and once allowed him to choose the plays for the evening. He chose Sheridan's 'School for Scandal' and 'the Critic', choices which went down well. The event was predicted to be 'a complete Bumper' and every off-duty officer from the garrison was expected to attend, as well as any non-commissioned officer who wished. In November 1826 Murray and Louisa were reported as being together at the County Tipperary seat of the Earl of Donoughmore, but not at the very splendid levee held by the Marquess of Anglesey, Lord Lieutenant and Louisa's brother, on 14 March 1828, when the great and the good of Dublin attended in force to present their compliments, alighting from a three hour queue of carriages. Murray was, by virtue of his status, one of the earliest to arrive, saving him from an impatient wait, even if it were in the comfort of his new conveyance. The following month Murray was granted leave of absence, perhaps an indicator that all was not well with Louisa, and command of the army devolved to Major General Sir Colquhoun Grant.

Louisa was not at the ball given by the Lord Mayor of Dublin on 1 May 1828, in honour of the Marquess. The Ladies Georgina and Agnes Paget, her nieces, were both among the guests, along with Murray. It is obviously strange that Louisa was not there and leads to the suspicion that on those occasions illness must have been the reason, and therefore possibly the cause of so many other notable absences.

Murray and Anglesey maintained a close relationship, as one might expect, and their paths would cross on many social and official occasions. Reilly and Co, of 14 Westmorland Street, were by special appointment, proud purveyors to their two households of 'Articles

7 S.G.P. Ward, 'Illustrated report on Murray Papers', *Journal for the Society for Army Historical Research*, Vol.10 (1931), p.206.

8 *Morning Post*, 18 December 1826,

9 *Southern Reporter & Cork Commercial Courier*, Saturday 11 November 1826.

of the very finest description, including genuine old cognac brandy, fine Jamaica rum, and prime old whiskey'.[10] The brothers-in-law provided plenty of custom without a doubt.

Murray benefitted from support in the highest places. There was mutual respect between him and the Duke of York, who was reported as speaking on his deathbed 'as he always has done, with the highest regard of an individual in whose talents, integrity and discretion he placed the utmost confidence and to whom he was personally sincerely attached'.[11] Most of Murray's support, however, particularly during these years, is attributable to Wellington, now Master General of the Ordnance, with a seat in the Cabinet: an appointment of some influence. It was likely to have been Wellington who secured for Murray the position of Lieutenant General of the Ordnance in 1824, and was closely involved in the Irish appointment.

There was a seemingly-common shuffling of positions among a small group of generals. Wellington, aware of Murray's domestic issues that had yet to reach their final conclusion, made sure that William Clinton, who would take over the Ordnance position from Murray would, if called upon, relinquish it back in Murray's favour should Murray find it impossible to take up the Irish post, owing to public reaction to any revelations from the divorce action, or the proceedings in London dragging on.[12] No wonder Murray wrote at the time that 'both at the Horse Guards and the Ordnance I have found myself to be in very friendly hands'.[13]

Perhaps conscious of the debt he owed the two men, he attempted to discharge those duties, in the case of Wellington, by agreeing to take on the role of Secretary of State for War and the Colonies in 1828, and remained loyal to his friend through the tumultuous years of political upheaval that followed. On the Duke of York's death, Murray was the instigator of the plan to erect, in the Duke's memory, the proud column that stands today where Regent Street meets The Mall. Following the fashion of the day, Murray suggested that the Duke's memorial should assume the form of 'a lofty pillar with a statue of the Duke upon the top, to be placed in some conspicuous and suitable position, perhaps... near the end of the Canal in St James's Park looking towards the Horse Guards'.[14]

Political upheaval was never far away, and shortly after Wellington took over the role as Commander in Chief following the Duke of York's death, he resigned that position and that of Master General of the Ordnance, following a change of government and its replacement by Canning's administration. Wellington felt he could not serve under the new leader. After a period of temporary patching, the idea of a military man becoming Secretary for War, also holding the position of Commander in Chief as part of his function, was mooted. Murray was considered for the role, at Wellington's suggestion, in May 1827, having in the meantime been re-elected again unopposed for Perthshire.

Ward's description of the extent to which various political and military minds were at work is illuminating:

10 *Saunders News-Letter*, 13 March 1828.

11 TNA WO 80/1, Taylor to Murray, Arlington Street, 31 December 1826.

12 Ward Draft, Ch.XVII, p.24.

13 Murray to Alexander Hope, 11 Old Burlington Street, 1 February 1825, Luffness Mss, GD 364/1/1286.

14 TNA, WO 80/1, Murray to Taylor, Dublin, 12 January 1827.

Field Marshal HRH Prince Frederick, Duke of York. (Anne SK Brown Military Collection)

> Murray's response is interesting. Like Palmerston, Wellington, Taylor, Hardinge and most other public men at that time, he was a disciple of Blackstone, [the Judge, Tory politician and author of *A Commentary on the Laws of England*] believing, as he said, that 'the genius of our government rests upon the mutual checks of departments', though sometimes, he thought, the universal application of the principle was carried too far for the good of the public service. In this instance his main objections to the union of the civil and military branches were, first, the inherent tendency of political influence to encroach upon military considerations, which could only act to the detriment of the army, and, secondly, the heavy share of criticism and odium to be incurred by the person in whom the business was united. If as you say, he wrote, even Palmerston, normally good-natured and good-hearted, has recently become harsh, that shows only too clearly the 'ungracious nature of the business'. He preferred the introduction of a Chief-of-Staff, who, acting in a way similar to the major-général in French armies, could conduct the business of the command in the name of the Crown. Nonetheless, in spite of his objections, he acknowledged that, if offered the post, he would accept it on the principle that his services belonged to the State, no matter how 'ungracious' it might be, and however presumptuous he might appear, in so closely following Wellington. As for his seat in Parliament, he considered that, since it was not a party seat, it did not inhibit his holding the appointment under any administration provided it introduced no legislation injurious to his constituents.[15]

In the event, in the way of such things, the initiative died. Murray's idea of a Chief of Staff, which was only taken up again early in the 20th century, proved too difficult to inject into the British system. Other political factors and plans took precedence. Wellington declined to return to Horse Guards despite pleas. A new plan, described by Ward, was floated by Canning.

> This plan consisted of placing the army command in commission under a Military Board composed of three members: the Adjutant-General and Quartermaster-General sitting under the presidency of a 'First Commissioner' with the assistance of a Military Secretary. Canning proposed that the important situation of First Commissioner should be held by none other than Murray, who would have been removed from Ireland to the English staff with the rank of General. The scheme had been drafted by Taylor, and examined by Torrens (A.G.) and Gordon (Q.M.G.), when all consideration of it was brought to an abrupt conclusion by the sudden and unexpected death of Canning on 8 August 1827, the fall of his government, and the return of Wellington to the Command-in-Chief.[16]

During this period of upheaval, there was regular correspondence between Wellington and Murray, with Wellington spelling out to Murray the reasons for his split with Canning. It

15 Ward Draft, Ch.XVII, pp.27-8.
16 Ward Draft, Ch.XVII, p.28.

certainly seemed that at the time Wellington needed to get a lot off his chest and it was to Murray, his trustworthy friend, that he turned. Murray had written a very supportive letter to him on his resignation, avoiding passing judgement on the political causes but leaving Wellington in no doubt as to his long-held personal loyalty:

> I know nothing of the political causes which have led to the present changes and have been very little of a politician and it is possible that my opinions upon some questions, if I were called upon to express them, might not have an exact concurrence with yours. But in whatever situation you may be placed, my personal feelings towards you can never alter. They have ben founded upon long experience of your friendship, upon a knowledge of your great qualities, which is the more fixed and certain because it had begun to be formed before you had mounted to so great a height as you have since reached and because, even after that had taken place, I had the best opportunity of being a very close observer of them, and lastly because I believe there is no one who either sets a greater value upon your services to the country or who can estimate more truly how much they are exclusively attributable to your own character and talents.[17]

Wellington replied with his explanation:

> Many thanks my dear Murray for your letter. I did not write to you when I resigned from my office of Commander in Chief as indeed I had little to say that was not in the papers. The fact is that I could not remain with the Gentleman as Minister. He was determined that I should not because he knew very well that I was too clear sighted not to see the juggle which would be going on; and that if I should possess the means of access to HRH, too honest not to tell him; and he likewise knew that I never spoke to the King in earnest upon any subject without making an impression. Therefore as long as he lived and was in office and I firmly believe that if he had lived to the Age of Methusalim, he would have continued in office, he would not have allowed me to approach the K. A little visit which I paid to HRH from S. Saye at his own suggestion created an earthquake in London.
>
> The offer made to me to return was conveyed in such terms both by the King and his Government as render it impossible for me to refuse. But I have accepted with an avowed difference of opinion in politics, as I was left to the Command of an army in the field. So I stand. The Administration is indeed in a wretched state.[18]

A few days later, having received further letter from Murray, Wellington again opened up to him:

> You are very right; political affairs in this country are in a very extraordinary situation… It is not in the power of any individual to remedy this state of things. I was

17 Murray to Wellington, Dublin, 3 May 1827, Wellington Papers, WP1/889/5.
18 Wellington to Murray, Lingslawe [?], 24 August 1827, Murray Papers, ADV MS 46.8.6.

> driven from the King's service by Mr Canning, for very obvious reasons (and I have been brought back). The truth is this – we would not remain in office with Mr Canning. The King knew it well.[19]

With the continuation of political manoeuvring it was inevitable that from time to time Murray would be considered for roles both military and quasi-military. There was talk of his becoming Master General of the Ordnance, the role in which he would end his life, but for which he had to wait. He was, on differing occasions, offered the Governor Generalship of India, Commander in Chief in India, and Commander in Chief in Canada. On one occasion he was erroneously reported as having been offered Command in Chief of the British Army. His affair and marriage to Louisa had seemingly no effect on Murray being considered suitable for these appointments, although her health did prevent Murray from a positive response to any overseas posting.

It was common for senior officers to seek to supplement their income, depleted in the aftermath of active service, with appointments to sinecures, and Murray was again fortunate in the support he had in high places. After completing his time at Sandhurst he was granted Governorship of Fort George, worth £475 a year. On Hope's death in 1823 he became colonel of the 42nd Highlanders (The Black Watch), until on Lyndoch's death in 1843 he was appointed to colonel of the 1st Foot (Royal Scots). His rank increased as time passed, and he became a lieutenant general on 27 May 1825, enabling his appointment to Ireland as Commander in Chief there, although he had held the rank locally elsewhere from time to time. He was promoted to full general on 23 November 1841.[20]

Murray's significance as an innovator, his role in developing the Quartermaster General's Department and military science, and the effective end, at least for the time being, of such new ideas are dealt with succinctly by Ward:

> In the wider context of the evolution of the Quartermaster-General's Department towards a General Staff, the effect of Murray's marriage on his career ensured that it never could be Murray who would foster the cause of Military Science. It is in any case unrealistic to expect politicians of that age to spend public money on arcane military sub-departments. Science had been a hot-house plant, encouraged in an emergency and allowed to droop in prosperity. The climate of peace, with its opportunities for retrenchment, was detrimental to its growth. Even Murray's period as Governor of Sandhurst was quite unremarkable for any attempt to reverse the current trend of economy. Willoughby Gordon, the Q.M.G almost throughout the forty years of peace, although a dyed in the wool 'Q' man was not a Scientific, and lacked the influence to resist the trend. Wellington, who had never been sympathetic to the Scientifics and even described the Wycombites as 'coxcombs and pedants', was alone in a position to promote their cause, but his powers in army matters were severely restricted until he actually exercised the command-in-chief from 1842 onwards, [he had also been C in C from January 1827 to January 1828]

19 Wellington to Murray, Stratfield Saye, 4 September 1827, Murray Papers, ADV MS 46.8.6.
20 Ward Draft, Ch.XVII, p.30.

by which time it was too late to expect innovation from him. As for Murray, from 1824 he held no situation in which he could have effectually sponsored the cause of Science, let alone for example introduce an Intelligence Department. The constitutional lawyers had brushed aside his suggestion of appointing a Chief of Staff; Canning's proposal of a First Commissioner had been shelved, both irrevocable moments. From then on Murray became, by force of circumstance, a predominantly political soldier, too preoccupied with other duties and too fettered by constitutional custom to intervene even if he had had the inclination.[21]

21 Ward Draft, Ch.XVII, pp.30-30b.

22

Perthshire Politics

Whilst Murray was still in the Peninsula, Patrick had raised the possibility of Murray standing for parliament to represent the Perth Burghs. Murray replied that he should, if there were a choice, prefer the County of Perthshire, where there was less need to be closely aligned to party. Nothing further happened. Then in 1820 he was offered the Glasgow Burghs 'at very little expense and probably no opposition'.[1] Again Murray declined. An opportunity to represent the County of Perth, a seat controlled by the Atholl interests, again surfaced in 1823, and this time Murray put himself forward, as we have seen. His circular letter to the electors, which was dated 12 March 1824, was run off on the press Lindenthal had introduced at the Horse Guards, and was sent out under cover of the Quartermaster-General's Office.

> Should the Freeholders be pleased to repose in my hands the important trust which it now rests with them to place where they think most proper, it shall be my endeavour at all times to prove to them that my zeal in the character of their Representative is not less strong than are those of ties of connection and of attachment which in so many ways have identified the interests of my family since its earliest existence with those of the County of Perth.[2]

His support looked solid. His stance was seen as independent enough to appeal to both Whig and Tory supporters. The election, in April, saw him duly elected unopposed, with broad support. A Perthshire Whig later recalled they were 'glad to obtain him' even though he was an opponent in politics, for he was supposed to be one of the most liberal of his party. And 'though but a small proprietor in the county, had claims to the respect and gratitude of his countrymen by successful military services'.[3]

There is no question but that Murray's affair and the attendant court proceedings did impact on his political ambitions, although he does not seem to have been too damaged, despite the efforts of some of his close Ochtertyre neighbours, particularly James Moray of

1 Lord Melville to Murray, Admiralty, 31 January 1820, Murray Papers, MS 21104.

2 Murray to the Freeholders of Perthshire, London, 12 March 1824, Moray of Abercairny Papers, GD24/1/419.

3 Fisher, D.R., 'Murray, Sir George', *The History of Parliament Online*, at www.historyofparliamentonline.org/volume/1820-1832/member/murray-sir-george-1772-1846.

Abercairny, who had intervened directly in the affair. Moray did his best to gain support among voters who might oppose Murray. By July 1824 when the Crim. Con. evidence was published in numerous newspapers, every lurid detail of the affair was out in the open. John Stuart, a son of the Earl of Moray, announced that he would stand against Murray at the next election, relying on support from those who might be shocked by Murray's affair. Ward illustrates the extent to which Murray's private life had become an issue, and ultimately how the scandal became increasingly irrelevant:

> The most revealing aspect of this development is the attitude adopted by some of the principals. Murray expressed himself hurt that 'a circumstance of a private nature' should be introduced into County politics. In his opinion Abercairny had 'not the smallest personal concern in it'. As for his own part in the affair, he thought 'the circumstances were such as to afford much ground for palliation' whenever they came to be fully explained. He complained to Lynedoch of his relatives' hostility and asked for his help in 'dissipating the cloud' which hung over him. In response, Lynedoch sounded one or two friends, eliciting the information that, however hostile Robert Graham and Maxtone of Cultoquhey might be, they were at least unlikely to vote for Stuart. To Cultoquhey, he deplored a situation in which 'the peace of the County should be disturbed by a contest now that it is represented with more ability than I ever remember to have been the case'- a handsome tribute coming from a former member. The adultery itself Lynedoch called 'an unlucky affair', for which, he said, Murray was 'much more to be pitied than blamed, all circumstances considered'.[4]

The storm subsided. The opposition withdrew. At the next election, which took place on 20 June 1826 and for which Murray came over from Dublin, he was again returned unopposed. Altogether he was elected six times for Perthshire – five times unopposed, once opposed – and he stood on two occasions when he was defeated. He was returned unopposed in June 1828, when, as the law then required, he submitted himself for election on accepting office in Wellington's government as Secretary of State for the Colonies.

In December 1829 the nobility and gentry of Perthshire felt it right to commission a portrait of their 'gallant representative' to be placed in the Town Hall in Perth. Sir Thomas Lawrence was considered the most natural painter for the commission. The painting and frame would together cost 800 guineas, and an initial subscription raised 500 guineas towards the cost. The portrait was unfinished at Lawrence's death and was completed by Henry Pickersgill. The original (there are a number of versions) was lent by Perth to its namesake in Western Australia in 1979 where it still hangs in the City Hall. It was also in that month that Murray and Lawrence were together elected as Councillors of the Royal Society to serve for the following year, though there is little evidence of any close involvement by Murray, and given the pressures on Lawrence and the number of part-finished works in his studio being anxiously awaited by patrons who had paid handsome deposits, it is unlikely that Lawrence would have spent much time there either.

4 Ward Draft, Ch.XVII, p.32.

Murray was again unopposed in the elections of August 1830 (caused by the death of George IV) and May 1831. At the general election later in 1831, called by Lord Grey in an attempt to gain the final support the Whigs needed to ensure success for the Reform Bill, Murray offered himself again for Perthshire as a man not averse to 'prudent ameliorations of our political system', but he did not specifically mention the Reform Bill. The Perthshire Whigs again had no one to put up against him and he was returned: professing support for moderate reform, but hostile to disruptive change which threatened the beneficial 'influence of property'. His lengthy speech of thanks, which was reproduced in *The Times*, ended with a fanciful and faintly ludicrous depiction of the 'ship of state', with 'monarchy at the helm, to guide her in her course, with aristocracy… as ballast, to keep her steady in a troubled sea, and with the favouring breath of the people to fill the sails'.[5]

The Spectator, recently launched as a liberal-radical magazine, and a strong supporter of Reform, offered this to him:

> Friendly Advice to Sir George Murray etc
> Saint George and a dragon to boot!
> Why Murray, man where are thy wits,
> Take breath and thy forces recruit
> Great dealer in palpable hits.
> Fierce was the flash of thine eye
> When thinking the Commons to flurry
> With the fire of the Scriptural cry
> The sword of the Lord and of Murray.[6]

He stood for Perthshire at the next general election, in the dying days of 1832, but was beaten by the Whig candidate, who held strong views on many issues, including repeal of the corn laws, banning sinecures, and any form of patronage. True to form *The Spectator* had something to say about Murray's attempts to be re-elected, by presenting himself as s friend of Reform: 'It is now evident that the professions hitherto made by Sir George are most hollow and insincere'.[7]

Now routinely opposed, he was again elected in April 1834, but in April 1835 he was defeated by Fox Maule, the future Lord Panmure. The extent to which politics had moved on during the years since Murray was first elected, is well illustrated by Ward's inimical words:

> Murray against Panmure! Two ages met in that election. Already by 1831 the new conditions created by the Industrial Revolution, of which the Reform agitation was one symptom, were throwing up even in the remote fastnesses of Perthshire a new kind of dedicated politician, implicated both emotionally and intellectually in the great questions of the day. Men of Murray's stamp, who assumed the responsibilities of political life as the accepted consequence of the station to which they had risen, were growing old-fashioned. The new men were as like as not ponderous,

5 Fisher, 'Murray, Sir George'.

6 *The Spectator*, 9 July 1831

7 *The Spectator*, 28 September 1832,

> blackcoated industrialists, who had made fortunes from the mills and, having distorted the features of society, entered Parliament to repair the damage by philanthropic legislation.[8]

In October 1834 Perthshire demonstrated its thanks to its MP by organizing a huge dinner in Perth in Murray's honour. Seven hundred attended and five hundred were turned away. The *Bucks Herald* reporter commented: 'always tranquil, sometimes cold in his manner and though I have seen him placed in sufficiently trying circumstances, I never saw him so mastered by his feelings as when he rose to return thanks for the kind manner in which his health had been drunk'.[9] Earlier in the year praise for the 'Tall and graceful figure with the commanding carriage' had flowed from the pages of the *Aberdeen Journal*: 'the best soldier speaker we have ever had the good fortune to hear, a man of sound and mature judgment, of great reflection, of much reading and exquisite tact and taste' He was 'almost the only Scotchman in the House of Commons who spoke and pronounced the English language with propriety and without the shadow of accent'.[10]

8 Ward Draft, Ch.XVII, p.33.
9 *Bucks Herald*, 25 October 1834.
10 *Aberdeen Journal*, 25 June 1834.

23

The Colonial Office

Viscount Goderich, a moderate Tory, too moderate to gain Wellington's approval, succeeded Canning as Prime Minister in 1827, and was preparing to recall Murray from Ireland, restore him to the Ordnance and give him a 'government' at the end of that year. Murray considered the rumours 'very flattering to me and very acceptable'. However, as he pointed out to Patrick in a letter from Dublin on 23 November 'I consider all political arrangements however to be very slippery things and until I am actually installed I do not mean to talk of the matter with any degree of certainty'.[1] Goderich's resignation in January 1828, after failing to keep a coalition with the Whigs intact and the King satisfied, meant that Murray remained in Ireland when Wellington became Prime Minister, at the King's request. He did not return to London till May 1828 to serve at Wellington's side, as a cabinet minister, and Secretary of State for the Colonies, the post becoming vacant after William Huskisson failed to support Wellington and Peel in a Commons vote on the Reform Bill. His years of loyalty had been rewarded.

Wellington's offer of the colonial post was recorded by Murray in a memorandum of a meeting with Wellington on 25 May 1828, there being a possibility up to the last moment that he might be appointed to the War Office in succession to Palmerston. He explained that he was quite satisfied where he was, or indeed with the War Office – in short to be made use of in any way. The Colonial Office seemed to him to be 'a higher one than I had any right to look at, or the public would consider me qualified to fill and what would be said about another military man with a high office'. Wellington assured him that he did not think the situation too high and felt the War Office not high enough. Murray was fit for the position 'and Mr Peel thought so too'. The appointment was confirmed by the King the next day and accepted by Murray that day in a letter from Mellor's Hotel.[2]

On Murray relinquishing his Irish Command, Louisa's brother Lord Anglesey wrote generously:

> I do assure you, I grieve to lose you as Commander of the Forces: that I should, however, have rejoiced most sincerely if you had taken the place of Chief

1 Murray to Patrick, Dublin, 23 November 1827, Murray Papers, MS 21102.

2 TNA, WO 80/2, Memorandum and letters 25 & 26 May 1828.

> Secretary for Ireland; that I am perfectly convinced that you will fill the situation to which you are appointed with advantage to your country and honour to yourself; and that in this my last declaration to you I am only repeating what I have often said, that whatever post may be assigned to you, whether it be civil or military, whether you be sent to govern an empire or remain to defend a kingdom or to fill a high official department, you will not be misplaced and will not be found wanting.[3]

Wellington himself described Murray 'as able and respectable a man as can be found in Parliament'.[4] It was inevitable though that in some circles the appointment met with criticism on the grounds of 'military government'.

Harriet Arbuthnot, the close confidante of Wellington, who took a lively interest in political affairs and who regularly gave Wellington her views on matters of the day, thought Murray would

> make an excellent Colonial Secretary. He is very clever, an excellent man of business, a very good speaker and, from having been in Canada, knows that colony (which is now so important) well and, in short, is in every respect well qualified.
>
> He is also quite unpledged, a new man who has never mixed up in any party squabbles and who can do his duty without looking to one side or the other.[5]

Lord Ellenborough, Lord Privy Seal and President of the Board of Control (overseeing the Honourable East India Company) reckoned:

> A better man could not have been found. He is able; a good man of business; a good speaker (as far as is known) and he brings a high established character into the service of the country. He is, besides, a Catholic [i.e a supporter of Catholic Emancipation]. My expectation is that in the next session he will be the most efficient man in the Commons.[6]

Lord Anglesey told Wellington that 'you have a very superior man in Murray. I wish he had fallen to my lot here'.[7]

However it soon became clear that Murray was, surprisingly perhaps, out of his depth. Not that he was in any doubt about the scale of the job and its challenges, as illustrated by a letter to Lord Dalhousie, until recently Governor General of British North America:

> The situation I have been placed in is not likely to be a very easy one, any more than that which you have quitted. Laborious duties & which is worse, very serious difficulties present themselves in all quarters.

3 Anglesey to Murray, private and confidential, Phoenix Park, Dublin, 30 May 1828, Murray Papers, ADV MS 46.8.12.

4 Fisher, 'Murray, Sir George'.

5 Fisher, 'Murray, Sir George'.

6 Fisher, 'Murray, Sir George'.

7 Fisher, 'Murray, Sir George'.

> I look at all that, however without much uneasiness, for having the situation to do, or to advise what appears to me best, under all circumstances for the public interest, I feel no anxiety beyond.[8]

At the time that Murray took office the list of Colonies comprised Upper and Lower Canada (the latter being populated largely with French inhabitants), Newfoundland, West Indies, Cape of Good Hope, Mauritius, Sierra Leone, New South Wales and Van Diemen's Land, Ceylon, India, Singapore, Malacca and Penang. In Europe, and technically included, were Heligoland, Gibraltar and Malta. Murray would, in 1829, claim Swan River Colony, which became Western Australia, as an addition to the list. Canada was on the verge of insurrection. The West Indies and the Cape were under intense scrutiny on slavery. The Dutch were causing problems in the Cape too. Ceylon was to be subjected to rebellion in 1830. Convicts and a lack of positive progress in New South Wales, never mind the individual complaints of the cartographer Thomas Mitchell, were time consuming. Sierra Leone was a philanthropic but unsuccessful attempt at colonization.

There were many who felt Britain's colonial ambitions an expensive distraction. Economic and sociological writers agreed that whatever the value of the colonies, the time was not far off when separation would inevitably arrive. A *Quarterly Review* article in 1829, when speaking of the new Swan River Colony, opined: 'In truth, it is pretty much with colonies as with children. We protect and nourish them in infancy, we direct them in youth, and leave them to their own guidance in manhood'.[9] Others viewed the Colonies as somewhere for Horse Guards to quarter its worn out general officers as governors. There was of course truth to this, and there were at the time so many retired officers with impeccable military records who were anxious to find positions where their talents might be put to good use, that it was perhaps inevitable that there was, for some time to come, a strong military bias in such appointments.

Canada was in constant need of direction, one observer having written in 1825: 'Every man of sense whether in the Cabinet or out of it, knows that Canada must, at no distant period, be merged in the American Republic'.[10] Murray disagreed.

For many years it had been an accepted fact of Whitehall life that the Colonial Office was run, not by the Secretary of State, but by permanent officials such as Sir James Stephen, Counsel there from 1825-1834. He was an official of the Church Missionary Society, and came from an evangelical background, his father being Wilberforce's brother in law. He was set against slavery and was a 'soft' colonialist. There were allegations that his 'evil influence' was the root cause of many of the problems in Canada. Yet it was accepted that he more than anyone virtually governed the colonial empire. Such were the workings of the department when Murray took office. If he tried to take more decision making and responsibility himself then he failed – or at least did not succeed sufficiently to satisfy Wellington. It seems to be the only time in Murray's career that he failed to engender that esprit de corps which he had achieved as Quartermaster General. He was to be uncomfortably caught between the demands of his Prime Minister and the workings of the government machine. One of

8 Murray to Dalhousie, London, 28 September 1828, Murray Papers, ADV MS 46.8.12.

9 *Quarterly Review*, Vol 39, January 1829.

10 *Edinburgh Review*, August 1825.

Murray's under secretaries said that he had never met with any public officer so inefficient as he.[11]

It is likely that, when Wellington accused Murray of serving up work that was produced by someone who did not have the interests of the government at heart, the drafting in question had been directed, or even created, by Stephen. Treated by Wellington as a barely competent senior clerk, Murray was soon overwhelmed by the mass of business which confronted him.[12]

Reviewing the copious quantity of correspondence that his department undertook day by day, one might be forgiven for thinking that it acted as a huge recruitment agency dealing with the endless requests for jobs for family members or acquaintances or friends of friends from all quarters, often as many as six or seven a day. The roles that were being filled ranged from ministers everywhere, assistant messengers at St James' Palace, surveyors in New South Wales, judges in Canada, to doctors in the Cape. Some of these roles fell directly under the auspices of the colonial department, and needed appointments; many were passed on to another department under cover of a relieved note. Murray was his usual cautious self, having made it clear earlier in his career that he did not approve of the system, although he did from time to time resort to it for his own extended family members. 'It is a rule I observe never to make a promise of an appointment & in every situation in which it has been my fortune to serve, I have found that my predecessors would have done well to have observed the same rule'.[13] His letters, declining to add his weight to so-and-so's application for a position in Ceylon or the Cape, are wonderful examples of polite negativity. One would hardly know, without reading the letters two or three times, that he was having nothing further to do with the request.

Not only were his own staff ready to criticize his performance, but increasingly his own social and political circle were expressing doubts as to his abilities and apparent lack of application. On 23 June Mrs Arbuthnot noted that he had not quite learnt his new duties, for on the 20th he had taken his seat dressed more 'a la militaire' than the Commons quite liked, with a black stock etc, and then left early to dine with Prince Esterhazy, the Austrian Ambassador, although colonial business was about to be discussed. She reflected that he would 'soon learn that the House takes precedence of dinners and do very well, I make no doubt'.[14] Meanwhile, Lord Palmerston's view was that: 'he makes an elegant speech upon preparation and with practice would make a useful debater, but it is too late in life for him to take up this exercise with hopes of excelling in it'.[15]

In June and July Murray defended the Governor of New South Wales, Sir Ralph Darling, against a charge of cruelty against two soldiers, denying accusations that favouritism existed in the government of New South Wales. This was to be a taste of the sort of issues that Murray was starting to wrestle with in his new position. The correspondence dealing with New South Wales is peppered with letters from Thomas Mitchell who, having been sent out to New South Wales to survey territory on the east coast of the continent, found his

11 Fisher, 'Murray, Sir George'.

12 Fisher, 'Murray, Sir George'.

13 Murray to Alexander Hope, Downing Street, 28 October 1828, Murray Papers, ADV MS 46.8.12.

14 Fisher, 'Murray, Sir George'.

15 Fisher, 'Murray, Sir George'.

efforts blunted by the Governor, and he did not hesitate to bring his many and long-winded concerns to the notice of his erstwhile mentor and patron back in London. Murray, over the two years of his tenure, endeavoured unsuccessfully to keep the peace between Mitchell and the Governor. The issues between the two men just kept multiplying. Mitchell was given the dual responsibility of surveying and engineering by Murray and was supported in this, probably overambitious, role by Murray's sending out additional surveyors. Darling was not properly consulted and objected in the strongest terms. Regular letters came in to Murray from Mitchell, who, when Darling was replaced by Richard Bourke, wrote at once to say how much better things were. Predictably, that did not last long and the whining letters eventually resumed: 'indeed I should prefer Darling, unjustly as he behaved to me'.[16] Most letters concluded with the expression of great thanks to Murray, and in one Mitchell hoped Murray would enjoy the pair of black swans which he was sending.[17] What might have been Lady Louisa's reaction if he brought them back to Belgrave Square from the office! Maybe it was not so bad, as Mitchell, perhaps encouraged by Murray's no doubt polite thanks which might have just arrived, despatched another three swans and some parrots on the long voyage to Murray's address under cover of a letter some six months later.[18]

Mitchell had finally completed his survey of New South Wales, a four year exercise which he said had taken its toll on his health and on his pocket as he had had to pay for so many things himself. The last straw seemed to be a refusal by Bourke to allow Mitchell to enjoy the income from the sale of the prints that he had had made. Murray, although no longer in office, had some sympathy with his plight and canvassed support in the highest places, with complete success, when, in December 1834 Wellington made the decision that he should be entitled to the income, while making it clear that the way Mitchell had gone about things was less than clever.

On the western edge of that continent the race was on against the French to establish a foothold and a colony, and Murray gave the necessary authority for possession to Captain James Stirling RN, who had inspected the coast of Western Australia and had returned to London in the same month as Murray's defence of Darling. Stirling had written to Murray, hardly believing his good fortune in the recent change of government that was likely to look more favourably on establishing another colony, and even more so the appointment of Murray to the Colonial Office.

Sir Thomas Mitchell in later life c.1870. (From the Collection of the State Library of New South Wales)

16 Mitchell to Murray, Sydney, 25 September 1834, Murray Papers, ADV MS 46.8.16.

17 Mitchell to Murray, Liverpool Plains, NSW, 5 December 1831, Murray Papers, ADV MS 46.8.16.

18 Mitchell to Murray, Sydney, 25 May 1832, Murray Papers, ADV MS 46.8.16.

Murray knew the Stirling family, from Lanarkshire, well. Everything looked very encouraging. Stirling informed him that

> His Majesty's right to that country has never been declared, and as it is reported that the French Government contemplates the formation of a settlement in New Holland, the apprehension is that an expedition proceeding there might find, on its arrival, the best positions occupied and its aim defeated, to the total ruin of the property... I take the liberty of suggesting that [the difficulties] may be obviated by despatching at once a ship of war to that quarter. Possession might thus be taken of the country, surveys commenced, and arrangements made for the reception of settlers.[19]

To Stirling's disappointment there was a somewhat lukewarm response to his proposals, probably on the basis of cost. Undeterred, Stirling set about trying to raise support for a private arrangement, as had worked in Georgia and Pennsylvania. This initiative too met with a less-than-encouraging response from Murray with the official line against such private endeavours, namely that Government needed to exercise control.

Stirling refused to give up, and after a number of meetings with colonial officials early in November 1828, obtained the approval he needed from Murray, who ordered a warship stationed at the Cape to proceed to the western coast of New Holland and take possession of the whole territory in the King's name.

> It having been resolved by His Majesty's Government to occupy the port on the western coast of New Holland at the mouth of the river called 'Swan River' with the adjacent territory for the purpose of forming a settlement there, His Majesty has been pleased to approve the selection of yourself to have command of the expedition appointed for that service and the superintendence of the proposed settlement.[20]

HMS *Challenger*, under Captain Fremantle, arrived in April 1829, and formally claimed the territory for Britain. Stirling, arriving shortly thereafter as the colony's first Governor, decided that the settlement be named Perth, in recognition of Murray's birthplace and constituency.

The attractions of the new colony were evident, and dozens of requests were soon being made to Murray to provide introductions to the new Governor. There are letters to Stirling from Murray in support of all kinds of hopeful settlers, including a Mr Thomson, who was heading out with his wife and no fewer than twelve children, seeking a better life, with Murray's letter of introduction in his pocket.[21]

A major issue needing Murray's attention was the governance of Canada, where he appointed Sir John Colborne, who had had a distinguished military career in the Peninsula

19 Stirling to Murray, late 1828, quoted in *Documenting Democracy*, at https://www.foundingdocs.gov.au/item-did-90.html.

20 Murray to Stirling, London, 30 December 1828, Frederick Watson (ed.), *Historical Records of Australia* (Melbourne : Library Committee of the Commonwealth Parliament, 1914-1925), Series 3, Vol 6, p.600.

21 Murray to Stirling, Downing Street, 29 April 1829, Murray Papers, ADV MS 46.8.13.

and at Waterloo, as Lieutenant Governor of Upper Canada, the situation that Murray himself had temporarily filled in 1815, at what was recognized as a difficult time in Canada. Colborne did indeed turn out to be as good a Governor of the province as Murray had hoped – a very successful start. Canada's fractious relationship with the USA, and its own impatience with colonial interference, gave rise to a substantial workload. So too did slavery in the various British colonies and attempts to introduce a new slave code.

Yet, despite some successes, in early January 1829 Mrs Arbuthnot wrote that Wellington now considered Murray 'a failure because he is so indolent and allows his under-secretaries to do all the business and govern him'. She added however, that he was 'a gentlemanlike, honourable man, very desirous of serving the Duke, and will I daresay improve'.[22] This 'indolent' tag is utterly uncharacteristic of Murray. He had never in his career been regarded as anything less that a driven perfectionist, an indefatigable operator in a similar vein to Wellington. Wellington had, in the field, always been able to rely on Murray's appetite for work, and at times the duties of the Quartermaster General were unending, but always performed with limitless energy. Yet in the colonial role he was found wanting. There were only a few newspapers that seemed to look beyond the political miscalculations that certainly plagued him, and his seemingly ambiguous position of loyalty to his Tory political master and his own more liberal, or at least independent, views. It is entirely possible that on slavery he had some sympathy for Stephen's views, but was nevertheless a minister and loyal servant of the Crown, part of a Tory administration, a division of loyalties which Murray would have found most uncomfortable. Nevertheless, it is clear that his performance, or at least that of his department, irritated Wellington.

The *Aberdeen Journal*, looking back in June 1834 over his Colonial Secretaryship, stated that Lady Louisa often

> had brought him his dinner in his carriage to the Colonial Office pretty much for the same reason that bricklaying labourers are served by the same fashion by their less elegant helpmates. In truth Sir George had not the leisure to return home, and rather than neglect the business of his office he would thus content himself with a hasty meal snatched between the conclusion of the business of that office and the commencement of the orders of the day in the House of Commons. Against the diligence of the ex Colonial Secretary we have never heard a complaint.[23]

On his varied brief, Murray argued against any diminution of resources for his department on the basis that, were colonies to be given up, there was a danger of a significant deterioration in the country's political standing in the world. He insisted on the need for a large military force in the West Indies, said caution must prevail on slavery abolition, and explained that ministers were eager to secure the Canadas by making them dependent on an extension of their own population. Whilst he was keen to be rid of Sierra Leone as soon as possible, it would be inhumane to abandon the colony precipitately. His position on most of these issues was notably more liberal than Wellington's, whose stance was more aligned with the 'Ultra' Tories.

22 Fisher, 'Murray, Sir George'.
23 *Aberdeen Journal*, 25 June 1834.

If there was plenty to occupy the politicians' minds on overseas matters, closer to home enormous upheavals were imminent in the shape of Catholic Emancipation and the Reform Act. Certainly, on the former, Murray's clear views were more aligned to the Whig position than many of his Tory colleagues would have found comfortable, while still trying to maintain a semblance of the old order. In July 1828 he had expressed to Lord Ellenborough his fears that Catholic emancipation would be delayed 'until the Catholics have gone as far as to make it impossible'. Now, six months on, Ellenborough thought he had 'put several points on the Catholic question extremely well' when he met him in the Cabinet Room on 20 January 1829, and he made contributions to the Cabinet's discussions of the details of the Relief Bill and the accompanying disenfranchisement measure.[24]

Murray's speech in support of the Government's policy of emancipation, on 5 March 1829, when he drew on his experiences in Ireland, received praise from all sides. It concluded:

> But what is the object of Civil Society? For what do Governments exist? It is not to side with one portion of the people, to oppress and destroy the other; it is for the peace and protection of the whole. For my part I can see no objection to the present measure; on the contrary I hail it as a bond of union, and as a pledge of security; and I regard it as the most certain means of confirming the tranquillity, of increasing the prosperity, and of extending the power of the Empire.[25]

Ellenborough thought he spoke 'admirably' and Mrs Arbuthnot 'beautifully', while the radical Whig Member John Cam Hobhouse reckoned he had delivered 'one of the most affecting and effective speeches ever heard, containing some finished eloquence of the highest character'. Lord Grenville, who had been Prime Minister in 1806, found the Whigs at Brooks's 'in great admiration' of his performance. Later in the month Murray went on to present petitions in favour of emancipation, and opposed an attempt to amend the Bill. He also welcomed the Edinburgh pro Catholic petition.[26]

More praise followed for another speech he made in the Commons, supporting Peel. Murray had stated in his speech that:

> In the Army there are no distinctions; no differences on account of religion. It is in civil society only that I have found such differences prevail. In the Army Catholics and Protestants dwell in harmony in the same tent; they march in the same ranks; they mount the same breach; and the only competition which is known between them is the competition of emulation to excel in courage, and in fidelity to their Country; and they fall together in the same field, they are laid together in the same grave, leaving behind them the same feelings of regret in the breasts of their surviving comrades, and carrying with them to another world, the same hopes in their common Redeemer.[27]

24 Fisher, 'Murray, Sir George'.
25 Speech to the House of Commons, 5 March 1829, Murray Papers, ADV MS 46.8.8.
26 Fisher, 'Murray, Sir George'.
27 Murray's Speech to House of Commons, 5 March 1829, Murray Papers, ADV MS 46.8.8.

Here was a cause that stirred something in Murray, and where he could demonstrate his support of the government's position. Illustrating his position from a military perspective clearly struck a chord with those who heard the speech delivered with passion. This was the Murray that his supporters had anticipated on his appointment, and they must have felt that, at last, he had come of age as a politician. Yet he had still to persuade the one that really mattered, namely Wellington, that he was in full command of his position at the Colonial Office.

Despite Murray's early success in impressing politicians of all hues in the House of Commons, by May 1829 the tone of Wellington's frequent notes to Murray on colonial affairs were starting to become more and more terse, in this case on the question of Demerara slaves: 'If the Order in Council has passed in its present form as it appears it has done there is no use in my objecting to it. But I thought I was to see the draft of it. It does not meet my views of the case'.[28] The business that was taking up large amounts of Murray's time and energy at this point, as indeed it had with earlier colonial secretaries, were the ongoing debates over slavery, the moves to remove some of its more cruel practices, and to establish some degree of human rights. The specific evils of the slave codes had to an extent been addressed in all slave colonies. It remained to gather up regulation into a consistent code of slave law. These came under numerous headings such as hours of labour, Sunday work, provision of food and clothing. Flogging of female slaves was to be prohibited and that of male slaves subject to restrictions. The system of a protector of slaves was to be introduced and returns would have to be made to him annually. Individuals who had been convicted for a second time for cruelty would cease to have the right to own slaves. The new code was designed around slavery in the West Indies, which gave rise to resentment in the Cape where colonists regarded the new provisions as an incitement to insurrection and Sir Lowry Cole, now Governor there, was obliged to issue an ordinance for the prohibition of meetings likely to endanger good order. The question arose as to how much discretion might be left to the colonial legislatures, rather than dictating from London. Murray tended towards allowing the colonies themselves to bring forward their own laws under the strict proviso that they would be left in no doubt as to the principles adopted in Westminster 'for the amelioration of the slave population, and for fitting that population by degrees to pass from a state of slavery to a state of freedom'.[29]

Wellington was prepared to move in step with much of the momentum on slavery but was more cautious than most, lest there be an unintended slide towards a more general debate on the whole question of the legitimacy or morality of the practice, which he would not countenance. He wrote to Murray, less than happy with the slant of the department's drafting

> I return the Slave Ordinance with some notes that have occurred to me upon the perusal of it.
>
> In general I should say that the Gentleman, whoever he may be, who has drawn up this Order in Council is a Partisan in favour of the Abolition of Slavery.

28 Wellington to Murray, London, 28 May 1829, Murray Papers, ADV MS 46.8.8.

29 Murray to Wellington, Downing Street, 19 August 1828, WP1/948/11.

Government must act upon the principle of carrying, with caution, fairly, the intentions of Parliament, but must avoid the extreme views of both Parties, and the hasty manner of the one and those of the other which are calculated to defeat the views of Parliament.[30]

The reference to 'the Gentleman, whoever he may be' is clearly directed at Stephen. Murray was deemed guilty of allowing the civil service to undermine the authority of an elected House.

A short report in the *Tipperary Free Press* of 26 December 1829 sheds a little light on the difficulties Murray must have been having reconciling his personal feelings with political party requirements and perhaps even with Wellington's deep seated views. The report is almost what one might suspect to have been planted with some ultimate aim. Certainly in today's political world it would be treated with some suspicion.

Sir George Murray, the Colonial Secretary, recently saw a distressed black man in the streets and, on humanely enquiring into his case, was answered that he was a free negro, who had left Jamaica to better his condition, and that he had served in the band of one of our regiments there. Finding his story to be true, Sir George procured him a pension of 1s. per day and his passage to his own country. But the captain of the ship refused to take him in his rags and tatters, which were certainly repulsive. This being communicated to Sir George, he clothed the unfortunate wretch and put him in a condition to join the ship, and to escape the unclothed, unfed and unhoused rigours of the approaching winter.[31]

During 1829 a good deal of business also centred on Canada, in particular the composition of the Houses of Assembly of Upper and Lower Canada and the appointment of judges, and these were the subject of long debates in the House of Commons. Murray was in constant communication not only with Wellington but also Robert Peel, the Home Secretary and future Prime Minister, devising political tactics. Correspondence flowed too between Murray and General Sir James Kempt, Governor General in Canada, on improving the militia system in Canada, and with Dalhousie, following his relinquishing the position in Kempt's favour. There was plenty to occupy the limited resources of the department, including plans to place an establishment on the Falkland Islands – the best time, it was considered, was the present, between the cessation of old Spanish power and consolidation of new governments in South America.

The work on the new slave code continued into the New Year, when Wellington again had cause to complain to Murray about what he saw as poor drafting by someone junior in Murray's office. Given the tangible evidence in the Murray Papers of Murray's own considerable and painstaking drafting exercises, it is entirely possible that Wellington was either unaware of the effort Murray was putting in to getting the final wording right, or was in

30 Wellington to Murray, London, 10 October 1829, Murray Papers, ADV MS 46.8.8.

31 *Tipperary Free Press*, 26 December 1829.

some way wanting to avoid having to point the finger of blame at his colleague. Either way he felt that it needed review by a qualified lawyer:

> I wish very much to see the Ordinance as amended before it will pass the Council.
> I must say in confidence that the Gentleman who draws these papers for your office serves the Government very ill. I wrote to the Lord Chancellor to beg him to look it over carefully, as it is impossible for the Government to act upon this or answer any question in the spirit of an authoritative party...
> We must look at it seriously by ourselves and oblige those under us to carry into execution our intentions and not their own fancies.[32]

Wellington's irritation was evident two days later – there had been considerable debate over the definition of 'Sunday' when applied to rest days for slaves. 'I understood that the Cabinet altered the 93rd clause; and made Sunday to be Sunday – that is from midnight on Saturday to midnight on Sunday. I should think it best to omit the clause altogether as being useless'.[33] Murray responded forcefully suggesting that Wellington's wording could, in the case of unscrupulous owners, deprive the slaves of two full night's sleep and felt that Sunday should be defined as commencing at 10 pm on the Saturday.[34] The exchange grew more heated later that same day, with Wellington's the final word:

> I am very sorry to differ from you. The Cabinet in my presence agreed to the alteration which I proposed in respect to Sunday. Before I left the room other business had been commenced...
> PS – I hope this will be settled before the Order is brought to Council on Tuesday.[35]

Murray was reported as being very quiet during a cabinet discussion on slavery a few days later. Ellenborough thought that he was overawed by the Duke having been under him for so long.[36] Perhaps he was fuming or sulking after the terse exchanges, which probably brought back memories of the Wellesley of 1809 in the Peninsula, the Wellesley who rarely delegated if he had time to attend to matters himself. Perhaps too there was a nagging doubt in his mind that his master was growing disappointed with his performance, despite his best efforts. To a man who had for so many years been in Wellington's total confidence on matters official and personal, it must have been devastating to be contradicted and upbraided so frequently. The 'reward' which Wellington had handed him was starting to taste bitter. According to Ellenborough, after a Cabinet meeting on 7 February, Murray, in a rare moment of criticism of Wellington in the presence of a third party 'expressed his surprise that the Duke should cling to the hope of reclaiming the Ultra Tories alienated by Catholic emancipation, for he would not get them and they were not worth having'.[37]

32 Wellington to Murray, London, 27 January 1830, Murray Papers, ADV MS 46.8.10.
33 Wellington to Murray, London, 29 January 1830, Murray Papers, ADV MS 46.8.10.
34 Murray to Wellington, Downing Street, 29 January 1830, WP1/1089/5.
35 Wellington to Murray, London, 29 January 1830, Murray Papers, ADV MS 46.8.10.
36 Fisher, 'Murray, Sir George'.
37 Fisher, 'Murray, Sir George'.

Shunned by royalty on account of his wife's earlier indiscretions, not only was his social life awkward, but Murray's future at the Colonial Office now became the subject of intense speculation. In April Ellenborough was told by Sir Henry Hardinge (whom he suspected of aspiring to the Office) that 'Murray does not do the business well' and would be 'very well satisfied to be Master General of the Ordnance',[38] though Ellenborough, strangely perhaps, doubted this. Wellington, now acutely aware of Murray's deficiencies in office, despite his successes in the Emancipation debate, was seemingly not prepared to defend him against criticism from elsewhere, including that from Mrs Arbuthnot. He would have liked to have moved him to a military post more suited to his talents; but he got angry with Mrs Arbuthnot when she badgered him on the need to strengthen the ministry's front bench in the Commons. Ellenborough dismissed Lord Rosslyn's notion that Murray would make an excellent Indian Governor General, because he would be too indolent.

The 'indolent' tag thus surfaces again. It is hardly a label that fits the man who once wrote to Augusta 'nothing makes me so happy as the thought that were several more hours added to the day, I should still find occupations sufficient for them all',[39] and to Isabella 'One cannot improve one's fortunes by indolence'.[40] But that was in 1802 when he was absorbed in military science, and 1809 when about to embark for Portugal with Wellesley. Perhaps Murray found politics and its attendant administration boring, and the ways of civilian life inefficient; a simple case of a soldier finding the transition difficult – and opted to leave the daily grind to his subordinates. Perhaps his mind was elsewhere; if Louisa was unwell that might provide an explanation, but given his apparent ability to apply himself fully to his duties even when dealing with the deaths of close colleagues and family, this seems less likely. Either way, his heart was not in it.

Despite Westminster's doubts about his suitability for the colonial role, Perthshire returned Murray unopposed and in absentia (pleading pressure of official business) at the General Election of 1830. When Mrs Arbuthnot again raised the issue of recruiting 'speakers' for the Commons, Wellington lost his temper, but admitted that 'in the department as a man of business', Murray was woeful.[41] He had found more cause to disagree with Murray, this time on Canadian affairs, where Wellington wanted to limit the powers of the Governor General:

> If you will be so kind as to refer to the 30th, 31st and 32nd Clauses... you will see that the Governor or Lt Governor has authority to declare according to his discretion...
>
> I am always very sorry to differ in opinion with any of my colleagues, particularly when I know that I am right.[42]

It would be surprising if Murray had not hungered for the good old days of straightforward soldiering in the Peninsula, when he knew that he had Wellington's full trust, where

38 Fisher, 'Murray, Sir George'.

39 Murray to Augusta, High Wycombe, 22 April 1802, Murray Papers, MS 21103.

40 Murray to Isabella, St Albans Street, 5 April 1809, Murray Papers, MS 21101.

41 Fisher, 'Murray, Sir George'.

42 Wellington to Murray, London, 27 June 1830, Murray Papers, ADV MS 46.8.10.

Wellington was often in the habit of following Murray's suggestions even when differing from his own instincts, and did not have to manoeuvre his way around London's social and political potholes. Murray was now on the receiving end of Wellington's ill-concealed impatience – an occurrence he would have witnessed many times in the case of officers who fell short of the commander's expectations. It must have been demoralizing for him. That their personal relationship remained seemingly unaffected is remarkable, but perhaps should not be so surprising given all that they had been through together.

By the end of September Wellington had made up his mind on replacing Murray, hard though he found the idea of disloyalty to a close military colleague. He had been persuaded that he needed to offer government places to Canning supporters, and to bring new blood on board. He decided to offer the Colonial Office to Palmerston and to compensate Murray with the colonelcy of the Blues and the promise of 'the first thing that falls vacant', surely an offer that Murray would have willingly embraced. However, the negotiations with Palmerston came to nothing, and Murray had to soldier on.

The other major preoccupation of Westminster was Reform, considered by many necessary to extend the franchise and eliminate political corruption, by replacing the numerous rotten boroughs, controlled by a very few landowners, with constituencies based more on the larger cities that were growing up, products of the Industrial Revolution. The measures were supported by the Whigs who recognized that the changes would create substantial support in Parliament, which would prop up the Whig aristocracy and keep them in office, regardless of the King's sentiments. These aristocrats were not promoting pure democracy but they did seek to recast the constitution to provide them with every chance of remaining in power and keeping the King under control. The support of the Radicals, republican sympathisers but essential Whig allies in this quest, created a prospect that terrified most Tories, traditionally loyal to the Crown.

Murray, more liberal than his Tory leader, who would not depart from what he regarded as the strictest interpretation of duty to King and Country, law and order, attempted to take a more moderate line, repeated that he was 'willing to listen… to the propositions that may be brought forward respecting it by others' and conceded that, while the 'great principles' of the constitution must remain inviolate, any particular detached portion of the system might 'from time to time undergo modification'. When his statement that he was 'perfectly willing that reform should take place' evoked opposition cheers, he reacted by saying that if Members thought he was going further than he had intended, he was sure that too great an extension of the franchise would be dangerous, and that a respectable and powerful aristocracy was essential to secure the country against the changes and convulsions that had happened in other countries.[43]

This speech, coming after an uncompromising declaration by Wellington in the Lords the previous evening, against all reform, caused a stir and created an impression that ministers were divided on the issue. Mrs. Arbuthnot thought that Murray 'did not mean to express any opposition to the duke', but that 'what he said was so ill-judged that it had the effect', while Ellenborough and Goulburn, who attributed the lapse to Murray's inexperience,

43 Fisher, 'Murray, Sir George'.

believed that he 'had done much injury'.[44] Wellington's speech, so blunt in its opposition to any reform, had the effect of uniting all shades of reformers. A planned dinner at the Guildhall for the inauguration of the Lord Mayor was cancelled against a backdrop of threatened violent disturbances. Reluctantly the Government decided that the risk of significant bloodshed was too great. Some felt the Government had lost its nerve. The new revolutions that had recently taken place in Paris and Brussels were very much in the cabinet's mind. A feeling was growing that timely concessions on issues such as Reform were less dangerous than uncompromising opposition to a rising tide of liberalism. There was considerable rioting in London on 9 and 10 November – for the most part contained by Peel's newly formed Metropolitan Police, avoiding the use of troops. The Government was defeated in the House of Commons on a relatively minor issue, demonstrating its inability to command a majority on Reform, and Wellington resigned on 16 November 1830.

The work of Wellington's government has often been underappreciated, it having introduced a range of progressive measures, both at home and in the colonies, of which any liberal administration would have been proud. He had handled foreign affairs deftly, and had shown delicacy in his reaction to the new revolutions in France, where the Bourbons had again been overthrown, and Belgium. There was however no escaping the fact that there was, as Muir puts it: 'a sharp shift in political outlook and attitudes which affected the press and part of the public in the 1820s and 1830s, and which led them to dismiss almost with contempt those who did not share their new found certainties'.[45] Wellington and Murray were both victims of that change.

44 Fisher, 'Murray, Sir George'.
45 Muir, *Fortunes of Peace*, p.400.

24

In Opposition

Murray went into opposition with Wellington as one of the more prominent members of the mainstream of the Tory party under Peel's leadership. In the Commons, on 13 December, he defended his and the late Government's record on slavery abolition, adding that precipitate emancipation would 'merely afford a sanction to the commission of murder… plunder and devastation'.[1] In a private letter written early in the New Year he again defended his stance on abolition of slavery and proposed emancipation very clearly. He was in favour of the former, but only gradually, and without compensation being paid to the slave owners. Immediate emancipation, he also argued, would lead to the likelihood of insurrection.

Without his ministerial income, money again became a worry. Wellington's defeat could not have come at a worse moment. Early in 1830, Murray had bought, and moved into, 5 Belgrave Square with his two Louisas – a residence perhaps more aligned to Lady Louisa's tastes than his own, and an address that satisfied her love of the new. That, however, had been a decision made against the good, if uncertain, income as Secretary of State. The last minute details and furnishing seem to have taken longer to finalise than planned, as Murray was due to entertain the cabinet to dinner early in March, but he had to enlist the support of his close neighbour at Apsley House who agreed to help him out by holding the dinner there instead. Not that Wellington himself seemed to be immune from financial concerns during that time. The costs of living at Apsley House were rising and 'I think that the Matter will end in my shutting up the House and living in a lodging'. He felt too that he was frequently cheated, and targeted for donations, which made him feel 'plundered' He was in fact extraordinarily generous in many directions.[2]

It was certainly not going to be cheap for Murray to run his new establishment. Nor was he the only Murray to be financially stretched – Patrick's financial affairs were now in the hands of trustees, a repeat of his father's circumstances and a situation not unfamiliar to generations of Ochtertyre Murrays both before and after. Murray wrote to his cousin Anthony at Dollerie on 20 January 1831, happy to hear that Patrick's trust seemed to be prospering, even in such difficult times, and even more importantly that his brother's debt to him was not in quite such a precarious state as he had feared. He went on:

1 Murray's speech, House of Commons Debate, 13 December 1829, quoted in Fisher, 'Murray, Sir George'.

2 Muir, *Fortunes of Peace*, p.452, citing letters Wellington to Mrs Arbuthnot 15 August 1832 and 12 December 1832.

> I find myself obliged to look much more narrowly into my pecuniary affairs more than I have ever been accustomed to do. In a great part of my life I had, as a single man, no cause for anxiety on that head, because I could shape my expenses to my income without any difficulty, or any inclination to consult but my own – and I always made my way, by good luck, to some Professional Appointment of emolument. Now, however I cannot so easily curtail my expenses at pleasure on a moment's notice, and the sphere of employment is much more narrowed than it used to be. A most heavy and unavoidable expense for many months past has been doctors fees, and apothecaries bills. However by parting with servants, and by giving up Carriage Horses, I hope to bring matters into such a shape as to keep clear of incurring debt.[3]

Louisa's health had not been good, which must have been an added worry on top of the stresses of his political life over the last two years. Her illnesses were to be a major factor in all major decisions made by Murray for the remainder of his career. Throughout the decade following his appointment as Secretary of State there are dozens of newspaper articles and society notices which refer to this dinner or that tour, or an escape to the country or another formal engagement, where Louisa'a name did not appear. Her narrow circle of friends, and perhaps the stigma of her affair with Murray, seem to have limited her social life. Yet such absences seem extreme and it is difficult not to give weight to the possibility that Louisa's health, as it had been in Ireland, was never without complications, and played its part in severely limiting her appearances. They did travel to Scotland in the shooting season together, but the society columns are devoid of what might be considered the usual pairing of husband and wife. The frequent invitations to Stratfield Saye and Peel's country home at Drayton Manor mostly seem to assume Murray would be coming by himself, although one from Peel is extended to include Murray's 'fair companions'.[4] Another from Peel in 1833 is 'for a few days moderate shooting' starting on 23 December.[5] So it does not look as though it was anything exceptional for Murray to be separated from his family at a this time of year, even given that Christmas was not yet accorded the importance that we are familiar with today. An exception to this was an invitation from the Whig George Grenville, nephew of Grenville the 1806 Prime Minister, inviting Murray and the two Louisas with great warmth to stay at Stowe in December:

> If you say that I have been riding about the country canvassing for Lord Grenville you may perhaps be right, if you say that I am naturally a very indolent being you certainly will not be wrong. Under the shade of these two palliatives I sit down to tell you how happy we shall all be to see you and your wife and daughter about the 17th or 18th, when we shall be certain of being at home, as my mother's birthday on the nineteenth is always the signal for the commencement of our family rendez-vous. For myself, I hope I need not say how happy I shall be to welcome you to the Museum, how cheerily my bugle horn, and post horn, will blow in token of salute

3 Murray to Anthony Murray, Belgrave Square, 20 January 1831, Private Collection.

4 TNA, WO 80/3Peel to Murray, Drayton, 15 November (No year).

5 Peel to Murray, Drayton Manor, 17 December 1833, Murray Papers, MS 21104.

> or with what an unusual air my wig, hat, nose and spectacles will sit upon my head on the day of your arrival.[6]

The new house in Belgravia inevitably attracted curious family visitors – Joanna Churchill and Anthony Murray's sister were staying at the time he was writing about his finances, and Patrick had warned him that he was coming up to London the following month with two of his daughters. Murray was not clear quite why, as Patrick rather typically had not told him, and Murray had some concern that it was merely an excuse to spend some money that his trustees had allowed him.

The new Government's Reform Bill was much more radical than anyone expected. In the Commons Murray spoke briefly from the opposition benches against the English bill, on 18 March, and voted against its second reading after asserting that the Irish bill would 'excite as much dislike in its details, as the Scottish bill has excited in Scotland'. He conceded that large numbers of people of Scotland favoured the measure, but insisted that 'the wealth and influence of the country' were hostile, being particularly alarmed by the proposal to enfranchise tenants, which he said would damage the agricultural interest by encouraging landlords to shorten leases and lead to the creation of fictitious votes. He was also concerned that Scotland would be left more poorly represented proportionately than England. His view, which became a recurrent theme of his, was that the larger Scottish counties (including Perthshire) should be entitled to two members each and Scottish towns of over 22,000 inhabitants (including Perth) to separate representation. He also supported enfranchising the Scottish universities, giving the church a voice, and objected to a description of the Scottish counties under the present system as 'rotten'. Before supporting the Tories' wrecking amendment to the Reform Bill, his preference being for a slower, more measured introduction of reform, in both England and Scotland, he said that the effect of reform would be to 'subject the people, to a dangerous degree, to the influence of those plausible harangues which have so often deceived and misled them'.[7]

Having now a substantial majority, the Whigs were assured of success in the Commons. On the second reading of the reintroduced English Reform Bill, in July 1831, Murray denounced it as 'a measure, the tendency of which is likely to give rise in this country to those dangerous and revolutionary convulsions with which we have seen other nations so much shaken'.[8] He regarded the Scottish Reform Bill on its second reading, as even more dangerous than the English:

> I never was an enemy to all reform; and I have... been ready to admit of the expediency of some modification in the Scottish system... But I do object to the utter abandonment of the principle of representation which has ever existed in that country.[9]

Ellenborough found him 'much elated' by the defeat of the English Reform Bill in the Lords, and on 10 October suggested him to Hardinge as a possible Leader of the Commons in a

6 Grenville to Murray, Stowe, 3 December (No year), Murray Papers, MS 21192.
7 Fisher, 'Murray, Sir George'.
8 Murray's speech, House of Commons Debate 5 July 1831, quoted in Fisher, 'Murray, Sir George'.
9 Murray's speech, House of Commons Debate 23 September 1831, quoted in Fisher, 'Murray, Sir George'.

5, Belgrave Square, Murray's Belgravia house. (Author's photo)

possible provisional government. Murray voted against the second reading of the revised English Reform Bill on 17 December 1831. The bill was passed in the Commons but again failed in the Lords.

The hotly contested bill became the cause of major political and social upheaval during 1832. Grey put pressure on William IV to create enough Whig Peers to ensure success in the Lords, but the King refused and Grey resigned. The King remained at St James's Palace during April and May out of a desire to be at hand during the crisis. In the midst of it all at least Murray was able to enjoy himself amongst many old colleagues when the King and Queen gave what was described as 'a grand dinner' for the Knights Grand Cross of the Bath in the Palace banqueting room. Doubtless many stories of the long years in the Peninsula were well rehearsed among the dazzling array of generals who were present that evening.

During May, when Wellington, at the invitation of the King, following Grey's resignation, tried to form a ministry to carry a limited measure of reform, Murray remained loyal to the duke and, according to Ellenborough, was willing, under duress, to become Leader of the Commons, although he was very reluctant to do so. Peel refused to serve, not wishing to be take responsibility for implementing reform although he had long regarded it as inevitable. Parts of the country descended into chaos and many feared revolution. Arrangements by activists for barricading Birmingham, Manchester and other cities were put in hand. The Army was ordered to prepare for action. There was a run on the Bank of England. Some reformers were convinced that Wellington was planning a coup d'etat. Only Wellington's veterans, Hardinge and Murray, seemed eager to serve next to him. Rumours that Wellington was to be assassinated on his way to Parliament spun out of control. There were calls for the abolition of the aristocracy and the monarchy. In the rowdy debate of 14 May, Murray, taking a different position from Peel, denied that it would be 'inconsistent' in men such as himself to take office to carry limited reform. He argued that 'the only line which it became the House to follow was to support the Crown'.[10]

Despite Wellington's offer of moderate reform, he was unable to form a government. The King had no option but to recall Grey. The King even reluctantly agreed to the creation of enough Whig Peers to allow success in the Lords. Wellington recognized this as the moment of defeat, and encouraged his supporters in the House of Lords to drop their opposition. The Great Reform Act received Royal Assent on 7 June 1832. But the country had come very close to revolution. Wellington continued for a while to be the target of rough treatment in the popular press and violent abuse on the streets, and at Apsley House. Murray too attracted hostility although not directly, when, in December that year, whilst at a meeting of his supporters in Perthshire, a number of farmers had their stockyards set on fire.

We know little of Murray's activities over the following nine months or so, other than that he was active in the Commons. On 5 March 1833 Ellenborough, who had been speaking to Sir John Hobhouse wrote to Murray – he had been discussed; 'Would you go to India as Governor General? W Bentinck has not yet signified to his intention of returning, but I believe he may be expected to leave India by the end of this year'. Murray replied from Sunninghill the very next day:

> The suggestion that it contains is most gratifying to me as a mark of your friendship and good opinion, but I do not think that the arrangement you point to would be suitable for me. In the first place it is rather too late in life for me to enter upon so great an undertaking…
>
> There are also some domestic considerations which would make me backward in indulging in the view that you place before me. These I shall mention to you when we meet – I am to dine at Gloucester House on Saturday next and I shall call for you within that day or the day following.[11]

10 Murray's speech, House of Commons Debate 14 May 1832, quoted in Fisher, 'Murray, Sir George'.

11 TNA, WO 80/4, Ellenborough to Murray, 8 Waterloo Place, 5 March 1833 and Murray to Ellenborough, Sunninghill 6 March 1833.

Ellenborough again tried to tempt Murray towards India a year later, soon after Murray had been appointed as Master General of the Ordnance. He felt that, in the twelve months that had elapsed, perhaps those domestic considerations might have changed. They had not, or at least not enough for Murray to accept. Later, in May 1838, he was to be offered Command in Chief in India, only to refuse again.

There is evidence of illness getting the better of Murray around this time. Many of his letters to his agent in Edinburgh, George Smythe, mention the fact, and apologise for delays in correspondence, but lack further elaboration. Murray was appointed President of the recently formed Geographical Society, (later The Royal Geographical Society) in succession to Lord Goderich, although he rarely attended and in two years of presidency only chaired two council meetings. He was, however, was in office at the time that Sturt, after naming the newly discovered Murray River in his honour, published his report in the 1834 *Journal* of the Society.

He regained his Perthshire seat at a by-election in May 1834, having also been invited to stand for the Western Boroughs, by which time the popular tide had turned against the Whigs, forcing Grey's resignation, and his replacement by Lord Melbourne, who was himself dismissed by the King in November 1834. Wellington gave way to Peel to lead the Tories, now back in power. Murray was appointed Master General of the Ordnance in Peel's short-lived first ministry, a post to which he was well suited.

He lost his seat at the 1835 general election. Nevertheless during the short period of Peel's first administration, the Tories re-established themselves after the humiliations of 1832. Radicalism had become exhausted and many liberals disillusioned by Whig government. Even so, Wellington, and probably Murray, continued to be worried about the risk of revolution. It was clear though that Murray would not be standing for Perthshire again, although he offered himself later for both Westminster and Manchester. Another familiar attack in *The Spectator* in August 1836 read: 'It is known everywhere that he is not a man of his word. Neither Whig nor Tory, nor Radical can have confidence in Sir George Murray'. In December 1836, in a final broadside, it stated: 'For an adroit person, not overgifted with principle, Sir George Murray plays his cards very badly. He has lost Perthshire irretrievably we presume, and as for his chance in Westminster it is very small indeed'.[12]

With no political responsibilities, or indeed Westminster income, the three or four years following the loss of his seat in Parliament must have been a period of considerable worry. As far back as 1831 he had been forced to trim his lifestyle, as a result of large doctors' bills for Louisa and the cost of running his substantial house. These pressures must now have reasserted themselves in full measure. A part of his time at least was spent in a battle of words with William Napier, the Irish officer who had seen service in the Peninsula, and who later wrote a history of the war. This necessitated the collating of as much evidence as Murray could from his own Peninsular colleagues to counter what he saw as Napier's ill-informed and inaccurate history of the campaign. Satisfying though this might have been, it was not remunerative. Perhaps his re-visiting of many of the events of those years might have rekindled his own idea, lying fallow for so long, of writing his own history, although there is no evidence of this being committed to paper, and in any case he was no doubt still

12 *The Spectator*, 20 August and 17 December 1836.

adhering to his principle of not writing anything critical of Wellington during his lifetime. However, freed from the tedium and cares of office, he would certainly have been keen to pursue some interest or other. Opportunities still presented themselves.

On 11 August 1838 he was approached by Lord Glenelg with yet another invitation to a prestigious position:

> I venture to address you on a subject of great interest and importance. Sir John Colborne is about to retire from Canada – and it is of course a matter of much anxiety to my colleagues and myself how we can replace him at this most critical time I am desired to ask you if it would suit your views to accept that command – most truly do I hope it may be our good fortune to place such a trust in such hands.[13]

Murray replied firmly next day, allowing no time for second thoughts: 'domestic considerations to which I attach much importance would render it undesirable to me at present to be called upon to assume the command of the troops stationed in Canada'.[14]

It was an exact replica of the exchanges over India. Louisa's health was surely the major issue which would have made such a posting unworkable, but the fact that Murray was approaching seventy, and also perhaps not in the best of health, must also have been on his mind. In a letter dated 28 September 1839 to his aunt Joanna Churchill, he went into some detail on the continuing concerns over Louisa's health. Even though she seemed better over the last few days,

> she does not seem to feel herself quite equal to go from home with confidence. And I am the less disposed to urge her doing so because I saw upon occasion of her last attack how important it was that I had had it in my power to have immediate recourse to Mr [illegible – presumably her doctor]. I am going on Monday to pay a short visit to Sir Robert Peel and when I return I shall see, if the weather is fair, whether we cannot come to see you.[15]

Murray contested, it need hardly be said unsuccessfully in view of the changes in the country, two English constituencies. In the general election caused by the death of William IV in June 1837, he stood for Westminster, won the previous month for the Tories. In September 1839 and June 1841 he again stood, as one of four candidates for the newly enfranchised constituency of Manchester, which returned two members. Sir James Graham, the colleague who wrote of the peculiar circumstances which made Murray 'unhappy and unfortunate', while respecting his ability, considered him a highly unsuitable person to contest constituencies like Manchester.[16] He was better suited to the Horse Guards. He was right.

13 Glenelg to Murray, George Street, 11 August 1838, Murray Papers, MS 21104.
14 Murray to Glenelg, Belgrave Square, 12 August 1838, Murray Papers, MS 21104.
15 Murray to Mrs Churchill, Belgrave Square, 28 September 1839, Murray Papers, MS 21101.
16 Ward Draft, Ch.XVII, p.34.

Contemporary cartoon of Murray's Election Campaign 1837. (National Portrait Gallery)

> When pressed, he makes dangerous concessions to political adversaries, and wants that high courage of resistance in the conflict of opinion which so eminently distinguishes him in the field.
>
> In revolutionary times – and on them our lot is cast – the surrender of first principles is the greatest of all dangers. To have carried Manchester would have been poor recompense for the loss of the vantage-ground on which we have hitherto defended the existing Corn Law and the amended Poor Law. To have lost Manchester, and gratuitously to have weakened these defences is indeed a misfortune, and I hope that Sir George Murray will renounce the temptations which these popular constituencies hold out to the ruin of a man who is not resolved to make no concession for the purpose of winning their favour.[17]

Graham's point, that Murray was too ready to compromise to curry favour with his audience, while perhaps true to a certain extent, also hints at the difficulty that Murray experienced

17 Sir James Graham to Charles Arbuthnot, Netherby, 12 September 1839, Aspinall (ed.), *Correspondence of Charles Arbuthnot*, p.207.

as a politician – namely that he was a moderate in a Tory party which felt that the whole country, its institutions, its aristocracy, and its monarchy was under threat, and any weakness towards the agitators was dangerous. Murray was always on the liberal side of Tory politics, to the extent that there was such a thing, and never shared Wellington's views, for instance, on the need for outright opposition to voting reform, a stance that Murray considered dangerous. He held similar views on any dragging of feet on Catholic Emancipation. He had even from time to time received the enthusiastic praise of the Whig establishment for his speeches, some of which took a distinctly independent line. Neither Murray nor Patrick felt entirely comfortable in being part of, and thus expected to be unquestioningly loyal to, the Tory party, although both would have recognized that they owed their appointments to it.

Ward summed up the inevitable march of public opinion away from the likes of Wellington and Murray. Times had changed:

> The new electorate had entirely forgotten anything it ever knew of Lady Louisa Erskine. The missiles it directed at Murray in the market square of Crieff in 1832 and at the hustings in Westminster were inspired by political, not moral, motives. It had scant respect for Peninsular generals. It was preoccupied with the Corn Laws and Free Trade and conditions of labour in the mills. None of these were issues to which Murray, who refused invitations to attend the opening of the Liverpool and Manchester Rail Road on 15 September 1830 and the launching of Brunel's *Great Britain* on 19 July 1843, and never, so far as can be seen, set foot in a factory, could contribute opinions or experience of any value.[18]

Murray seemed fundamentally unsuited to modern politics, despite instances of some first-rate speeches, and evidence of some good decisions, including the claiming of Swan River for Britain, and the appointment of Sir John Colborne as Governor General of Canada. He was as loyal to Peel, whose company he clearly enjoyed, as he had been to Wellington, to the extent of agreeing to stand in unwinnable seats. Regrettably, his spark, his ability to get things done without fuss, even his self-confidence perhaps, all seem to have deserted him from the moment he walked up Downing Street to his new office.

18 Ward Draft, Ch.XVII, p.33.

25

Literary Work

During 1836 and 1837 William Napier, once a Peninsular officer and later an historian, was immersed in finalising his *History of the War in the Peninsula*, four volumes already having been published, regarded by many as extraordinarily pro-French and anti-Spanish. He approached Murray with the request for a loan of the maps, produced by Mitchell, many of which were in Murray's possession. Some were still incomplete, being worked on by Mitchell. Murray declined to hand them over. Battle commenced between the two men, resulting in a flurry of letters to and from Murray's old Peninsular comrades, who had to dredge up what recollections they could, from their desks and memories, of incidents and battles in an effort to discredit Napier's commentary and his views, which were, in many cases, at odds with Murray's. Murray's attack on Napier took the form of articles in the *Quarterly Review*, a Tory-leaning journal founded by Napier's publisher, John Murray, in 1809, written anonymously although clearly by him. In the articles Murray was heavily critical of Napier's inaccuracies. Murray's stance was that he would gladly furnish Napier with individual plans, maps, et cetera, which related to particular actions in the Peninsula, but would not make available to him the full series of maps that had been so painstakingly created by Mitchell under Murray's direction. However, public funds had been involved in the maps' production. Between 1814, when Mitchell was sent into Spain by Murray, and 1824, a total of £5,167 of taxpayers' money had been spent. So it was perhaps not unreasonable for Napier to consider that the maps should be made available to him, or indeed anyone, for a history of the war. Ironically, particular criticism meted out by Murray centred on the poor quality of the maps in Napier's work. Napier complained that Murray had consistently put obstacles in his way.

In February 1837 Murray was forced to pen a letter to the *Morning Chronicle* contradicting reports that he had taken away certain military plans from the Quartermaster General's office, specifically to prevent Napier gaining access to them. Napier also accused John Murray, his publisher, of being under Murray's influence and being reluctant to publish subsequent volumes of his work.

Murray was not, however, even with support of powerful allies, able to brush Napier's complaints aside, and in December 1837 he was obliged to furnish a formal memorandum, to be read out by Fitzroy Somerset in the House of Commons the following month, detailing the circumstances surrounding his possession of the Mitchell maps. The gist of the memorandum, drafted by Murray, under both time and moral pressure, was that the whole mapping exercise would never have been commissioned without his desire to have a full and true record of the Peninsular War. Murray also stated that Mitchell, since his return from New South Wales, was working on putting the final touches to his Peninsular work, and the intention was to complete the plans and publish them without any further charge to the public. Arrangements had been made with Mr Wyld of Charing Cross.

Looking at all the evidence, it is hard to escape the impression that, despite the passage of time, Murray still harboured ideas of writing his own history of the campaign. He certainly had ready access to a mass of official material as well as private correspondence among the senior combatants, politicians, and Horse Guards. His central role, and closeness to Wellington, would have been invaluable. Nobody other than Wellington himself had the knowledge of so many facets of the whole military campaign, albeit without personal experience of 1812 when Murray was back in England. It is equally probable that he would have been granted access to French military records; he had built up an excellent rapport with the French War Ministry during his time as chief of staff in Paris, and would still have influential friends across the Channel. Yet he had always maintained that it would be impossible for him to produce a history, deserving of the highest degree of truth and accuracy, as this would, at times, inevitably, be critical of Wellington. Murray was simply not prepared to level such criticism at his close friend and fellow soldier during the Duke's lifetime. Equally, however, he was not going to let an upstart such as Napier steal his unwritten thunder by arming him with the essential tools to make accurate sense of many aspects of the conflict. In March 1837 Murray wrote to Sir John Colborne requesting some information on Napier's work, and Colborne replied that he recalled having conversations with Napier as early as 1825, but suggested that at that time Napier's aims were likely restricted to Moore's campaign. He made it clear that Murray had pointed out to him around that time that he (Murray) would never relinquish the hope of being able to write the history of the Peninsular War, but such a move would take a lot of time, which he did not currently have. Wellington, too, was asked by Murray for his recollections of Napier and his intentions. Wellington replied that Napier had been a frequent visitor to Colonel Sir Guy Campbell, a close neighbour at Stratfield Saye, and Wellington had spent time with him, probably around 1820, but could not recall if he had said anything about writing a history. This seems unlikely given that Wellington provided Napier with a number of documents to help with his writing.

Napier's *History* was published in six volumes between 1828 and 1840. Murray wrote four lengthy articles in the *Quarterly Review*, with many detailed criticisms, largely accusations of distorting the facts and attacking what he saw as Napier's biased comparisons of the French and Spanish. Referring to Napier's earlier robust defence before the fifth volume made its appearance, Murray mounted a further scathing attack:

> We propose to expose hereafter the flippancy, the want of candour – to use no less cautious expression – by which Napier's Answer is characterised. He is, we find, not an exception to the general rule that those who are most profuse of censure towards others are always the most sore under anything like freedom of comment upon themselves. We shall at our leisure continue our examination of this equally pompous, flagitious and shallow history.[1]

1 *Quarterly Review*, April 1836, pp.131-219; June 1836, pp.437-489; December 1836 pp.492-542; January 1838, pp.51-96.

The jealously-guarded plans and maps were eventually returned to Horse Guards on 12 August 1840, having been kept safely out of Napier's reach.

As long ago as 1814, Murray, perhaps anticipating publication of his own history, recognized at that moment he had, in his own department, a man of prodigious talent who would happily spend years producing the most intricate and elaborate maps of the major movements and battles, around which Murray might eventually build his own work. The product of Mitchell's extraordinary work would form the basis of Wyld's Atlas, published in 1841, its full title being *Maps & Plans of the Principal Movements & Battles and Sieges in which the British Army was engaged during the war from 1808-1814*. The atlas measures 865 mm by 700 mm, and has been described as being more like a piece of furniture than a book. It contains some fifty maps and plans of the actions in which the British, Portuguese and Spanish armies were engaged with the French in the Peninsula. The lengthy memorandum introducing the atlas, including most of his orders circulated before the major actions, was written by Murray and is the closest Murray came to writing detailed accounts of the more important events of the war. While the memorandum itself might have little interest for cartographers, the orders illustrate Murray's extraordinary grasp of the complex manoeuvres necessary to move large bodies of troops into the positions demanded by Wellington's battle plans.

Murray made it quite clear that he had no desire to profit in any way from the work he was contributing towards publication of the atlas. In his letter to Mitchell in August 1837 he stated that 'I had no view whatever to profit from the business, but exclusively to the truth of history, and the just credit of all parties'. Wyld acknowledged Murray's generosity by saying that this would enable him to procure material from abroad, complete bits where necessary, and work towards perfection. Murray and Mitchell were to work closely on the atlas and its accompanying memorandum, and Murray asked Mitchell to take charge of certain elements 'which I had proposed to assign to the draughtsman to be furnished to me by Mr Wyld'. He wanted the final result to be 'a National Military Work and not purely a commercial enterprise'.[2] Mitchell had come across an anaglyptagraph, a new invention, allowing representation of heights in true relief by engravings in steel and copper from models. By April 1839 Mitchell realised that, as fine a result the anaglyptograph gave, there was not sufficient time to complete all the maps by this method. He wrote to Murray:

> I find no difficulty at all likely to prevent the publication now by the most expeditious means. This appears to be zincography, for although the method of modelling seems by far the best, and I have made great progress in that art, I cannot hope to complete the whole in that manner before the time when I must return.[3]

Mitchell would have to agree his remuneration with Wyld direct, which, inevitably, resulted in an argument, with Murray called upon to adjudicate, adding to an immense volume of correspondence among Wyld, Murray, Mitchell, and the various artists employed in the project, which got into its stride in July 1839.

2 Murray to Mitchell, (draft letter) Belgrave Square, 28 August 1837, Murray Papers, ADV MS 46.8.17.

3 Mitchell to Murray, Brompton, 27 April 1839, Murray Papers, ADV MS 46.8.18.

Mitchell applied his unending patience and skill in the immensely intricate work, agonizing over the width of lines drawn to represent the varying armies' cavalry and infantry, completed to scale with extraordinary precision, after clearing the issue with Murray. Murray had earlier provided Mitchell with sketches done by eye, which Mitchell commented had needed little alteration even when he had his compasses in hand. Mitchell approved of Murray's agreement to bright colours, noting that 'the brightest scarlet and the richest ultramarine shall be used for the English and French respectively'.[4] A problem was looming however, namely the fact that the period of leave that had been granted to Mitchell had expired and he should have been on his way back to New South Wales. He applied to the Colonial Office for an extension, got nowhere with Stephen, and begged Murray to intervene. Murray took up the case with Lord Normanby, the Secretary of State. Even then the application seemed to have got lost and Mitchell was still anxiously awaiting a letter in February 1840 by which time he was long overdue. A three month extension was in time granted, but that would soon be eaten into, and the anxiety would return.

Mitchell fell out with Wyld over the issue of copyright, and a stand-off resulted. Lawyers became involved. Murray intervened to prevent complete breakdown of the project and drafted a memorandum dealing with the points in dispute. Cleared with Mitchell's lawyers, Wyld accepted the terms, broadly giving him ownership of the atlas when complete, but not of the maps that comprised it, which Murray stressed were not his to give away. If there was any delay in publication, Murray would have no hesitation in finding a new publisher and Wyld would get nothing. Meanwhile Murray was engaged again in a wide exercise tracking down all those who had served with him in the Peninsula to prise from them any material that might be of use. By now many of the generals were ageing rapidly, and answered in shaky hands that they were sure they had something somewhere but were not sure where. They all did their best to help, although many confessed that they simply could not remember events so far back. Wellington was, of course, among those from whom Murray requested material: 'I must have had all the information that you require. God knows what I have now! You may have whatever there is', he wrote.[5] In the midst of all the pressure to get the atlas completed and published before Mitchell was forced to leave the country, Murray found himself called upon to stand for Parliament again, this time for Manchester, a seat that realistically he was never going to win. He left town for Manchester on 3 September, with encouragement from Peel. After the election Peel again wrote to Murray: 'You approached near enough success to justify the attempt you made, and failure under such circumstances, is, I am confident, far preferable to forebearence altogether'.[6]

Murray was bidden to stay at Drayton at the end of the month, perhaps to discuss a future appointment in the Government, but still kept in touch with Mitchell to whom plans had been sent as soon as they came into Murray's hands.

By March 1840 much of the hard preparatory work had been completed. Mitchell now turned yet again to Murray for support in his claim to what he saw as his just reward for all the work and sacrifice he had made in surveying New South Wales, namely a grant of land. He wanted a mere 150,000 acres or so to raise sheep to support his family, but if the governor

4 Mitchell to Murray, 3 Upper Queen's Buildings, Brompton, 22 July 1839, Murray Papers, ADV MS 46.8.18.

5 Wellington to Murray, Stratfield Saye, 8 December 1839, Murray Papers, ADV MS 46.8.18.

6 Peel to Murray, Drayton Manor, 16 September 1839, Murray Papers, ADV MS 46.8.18.

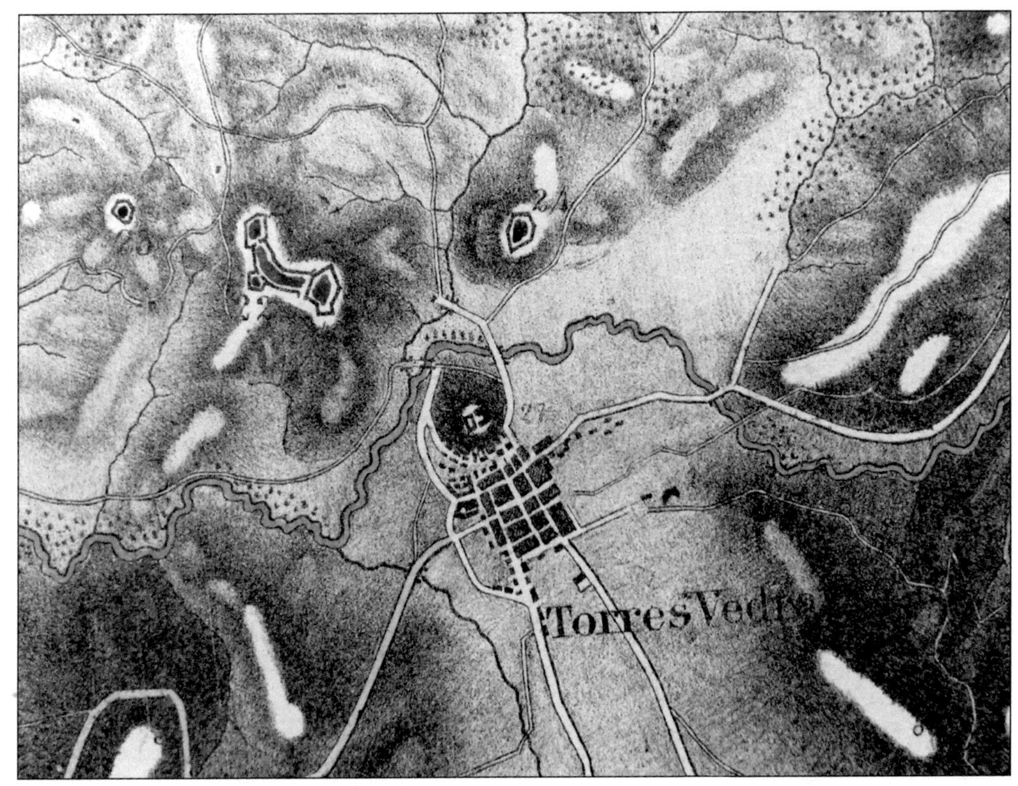

A typical Mitchell map in Wyld's Atlas – part of the Lines of Torres Vedras.
(Author's photo from Murray Papers in The National Library of Scotland)

generalship of Van Diemen's Land should be available then he would like to be in the frame for consideration for this too.

By the end of June the maps to go into the atlas were close enough to completion to allow an inspection by Wellington, and all the plans were returned to Murray in early August. The *Era* reported the impending publication:

> [A]n interesting work… is about to be published by Mr Wyld of Charing Cross. The troops have been placed in their respective positions in the plans made under the direction of Lt. General Sir George Murray, who has also contributed many original documents and explanations, and by whom the letterpress is superintended. The maps are chiefly from zincographical drawings… The work will be interesting to military men and generally useful.[7]

It looked as though publication might, if all started to fall into place and Wyld played his part professionally, eventually happen, and Mitchell would at last be able to take passage back to New South Wales with his family. However, on returning home from dinner one

7 The *Era*, 21 June 1840.

evening he was arrested by sheriff's officers for a debt of £306 at the suit of a Mr Fairbairn, one of the artists who had been working on the atlas who had not been paid. His solicitor managed to arrange bail, sparing his client a night in jail. Eventually Wyld settled the claim from Fairbairn in an amount of £270. By now the prospect of publication seemed to Mitchell to be 'all but hopeless'. However, in case it ever happened he was a bit disappointed with a small but important matter. It did not seem to be evident from the drafts of Murray's memorandum that was to accompany the maps, that his brevet rank of lieutenant colonel and his CB (Companion of the Bath) were to be publicised. He felt they should be, given all the effort and time he had applied. Events were constantly conspiring against him. He was badly out of pocket as regards his colonial work, and now too in London. His request for a grant of land had been turned down. Final touches still needed to be applied to the work on the Atlas. He had to be on board the *Mary Bannantyne*, which was due to sail on 8 September. On 18 September he was still writing anxious letters from Hans Crescent. He had still not sailed on the 20th. By the 25th he was on board, and, with a copy of Murray's nephew's handsome book of *Sketches of Scotland*, sent to him by Murray, in his luggage, wrote a final letter to his mentor, He sailed, he wrote,

> with the recollection which I shall carry with me to the Antipodes – of your great kindness – like that of a father – and the wisdom of your advice. These convince me that you were satisfied with me, an object of the first importance with me from childhood. My family unite with me in earnest prayers for the health and welfare of Lady Louisa, Miss Murray, and you.[8]

It is a generous letter from a man whose character so often steered him head first into confrontation with those with whom he had to work. Meticulous and extraordinarily talented, Mitchell has left us with the most beautifully executed maps and drawings of the Iberian Peninsula and New South Wales. There is no doubting the immense time and application that went into all of his projects, and from a distance it does seem that he was perhaps treated poorly by many, who were throughout his career in positions where they would have been able, had they so wished, to make life very much better for him. Yet there is no escaping the fact that he did manage to fall out with almost everybody he had dealings with. The letters he wrote to Murray cover the period from 1814, when he was despatched back to Spain to complete the maps and plans of the big Peninsular actions, through 1828-30 when Murray was Colonial Secretary, to the time he spent in London completing the Peninsular work and Wyld's Atlas. To describe the letters as long and unhappy is to do them a disservice. Murray must have dreaded receiving them. There is hardly one out of dozens that does not contain a litany of injustices, real or perceived, with requests for Murray to intervene on his behalf.

Interestingly Murray rarely seemed to lose patience. Perhaps he genuinely sympathised with the treatment Mitchell received from people. He would certainly have recognized that here was a man of vast talent and seemingly endless patience in the pursuit of perfection.

8 Mitchell to Murray, *Mary Bannantyne*, 25 September 1840, Murray Papers, ADV MS 46.8.18.

And Murray admired perfection, especially in the production of plans and maps. Ward in his paper on Wellington's Headquarters in 1957 agreed:

> Wyld's Atlas... is an elaborate and monumental work of almost unimpeachable accuracy which has by some means or other escaped recognition as a prime source of the topography of the war. If it is evidence of the intense activities of the topographers of Wellington's Army it can also be looked upon as the last manifestation of the old QMG Department's preoccupation with military topography, military science and military history.[9]

It was not until November 1842 that Mitchell was to see a copy in Sydney. He wrote at once to Murray to express his disappointment that Wyld had made no acknowledgment of his part in the production of the Pyrenees map and that Wyld should have substituted his dedication 'to The British Army' with the dedication composed by Murray. All the irritations and problems he had encountered with Wyld were vividly recalled, with regret 'that this National work' should 'have fallen into such hands'. Mitchell's last words on the matter were rather typical: 'I take some comfort here in the belief that we have no men at Botany Bay so morally bad as Wyld of Charing Cross'.[10]

Murray's involvement with the creation of the atlas and its problems took up a great part of his time during 1839 and 1840. By 1841 he was again in office as Master General of the Ordnance and, true to form, his new appointment resulted in a deluge of requests from all sorts, relations and complete strangers, but all most deserving and talented, at least in the authors' opinions, seeking jobs in the various departments which comprised the Ordnance's domain. They were, as in the case with such pleas received by Murray in the Colonial Department, dealt with efficiently but without much favour.

Early in 1843 the Duke of Marlborough's family lawyer was tasked with sorting out family papers. At the bottom of a chest containing wills and family deeds, he came across a number of volumes (there were eventually 29 discovered) of the first Duke of Marlborough's diaries, letters, and despatches. The current Duke contacted Murray and asked if he might be interested in them, and perhaps to act as editor in their publication. John Murray agreed to publish and the necessary financial arrangements were drawn up in short order. Murray wrote to Marlborough on 10 August, when the exercise was getting under way. He was keen to have published as many as possible of the letters and despatches and allow them to show the fullest picture of the man, rather than merely have an arbitrary selection.

> The more the Duke of Marlborough is allowed to be his own biographer the higher he will stand in the estimation both of the present and future generations. It has given me sincere satisfaction to have seen that the means exist of doing that justice to a truly great man; and it is an additional pleasure to me that he belongs to a family whose membership I have the good fortune to enjoy.[11]

9 Ward, *Wellington's Headquarters*, p.110.

10 Mitchell to Murray, Sydney, 2 November 1842, Murray Papers, ADV MS 46.9.4.

11 Murray to Marlborough, Ordnance Office, 10 August 1843, Murray Papers, ADV MS 46.9.24. Murray was related by marriage, his aunt Joanna having married Charles Churchill

Murray enlisted the assistance of one or two people he knew in the literary world, including Charles Macfarlane, a well-known Scottish writer of historical biographies and novels, but did the basic editing work himself. Given that many of the letters and despatches were in French, he was well equipped to deal quickly and efficiently with the task in hand. In the Murray Papers, among his painstakingly written drafts and annotations, is his reader's ticket for the British Museum dated 1 March 1844.

Murray, unsurprisingly, was determined that the work should include maps: 'Good maps would add very much to the interest of the work, and to the satisfaction of the generality of readers. Three maps should be sufficient'.[12] He detailed what areas he felt these maps should cover. By August of that year the proof of the first sheet of the despatches was ready and the first volume of five was published in February 1845, a work of which Murray must have been justly proud, and which is of equivalent interest and importance to many military historians as *Wellington's Dispatches*, which Murray himself had reviewed for the *Edinburgh Review* in 1838. Although contemporary reviews seem not to exist, a recent author writing on Marlborough is in no doubt as to the quality of the work:

> The immensely valuable, voluminous Letters and Despatches of the Duke of Marlborough collected and edited by General Sir George Murray... are an indispensable contemporary resource...Copies are scarce but are well worth the effort to find.[13]

12 Memorandum, Belgrave Square, 31 July 1843, Murray Papers, ADV MS 46.9.24.
13 James Falkner, *Marlborough's Battlefields* (Barnsley: Pen & Sword, 2008), p.249.

26

Master General of the Ordnance

Murray flourished in the role of Master General of the Ordnance, to which Peel appointed him at the start of his first administration in 1834, although his government was only to last for a matter of months. He was soon dealing enthusiastically with matters that were far more familiar to him: the business of the military academies at Sandhurst and Woolwich, where competition for places were intense; the economic use of redundant fortifications; the ongoing debate on corporal punishment in the army and comparisons with disciplinary methods in other European armies; the fair level of pensions to be paid to wounded veterans, where again differences with counterpart armies were closely examined. In this case it was immeasurably better to have fought and been wounded in the British Army than the French. The detailed estimates of costs, budgets and the inevitable correspondence with the Treasury played a large part in his working life.

Murray's duties included that of examiner for admission for Gentlemen Cadets to Woolwich, which took entrants at age 14 or 15, who were required at that stage in their education to be qualified in common arithmetic, vulgar and decimal fractions, the extraction of the square root, English grammar and parsing, French translation of dialogue, and translating Caesar's *Commentaries*. Those nervous candidates would no doubt have been thoroughly tested by Murray on their French and Caesar's military methods. Future progress in the service would be enhanced if the young men could draw, so they would have also been quizzed by the ex-Quartermaster General, with his unrivalled interest in the matter, on their understanding of maps and mapping.

However, the defence of the realm was the more pressing matter. During his second appointment, which started in 1841, Murray and Peel became embroiled in a long drawn out correspondence involving a Captain Warner who was persuasive enough to attract considerable interest in a pair of inventions – the invisible shell and the long range shell, both, he claimed, with massive destructive power. He demonstrated both in the presence of large crowds including Peel and Murray as well as many other politicians, successfully destroying target ships on two separate occasions. Murray was sceptical of the claims, particularly when Warner insisted on a guarantee from the government that it would pay him the vast sum of £400,000 if either of his weapons were successful against a target at a distance of six miles offshore. On Murray's recommendation Peel refused to entertain Warner any further and the matter never proceeded. It was generally thought that some form of underwater mine or bomb on board was responsible for the earlier successful trial.[1]

More prosaic matters occupied Murray's second spell at the Ordnance Office. Sir James Graham, then Home Secretary, who was trying to introduce a new Factories Act, limiting the hours of factory work for children and increasing compulsory hours of education, against fierce opposition of many in the north, wrote to Murray on 22 July 1843:

> I am afraid that coming events portend a storm; and I am most anxious to have the Yeomanry in the manufacturing districts armed with carbines with percussion locks as soon as possible. A contract for 10,000 of these arms to be delivered immediately would appear to me to be a prudent measure.[2]

Later that year, in October, Graham again asked Murray for armed support, this time for two additional companies of artillery in Ireland to support Blakeney, the military commander, against a background of imminent civil war with supporters of Daniel O'Connell determined to break the 1801 Union with Britain. Peel was also anxious that the army should be ready and sufficiently armed to snuff out any hint of insurrection:

> I think there should always be in store, prepared for any contingency, a considerable supply of small arms. Could you not quietly give such directions as would expedite manufacture, without directing public attention to the fact.[3]

So Murray continued, after all these years in uniform and parliament, to be involved in protecting the British State against malign influences from abroad and within. He was faced with the seemingly unending challenges of ensuring the safety of British citizens, everlasting issues that had filled Wellington's life too. He still commanded great respect in the corridors of power.

As in his earlier appointment to the Ordnance, there were plenty of ancillary topics to occupy Murray's time, from correspondence on new percussion shells and the necessary improvements to the defences of the colonies, to expenses claims from the creator of a model of Waterloo – if necessary, to get paid, the creator emphasized that he would effect alterations to show the Prussians in a less prominent position – to the usual, and never ending requests from relatives and colleagues seeking favours on behalf of acquaintances and servants. One request was from a man who had, if Murray might remember, done Lady Louisa's and Miss Murray's hair in the Pantechnicon.[4] Maybe Murray might have a position for him in his household? There were plenty more from parents of young gentlemen who had failed the entrance exam for Woolwich; in one case it must clearly be a mistake as the boy had 'fagged both day and night' for ages; in another a 'shy, timid boy who gets easily

1 Murray to Peel, Ordnance Office, 1 June 1843, Luffness Mss, GD18/3548. See also Peel Papers, British Library, 40508.

2 TNA, WO 80/4, Graham to Murray, H.O, 22 July 1843.

3 WO 80/3, Peel to Murray, Whitehall, 24 August 1844.

4 Pantechnicon is Greek for 'pertaining to all the arts and crafts'. It was originally the name of a large establishment in Motcomb Street, Belgrave Square, opened around 1830. It combined a picture gallery, a furniture shop, and the sale of carriages, while its southern half was a sizable warehouse for storing furniture and other items.

flurried' had failed, despite extra tuition. The father dreaded the effect on his wife who had already cost him dearly in necessary visits to watering places on account of her very bad health. Seventy places were available each year.

At the time of his death Murray had on his desk a waiting list of five hundred. Further up the scale were the requests for Murray to put individuals forward for knighthoods. Most of these, which arrived daily in huge numbers, were politely declined. Other issues under scrutiny at the time included duelling and the Army's stance on it. Murray wrote to Hardinge, with some drafting to place responsibility on the shoulders of the seconds to dissuade the principals from a rash pursuit of honour:

> I have suggested a little alteration in the two proposed articles, but whether for the better or otherwise I really do not know:
>
> You will see that I seek to make the Principals responsible for not accepting the advice of the Seconds and the Seconds responsible if they do not tender advice. And it is also intimated to the Seconds that it is their duty to suggest such an adjustment as shall be consistent with the honour of both parties and not for each merely to endeavour to obtain some advantage for his own friend.[5]

By this time the duties attaching to the 450 year old office had become so diverse, with both civil and military responsibilities, that it is no surprise that within a few years of Murray's death the office ceased to exist.

After being approached twice for the governor generalship of India, Murray's name was again in the frame, along with Hardinge's and Graham's, when Peel was faced with filling the position following the recall of Ellenborough in April 1844. Either of the former, he wrote, would be acceptable to the public. Graham could not be spared from the Home Office. It was Hardinge who accepted the honour. Murray's health was by now failing, and if he had been offered it, he would certainly have declined yet again.

One day late in 1844 Murray was at the Ordnance Office described as 'ill, very ill' by Charles Macfarlane, who had lately been assisting him with the editing of *Marlborough's Despatches*. Murray was due to attend a Committee of Taste to which he had been appointed.

> I wish I were not going; I would much rather stay here and talk over the Marlborough Despatches with you. It does seem to me that this committee does hardly anything that is right. If twenty or thirty architectural Plans and designs be brought before them it is the toss-up of a halfpenny that they do not choose the very worst and the most expensive. Was there anything worse than the Nelson Column, with the queer statue a-top of it, that looks like a man with a tail! I think, that I shall cry off. I am sick of voting in minorities, and of seeing things adopted of which I can not approve. It is the old English story: there are on the Committee men of indisputable taste and ability, men quite incapable of being swayed by partialities or prejudices, or self interested motives; but these men are not regular in their attendance, or strenuous in their exertion; while, on the other hand, a set of inferior individuals,

5 TNA, WO 80/13, Murray to Hardinge, Ordnance Office, 5 September 1844.

> inferior not only in taste but also in other qualities, are constant in their attendance at the Board, and by coalescing and clubbing together, they generally manage to carry everything their own way...
>
> The Duke laughed at me for accepting the nomination. If I had taken the Duke's advice, I should never have been on the Committee of Taste. The Duke's plain common sense always leads, and always did lead him right. One of his maxims has been never to undertake work with your arms tied; another, never to seek reputation, or the power of doing good or preventing evil, as a member of a committee or any such body! For though you will get neither credit nor praise for what it does well, you will not escape blame for what it does ill.[6]

He had had his fill of politics and committees, and the lack of application by men of his kind. It is the rant of an exhausted man, suffering from frequent and debilitating rheumatic attacks, who had recently seen the world change and the rise to power of people and ideas very different to his own.

Murray worked on at the Ordnance Office, dealing, amongst his varied responsibilities, with yet more correspondence from Mitchell, now seeking Murray's support in his desire to be appointed Governor of New South Wales,[7] until he no longer had the strength to continue, in the last months carrying out his duties from Belgrave Square.

Towards the end of his working life Murray kept up a regular official dialogue with Wellington, against a background of a continuing military threat from the continent. The exchanges were forthright and friendly. The principal dockyards were an obvious target and Murray told Wellington that he had written to Peel with his reports on their defence. 'My object in taking this course is that Government may be aware of the deficient nature of our defences, before the large demands for money are made which will be necessary for their general improvement'.[8]

Murray and Wellington continued to consult each other as to their ideas on the defence of the south-east against the threat of invasion. Murray dug out, at least from his memory, his ideas formed as long ago as 1803 and 1804, when Napoleon was staring across the channel from Boulogne, and he had carried out extensive reconnaissance of the southern counties and coastline to advise on defensive preparations. His thoughts for London had been that there should be a broad and steep ditch and bastioned rampart protecting the north of the city as far as Willesden, and in the south as far as Norwood. The right would be on the river a little above Vauxhall Bridge and the left end connected with the river a little below Deptford where the Lewisham river joined with the Thames. His latest idea was to create a separate system of defences at Hampstead, Campden Hill, and Stamford Hill to meet the Essex defences at Bow Creek. The docks would need a separate system of defence.[9] This work would continue unabated when Anglesey took over the Ordnance from Murray on his death.

6 Charles Macfarlane, *Reminiscences of a Literary Life*, (London: John Murray, 1917), pp.234-5.
7 TNA, WO 80/4, Mitchell to Murray, Sydney, 9 July 1844.
8 Murray to Wellington, Ordnance Office, 29 November 1844, Peel Papers, MS 40460.
9 Murray to Wellington, Belgrave Square, 8 November 1845, Murray Papers, ADV MS 46.9.16.

The French threat and parallel internal insurrection had been a constant throughout Murray's entire life. In his advancing years Murray enjoyed applying his long experience in advising on the continuing preparations to protect the nation. It was in his blood, as it was Wellington's. As Wellington warmly put it in a letter to Murray from Walmer:

> This letter will show you that your mind and mine are perfectly on the same road as regards general principles – I know well that which we may have to undertake; the defence of this country from invasion, plunder and even conquest must be well considered, its objects, its means of execution, its probable results, and every difficulty must be provided against and surmounted. This is the way we worked together successfully heretofore, and by the blessing of the Almighty, old as we are, I hope that by adhering to the correct course we shall be successful again.[10]

10 TNA, WO 80/8, Wellington to Murray, Walmer, 20 September 1845.

27

Politics, Society, and Family

Murray's periods in political office may not have been the most enjoyable or the most successful years of his life, but, despite the criticism levelled at him from many quarters, including of course, Wellington, he did command respect amongst other Members of Parliament, including Peel, Hardinge, and Graham. Wellington never allowed the pressures he was under to publicly undermine his Colonial Secretary, and remained grateful to him for the loyalty Murray showed throughout the years of political upheaval. Fully aware that Murray's talents lay outwith the mainstream of politics he pushed, whenever the opportunity presented itself, for Murray to be given a more military role. Hence he persuaded Peel, if he needed persuading, that he should appoint Murray to be Master General of the Ordnance in 1834, an appointment that was short lived as a result of Peel's government falling. He also had Murray in mind as Leader of the House, but that initiative also came to nothing.

If Murray was so much less successful as a politician than a soldier, and equally seemed to take little enjoyment from his time in the House of Commons, why did he continue for so long to put himself forward for roles, and seats in Parliament that were unlikely to provide anything in the way of satisfying second career? The first reason is his sense of duty. Duty to his country, duty to his monarch, duty to his Perthshire constituents, and, in particular duty to Wellington. Murray was never afraid to acknowledge his obligations to the Duke. He recognized that while Wellington had the power he would use it to place Murray's claim in front of those who might make things happen, and even more if he could make such things happen himself. One cannot imagine Murray agreeing to take on the colonial role without weighing up the factors which might impact on his life, and his own satisfaction. Whatever misgivings Murray had, it was enough that Wellington asked him, and demonstrated confidence in him.

Yet Murray was very well aware of the pressures and pitfalls of Westminster, as the letter to Dalhousie on his appointment shows, and all the more so at such a time of political change. Even so he must have felt he had the skills to handle them. He was not coming to an office of state from the relative backwater of Perthshire. He had taken an active interest in politics from the early days in the Peninsula, and, indeed, even earlier than that. He had been very closely involved in the political decision making that lay behind the Swedish expedition with Moore, had spoken bluntly to the British Cabinet and made it clear that what they had asked of Moore was idiotic. The message hit home. He was close enough to the political machinations that sent the four senior generals to Portugal, almost certain to result in confusion if not worse, and was highly critical of it. His time in Portugal and Spain was peppered with political discussions with his brother, himself an MP. He enjoyed teasing his sister, following her marriage to an active Whig. He was careful to read balanced newspapers, to the extent there were any. He was aware of the constitutional issues which governed the relationship between the Monarch, the Regent, and Parliament. He had fought for twenty five years against a country that wanted to replace its unwholesome monarchy, only to discover something equally unpalatable. No one could consider Murray anything other than politically aware.

Many of his political colleagues recognized that Murray would flourish in a more military role if one could be found – and it was, twice, in the form of Master General of the Ordnance, both instances at Peel's invitation, the first time, in 1834, when he had a seat in the Cabinet, and latterly in 1841, a post he held till his death. 'It is', he said, when he held it without a seat in the Commons, 'the one of all the high situations connected with the government of the country which I like the best, and', he added significantly, 'my not being associated with Parliament, and scarcely with politics, renders it the more agreeable to me'.[1]

Strong as his sense of duty certainly was, Murray would have been constantly reminded of his financial position. Ochtertyre was never in a position to support more than the Baronet and his immediate family. Patrick, although seemingly not any better with money than many Lairds of Ochtertyre, recognised the need to make a decent living for himself in the law, as Baron of Exchequer, in politics as MP for Perth, and in an important position in the India Office. These good sources of income were seemingly insufficient, even when added to whatever income the estate produced, to avoid Patrick's affairs from ending up in the hands of trustees. Fortunately his two sisters had found 'good' husbands, and would not have been a drain on Ochtertyre for long. The same went for Murray's mother, Augusta, albeit for different reasons. So it might not have been too unusual for some money to have been available in times of need from the Ochtertyre coffers. On the contrary it was Murray who ended up supporting Patrick, and who had to wait for the trustees to pay back the debt bit by bit. There were plans drawn up to make some major additions and cosmetic alterations to Ochtertyre when the house was barely twenty years old, shortly after Patrick inherited from his father. These ideas of adding castellated battlements came, thankfully, to nothing, perhaps because even at that stage there was a recognition that the estate was hardly flourishing, and money scarce.

Murray's nephews, particularly those who had chosen a military career and had received his help in procuring commissions, came to him frequently as a kind of father confessor. The familiar pressures were evident in one nephew's life. John Murray had inherited the Gartshore estate in Kirkubrightshire as a result of the marriage, in 1741 of Helen, daughter of James Hamilton, to Sir Patrick Murray, Murray's grandfather, and from that time assumed the suffix Gartshore. In 1833 Ravelston House in Edinburgh had come into the Murray family as a result of Helen Keith, an only child of Sir Alexander Keith of Ravelston and Dunnottar, marrying Sir William, Murray's nephew, Gartshore's brother. Sir William prefixed Murray with Keith to become William Keith-Murray.

1 Murray to Brisbane, Ordnance Office, 23 October 1841, Murray Papers, ADV MS 46.9.12.

The next Ochtertyre Baronet, Patrick, sold Ravelston to his uncle John, which resulted in Gartshore Estate, once earmarked for Murray, being sold and the Murray Gartshore family keeping Ravelston, an altogether easier house. Gartshore might perhaps have provided a suitable marital home for Murray and Louisa, and Murray could have still followed his political career from there. Such imaginings were certainly far from Murray's thoughts when remarking that he was glad the Gartshore estate had not come his way, as he planned the expulsion of Massena from Portugal. By 1844 the burden of running both establishments was obvious when John Murray Gartshore wrote to Murray telling him that he 'must live still more economically' and had had to part with his indoor manservant, the son of an old artillery pensioner. He wondered if Murray had a place in his department for this loyal retainer.[2]

Murray's income from his various appointments, his colonelcies, and any military pension was simply insufficient to meet the new expenses which were the inevitable result of his decision to marry Louisa. Even if there were to be another war, and an active military command, his new wife would expect a lifestyle which military pay alone could not hope to provide. The Belgravia mansion, much grander than Murray would have sought in other circumstances, was always going to be a very heavy drain on his finances.

One avenue might provide Murray with an income, if not equal to the Torrie income that Louisa had become used to, still enough to carry on the lifestyle which they aspired to. That was a political career. Even if Murray had doubts about his own suitability for the colonial role, which paid £6,000 a year, and the evidence is that he felt he could succeed in it, he was never going to refuse, the more so because it would seem disloyal to Wellington. However, money became of prime concern in the years following his command in Ireland.

It is equally certain that there were others suffering from the same financial worries as Murray, who did not have the support of such eminent colleagues as Wellington and Peel. It was important in many social circles to maintain the illusion of solid financial comfort, however difficult. Murray had always been careful with money, and certainly was aware from an early stage that his brother had less financial skill than he. Not for Murray the easy route of borrowing and turning a blind eye to mounting debt. He had fretted about the debt incurred to acquire Drumlandrick, and during the Peninsular years had made it a priority to eliminate it. When the time came to confront the problem of outgoings exceeding income, on going into opposition with Wellington, he at once looked to reducing his overheads by disposing of servants and a carriage.

Wellington and Murray were both painted by Sir Thomas Lawrence a number of times in their lives. Lawrence and Murray became close friends. Louisa would also have known the man who painted most of the important society figures, as Erskine also sat to Lawrence. Murray's first sitting was in 1812, as a newly-promoted major general, when he was back in London after returning from the Peninsula. Lawrence painted him again in 1829, suggesting that the character in the face was more pronounced 'although it may have increased age, it has likewise had increased working of intellect, which is always advantageous to the physiognomy of man'.[3] The portrait is very similar to one painted at the same time of Wellington

2 John Murray Gartshore to Murray, Gartshore, 10 January 1844, Murray Papers, ADV MS 46.9.8.

3 Lawrence to Murray, Russell Square, 1 March 1829, Murray Papers, MS 21104. Lawrence also painted Wellington again in 1829 – like the Murray portrait it is head only, unfinished because of his death in 1830, and very similar in style

and both remained unfinished on Lawrence's death. There are many references to Murray's physical appearance around this time, mostly gushingly flattering.

The son of one of his constituents recalled a glimpse he had of him when he called to ask for his father's vote in the election of 1832:

> [A] tall, rather thin, elderly gentleman, dressed in a blue military overcoat that looked as if it had seen the firing of redhot-shot at the French boats when navigating the Adour. He had a highly cultivated air, a mild expression and altogether a very winning countenance, with manners entirely devoid of affectation. My father declined to support him, but he had been so long a Volunteer under Sir Patrick Murray that the refusal cost him a pang. He denied cordially and civilly, and his denial was courteously regretted.[4]

A third portrait, at the behest of Murray's constituents in Perthshire, was started by Lawrence but on his death fell to Henry Pickersgill to complete, and it accurately fits the description given by the constituent.[5]

When daughter Louisa was about 2½, in October 1824, Murray and Lady Louisa asked Lawrence if he would paint a portrait of her. Lawrence was delighted, and wanted to get started as soon as sittings could be arranged. 'I know how soon the sort of peculiar beauty, (the peculiar character of it) which your daughter has I fear must change! Something very delightful may remain, but not so rare'. He wanted 'to snatch (and I hope for some century or so secure) this fleeting beauty and expression, so singular in the child, before the change takes place that some few months may bring'.[6]

The price, Lawrence warned Murray, would be 300 Guineas for a half-length, in advance. Although initially saying that it would not be possible to complete the picture until late 1825, he worked unusually fast, with a number of sittings, and the portrait was ready at the end of March. It has become one of the best recognized of Lawrence's work, and he regarded it as 'one of the happiest of my labours', adding 'I know of no work by which my own reputation would be better supported'.[7] It is now familiar to us from the image on playing cards, biscuit tins, and jig saws, generally labelled 'Miss Murray' or 'A Child with Flowers'. The following year it was exhibited at the Royal Academy, simply labelled 'A Child'. There was no public link to the parents. Then Lawrence's delight at the quality of the portrait must have got the better of him, as he allowed an engraver, William Humphreys, to publish a print of it in a publication called 'the Bijou' early in 1828. This time there must have been some reference to whom 'the Child' belonged. Murray and Louisa having been married in April 1825, there was no way, assuming she was born in their wedlock, that she could realistically have been more than about 18 months old at the time of the painting from which the print derived. Yet clearly she was a good deal older. Murray and Louisa were, in the circumstances, very forgiving of Lawrence. Whatever damage had been done in society could not be undone, the

4 Peter Robert Drummond, *Perthshire in Bygone Days* (London: Whittingham & Co, 1879), p.77.

5 At least four versions exist, including one in the Scottish National Portrait Gallery, and another, full size, in the City Hall in Perth, Western Australia.

6 Lawrence to Murray, Russell Square, 28 October 1824, Murray Papers, MS 21104.

7 Lawrence to Murray, Russell Square, 23 February 1829, Murray Papers, MS 21104.

friendship did not seem to suffer, and Murray was a pallbearer at Lawrence's grand funeral in St Paul's Cathedral in 1830.

Whatever embarrassment may have been caused by the careless handling of the portrait, there was more to come, this time at the hands of royalty. At the prorogation of Parliament in July 1830, Murray, as Colonial Secretary, brought his daughter to be presented to Queen Adelaide, less than a month after she had become Queen upon her husband William IV succeeding as monarch. We do not know for sure what was said, other than that she seems to have been very rude to Murray, defending her attitude later by insisting that it was very painful but necessary. It was remarked by some that as the Queen was attended at the audience by one of her husband's illegitimate daughters by the actress Mrs Jordan, she had chosen a bad moment to make a point about morality.[8]

The Murrays would have been conscious of the way that British society, its attitudes changing, was now starting to look upon the sort of behaviour that in the Georgian and early Regency periods had been openly acceptable. The code of morals that we often associate with the Victorians was already becoming evident. Murray's and Louisa's social lives were carried on quietly. Louisa, judging from newspaper columns covering society events and letters of invitation from Murray's political and military acquaintances, does not seem to have accompanied Murray much to dinners, balls or country weekends. However, they did not cut themselves off completely from society. Louisa maintained her close friendship with Princess Sophia, the 5th daughter of George III, who, in her miniscule hand, on the occasion of one of Louisa's attacks, addressed Murray as 'Dear Kind Sir George'.[9] Murray was well-known to, and at ease with, other members of the extended Royal Family. There was some contact with the young Princess Victoria, and perhaps the young Louisa and Victoria spent time in each other's company given Louisa's court connections, being quite close in age. A letter from the future Queen, written from Claremont, where Victoria used to visit her uncle Leopold, on 19 November 1830, a few months after the incident with Queen Adelaide, could have been referring to any sort of event or correspondence:

> I must thank you with my own hand for your attention, an attention it is extremely agreeable for me to receive. I was very glad to hear the continued good accounts of the Lady Louisa. Believe me, always to be with much esteem, dear Sir George Murray, your very sincere friend, Victoria.[10]

Victoria was only 11, it is written in a beautifully neat hand, and is a mature note, at least by today's standards.

Louisa no doubt kept in touch with other friends from her previous married life, at least those who felt they could be seen to be supportive of her in her new life, but the years half hidden away, between 1818 and 1825, and the birth of an illegitimate daughter, must have made for great difficulties in maintaining close friendships. She still was prepared to use her social standing and her contacts to advantage if necessary, including asking Wellington for an invitation to a ball at Apsley House for a niece, and assistance with a pension for one of

8 Ward Draft, Ch.XVII, p.38.

9 Princess Sophia to Murray, 3 April (No year), Murray Papers, MS 21104.

10 Princess Victoria to Murray, Claremont, 19 November 1830, Murray Papers, MS 21104.

her domestic servants.[11] As far as her own pension was concerned – which she declined to surrender and continued to receive despite her affair and remarriage, to a man now holding an important office of State – this was to become a matter of public knowledge, as a result of publication of the details by William Cobbett, a radical journalist whose *Political Register* was mostly read by the working classes, but seemingly to no ill effect.[12]

From the moment Louisa was abandoned by Erskine, Murray's career followed a very different path to that which arguably he was well qualified to pursue. He would not consider a governor general's position overseas on account of Louisa's delicate health, which meant his choices were limited to serving in Britain, unless an opportunity arose for short term military campaigning and there is no evidence that this was ever contemplated. On the basis of his comments made during his years on active military service, he would probably not have regretted missing out on much of London's social scene. Sitting too long at dinner was, for him, a waste of time. He would have relished, from time to time, the opportunity to discuss matters military, and exchange views on the continuing threat from revolutionary factions, with the many colleagues he had fought with and who remained firm family friends. He accepted invitations to Stratfield Saye, to shoot at Drayton, Peel's house, and from others, but rarely with Louisa.

Murray had a large library, and no doubt read a good deal when at home. His writing, those articles in the *Quarterly Review* castigating Napier, his memorandum to Wyld's Atlas, his reviews of *Wellington's Dispatches*, his editing of *Marlborough's Despatches*, would all have filled the time in a very satisfying way. Murray's history of the Peninsular War was never started. If he felt that criticism of Wellington whilst alive would have been a significant element of any work of his then that would presumably have been enough to force the idea of publication from his mind.

There are hardly any real clues to the day to day lives of Murray and Louisa in the Murray papers. The only glimpses we get are those where letters make mention of Louisa's health, and there are only a couple of them. It was no doubt a major problem, but again the detail is not there to allow an informed judgment as to what might have been the cause of her problems. But there is no evidence of Murray ever regretting the limitations it placed on their lives or his career. Despite the lack of information as to their domestic lives, we do get a glimpse of the strength of the marriage and Murray's intense feelings for Louisa during her last illness and on her death on 23 January 1842. Throughout the last two or three months Murray would work at the Ordnance office in the mornings and was at her bedside for the rest of the day. He wrote to Peel on the morning of her death:

> You will learn with grief that the loss which I have for some time anticipated has arrived this morning. Lady Louisa ceased to live a little after 4 o'clock this morning. There was no struggle, nor the slightest appearance of any bodily suffering. Lady L's mind had long been prepared, and in a state of the most perfect contentment under anticipation of the event which has just occurred. These are the consolations upon which I pray that my thoughts shall dwell.[13]

11 Wellington to Louisa, London 7 &9 June 1837, quoted in Ward Draft, Ch.XVII, p.40.

12 *Political Register*, 11 August 1832.

13 Murray to Peel, Belgrave Square, 23 January 1842, Peel Papers, Add MS 40501.

Following her death, for about two months, much of his business was conducted from Sunninghill. He spent the whole of that summer staying with friends, at Gordon Castle, Fochabers (the Duke of Gordon), Inverary castle (the Duke of Argyll), in Edinburgh, at Leamington (his sister) with the Peels at Drayton, as well as Ochtertyre. He made his way back to Belgrave Square in November after a short stay at Farrer's Hotel, just round the corner, while his own house, completely redecorated, was made ready for him. There are no letters that give us any clue as to what he was suffering.[14]

During his months of social seclusion after Louisa's death, Murray was at Ochtertyre to welcome the young Queen Victoria on her visit with Prince Albert to Strathearn. Patrick had died in 1837 and it fell to his son, the new Baronet, Sir William, to provide a mounted guard of honour for the royal party as it approached Ochtertyre, against the background of a 21-gun salute, and to orchestrate the celebratory fireworks in the evening. It is hard to imagine Murray himself not getting directly involved in the turnout of the men and organization of the explosions. The royal party, Murray, various dukes and earls, and past and present Prime Ministers including Peel, moved on to Drummond Castle where the royal couple stayed the weekend. That evening Murray attended a dinner in the company of a glamorous array of Scottish aristocrats. The weekend was a mixture of flying royal visits to local houses including Abercairney, Monzie, and Ochtertyre, with some stalking for Prince Albert at Glenartney about 12 miles away. The visit concluded with a Ball in a specially erected pavilion at the Castle, this time Murray being accompanied by 'Miss Murray'. No regal snubs on this occasion.

As a parent he showed himself a fond and proud father. He circulated his daughter's one known literary composition, 'The Tale of Waterloo', among his friends for their opinions: to James Glassford, Henry Hobhouse, Sir Robert Inglis and Bishop Blomfield of London. As soon as she turned 21, she became engaged to Henry Boyce, Murray's aide de camp, a captain in the Life Guards and a grandson of the Duke of Marlborough. She married him handsomely at St George's, Hanover Square on 14 September 1843. There followed a 'sumptuous dejeuner' at Belgrave Square, during which the band of the 2nd Life Guards played. Murray, demonstrating his earlier military ability to find a quiet corner to compose a letter in the midst of mayhem, as he had done so often in the Peninsula, wrote to his niece Georgina who had married Anthony Murray of Dollerie in 1829:

> Although you will hear it from other quarters also I write a line to tell you that Louisa's marriage took place today, and we are just returned from the church. All went off well, but you were much missed. Love to Anthony and all the Flock.[15]

It was but a concise report, written one assumes while the celebrations were in full swing, containing the information that Murray felt necessary. In the absence of Lady Louisa to write a detailed, perhaps gossipy account of the occasion, he left it to others to tell the full tale. He was no doubt glad to see Louisa happily married, and to a soldier with impeccable

14 Ward Draft, Ch,XVII, pp.44-5.
15 Murray to Georgina Murray, Belgrave Square, 14 September 1843, Private Collection

connections. Still, losing both his wife and daughter within eighteen months of each other must have left Murray, now in his seventies, a lonely man.

Spending time in his native Perthshire and being able to stay at Ochtertyre probably helped Murray come to terms with Lady Louisa's death. He would likely, from time to time, have forced himself to recall his brotherly advice to Augusta on dealing with the death of loved ones when writing to her from his quarters on active duty many years earlier. One letter does survive that gives an idea of the very close love that Murray had for Louisa. It was from Julia, Lady Peel, the Prime Minister's wife. Lady Peel had known Murray since 1805, when Murray was Deputy Quartermaster General in Dublin and she was Julia Floyd, the attractive daughter of his commander. Her letter of condolence – the only one Murray seems to have preserved – is perhaps all the evidence we need. She wrote:

> My dear Sir George, I hope you will allow me the privilege of our long standing intimacy and friendship to intrude one word of sincere condolence to you at this moment when you are sorrowing from your late melancholy bereavement. I know that no words can soothe such a grief as yours for the loss of a dear domestic tie, but I cannot resist expressing my sorrow for yours. I trust it will in part console you to reflect how kind and affectionate your attendance has been, and that circumstance combined with so much fortitude and Christian resignation, must have comforted and even cheered, the last hours of her who is gone and whose loss you deplore.[16]

16 TNA, WO 80/3, Lady Peel to Murray, Whitehall Gardens, 25 January 1842.

28

An Understated Life

Murray died four years after Louisa, on 28 July 1846. Illness had prevented him for many weeks from leaving home. Wellington was a frequent visitor towards the end. Augusta, to whom he had been so close, had died earlier in the year in Leamington. She is buried in Greyfriars Cemetery, Edinburgh. In her will she left to Murray a portrait of General Sir Lowry Cole, one of his closest friends and Peninsular colleagues. Why she had the portrait is not clear but Murray would surely have been thrilled to hang it at Belgrave Square, even if only for a very short time.

Murray's funeral took place on 5 August in the chapel at Kensal Green cemetery, opened in 1833 and a fashionable place to be buried. It was a low-key, private affair, although attended by a number of dignitaries including Wellington, Anglesey, and Peel. A number of surviving officers of the Peninsular and Waterloo campaigns also attended. The carriages of the Duchess of Kent (the Queen Mother), Mary, Duchess of Gloucester (daughter of George III) and Adolphus, Duke of Cambridge (son of George III) were also sent with their curtains drawn. The distinguished guests outnumbered the family, who were led in mourning by Louisa's husband Henry Boyce. At about 11 the silent cortege left Belgrave Square, in the rain, at walking pace. The elaborate coffin with its 'dazzling furniture' was covered in purple velvet, and the bad weather continued with dramatic bouts of thunder and lightening throughout the service. The Rev. Arthur Isham, Murray's niece Charlotte's husband, led what the newspapers reported to be a funeral appropriate to the nature of the deceased. Murray was buried in the family vault alongside Lady Louisa.[1]

Murray, like most of his fellow officers throughout the long years of the Peninsular War, had maintained an unwavering admiration for Wellington's undoubted skills as a commander without necessarily agreeing with him on all aspects of the war. He had been very close to other commanders of equal or more senior rank to Wellington before the start of the campaign and was in a position to compare them. He had served alongside Abercromby and Moore, very different men but individuals with whom Murray developed a close bond. Both died in battles where Murray was present. With Moore in particular Murray could not help but become very close. The Swedish initiative in 1808 required extraordinary tact and diplomacy and Murray succeeded, at least, in ensuring Britain was not drawn into a

1 Kensal Green 3368, Catacomb B, vault 93, Compartment 4 below the Cemetery Church.

flawed military campaign which could only have had serious repercussions for the army, and perhaps seriously weakened the campaign in the Peninsula. He was delighted to be chosen as Moore's Quartermaster General after Cintra and was deeply affected by his death at Corunna. The months that he spent assisting Moore in his planning, and dealing with the many changes of those plans, necessitated in part by the poor level of intelligence at that time, must have resulted in a close bond even before the horrors they faced together on the retreat to the coast. He would have no doubt discussed with Moore the justification for Wellington's impatience after Vimeiro, but would also have recalled his own relationship with Wellington at Copenhagen, which is where their close working partnership started to form. He would not necessarily have agreed with all Moore might have had to say about Wellington, as some professional jealousy was to be expected.

So by the time he was called to Wellington's side in 1809 Murray was well aware of the human side to the heroes of the day. He would probably have been equally happy to serve under either Moore or Wellington, but would have felt more naturally at ease with Moore, the less reserved of the two. At the outset there is no doubt that, despite Murray's excitement at operating at a very senior level alongside Wellington, he was disappointed that he was not given more latitude, especially in the development of the intelligence side of the department's responsibilities. Murray was a more 'modern' soldier than Wellington, having embraced the scientific approach which Wellington, at least in the early stages of their relationship, distrusted. It certainly seems that Wellington simply did not fully appreciate Murray's quiet, but very effective, contribution until he was denied access to it, on Murray's return to Britain in 1812, disillusioned with his lack of progress in the promotion game. Promotion, when it did arrive, a double jump from lieutenant colonel to brigadier general to major general in the space of a few short months, suggests a recognition in high places that the army could not afford to lose Murray, and perhaps a belated effort by Wellington himself to secure the advancement that Murray firmly believed was due to him.

Murray's linguistic and diplomatic skills were of immense assistance to Wellington. Wellington, quite justifiably in most cases, simply could not bring himself to deal at length with the Spanish, and much was left to Murray to sort out. The volume of paperwork and correspondence that flowed between the Quartermaster General and the Spanish, in French, particularly after 1812, is indicative of the additional work that was involved and the increased diplomacy required to maintain a united force under one command.

The two men were not that different in the way they dealt with problems, in that they both believed strongly in a straightforward common sense, at times pragmatic, approach to most issues, but always alert to factors and risks that might have a bearing on an outcome, although each would recognise in the other the different way in which those risks were dealt with. Murray, the more cautious of the two, would leave less to chance, a requirement for an effective Quartermaster General. They both exemplified total commitment to the job in hand and were forceful in their demands for a proper execution of their instructions. It was this common approach which was to engender a degree of trust between the two that was extraordinary, and which survived right to the end of Murray's life, despite Wellington's disappointment at his apparent lack of application in his Colonial Secretary's role.

Even before Murray left Portugal for home at the end of 1811, ready, if necessary, to quit the army, Wellington had involved him in his strategy based on the defensive lines of Torres

Vedras, in the knowledge that a French army, poorly supplied, could not sustain itself long enough to overcome the hastily but craftily engineered defences. The fact was that Murray, despite being one of the very few who was privy to Wellington's plans, nevertheless did not share his commander's confidence in their ultimate success. He could see no reasonable outcome other than eventual evacuation by sea and the continuation of the guerrilla war which he had been advocating, supported by the Royal Navy. Napoleon's war machine was simply too large and there was no chance that the very much smaller British army, even with Spanish and Portuguese support, would be able to match the French in the longer term. The only factor that Murray was prepared to admit could make a difference was the defeat of Napoleon in Northern Europe, or at least a series of setbacks that would suck French troops from the Peninsula. Such setbacks took a long time coming. Meanwhile guerrilla and intelligence-led actions increased under Murray's department, and certainly played a significant part in pinning down French armies in differing parts of the Peninsula: following the French retreat from the Lines, he was forced to accept that his pessimism was overdone.

There was an edge to Murray's letters around this time that is unusual. He felt let down, particularly by Horse Guards, and the rules on promotion. Did he also feel that Wellington should have done more to press his case? It looks as though, having made his opinions known to Wellington, they were acted upon at Horse Guards with extraordinary swiftness, which suggests some influential input. Certainly Murray's replacement, Willoughby Gordon, allowed Wellington to make comparisons, and there was no shortage of senior officers, used to Murray's efficiency and ready access to Wellington, who were desperate to have him back. To Wellington himself, at last, came a realisation that Murray was an asset of huge value, who could be used to great effect were he to return to his side. The pleas from Portugal, and from closer to home in the shape of the Duke of York, persuaded Murray to overcome his earlier irritation and his desire to be closer to troops in the field, and return to his active duties as Quartermaster General. The reception he got when arriving back at Freineda from Wellington and his senior colleagues as well as the soldiers, must have given him enormous satisfaction, and he set about his work to plan the advance into Spain with impatient gusto. The result was the rapid advance through Spain and into France and clear victories at the battles of Vitoria, the Pyrenees, Nivelle and Toulouse, much of which success can be credited to Murray personally.

From this moment Murray was working on a different level with Wellington. Not only was he living and working alongside his commander on a daily basis, but he was going well beyond his earlier role. There is plenty of evidence that he would at times make operational decisions without first referring them to Wellington, sometimes as demanded by circumstances when, for example, Wellington was absent during the Battle of the Pyrenees. These were commander's decisions on the field of battle, to which must be added the enormous amount of preparatory work, for example in the four pronged advance into Spain, which Murray was responsible for, whenever the army had to move. This was a war of marching and countermarching, mostly through areas ravaged by years of conflict, as much as battles and sieges; of advancing and retreating as became necessary in the face of overwhelming numbers. Murray was a master of this. The operational methods of the two men became almost as one, as Wellington's confidence in his Quartermaster General increased.

Despite the ability of the Spanish to underplay the British role in driving Napoleon's vast armies from their country – they seemed often to be in denial about the existence of any force other than heroic Spanish troops – Wellington had achieved extraordinary success with very limited resources, indeed a British army which never exceeded 40,000 men. Nevertheless assistance was provided in many forms, if not always reliably or willingly, by the Spanish and Portuguese, and Murray was always loathe to criticise the soldiers, as opposed to their leaders.

The arrangements at headquarters were extraordinarily low key – there was none of the formality or bling that was evident at French headquarters. Wellington and Murray worked together, almost every single day when they were both at headquarters, and when they rode together to visit parts of the allied armies, or on diplomatic duties. They both recognised the need to be seen out and about maintaining close contact with the various parts of the army. This was as much appreciated by those in the field and they both took a keen interest in ensuring the welfare of the men, although by the standards of today what the men were expected to put up with was hard to imagine – it was only very late on in the war that the soldiers were routinely provided with tents, and supplies were frequently interrupted. The very basics like shoes and greatcoats constantly needed to be replaced, and Murray's orders demonstrate an impatience to get the men properly equipped as soon as possible. Significantly, they were for the most part better fed than the French, who were mostly required to feed themselves from whatever was available in the countryside. This proved critical, and the French were forced to abandon a number of initiatives when they simply ran out of food and had to move to survive, as Wellington correctly predicted at Torres Vedras. As the war progressed the British supply lines improved, based on a system of depots and mules to carry the basic biscuit to the front. This was supplemented by bullocks, which were slaughtered as required, and local produce, paid for mainly in cash. At its peak Wellington's army consumed 44 tons of biscuit per day, much of it imported from America. From 1808-1814 there were 13,500 individual ship voyages in 400 convoys connecting the Peninsula with England, support acknowledged by Wellington as critical to his success. Murray's role did not extend as far as supplying the troops – this was the province of the Commissariat, who, after a hesitant start, acquitted themselves admirably considering the difficulties, particularly the distance from home, the weather, and poor roads.

Wellington, like many great leaders, was feared by many of his generals. They had their divisions and brigades to command and were often some distance from headquarters, even when not actively engaged in operations, as billeting and supplies demanded. Most of their communication with their commander was by orders passed through Murray. Murray was a very effective conduit between them. His charm was clearly an asset and his skills both at the highest level, when on official diplomatic duties, or within the layers of the army were recognised early on. Wellington was brusque and would ruffle feathers. Murray would soothe and reassure. It was his capacity for getting the best from people that distinguished him. By chance it is not one of his British officers who most vividly recorded the impression this capacity made on those who worked for him, but a Dane, Captain Abrahamson, who was attached to Murray during the occupation of France. He himself was to become Quartermaster General in his own country's service. His farewell letter to Murray when the allied army was breaking up is a generous tribute:

> The kindliness with which you invariably treated those who were placed under your direction, the promptitude with which you despatched all business, the precise and

> rapid pace of all the operations connected with the duties of your department – all these characteristics, which are the essence of good management, have distinguished your own administration and have left the most lively impression upon all the officers who have had the good fortune to make your acquaintance. The more we reflect upon the correctness of your judgement and the obliging dignity in the consideration you ever showed to your subordinates, the more we intend to look on you as our model should we ever be called on to undertake duties comparable with those which you have discharged in so distinguished a manner.[2]

From very early in his career, perhaps helped by his command of French, Murray was given the diplomatic roles in the midst of military campaigns – negotiating with the Turks at Jaffa, with the Danes at Copenhagen, with the Swedish king alongside Moore, opposite Junot and Kellermann at Lisbon, assisting Hope in setting up the Portuguese Regency, and finally at Toulouse. All of these roles, with the exception of Toulouse which was a local part of a much bigger armistice, were significant international events with repercussions. Even after Toulouse it was Murray who was left to negotiate and liaise with the French authorities to repatriate the British, Spanish, and Portuguese armies from France without incident.

Wellington grew to recognise the importance of Murray's application of those skills, in areas where his own natural impatience would often have become an issue. Despite their differences, and each would have recognised these in the other, there were similarities in temperament and background which bound the two men together. Both had an appetite for immense hard work – the only times that Murray complained were when he had not enough to do. He had to run a department which was tiny given its responsibilities and the diversity of activities. Any truly able officers were posted with various divisions to be Murray's eyes and ears in every part of the country where the allies were active, leaving a skeleton at headquarters. Both Murray and Wellington were able to ride hard and fast, day after day, checking on the armies and taking note of the roads and local infrastructure, and assessing what might be a problem if cavalry or artillery needed to be moved fast in an emergency. Both recognised the value of intelligence, of every kind, and Murray was given authority to develop this area, particularly using George Scovell and his Corps of Guides to provide good quality information in addition to that coming in from locals, French deserters, and intercepted letters and orders. This initiative was vastly more effective than anything the French could achieve. Their treatment of the population saw to that.

The two men had an eye for detail, could not stand pomposity, and fought uphill battles against the old-fashioned army methods, particularly when it came to appointments and promotions. Wellington was initially suspicious of the new scientifics, graduates of the new Staff College, where Murray had spent a few short months, as he felt that this new breed could emulate the rapid rise to individual power that Napoleon had achieved, and that was dangerous. Better to stick to those from good families who understood the dangers that could throw a nation into chaos and bloodshed, as demonstrated so clearly by the French example. Yet gradually, perhaps as he became exasperated by the 'gallant officers' that were inflicted on him by Horse Guards, this view changed. Murray was fine: he came from a not

2 Quoted, without citation, in Ward Draft, Ch.IX, p. 44.

dissimilar background to Wellington himself – minor aristocracy, not English establishment. Socially they might be described as equals, and as such would have been easy in each other's company, at least when they were alone, although in the early days one can detect a respectful distance being kept – perhaps because until Murray achieved his promotion to major general there was a marked gap between the two – one a lieutenant general, the other a mere lieutenant colonel.

It is not presumptuous to suggest that there was no one in Wellington's entire circle, military, personal, or political to whom he was as close and whom he trusted more. Murray was commonly said by the cognoscenti at headquarters to be the only individual 'received into the unlimited confidence of Lord Wellington'.[3] Wellington was in the Peninsula for five years. There were, seemingly, few personal visits from friends at home. His wife Kitty led a lonely existence in London, excited by her husband's triumphs and regular elevations up the peerage, but more and more irrelevant in Wellington's life. He had a good relationship with most of his senior generals but not necessarily close – Graham and Hill were perhaps the most trusted. Some he barely suffered, such as the unfortunate William Erskine. He never got close to his Spanish or Portuguese counterparts, and Murray no doubt had often to sort out awkward situations with them. There is evidence that he did not get on that well with his brothers. There is little written about any liaisons with local ladies in the Peninsula although there must have been plenty. Similarly nothing survives in Murray's papers or letters that point to his having mistresses, or seducing or being seduced by the comely daughters of the local population. It is impossible to imagine that Murray would not have had the opportunity and plenty of offers. Wellington clearly did.

Wellington liked Murray, trusted him, admired his abilities, used him in situations where he himself was less suited, and employed him in every aspect of the campaign, next to him, day in, day out, rarely separated, for the duration of the war, save for the unfortunate period in 1812 where Willoughby Gordon was foisted on him. Murray's return as a major general gave both men the opportunity to reach even greater effectiveness as a team. Wellington was much happier to delegate at important moments. Murray had the confidence and seniority to make the most of this and felt able to speak out and challenge Wellington's views and plans. The new relationship worked well; in Larpent's words 'Murray was decidedly the second man' and 'the life and soul of the army next to Lord Wellington'.[4] Vitoria was the first hard evidence of this, and from that moment it is clear that Murray was allowed a good deal of latitude in making plans and issuing orders to the army, split as it became in various locations in and around the Pyrenees. Wellington no longer had to be in three places at once – two was now what he strove to achieve. It is hard to see how the campaign in the Pyrenees, and the advance into France would have turned out were it not for the two men dovetailing so effectively.

'The most complicated arrangements are those which must be made out when there is least time and the least tranquillity', wrote Murray to Augusta.[5] Ward's opinion of Murray's skills is clear:

3 Sir Richard Drake Henegan, *Seven Years Campaigning in the Peninsula and the Netherlands from1808-1815* (London: Henry Colburn, 1846), p.316.
4 Larpent (ed.), *Private Journal*, p.188.
5 Murray to Augusta, Villafranca, 13 May 1811, Murray Papers, MS 21103.

> In these circumstances, when there were perhaps eight infantry divisions to take care of, several cavalry brigades, detached corps, brigades of artillery, baggage, headquarters, regiments joining, picquets, outposts – in these circumstances it would have been easy to 'lose' a formation or detachment and overlook it. Yet in five years of constant campaigning not one instance of such a lapse seems to occur. He once refers to the 88th as the 87th; he once forgets the name of La Baneza as a commissariat station; but otherwise there are probably not more than around half a dozen small slips in his orders over the whole period, none of any significance. His attention is so concentrated that he can ignore the distractions and make his pen flow on without erasures or second thoughts. Such corrections as are to be found are probably those made after consultation with Wellington. They are not lapses of mind.
>
> Though it is always difficult to gauge time, there is every reason to suppose that he despatched his business with very great rapidity. He told his sister that writing letters to her made no more difference to him than 'a quarter of an hour, or somewhat more occasionally'. Such letters amount to two quarto sheets or more written on both sides, which take about thirty minutes merely to roughly transcribe. If he could write and compose at such speed, some idea can be had of the pace at which he could work.[6]

Ward also makes no secret of his admiration for Murray's industry:

> The clear headedness with which he kept court and directed the complex movements of a large number of formations in the passes of the Pyrenees enabled Wellington to thwart Soult's dangerous counter – offensive in the last days of July 1813. His elaborate instructions for the 'set piece' battles of the Bidassoa and the Nivelle carried the army into France. Some idea of the magnitude of the work involved may be gathered from the Memoir annexed to an Atlas of the War where Murray's Arrangements are printed from the edited text. It is impossible to come away from the original document without a profound admiration for the speed and accuracy of his business methods.[7]

Wellington hated staff coming to him with memoranda, and it can be assumed that Murray reported to Wellington on most occasions with the location of the relevant elements of the army, and who was on the move, arranged in his head. It is significant that almost all of the memoranda of this description date from a period where Murray was not Quartermaster General. Both De Lancey and Gordon were ponderous by comparison and one can almost hear the sighs of desperate impatience behind Wellington's scribbled responses to explanations of delays.

Although the tone of their written communications is formal, this is what would be expected in the military of the time. There are a number of more personal letters between

6 Ward Draft, Ch.IX, p.39.

7 Ward, 'Report on Murray Papers', p 201.

Wellington and Murray that provide an insight into the friendship that developed between the men. One should not forget that they had worked together very closely at Copenhagen in 1807 – almost to the extent of taking control of events from Cathcart. That close affinity was again on display at Vimiero when Wellesley, as he then was, was superseded by Burrard and then Dalrymple, his plans to pursue the French to a possible defeat brought to a shuddering halt. We then see Wellesley and Murray acting together – Wellesley using Murray as a go-between in an effort to get Dalrymple to agree his plan. This was about to be realised when everything changed with Kellermann's arrival, with proposals for an armistice, which led to the notorious Convention of Cintra. When Wellesley opted to return to England, declaring it was impossible for him to continue in such circumstances and under such ineffective command, the last thing he did was write to Murray saying, after expressing his anger, how much he had hoped to see him before he left, and was there anything he could do for him in London? It was the letter of a man who already was a close friend.

This personal friendship developed over the time the two of them worked together, as they must have done almost every day. Headquarters were occasionally stationary for months on end, as in the case of Freineda near the Spanish border, but often only for a few days or even a day at a time when the army was advancing. Mostly it was a low-key operation – a few houses in a village square. Wellington naturally had the best quarters that were available. His staff, Murray included, had to make do with whatever might be left. Wellington would use his for receiving a constant flow of visitors. Murray would be with him for a part of each morning bringing him up to date on the movements of the army, the latest intelligence on the enemy, or more humdrum issues such as the lack of shoes for the men or forage for horses. Both men wrote prodigiously, one assumes late into the night. In addition to all the military correspondence and orders Murray wrote with unceasing regularity to his brother and sister with his views on the military situation or the wider political scene. Often these letters from Murray, especially those to Augusta, are very descriptive, sensitive pieces on nature and the scenery, many philosophical on the nature of man and war. It is harder to visualise Wellington using this important release valve to unburden himself, certainly not to Kitty.

Was it Murray, then, who would have to soak up the ranting of his boss when things were not going well with a siege, or when politicians in London were seemingly unsupportive of his efforts, or when idiotic generals made a mess of things again, or when another pack of Spanish lies was unearthed? Was it Murray who had, quietly and without fuss, to fill in the gaps in Wellington's plans which might have been overlooked, or to calm his commander after the Royal Navy insisted on doing things their way, or come up with an answer when the rains fell and the artillery could not move as planned? Probably. He was, after all, the closest.

When Murray was in London in 1812 he kept in contact with and visited Kitty, who clearly adored him and loved the close bonds that she knew tied the two men together. Perhaps because she herself was unable to get close to her hero husband she viewed Murray as a kind of substitute confidante, and saw in him a person to whom Wellington could unburden himself, knowing her husband's reticence at allowing himself to become too close to anyone.

The urgency with which Murray was contacted by London, soon after his arrival in North America, on Napoleon's escape from Elba, giving him the choice of remaining in Canada or returning to resume the fight alongside Wellington, underlines the feeling in royal circles and Whitehall, probably prompted by Wellington, that what was needed to finish the job was the old partnership, the Duke and his Quartermaster General. There is the tantalising reference in a letter written by Wellington, referring to an earlier letter, never received by Murray, in which Wellington stated that if Murray had received the earlier one, he would never have left for Canada. Murray was very much part of Wellington's plans at that stage, even though there was no apparent likelihood of an immediate resumption of the war.

In the days leading up to Waterloo, the scant preparations for confronting the newly-energised Napoleonic army, and the deployment of troops and liaison with allies left a good deal to be desired, and Wellington made no bones about wishing Murray had been there. Might the allies have been better prepared and coordinated had Wellington had Murray with him?

It was Murray's idea that he should be chief of staff to the 150,000-strong Allied Occupation Force in France in between 1815 and 1818. His patience with difficult allies and the French no doubt took much of the pressure off the commander in chief. No such position existed in the British Army at the time, but it worked perfectly for the role that Murray would play. Paris and Cambrai were certainly a welcome relief after so many years of brutality and hardship. Both men revelled in their freedom and popularity. In Murray's case it was the start of the love affair that would result in years of personal difficulties and would change his life. Wellington, too, sailed close to the wind, and was thought to have had a number of affairs.

The two men were exemplary in their loyalty to one another. At the end of the occupation regiments were disbanded and officers and men left without employment, at best on half pay. This would have been embarrassing for Murray who had nothing to fall back on; he was a professional soldier, having spent more than 25 years serving in the military. He had no reliable personal wealth. The finances of Ochtertyre were less than healthy, not that he would have countenanced living off his elder brother, and suitable positions for senior officers were at a premium. Wellington, by now at the height of his popularity, could make anything happen if he so desired. Hence Murray's appointment as commander in chief in Ireland, his governorship of Sandhurst, his colonelcies of two regiments, his appointment as Master General of the Ordnance and most important of all, his appointment to the office of Secretary of State for War and the Colonies in 1828.

This would prove the biggest test of the men's loyalty. For whatever reason Murray's performance fell well short of what he had achieved in every other post he had ever held. Wellington's patience was stretched to the limit, and he reluctantly planned to replace him, when events intervened. Although Murray remained one of very few who supported Wellington as Prime Minister, and in opposition to the Whig administrations through the turbulent period between 1828 and the mid-1830s, he could never be quite as intransigent as Wellington in his attitude to the massive changes that were taking place in the country. Murray was very much on the liberal flank of the Tory party, a stance acknowledged by his Perthshire political opponents who were happy to allow him to be elected unopposed. Along with Patrick, Murray regarded himself as an independent and was happy to see a real, if limited, move to reform, and fully supported Catholic Emancipation. The alternative to reform he saw as revolution, and reform was overdue. Wellington took the Ultra Tory view that the risk of revolution was so great that it was necessary to avoid any major disruption of the status quo, which would lead to greater demands, and to maintain a fierce loyalty to the Crown and the established order. Chaos was the alternative. He had given his all in the fight against revolutionary France and would not allow the same fate to befall Britain and its constitutional monarchy.

There is probably some truth that Murray, during his time as a politician, was worn down by the dramas and costs associated with his affair with Lady Louisa, the secretive birth of his daughter, his rejection by many in London society as a result, the worries of maintaining a lifestyle which matched Louisa's expectations, as well as the understandably difficult transition from military life to civilian ways, the political negotiations, the glare of publicity, the committees. He probably longed for the simpler military life, the obeying of orders and the dignified treatment of a defeated opponent. Described as 'indolent' on more than one occasion in connection with his colonial duties, idleness was certainly not a feature of his character prior to this. Something had changed, or at the very least he was simply bored with the political obligations to which he was expected to adhere, and knew that he was not in a position to leave it behind, both out of loyalty to Wellington and financial necessity.

In the political world his talents were much more suited to the role to which he was appointed by Peel, that of Master General of the Ordnance. This was as much a military position as political. Murray found his old spark and applied himself diligently to the defences of Britain, Ireland and the colonies in the face of renewed threats.

Wellington had, of course, a vast array of admirers, and a life brim-full of duties both political and military. Indeed he complained of the amount of work and detail expected of him, no doubt, as ever, finding it difficult to delegate, although in truth in most cases this would have been impossible. He maintained contact with many of his senior officers from the Peninsula and Waterloo, but never seemed especially close to any. Murray remained a close friend in the years after active military service. Wellington, who only had sons, which Lady Shelley felt was 'so unlucky', had excellent relations with his nieces, his women friends and, later, with his daughters-in-law. He agreed to be Louisa's godfather, and probably enjoyed spoiling her as a result.

Murray was always welcome at Stratfield Saye, where he had his own room. Wellington had many of the rooms decorated with prints, 'every bed Room in the House full of them', some Russian, many Portuguese and military, as he proudly pointed out to Harriet Arbuthnot, who was also a very regular visitor with an earmarked room. Murray's room must surely have been a military or Portuguese one. Little evidence of such occasions survives, and Wellington's social life is largely recorded by women. Much of his entertaining was inevitably political and society, rather than among old soldiers, and whilst he did not seek them out he was glad of their uncomplicated company and welcomed them generously when the opportunities presented themselves. Charles Arbuthnot once remarked to his son, Charles: 'I never see the Duke in roaring spirits but when his old military associates are around him'.[8] Whilst there is little in the archives documenting social occasions enjoyed by the two men, other than in the company of many others, Murray would of course be present at most if not all of the dinners involving his Peninsular officers, as well as all the functions necessarily involving the Cabinet or Ministers of State during the time Wellington and he were in government. But the invitations to Stratfield Saye were over and above the official

8 Aspinall (ed.), *Correspondence of Charles Arbuthnot*, p.172.

London occasions, and the two would have relished the exercise, fresh air and unforced camaraderie that exists between men who have known each other for many years, who have shared intense experiences, and who recognise each other's strengths and weaknesses. The trust and mutual respect between the two men ran deep. Murray's advice continued to be sought, especially on defence issues, right up to his death. Murray was certainly one of a very close circle of friends, perhaps the only one, who could claim uninterrupted friendship and mutual loyalty from the moment of the decision to take control of a situation, caused by poor command on the expedition to Copenhagen in 1807, to the very end of his life 39 years later.

There is no doubt that Murray was an exceptional soldier, without whom Wellington's job would have been even more arduous. His contribution to the successful outcome of the Peninsular War, and his closeness to Wellington, has never been fully explored by historians, with the obvious exception of Ward, who was seemingly intent on publishing what would have been a lengthy and immensely detailed biography, and whose research has been widely used by authors writing about the Peninsular Campaign. Murray's importance certainly was very clearly acknowledged in the highest echelons at the time. A glittering array of decorations from grateful monarchs and allies, as far apart as Russia and Portugal, is evidence of that.

It is perhaps ironic that whilst generally regarded as a less than inspired politician and Secretary of State, it is as a result of that part of his life that we have plenty to remember him by, including Australia's best known river, Perth in Western Australia, Mount Ochtertyre in Victoria, Murray House (a government building in Hong Kong), a Martello tower, and numerous places and street names in Canada, and surely many more. There are cartoons, and scathing articles in the *Spectator*, and other, Whig, journals. There are, of course official records of all his parliamentary activities and speeches. Wyld's Atlas and the Marlborough Despatches are of significant historical value.

There are many generals who fought with Wellington against Napoleon who were respected and trusted by him – Graham, Hill and Hope all can claim to be thus recognised. But their influence waned after the battles were fought and won. There were a few in the political arena who can claim similar recognition, but given the fickle nature of politics they merely had their moments, or at least only became part of Wellington's life at quite a late stage. There were of course numerous friends and confidantes in the society into which Wellington was thrust after Waterloo. Harriet and Charles Arbuthnot and Lady Shelley lead the pack. Again, although of significant importance and influence, especially in the case of the Arbuthnots, they came upon the scene only in the post military era. Kitty, although married to him for 25 years, never occupied a position of trust or intellectual admiration, hence, perhaps, Wellington's search for women outside marriage, in most cases platonic, to whom he could confide, with whom he might discuss robustly, and from whom he could expect uncomplicated honesty.

Murray's and Wellington's lives were intertwined over a period of almost 40 years, during a seemingly endless war involving moments of testing intensity, and in the years of fundamental social and constitutional change that followed, the whole overshadowed by the awful possibility of descent into bloody revolution. At times during their military careers Wellington needed Murray more than Murray needed Wellington. That position was certainly reversed in the political years that followed. Their mutual respect and friendship, two men at ease with each other, for the most part ignoring the inescapable fact that throughout those years Murray was the subordinate, survived a period of history that matches any other for excitement, glamour, uncertainty, danger, and upheaval.

It would be easy to see Murray as just a part, albeit an important part, of the canvas, dominated by Wellington. Described by Tennyson as 'the last great Englishman', in his time Wellington had no equal. Certainly there were many who owed the success of their careers to the great man. There were others whose lights might have shone brighter were it not for the dominating presence of the chief. Murray owed as much as most to Wellington's support, but there is no doubting that he had fully earned Wellington's hard won admiration. Murray was supremely gifted, proud of his Scottish roots, with an impressive intellect and a true sense of duty and loyalty to those around him. As a soldier he was hugely admired by allied commanders, brother officers, and men, who missed his presence at some critical moments. As a politician he applied himself as he felt right – often torn between his conscience and the realities of the brutal political world in which he found himself, pilloried by an unforgiving press when he tried to please too many factions at once. His talents as the best staff officer in Europe were recognised by foes, as well as in the corridors of military and political power in London. When diplomacy and negotiating skills were required at great moments in the military struggle against France, Murray was summoned and entrusted with getting the best from the situation.

Napoleon's escape from Elba was the most important turning point in Murray's life. Had he not elected to race back from Canada, to be at Wellington's side, he would probably have cemented himself into the role of commander in chief of the North American forces or in the position of governor general there. He would not have succumbed to Lady Louisa's charms in Paris. He would have avoided the only part of his career that he really did not enjoy, Westminster politics. He might have returned to England perhaps to be Master General of the Ordnance, after serving either politically or militarily in India, Canada, Ceylon, or the Cape. His ability to deal with different people with sensitivity, and his common sense approach would have suited any of these roles, in countries where the older principles still meant something and where the uncomfortable tide of liberalism, stemming from the rise of industrialisation, was still some way off. He might still, perhaps with more money than he ever seemed to have, have found time to write his Memorandum to Wyld's Atlas, maybe even persuading Wellington that a full and accurate history of the Peninsular War was crying out to be written. Whatever life provided in the way of opportunities, Murray would have made his mark on them, albeit in that quiet reserved manner that was his trademark.

Were anyone to have lavished overblown praise on him for his contribution to the defeat of Napoleon, he would have acknowledged to Augusta that she would no doubt enjoy bringing him back to his senses. He would have been content to receive the deep appreciation of his fellow soldiers, his commander, and those who needed educating back at Horse Guards. He would have been happy to see Wellington receive the many accolades he did, but might equally, perhaps riding out at Stratfield Saye, have shared some jokes about episodes they both had lived through which merited less glorification. He would have been content in the knowledge that he had served his country well in many campaigns over long and physically demanding years, was loved and admired by many, had handled the social difficulties caused by his marriage to Louisa with dignity and sensitivity, and had had the chance to apply his academic skills in two notable literary works. No more fuss than that.

He would, perhaps most of all, have been touched by Wellington's acquisition of the portrait of him by John Prescott Knight to hang at Apsley House, where it remains today. This was possibly painted originally for the Board of Ordnance, but purchased by Wellington in 1847 from the artist for 60 guineas. Wellington had made a point of surrounding himself with portraits of as many of his Peninsular and Waterloo generals as he could. He had never managed to acquire a suitable portrait of Murray. That omission was rectified with Knight's portrait, painted shortly before Murray's death. It is not a bold military picture as are so many of those on the walls there, but a much more thoughtful painting of an alert, sensitive, intelligent man, albeit in his old age, still with those keen blue eyes, an image that would have constantly reminded Wellington of those many arduous and dangerous years alongside each other in military conflict and political life, and of their close, loyal comradeship.

Appendix I

Murray's Medals and Decorations

The Imperial Austrian Order of Leopold (plus two Stars)
The Order of St Alexander Newski of Russia (plus Star)
The Star of the Grand Cross of the Order of Guelphs of Hanover.
The Order of the Crescent of the Imperial Ottoman Empire, second class (The Star and Crescent set in Brilliants – this Order is of great rarity)
The Order of the Tower and Sword of Portugal (plus two Stars)
The Military Order of St Henry of the Kingdom of Saxony (plus two Stars)
The Military Order of Maximillian Joseph
The Peninsular Gold Cross with six Bars (only three Crosses with six clasps, as this one has, were granted)
The Peninsular Gold Medal for Corunna and Talavera
Knight Grand Cross of the Military Order of the Bath (plus Star KB, plus Star GCB)
The Order of the Red Eagle of Prussia (plus two Stars)

A number of valuable items gifted to Murray by grateful nations were sold at Christies in 1891 following his daughter Louisa's death. Among them were:

An oblong octagonal gold box with a miniature of Louis XVIII, by whom it was presented.
A gold box with a miniature of the King of Sweden.
A blue and gold box formerly set with Brilliants presented by the Sultan.
A black and gold enamel box and watch with Royal Arms and Garter.
An oval gold box encrusted with lapis lazuli, agate etc.
A chased silver box presented with the Freedom of City of Cork (bought by Mary Murray Gartshore).

Appendix II

The Convention of Cintra

DEFINITIVE CONVENTION FOR THE EVACUATION OF PORTUGAL BY THE FRENCH ARMY AUGUST 30, 1808

The Generals commanding in chief the British and French armies in Portugal, having determined to negotiate and conclude a treaty for the evacuation of Portugal by the French troops, on the basis of the agreement entered into on the 22nd instant for a suspension of hostilities, have appointed the under-mentioned officers to negotiate the same in their names; viz. — on the part of the General-in-Chief of the British army, Lieutenant-Colonel Murray, Quarter-Master-General; and, on the part of the General-in-Chief of the French army, Monsieur Kellermann, General-of-Division to whom they have given authority to negotiate and conclude a Convention to that effect, subject to their ratification respectively, and to that of the Admiral commanding the British fleet at the entrance of the Tagus.

Those two officers, after exchanging their full powers, have agreed upon the articles which follow:

1. All the places and forts in the kingdom of Portugal, occupied by the French troops, shall be delivered up to the British army in the state in which they are at the period of the signature of the present Convention.
2. The French troops shall evacuate Portugal with their arms and baggage; they shall not be considered as prisoners of war; and, on their arrival in France, they shall be at liberty to serve.
3. The English Government shall furnish the means of conveyance for the French army; which shall be disembarked in any of the ports of France between Rochefort and L'Orient, inclusively.
4. The French army shall carry with it all its artillery, of French calibre, with the horses belonging to it, and the tumbrils supplied with sixty rounds per gun. All other artillery, arms, and ammunition, as also the military and naval arsenals, shall be given up to the British army and navy in the state in which they may be at the period of the ratification of the Convention.
5. The French army shall carry with it all its equipments, and all that is comprehended under the name of property of the army; that is to say, its military chest, and carriages

attached to the Field Commissariat and Field Hospitals; or shall be allowed to dispose of such part of the same, on its account, as the Commander-in-Chief may judge it unnecessary to embark, In like manner, all individuals of the army shall be at liberty to dispose of their private property of every description; with full security hereafter for the purchaser.

6. The cavalry are to embark their horses; as also the Generals and other officers of all ranks. It is, however, fully understood, that the means of conveyance for horses, at the disposal of the British Commanders, are very limited; some additional conveyance may be procured in the port of Lisbon: the number of horses to be embarked by the troops shall not exceed six hundred; and the number embarked by the Staff shall not exceed two hundred. At all events every facility will be given to the French army to dispose of the horses, belonging to it, which cannot be embarked.
7. In order to facilitate the embarkation, it shall take place in three divisions; the last of which will be principally composed of the garrisons of the places, of the cavalry, the artillery, the sick, and the equipment of the army. The first division shall embark within seven days of the date of the ratification; or sooner, if possible.
8. The garrison of Elvas and its forts, and of Peniche and Palmela, will be embarked at Lisbon; that of Almaida at Oporto, or the nearest harbour. They will be accompanied on their march by British Commissaries, charged with providing for their subsistence and accommodation.
9. All the sick and wounded, who cannot be embarked with the troops, are entrusted to the British army. They are to be taken care of, whilst they remain in this country, at the expense of the British Government; under the condition of the same being reimbursed by France when the final evacuation is effected. The English government will provide for their return to France; which shall take place by detachments of about one hundred and fifty (or two hundred) men at a time. A sufficient number of French medical officers shall be left behind to attend them.
10. As soon as the vessels employed to carry the army to France shall have disembarked it in the harbours specified, or in any other of the ports of France to which stress of weather may force them, every facility shall be given them to return to England without delay; and security against capture until their arrival in a friendly port.
11. The French army shall be concentrated in Lisbon, and within a distance of about two leagues from it. The English army will approach within three leagues of the capital; and will be so placed as to leave about one league between the two armies.
12. The forts of St. Julien, the Bugio, and Cascais, shall be occupied by the British troops on the ratification of the Convention. Lisbon and its citadel, together with the forts and batteries, as far as the Lazaretto or Tarfuria on one side, and fort St. Joseph on the other, inclusively, shall be given up on the embarkation of the second division; as shall also the harbour; and all armed vessels in it of every description, with their rigging, sails, stores, and ammunition.

    The fortresses of Elvas, Almaida, Peniche, and Palmela, shall be given up as soon as the British troops can arrive to occupy them. In the mean time, the General-in-Chief of the British army will give notice of the present Convention to the garrisons of those places, as also to the troops before them, in order to put a stop to all further hostilities.

13. Commissioners shall be named, on both sides, to regulate and accelerate the execution of the arrangements agreed upon.
14. Should there arise doubts as to the meaning of any article, it will be explained favourably to the French army.
15. From the date of the ratification of the present Convention, all arrears of contributions, requisitions, or claims whatever, of the French Government, against the subjects of Portugal, or any other individuals residing in this country, founded on the occupation of Portugal by the French troops in the month of December 1807, which may not have been paid up, are cancelled; and all sequestrations laid upon their property, moveable or immoveable, are removed; and the free disposal of the same is restored to the proper owner.
16. All subjects of France, or of powers in friendship or alliance with France, domiciliated in Portugal, or accidentally in this country, shall be protected: their property of every kind, moveable and immoveable, shall be respected: and they shall be at liberty either to accompany the French army, or to remain in Portugal. In either case their property is guaranteed to them; with the liberty of retaining or of disposing of it, and passing the produce of the sale thereof into France, or any other country where they may fix their residence; the space of one year being allowed them for that purpose. It is fully understood, that the shipping is excepted from this arrangement; only, however, in so far as regards leaving the port; and that none of the stipulations above-mentioned can be made the pretext of any commercial speculation.
17. No native of Portugal shall be rendered accountable for his political conduct during the period of the occupation of this country by the French army; and all those who have continued in the exercise of their employments, or who have accepted situations under the French Government, are placed under the protection of the British Commanders: they shall sustain no injury in their persons or property; it not having been at their option to be obedient, or not, to the French Government: they are also at liberty to avail themselves of the stipulations of the 16th Article.
18. The Spanish troops detained on board ship in the port of Lisbon shall be given up to the Commander-in-Chief of the British army; who engages to obtain of the Spaniards to restore such French subjects, either military or civil, as may have been detained in Spain, without being taken in battle, or in consequence of military operations, but on occasion of the occurrences of the 29th of last May, and the days immediately following.
19. There shall be an immediate exchange established for all ranks of prisoners made in Portugal since the commencement of the present hostilities.
20. Hostages of the rank of field-officers shall be mutually furnished on the part of the British army and navy, and on that of the French army, for the reciprocal guarantee of the present Convention. The officer of the British army shall be restored on the completion of the articles which concern the army; and the officer of the navy on the disembarkation of the French troops in their own country. The like is to take place on the part of the French army.
21. It shall be allowed to the General-in-Chief of the French army to send an officer to France with intelligence of the present Convention. A vessel will be furnished by the British Admiral to convey him to Bourdeaux or Rochefort.
22. The British Admiral will be invited to accommodate His Excellency the Commander-in-Chief, and the other principal officers of the French army, on board of ships of war.

Done and concluded at Lisbon this 30th day of August, 1808.

[Signed] Murray, Quarter-Master-General. Kellermann, Le Général de Division.

We, the Duke of Abrantes, General-in-Chief of the French army, have ratified and do ratify the present Definitive Convention in all its articles, to be executed according to its form and tenor.

[Signed] The Duke Of Abrantes. Head-Quarters, Lisbon, 30th August, 1808.

ADDITIONAL ARTICLES TO THE CONVENTION OF THE 30TH OF AUGUST 1808

1. The individuals in the civil employment of the army made prisoners, either by the British troops, or by the Portuguese, in any part of Portugal, will be restored, as is customary, without exchange.
2. The French army shall be subsisted from its own magazines up to the day of embarkation; the garrisons up to the day of the evacuation of the fortresses.

   The remainder of the magazines shall be delivered over, in the usual form, to the British Government; which charges itself with the subsistence of the men and horses of the army from the above-mentioned periods till they arrive in France; under the condition of their being reimbursed by the French Government for the excess of the expense beyond the estimates, to be made by both parties, of the value of the magazines delivered up to the British army.

   The provisions on board the ships of war, in possession of the French army, will be taken in account by the British Government in like manner with the magazines in the fortresses.

   The General commanding the British troops will take the necessary measures for re- establishing the free circulation of the means of subsistence between the country and the capital.

Done and concluded at Lisbon this 30th day of August, 1808. [Signed] Murray, Quarter-Master-General Kellermann, Le Général de Division.

We, Duke of Abrantes, General-in-Chief of the French army, have ratified and do ratify the additional articles of the Convention, to be executed according to their form and tenor.

The Duke of Abrantes. (A true Copy.) A.J. Dalrymple, Captain, Military Secretary.

Bibliography

Archival Sources

British Library
- Hill Papers
- Liverpool Papers
- Moore Papers
- Murray Correspondence
- Napier Papers
- Peel Papers
- Wellington Papers
- Willoughby Gordon Papers

Hartley Library, University of Southampton
- S.G.P. Ward Papers
- Wellington Papers

Lambeth Palace Library
- Erskine v Erskine Papers

National Archives, Kew
- Admiralty Papers (ADM1 and ADM51).
- Brownrigg Papers (WO133)
- Murray Papers (WO79-80)
- Scovell Papers (WO37)

National Archives of Scotland, Edinburgh
- Hope of Linlithgow Papers
- Hope of Luffness Papers
- Leith Hay Papers.
- Moray of Abercairny Papers

National Library of Scotland
- Murray Papers (including Murray Gartshore Papers).

Public Record Office of Northern Ireland
- Castlereagh Papers

West Yorkshire Archive Service, Leeds
- Canning Papers

Published Primary Sources

Anon., *Minutes of Proceedings of the Court of Inquiry upon the Treaty of Armistice and The Convention of Cintra* (London: Samuel Tipper and John Booth, 1808).
Anon., *Report of the Manuscripts of Earl Bathurst* (London: HM Stationery Office, 1923).
Aspinall, A. (ed.) *The Correspondence of Charles Arbuthnot* (London: Royal Historical Society, 1941).
Buckham, E.W., *Personal Narrative of Adventures in the Peninsula during the War in 1812-1813* (London: John Murray, 1827).
Buckley, R. (ed.), *The Napoleonic War Journal Of Captain Thomas Henry Browne 1807-1816* (London: Army Records Society, 1987).
Cole, M.L., & S. Gwynn (eds.), *Memoirs of Sir Lowry Cole* (London: Macmillan, 1934).
Glover, G., *Eyewitness to the Peninsular War and the Battle of Waterloo: The Letters and Journals of Lieutenant Colonel James Stanhope 1803 to 1825* (Barnsley: Pen & Sword, 2010).
Ellenborough, 1st Earl of, *A Political Diary 1828-1830* (London: R. Bentley & Son, 1881).
Gurwood, Lieut. Colonel (ed.), *The Dispatches of Field Marshal the Duke of Wellington, During his Various Campaigns in India, Denmark, Portugal, Spain, The Low Countries, and France* (London: John Murray, 1837-1839).
Henegan, Sir Richard Drake, *Seven Years Campaigning in the Peninsula and the Netherlands from 1808-1815* (London: Henry Colburn, 1846).
Maurice, J., (ed), *The Diary of Sir John Moore*, (London: Edward Arnold, 1904).
Larpent, Sir George (ed.), *The Private Journal of Judge Advocate Larpent* (Staplehurst, Spellmount, 2000).
Moore, J.C., *A Narrative of the Campaign of the British Army in Spain commanded by His Excellency Sir John Moore* (London: Joseph Johnson, 1809).
Moore, J.C., *The Life of Lieutenant General Sir John Moore KB* (London: John Murray, 1833).
Moore Smith, G.C. (ed.), *The Autobiography of Lt. General Sir Harry Smith* (London: John Murray, 1903).
Muir, R, (ed.) *At Wellington's Right Hand. The Letters of Lieutenant-Colonel Sir Alexander Gordon, 1808-1815* (Stroud: Army Records Society, 2003).
Murray, Sir George, *Memoir annexed to an Atlas, containing plans of the principle battles, sieges, and affairs, in which the British Troops were engaged during the War in the Spanish Peninsular and in the south of France from 1808 to 1814* (London: James Wyld, 1841).
Murray, Sir George and Mitchell, Sir Thomas, *Maps & Plans of the Principal Movements & Battles and Sieges in which the British Army was engaged during the war from 1808-1814* ['Wyld's Atlas'] (London, James Wyld, 1841).
Schaumann, A.L.F., *On the Road with Wellington* (London: Greenhill Books 1999).
Sherer, M., *Recollections of the Peninsula* (London: Longman, Rees, Orme, Brown and Green, 1827).
Thiébault, P.C., *Mémoires du Général Baron de Thiébault* (Paris: E.Plon, Nourrit et Cie., 1895).
Tomkinson, J. (ed.), *Diary of a Cavalry Officer in the Peninsular War and Waterloo Campaigns* (London: Swan Sonnenschein & Co, 1895).

Ward, S.P.G., 'Illustrated Report on Murray Papers', *Journal for the Society for Army Historical Research* Vol.10 (1931), pp.34-39.
Walsh, T., *Journal of the Late Campaign in Egypt* (London: T. Cadell and W. Davies, 1803).
Watson, F., (ed.), *Historical Records of Australia* (Melbourne: Library Committee of the Commonwealth Parliament, 1914-1925).
Wellington, 1st Duke of, *Some Letters of the Duke of Wellington to his Brother, William Wellesley-Pole* (Camden Miscellany Vol. XVIII), (London: Royal Historical Society, 1948).
Wellington, 2nd Duke of (ed.) *Supplementary Despatches, Correspondence, and Memoranda, of Field Marshal Arthur, Duke of Wellington* (London: John Murray, 1858-62).
Wilson, Sir Robert, *History of the British Expedition to Egypt* (London: Egerton, 1803).

Secondary Sources

Annand, A, 'Major General Lord Macleod', *Journal of the Society for Army Historical Research*, Vol XXXVII, No.150. (Summer 1959), pp.21-27.
Burnham, R. and McGuigan R, *The British Army Against Napoleon* (Barnsley: Frontline Books, 2010).
Burns, Robert, *The Life and Work of Robert Burns* (Edinburgh: W&R Chambers, 1896).
Davies, Huw J., 'Moving Forward in the Old Style; Revisiting Wellington's Greatest Battles from Assaye to Waterloo', *British Journal for Military History*, Vol I, Issue 3 (June 2015), pp.2-23.
Drummond, P.R., *Perthshire in Bygone Days* (London: Whittingham & Co, 1879).
Falkner, J., *Marlborough's Battlefields* (Barnsley: Pen & Sword, 2008).
Fisher, D.R., 'Murray, Sir George', *The History of Parliament Online*, at www.historyofparliamentonline.org/volume/1820-1832/member/murray-sir-george-1772-1846.
Fortescue, J.W., *History of the British Army*, (London: Macmillan, 1899-1930).
Fraser, Sir William, *The Earls of Cromartie* (Edinburgh: Tanner Ritchie, 1876).
Gates, D, *The Spanish Ulcer*, (Cambridge Mass.: Da Capo Press, 1986).
Glenthoj, R., and M. Nordhagen Ottosen, *Experiences of War and Nationality in Denmark and Norway 1807-1815* (Basingstoke: Palgrave Macmillan, 2014).
Glover, M., *Wellington's Peninsular Victories* (London: Windrush, 2001).
Hague,W. *Pitt the Younger* (London, Harper Collins 2004).
Hastings, M. (ed), *The Oxford Book of Military Anecdotes* (Oxford: Oxford University Press, 1987).
Hill, J. *Wellington's Right Hand. Rowland Viscount Hill* (Stroud, Spellmount 2011).
Holmes, R. *Wellington – The Iron Duke.* (London, Harper Collins 2003).
Howard, M.R., *Death Before Glory: The British Soldier in the West Indies in the French Revolutionary and Napoleonic Wars*, (Barnsley: Pen & Sword: 2015).
James, L. *The Iron Duke* (London: Pimlico,1992).
Knight, R. *Britain Against Napoleon.* (London: Penguin Books, 2013).
Longford, E. *Wellington – The Years of the Sword.* (Herts, Panther 1971)
Longford, E. *Wellington – Pillar of State.* (London, Panther 1975)

Maurice, F., *History of the Scots Guards from the Creation of the Regiment to the Great War* (London: Chatto & Windus, 1934).
Macdonald J., *Sir John Moore, The Making of a Controversial Hero* (Barnsley: Pen & Sword, 2016).
Marshall-Cornwall, General Sir James, 'Our First Soldier President', *The Journal of the Royal Geographical Society*, Vol.151 Part 1 (March 1985), pp.138-147.
Muir, R., *Wellington – The Path to Victory 1769-1814* (New Haven:Yale University Press 2013).
Muir, R., *Wellington – Waterloo and the Fortunes of Peace 1814-1852* (New Haven: Yale University Press 2015).
Oman, Sir Charles, *A History of the Peninsular War* (Oxford: Oxford University Press, 1902-1930).
Robertson, I. *A Commanding Presence – Wellington in the Peninsula 1808-1814.* (Stroud: Spellmount, 2008).
Robertson, I. *An Atlas of the Peninsular War.* (New Haven: Yale University Press, 2010).
Snow, P. *To War with Wellington.* (London: John Murray, 2010).
Smith, R.H.P., "Getting Lost and Finding the Way: the Use, Misuse and Nonuse of Maps and Reconnaissance for Route Planning in the Peninsular War (1807-1814)", *Napoleon Series*, at www.napoleon-series.org/military/battles/Peninsula/GettingLost.pdf.
Smith, R.H.P., 'Peninsular War Cartography: A New look at the Military Mapping of General Sir George Murray and the Quartermaster General's Department', *Imago Mundi*, Vol 65, Part 2 (2013), pp.234-252.
Sweetman, J., *Raglan. From the Peninsula to the Crimea* (Barnsley: Pen & Sword, 2010).
Urban, M. *The Man who Broke Napoleon's Codes* (London: Faber and Faber 2001).
Ward, S.G.P., 'General Sir George Murray', *Journal of the Society for Army Historical Research*, Vol LVIII, No 236 (Winter 1980), pp.191-208.
Ward S.G.P., *Wellington's Headquarters* (Barnsley: Pen & Sword, 2017).
Woolgar, C.M. (ed.), *Wellington Studies II* (Southampton: Hartley Institute, University of Southampton 1999).

Index

From Reason to Revolution series – Warfare 1721-1815

http://www.helion.co.uk/series/from-reason-to-revolution-1721-1815.php

The 'From Reason to Revolution' series covers the period of military history 1721–1815, an era in which fortress-based strategy and linear battles gave way to the nation-in-arms and the beginnings of total war.

This era saw the evolution and growth of light troops of all arms, and of increasingly flexible command systems to cope with the growing armies fielded by nations able to mobilise far greater proportions of their manpower than ever before. Many of these developments were fired by the great political upheavals of the era, with revolutions in America and France bringing about social change which in turn fed back into the military sphere as whole nations readied themselves for war. Only in the closing years of the period, as the reactionary powers began to regain the upper hand, did a military synthesis of the best of the old and the new become possible.

The series will examine the military and naval history of the period in a greater degree of detail than has hitherto been attempted, and has a very wide brief, with the intention of covering all aspects from the battles, campaigns, logistics, and tactics, to the personalities, armies, uniforms, and equipment.

Submissions

The publishers would be pleased to receive submissions for this series. Please contact series editor Andrew Bamford via email (andrewbamford@helion.co.uk), or in writing to Helion & Company Limited, Unit 8 Amherst Business Centre, Budbrooke Road, Warwick, CV34 5WE

Titles

1. *Lobositz to Leuthen: Horace St Paul and the Campaigns of the Austrian Army in the Seven Years War 1756-57* (Neil Cogswell)
2. *Glories to Useless Heroism: The Seven Years War in North America from the French journals of Comte Maurés de Malartic, 1755-1760* (William Raffle (ed.))
3. *Reminiscences 1808-1815 Under Wellington: The Peninsular and Waterloo Memoirs of William Hay* (Andrew Bamford (ed.))
4. *Far Distant Ships: The Royal Navy and the Blockade of Brest 1793-1815* (Quintin Barry)
5. *Godoy's Army: Spanish Regiments and Uniforms from the Estado Militar of 1800* (Charles Esdaile and Alan Perry)
6. *On Gladsmuir Shall the Battle Be! The Battle of Prestonpans 1745* (Arran Johnston)
7. *The French Army of the Orient 1798-1801: Napoleon's Beloved 'Egyptians'* (Yves Martin)
8. *The Autobiography, or Narrative of a Soldier: The Peninsular War Memoirs of William Brown of the 45th Foot* (Steve Brown (ed.))
9. *Recollections from the Ranks: Three Russian Soldiers' Autobiographies from the Napoleonic Wars* (Darrin Boland)
10. *By Fire and Bayonet: Grey's West Indies Campaign of 1794* (Steve Brown)
11. *Olmütz to Torgau: Horace St Paul and the Campaigns of the Austrian Army in the Seven Years War 1758-60* (Neil Cogswell)
12. *Murat's Army: The Army of the Kingdom of Naples 1806-1815* (Digby Smith)
13. *The Veteran or 40 Years' Service in the British Army: The Scurrilous Recollections of Paymaster John Harley 47th Foot – 1798-1838* (Gareth Glover (ed.))
14. *Narrative of the Eventful Life of Thomas Jackson: Militiaman and Coldstream Sergeant, 1803-15* (Eamonn O'Keeffe (ed.))
15. *For Orange and the States: The Army of the Dutch Republic 1713-1772 Part I: Infantry* (Marc Geerdinck-Schaftenaar)
16. *Men Who Are Determined to be Free: The American Assault on Stony Point, 15 July 1779* (David C. Bonk)
17. *Next to Wellington: General Sir George Murray: The Story of a Scottish Soldier and Statesman, Wellington's Quartermaster General* (John Harding-Edgar)
18. *Between Scylla and Charybdis: The Army of Elector Friedrich August of Saxony 1733-1763 Part I: Staff and Cavalry* (Marco Pagan)
19. *The Secret Expedition: The Anglo-Russian Invasion of Holland 1799* (Geert van Uythoven)
20. *'We Are Accustomed to do our Duty': German Auxiliaries with the British Army 1793-95* (Paul Demet)
21. *With the Guards in Flanders: The Diary of Captain Roger Morris 1793-95* (Peter Harington (ed.))
22. *The British Army in Egypt 1801: An Underrated Army Comes of Age* (Carole Divall)
23. *Better is the Proud Plaid: The Clothing, Weapons, and Accoutrements of the Jacobites in the '45* (Jenn Scott)
24. *The Lilies and the Thistle: French Troops in the Jacobite '45* (Andrew Bamford)
25. *A Light Infantryman With Wellington: The Letters of Captain George Ulrich Barlow 52nd and 69th Foot 1808-15* (Gareth Glover (ed.))
26. *Swiss Regiments in the Service of France 1798-1815: Uniforms, Organisation, Campaigns* (Stephen Ede-Borrett)

27 *For Orange and the States! The Army of the Dutch Republic 1713-1772: Part II: Cavalry and Specialist Troops* (Marc Geerdinck-Schaftenaar)

28 *Fashioning Regulation, Regulating Fashion: Uniforms and Dress of the British Army 1800-1815 Volume I* (Ben Townsend)

29 *Riflemen: The History of the 5th Battalion 60th (Royal American) Regiment, 1797-1818* (Robert Griffith)

30 *The Key to Lisbon: The Third French Invasion of Portugal, 1810-11* (Kenton White)

31 *Command and Leadership: Proceedings of the 2018 Helion & Company 'From Reason to Revolution' Conference* (Andrew Bamford (ed.))

32 *Waterloo After the Glory: Hospital Sketches and Reports on the Wounded After the Battle* (Michael Crumplin and Gareth Glover)

33 *Fluxes, Fevers, and Fighting Men: War and Disease in Ancien Regime Europe 1648-1789* (Pádraig Lenihan)

34 *'They Were Good Soldiers': African-Americans Serving in the Continental Army, 1775-1783* (John U. Rees)

35 *A Redcoat in America: The Diaries of Lieutenant William Bamford, 1757-1765 and 1776* (John B. Hattendorf (ed.))

36 *Between Scylla and Charybdis: The Army of Friedrich August II of Saxony, 1733-1763: Part II: Infantry and Artillery* (Marco Pagan)

37 *Québec Under Siege: French Eye-Witness Accounts from the Campaign of 1759* (Charles A. Mayhood (ed.))

38 *King George's Hangman: Henry Hawley and the Battle of Falkirk 1746* (Jonathan D. Oates)

39 *Zweybrücken in Command: The Reichsarmee in the Campaign of 1758* (Neil Cogswell)

40 *So Bloody a Day: The 16th Light Dragoons in the Waterloo Campaign* (David J. Blackmore)

41 *Northern Tars in Southern Waters: The Russian Fleet in the Mediterranean 1806-1810* (Vladimir Bogdanovich Bronevskiy / Darrin Boland)

42 *Royal Navy Officers of the Seven Years War: A Biographical Dictionary of Commissioned Officers 1748-1763* (Cy Harrison)

43 *All at Sea: Naval Support for the British Army During the American Revolutionary War* (John Dillon)

44 *Glory is Fleeting: New Scholarship on the Napoleonic Wars* (Andrew Bamford (ed.))

45 *Fashioning Regulation, Regulating Fashion: Uniforms and Dress of the British Army 1800-1815 Vol. II* (Ben Townsend)

46 *Revenge in the Name of Honour: The Royal Navy's Quest for Vengeance in the Single Ship Actions of the War of 1812* (Nicholas James Kaizer)

47 *They Fought With Extraordinary Bravery: The III German (Saxon) Army Corps in the Southern Netherlands 1814* (Geert van Uythoven)

48 *The Danish Army of the Napoleonic Wars 1801-1814, Organisation, Uniforms & Equipment: Volume 1: High Command, Line and Light Infantry* (David Wilson)

49 *Neither Up Nor Down: The British Army and the Flanders Campaign 1793-1895* (Phillip Ball)

50 *Guerra Fantástica: The Portuguese Army and the Seven Years War* (António Barrento)

51 *From Across the Sea: North Americans in Nelson's Navy* (Sean M. Heuvel and John A. Rodgaard)

52 *Rebellious Scots to Crush: The Military Response to the Jacobite '45* (Andrew Bamford (ed.))

53 *The Army of George II 1727-1760: The Soldiers who Forged an Empire* (Peter Brown)

54 *Wellington at Bay: The Battle of Villamuriel, 25 October 1812* (Garry David Wills)

55 *Life in the Red Coat: The British Soldier 1721-1815* (Andrew Bamford (ed.))

56 *Wellington's Favourite Engineer. John Burgoyne: Operations, Engineering, and the Making of a Field Marshal* (Mark S. Thompson)

57 *Scharnhorst: The Formative Years, 1755-1801* (Charles Edward White)

58 *At the Point of the Bayonet: The Peninsular War Battles of Arroyomolinos and Almaraz 1811-1812* (Robert Griffith)

59 *Sieges of the '45: Siege Warfare during the Jacobite Rebellion of 1745-1746* (Jonathan D. Oates)

60 *Austrian Cavalry of the Revolutionary and Napoleonic Wars, 1792–1815* (Enrico Acerbi, András K. Molnár)

61 *The Danish Army of the Napoleonic Wars 1801-1814, Organisation, Uniforms & Equipment: Volume 2: Cavalry and Artillery* (David Wilson)

62 *Napoleon's Stolen Army: How the Royal Navy Rescued a Spanish Army in the Baltic* (John Marsden)

63 *Crisis at the Chesapeake: The Royal Navy and the Struggle for America 1775-1783* (Quintin Barry)

64 *Bullocks, Grain, and Good Madeira: The Maratha and Jat Campaigns 1803-1806 and the emergence of an Indian Army* (Joshua Provan)

65 *Sir James McGrigor: The Adventurous Life of Wellington's Chief Medical Officer* (Tom Scotland)

66 *Fashioning Regulation, Regulating Fashion: Uniforms and Dress of the British Army 1800-1815 Volume I* (Ben Townsend) (paperback edition)

67 *Fashioning Regulation, Regulating Fashion: Uniforms and Dress of the British Army 1800-1815 Volume II* (Ben Townsend) (paperback edition)

68 *The Secret Expedition: The Anglo-Russian Invasion of Holland 1799* (Geert van Uythoven) (paperback edition)

69 *The Sea is My Element: The Eventful Life of Admiral Sir Pulteney Malcolm 1768-1838* (Paul Martinovich)

70 *The Sword and the Spirit: Proceedings of the first 'War & Peace in the Age of Napoleon' Conference* (Zack White (ed.))

71 *Lobositz to Leuthen: Horace St Paul and the Campaigns of the Austrian Army in the Seven Years War 1756-57* (Neil Cogswell) (paperback edition)

72 *For God and King. A History of the Damas Legion 1793-1798: A Case Study of the Military Emigration during the French Revolution* (Hughes de Bazouges and Alistair Nichols)

73 *'Their Infantry and Guns Will Astonish You': The Army of Hindustan and European Mercenaries in Maratha service 1780-1803* (Andy Copestake)
74 *Like A Brazen Wall: The Battle of Minden, 1759, and its Place in the Seven Years War* (Ewan Carmichael)
75 *Wellington and the Lines of Torres Vedras: The Defence of Lisbon during the Peninsular War* (Mark Thompson)
76 *French Light Infantry 1784-1815: From the Chasseurs of Louis XVI to Napoleon's Grande Armée* (Terry Crowdy)
77 *Riflemen: The History of the 5th Battalion 60th (Royal American) Regiment, 1797-1818* (Robert Griffith) (paperback edition)
78 *Hastenbeck 1757: The French Army and the Opening Campaign of the Seven Years War* (Olivier Lapray)
79 *Napoleonic French Military Uniforms: As Depicted by Horace and Carle Vernet and Eugène Lami* (Guy Dempsey (trans. and ed.))
80 *These Distinguished Corps: British Grenadier and Light Infantry Battalions in the American Revolution* (Don N. Hagist)
81 *Rebellion, Invasion, and Occupation: The British Army in Ireland, 1793-1815* (Wayne Stack)
82 *You Have to Die in Piedmont! The Battle of Assietta, 19 July 1747. The War of the Austrian Succession in the Alps* (Giovanni Cerino Badone)
83 *A Very Fine Regiment: the 47th Foot in the American War of Independence, 1773–1783* (Paul Knight)
84 *By Fire and Bayonet: Grey's West Indies Campaign of 1794* (Steve Brown) (paperback edition)
85 *No Want of Courage: The British Army in Flanders, 1793-1795* (R.N.W. Thomas)
86 *Far Distant Ships: The Royal Navy and the Blockade of Brest 1793-1815* (Quintin Barry) (paperback edition)
87 *Armies and Enemies of Napoleon 1789-1815: Proceedings of the 2021 Helion and Company 'From Reason to Revolution' Conference* (Robert Griffith (ed.))
88 *The Battle of Rossbach 1757: New Perspectives on the Battle and Campaign* (Alexander Querengässer (ed.))
89 *Waterloo After the Glory: Hospital Sketches and Reports on the Wounded After the Battle* (Michael Crumplin and Gareth Glover) (paperback edition)
90 *From Ushant to Gibraltar: The Channel Fleet 1778-1783* (Quintin Barry)
91 *'The Soldiers are Dressed in Red': The Quiberon Expedition of 1795 and the Counter-Revolution in Brittany* (Alistair Nichols)
92 *The Army of the Kingdom of Italy 1805-1814 : Uniforms, Organisation, Campaigns* (Stephen Ede-Borrett)
93 *The Ottoman Army of the Napoleonic Wars 1798-1815: A Struggle for Survival from Egypt to the Balkans* (Bruno Mugnai)
94 *The Changing Face of Old Regime Warfare: Essays in Honour of Christopher Duffy* (Alexander S. Burns (ed.)
95 *The Danish Army of the Napoleonic Wars 1801-1814, Organisation, Uniforms & Equipment: Volume 3: Norwegian Troops and Militia* (David Wilson)
96 *1805 - Tsar Alexander's First War with Napoleon* (Alexander Ivanovich Mikhailovsky-Danilevsky, trans. Peter G.A. Phillips)
97 *'More Furies then Men': The Irish Brigade in the service of France 1690-1792* (Pierre-Louis Coudray)
98 *'We Are Accustomed to do our Duty': German Auxiliaries with the British Army 1793-95* (Paul Demet) (paperback edition)
99 *Ladies, Wives and Women: British Army Wives in the Revolutionary and Napoleonic Wars 1793-1815* (David Clammer)
100 *The Garde Nationale 1789-1815: France's Forgotten Armed Forces* (Pierre-Baptiste Guillemot)
101 *Confronting Napoleon: Levin von Bennigsen's Memoir of the Campaign in Poland, 1806-1807, Volume I Pultusk to Eylau* (Alexander Mikaberidze and Paul Strietelmeier (trans. and ed.))
102 *Olmütz to Torgau: Horace St Paul and the Campaigns of the Austrian Army in the Seven Years War 1758-60* (Neil Cogswell) (paperback edition)
103 *Fit to Command: British Regimental Leadership in the Revolutionary & Napoleonic Wars* (Steve Brown)
104 *Wellington's Unsung Heroes: The Fifth Division in the Peninsular War, 1810-1814* (Carole Divall)
105 *1806-1807 - Tsar Alexander's Second War with Napoleon* (Alexander Ivanovich Mikhailovsky-Danilevsky, trans. Peter G.A. Phillips)
106 *The Pattern: The 33rd Regiment in the American Revolution, 1770-1783* (Robbie MacNiven)
107 *To Conquer and to Keep: Suchet and the War for Eastern Spain, 1809-1814, Volume 1 1809-1811* (Yuhan Kim)
108 *To Conquer and to Keep: Suchet and the War for Eastern Spain, 1809-1814, Volume 2 1811-1814* (Yuhan Kim)
109 *The Tagus Campaign of 1809: An Alliance in Jeopardy* (John Marsden)
110 *The War of the Bavarian Succession, 1778-1779: Prussian Military Power in Decline?* (Alexander Querengässer)
111 *Anson: Naval Commander and Statesman* (Anthony Bruce)
112 *Atlas of the Battles and Campaigns of the American Revolution, 1775-1783* (David Bonk and George Anderson)
113 *A Fine Corps and will Serve Faithfully: The Swiss Regiment de Roll in the British Army 1794-1816* (Alistair Nichols)
114 *Next to Wellington: General Sir George Murray: The Story of a Scottish Soldier and Statesman, Wellington's Quartermaster General* (John Harding-Edgar) (paperback edition)